THEODERIC AND THE ROMAN IMPERIAL RESTORATION

This book provides a new interpretation of the fall of the Roman Empire and the "barbarian" kingdom known conventionally as Ostrogothic Italy. Relying primarily on Italian textual and material evidence, and in particular the works of Cassiodorus and Ennodius, Jonathan J. Arnold argues that contemporary Italo-Romans viewed the Ostrogothic kingdom as the Western Roman Empire and its "barbarian" king, Theoderic (r. 489/93–526), as its emperor. Investigating conceptions of Romanness, Arnold explains how the Roman past, both immediate and distant, allowed Theoderic and his Goths to find acceptance in Italy as Romans, with roles essential to the empire's perceived recovery. *Theoderic and the Roman Imperial Restoration* demonstrates how Theoderic's careful attention to imperial traditions, good governance, and reconquest followed by the re-Romanization of lost imperial territories contributed to contemporary sentiments of imperial resurgence and a golden age. There was no need for Justinian to restore the Western Empire: Theoderic had already done so.

Jonathan J. Arnold is Assistant Professor of Ancient and Medieval History at the University of Tulsa. His research and publications focus on issues of culture and identity, travel and communication, and the legacy of Rome in the late antique and early medieval West, particularly in Gaul and Italy. He has written entries for a number of encyclopedic works, including the *Oxford Dictionary of the Middle Ages* and the *Oxford Dictionary of Late Antiquity*, and his articles appear in the *Journal of Late Antiquity* and *The Battle of Vouillé, 507 CE: Where France Began*.

THEODERIC AND THE ROMAN IMPERIAL RESTORATION

Jonathan J. Arnold
University of Tulsa

CAMBRIDGE
UNIVERSITY PRESS

CAMBRIDGE
UNIVERSITY PRESS

32 Avenue of the Americas, New York NY 10013-2473, USA

Cambridge University Press is part of the University of Cambridge.

It furthers the University's mission by disseminating knowledge in the pursuit of education, learning, and research at the highest international levels of excellence.

www.cambridge.org
Information on this title: www.cambridge.org/9781107054400

First published 2014

Printed in the United States of America

A catalog record for this publication is available from the British Library.

Library of Congress Cataloging in Publication data
Arnold, Jonathan J., 1980–
Theoderic and the Roman imperial restoration / Jonathan J. Arnold.
    pages   cm
Includes bibliographical references and index.
ISBN 978-1-107-05440-0 (hardback)
1. Theoderic, King of the Ostrogoths, 454–526.   2. Ostrogoths – Italy –
History.   3. Ostrogoths – Italy – Biography.   4. Goths – Kings and rulers –
Biography.   5. Italy – Kings and rulers – Biography.   6. Italy – History – 476–774.
7. Rome – History.   8. Restorations, Political – History – To 1500.
9. Imperialism – History – To 1500.   I. Title.
DG507.A76   2014
945'.01092–dc23 [B]   2013044146

ISBN 978-1-107-05440-0 Hardback

For Claude Henry "Bob" Davies (1919–2013)
Cineri gloria sera venit

CONTENTS

Acknowledgments   *page* ix

List of Abbreviations   xi

Introduction   1

PART I AN EMPIRE TURNED UPSIDE-DOWN   9

1   Ennodius the Ligurian   11

2   Cassiodorus the Calabrian   37

PART II EMPEROR THEODERIC   57

3   *Princeps Romanus*   61

4   The Imperial Image   92

PART III ITALO-ROMANS AND ROMAN GOTHS   117

5   Men of Mars   121

6   *Rex Genitus, Vir Inlustris*   142

PART IV *ITALIA FELIX*   175

7   Italy Revived   179

8   Rome Rejuvenated   201

– Contents –

PART V *RENOVATIO IMPERII*   231

   9 Becoming Post-Roman   235

  10 *Gallia Felix*   262

Epilogue   295

Bibliography   303

Index   335

ACKNOWLEDGMENTS

It is difficult to express the deep gratitude that I feel toward those who have played their parts in the various stages of this book. First and foremost, I am grateful to the University of Michigan, the "gymnasium of scholarly learning" (to borrow from Ennodius), where I was privileged to meet and learn from many gifted and inspiring individuals. The most important and influential of these were the members of my dissertation committee, Ray Van Dam, Paolo Squatriti, Diane Hughes, and Bruce Frier. Ray, in particular, has continued to provide sagacious advice, proving himself far more than a dissertation chair – a valued mentor, colleague, and friend. Likewise, the University of Michigan has continued to support my endeavors, sponsoring my research as a visiting scholar twice since my departure and proving itself more than worthy of the term "nourishing mother" (*alma mater*).

Other scholars have left their marks on this book in different ways, commenting on related papers and publications, exchanging correspondence, or simply providing friendly encouragement, advice, or banter. These include Ralph Mathisen, Deborah Deliyannis, Bernard Bachrach, Danuta Shanzer, Walter Goffart, Paul Dutton, and Anthony Kaldellis. Not to be forgotten are also the anonymous readers for Cambridge, whose thorough and learned comments on the manuscript, though not always adopted, were extremely helpful and made this book infinitely better than it otherwise would have been.

Next I turn to the University of Tulsa, Oklahoma's own "citadel of eloquence" (to borrow again from Ennodius). I thank my colleagues in the History Department for their support, sound advice, and excellent collegiality, all of which make Chapman Hall a very pleasant place to work. I also thank the staff at McFarlin Library, particularly Steve Nobles and the Interlibrary Loan Department, who proved instrumental in obtaining the materials needed to finish this book. Likewise, I owe a very great

ix

deal of thanks to the Office of Research and Sponsored Programs at TU. Through its assistance, I was able to acquire funding for my research, including an Oklahoma Humanities Council Scholar Research Grant and two University of Tulsa Faculty Development Summer Fellowships. Last, I have to thank my students: Few will ever read this book (unless I assign it!), but teaching them has made me a far better scholar.

Finally, to my family and personal friends, who have supported me in their own ways and waited what seems like an eternity for this book to be finished: to Mom, Dad, Ben, Jamie (hey, bud, you made it into the book!), Charlie, Jen, Hannah, Creighton, Matt, my dear wife, Raven, and Grandpa Bob, to whom this book is dedicated. Bob never got to hold this book, but I know he would be proud.

ABBREVIATIONS

AA	Auctores Antiquissimi.
AnonVal	*Anonymi Valesiani pars posterior.*
CassChron	*Cassiodori Senatoris Chronica ad a. DXIX.*
CassOratReliquiae	*Cassiodori Orationum Reliquiae.*
CCCM	Corpus Christianorum. Continuatio Mediaevalis.
CCSL	Corpus Christianorum. Series Latina.
CIL	*Corpus Inscriptionum Latinarum.*
CSEL	Corpus Scriptorum Ecclesiasticorum Latinorum.
CTh	*Codex Theodosianus.*
Ep.	*Epistulae.*
Fiebiger 1	*Inschriftensammlung zur Geschichte der Ostgermanen.*
Fiebiger 2	*Inschriftensammlung zur Geschichte der Ostgermanen. Neue Folge.*
Fiebiger 3	*Inschriftensammlung zur Geschichte der Ostgermanen. Zweite Folge.*
Frag.	*Fragmenta.*
HA, DAur	*Historia Augusta, Divus Aurelianus.*
HA, TT	*Historia Augusta, Tyranni Triginta.*
Hist. Goth.	*Isidori Iunioris episcopi Hispalensis historia Gothorum Wandalorum Sueborum ad. a. DCXXIV.*
ILS	*Inscriptiones Latinae Selectae.*
LHF	*Liber Historiae Francorum.*
LL	Leges (in Folio).

LTUR	Steinby, Eva Margareta, ed. *Lexicon Topographicum Urbis Romae.*
Marc. Com.	*Marcellini v.c. comitis Chronicon ad a. DXVIII.*
MGH	Monumenta Germaniae Historica.
NMaj	*Novellae Maioriani.*
NVal	*Novellae Valentiniani.*
PanTh	Ennodius, *Panegyricus dictus clementissimo regi Theoderico.*
PL	Patrologiae cursus completus, series Latina.
PLRE	Martindale, J. R. *The Prosopography of the Later Roman Empire.*
SC	Sources chrétiennes.
SRL	Scriptores rerum Langobardicarum et Italicarum Saec. VI–IX.
SRM	Scriptores rerum Merovingicarum.
TLL	*Thesaurus Linguae Latinae.*
TTH	Translated Texts for Historians.
VE	Ennodius, *Vita Epiphanii.*

INTRODUCTION

A Happy Year

In 511, for the first time in more than two generations, a Gallo-Roman was consul at Rome. The event would have shocked and delighted former Gallo-Roman statesmen like Sidonius Apollinaris, who had claimed decades earlier and in the midst of western imperial collapse that worthy Gallo-Romans would no longer hold such offices.[1] For Sidonius and countless others, the future of Gaul seemed to lie with "barbarian" kings, and by the early sixth century Italo-Romans like the young Cassiodorus Senator were in agreement, openly declaring that his generation had only *read* of a Roman Gaul and in utter disbelief.[2] By 511, however, a series of unexpected events had unfolded in the West, suddenly reuniting Italy with its long-lost Gallic province. Italy's sovereign welcomed these newly "liberated" provincials back to their ancient homeland, to the Roman Empire, and invited them to wrap themselves again in the "morals of the toga." He informed the western Senate that the Gauls had "gloriously regained Rome" and told those in Constantinople that Rome had reclaimed "her very own nurslings," the senators of Gaul.[3]

Yet this was not a solitary or confined incident; it was, in fact, a capstone to a series of rebounds and recoveries witnessed in Italy for more than a decade. Even before this consulship, Italo-Romans had been applauding the restored status of the Roman state and lauding their *princeps* as "forever Augustus" and a "propagator of the Roman name."[4] Portions of Italy, recently ravaged,

---

[1] Sidonius, *Ep.* 9.14.
[2] *CassOratReliquiae*, p. 466, ln. 17–20, with Chp. 9.
[3] *Variae* 2.1, 2.3, and 3.17, with Chp. 10.
[4] For *princeps*, Chp. 3. For Augustus and propagator, Fiebiger 1, #193 (*ILS* 827 and *CIL* 10 6850–2), with Chps. 3 and 10. For status, *VE* 51 and 81, and *PanTh* 5, with Chp. 1 and the Introduction to Part IV.

were said to "live again," while "unforeseen beauty" was hailed as coming forth "from the ashes of cities." Rome too, once decrepit and "slipping in her tracks," was described as youthful and her Senate's crown as "wrapped with innumerable flowers."[5] Nor was Italy the only beneficiary, as regions of the Balkans, lost in the fifth century, had been reclaimed by valiant soldiers, "returning Roman powers to their [former] limits" and making the Danube Roman again.[6] By 511, the western Roman Empire appeared to be resurging and reclaiming its rightful place. It was fitting, therefore, that the Gallic consul granting his name to this year was named Felix, "the happy one"; sentiments of a golden age had been on the lips of many, and with Gaul now restored, it seemed as if its blessings would never end.[7]

Despite all the celebration and jubilance, however, these events received little commentary outside the confines of Italy and have remained relatively obscure to this day. Moreover, to those with even a basic knowledge of late Roman or early medieval history, such anecdotes must seem bizarre. After all, the soldiers responsible for restoring Rome's lost provinces were not Romans but Ostrogoths, cousins of the same "barbarians" who infamously sacked Rome in 410 and went on to wrest portions of Gaul and Spain from the western empire. Likewise, Italy's sovereign, if afforded that title, was not a Roman *princeps* or *Augustus*, but a barbarian *rex*, a king with a hopelessly un-Roman name, Theoderic. Finally, the state to which they belonged was not the western Roman Empire. That empire had ceased to exist decades earlier, in 476, when a barbarian generalissimo named Odovacer deposed its final emperor and established a kingdom of his own. Instead, this was Ostrogothic Italy, a kingdom founded when Theoderic himself personally slew Odovacer in 493 but fated to be liberated by and restored to the real Roman Empire (the eastern or Byzantine Empire) during the reign of Justinian (527–565). How could Italo-Romans have been so mistaken? And why were they celebrating the very barbarians who, according to Romans elsewhere, had conquered them and held them in captivity?

BARBARIANS AND LATE ANTIQUITY

"Barbarian" is a term that will acquire much complexity in the chapters that follow. Yet it is understandable why conventional "barbarians"

---

[5] For Italy, *VE* 141 and *PanTh* 56, with Chp. 7. For Rome, *PanTh* 56–7, with Chp. 8.
[6] For powers, *PanTh* 69, with Chp. 5; for Danube, *Variae* 11.1.10, with Chp. 2
[7] See Ennodius, *PanTh* 93, #458.10 (*In Christi Signo*), and *CassOratReliquiae*, p. 466, ln. 17–18, with Chps. 8 and 10.

like the Franks, Vandals, and Goths have dominated modern studies of the late Roman and early medieval West. Not only do Roman sources describe them as the traditional nemeses of the Roman Empire, but they also played a fundamental role in the transformations witnessed over the course of the late fourth, fifth, and sixth centuries. At times they acted as the primary agents of imperial decline, sacking cities like Rome, dismantling provinces, and establishing their own kingdoms; at other times, they cast their lots with the empire and attempted to forestall its collapse. In the process and in the immediate aftermath, their impact was significant, contributing to new identities and polities that would define the societies of the early medieval West and, by extension, the modern nations of Western Europe.

Scholars generally agree on these basic points, but their interpretations of this period, emphases, and overall tones have varied greatly over the years, providing an important historiographical context and point of departure for the present study. The most traditional of narratives envision this period from the perspective of a unified Roman Empire and Roman civilization. Privileging both, they offer a crisis or conflict model, a clash of civilizations where stereotypically savage barbarians insert themselves into the Roman world by violent means, disrupt and dismantle the empire, and, at their very worst, even destroy Roman civilization.[8] Here, as might be expected, Romans appear as victims, the empire and its institutions collapse, and a decisive cultural break, often with moral implications, ushers in the Dark Ages. If there is continuity beyond the fifth century, it is dismal in comparison with the greatness of Rome.

Such "disruption" models have existed since the era of Justinian himself and have even witnessed a minirevival in recent years.[9] But the last fifty years have also provided a number of alternatives. Most broadly, the advent and popularization of a new periodization known as "late antiquity" has challenged the very idea of a decisive break between the "ancient" and "medieval" worlds, envisioning a gradual transformation beginning as early as the second century and ending as late as the ninth. Here, instead

---

[8] See, for instance, Musset (1965) or, most recently, Ward-Perkins (2005).

[9] For the fall of Rome in Justinian's day, Croke (1983); Goffart (2006), 51–4; and Goltz (2007). Modern understandings trace their origin to the Italian Renaissance, when terms like "Dark Ages" and "Middle Ages" were first coined, and by extension to the European Enlightenment, which privileged (classical) reason over (medieval) superstition and viewed human history in terms of progress. Gibbon's monumental *The History of the Decline and Fall of the Roman Empire* (1776–88), the product of Enlightenment thinking, continues, both directly and indirectly, to influence. See Pocock (2003). For the recent revival, Ward-Perkins (2005) and, less negatively, Heather (2006).

of high politics, cultural, religious, and intellectual histories are the norm, while the traditional boundaries of the Roman Empire are often eschewed in favor of micro- and macroregions that focus on a particular province or community or extend broadly from the Mediterranean to places as distant as the Indus or Scandinavia.[10]

Not surprisingly, so dynamic a way of imagining the late ancient and early medieval worlds has had an impact on accounts of barbarians and the fall of Rome, and many new paradigms have emerged.[11] Some of the most radical have simply replaced traditionally Romanocentric approaches with an emphasis on barbarians and barbarian kingdoms. Studies of this sort have endeavored to "liberate the barbarians" from what is seen as unfair Roman and modern biases, attempting to study these peoples in their own right and on their own terms. Members of the so-called Vienna School, for example, have utilized ethnogenesis theory in an effort to shed further light on barbarian origins, investigating the process whereby once-disparate tribes coalesced and formed into the larger confederacies of late antiquity. In their view, ethnogenesis informed and created the "tribal" memories and identities of peoples like the Franks and Theoderic's Goths, memories and identities that accompanied them when they entered Roman soil and contributed to the new, "national" identities of early medieval Europe. Ethnogenesis, in other words, transformed barbarians and Romans, forging a new world order.[12]

Other scholars, while still privileging barbarian ethnicity or identity, have criticized ethnogenesis models, both questioning the written sources that are used as evidence for tribal memory and accusing modern advocates of having nationalistic motives of their own.[13] These scholars propose, instead, that the barbarians of late antiquity were the products of the Roman frontier and a mixed Romano-barbarian military aristocracy. They treat the frontier as a broad zone, imagining that it fostered interaction, cooperation, and even synthesis between "barbarians" and "Romans" long before the political transformations of

[10] Brown's *The World of Late Antiquity* (1971) remains a standard point of departure. Shorter and more recent introductions can be found in Bowersock et al. (1999), vii–xiii; Brown (2003), 1–33; James (2008); Marcone (2008); and Clark (2011). For a critique, Ward-Perkins (2005), 169f.

[11] For recent discussions, Pohl (1997), 1–12, and (1998a), 1–15; and Mathisen and Shanzer (2011), 1–11.

[12] The classic work is Wenskus (1961). Wolfram, Pohl, and Geary are more recent representatives of this school of thought, Geary (2002) being especially useful for novices. See also the essays in Wolfram et al. (1990). For a critique, see the following note.

[13] See, most recently, Goffart (2006) and the collection of essays in Gillett (2002). Gillett (2006) provides a useful and accessible introduction for those unfamiliar with the debate.

the fifth century.[14] In their view, the arrival of the barbarians had clear political repercussions, but the cultural seeds of the Middle Ages had already been sown.

A final model, more Romanocentric in its approach, has emphasized accommodation. Here, scholars have focused on either the legal and constitutional mechanisms that allowed for barbarian rule in the West or the sociocultural mechanisms that provided Roman elites with alternatives to Romanness and Roman political rule. Such legal and constitutional analyses often stress the ordered settlement of barbarians on Roman soil, challenging models of "disruption" and demonstrating greater and lesser degrees of political continuity within the barbarian kingdoms.[15] The sociocultural analyses, on the other hand, tend to focus on the reactions of individual Romans to the advent of the barbarians. Here, fifth-century Gaul frequently serves as the model, with Gallo-Roman elites like Sidonius Apollinaris gradually becoming "post-Roman" and then "medieval" through mass exodus to the church or (less frequently) by holding offices in barbarian regimes.[16] Accommodation, in short, eases the fifth-century West into the Middle Ages, while still allowing for a degree of crisis and disruption.

FROM OSTROGOTHIC ITALY TO ROMAN RESTORATION

In general, the scholarship dealing with Ostrogothic Italy, the barbarian kingdom that will be the focus of this book, has fit within the interpretive schemes just discussed. Those interested in disruption models have emphasized the otherness and "barbarian" status of Theoderic and his Goths, or pointed toward "un-Roman" activities within the Ostrogothic kingdom.[17] Those interested in understanding the Ostrogoths on their own terms have relied on ethnogenesis or frontier models, both benefiting

---

[14] For this view of the frontier, Whittaker (1994) and Burns (2003). For the military aristocracy, Demandt (1989) and Goffart (2006), 188–92.

[15] For legal settlement based on taxation, Goffart (1980) and (2006), chp. 6. For constitutionality, Barnwell (1992). Both treat developments in the West broadly.

[16] The classic treatment is Stroheker (1948), which focuses primarily on the lay aristocracy. More recent works, such as Van Dam (1985) and (1993) and Mathisen (1993), have emphasized the Christianization of Gallo-Roman society. The collected essays in Drinkwater and Elton (1992) and Mathisen and Shanzer (2001) utilize both approaches.

[17] Cf. MacPherson (1989) and Ward-Perkins (2005), 72f.

from studies in disciplines like archaeology and linguistics;[18] or, rather differently, they have challenged the very idea of Gothicness, suggesting that in the Ostrogothic kingdom "Goths" and "Romans" were merely ideological constructs that served propagandistic purposes.[19] Finally, those interested in accommodation narratives have explored a number of topics, including the legal mechanisms of Gothic settlement in Italy, the constitutional position of Theoderic vis-à-vis Constantinople, and the collaboration of the senatorial aristocracy with the Ostrogothic regime.[20] A recent proliferation of studies treating contemporary authors and their works, moreover, has granted greater insight into the reactions of certain individuals at this time.[21]

Such developments would seem to suggest that a synthesis is warranted, but this is not the purpose of this book. Indeed, though the present study is informed by the preceding models and subscribes to a late antique view, its purpose is to take the fields of "Ostrogothic Italy" and "barbarian studies" in an entirely different direction by suggesting a new type of accommodation model. Set within the context of Roman imperial decline and the emergence of "barbarian kingdoms," this book is unapologetically "Roman," "Italo-Roman" to be more specific, in its orientation. It is not, therefore, a history of Ostrogothic Italy or the Goths, but a study of

[18] Cf. Burns (1984); Wolfram (1988); and Heather (1996); as well as the topical essays collected in *Teoderico il Grande e i Goti d'Italia* (1993); Bierbrauer et al. (1994); Carile (1995); and Barnish and Marazzi (2007).

[19] For this thesis, see especially Amory (1997). For a recent critique, Heather (2007). Cf. Goffart (1988), part 2, and (2006), chp. 4, who argues for a similar kind of propagandistic construction of Gothicness in the eastern Roman Empire.

[20] For the argument that the Goths were given tax revenues rather than land, Goffart (1980), chp. 3. For critiques, Barnish (1986) and Heather (2007). See also Chp. 7 of this study. The literature on Theoderic's constitutional position is vast, much of it cited in Chp. 3. For collaboration, Momigliano (1955); Moorhead (1978a); O'Donnell (1981); Barnish (1988); and Giardina (1993).

[21] The most important of these individuals are Cassiodorus and Ennodius. The former has received much more attention than the latter. For recent studies, O'Donnell (1979) and the collected essays in Leanza (1986). The partial translations of Cassiodorus' *Variae* found in Barnish (1992) likewise provide a needed alternative to the useful, but ultimately unsatisfying summations of Hodgkin (1886), which continue to be cited in modern works as if accurate translations. More recently, studies of Ennodius have also flowered, though most not in English. Kennell (2000); the proceedings of the *Atti della Giornata Ennodiana* (2001–6); and Schröder (2007) can now be consulted for treatments of his life and works. With respect to his *Life of Epiphanius*, an Italian translation with commentary superior to that of Cook (1942) is now available in Cesa (1988). Ennodius' extremely important *Panegyric to King Theoderic* now has two newer editions in the works of Rohr (1995) and Rota (2002), both of which include translations and extensive commentary in German and Italian, respectively. Finally, his letters are becoming available in French via the Budé editions of Gioanni (2006–10).

Romanness and the Roman Empire that fully accepts Theoderic's reign (489/93–526) as a continuation of Roman history. It does not, then, like the teleological models discussed previously, look forward to the medieval future and attempt to explain the transition from antiquity to the Middle Ages. Instead, its chronological scope is far narrower and it looks backward to the Roman past, immediate and distant, in an attempt to explain the continuities and changes, all overwhelmingly Roman and imperial in nature, of the Theoderican era.

One of its principal purposes, therefore, is to complicate quite considerably notions of "barbarian" and "Roman" during this period, providing new models for the understanding of both and demonstrating in the process how Theoderic and his Goths found acceptance as "Romans." Another purpose, in keeping with the first, is to draw attention to the full extent to which the "Ostrogothic" state presented itself and was perceived by its own inhabitants as the western Roman Empire. "Ostrogothic Italy," this study claims, is a misnomer, an unfortunate but convenient inaccuracy that renders "barbarian" an Italy that remained proudly Roman in its self-identification, regardless of external perceptions. Finally, a third underlying purpose is to demonstrate that Theoderic and his Goths not only fit within these understandings of Romanness and a Roman Empire, but were also essential to it, their unique roles contributing to the contemporary beliefs of imperial resurgence, blessedness, and a golden age already encountered earlier. Theoderic's Italy, then, was not a mistake; nor were the Romans of Italy yearning to be liberated by the only real Roman Empire, based in Constantinople. It was a true Roman Empire that presented itself as such and exceeded the expectations of many of its Roman inhabitants; and it would have persisted in its Roman identity, had it not been for the unforeseeable intervention of the east Roman state.[22]

The book itself is divided into five parts, each with two chapters, and addresses these ideas both diachronically and thematically. Part I introduces Magnus Felix Ennodius and Magnus Aurelius Cassiodorus Senator, two Italo-Romans whose sentiments remain paramount throughout this study. It focuses on their respective backgrounds and impressions of the fifth-century "decline and fall" of the western empire, the role of "barbarians" and "Romans" in the process, and their shared understanding that the empire persisted, despite the deposition of its emperor in 476. Part II shifts away from a purely Ennodian or Cassiodorean reading, examining the highly traditional mechanisms that allowed Theoderic to fit within the idea of a revived and resurging Roman Empire. It investigates his position

---

[22] Cf. Sirago (1986), 198; Schäfer (2001), 196–7; and O'Donnell (2008).

as the independent ruler of the West, the titles and epithets that he used and had applied to him by his subjects, and his regular employment of imperial iconography and regalia. It suggests that Italo-Romans wanted their own emperor, a *princeps* reminiscent of Augustus or Trajan, and concludes that Theoderic conformed to their expectations. Part III addresses the issue of "Gothicness" in Theoderic's realm, demonstrating how Goths were transformed into civilized defenders and avengers of the Roman Empire and how Theoderic's uniquely royal and east Roman credentials served to legitimize him as a proper imperial successor. Part IV focuses on the positive changes that Italo-Romans witnessed at home during the long reign of Theoderic, acts of benefaction that contributed heavily to contemporary sentiments of blessedness and a golden age. It demonstrates that the celebratory language of the day was not empty rhetoric, and using case studies from Liguria, the city of Rome, and other Italian regions, it draws attention to how sound leadership and needful patronage could validate "Gothic" imperial succession at a local level. Part V, finally, complements Part IV by looking at the positive changes that Italo-Romans (and others) witnessed in matters abroad. It focuses on the role of non-Italian lands in Theoderic's Roman Empire, using Gaul, a region for which there is abundant evidence, as an extensive case study. It treats Gaul's complex historical relationship with Italy; Italian perceptions of Gallic continuity, captivity, and barbarization in the aftermath of Roman rule; and the intervention of the Theoderican regime, which ultimately led to a Gallic restoration and the consulship of Felix.

Part V thus concludes where the Introduction begins: with the "happy year" (*felix annus*) of the consul Felix, an event that was emblematic of the wonders of the Theoderican era and the proudly Roman identity of "Ostrogothic Italy." To some, however, this may seem a strange place to end the account. After all, Theoderic continued to rule until his death in 526, while his empire persisted without him, and in various incarnations, until its final "reconquest" by the armies of Justinian in 555. An Epilogue, therefore, follows the final chapter of this book, providing a rationale and tying up some proverbial loose ends. Most studies of Ostrogothic Italy conclude with a discussion of its doomed future, seeing the final years of Theoderic's reign as the beginning of the end. But in 511, and even as Justinian's armies were marching on Ravenna, the Roman past, which now included Theoderic and his Goths, continued to inform Italy's present, while Italy's future remained unknown.

PART I

AN EMPIRE TURNED
UPSIDE-DOWN

A Shadow Empire

Rome did not fall in a day.[1] It took the better part of a century, and, indeed, the Gallo-Roman perspective on this process is well documented, not least owing to the survival of fifth-century works by "representative men" like Sidonius Apollinaris.[2] In Gaul, Roman aristocrats like Sidonius watched as barbarian Visigoths and Burgundians slowly whittled away at those enclaves still claimed by the Roman Empire. They continued to participate in the imperial administration, to be staunchly "Roman," and to hope for imperial resurgence into the twilight of Roman rule. Though eventually resigning themselves to their lots and adapting, many nonetheless expressed horror and disbelief when the crumbling western empire, reduced to Italy, finally abandoned them.[3] How exactly the Roman inhabitants of Italy reacted to this situation, on the other hand, is difficult to ascertain. Surely, if Gallo-Romans could feel betrayed, Italo-Romans must not have felt much better. Italy, the ideological heartland of the Roman Empire, had witnessed disappointments of its own: barbarian invasions, internal strife and civil wars, and finally the loss and even willful abandonment of long-held provinces like Gaul. Though the central administration endeavored to reassert itself, it was ultimately unable. Developments like these must have been shocking and humiliating to contemporary Italo-

---

[1] In fact, it will be suggested in Part I that Rome never fell, at least as far as certain Italo-Romans were concerned.

[2] Treatments of fifth-century Gaul rely heavily on Sidonius' works. See, among others, Stroheker (1948); Van Dam (1985); Mathisen (1993); and Harries (1994).

[3] Sidonius, *Ep.* 7.7 provides an excellent example. On the "crisis" and reaction of the Gallo-Roman aristocracy in general, see Mathisen (1993) and the collected essays in Drinkwater and Elton (1992).

9

Romans, yet a "representative man" like Sidonius fails to shed light on the matter, ushering in Italy's "dark ages" with blackening silence.[4]

This long silence, however, is soundly broken by a number of important individuals who emerge from the shadows at the turn of the sixth century. Classically trained and traditionally elite in outlook, these men were heirs to Rome's grievous past and direct beneficiaries of its present fortunes. More than simply living through change, they were molded by it, enthusiastically celebrating the tidings of Theoderic's reign and looking forward to a bright future. Most noteworthy among them were Magnus Felix Ennodius, a north Italian churchman, and his younger contemporary, Magnus Aurelius Cassiodorus Senator, a southern Italian bureaucrat. Their collective writings are extensive, and though their ornate styles have often befuddled even the best of Latinists,[5] their works provide invaluable evidence for Italian sentiments at this time.

Here, in the two chapters that follow, their individual backgrounds and perspectives on the past will be treated in an effort to understand contemporary enthusiasm for Theoderican rule. Though from opposite ends of the Italian Peninsula, following dissimilar career paths, and writing for different audiences and with different purposes in mind, Ennodius and Cassiodorus agreed on much. Imperial leadership had failed during the fifth century; provinces had been lost, and not just to stereotypically savage barbarians but also to an increasingly rapacious eastern Roman Empire; and amid the chaos, Roman society had begun to decay. Within this milieu of decline, Romanness, according to them, became negotiable, a factor that allowed fifth-century "barbarians" to appear at times more Roman than certain "Greek" emperors dispatched from Constantinople. Finally, and despite these calamities, both Ennodius and Cassiodorus agreed on a fundamental point: 476, the traditional date for the fall of the western empire, was meaningless. Odovacer's position may have been ambiguous, but his realm was not. There was still a western Roman Empire, separate from its eastern counterpart, and, according to these two Italo-Romans, it waited for a proper Roman emperor to rule it.

---

[4] Granted, this period in Italian history is not without its evidence, but what does exist is rather sparse in nature, composed mostly of short inscriptions, coins, and chronicle entries. Compared to the plethora of literary sources from contemporary Gaul, many of a deeply personal nature, Italy truly is bleak. Still, "dark ages" is a term used here for ironic and rhetorical effect. The evidence for Italo-Roman sentiments during the late fourth and early fifth centuries, on the other hand, is more substantial. See, for instance, Paschoud (1967).

[5] Ennodius' style may explain why his works (with few exceptions) never gained much popularity in the Middle Ages and, indeed, continue to be overlooked. See Rohr (1994), 95–6 and (1999), 261–2, who comments on the twelfth-century assertion of Arnulf of Lisieux that Ennodius was really Innodius: "the entangled knot."

1

ENNODIUS THE LIGURIAN

Magnus Felix Ennodius, or simply Ennodius, was a prolific author, whose writings straddle a number of genres, including private epistles, panegyric, hagiography, orations, and epigrams. Though later bishop of Pavia and papal envoy to Constantinople, he penned his works while serving as a subdeacon and then deacon in Milan, between 495 and 513.[1] This timing is extremely important, as it coincides almost exactly with the period during which lofty claims of Roman restoration began to circulate. Ennodius, as a classically trained rhetorician, a reader and admirer of Sidonius' works,[2] and an eyewitness to the changes that had occurred both before and during Theoderic's reign, was especially susceptible to these ideas, proving himself a steadfast and consistently loyal adherent.

Ironically, however, this much needed "representative" of the Italo-Roman perspective was not an Italian by birth, but a member of a Gallo-Roman family with extended kin on both sides of the Alps. Ennodius had spent his early childhood within the vicinity of Arles, relocating while still a child to Pavia when he was orphaned sometime in the late 470s or early 480s.[3] He may have been too young, therefore, to comprehend fully the transformations of his youth. But it was at about this time that Sidonius had

---

[1] The exact chronology of Ennodius' career is uncertain. It began at Pavia (Ticinum) during the episcopate of Epiphanius, under whose direction he may have reached the rank of subdeacon. Following Epiphanius' death (c. 496/9), he was transferred to Milan, where he remained until his episcopal ordination (c. 513/15). The dating of his works, however, is more certain. Only #43 can be placed before the sixth century, whereas the majority of the extant corpus dates to the period 501–13 and was written at Milan. See Kennell (2000), 6–18; Bartlett (2003); and the introduction in Vogel's *MGH* edition (*AA* 7). Vogel's numbering system (rather than the artificial divisions by genre employed in Hartel's *CSEL* edition) has been used throughout.

[2] Ennodius imitated or outright copied passages from Sidonius' poetry in his *dictio* on the occasion of Epiphanius' birthday (#43), his earliest extant opus (c. 495).

[3] See #438, with Kennell (2000), 5–8, and Vogel's *MGH* edition, p. II-V.

given up on the Roman Empire, and likewise that the government of Italy had ceded the remnants of its Gallic possessions to the Visigoths.[4] A true testament to the interconnectedness of Provence and Liguria,[5] Ennodius was able to keep his transalpine ties, despite changing political climates and attitudes and the formidable barrier posed by the Alps. And these ties, as will be seen in a later chapter, provided him with a unique perspective vis-à-vis Gaul and its Roman inhabitants, men like the consul Felix.[6] Still, though well aware of his origins and on intimate terms with certain Gallic individuals, Ennodius was not a Gallo-Roman.[7] The majority of his life, including his youth and formal education, had been spent on the Italian side of the Alps; his closest friends and patrons were Italo-Romans, often from the noblest senatorial families;[8] and, most importantly, he identified with Italy and Liguria foremost.[9]

This north Italian upbringing had consequences for the deacon's impression of the world. Since the late third century, northern Italy had played host to emperors and their courts, providing local aristocrats like Ennodius and his peers with access to their patronage and ennobling offices of state. Ennodius' own Milan and later Pavia featured imperial and then royal palaces,[10] while the more permanent court at Ravenna, which developed into a true capital over the course of the fifth century,

---

[4] Sidonius, *Ep.* 7.7 is conventionally dated to 474/5, while Odovacer appears to have yielded Provence to Euric late in 476.

[5] The term *Liguria* is used in reference to the late Roman province of Liguria, which must not be confused with the modern Italian region of the same name. Late Roman Liguria encompassed much of modern Piedmont and portions of Lombardy, with its capital at Milan.

[6] See Chp. 9.

[7] See Kennell (2000), 18. His north Italian weltanschauung and career have led some to suggest a Ligurian birthplace at Milan, a possibility that Ennodius appears to deny in #311 (see the *MGH* edition, p. III). Regardless, Ennodius' Gallic origins should not be overemphasized. Despite descent from a Gallo-Roman family and likely birth at Arles, he also had family ties to Liguria, including an aunt. Moreover, though maintaining ties with Gallic correspondents, Ennodius at times viewed Gaul and Gauls with traditional Italo-Roman contempt. See Chp. 9.

[8] For Ennodius' connections, Näf (1990), 104–6; Moorhead (1992), 155–8; Kennell (2000), 31f.; and Gioanni (2006), LXVII–LXXIII. The most important of these was the illustrious senator Faustus Niger (*PLRE* 2, 454–6), Ennodius' patron and relative, to whom the greatest number of his letters are addressed. See also Gioanni (2003), who is keen to point out Ennodius' role as an intermediary among the elites at Rome, "new men," the church, and the court at Ravenna.

[9] Cf. Bartlett (2001), 201–16, on Ennodius' understanding of Christianity as more typically Italian than Gallic. These sentiments, as will be demonstrated throughout, extend far beyond the ecclesiastical realm.

[10] On Milan and Pavia, Matthews (1975), chp. 8; Clemente (1984); and Cracco Ruggini (1984); more broadly Wickham (1981), 10–11, and (2005), 33–4. These two cities also had munitions factories, a mint, and walls that were put to good use in late antiquity. For their importance in Ennodius' day, see later discussion and Chp. 7.

could be visited with relative ease thanks to the Po and its tributaries.[11] The presence of emperors and imperial courts had other consequences as well. Northern Italy became increasingly militarized and frontierized, and the soldiers and armies that were attracted to emperors, both Roman and barbarian, friendly and hostile, became regular (and often unpleasant) phenomena.[12] Alaric and his Visigoths, for example, were neither the first nor the last barbarians to run amuck in this region, pillaging its fields and burning its cities.[13] And even before the fifth century, more than one civil war had pit Roman army against Roman army, with the Alps functioning as a backdrop.[14]

These environmental factors, as will be seen, played an important role in the development of Ennodius as a person: his tastes, biases, and expectations. His birth and education, however, were similarly (and in some cases even more) influential. Indeed, Ennodius was raised with a traditionally aristocratic and northern Italian outlook, believing that Italy, and more specifically Rome, was the heartland of Roman civilization. Years of training in Latin grammar and rhetoric strengthened these ideas, while the study of classical works by authors like Cicero and Virgil helped to instill notions, albeit anachronistic, of republicanism and liberty (*libertas*). A veritable prerequisite of Romanness, liberty was essential to Ennodius and his class' identity and entailed important expectations.[15] Most notable among these was the understanding that Romans were culturally and morally superior to barbarians, and that emperors were not to be despots but *principes* (first citizens), who worked in partnership with the senatorial aristocracy.[16] This elite upbringing and rhetorical education also instilled

---

[11] For the rise of Ravenna, Mazza (2005); Pani Ermini (2005); and Deliyannis (2010), chp. 3. For the ease of travel, Sidonius, *Ep.* 1.5. Cf. Ennodius, *VE* 183–4 and #423, where the Po serves as an obstacle.

[12] For more on the frontierization of the Italian Alps, see Chp. 9.

[13] Just a few years before their invasion, for instance, the Goth Radagaisus had crossed the Julian Alps and devastated northern and west-central Italy, including such cities as Pollenzo and Florence. Later, in 452, Attila and his Huns attacked Milan, Aquileia, and other cities. And in 464 a group of Alani, led by Beorgor, was active near Bergamo.

[14] The latter half of the fourth century witnessed a number of civil wars in the region, including those from 351–3 (Magnentius vs. Constantius II); 387–8 (Magnus Maximus vs. Valentinian II and then, in retaliation, Theodosius); and 394 (Theodosius vs. Eugenius/Arbogast). Later, in the fifth century, the civil wars intensified and spread to Rome. Alaric, fighting on behalf of Priscus Attalus, besieged Ravenna and took most of Aemilia and Liguria between 409 and 410. Later northern skirmishes are attested in and around Ravenna in 424/5 (Valentinian III vs. John); near Rimini in 432 (Aetius vs. Boniface); at Piacenza in 456 and 476 (Avitus vs. Ricimer and Orestes vs. Odovacer); and at Tortona in 461 (Majorian vs. Ricimer).

[15] See Dauge (1981), 534–7; Moorhead (1987); Barnish (2003); and Gioanni (2003), 48–9.

[16] For an elaboration, Chp. 3 and Part III.

in Ennodius a deep appreciation for the art of proper speaking ("sweet speech") and the conviction that its possession defined an individual as nobly Roman.[17] Altogether, these ideas served to reinforce the hoary belief that Rome was the mistress and the center of the world (*caput mundi*), not simply the ideological capital of the Latin West, but the true source of Latin eloquence and Romanness. Rome was "parent city of the world," "mother of cities," "friend to the liberal arts," and "birth place of knowledge and erudition."[18] Finally, Ennodius' reverence for Rome was mirrored in his personal devotion to its bishop, whom he saw as the undisputed head of the church, infallible, and answerable to God alone.[19] This was the only bishop worthy of the title "father" (*papa*), and his see, which defended the faith of St. Peter, was a nourishing mother, just like Rome.[20] For Ennodius, then, service in the church did not weaken venerable ideas about Rome; it strengthened them.[21]

With the exception of his views on the papacy, these were very traditional sentiments, but they were also painfully inconsistent with Ennodius' recollection of the Italy of his youth. For him, to reflect upon the

---

[17] On sweet speech in Ennodius' opera, Kennell (2000), chp. 2 especially. Its role as an indicator of Romanness, attested in Sidonius, *Ep.* 5.5 and 8.2, will be discussed later and at length in Chp. 9. See, more broadly, Heather (1994), 182–6.

[18] For center of the world, *Libellus pro Synodo* (#49) 120: "mundi caput Romam"; mistress of the world, *PanTh* 30: "orbis domina ... Roma"; parent city, *Libellus pro Synodo* 128: "orbis parentem urbem"; mother of cities, *PanTh* 56: "illa ipsa mater civitatum Roma"; friend to the liberal arts, #290.1: "urbem amicam liberalibus studiis"; birthplace of knowledge, #282.2: "natalem scientiae sedem Romam"; birthplace of erudition, #225.2: "Romam, in qua est natalis eruditio." Cf. Delle Donne (2001), 12f.

[19] See especially Ennodius' *Libellus pro Synodo*, with Lumpe (1969); Navarra (1974), 317–18; Kennell (2000), 199–201, and (2001); and Gioanni (2001). This composition is generally seen as one of the most important early documents articulating notions of papal primacy and infallibility. Ennodius' private letters reiterate these ideas. See Gioanni (2003).

[20] For Ennodius' almost exclusive use of the term *papa* (pope) for the bishop of Rome, see Lumpe (1969), 26–7. Sidonius, by comparison, regularly addressed his episcopal correspondents as "dominus papa." For Peter and Rome, see (for instance) #8.11, *Libellus Pro Synodo* 21 and 24, and #458.4 (*In Christi Signo*), along with Ennodius' epitaph (*CIL* 5 6464 = *ILS* 2952), partially cited in the following footnote. For nourishing see, *Libellus pro Synodo* 120: "Romam ... nutricem pontificii cathedram."

[21] But cf. Vandone (2001), who suggests that Ennodius struggled with his role as a classically trained litterateur and churchman. He concludes that Ennodius eventually reconciled the two by using his literary skills in the service of the faith. Ennodius' epitaph (*CIL* 5 6464 = *ILS* 2952), discussed in Polara (2006), would seem to support this view. It celebrates Ennodius as a kind of bishop-poet (*vatis*), "potent with eloquence" (*pollens aeloquio*), who "restored innumerable people to Christ" ("restituit Cristo innumeros populos") and "returned churches to the Faith of Peter" ("fidem Petri reddedit aeclesiis"). See also Gioanni (2001), 254f., who speculates that Ennodius may have penned letters on behalf of Popes Symmachus and Hormisdas before his missions to Constantinople.

late fifth century was to remember a time when the world had been turned upside-down and expectations denied. Romans had become barbarians; emperors, despots; rusticity and a lack of erudition, virtues; and Rome, once the invincible mistress of the world, severely battered and poised to collapse. Rome and Romanness had been placed in peril, and in the process Roman provinces, especially Liguria, had suffered countless misfortunes. But despite these vicissitudes, the Roman Empire had endured. The deposition of the last western emperor in 476 failed to resonate with Ennodius as a pivotal moment: One poor ruler simply replaced another. Moreover, decline had set in long before this, long before Ennodius had even been born, and it persisted, in his opinion, long after Odovacer became king. Indeed, Ennodius was convinced that he had grown up in a Roman Empire denuded of its territories and ruled by a series of unworthy and often savage men, an "Empire of Italy," as he sometimes referred to it. But it had been in this sordid state for decades, lingering on until Theoderic and his Goths arrived and rescued it.

Nowhere is this conception of catastrophic continuity more clearly expressed than in two of Ennodius' more substantial works, the *Panegyric to Theoderic* and the *Life of Epiphanius*.[22] A discussion of the latter, which includes a more extensive treatment of the fifth century, now follows.

THE SAINTLY ORPHEUS

The *Life of Epiphanius*, written between 502 and 504, was intended as a tribute to the holy man described within and by extension his see of Pavia. It was thus not an official piece of Theoderican propaganda, but a work of hagiography that endeavored foremost to praise Epiphanius (c. 438–97) as a hero of God by drawing attention to his saintly virtues, miracles, and imitation of Christ and his apostles.[23] Epiphanius, therefore, was the central figure in this work, but he was also a different kind of saint from those usually encountered in contemporary pieces of hagiography. Less

---

[22] For modern understandings of continuity and catastrophe in post-Roman northern Italy, see Ward-Perkins (1997), who juxtaposes the interpretations of "positive" continuists with "negative" catastrophists. Ennodius himself was a negative continuist, at least when it came to the fifth century.

[23] For assessments, see the introductions and notes in the translations of Cook (1942) and Cesa (1988), along with the important studies of Navarra (1974); Pietrella (1984); and Herrmann-Otto (1995). Delle Donne (2001), 8–9, questions the hagiographical nature of this work and characterizes it as a kind of political manifesto that sought to celebrate not only Epiphanius but also Theoderic. This goes too far, however, not least because Theoderic is absent from more than half of the account.

like Martin of Tours and more like Ambrose of Milan, he was a worldly and pragmatic bishop, whose holiness was derived from numerous acts of pious intervention, peacemaking, and diplomacy, rather than a plentitude of miracles.[24] As his *Vita* will soon demonstrate, such holy acts of intercession regularly forced Epiphanius to contend with some of the greatest figures of his era, often with wondrous results. And as a consequence, many of the defining episodes in Ennodius' account revolve around key events from the final decade of western imperial rule. These were tumultuous times, and while Ennodius' depiction of fifth-century woes was limited, at least in this work, to the incidental experiences of Epiphanius, a consistent image emerges, finding echoes in his other works.

Ennodius began his *Life of Epiphanius* with the expected topoi of the hagiographical genre. A miracle was associated with the saint's infancy; there were prefigurations of his later, more defining feats during his teenage years; and his pious virtues eventually allowed him to ascend the ecclesiastical cursus with ease, becoming bishop of Pavia by popular acclaim.[25] Once bishop, Epiphanius was inevitably drawn into the politics and intrigues of the late imperial period. Liguria, after all, was a staging ground for Italian-led campaigns in Gaul, of which there were a number during Epiphanius' lifetime,[26] and a source of grain for the nearby imperial court and its army. Milan was by far a more prestigious city, but Pavia's fortunes were rising, and its greater proximity to Gaul made its bishop an obvious choice should an ambassador of goodwill be needed there.[27]

Epiphanius' first major trial, however, concerned a matter of internal discord, a clear indication that all was not well in fifth-century Italy. This particular episode was set in the reign of the emperor Anthemius (467–72), traditionally seen as the last truly effective emperor of the West. An easterner, Anthemius had been made emperor at Constantinople and then sent to Rome in the hope that his military expertise would be put to good use against the Vandals in North Africa and the Visigoths in Gaul and Spain.[28] An outsider, the new emperor had attempted to win an Italian home base

---

[24] For this kind of late antique holy man, Navarra (1974), 326–9; Pietrella (1984), 220f.; and Herrmann-Otto (1995). The biographies of saints like these tend to have a more secular feel and comparatively few miracles, but this should not deceive a modern reader: They are still hagiographical.

[25] VE 7–42.

[26] See Stroheker (1948), chp. 2 especially.

[27] The use of bishops as peacemakers was common at this time. See Herrmann-Otto (1995), 212–14; Gillett (2003), 113f.; and Schwarcz (2004), 37–40.

[28] A joint East-West expedition against the Vandals in 468, however, proved disastrous. See Kaegi, (1968), 36–44, and Williams and Friell (1999), 173–5.

through a marriage alliance with the Gotho-Sueve ("barbarian") Ricimer, the current generalissimo of the West and an emperor-maker who had ruled alone in the eighteen months prior to Anthemius' accession.[29] Ricimer was a domineering figure, and though Sidonius Apollinaris himself had lauded the union of both houses while in Rome,[30] it had failed to establish concord between these two headstrong men. Envy and equal dignity became a cause of discord, according to Ennodius, and the "status of Italy wavered in peril."[31]

Ostensibly, at any rate, this would seem to have been a clear case of an overmighty barbarian general challenging the Roman order, a cause traditionally cited for the fall of the western empire. Ennodius, however, did not depict it as such, his account demonstrating the full extent to which traditional expectations had been inverted. According to Ennodius, both emperor and general were consumed with madness.[32] Yet, as civil war seemed imminent, the nobility of Liguria turned not to the emperor, but to Ricimer as their patron and protector. With tears in their eyes they begged him to seek peace, and Ricimer, surprisingly, yielded before their supplication. "Soothed" and "deeply moved by their tears,"[33] he promised that he would seek reconciliation with the emperor, yet added that success seemed improbable. "Who is there," he asked, "who can win over that enraged Galatian," whose wrath yields to no "natural moderation?"[34] Such wrath, Ricimer feared, would render his petition useless, but the nobles of Liguria responded that Epiphanius, the account's hero, should be chosen for the task, since he could tame "even rabid beasts."[35] Epiphanius, they claimed, was worthy of veneration by every Catholic, Roman, and even "the Greekling," Anthemius.[36] And true to their advice, Ricimer himself venerated the saint upon his arrival, choosing him immediately for the mission.[37]

---

[29] For Ricimer, *PLRE* 2, 942–5 (Fl. Ricimer 2). For this interregnum, which was not the first time Ricimer had ruled alone, MacGeorge (2002), 233–4.

[30] See *Carmen* 2, with Chp. 6.

[31] For envy, *VE* 51: "invidia et par dignitas causa discordiae"; for peril, *VE* 52: "Nutabat status periclitantis Italiae." The Latin text used throughout is from Cook (1942), which utilizes Vogel's *MGH* edition as its basis.

[32] *VE* 52: "Surrexerat enim tanta rabies atque dissensio, ut mutuo bella praeparent."

[33] *VE* 53: "Mulcetur Ricemer et velle se reparare concordiam permotus multorum fletibus pollicetur."

[34] *Ibid*.: "'Quis est qui Galatam concitatum revocare possit et principem? Nam semper, cum rogatur, exuperat qui iram naturali moderatione non terminat.'"

[35] *VE* 54: "'cui et beluae rabidae colla submittunt.'"

[36] *Ibid*.: "'quem venerari possit quicumque si est catholicus et Romanus, amare certe, si videre mereatur, et Graeculus.'"

[37] *VE* 58: "ad Ricemerem patricium perrexit, a quo simul visus et electus est."

Paradoxically, then, this initial exchange served in Ennodius' narrative to transform the barbarian Ricimer into a benevolent, moderate, and surely "Roman" ruler, in stark contrast with the emperor, who was described as an unyielding savage and rabid beast. Anthemius, it seemed in Liguria, was the real barbarian, and beyond his disposition, his foreignness was underscored by his Galatian and pejoratively Greek origins.[38] But when Epiphanius arrived in Rome and was rather reluctantly received by the emperor, another demonstration of the backwardness of this period was presented, this time by Anthemius. Ricimer, in his eyes, was the real barbarian, and the emperor, proud of his own Roman lineage, had been dishonored by a traditionally deceitful savage. The mere act of sending Epiphanius, well known in Rome for his eloquence, qualified as a crafty ruse, apparently the only possible means of rendering Ricimer's "immoderate and unreasonable proposals" acceptable.[39]

In addressing the emperor, Epiphanius likewise manipulated these expected categories. Playing on origins, he urged, "your Italy and the patrician Ricimer sent my smallness, concluding that a Roman would grant, as a gift to God, that peace for which even a barbarian begs."[40] He then suggested to the emperor that the best way to prove his valor was to contend with his own anger, to earn a "triumph without blood" and thus "shame the very fierce Goth with kindness."[41] The implications of these words are revealing: It was the barbarian Ricimer who had come to speak on behalf of the emperor's Italy. He offered "Roman" peace with the common good in mind, while the emperor appeared concerned with bellicose thoughts of victory and valor. Moreover, though a "fierce Goth," it was Ricimer who

---

[38] Galatian was more than just a reference to Anthemius' eastern origins, since (despite Hellenization) the Galatians were understood in antiquity to be Gallogrecians and hence only semicivilized. See Mitchell (1993), with Cook (1942), 162, and Cesa (1988), 152. For *Graeculus*, Näf (1990), 118; O'Flynn (1991); and Isaac (2004), 401–3. Näf suggests that, while Ennodius seems to favor Ricimer, his Epiphanius remains neutral.

[39] For crafty ruse, *VE* 60: "'Callida mecum Ricemer et in legationibus suis arte decertat.'" For immoderate and unreasonable, *VE* 61: "'cuius scio votorum intemperantem esse personam et in condicionibus proponendis rationis terminum non tenere.'" Anthemius' fears seem, to some extent, well founded, since the *adventus* of Epiphanius at Rome and his obvious holiness had already rendered the Romans dumbstruck. See *VE* 59.

[40] *VE* 64: "'Hoc ergo Italia vestra freta iudicio vel Ricemer patricius parvitatem meam oratu direxit, indubitanter coniciens quod pacem Romanus deo munus tribuat quam precatur et barbarus.'"

[41] *Ibid*.: "'Erit enim triumphus vestris proprie profuturus annalibus si sine sanguine viceritis. Simul nescio quae species fortior possit esse bellorum quam dimicare contra iracundiam et ferocissimi Getae pudorem onerare beneficiis.'" The reference to Ricimer as "Getic" in origin is a rather classicizing way of calling him a Goth (see later discussion). Ricimer, as intimated earlier, was actually of mixed barbarian origins, his father a Sueve and his mother a Visigoth.

had already proven himself merciful and kind, while Anthemius, still truly angry, had to be provoked to kindness. In this depiction of Epiphanius' initial audience with the emperor, therefore, Ennodius yet again suggested who the barbarian really was.

These implications, intended to shame the emperor, were lost on Anthemius, however, whose outrage was fueled by more traditional assumptions of Roman dominance over barbarians, as well as the personal insults that he had suffered at the hands of his son-in-law. Indeed, the noble marriage alliance lauded by Sidonius for linking East and West was thoroughly denigrated by the Greek emperor, who claimed that it had shamed both his house and the state.[42] Pleading with Epiphanius, he demanded to know which of his imperial predecessors, for the sake of peace, had included a daughter "among the gifts to a skin-clad Goth," implying that such an occurrence had been unprecedented.[43] Romans were not supposed to mix with barbarians, and he alone had made the ultimate sacrifice on behalf of the state, sparing not even his blood from barbarian filth.[44] Ironically, of course, the very Italo-Romans for whom Anthemius had played the martyr had only recently disparaged him as both a savage and a little Greek. But the emperor was unaware, and regardless, his sacrifice had been in vain, for "the greater the gifts" he showered upon his son-in-law, the "more serious an enemy he appeared."[45] Ricimer, he avowed, had plotted against the state on numerous occasions, even scheming against his life. He was thus an "enemy of the state in the garb of friendship"[46] and needed to be treated appropriately.

War, it seemed, was unavoidable. But true to his saintly powers, Epiphanius miraculously mollified the emperor, who agreed to a shaky peace. Even then, however, Anthemius remained convinced of his

[42] That Sidonius appears unconcerned with such miscegenation may be reflective of a greater tolerance for barbarians in fifth-century Gaul. Marriage between elite barbarians and the Roman (even imperial) aristocracy, however, was actually quite common from the fourth century onward. See Demandt (1989). *Variae* 5.14.4 also demonstrates that mixed marriages were common at a nonelite level.

[43] *VE* 67: "'Quis hoc namque veterum retro principum fecit umquam ut inter munera, quae pellito Getae dari necesse erat, pro quiete communi filia poneretur.'" But again, it was not unprecedented for a Roman princess to be married to a barbarian prince, the best "Gothic" example being Galla Placidia, who married the Visigothic king Athaulf amid great fanfare in Narbonne. See the introduction to Part III. More recently Huneric, a Vandal prince, had married the daughter of Valentinian III, Eudocia.

[44] *VE* 67: "'Nescivimus parcere sanguini nostro.'" Cf. the discussion of Ennodius' nephew Parthenius in Chp. 9.

[45] *VE* 68: "'quotiens a nobis maioribus donis cumulatus est Ricimer, totiens gravior inimicus apparuit.'"

[46] *VE* 69: "'Hunc intestinum sub indumento amicitiarum inimicum sustinebimus.'"

suspicions concerning Ricimer. Alluding to his rival's innate barbarism, he even suggested that perhaps Epiphanius himself had been fooled by "the cunning of his customary trickery"[47] and promised to renew hostilities should his fears prove founded.

Getic Murmurs

A brutal civil war between Ricimer and Anthemius did eventually break out, but it received no treatment in the *Life of Epiphanius*, doubtless because its greatest casualty was not Epiphanius' Liguria but central Italy, where Ricimer put Anthemius on the defensive.[48] In passing, Ennodius simply informed his audience that the two had died and that Anthemius had been succeeded by Olybrius, who soon also died.[49] Only a brief anecdote concerning the reign of his successor, Glycerius, was then provided, but these shorter entries were then followed by a much more extensive treatment of an episode from the reign of Julius Nepos (474–5), yet another imperial appointee from Constantinople.[50]

Related by marriage to the eastern imperial family and master of soldiers in Dalmatia, Nepos had been commissioned by the eastern emperor Leo to depose Glycerius, who was viewed in the East as a usurper.[51] In his account, Ennodius devoted no space to what must have been a confusing situation, a replay of sorts of the conditions witnessed before the advent of the preceding "Greek" emperor, Anthemius.[52] Unlike Anthemius, however, whose Romanness and qualities as a leader Ennodius implicitly questioned, Nepos was eventually treated sympathetically, if not favorably, in the *Life of Epiphanius*. Indeed, in this particular episode Nepos became the victim, while Italy ceased to be the proxy whereby the status of the Roman Empire was measured. Instead, Gaul took its place, and the

---

[47] *VE* 70: "'Postremo si solitae calliditatis astutia etiam te fefellerit certamen iam vulneratus adsumat.'" Both *astutia* and *calliditas* were the mark of a barbarian. See Dauge (1981), 748.

[48] For details, Jones (1964), 243; MacGeorge (2002), 253–7; and Heather (2006), 425.

[49] *VE* 79: "Defuncto tunc Ricimere vel Anthemio successit Olybrius, qui in ipsis exordiis diem clausit extremum." This one-sentence entry seems worth quoting, since it reiterates the point that the *Life of Epiphanius* is specifically centered on Epiphanius, while politics serves as an important backdrop.

[50] The anecdote, recorded in *VE* 79, concerned securing a pardon for a man who had insulted the bishop's mother.

[51] For Nepos, *PLRE* 2, 777–8 (Nepos 3). For his relations with the eastern court and unique position in Dalmatia, MacGeorge (2002), 40–62.

[52] Anthemius' predecessor, Libius Severus (461–5), a "puppet" of Ricimer, had also not been recognized in the East. It was during the eighteen-month interregnum that followed his death that Ricimer had acted as sovereign in the West.

rise of Euric's Visigothic kingdom at the expense of Nepos' Roman Empire became the motif reiterated throughout, providing a sobering glimpse into the Italo-Roman side of the situation deemed by Gauls like Sidonius as "betrayal."

Euric had been on the move against the empire since the early 470s, perhaps in response to the rapid imperial turnover and civil wars in Italy at the time.[53] When Nepos arrived on the scene in 474, the Visigoths had already laid claim to most of Aquitania Prima as well as the important maritime cities of Arles and Marseille. Their principal rivals and imperial allies, the Burgundians, had refused to check their advances,[54] and Gothic raiders had even made forays into Italy itself.[55] The perspective from Italy was no doubt bleak at this point, not just because more territories had been lost, but because Italy was clearly exposed. Within the confines of his hagiographical treatment, Ennodius described a situation in which the central imperial authority ardently desired to reclaim its lost territories and assert its dominance in the West but understood that it lacked the strength to challenge this new order and so reluctantly (but of necessity) nodded assent in order to survive. Epiphanius himself played an essential mediatory role in the process, securing a truce perhaps even more humiliating in retrospect than at the time. And in recounting the events, Ennodius depicted once more a world of inversions, where traditional expectations had been denied.

There was no room in this account for the nuances encountered earlier in the *Vita*. The king of the Visigoths and (by extension) the Visigoths themselves were stereotypically antithetical barbarians. Ennodius introduced them by explaining that dissension had arisen between Nepos and the "Getic nurslings of Toulouse, whom Euric governed with cruel despotism."[56] From the beginning, this association of the Visigoths with the classical Getae found in the pages of ancient works like Herodotus suggested, despite its common usage in late antique sources, that certain "facts" could be assumed about them. The most obvious of these

---

[53] For a reappraisal of Euric's "empire-building" policy, see Gillett (1999). For the more traditional view of Euric as anti-imperial, Wolfram (1988), 182f., and Heather (1996), 189f.

[54] This refusal probably stemmed from the fact that their king, Gundobad, had been the driving force behind the accession of Glycerius. See MacGeorge (2002), 272–5.

[55] See Jordanes, *Getica* 284 and *Romana* 347, with Wolfram (1988), 188. In fact, these Gothic raiders were "Ostrogoths" under the leadership of King Vidimir and had invaded Italy in 473 from Pannonia, not Gaul. Interestingly enough, they later joined forces with Euric in Gaul and became assimilated to his Visigoths. For the possibility that they had been invited to Italy by Glycerius, MacGeorge (2002), 272.

[56] *VE* 80: "Tolosae alumnos Getas, quos ferrea Euricus rex dominatione gubernabat."

was that they were a warlike, barbarous people originating outside the boundaries of the Roman Empire, specifically in trans-Danubian Scythia.[57] The claim that Euric governed them cruelly,[58] that is, in stark contrast with civilized, Roman conceptions of *libertas* and *humanitas*, reiterated their barbarism. More importantly, these savage qualities provided a rationale for why a disagreement had arisen between Nepos and Euric. According to Ennodius, Nepos had recently restored lands across the Alps to his "Italian Empire," and the Goths, "scorning their recovery," had continually attacked them.[59] On the one hand, Euric and his Goths believed they had a claim to these lands by right of conquest, and, on the other, Nepos argued that he had to "vindicate the boundaries committed to his rule by God," since to forfeit them to the Goths would lead to further losses.[60]

Though clearly casting Euric and his Goths as savages, Ennodius likewise claimed, as in the case of Anthemius and Ricimer, that both parties were blameworthy. Nepos and Euric, in his opinion, were both driven by "the excitement derived from an eagerness for conquest,"[61] and it was this unwillingness to back down that had perpetuated their dispute. Initially, then, Julius Nepos had appeared as much an enraged and bellicose easterner as his predecessor, sharing his concern for military glory. To Nepos' credit, however, he soon had a change of heart, ardently desiring to make overtures to the enemy. Time and a lack of success had caused him to alter his position, and he now summoned the nobles of Liguria (*Liguriae lumina*) to his counsel. The advice of these bright men, the emperor hoped, would help him to "revive the status of the declining Republic" and "restore its stability, then despaired of, to its ancient height."[62] The move was significant, transforming the warlike, semibarbarous Nepos into a truly Roman

---

[57] For a discussion of these broad generalizations, Pohl (1998b).

[58] *Ferrea*, literally "iron," suggests an unyielding, stern, or even cruel quality. Its use as a descriptive adjective to characterize weapons complements the martial language later used to describe Euric.

[59] *VE* 80: "dum illi Italici fines imperii, quos trans Gallicanas Alpes porrexerat, novitatem spernentes non desinerent incessere." Cook (1942), 65, and Cesa (1988), 94, take *novitatem* to refer to the "new" emperor, rather than to Nepos' restored territories in Gaul (presumably in Provence). See Harries (1994), 236–8, for Nepos' Gallic policies, which indirectly led to his deposition.

[60] *VE* 80: "Nepos, ne in usum praesumptio malesuada duceretur, districtius cuperet commissum sibi a deo regnandi terminum vindicare."

[61] *Ibid.*: "Dum neutrae partes conceptum tumorem vincendi studio deponunt."

[62] *VE* 81: "Quorum possit deliberatione labans reipublicae status revivescere et in antiquum columen soliditas desperata restitui." The importance of the Ligurian nobility in this episode may seem bizarre but is derived from this region's proximity to Nepos' court and strategic value with respect to Gaul. Its centrality also reflects Ennodius' personal ties to the region.

emperor acting with moderation on behalf of the common good. The contrast with Anthemius is unmistakable, so too the contrast with Ricimer, who required tears and supplication in order to act.

Nepos' Ligurian advisers eventually assembled and unanimously selected the bishop of Pavia, Epiphanius, as the ambassador most suited to carry the olive branch over the Alps. According to Ennodius, the soldier of Christ accepted the burden with joy, arriving at Toulouse weak from the rigid spiritual exercises that he had undertaken during his journey.[63] At Toulouse he was quickly taken before Euric, whose court was moderated by Leo, a Gallo-Roman correspondent of Sidonius, praised by Ennodius for his oratorical skills.[64] Romanness, it seemed, could still survive in Euric's Gaul, but only, as this episode eventually made clear, through the learning of men like Leo.[65]

Negotiations with the king began with Epiphanius appealing to Euric's love for military glory, while also reminding him of his duties as a Christian. He assured Euric that "the fame of valor" rendered him "terrible to the ears of many"; that his swords oppressed "neighboring regions with continual devastation" and "reaped a harvest of enmity"; but that, nonetheless, his "horrible desire to wage war" had scarcely been pleasing to God.[66] Indeed, Epiphanius warned Euric that his mighty swords would be rendered useless, should he persist in offending the Lord of Heaven,[67] advising the king to "defend his own possessions more diligently" by not seeking after those of another.[68] The bishop then continued by pressing the case of Nepos, who, he informed Euric, had been entrusted with the "rule of Italy" through "divine ordination."[69] Nepos' divine right, therefore, remained a rationale, and though reduced for a second time in Ennodius' opus to merely the ruler of Italy, Epiphanius' final remarks served to remind Euric, and more importantly Ennodius' audience, that this was not the way the situation was supposed to be.

---

[63] VE 82–4.

[64] See Sidonius, Ep. 4.22 and 8.3. For Ennodius' praise, VE 85: "Leo nomine, quem per eloquentiae meritum non una iam declamationum palma susceperat." See also PLRE 2, 662–3 (Leo 5).

[65] For more on this theme, Chp. 9.

[66] VE 86: "'quamvis te … multorum auribus reddat virtutis fama terribilem, et gladii, quibus finitimos continua vastitate premis, segetem quandam inimici germinis metant, nullam tibi tamen superni gratiam numinis dira bellandi praestat ambitio.'"

[67] Ibid.: "'nec ferrum fines tuetur imperii si caelestis dominus offendatur.'"

[68] VE 87: "'Deinde perpendere nos convenit quod nemo diligentius propria tuetur quam qui aliena non adpetit.'"

[69] VE 88: "'Nepos, cui regimen Italiae ordinatio divina commisit.'"

You know ... with what border the ancient inhabitants of our dominions were demarcated and with what patience these lands [of yours] endured serving the rulers of those [lands of ours]. Let it suffice that [Nepos] has chosen, or at any rate allows himself to be called your friend, when he deserves to be called your master.[70]

Barbarians like Euric were supposed to be servants of the empire, their subordination a constant theme in imperial panegyric and propagandistic imagery. The Visigoths, in particular, had been granted a special position within the Roman Empire as federate allies, theoretically independent residents, yet bound by their treaties to provide military aid. Nepos assumed that Euric understood this historical relationship. There had been a specific border, and Euric's predecessors had respected it and heeded the orders of prior Roman emperors. But in 474 the situation was markedly different. The Roman Empire's position had declined to such an extent that, though confident in Roman superiority, it was necessary for Nepos to behave as an equal.[71] This very concession, shocking and painful, flew in the face of centuries of Roman ideology.

On the other hand, these remarks were potentially quite insulting to the Visigothic king: How dare the emperor call him a slave unworthy of friendship? Nepos was in the weaker position, begging for peace, not the other way around. As with Anthemius, however, the implications of Epiphanius' words appeared lost on Euric, who failed to comment on them directly. Instead and in true barbarian fashion, he broke off into "I know not what barbarous murmur" and availed himself of an interpreter.[72] Using this go-between, the king then gave a speech that validated those martial themes already associated with his person. "Although armor is scarcely absent from my chest," he explained, "a shield constantly covers my hand, and my side is protected by my sword, nonetheless I have found a man who

---

[70] *Ibid.*: "'Nostis in commune, quo sit dominiorum antiquitas limitata confinio, qua sustinuerint partes istae illarum rectores famulandi patientia. Sufficiat quod elegit aut certe patitur amicus dici, qui meruit dominus appellari.'" Reydellet (1981), 157, interprets the passage similarly, but see Cook (1942), 96, with Cesa (1988), 171–2, for a slightly different reading.

[71] Such equality is in fact anticipated by Ennodius, who refers to Euric and Nepos as *reges* in VE 81. For the significance, see later discussion.

[72] VE 89: "Gentile nescio quod murmur infringens." This *gentile murmur* may not be a reference to the Gothic tongue, however, since Ennodius claims in another work that his Gallic nephew, Parthenius, spoke with a similar impediment (see Chp. 9). Perhaps, like Parthenius', Euric's Latin (a language he surely knew) was unrefined and the interpreter (Leo?) simply presented his words in a more stylized manner. Cf. Kennell (2000), 139. It is also possible that Euric feigned ignorance of Latin, much as contemporary Vandals seem to have done in North Africa. See Conant (2012), 62–3.

can conquer me, armored as I am, with words."[73] A man of war, he had been moved by Epiphanius' gift of speech, which he described as a specifically Roman weapon that could substitute for a shield and javelin and pierce its adversary deep in the heart.[74] Charmed, the once savage Euric agreed to come to terms, bested by the soothing words of an envoy whose persona was "greater than the power of the one who had sent him."[75]

The strict polarization between "Roman" and "barbarian" in this episode is blatant and over the top, but also highly suggestive. On the one hand, Epiphanius was transformed into a new Orpheus, taming the savage beast with sweet speeches in lieu of music. His eloquence, the mark of a noble Roman, could win out amid barbarian swords. As a stereotypical barbarian who literally spoke gibberish, on the other hand, Euric could not have been a better savage. He was covered in the instruments of war and, when it came time to praise the bishop's "Roman" talents, could only do so by analogy to the battlefield. He might be pacified and charmed into a beneficial peace, but so long as Euric and "real" barbarians like him reigned supreme in Gaul, the fate of this land and neighboring Italy remained in question.

Still, Gaul was not the worst of Italy's problems. Italy, too, the *Life of Epiphanius* has already shown, had savages of its own to deal with, often lurking in not-so-obvious places. One such barbarian, Odovacer, would even put Nepos' "Italian Empire" out of its misery and declare an end to the western Roman Empire once and for all. No one in Italy, however, seemed to notice.

THE FALL OF ROME?

Thus far a close reading of the *Life of Epiphanius* has demonstrated Ennodius' impression of the period immediately preceding his lifetime, presenting a picture of a western Roman Empire in turmoil and unapologetically Italian in its orientation. Such fifth-century woes are traditionally understood to have reached their nadir shortly after the truce established

[73] *VE* 90: "'Licet pectus meum lorica vix deserat et adsidue manum orbis aeratus includat necnon et latus muniat ferri praesidium, inveni tamen hominem qui me armatum possit expugnare sermonibus.'"

[74] For moved, *VE* 89; for weapons, *VE* 90: "'Fallunt qui dicunt Romanos in linguis scutum vel spicula non habere. Norunt enim et illa quae nos miserimus verba repellere et quae a se diriguntur ad cordis penetralia destinare.'"

[75] *VE* 91: "'Facio ergo, venerande papa, quae poscis quia grandior est apud me legati persona quam potentia destinantis.'" It should be noted that this is one of the few instances where Ennodius used *papa* for a bishop other than the bishop of Rome.

(with Epiphanius' saintly intercession) between Euric and Nepos. It was at this time that a series of civil wars once again rocked Italy, ultimately leading to the deposition of the last western emperor, Romulus Augustus. The events themselves are important, but for the present purposes only a cursory recounting is warranted.

In 475 Julius Nepos was forced to abandon Italy altogether, seeking the safety of his native Dalmatia. Though he was technically still emperor, for all intents and purposes his reign in the West had ended.[76] In Italy, Nepos was replaced by Romulus Augustus, the young son of his principal rival and master of soldiers, Orestes.[77] The little Augustus,[78] who was never recognized in the East, reigned as a figurehead for his father for less than a year, during which time questions of payments to his soldiers escalated to the point of violence. When civil war erupted in August of 476, Odovacer, a military man of barbarian origins,[79] became the champion of the mutiny, promising the soldiers payment in the form of land if victorious. Orestes was quickly defeated and killed, little Romulus deposed but spared, and Odovacer, as master of Italy, wrote to Emperor Zeno at Constantinople officially announcing that the West no longer required its own emperor. He would rule, instead, as a king and patrician, subordinate to the emperor. So fell the western Roman Empire.[80]

These events conventionally provide an important (and convenient) terminus for accounts of Roman history, though they appear to have had little resonance in Western eyes.[81] Indeed, the end of the Roman Empire

[76] He was still recognized as the legitimate western emperor in Constantinople, and Odovacer would later recognize Nepos as the sovereign of the West (at least until 480, when the exiled emperor was assassinated). Nonetheless, he was never able to exercise real authority in the West, and Italo-Romans like Ennodius and Cassiodorus clearly thought that his flight in 475 had ended his reign. See later discussion and Chp. 2.

[77] Ironically the soldiers that Orestes had been granted were intended for a campaign against the Visigoths in Gaul. See MacGeorge (2002), 275–9, with *PLRE* 2, 811–12 (Orestes 2). Even more interesting, Orestes had once served as a secretary to Attila the Hun, a fact that may explain his desire to elevate his son as emperor, since he himself may have been considered "too Hunnic."

[78] Romulus is referred to as *Augustulus* (little Augustus) in a number of sources. See *PLRE* 2, 949–50 (Romulus Augustus 4).

[79] His exact origins are disputed. See Macbain (1983), with *PLRE* 2, 791–3 (Odovacer). For the possibility of an imperial connection, Chp. 3.

[80] For reconstructions, Bury (1958), vol. 1, 405–9; Demougeot (1978), 371–2; and MacGeorge (2002), 281–93. Greater elaboration (with references) can be found in Chp. 3.

[81] This has not gone unnoticed. See, among others, Wes (1967), chp. 3; Momigliano (1973), 397–418; Irmscher (1978); Markus (1982); Croke (1983), 81–119; Zecchini (1985); Krautschick (1986), 355f.; Barnwell (1992), 134–5; Moorhead (1992), 7–8; and Goltz (2007). Some have argued that Eugippius, *Vita Severini* 20 (written in Italy c. 511), provides the earliest western reference to the fall of the western empire. However, the passage seems to refer to only the end

in 476 would have fit rather nicely into the version of history presented and discussed so far in Ennodius' *Life of Epiphanius*, with decline leading, as it does in many modern accounts, to collapse. But this was not reality as Ennodius imagined it. For him and other Italo-Romans, Odovacer was simply a replacement for the young Augustus, and in some instances even an improvement of sorts.[82] Continuity, therefore, typified the contemporary (or, in Ennodius' case, near-contemporary) understanding in Italy of the so-called fall of the Roman Empire.[83] This continuity, moreover, was largely characterized by the persistence of two important fifth-century conditions, which would play fundamental roles in later perceptions of resurgence and fecundity during the era of Theoderic.

First, as far as Italo-Romans like Ennodius were concerned, the western empire as a political institution never ceased to exist. The political changes ushered in by the events of 476 were essentially meaningless to them, a reality demonstrated by the fact that they continued to refer to their government as the Roman Empire or Republic.[84] Indeed, contemporary

of Roman rule in Noricum, since in *Vita Severini* 31 and 40 Eugippius refers to Odovacer's evacuation of Noricum (488) as a relocation to a "province on Roman soil" (*romani soli provinciam*) and "Roman province" (*romanam proviniciam*). The eastern perspective on these events is a slightly more complicated matter. The earliest Byzantine commentator, Malchus of Philadelphia (c. 500), continued to hold Nepos as the reigning emperor of the West and Odovacer as his subordinate. See Malchus, frag. 10, with Chp. 3. There are some interesting (but not decisive) notices in the fragments of Eustathius of Epiphaneia (c. 503 and cited by Evagrius Scholasticus, *HE* 3.27) and Damascius' *Vita Isidori* (c. 517), but it was not until the Justinianic era that a Byzantine source, the *Chronicle of Marcellinus Comes*, explicitly referred to the "fall" of the western empire. Moreover, in Marcellinus' case both 454 and 476 were proposed as dates.

[82] For one of these other Italo-Romans (Cassiodorus Senator) see the following chapter. For Eugippius, who seems to have had important senatorial contacts that may have even included Romulus Augustus, see (with caveats) Markus (1982) and Zecchini (1985), 21f. For his sympathetic position on Odovacer, *Vita Severini* 7, 32, and 44, along with 31 and 40 (cited in the above note). For a more sympathetic interpretation of the era of Odovacer in general, Stein (1949), vol. 2, 39–54; Chastagnol (1966); Moorhead (1992), 8–9 and 29–31; and Cesa (1994) and (2001).

[83] Cf. Näf (1990), who suggests that Ennodius was aware of the fall of Rome, but believed in its afterlife and later revival under Theoderic.

[84] The terms *Imperium Romanum*, *Res publica Romana*, and even *Regnum Romanum* are pervasive and used synonymously in Italian sources from this period. See later discussion, with Prostko-Prostyński (1994a), 77–80, and Rota (2002), 245–6. Heather (2006), 432f., argues that the institutions of the western empire themselves ceased to exist, the office of emperor the most conspicuous example. Hence, to his mind, so too did the western empire. There was, however, much institutional continuity after 476, the most important example of which was the Senate at Rome, which continued to be populated by the same aristocratic families. See Chastagnol (1966); Barnish (1988); Moorhead (1992), 7–11; and Barnwell (1992), 140f., with Chps. 5 and 8. Moreover, "real" continuity is moot, for the fact of the matter is that Italo-

Italo-Romans appear to have had little trouble reconciling a king or kingdom with their empire, and though perhaps bizarre to the classically trained, this is quite understandable. Already in Augustus' time the principate had been viewed by some as merely a monarchy in disguise, and by the fifth century royal language was regularly and unapologetically applied to emperors and their empire.[85] Odovacer's imperial predecessors were thus, more or less, just as "royal" as he was and, as the case of Anthemius suggests, perhaps even more barbarous.[86] Second, the sense of this Roman Empire as moribund and decadent endured. Thus, though the Roman Empire survived 476, it did so in what was perceived to be a rather sorry state. Weak fifth-century leadership had deprived the empire of its provinces and allowed the barbarians to dishonor the Roman name. Individual emperors, likewise, had behaved no better than their savage enemies, thinking selfishly of personal dignity and not the common good. Their actions had pitted Roman against Roman in one civil war after another, contributing further to the internal decay of what remained of the western empire.

In their works, both Ennodius and, as the following chapter will show, Cassiodorus make it abundantly clear that these two characteristics typified the period leading up to the advent of Theoderic. For them, and doubtless others, the Roman Empire, reduced to Italy, simply languished from one fifth-century ruler to another, until Theoderic, a kind of savior, assumed command. A continued close reading of the *Life of Epiphanius*, later supplemented by Ennodius' *Panegyric to Theoderic*, will now occupy the remainder of this chapter, providing greater insight into the reign of Odovacer and the origins of the Theoderican "golden age." What follows is by no means intended to be an accurate appraisal of the Odovacrian era, but instead a discussion of one interpretation of that period, written by a partisan (but not an official propagandist) of the Theoderican government, who believed that a Roman renovation and restoration had been achieved.

Romans continued to believe that their state was the western empire. Modern criteria like Heather's need not apply.

[85] Provided the views found in Tacitus, *Annals* 1.9–10, are a reflection of early first-century (AD) sentiments and not those of Tacitus and his contemporaries. On the use of royal language in late antiquity, Suerbaum (1961), 147f.; Wolfram (1967), 33f.; Reydellet (1981), 25f.; and Fanning (1992) and (2003). For more on this royal language, see later discussion.

[86] Other "barbarian" emperors (legitimate and illegitimate) had also paved the way. These included Maximinus Thrax (Goth-Alan), Magnentius (Briton-Frank), and Silvanus (Frank). But see Chp. 5 for a complication of the idea of barbarian, which might suggest that a number of other "Roman" emperors could also have been considered as such.

THE ODOVACRIAN INTERLUDE

In his *Life of Epiphanius* Ennodius introduced the events of 476 shortly after the Visigothic embassy recounted earlier. He completely passed over Orestes' revolt against Nepos and likewise provided no details concerning the elevation of his son, Romulus, to the purple. Instead, he simply described Orestes as the patrician of Italy and claimed that Odovacer had marshaled an army against him (not his son).[87] Despite the apparent ambiguity of Orestes' position and his prior, unmentioned role as a usurper against Nepos, Ennodius cast him in the role of a legitimate power in Italy, for Odovacer's revolt was portrayed as a crime and inspired by the adversary himself, the devil.[88] In Ennodius' account, the civil war that followed became yet another proving ground for the holy man, but the central position of Italy, whose safety had figured so prominently in earlier episodes, was abandoned in favor of the more local perspective of the bishop's see. Pavia, not Italy or the Roman Empire, suffered, transforming the "fall" of the Roman Empire into a trial designed specifically by the devil to defeat the hero of God. "Men enflamed with a passion for plunder" rushed upon Epiphanius' house, ransacked it like "cruel barbarians," and seized captives from the local nobility, including the bishop's own sister.[89] Both of the city's churches were destroyed by fire and "the entire city burned as if a funeral pyre."[90] Pavia literally became hell on Earth, populated by the dead and plagued by evil forces (barbarians). But true to hagiographical expectations, Epiphanius was somehow able to inspire fear and dread in these barbarians, ransoming captives and beginning the processes of rebuilding even as the city burned.[91]

With the death of Orestes, however, the situation in Pavia appeared to return to normal, so normal, in fact, that it is difficult to find evidence of

---

[87] *VE* 95: "Exercitum adversus Orestem patricium erigit et discordiae crimina clandestinus supplantator interserit."

[88] For the devil, *VE* 95: "scelerum patrator inimicus ... Odovacrem ad regnandi ambitum extollit." Hence, though Odovacer himself raised the army, the devil instigated him. The "adversary" as the devil is quite common in hagiographical treatments, paralleling the life of Christ and the archetypical holy man, Anthony.

[89] *VE* 97: "Currunt ad ecclesiae domum, totis direptionis incendiis aestuantes.... Pro nefas! thesauros cruda barbaries quaerebat.... Diripitur etiam sancta eius germana et seorsum ab eo captivitatis sorte deducitur." Also taken into captivity at this time was the noble matron Luminosa.

[90] *VE* 98: "O dolor! utraeque ecclesiae flammis hostilibus concremantur, tota civitas quasi rogus effulgurat."

[91] For this, *VE* 98–100. For other instances where Epiphanius liberated captives, Chp. 7.

any change at all. Whatever Odovacer's actual constitutional position,[92] Ennodius' language makes it clear that he viewed the king as no different from his imperial predecessors, commenting in a rather formulaic style, "after him [i.e. Orestes], Odovacer was admitted into royal power."[93] Removed from its literary context and at an initial glance, of course, this statement seems to suggest that Ennodius did perceive a difference between Odovacer and the Roman emperors preceding him.[94] His use of *regnum* in this instance is especially important, since the term in its simplest English translation means "kingdom" and a kingdom is ruled by a king (*rex*), exactly the title Odovacer appropriated for himself. In contrast, the Roman Empire was traditionally referred to as the *imperium* (empire) or *res publica* (republic) and ruled by an *imperator* (emperor), *princeps* (first citizen/prince), or *Augustus* (Augustus). As intimated previously, however, the problem for modern readers is that in later Latin the distinctions among all these terms were becoming increasingly blurred. In the early imperial period the idea of a *princeps* as something other than a monarch had been a fundamental element to the fiction of a revived republic. But time had slowly changed this. Outside Rome, especially in the Greek East, for instance, it had already become common in the first century to call the emperor king (*basileus*) and his empire the kingdom of the Romans (*Basileia ton Rhomaion*). These Greekisms no doubt influenced Latin over the centuries, as did the increasingly despotic nature of imperial rule (complete with new titles) witnessed especially after the third century. Christianization, likewise, played an important role, providing new models of rulership that made Old Testament kings like David and Solomon archetypes for Christian emperors. Finally, the highly stylized Latin of the fifth and early sixth centuries, which required linguistic flexibility and a plethora of creative synonyms, aided in the breakdown of barriers. In short, by the fifth century it would have been rather natural to hear the Roman Empire referred to as a *regnum* and *res publica* in the same work; the emperor as *princeps*, *dominus*, and *rex*; and his exercising of official powers as *regnare*, *dominare*, and *imperare*.[95]

---

[92] A subject of some debate, but see Chp. 3.

[93] *VE* 101: "Post quem adscitus in regnum Odovacris."

[94] See Cook (1942), 197, and Cesa (1988), 178.

[95] Examples of this kind of language will be encountered throughout, but again, see the important studies of Suerbaum (1961); Reydellet (1981), 25f.; and Fanning (1992) and (2003). As will be seen, these terms could be used interchangeably; hence, though it might be expected that a "princeps imperat imperium/rem publicam," one might just as easily find that a "princeps regnat rem publicam."

This ambiguity of imperial terminology in fifth- and sixth-century Italy will have greater implications later on, particularly because the use of many of these terms still tended to be the prerogative of the imperial court and a sign of its Romanness.⁹⁶ In the *Life of Epiphanius*, at any rate, it is quite clear that using such royal language in reference to emperors was more than natural, since Ennodius did so on multiple occasions. Two of the most telling instances were rather formulaic expressions of the assumption of power by emperors, and as such they resemble the statement encountered earlier concerning Odovacer. In one, the emperor Glycerius was said to have been "admitted into royal power," while in the other Ennodius claimed that "Nepos came into royal power after him [i.e. Glycerius]."⁹⁷ In addition, Nepos actually had royal language applied to him elsewhere, at one point even referring to himself and Euric as *reges*.⁹⁸ Ennodius' statements concerning the assumption of royal power by Odovacer, therefore, cast him as nothing more than one in a long line of ambiguous rulers of the western empire (Italy).⁹⁹

What was different about Odovacer, however, was the *Life's* comparatively positive depiction of his reign, which only hinted at certain problems later criticized in Ennodius' panegyric.¹⁰⁰ Just as before, this portrayal was limited by the necessities of the hagiographical genre and thus restricted to Epiphanius' personal interaction with Odovacer and his agents; and, as before, the perspective remained predominantly Ligurian and episcopal in tone. Yet through his benefaction to this region, its churches, and its holy man, Odovacer was able to become a subject of praise in Ennodius' narrative, implicitly surpassing rulers like Anthemius, who seemed (at least to the Ligurian nobility) to have had Liguria's ruin in mind. In fact, Ennodius only partially blamed the new ruler for his disastrous coup¹⁰¹ and explained that, once hostilities had subsided, Odovacer "began to honor the eminent man [i.e. Epiphanius] with such worship that he surpassed

⁹⁶ See Chp. 3.
⁹⁷ *VE* 79: "post hunc Glycerius ad regnum ascitus est"; *VE* 80: "post quem ad regnum Nepos accessit." Cf. *VE* 101 (cited previously) for Odovacer.
⁹⁸ For *reges*, *VE* 81. For Nepos' view that God ordained him to rule (*regnandi*) the Roman Empire, *VE* 80.
⁹⁹ Cf. Reydellet (1981), 154–6, who suggests that Ennodius substituted royalty for "la notion d'Empire," transposing the *regnum Italiae* of the early sixth century back upon the Roman Empire of the late fifth century. Delle Donne (2001) accepts this view, but their distinction between *regnum* and *imperium* seems artificial.
¹⁰⁰ Cf. Pietrella (1984), 219–20, and Herrmann-Otto (1995), 208.
¹⁰¹ After all, he had been inspired by the devil. But cf. *VE* 109, which describes Theoderic's arrival as ordained by heaven ("dispositione caelestis imperii"), along with the commentary in Cesa (1988), 174.

all his predecessors in kindness."[102] His royal favors, combined with the general peace of his reign, benefited the bishop's see and flock. Pavia's two churches, which had been ruined during the course of the civil war, were rebuilt, and Epiphanius succeeded in securing a five-year exemption from fiscal tribute for the city.[103] Numerous embassies from the city were also received by the king, who, judging from Ennodius' comments earlier, must have ruled in Epiphanius' favor on many occasions.[104]

Indeed, in the *Life of Epiphanius*, only a brief episode specifically tarnished Odovacer's fifteen-year reign, aside from, of course, the ruinous civil war that had put him on the throne. Ennodius claimed that Odovacer's praetorian prefect of Italy, Pelagius, had been particularly oppressive and that his "love of malice" had acted "for the ruin of the landowners of Liguria."[105] The prefect had apparently abused his right of *coemptio*, doubling the burden of tribute owed by the Ligurians and rendering it unbearable.[106] Once again, the situation afforded Epiphanius an opportunity to intercede, and though only the scantest details were provided, Ennodius' short entry is revealing: "For the sake of all in need, he [Epiphanius] went quickly, asked, and obtained."[107] The swiftness of this resolution seems as much a tribute to the hero's willingness to seek help as Odovacer's to provide it.

Rapacious Disregard

Ennodius' treatment of the era of Odovacer in the *Life of Epiphanius* demonstrates well his understanding of continuity beyond 476. In this work, Odovacer appeared, at best, an emperor himself, since emperors from a fifth-century Ligurian perspective were little more than kings, or, at worst, a surrogate. The second aspect of continuity discussed earlier, that of decadence, however, barely made an appearance in this work's treatment, no

---

[102] VE 101: "tanto cultu insignem virum coepit honorare ut omnium decessorum suorum circa eum officia praecederet." Doubtless, *omnium decessorum* demonstrates the perceived equality of the respective positions of Odovacer and his imperial predecessors.

[103] For the churches, VE 101–5. For the exemption, VE 106.

[104] VE 109: "post multas tamen quas apud Odovacrem regem legationes." But see later discussion and Chp. 7 for a critique.

[105] VE 107: "in perniciem Liguriae possessorum Pelagi, qui ea tempestate praetorio praefectus erat, repositus malitiae ardor efferbuit."

[106] *Ibid.*: "Nam coemptionum enormitate gravissima tributa duplicabat reddebatque onus geminum quod simplex sustineri non poterat." For *coemptio*, see Cook (1942), 197–8, and Cesa (1988), 181.

[107] VE 107: "pro cunctorum necessitate alacer ambulavit poposcit obtinuit." Cf. VE 58 (cited earlier).

doubt owing to the rather limited criteria by which Odovacer's reign was described. Liguria, in fact, appeared to flourish under a kind of Odovacrian peace and its holy man to have been quite successful at securing the new ruler's benevolence. Compared to the cycle of civil wars witnessed in the last decades of the Roman Empire and featured as a backdrop to prior episodes in the *Vita*, this really was an improvement. But there are cracks in the veneer, and upon closer scrutiny, Odovacer's role appears perhaps too passive throughout and more akin to apathy than benevolence. Indeed, in Ennodius' short treatment, Odovacer never took the initiative, and his kindness, though available, always required seeking. In this way, he was more like Ricimer and Anthemius, who required courting, and less like the sympathetic Nepos, who acted out of personal conviction. To his credit, Odovacer was quick to intercede when approached, but his inactivity could have dire consequences, allowing agents like Pelagius to abuse his subjects and potentially tarnish his name.

While these critiques of Odovacer were not explicitly made in the *Life of Epiphanius* and must be teased out, they are nonetheless in accord with the more specific comments on his reign found in Ennodius' *Panegyric to Theoderic*, an unofficial but extremely traditional and rhetorical composition that was written and perhaps delivered early in 507.[108] Ennodius' motivation in writing this work is unknown, but unlike the *Life*, its purpose (as a composition) was to praise the current ruler, Theoderic, who had invaded Italy and then deposed and killed Odovacer.[109] Naturally, a rather effective way of accomplishing this was to disparage the preceding regime, an act that Ennodius, as a genuine and loyal partisan of Theoderic, proved more than willing to do.[110] The Odovacer of the *Life*

[108] For the date, see the editions of Rohr (1995), 17–26, and Rota (2002), 22–5, along with their relevant articles. The work is "unofficial" insofar as it does not seem to have been commissioned by the Theoderican regime. On its traditional nature, see the same, along with Ficarra (1978) and Delle Donne (1998). There is some debate as to whether it was ever recited and, if so, whether Theoderic would have understood it. See the following note.

[109] Some have suggested that it was commissioned by the church of Pavia, Milan, or Rome as a means of thanking Theoderic for his support of Symmachus during the Laurentian Schism; others have seen it as an attempt on Ennodius' part to win Theoderic's favor in the case of his recently disgraced relative, Faustus Niger; still others place its recitation in the aftermath of an important embassy (perhaps of the Byzantines or Alamanni); and still others have suggested that the work was spontaneous or perhaps simply a rhetorical exercise by Ennodius. See Rohr (1994) and (1999), 270–4; Delle Donne (1998), 73 and 77–8; and Rota (2001a), 204–6, and (2002), 25–35, who also discuss whether the work was recited.

[110] Indeed, and despite the embellishments of the genre, Ennodius believed what he wrote in his panegyric, as his public and private works (which will be encountered throughout this study) fully demonstrate. Cf. Rota (2001a), 207–8, who concludes similarly. Delle Donne (1998), 77 and 83–4, is also keen to point out that, while the panegyric echoes the official propaganda

of Epiphanius, for instance, had kept a sinking ship of state afloat, but in the *Panegyric* the condition of that ship appears less than sturdy. In the *Life*, likewise, Odovacer himself had been kindly (at least to Epiphanius), but his governance passive and one of his agents particularly corrupt. In the *Panegyric*, however, it becomes clear that such corruption was not the exception, but the rule and that greediness extended as high up as the king himself. The *Panegyric* even claims that the Odovacrian peace, during which Pavia seemed to benefit in the *Life*, was a sham, for the presumed loyalty and bravery of Odovacer's soldiers were purchasable and could falter at a whim. These problems, moreover, were imagined to extend beyond the administration of Odovacer, trickling down to Italo-Roman society as a whole. Decline, per usual, begot decline in a domino-like fashion. And though Ennodius' panegyric was propagandistic in nature and full of expected embellishments, it nevertheless provided an image of the past, however distorted, that was based in reality and made sense of Italy's current gold age.[111]

Rather depressingly, Ennodius introduced Odovacer's Italy in his panegyric as a once "mighty land that had grown weak through the worthlessness of its governors."[112] Odovacer himself, though not specifically named, was described as a "ravager of the state" who had "brought failure to the public resources," despite an "undefiled peace," and had increased his treasury not so much "through taxation as rapine."[113] Such a "tyrant" and "poor master," Ennodius claimed, had "driven private assets into difficulty" and "provoked hatreds through his extravagance."[114] If this was not bad enough, the peace and stability secured by Odovacer's revolt in 476 had also proven shaky. The king could still command his legions, but he did so "cold with fear."[115] "Obedience," Ennodius explained, "was

of the Theoderican regime, it likewise manipulates that propaganda in an attempt to influence its recipient. Such manipulation was common to panegyrists, who subtly insinuated to their rulers how they ought to behave. Cf. Ficarra (1978), 254.

[111] See Nixon and Rodgers (1994), 33–5, on the value of panegyrics as historical sources. Cf. Rota (2001a), 203.

[112] *PanTh* 23: "per gubernantium vilitatem potens terra consenuerat." The Latin text used throughout is from Rohr's 1995 *MGH* edition, though the edition of Rota (2002), which differs in punctuation in some places, as well as Vogel's *MGH* edition, were consulted.

[113] *PanTh* 23: "Iam attulerat publicis opibus pax intemerata defectum, cum apud nos cottidianae depraedationis auctus successibus intestinus populator egeret, qui suorum prodigus incrementa aerarii non tam poscebat surgere vectigalibus quam rapinis."

[114] *PanTh* 23–4: "Saeviente ambitu pauper dominus odia effusione contraxerat.... Tunc enim aulae angustia in artum res privatas agitabat, nec micare usquam scintillas famulantum extinctus tyranni fomes indulserat." Cf. *AnonVal* 60, with Chp. 7.

[115] *PanTh* 24: "nam ire ad nutum suum legiones et remeare pavore algidus imperabat."

suspect," and Odovacer's lowly origins and assumption of power through a military coup exacerbated his suspicions. If he could seize power, he believed, any soldier could, and because his own officers were aware of this fact, "they feared that for which they were being feared."[116]

Beyond this mutual distrust, Ennodius denigrated the king's soldiers for their cowardice and infidelity in battle. He referred to them initially as a "faction of men apt to flee"; later he asserted that while engaging Theoderic's army their "pledges of loyalty faltered from prior decay and the feebleness of their limbs failed to complete their promised attacks."[117] In a final engagement Odovacer was even depicted trying to ply his "lax soldiers" with fine trappings and payments, attempting to buy their loyalty once more.[118] Odovacer himself, likewise, was described as a coward throughout the account. At one point Ennodius declared to the long-dead king, "the battle consumed your lines while you watched, not toiled."[119] The contrast with Theoderic, who twice in the course of the panegyric fought heroically alongside his troops, is unmistakable.[120]

But the reign of Odovacer, as intimated earlier, had repercussions beyond this weakening of the army and bankrupting of public and private assets. Not only had the venerable institutions of the Roman Empire suffered under Odovacer's poor stewardship, but Rome and the Roman way of life had suffered as well. Ennodius described the city of Rome, Romanness' greatest representative, as old and decrepit in the period leading up to, and in the immediate aftermath of, Theoderic's invasion. At one point he specifically addressed a personified Eternal City and beckoned her to come to Theoderic, "unmindful of your old age" and "trembling in your slipping footsteps."[121] The beleaguered and war-weary Rome of earlier panegyrics had at last succumbed to a long-overdue senescence, neglected by an impious Odovacer.[122]

---

[116] *Ibid.*: "suspecta enim est oboedientia quae famulatur indignis, et quotiens praelatos convenit conscientia stirpis ultimae, et illud metuunt, quod timentur." But see Cesa (1994), 312, who hypothesizes that Odovacer may have been of noble blood.

[117] For faction, *PanTh* 25: "pars fugacium proelia concitavit"; for faltering and feeble, *PanTh* 37: "adhuc tuorum dexterae de praecedenti tabe titubabant nec peragebat votivos impetus membrorum inbecillitas."

[118] *PanTh* 39: "Dum apud Veronam tuam apparatu nobili laxis manibus pugna instruebatur inpendiis." Cf. Rohr (1995), 225, and Rota (2002), 332.

[119] *PanTh* 38: "Interea acies tuae aspectu consummant proelia, non labore."

[120] See *PanTh* 31–5 (against the Gepids) and 42–7 (against Odovacer).

[121] *PanTh* 48: "Illic vellem ut aetatis inmemor, Roma, conmeares. Si venires lapsantibus tremebunda vestigiis, aevum gaudia conmutarent."

[122] See, for instance, Sidonius' *Pan. on Avitus*, ln. 45–60, and *Pan. on Majorian*, ln. 35–50. The Rome featured in these works, a likeness of Minerva, is still youthful, capable of brandishing a spear, and pugnacious. The theme of Rome as battle-weary and elderly, however, has

The Romans, themselves, on the other hand, and by this Ennodius meant Italo-Romans, were depicted as victims of poor policies. Theoderic's predecessors, not just Odovacer, had "loved ignorance, and never did what was praiseworthy."[123] Moreover, eloquence, an ideal so important to classically trained rhetoricians like Ennodius, an indicator of Roman nobility and a weapon of sorts particularly effective against uncouth barbarians like Euric, had been abandoned, replaced by the plow. Under Odovacer, it was bemoaned, "bodily strength negated whatever [eloquence's] expertise once bestowed."[124] Just as in the *Life of Epiphanius*, therefore, Romans were imitating barbarians; only now the phenomenon had become endemic. This lack of appreciation for educated men had also led to further corruption and decline; without erudition "the outcome of lawsuits gave way to chance and no value was given to written accounts."[125] "Everywhere," Ennodius concluded, "one massive sadness oppressed us, since inactivity was impairing the faculties of eloquent men; rapacious disregard was stealing away the ostentation of our elders, while the youth were not incited to excel at anything worthy of pursuit."[126]

Before the arrival of Theoderic, Ennodius' panegyric ultimately suggests, Italo-Roman society had been doomed.

precedents in earlier panegyrics. See Roberts (2001), 535–6. Odovacer, of course, did not neglect Rome entirely. See Stein (1949), vol. 2, 43f.; Chastagnol (1966), 52–6; and Moorhead (1992), 9 and 29.

[123] *PanTh* 76: "Amaverunt praecessores tui inscitiam, quia numquam laudanda gesserunt."

[124] *Ibid.*: "Sordebat inter aratra facundissimus et, quod peritia dederat, vis negabat." The lack of regard for education cannot be confirmed, though see Cassiodorus' comments in Chp. 2. For Theoderic's support of letters and lettered men, Chp. 8.

[125] *PanTh* 77: "In casu negotiorum nutabat eventus, quando litteris genius non dabatur."

[126] *Ibid.*: "Unus ubique ingenia maeror oppresserat, quia adterebant otia eloquentium facultates; pompam seniorum edax neglegentia possidebat nec accendebatur tiro aemulatione sectanda."

2

CASSIODORUS THE CALABRIAN

To this point Part I has relied exclusively on the writings of Magnus Felix Ennodius, a classically educated churchman of Gallo-Roman origins with a north Italian (Ligurian) outlook. Ennodius has acted more or less as the voice of Italo-Roman aristocratic malaise vis-à-vis the decline of Roman power during the course of the fifth century. Relevant passages from his most extensive works, the *Life of Epiphanius* and *Panegyric to Theoderic*, have been closely examined, providing a specific and coherent interpretation of this period. In Ennodius' version of the past, influenced in part by his own experiences, there were key factors that had contributed to overall notions of decadence and decline. The empire, he believed, had been denuded of its provinces and stripped of its honor by savages; it was feeble and weak with old age; it was a ship of state piloted by un-Roman, inept, and greedy rulers; and, though never falling in the traditional sense of the term, its sorry condition had persisted, eventually leading to social decay that extended to the masses.

Despite the coherence of this picture, it might easily be argued that this version of the past was unique to Ennodius and possibly even exceptional. Indeed, perhaps Ennodius should not be considered representative at all: The very notion of one individual representing the entirety of Italo-Roman society is dubious, not least because Italy and its Roman population were both quite diverse.[1] Among Ennodius' aristocratic peers, for instance, regional and familial origins differed, as did cultural leanings, chosen career paths, and personal loyalties, which could vary considerably when it came to political and ecclesiastical leadership, theological positions, and circus factions.[2] As a classically trained churchman of

[1] See, in general, Wickham (1981), 9–14, and Giardina (1997).
[2] See Pietri (1981) and Burgarella (2001), 144–57. Divisions of this sort occasionally inspired acts of violence in the city of Rome. For examples and Theoderic's response, Chp. 5. Even individual

Gallic origins and a proud inhabitant of the progressively frontierized province of Liguria, Ennodius himself is even indicative of this diversity. But an identity of this sort should not necessarily suggest that he was out of touch with mainstream aristocratic ideas, especially given his noble blood, traditional education, and powerful connections at Rome. This is not to say that Ennodius' understanding of the past was the only one in circulation; far from it.[3] But many of his sentiments do find harmony with the opinions evidenced in other Italian sources. These corroborating sources will be encountered in various ways throughout this study, but for the present the most important and most extensive in their treatment are the works of Magnus Aurelius Cassiodorus Senator, a second "representative" man.

A younger contemporary of Ennodius, Cassiodorus was a native of the seaside town of Squillace, located in the province of Lucania and Bruttium (modern Calabria) in southern Italy. He was born to a politically active family around 485 and perpetuated its tradition of public service under Theoderic and his successors. His illustrious career spanned the period between 504 and 537/8, during which time he loyally served as a consiliarius, quaestor, consul, corrector, master of offices, and praetorian prefect of Italy.[4] Like Ennodius, he was a classically trained rhetorician and prolific author, who composed numerous works, many in the service of the state.[5] Like Ennodius, his training and aristocratic connections imparted similar expectations of Roman order. Like Ennodius, he was a spiritual man, who developed important relations with the popes at Rome and eventually

---

family members were not immune, as Moorhead (1984a) so nicely demonstrates in the case of four Decian brothers.

[3] There are known partisans of Odovacer, for instance, who stood by him until the bitter end. The most notable was Petrus Marcellinus Felix Liberius, a friend and patron of Ennodius who will be encountered throughout this study. See Chp. 5, n. 59, for an overview of his career. Doubtless, men like Liberius would have been much more sympathetic to the reign of Odovacer, despite serving Theoderic and his immediate successors loyally. Cf. Moorhead (1992), 29–31, and Cesa (1994), 315–16.

[4] On Cassiodorus' career, O'Donnell (1979), 20–32; Krautschick (1983); Barnish (1992), xxxix–liii; and Giardina (2006). Though some have faulted Cassiodorus for being an opportunist, most generally do not doubt his loyalty to the Theoderican regime. For his loyalties after Theoderic's death, see the Epilogue.

[5] These works, which will be encountered later, included official letters (Variae), orations (surviving in fragments), a chronicle, and a (lost) history. For his later works, which were more spiritual and educational in tone, O'Donnell (1979), 103f.; Aricò (1986); and Barnish (1989).

retired to a monastery.[6] And like Ennodius, he was deeply attached to the region of his birth.[7]

Yet, unlike Ennodius, Cassiodorus was born just a few years before the Ostrogothic invasion of Italy, and as a consequence his understanding of the pre-Theoderican era was not derived from personal experience. Instead, it drew its inspiration from external sources: from the books that he read and most importantly, at least in his younger years, from the opinions of family and friends who had lived through this period, contemporaries of Epiphanius.[8] Their recollections, the remembrance of southerners, would have been quite different from the impressions of an individual from the north, where a great deal of the violence and disruption of the fifth century had occurred. Situated as they were at the opposite end of Italy, southerners were far removed from the world of high politics and intrigue that surrounded Ennodius and Epiphanius. Theirs was a land not of cities like Milan and Pavia, or of emperors, armies, and barbarians, but of great estates and powerful magnates, who increasingly abandoned decaying cities and city politics in favor of their villas. Here, since the fourth century, many had expanded their holdings, intensified production, and grown rich from slave and dependent labor, acquiring greater local and regional influence owing to the demands of Rome and the imperial court.[9] The crises of the fifth century, especially the loss of North Africa to the Vandals, had only increased the value of their products and support, and as Sicily and southern Italy became the pantry, so to speak, of an increasingly desperate Roman Empire, they were left to their own devices and spared the turmoil of incessant war.[10] There remained, of course, agents of the central

---

[6] Unlike Ennodius, he may have supported Laurentius during the Laurentian Schism. He was intimate with the scholar-monk Dionysius Exiguus and later, in the mid-530s, attempted to found a Christian school at Rome with the assistance of Pope Agapitus. On his monastery at Vivarium, see later discussion.

[7] See, for instance, *Variae* 12.15 for an encomium of Cassiodorus' home region. Cf. *Variae* 11.14, for a similar laudation of the region around Como, an area disparaged by the northerner Ennodius in a letter to the senator Faustus (#10).

[8] See later discussion for Cassiodorus' reading (and alteration) of the *Chronicle* of Prosper of Aquitaine. The books that Cassiodorus read likewise made an impression on his feelings about Gaul. See Chp. 9. This is not to say that books and family members did not make an impression on Ennodius. But at sixteen years old, Ennodius could (and did) decide for himself what to make of Theoderic's invasion, while Cassiodorus, a mere four-year-old, could not.

[9] See especially Noyé (1996).

[10] *Ibid.*, with Cracco Ruggini (1986), 246–8; Christie (1996), 263–4; and Barnish (1987). Cf. Wickham (2005), 204f., who emphasizes the long-term impoverishment of this region as a result of a the severing of the Italy-Africa link.

authority, such as governors and counts, stationed in various cities. And likewise, armies and barbarians, usually marauding Vandals, occasionally passed through the region.[11] But compared to Ennodius' Liguria, Bruttium and Lucania was an independent safe haven, plagued more by internal corruption and local factionalism than any outside threat.[12]

Generally speaking, then, these southern gentlemen had prospered over the course of the fifth century, and the Cassiodori were not an exception. Their power and influence had grown significantly at this time, and they expanded their holdings to include large estates throughout the region, including Sicily.[13] Yet in other ways the Cassiodori were less typical, and this too was an important factor in the formation of Cassiodorus as a person. For one, despite multiple generations of naturalization, the Cassiodori were eastern transplants, possibly from Syria, and they continued to have contacts and even family members in the Greek-speaking world. This, no doubt, helped to inform Cassiodorus' appreciation of Greek culture and colored his impression of matters eastern.[14] More importantly and more influentially, the Cassiodori had held high office as a means of augmenting their authority, both locally and beyond, at a time when many southern magnates were shunning curial and imperial service. Cassiodorus' great-grandfather, for example, had acquired the rank of *vir inlustris*, the highest of the senatorial grades, and was sufficiently well established to amass and lead a private army in the face of a Vandal raid. His grandfather, likewise, had served as a tribune and notary under Emperor Valentinian III, acting as an envoy to the court of Attila and obtaining illustrious rank. And his father, finally, had held two countships under Odovacer and had acquired

[11] For a Vandal incursion involving Cassiodorus' great-grandfather, see later discussion. Though a threat to southern Italy, Vandal aggression was more regularly directed toward Sicily and had ceased altogether by the reign of Odovacer. See Saitta (1987), 365–81; Kislinger (1994); and Goltz (1997).

[12] For local factionalism and the largely "hands-off" policy of the central administration (continued under Theoderic), Cracco Ruggini (1986); Saitta (1987), 381f.; and Noyé (2007). During Theoderic's reign, Goths and Gothic officials were concentrated in the north of Italy, though there were a few notable garrisons at key locations (nearly all urban) in the south. See Bierbrauer (1973), 12–15, and Azzara (2006), 9–10. Such conditions rendered southern Italy a frontier of sorts.

[13] For the fifth-century rise of the Cassiodori, O'Donnell (1979), 17–20, and later discussion. Their most extensive holdings were in Calabria at Squillace, where Cassiodorus later founded the joint monastic communities of Vivarium and Castellum. He also may have founded a similar community at Taormina in Sicily. See Barnish (1989), 166.

[14] For Syria, O'Donnell (1979), 15–17 and 267–8, and Barnish (1992), xxxvii. For Cassiodori in the East (Heliodorus), Chp. 6. For Cassiodorus' appreciation of Greek culture, O'Donnell (1979), 16–17 and chp. 6, and Garzya (1986). It is unclear how much Greek he knew, though his origins in the south of Italy (*Magna Graecia*) are suggestive.

a governorship in Sicily. He was credited with handing this province over to Theoderic peacefully and was later rewarded with another regional governorship in southern Italy, the office of praetorian prefect, and a patriciate.[15]

This, then, was a family with strong roots in the south, but also important contacts to the north that were derived from generations of participation in the imperial administration.[16] Contacts like these would have exposed its members, including a young Cassiodorus, to the world of high politics and intrigue featured in the *Life of Epiphanius*. Unlike most southerners, they had lived and worked, from time to time, in Ravenna and Rome and participated in the empire's struggles firsthand. They understood the manifold crises and disappointments of the fifth century and, though never fully a part of Ennodius' world, they were aware of it and could sympathize with its concerns. Moreover, their own successes, though a source of pride, had not come easy. Only in the era of Theoderic had this family's long history of loyal service really been recognized and given its proper remuneration. Only under Theoderic had the Cassiodori reached their zenith, a patent reminder that times had not always been so felicitous for this noble house and that its sacrifices, until recently, had gone underrewarded.

Like Ennodius, therefore, Cassiodorus found good reason to disapprove of the fifth century. He may have even helped to popularize the relative neologism *modernus* (modern) as a means of separating his own, contemporary era of blessedness from the gloomier epoch preceding it.[17] But for him, fifth-century disappointments were not simply a matter of lost prestige or territory for the Roman Empire, though both, as will be seen, were important. Instead, and true to his origins and chosen career path, the status of the empire was directly related to the honor and standing of its traditional office-holding nobility, of families like his own. The situation

---

[15] Much of this information is described by Cassiodorus himself in *Variae* 1.3 and 1.4. See also O'Donnell (1979), 18–20, and Barnish (1992), xxxvii–xxxix, with *PLRE* 2, 263–5 (Cassiodorus 1–3).

[16] Cf. Barnish (1992), xxxvii. The *Anecdoton Holderi* (or *Ordo Generis Cassiodororum*) may even suggest that this family had established marriage ties with the powerful Anicii clan, since it implies that Cassiodorus claimed kinship with Symmachus and Boethius. See Momigliano (1955), 215–16, and (1960), 243–4, and Barnish (1992), xxxviii. As tantalizing as this may be, the *Anecdoton* should be used with caution, since it is a self-described "excerpta" of a lost document. Its claims of kinship, therefore, may be fictive or the unintended product of excerption. See Usener (1877); O'Donnell (1979), 13–15 and 259–66; Martino (1982), 33–6; Krautschick (1983), 78–84; Dolbeau (1983); Viscido (1985) and (1986a); and Galonnier (1996) and (1997).

[17] On *modernus*, Freund (1957) and Moorhead (2006). For blessedness, Chp. 10.

in Italy was thus not quite as Ennodius had presented it. Society had not simply abandoned its core values through a steady process of attrition, imitating its increasingly "barbarized" leaders. Instead, the leadership itself was to blame for ceasing to promote those men who actually cherished these values, among whom Cassiodorus counted his ancestors. The Cassiodori and those like them, in other words, had not become barbarians. But the net result was still an impression of a fifth-century empire badly in need of resuscitation and desperate for a *pius princeps*, a dutiful ruler.

Two of Cassiodorus' works, his lesser *Chronicle* and larger *Variae* collection, make this abundantly clear, demonstrating that, while not in complete agreement, Cassiodorus was sympathetic to Ennodius' views.

Cassiodorus the Historian

It is well known that Cassiodorus wrote an extensive history, designated by him as a "Roman history of the Goths," that unfortunately does not survive.[18] Begun and finished sometime between 519 and 533,[19] in the two decades following Felix's consulship, it consisted of twelve books and contained, among other topics, a royal genealogy of the Amal house, the royal clan of Theoderic.[20] Though the scholarly conjecture and debate concerning this lost work are tremendous, there is little doubt that, as an official work commissioned by Theoderic, it had the main purpose of eulogizing the king and his family and drawing attention to the benefits of his reign. The work, therefore, would have contained information relevant to an official or semiofficial understanding of the past, one endorsed by Cassiodorus, that contrasted the golden age of the present with earlier (but comparatively recent) catastrophes. Had it survived, it would have been an invaluable source for this period. But since it has not survived, scholars

---

[18] *Variae* 9.25.5: "Originem gothicam historiam fecit esse romanam." Its relationship to the *Getica* of Jordanes will not be treated here. But see Chp. 6 for relevant bibliography.

[19] The *History* postdates Cassiodorus' *Chronicle* (discussed shortly), which was completed in 519, and *Variae* 9.25 demonstrates that it was in circulation by 533. When during this period (519–33) it was begun and then finished is uncertain. The *Anecdoton Holderi* claims that it was commissioned by Theoderic, providing a date as late as 526, but its reliability is unclear. Some scholars have even suggested that it was only partially completed in 533 and that Cassiodorus continued editing and updating the work as late as the early 550s. Such hypotheses, however, are highly speculative and should probably be rejected. See Momigliano (1955); Bradley (1966); O'Donnell (1979), 43–5; Luiselli (1980), 228–9; Krautschick (1983), 26f.; Barnish (1984); Croke (1987), 117, and (2005a), 473; and Weißensteiner (1994).

[20] For twelve books, *Variae*, praef. 11; *Anecdoton Holderi*; Jordanes, *Getica* 1 and 315. For Amal genealogy, *Variae* 9.25.5 and 11.1.19, with Chp. 6.

must rely instead on a lesser historical work, a prototype of sorts for his lost history, namely, Cassiodorus' *Chronicle (Chronica)*.[21]

This work, like Cassiodorus' history, was an official commission, but presumably much less ambitious or original. Composed in 519, in celebration of the consulship of Theoderic's son-in-law and intended heir, Eutharic, it provided an abbreviated history of the world from creation to the present. It was thus a universal history, written in the style of previous world chronicles, that quickly developed into a "consular" history and culminated with the blessings of the Theoderican era.[22] Most of this work was excerpted from earlier chronicles, verbatim.[23] And later portions, while original to Cassiodorus, are generally straightforward. Yet some entries are indeed noteworthy and do, in fact, provide glimpses into Cassiodorus "the historian," his conception of the past, and (as will be seen in later chapters) its contrast with the present.

It is revealing, first of all, to note that the terminology used throughout the *Chronicle* is just as vague as contemporary sources when it comes to the empire and its emperors. Emperors, according to Cassiodorus, exercised royal and imperial power (*regnare* and *imperare*); their realms were both a kingdom and empire (*regnum* and *imperium*); and their titles were interchangeable, including *imperator*, *Augustus* (or the lesser *Caesar*), and *princeps*. Eastern and western portions of the Roman Empire, moreover, were generally distinguished from one another, often in revealing ways. Cassiodorus' entries for the years 457 and 474 provide cases in point. In the first, Leo was said to receive the "empire of the east" (*Orientis imperium*), and Majorian the "empire of Italy" (*Italiae imperium*). In the latter, Zeno succeeded Leo in the empire (*in imperium*) and ruled (*regnavit*) for seventeen years; while at Rome Nepos succeeded Glycerius in the kingdom (*in regno*).[24] Still other notices were more conventional. Hence, the entry

---

[21] Cf. O'Donnell (1979), 36f.

[22] It is difficult to accept the conclusion that Cassiodorus' chronicle is simply a consular chronicle, despite its author's claim to have composed "consules in ordinem." The chronicle begins with Adam and continues with Assyrian kings and then Latin and Roman kings (none of whom was a consul). It is true that the preponderance of the chronicle is concerned with the listing of consuls, but this is also the case in the rather Romanocentric Christian world chronicles on which Cassiodorus based his own. Cf. O'Donnell (1979), 37, and Luiselli (1980), 226. For a broader discussion, which supports the position taken in this note, Croke (2001).

[23] The work is heavily dependent on the *Chronica* of Jerome and Prosper of Aquitaine, as well as an epitome of Livy. See the introduction in Mommsen's *MGH* edition (1894), 111–13.

[24] *CassChron*, anno 457: "His conss. Marciano defuncto LEO Orientis, Maiorianus Italiae suscepit imperium"; and *CassChron*, anno 474: "cui ZENO successit in imperio, qui regnavit annis XVII.... Eo etiam anno Romae Glycerio Nepos successit in regno."

for 467 recorded that the emperor (*imperator*) Leo sent Anthemius to Italy, where he received the empire (*imperium*).[25]

Cassiodorus and Ennodius, therefore, agreed on terminology, and this is not surprising given that they were contemporaries whose styles were derived from a similar education. Yet Cassiodorus' depiction of fifth-century events in this source was more traditional than Ennodius', and not simply because a chronicle, unlike a panegyric or work of hagiography, hardly allowed for nuance. In fact, in a few instances, Cassiodorus showed some originality by making minor alterations to his original sources, intending to cast the Goths in a more favorable light. Thus, he inserted a brief comment on Alaric's mercy during the sack of Rome, a commonplace by the time he was writing, and noted other instances of Gothic service on behalf of the empire.[26] Notices like these, however, were exceptions rather than the rule. Generally speaking, and quite different from the world encountered in the preceding chapter, the barbarians featured in Cassiodorus' *Chronicle* were the traditional foes of the empire, whose savagery and deceit had cost it dearly over the course of the fifth century.

The Vandals, the barbarians who posed the greatest threat to Cassiodorus' (southern) Italy, provide a noteworthy example. The *Chronicle*'s treatment of their depredation is derived from an earlier source, but as a major abbreviation of that source, it demonstrates that Cassiodorus actually *read* this work and chose from its contents judiciously. Sparing in details, his entry for 439 simply records that the Vandal king Gaiseric had captured Carthage through a "false peace," at a time when "nothing was feared concerning his friendship."[27] The next year Gaiseric "violently afflicted Sicily," and the year after this, and much to the empire's discredit, a punitive expedition was conducted, quite revealingly, by an eastern Roman emperor who made war "ineffectively."[28] Next, the entry for 442 records that the

---

[25] *CassChron*, anno 467: "His conss. Anthemius a Leone imp. ad Italiam mittitur, qui tertio ab urbe miliario in loco Brontotas suscepit imperium."

[26] See the comments in Mommsen's *MGH* edition (1894), 113–14, with O'Donnell (1979), 38–41, and Moorhead (1999), 255–8, which provide other instances of Cassiodorus' deliberate (but minor) distortions regarding the Goths (e.g. downplaying Gothic Arianism). Cf. Luiselli (1980), 226–7, who, while acknowledging these distortions, is keen to point out that in most entries the Goths are treated no differently from other barbarians.

[27] *CassChron*, anno 439: "Ginsericus, de cuius amicitia nihil metuebatur, Carthaginem dolo pacis invadit." Cf. Prosper of Aquitaine, 1339, which is twelve lines long in the *MGH* edition and elaborates on the Vandals' cruelty and impiety during Carthage's capture.

[28] *CassChron*, anno 440: "His conss. Ginsericus Siciliam graviter affligit"; and anno 441: "His conss. Theodosius imp. bellum contra Vandalos inefficaciter movit." Cf. Prosper of Aquitaine, 1342 and 1344. The former is seven lines long, while the latter is four lines and lacks the adverb *inefficaciter*.

western emperor, Valentinian III, made peace with Gaiseric and granted the Vandals a larger portion of Africa.[29] And while this seems to have secured an important respite from Vandal expansion for more than a decade (they cease to be mentioned), by 455 that peace had failed, the Vandals had sacked Rome itself, and Cassiodorus, having just described the intervening devastations caused by Attila and his Huns, summarized the rather melodramatic source at his disposal by simply writing that, "in the same year, through Gaiseric, Rome was emptied of all its riches."[30]

The *Chronicle*'s treatment of fifth-century emperors is similarly traditional, casting them as unquestionable and legitimate heads of state, deserving of their subjects' respect, but failing to live up to expectations. An excellent example of this can be found in Cassiodorus' treatment of Ricimer, a treatment that is original to his work. While Ennodius had depicted this generalissimo in a sympathetic light, Cassiodorus took a position analogous to the one expressed by Anthemius in the *Life of Epiphanius*. In his view, Ricimer was indeed a crafty barbarian and an enemy of the state. Restricted to just a few short sentences, the Ricimer of the *Chronicle* is an overwhelmingly negative entity, who contributed personally to the ruin of the western empire. He made and unmade emperors at will, implicitly mocking the imperial office, and was blamed explicitly for the deaths of multiple emperors. Majorian and Severus were murdered, according to Cassiodorus, the latter poisoned by the "deceit of Ricimer."[31] His role in the death of Anthemius, likewise, received a serious rebuke. "After he made Olybrius Emperor at Rome," Cassiodorus recorded, "the patrician Ricimer killed Anthemius contrary to the reverence owed to a *princeps* and the laws of affinity."[32] The act itself he labeled specifically as a crime (*scelus*), and no doubt, if featured in Cassiodorus' nonextant history,

---

[29] *CassChron*, anno 442: "Cum Ginserico ab Augusto Valentiniano pax confirmata et certis spatiis Africa inter utrosque divisa est." Cf. Prosper of Aquitaine, 1347. Aside from spelling differences, the entries are the same, though 1348 continues by treating a conspiracy against Gaiseric in the same year.

[30] *CassChron*, anno 455: "Eodem anno per Ginsericum omnibus opibus suis Roma vacuata." Cf. Prosper of Aquitaine, 1375, where, at 31 lines, the account is extremely detailed. It concludes with the portion adapted by Cassiodorus (p. 484, ln. 27–31), itself an abbreviation of a longer sentence.

[31] *CassChron*, anno 461: "His conss. Maiorianus inmissione Ricimeris extinguitur, cui Severum natione Lucanum Ravennae succedere fecit in regnum"; and anno 465: "His conss., ut dicitur Ricimeris fraude, Severus Romae in Palatio veneno peremptus est." The Lucanian origin is a nice touch, betraying Cassiodorus' affinity for the region.

[32] *CassChron*, anno 472: "His conss. patricius Ricimer Romae facto imperatore Olybrio Anthemium contra reverentiam principis et ius adfinitatis cum gravi clade civitatis extinguit. Qui non diutius peracto scelere gloriatus est XL dies defunctus est."

the Ricimer depicted here would have seemed almost the alter ego of the concerned patron of Liguria encountered in the *Life of Epiphanius*.

Cassiodorus and Ennodius, therefore, disagreed on certain, finer points of fifth-century history. But despite such differences, Cassiodorus' *Chronicle* demonstrates that he too understood the situation to have been "contrary" (literally *contra*) to the way that it should have been, echoing Ennodius' sentiments of a world of inversions. Just a few carefully chosen words reveal his loyalties toward the empire and its emperors, even "little Greeks" like Anthemius, and just a few carefully chosen words betray his rather traditional, and indeed the official, perspective on the barbarian enemies of Rome and the devastation that they had caused.

And yet, one- and two-sentence entries in a chronicle are admittedly little on which to base such conclusions, and so further corroboration is desirable. As already suggested, the *Variae* collection can serve in just this capacity. Here, Cassiodorus' disappointment with the fifth century, and especially its leadership, becomes much clearer, and critiques bearing greater resemblance to those made by Ennodius can be readily discerned.

THE *VARIAE*

The *Variae* is a collection of 468 official documents written by Cassiodorus and spanning the period of his public career. Its contents, divided into twelve books, range from letters and edicts to formulas and veritable panegyrics. Most of these were composed in the name of Theoderic and his successors and are thus invaluable sources for the history of "Ostrogothic" Italy. As such, they reflect the official position of the Ravenna government and the individuals for whom they were composed, rather than necessarily those of Cassiodorus. As he put it in a formula, his duties had placed him "on intimate terms with [their] thoughts," and he had internalized "the desires of [their] minds." He assumed "the words of the sovereign," becoming the "mouth of the *princeps*." And, of necessity, he spoke "with gravity and embellishments," saying what he knew his masters felt, so that his orders were "thought to have come from [them]."[33]

---

[33] *Variae* 6.5.2: "Haec nostris cogitationibus necessario familiariter applicatur, ut proprie dicere possit quod nos sentire cognoscit: arbitrium suae voluntatis deponit et ita mentis nostrae velle suscipit, ut a nobis magis putetur exisse quod loquitur." For mouth and gravity, *Variae* 6.5.3: "graviter et ornate dicere, ut possit animos iudicum commovere, quanto facundior debet esse, qui ore principis populos noscitur ammonere"; with *Variae* 6.5.6: "sic ore nostro glorificatus eloquere." These citations are derived from a formula for the appointment of a quaestor, in which capacity (even when not holding this office) Cassiodorus composed the majority of his *Variae*. According to Maas (1986), 27, quaestors like the emperor Justininian's own Tribonian

Cassiodorus' role in these documents, therefore, was largely cosmetic and stylistic, and this is confirmed to some extent by the existence of official Theoderican correspondence not written by him, but espousing similar ideologies.[34] Yet Cassiodorus' long and loyal service to the Ravenna government, even in adverse times, suggests that the ideas encapsulated in the *Variae* were not terribly different from his own.[35] Indeed, his choice to edit and publish the collection is revealing; so too the time of its publication, 537/8, when Justinian's armies had already conquered much of Italy and the situation was going downhill fast. As a whole, then, the *Variae* can be read as an apology of sorts for Gothic rule and Italo-Roman collaboration, despite the absence of this specific motivation in Cassiodorus' preface.[36] Certain items seem deliberately selected and placed within the collection, and, if accidental, the impression is still overwhelmingly positive, casting Theoderic especially in a legitimate and thoroughly Roman light, just as Cassiodorus had viewed him and wanted him to be viewed.[37]

Moreover, and more telling, Cassiodorus dedicated the last two books of the *Variae* to documents penned in his own name while serving as praetorian prefect of Italy, lest, as he claimed, "I, who have spoken as the king's mouth, should go unrecognized [for what was spoken] in my own name."[38] And these, though still official in nature, provide important insights into his expectations and understandings of the period, rather than simply

(c. 535–40) lent their literary skills to the practical needs of their sovereigns. The result was "not merely the consequence of individual stylistic idiosyncrasy but ... [a] collaborative effort at the highest level." Cf. Sirago (1986), 180–1.

[34] These are collected in the so-called *Epistulae Theodericianae Variae* and in the royal precepts of the *Acta Synhodorum Habitarum Romae*, portions of which are cited throughout.

[35] Moorhead (1999), 246f., provides a similar interpretation of the *Variae* as an expression of Cassiodorus' and his sovereign's views, while Krautschick (1983), 118f., even sees Cassiodorus as a driving force behind the policies of Amalasuentha's reign.

[36] *Variae*, praef. 9, however, does come close to making this claim, citing a desire on Cassiodorus' part to record for posterity the many royal favors shown to men who were worthy to receive illustrious dignities. Cf. Gillett (1998), who denies the apologetic/propagandistic nature of this work and suggests that its contents are not necessarily a reflection of Cassiodorus' loyalties. Gillett sees the work as an epistolary collection intended for Cassiodorus' bureaucratic peers, a demonstration of his own career and talents, and a model of style for others. Cf. Giardina (2006), 29–39. It seems best to conclude (as the preface suggests) that the work served many purposes.

[37] Krautschick (1983) concludes similarly and sees the selection of materials as quite deliberate. But see the introduction to Barnish (1992), xvi–xvii, who provides a list of "cracks beneath the surface" that Cassiodorus failed to cover up adequately. Barnwell (1992), 166f., and Bjornlie (2009) even go so far as to suggest that these documents are not entirely authentic (the former much more than the latter), making the contents all the more intentional and constructed.

[38] *Variae* 11, praef. 4: "ut qui decem libris ore regio sum locutus, ex persona propria non haberer incognitus."

those of his masters. Significantly, one of these very documents contains Cassiodorus' most vivid treatment of the fifth century and its woes. Here, like his Ligurian contemporary, he presented a version of the past where imperial ineptitude had cost the empire provinces and prestige, and where sixth-century reprisals had avenged such injuries.

The context was an encomium, an original work written in the style of a panegyric and delivered before the Senate at Rome in 533.[39] Its subject was Amalasuentha, the daughter of Theoderic, who was then acting as regent for her young son, Athalaric. This was not the first time that Italy or its empire had been ruled by a woman, and true to the expectations of his genre, Cassiodorus took the opportunity to draw comparisons.[40] A century prior, Galla Placidia, the daughter of Theodosius I, had also served as regent for a purple-clad son named Valentinian. But while, in hindsight, she had largely failed to live up to her noble lineage, Amalasuentha was depicted as exceeding, by far, all expectations. The former, in Cassiodorus' view, had played a fundamental role in the ruin of the Roman Empire, the latter in its continued florescence under a Gothic aegis.

A Placid Empire

Obviously, Cassiodorus' objections to the regency of Placidia should not have been based on gender, since the comparison being made was between two women. Nevertheless, the Roman view of women as naturally weak and fickle (*infirmitas* and *levitas sexus*) did subtly underlie his critique. It was evident, in Cassiodorus' estimation, that both women's gender-specific qualities were demonstrably opposed and with consequences for their respective reigns. Though Placidia was praised foremost for being "glorious in her imperial lineage" and for rearing a "purple-clad son" (fundamental roles for an imperial matron), she was denigrated for her rather feeble administration of the empire.[41] "Feeble," construed by the adverb *remisse*, was a clever word choice on Cassiodorus' part. On the one hand, it suggested the weakness understood to be innate in all womankind

---

[39] For an analysis, Romano (1978), 32–5, and Fauvinet-Ranson (1998). The latter suggests (p. 278) that Cassiodorus' panegyric may not have been given at Rome, but sent to the Senate while he was serving as praetorian prefect in Ravenna.

[40] On the expectation, Menander Rhetor, *Peri Epideiktikon (Basilikos Logos)* 377.

[41] *Variae* 11.1.9: "Placidiam mundi opinione celebratam, aliquorum principum prosapia gloriosam purpurato filio studuisse percepimus, cuius dum remisse administrat imperium, indecenter cognoscitur imminutum." Domenico (1978), 34, rightly points out that by drawing attention to Placidia's noble house, Cassiodorus was indirectly praising Amalasuentha's own pedigree. For the legitimizing role of Amal descent, see especially Chp. 6.

(*infirmitas*) and, on the other, its ancillary meaning of "peacefully" or "placidly" (*placide*) played quite nicely upon Placidia's own name.[42] In keeping with this idea, Cassiodorus complained that Placidia had destroyed her soldiers "with too much peace,"[43] later commenting that long periods of peace "soften" (*molire*) soldiers;[44] this softness, too, was a condition of the feminine sex, suggesting a kind of feminization of the empire's once valiant and manly soldiers. Placidia's placidity, then, had seriously undermined the Roman Empire's ability to assert or even defend itself.

In contrast to Placidia's softness and weakness, Amalasuentha was a perfect combination of the masculine and feminine qualities necessary for a female ruler. Her foresight, a virtue inherited from her father,[45] had prevented an excess or a lack of warfare from having a negative effect on the disposition of her soldiers. As a result, Cassiodorus claimed, "our soldiers terrify our enemies,"[46] a situation rather different from that of the fifth century. The extent of this terror was phenomenal and treated at length by Cassiodorus, his references to fearful or subservient Franks, Burgundians, and even Byzantines no doubt reminding his audience that in fairly recent times these very foes had posed serious threats to Italy.[47] Such valor, by its very Latin name, *virtus*, was a condition of manliness obviously alien to Placidia and her times, but now embraced by the Amal princess. Amalasuentha, however, was also a mother and, just as Placidia, had served as a conduit for royalty through her childbearing capacity. Her dual role as both *mater patriae* and *pater patriae* was, hence, nothing short of a miracle. Cassiodorus went so far as to exclaim, "Behold, under God's watch our happy mistress has done what is excellent for both sexes, for she has begotten for us a glorious king and defended a very extensive empire with the fortitude of her mind."[48] Her embodiment of masculine and feminine roles was a patent reminder of the marriage of Goths and

---

[42] Cf. Fauvinet-Ranson (1998), 299.

[43] *Variae* 11.1.9: "militem quoque nimia quiete dissolvit."

[44] *Variae* 11.1.10: "Qui [i.e. exercitus] provida dispositione libratus nec assiduis bellis adteritur nec iterum longa pace mollitur."

[45] *Variae* 11.1.19: "enituit ... sapientia, ut iam vidistis, inclitus pater [i.e. Theoderic]." For the connection between *sapientia* and *providentia*, both virtues associated with emperors, Nixon and Rogers (1994), 10–12, and Rota (2002), 96. Foresightedness and wisdom are attributed regularly to Theoderic in the sources. Cf. *Variae* 3.41, 4.5, and 4.19; *PanTh* 51; *AnonVal* 61; Jordanes, *Romana* 349; and Procopius, *Wars* 5.1.27.

[46] *Variae* 11.1.10: "Sub hac autem domina ... noster exercitus terret externos."

[47] See *Variae* 11.1.10–13, along with the Epilogue. For similar references from the reign of Theoderic, Chps. 5, 9, and 10.

[48] *Variae* 11.1.14: "Ecce praestante deo felix domina quod habet eximium uterque sexus implevit: nam et gloriosum regem nobis edidit et latissimum imperium animi fortitudine vindicavit."

Romans that had rescued and reinvigorated the Roman Empire: a union of wise, yet effeminate and decadent Romans with manly and courageous, but unruly Goths.[49] In contrast, Placidia's reign stood for the decadence and decline of the fifth century, a time of proud Roman leadership that was ultimately ineffectual and weak.

Cassiodorus' critique also extended beyond the specific qualities of these two rulers. Like Ennodius, he believed that the loss of territory long held by the West was indicative of the incompetent management characteristic of the fifth century, management that had dealt a serious blow to Roman prestige. But, whereas Ennodius' *Life of Epiphanius* had emphasized the loss of Gaul to the archetypically barbarous Euric, Cassiodorus focused on the predation of Illyricum not by barbarians but by other Romans, namely, the "Greeks" at Constantinople.[50] Cassiodorus, of course, was by no means hostile to Greeks or Greekness and clearly viewed both eastern and western courts as legitimate sources of Roman power.[51] But his portrayal of these events reiterates the tension between western and eastern Romans already encountered in the Anthemius episode of the *Life of Epiphanius* and hinted at in his *Chronicle*. As a westerner and a native Latin speaker with south Italian sympathies, he naturally sided with the West whenever conflict arose between both empires. And in this particular episode, since Italy's sphere of influence had been violated by the East, the eastern Romans were portrayed as usurpers and betrayers of their western consorts. Their presumption was outrageous. But Placidia's weakness had allowed for it, and it was she, therefore, who received Cassiodorus' rebuke.

The particular straits into which Placidia and young Valentinian III had fallen received no mention in the account, despite Cassiodorus' awareness of them, likely because this might have justified her actions.[52] Only recently, in 423, had they fled from the hostile western emperor, Honorius, seeking refuge in Constantinople at the court of Theodosius II. The following year,

---

[49] For an elaboration, Chp. 5.

[50] And this despite the fact that there were plenty of barbarians in the region who had played a role in the empire's decline. See Lemerle (1954), 277–81, and Šašel (1979). Indeed, other sixth-century Italians drew attention to these very barbarians in their works. Cf. Ennodius, *Vita Beati Antonii* 12–13, and Eugippius, *Vita Severini*, where they are ubiquitous.

[51] The language of his *Chronica* makes this abundantly clear, referring to both realms as the "occidentale" and "orientale imperium," respectively. Theodosius II, who ruled from Constantinople, moreover, is said to have ruled the "Romanum imperium" alone ("solus," i.e. both east and west) until appointing Valentinian III as his Caesar (later referred to as an Augustus). Cf. *CassChron*, anno 423 and 424.

[52] For Cassiodorus' awareness, *CassChron*, anno 423–5, with Fauvinet-Ranson (1998), 298–9.

Honorius had died and a usurper with no dynastic ties to the house of Theodosius had been proclaimed emperor in Ravenna. It was unclear how Theodosius would respond to these developments, but Placidia was desperate to secure Valentinian's recognition as the rightful western emperor and needed military assistance to press their case. She thus offered to cede to the eastern empire portions of Illyricum and, in exchange, acquired recognition, an east Roman army, and a bride from the house of Theodosius for her son, binding East and West further through a dynastic alliance.[53]

The bargain was quite effective for Placidia's purposes, but in retrospect, Cassiodorus was unimpressed. The act, he claimed, had "indecently impaired the [western] Empire,"[54] and Placidia had "acquired a daughter-in-law through the loss of Illyricum and caused a division lamentable to the provinces."[55] It mattered not from his early sixth-century perspective that peace and harmony had been restored, since this "harmony" was viewed as a state of inequality that had meant a loss of territory and face to the East.[56] Cassiodorus could justifiably conclude, therefore, that Valentinian "had endured, while protected by his mother, what scarcely could have been suffered without her,"[57] and continue in his encomium of Amalasuentha by celebrating her reconquest of some of these very lands. "Contrary to the will of the eastern emperor," he exclaimed, Amalasuentha "had made the Danube Roman (again)."[58]

CASSIODORUS AND ODOVACER

Thus far the examination of Cassiodorus' works has demonstrated the broader appeal of some of Ennodius' sentiments concerning the status of the empire during the fifth century. Though neither wholeheartedly agreed with the other, and sometimes, owing to their individual backgrounds, they even patently disagreed, both found common ground in their general

---

[53] For reconstructions, Bury (1958), vol. 1, 221–5; Kaegi (1968), 19–23; and Heather (2006), 258–60. The fact that Theodosius II had not recognized Valentinian III's father, Constantius III, as emperor presumably rendered his aid even more uncertain.

[54] *Variae* 11.1.9: "administrat imperium, indecenter cognoscitur imminutum."

[55] *Ibid.*: "amissione Illyrici comparavit factaque est coniunctio regnantis divisio dolenda provinciis."

[56] Despite the fact that lands in the Balkans had switched from the western to eastern empire, and vice versa, a number of times before this. See Demougeot (1981).

[57] *Variae* 11.1.9: "Pertulit a matre protectus quod vix pati potuit destitutus."

[58] *Variae* 11.1.10: "contra Orientis principis votum Romanum fecit esse Danuvium." For commentary, Fauvinet-Ranson (1998), 287. Certain lands along the Danube had already been reclaimed by Theoderic during the Sirmian War, an act that was likewise praised for its restitutive effect. See *PanTh* 69, with Chp. 5.

assessment of the outrages of this period. Whether emperors were lazy, weak, barbarous, or all of the above, the simple fact was that they had failed the state, the greatest expression of this being the loss of provinces and, by association, prestige for the Roman Empire (embodied for them in Italy). In Ennodius' estimation, the Roman Empire continued well beyond 476, but so too did its concomitant miseries. Cassiodorus shared this vision, presenting a history of fifth-century decadence that culminated with the reign of Odovacer and was decisively ended by the glorious advent of Theoderic.

Since it doubtless would have provided important details as to the nature of Odovacer's reign, it is once again particularly unfortunate that Cassiodorus' official history does not survive. Nevertheless, both the *Variae* and the *Chronicle* suggest that his impression of Odovacer was just as ambiguous as Ennodius', viewing him more or less as a successor to the western emperors. Most telling, perhaps, is the world chronicle genre itself with its divisions into nations and eras. Had Cassiodorus imagined that 476 represented a decisive break, a new heading would have been necessary. That Odovacer's and later Theoderic's reign fell under the rubric "Imperatores Romani" surely implies that the chronicler's impression was one of continuity.[59] Likewise, in the few references to Odovacer and his reign found in the *Variae*, Cassiodorus seems to echo this understanding of continuity, referring to Odovacer tellingly as a *princeps* and his realm as the *res publica*.[60]

It is nonetheless clear from the chronicle entry for 476 that Cassiodorus was aware of certain differences between Odovacer and his predecessors. Specifically, Cassiodorus wrote that Odovacer had "assumed the name of king, though he employed neither purple nor the imperial insignia."[61] The title "rex," of course, should not be alarming, since, as demonstrated previously, kingship was thought by fifth- and sixth-century Italo-Romans to be wholly consistent with imperial rule. What was strange, then, was not that Odovacer had taken the name of king, but that he refused to adopt the proper attire of one, that is, imperial purple and insignia.[62] Cassiodorus

---

[59] Cassiodorus' division and calculation of Roman history at the end of this work is also revealing, reckoning the present era from Brutus and Tarquinius to Eutharic.

[60] See *Variae* 5.41.5 and 8.17.5 (discussed later). For more on this "princely" language, Chp. 3.

[61] *CassChron*, anno 476: "His conss. ab Odovacre Orestes et frater eius Paulus extincti sunt nomenque regis Odovacar adsumpsit, cum tamen nec purpura nec regalibus uteretur insignibus." Considering the interchangeability of royal and imperial language in the chronicle and the reference to purple, *regalibus insignibus* appears to imply imperial (rather than royal) insignia. Cf. Barnwell (1992), 134, and MacGeorge (2002), 292.

[62] Cf. Fanning (2003), 51.

might have seen this as especially bizarre, given that in an earlier entry he had been keen to point out the various styles of adornment historically adopted by Roman emperors.[63] Odovacer's decision to avoid these trappings, therefore, was an obvious break with a particular ornamental tradition. It was backward but perhaps did not extend beyond this. Indeed, rather than an indication of subservience or deference to the eastern emperor, which was, in fact, Odovacer's actual intention,[64] this peculiar manifestation of royalty (or lack thereof) stood in Cassiodorus' eyes as a witness to the inappropriateness and illegitimacy of his rule. A ruler who refused to dress as one was perverse, and Odovacer's choice of attire was thus a further indication of the disrespect for tradition felt to be ubiquitous at the time.[65] That Cassiodorus refused to associate Odovacer with any title for the remainder of his chronicle no doubt seconded this sentiment, echoing, at the same time, the official Theoderican (and east Roman) position that Odovacer was a usurper.[66]

Usurpation, however, was a common enough phenomenon throughout the history of the empire for its occurrence to be an unfortunate, yet inevitable, condition of Roman rule.[67] So, while the Odovacer depicted in Cassiodorus' *Chronicle* was indeed a usurper, this fact alone disqualified neither his realm from being the western Roman Empire nor him from being its ruler. Cassiodorus' impression was not, therefore, that the western empire continued to exist by virtue of the survival in Dalmatia (at least until 480) of its deposed emperor, Julius Nepos. Nor did he maintain that Italy retained its imperial status because the eastern emperor Zeno nominally ruled over it.[68] While both views acquire some support in other sources,[69] they utterly fail in reaching accord with the versions of the past endorsed by either Ennodius or Cassiodorus. For Cassiodorus,

[63] *CassChron*, anno 298: "His conss. primus Diocletianus adorari se iussit ut deum et gemmas vestibus calciamentisque conseruit, cum ante eum omnes imperatores in modum iudicum salutarentur et chlamydem tantum purpuream a privato habitu plus haberent." The entry is derived (nearly verbatim) from Jerome's *Chronica*.
[64] See Chp. 3.
[65] The same was implied of cross-dressing emperors like Gaius in the first century, or emperors who donned Dacian attire like Galerius in the fourth.
[66] For this observation, Wes (1967), 69.
[67] The years 469 through 476 in Cassiodorus' chronicle feature coups in nearly every entry; nor are these restricted to the West. In general, the term "usurper" was (and is) highly subjective, for legitimization could be acquired through a number of avenues, perhaps the most obvious being victory. Cf. Cullhed (1994), 89f.
[68] For such views, Bury (1958), vol. 1, 408; Kent (1966); Wes (1967), 52f.; and Moorhead (1992), 8.
[69] See Chp. 3 and Wes (1967), 52f., especially.

Nepos' deposition had decisively ended his imperial claims in the West, and Romulus Augustus was his legitimate successor.[70] Moreover, the wording of his chronicle implies that the emperors residing in Constantinople during Odovacer's reign only ruled the eastern empire, a fact surely suggesting that a western empire existed and was thus ruled by Odovacer.[71] In short, Cassiodorus' Odovacer may have been poorly dressed and an illegitimate tyrant, but neither was a novel experience for the western empire; neither necessitated its collapse; and neither resulted in a loss of western independence to Constantinople.

A Sterile Remunerator

Of course, as before, there is great danger in inferring too much from one-line entries in a chronicle, no matter how tempting. Still, the *Variae* contains more specific claims about the reign of Odovacer that would seem to validate the conclusions drawn thus far. Its more elaborate treatment also hints at Cassiodorus' personal grievances against this era and consequently supports the themes of decline, continuity, and decadence that have been discussed throughout. Two letters, one dating to 524 and the other 527/8, are of paramount importance, though they must be used with caution, since they were written in the name of Theoderic and his successor, Athalaric, rather than Cassiodorus himself. In their original context, therefore, they would have reflected the official position of the monarchs for whom they were composed, and those reading or hearing them would have accepted them as such. But since the *Variae*, as a collection, was consciously and deliberately assembled by Cassiodorus; since his other works generally demonstrate his approval of the official position; and since the contents of these two letters, as will be seen, were relevant to Cassiodorus as a person, it seems fair to suggest that the ideas espoused within were not very dissimilar from his own.

Both letters were official announcements conferring high office to the brothers Cyprian and Opilio, whose father, also called Opilio, had served in a lesser capacity during the reign of Odovacer.[72] Both letters, naturally enough, treated the qualities of these two brothers at length. And both used

---

[70] *CassChron*, anno 475: "Eodem anno Orestes, Nepote in Dalmatias fugato, filio suo Augustulo dedit imperium." Moreover, had Nepos been regarded as the reigning emperor in exile, reference to him would have been made in later entries. Nepos, however, fails to appear again in the chronicle. Cf. Wes (1967), 68.

[71] *CassChron*, anno 491: "Cui ANASTASIUS in orientali successit imperio."

[72] For more on Opilio and his sons, Chp. 5, with *PLRE* 2, 807–8 (Opilio 3–4) and 332–3 (Cyprianus 2).

their discussions as an opportunity to reflect upon the changes ushered in under Amal rule. Much like Cassiodorus' own familial experiences, only more extreme, these brothers had risen to heights far exceeding those of their father, a man whose merits, it was believed, should have afforded a similar level of success, but whose sovereign had failed to reward him adequately. Such injustices, these dispatches suggest, were typical of the reign of Odovacer, while the achievements of the brothers Opilio and Cyprian (and by extension Cassiodorus) were further proof of the glory of "modern" times.

The earlier letter, written to Cyprian and more detailed in its treatment, introduced the elder Opilio as a man living "in sordid times," who "would have been promoted much more, had his faith not lain dead under the most greedy sterility of its remunerator."[73] This statement hints at the greediness and distrust of the era already encountered in the works of Ennodius, though the missive continues by claiming that Odovacer was a "weak benefactor," who could literally do no better.[74] Similar ideas were expressed in the second letter, where the Senate was reminded of the specific qualities that had made the elder Opilio worthy: his fame in battle, the highest nobility of his character, and his preservation of ancient (Roman) virtues. Playing upon the adjective *clarus*, which meant "famous" but was also a rank conferred by holding certain offices, this royal announcement maintained that Opilio had never obtained this distinction under Odovacer, but was a *clarus* nonetheless through his merits.[75] Opilio's achievements were thus "extraordinary, since the *princeps* was not attentive in those times."[76] And he was worthy of esteem, "since there is an abundance of great praise in having earned offices, however mediocre, in a time of scarcity for the Republic."[77]

Odovacer, therefore, had failed to reward deserving men, and this failure was seen as characteristic of his reign. But it had ultimately served to glorify neglected officials like Opilio and, later, Theoderic himself, who recognized such virtues and promoted honorable men to the highest of offices.[78] Indeed and fortunately for Opilio, his sons, and those like them,

[73] *Variae* 5.41.5: "Nam pater huic ... Opilio fuit, vir abiectis quidem temporibus ... qui multo amplius crescere potuit, nisi fides eius sub avidissima remuneratoris sterilitate iacuisset."
[74] *Ibid.*: "Quid enim conferre poterat tenuis donator?"
[75] *Variae* 8.17.1: "Pater huic manu clarus ac summa fuit morum nobilitate conspicuus, quem nec ferventia bella respuerunt et tranquilla otia praedicarent, corpore validus, amicitia robustus aevi antiquitatem gestabat, abiectis saeculis Odovacris ditatus claris honoribus."
[76] *Variae* 8.17.2: "his temporibus habitus est eximius, cum princeps non esset erectus."
[77] *Variae* 5.41.5: "Quia magnae abundantia laudis est in penuria rei publicae vel mediocria munera meruisse."
[78] This is a common theme in the *Variae* and likewise eulogized in Ennodius' *Panegyric*. For more examples and their significance, Part IV.

including the Cassiodori, much had changed since the days of Odovacer. Cyprian, according to one letter, now "surpassed his ancestors in the happiness of his era," and this, it was asserted, "must be associated with our [i.e. present] times. The measure of successes among our subjects is as great as the difference in lords."[79]

Looking back on the fifth century, on a Roman world turned upside-down and denied its traditional expectations, it could seem as if many wrongs had been righted under Theoderic's watchful guidance.[80] The empire, though denuded of territory, stripped of its honor, and poorly governed, had persisted, waiting to be rescued, while its Romans had lost their way or, if still paragons of ancient virtues, had ceased to receive the recognition they deserved. And then, in 489, Theoderic had arrived. To Ennodius, the reasons were obvious, and he expressed his elation on a number of occasions, both private and public: Theoderic's advent was most desired and had resuscitated Italy;[81] he was sent by God and looked to Roman prosperity;[82] and, as he told his *pius princeps* in 507, "Rome, the mistress of the world, demanded you for the restoration of her status."[83] For Cassiodorus, the reasons were perhaps less clear, but their outcome just as praiseworthy: A "most fortunate and very brave lord" had entered Italy and defeated Odovacer in a "remarkable struggle," and following this, his wonders had never ceased.[84]

---

[79] *Variae* 5.41.6: "Vicit iste maiores suos felicitate saeculorum et, quod amplius evectus est, nostris est temporibus applicandum. Talis quippe est in subiectis mensura provectuum, qualis fuerit et distantia dominorum."

[80] For more on this, *CassOratReliquiae*, p. 465, ln. 9–19, with Chps. 8 and 10.

[81] *Eucharisticon* (#438.20): "tempore quo Italiam optatissimus Theoderici regis resuscitavit ingressus."

[82] For God, *VE* 109: "Dispositione caelestis imperii ad Italiam Theodericus rex ... commeavit." For Roman prosperity, *PanTh* 25: "causa discordiae, dum ... Romana prosperitas invitavit."

[83] *PanTh* 30: "te orbis domina ad status sui reparationem Roma poscebat."

[84] For most fortunate, *CassChron*, anno. 489: "His cons. felicissimus atque fortissimus dn. [i.e. dominus noster] rex Theodericus intravit Italiam." For remarkable struggle, *Ibid.*, anno 491: "Hoc cons. Odovacar ... a dn. [i.e. domino] nostro rege Theoderico memorabili certamine superatur." For wonders, see the remaining portions of Cassiodorus' *Chronicle*, with Chp. 8.

PART II

EMPEROR THEODERIC

ORDER FROM CHAOS

Embarking from the Balkans in 488 with a mixed group of peoples conveniently (but misleadingly) labeled Goths, Theoderic arrived in Italy the following year with perhaps twenty thousand warriors and eighty thousand noncombatants.[1] Conflict ensued for the better part of four years and unfolded much like the other civil wars that had typified the fifth century. Loyalties varied on regional and personal bases and were often fickle. Cities like Milan and Rome switched sides or suffered the alternating domination of one faction over another. Others, like Ravenna and Pavia, had sides chosen for them through their occupation by "defending" or "invading forces." Still others remained neutral, awaiting an outcome. The Po Valley, where Odovacer's base of operations had been located and where Theoderic's army had initially entered the Italian Peninsula, witnessed the greatest amount of disruption and destruction.[2] Verona, Ravenna, Pavia, Milan, Cremona, and Trent were among those cities most

---

[1] Numerical estimates have varied considerably. See Burns (1978a); Wolfram (1988), 279; Schäfer (2001), 182–3; and Heather (2007), 36–40. The term "Goths" is misleading because non-Goths, including Rugi, Sarmatians, and individual Romans, were among those who accompanied Theoderic. Moreover, Theoderic's "Goths" were of mixed origins. Some were Thracian, others Pannonian, and many had only recently placed themselves under Theoderic's authority. See Claude (1978a), 3–4, and (1980), 151–5; Burns (1982), 101; Sirago (1986), 186–7; and Heather (1995), 145–51. Later these "Goths" were augmented by the remnants of Odovacer's polyethnic army and certain Gepids. See Cesa (1994), 315. Heather (2007) seems right to point out the overwhelmingly "Gothic" nature of Theoderic's "Goths," but see Part III for a complication of "Gothic." See also *PanTh* 26–34 for an epic account of their migration, with Löwe (1961), who suggests their route betrays the careful planning of an imperial general.

[2] See Chp. 7 for greater detail.

notably affected, but the chaos and disruption of these years extended far beyond this theater of war, even as far south as Sicily.[3]

Years would be required to undo the damage. And as the dust was settling in 493 and Theoderic was just beginning to assert control, the fate of Italy and its inhabitants remained in doubt. There was little indication that this barbarian general, sent by the emperor in Constantinople to liberate the West from Odovacer's tyranny, would prove any different from his immediate fifth-century predecessors. Other barbarian generals and even emperors had been sent from the East before, often with disastrous results. Yet within less than a decade of his triumph over Odovacer, Theoderic would be hailed as a new Trajan and Valentinian;[4] would celebrate in true imperial style his *tricennalia* (or *decennalia*) at Rome; would honor the Senate and people; and would begin a series of massive renovation projects hailed by contemporary Italo-Romans as "surpassing ancient wonders."[5]

Theoderic's invasion may have devastated Italy, but he would personally intervene, reviving Italy and reasserting the *status*, despaired of in the fifth century, of the Roman Republic.[6] Moreover, and as Part II will demonstrate, he would conform to the style of rulership expected by his subjects, departing from the ambiguousness of Odovacer's reign. The Romans of Italy had wanted their own emperor, but a ruler who intentionally avoided imperial regalia and titulature, and who claimed to be a mere subject of the eastern emperor, failed to live up to such expectations. Theoderic, these chapters will argue, was different. Whatever his intended position in 488, he presented himself throughout his reign as the sovereign of an independent western Roman Empire, as the colleague of the eastern Roman emperor, and as a ruler who borrowed from many imperial traditions, but who ruled, foremost, in the style of Augustus: as a *princeps* (first citizen). His subjects, it will be shown, enthusiastically accepted this position, which contributed to contemporary conceptions of restoration

---

[3] For general accounts, Courcelle (1948), 168–7; Burns (1984), 72; Wolfram (1988), 278–84; and Moorhead (1992), 17–27. For Sicily, O'Donnell (1979), 18–19; Cracco Ruggini (1986), 245–6; and Noyé (2007), 191–2.

[4] *AnonVal* 60, discussed more fully in Chp. 3. The reference to Trajan is obvious, that to Valentinian less so. Some have suggested Valentinian III, since, like Theoderic, he heavily patronized the city of Ravenna (where the chronicler was likely a resident) and paid respect to St. Peter's during an *adventus* at Rome. Others have suggested Valentinian I, since he was also a tolerant Arian ruler and played a similar role in a papal schism at Rome. Cf. Ensslin (1959), 107 and 111; Burns (1982), 99–100, and (1984), 68; Rohr (1998); and Vitiello (2004), 108–14.

[5] See *CassChron*, anno 500, and *AnonVal* 60, with Chp. 8.

[6] For destruction, Ennodius, *Eucharisticon* (#438.20): "cum omnia ab inimicis eius inexplicabili clade vastarentur"; for status despaired, *VE* 81, with Chp. 1; for status restored, *PanTh* 5: "Salve, status reipublicae," with the Introduction to Part IV.

and renewal in significant ways. And while less important from a strictly Italo-Roman perspective, the eastern emperors also acknowledged it. Despite some friction, they even granted Theoderic the very insignia that Odovacer had remitted to Constantinople in 476, traditional symbols of Roman power that Theoderic wore and that provided visual confirmation of his imperial status.

3

PRINCEPS ROMANUS

ODOVACER THE PATRICIAN

There is a tendency to place Odovacer and Theoderic within the same constitutional context and to see Theoderic and his policies as largely an extension of his predecessor.[1] While to some extent this was the case, their reigns and positions were nonetheless quite different, both in substance and in ideology, and these differences had important consequences for contemporary receptions of their respective reigns.

Italo-Romans like Cassiodorus and Ennodius, for instance, had understood Odovacer's position vis-à-vis the Roman Empire and Italy rather ambiguously: He was undeniably the ruler of Italy and certainly the successor of Romulus Augustus, but also an obvious usurper, who refused to clothe himself in a manner befitting his station.[2] Odovacer himself, however, had generally not made any claims to imperial succession, and if so, only after Constantinople had sent Theoderic to depose him.[3] From the very beginning, he had asserted that he was the subject of the eastern emperor Zeno. The West, senatorial ambassadors had suggested on his behalf in 476, no longer required its own emperor, and he, content to rule as Zeno's representative, simply asked for the title and rank of a

[1] Standard discussions, which continue to serve as points of departure, include Mommsen (1889), 505f.; Stein (1949), vol. 2, 116–19; Ensslin (1959), 74f.; and Jones (1962). For more, see later discussion.

[2] See Part I.

[3] The evidence for Odovacer's reign is scanty, but a fragment of the history of John of Antioch (frag. 307) claims that he appointed his son, Thela (Thelanes), as a Caesar during Theoderic's campaign, perhaps an indication that ties with Constantinople had been severed and that Odovacer was willing to go his own way. His later treaty with Theoderic (see later discussion) would be consistent with such an interpretation. For Thela/Thelanes, *PLRE* 2, 1064, with Schmidt (1933), 335; Wolfram (1979), 21–2, and (1988), 282–3; Moorhead (1992), 23; Cesa (1994), 320; and Kosiński (2010), 179.

patrician.[4] Odovacer's idea had been to function like other fifth-century generalissimo-patricians, such as Stilicho, Ricimer, and Orestes, only now unimpeded by a resident emperor.[5] And as a sign of his obedience and commitment to a single empire with a single emperor, he had even sent Romulus Augustus' imperial insignia to Constantinople, providing a more reasonable explanation for their noticeable absence from his attire.[6]

Such proposals, however, were problematic from the perspective of Constantinople and only partially, if temporarily, acceptable. On the one hand, the emperor whom Odovacer had deposed and whose regalia he had remitted to Constantinople had never been recognized in the East. Romulus was a usurper, and Zeno still technically had an imperial colleague in the person of the exiled (but still active) Julius Nepos, whose own ambassadors were courting assistance at the time. On the other hand, Zeno's reputation had been tarnished recently by a coup, perhaps at the hands of a relative of Odovacer.[7] He was, thus, understandably sympathetic to Nepos' cause but lacked the resources to assist him. Moreover, Zeno could not have failed to appreciate the value of Odovacer's offer, for it would have made him ruler of the entire Roman Empire, a prestigious feat not achieved since Theodosius the Great.[8] Choosing a sort of middle ground, therefore, the eastern emperor responded to Odovacer by addressing him as a patrician, apparently agreeing to the requested rank, but also instructing him to accept his patriciate from Nepos and to be obedient to him.

The Byzantine perspective, then, at least in 476, was that Nepos would continue to rule the West, albeit from Dalmatia, and that Odovacer would be his patrician and representative in Italy. Odovacer, moreover, appears to have complied, minting his coinage in Nepos' and later Zeno's name and invading Dalmatia as Nepos' avenger after the exiled emperor's assassination in 480.[9]

---

[4] See Malchus, frag. 10, with Schmidt (1933), 319–21; Wes (1967), 72–3; Cesa (1994), 317, and (2001), 47–8; and Burgarella (2001), 121–5.

[5] For such "generalissimo-patricians" and a complication of Odovacer's status as one, see later discussion. This kind of military patrician was different from the senatorial patricians that often functioned as diplomats. See Mathisen (1986) and (1991).

[6] *AnonVal* 64 (cited later), with *CassChron*, anno 476, discussed in Chp. 2.

[7] It has been suggested that Odovacer was the nephew of Verina, Zeno's mother-in-law, who played an important role in the revolt of Basiliscus. See Krautschick (1986), 349, with Cesa (1994), 311; Prostko-Prostyński (1994b); and MacGeorge (2002), 284–5.

[8] Though there were shorter interregnum periods during the fifth century, when the eastern emperor technically ruled both halves of the empire. The eighteen-month interregnum separating the reigns of Libius Severus and Anthemius is a case in point. See Wes (1967), 54–5.

[9] For Nepos' coins, Kent (1966), with Moorhead (1992), 8; for Zeno's coins, Kraus (1928), 52f. For the invasion of Dalmatia, Cesa (1994), 317–18, with a critique in the Introduction to Part V.

THEODERIC AND ZENO

Perspectives changed after Nepos' death, and Odovacer's position with respect to Constantinople became more tenuous. He continued to nominate consuls who were recognized in the East and even made Zeno a partner in his victory over the Rugi in 487.[10] But by 488, a falling-out had occurred, and Zeno and Theoderic had reached an agreement. The exact details are less than certain, but it is clear that this agreement had stipulated that Theoderic was to go to Italy and depose Odovacer. Later Byzantine sources actually question Zeno's involvement, and the earliest Italo-Roman reference, found in Ennodius' *Panegyric*, cites vengeance as Theoderic's rationale.[11] But Theoderic, who was then acting as Zeno's *magister militum praesentalis* in the Balkans, had a long history of service in the East. More than just another "barbarian" king with a token military title, he was a highly decorated patrician, who had served as ordinary consul in 484 and received manifold honors from the eastern emperor, including an equestrian statue in the capital.[12] The two had not always been on friendly terms, but Theoderic had already offered to undertake a similar mission nearly a decade earlier.[13] And this history, combined with a recent outbreak of hostilities between the two, rendered an official commission against Odovacer mutually beneficial.[14] Not only was it prudent

[10] See McCormick (1977). Zeno had actually incited the Rugi against him, but Odovacer, true to his role as a subordinate, sent tokens of his victory to the emperor.
[11] See Moorhead (1984b). Byzantine sources that question Zeno's involvement (citing instead Theoderic's fear of Zeno) include Eustathius (frag. = Evagrius Scholasticus, *HE* 3.27); John Malalas 5.9; and John of Nikiu 47–50. For vengeance, which seems to have stemmed from Odovacer's slaughter of Theoderic's relatives (*parentes*) and mismanagement of Roman affairs, *PanTh* 25, with Delle Donne (2001), 10–11. Doubtless these relatives were the same Rugi whom Odovacer had defeated in 487. Cf. McCormick (1977), 215–17; Moorhead (1992), 10–11; Cesa (1994), 319; and Rohr (2006), 49.
[12] For a more extensive discussion, see Chp. 6.
[13] For the mission (an offer to restore Nepos), Malchus, frag. 20, ln. 216–21. For their on-again, off-again relationship, Ensslin (1959), 39–57; Wolfram (1988), 70–8; and Heather (1991), 275f.
[14] For the recent hostilities, John of Antioch, frag. 306, with Heather (1991), 304–5. Theoderic had marched on Constantinople in 487 and blockaded the city. However, Zeno sent gifts along with Theoderic's sister, then living in the city and on good terms with the imperial family. Negotiations presumably followed thereafter. For mutually beneficial, Procopius, *Wars* 5.1.11, with Moorhead (1992), 17–19, who places Zeno's decision within the Roman tradition of encouraging barbarian groups to fight against each other. This is a somewhat problematic interpretation considering Procopius' own statement that Theoderic's senatorial dignity influenced Zeno's decision (see later discussion). Heather (1991), 305–7, and (1996), 217–18, suggests a bit more cautiously that both Theoderic and Zeno were looking for a solution and cites the Malchus fragment (see previous note) as evidence for Theoderic's earlier interest in western affairs. This is true, though Malchus also demonstrates that Theoderic preferred to move to Constantinople and live as a Roman.

for Zeno to remove an ambitious and potentially dangerous general from the vicinity of Constantinople, but it was better, as many east Roman sources claimed, to allow an individual with Theoderic's illustrious credentials, one with a senatorial dignity and familiar to the emperor, to rule in Odovacer's place.[15]

Unlike Odovacer, then, Theoderic was intended from the very beginning to function as a legitimate representative of imperial power in the West. The available sources, however, disagree as to the exact nature, function, and intended duration of his position; and this has led to much modern scholarly speculation, often based on non-contemporary and non-Italian sources. The mid-sixth-century Byzantine historian Procopius, for instance, whose account is generally favored, seems to suggest that Italy was to remain a separate entity from the eastern empire and be ruled directly by Theoderic. Zeno, according to Procopius, "advised Theoderic to go to Italy, come to blows with Odovacer, and procure for himself and the Goths the Western domain."[16] Yet even his account, as straightforward as it seems, is far from conclusive, since within just a few lines (and on later occasions) Procopius described Theoderic as a *tyrannos* (usurper/tyrant) and cited his usurpation as a *casus belli*.[17] To Gothic envoys, who clearly disagreed with this understanding, Procopius made the general Belisarius pose the question, "Why would the emperor have been concerned to replace a tyrant with a tyrant?" And providing his own answer, he concluded that Zeno had sent Theoderic, "not to hold the dominion of Italy himself ... but to free it and make it obedient to the emperor."[18]

Jordanes, another Byzantine historian and a contemporary of Procopius, provides yet another interpretation. In his *Getica* he described Odovacer as a tyrant unfamiliar to Zeno and oppressing the Senate and a portion of the republic. Italy, in this version, remained a part of Zeno's empire and Theoderic asked permission to depose its unlawful ruler, stipulating that if victorious, he would possess "that kingdom" through Zeno's bestowal as a "gift and present."[19] Jordanes' understanding of the situation, therefore, appears to have been that Theoderic would rule Italy as a kind of client or federate kingdom, independent of Constantinople's

---

[15] Cf. Procopius, *Wars* 5.1.9–11, and Jordanes, *Getica* 291 and *Romana* 348–9 (cited later), where Theoderic's services in the East and personal relationship with Zeno are provided as rationales.

[16] Procopius, *Wars* 5.1.10.

[17] *Ibid.*, 5.1.29 and 5.5.8–9.

[18] *Ibid.*, 6.6.23–4.

[19] *Getica* 291: "haut ille, quem non nostis, tyrannico iugo senatum vestrum partemque rei publicae captivitatis servitio premat. Ego enim si vicero, vestro dono vestroque munere possedebo."

control, but certainly owing much to Zeno's act of bestowal. Roles were essentially reversed in Jordanes' *Romana*, but the same basic premises hold true. Here Zeno commended to Theoderic, described as his *cliens*, the Senate and people of Rome, shorthand for the republic itself, and Theoderic then proceeded to Italy in the capacity of a barbarian king and former Roman consul.[20] This consular status linked Theoderic to the eastern court, yet Jordanes described his subsequent domain as concurrently a barbarian kingdom (*regnum gentium*) and Roman principate (*principatus romani populi*), both terms implying a certain degree of autonomy from Constantinople.[21]

Jordanes and Procopius, therefore, agreed and disagreed on certain details, and at times their own accounts even contradicted themselves. Both concurred that Theoderic had ruled Italy independently of the eastern emperor. However, Jordanes suggested that this had always been the agreement, while Procopius, at least in some places, cast some doubt. A third source, a short historical excerpt known by many names but here referred to simply as the *Anonymus Valesianus*, provides yet another perspective, this time Italian rather than Byzantine.[22] The work is not without its problems, though. As an excerpt from a larger (lost) chronicle, for instance, it is not entirely clear how complete or incomplete it is. More alarming, its account is so bipolar in its treatment of Theoderic, its first half praising him overtly in the style of Ennodius or Cassiodorus and its second providing a scathing (and at times repetitive and contradictory) rebuke, that some scholars maintain that it is the work of two authors or that a rather clumsy author combined two independent sources, one pro-Theoderican, the other anti-Theoderican.[23] Still, and despite such problems, the

---

[20] *Romana* 348–9: "Maluit Theodorico ac si proprio iam clienti eam committi ... ad partes eum Italiae mandans, Romanum illi populum senatumque commendat. Obansque rex gentium et consul Romanus Theodoricus Italiam petiit." The reference to Theoderic as a *cliens* surely refers to his current status in 488, rather than his intended status as ruler of Italy, contra Demougeot (1978), 374, and Moorhead (1984b), 263, and (1992), 50.

[21] *Romana* 349: "regnum gentis sui et Romani populi principatum prudenter et pacifice per triginta annos continuit."

[22] The title is derived from Henri Valois, who published it, along with a similar excerpt treating the reign of Constantine, in 1636. Its most common names are *Anonymi Valesiani pars posterior*, *Chronica Theodericiana*, and *Excerpta Valesiana II*. *Anonymus Valesianus* is the most conventional, though the third title is probably the most appropriate, not only because its earliest manuscript (ninth century) provides the heading *Item ex libris Chronicorum inter cetera*, but also because it lacks a proper introduction and conclusion and treats non-Theoderican material extensively (more than 30% of its contents). Cf. Croke (2001), 352–3. The Latin edition of Moreau (1968) has been used throughout.

[23] For multiple authorship, see the introduction to the edition of Cessi (1912/13); Tamassia (1913); Bury (1958), vol. 1, 423 (n. 1); Moreau (1968), VII–VIII; and Morton (1982). In his *MGH*

strengths of this source are twofold. First, and regardless of authorship, many of its details represent an earlier tradition, derived from the western court at Ravenna and independent of the milieu of "reconquest" and war that so clearly influenced Procopius and Jordanes.[24] Second and much more importantly, the *Anonymus* provides a very specific, though convoluted, description of the pact made between Theoderic and Zeno in 488, as well as much greater detail concerning Theoderic's intended position and how it changed over the course of his Italian campaigns.

A cautious reading of the *Anonymus Valesianus*, therefore, which takes into account the later claims of Jordanes and Procopius, can help to provide a hypothetical reconstruction of the nature of Theoderic's rule, ultimately demonstrating just how different it was from Odovacer's, both in origin and in content.

FROM *PRAEREGNARE* TO *REGNARE*

To begin, the author of this source stated the intended conditions of Theoderic's rule rather plainly. He was supposed to travel to Italy and, if he defeated Odovacer, he would rule in place of the emperor until Zeno himself should arrive. Theoderic, acting as a patrician, would thus defend Italy for the emperor.[25] Still, whether Zeno actually planned to

---

edition, Mommsen (1892) assumed sole authorship, while Adams (1976); Barnish (1983); and Zecchini (1993) have since made strong arguments in favor of a single author, emphasizing the work's unity of style and language, repeated tropes, and the fact that Greco-Roman (and biblical) biographies provide similarly bipolar accounts. Their points are valid, but not decisive. Not only is the work, as it survives, an excerpt and thus incomplete, but its unity might be simply the product of a third author (or even later editor), who was far less clumsy than Cessi or others imagined. Cf. Croke (2001), 353–5, who favors sole authorship but is sensitive to other possibilities.

[24] The work is grouped among the so-called *Consularia Italica*, a collection of related late antique *fasti* from various Italian municipalities, and its first (pro-Theoderican) half is commonly believed to have been derived from a (now-lost) source close to the Theoderican court at Ravenna. Its actual date of composition, however, is far from clear and rendered all the more difficult given its incomplete nature. Proposed dates have ranged from shortly after Theoderic's death, to the 540s or even 550s (the same context as Jordanes and Procopius). See earlier references. Since Athalaric's succession is mentioned without negative commentary (*AnonVal* 96) and references to Justinian are lacking throughout, an earlier date seems probable.

[25] *AnonVal* 49: "Cui [i.e. Zenoni] Theodericus pactuatus est, ut, si victus fuisset Odoacar, pro merito laborum suorum loco eius, dum adveniret, tantum praeregnaret. Ergo superveniente Theoderico patricio de civitate Nova cum gente Gothica, missus ab imperatore Zenone de partibus Orientis ad defendendam sibi Italiam." The Latin of this passage is admittedly vulgar, allowing for other possible interpretations. Cf. Prostko-Prostyński (1994a), 103–5. Though a later, eighth-century source, see also Paul the Deacon, *Historia Romana* 15.14, who claims that Zeno granted Theoderic Italy and the Senate and people of Rome via a mandate (*pragmaticum*)

go to Italy in the aftermath of a Theoderican victory is questionable,[26] especially since this was not the first time that he had sent a patrician to depose a western usurper. In fact, as the *Anonymus Valesianus* understood it, Julius Nepos had come to Italy in exactly the same capacity, deposed Glycerius, and then himself been made emperor at Rome.[27] It would not be unreasonable, therefore, to suggest that Zeno had no intention of leaving Constantinople and that Theoderic was intended to function indefinitely as his subordinate in Italy. His loyalty would have been assured by the potential of being recalled or replaced by yet another eastern patrician. Moreover, this position would have been a logical extension of Theoderic's current (and official) capacity in the East as a *magister militum praesentalis* and patrician and would have fit well in the West, where such titles had long since become the prerogative of the senior ranking military commander.[28] Alternatively, Zeno may indeed have intended to travel to Italy, not to relieve Theoderic of his duties, but to sanction his reign officially and invest him with the insignia of his office. Some decades earlier, the emperor Theodosius II had planned to do just this after the victory of Valentinian III, not yet an Augustus, over the usurper John.[29] What seems

---

and the gift of a sacred robe (*sacri ... velaminis dono*). For "pragmaticum" as a legally binding mandate, König (1994), 152, and Prostko-Prostyński (1994a), 108. Paul and the *Anonymus Valesianus* may share a common source, but this is speculative, and so his history should be used with caution.

[26] Cf. König (1994), 153, who takes the possibility seriously, and Haarer (2006), 73–4, who claims direct intervention was "out of the question."

[27] *AnonVal* 36: "Igitur imperante Zenone Augusto Constantinopoli, superveniens Nepos patricius ad Portum urbis Romae, deposuit de imperio Glycerium et factus est episcopus et Nepos factus imperator Romae." Cf. *Marc. Com.* 467 (on Anthemius). There is, therefore, no justification for assuming that Theoderic's patrician status was specifically "barbarous" in nature, i.e. a form of rulership reserved for the "barbarian" generalissimos of the West. Cf. Moorhead (1992), 36, and Wolfram (1979), 2.

[28] On this special "patricius et magister militum praesentalis" in the West, Ensslin (1931); Demandt (1970); Wolfram (1979), 20; and Mathisen (1991). Such figures, often described as "vice-emperors," included "barbarians" like Ricimer and Gundobad, but also "Romans" like Ecdicius (Sidonius' brother-in-law) and Orestes. Despite sometimes being grouped with these individuals, Odovacer was a departure, since he never served as *magister militum*. Cf. Demougeot (1978), 373; Burns (1982), 105; and Cesa (1994), 314. Mommsen (1889), 505–9, suggests that both Odovacer and Theoderic, as *reges*, assumed the powers of a *magister militum*, rendering that position (and its title) unnecessary. But other *magistri*, such as Tufa, Libila, and Aemilianus, are attested during their reigns. See Prostko-Prostyński (1994a), 39–40, with *PLRE* 2, 15 (Aemilianus 5), 681, and 1131. After Theoderic's death, the position reemerged with the shortened title *patricius praesentalis* and was open to both Goths and Romans. It may have been the basis for later exarchs. See Ensslin (1936), 244–9, modifying Mommsen (1889), 506–7 and (1890), 185–6; for a critique, Prostko-Prostyński (1994a), 55–6.

[29] See Socrates Scholasticus, *HE* 7.24, with Kaegi (1968), 19–23. Theodosius even set out for Italy but was forced to return to Constantinople and sent the patrician Helion in his stead.

certain, at any rate, is that, at least before Zeno's arrival, Theoderic was not supposed to rule Italy outright or even necessarily claim a royal title. He would remain a patrician and, as such, was only to *praeregnare*, a verb first attested in the *Anonymus Valesianus*, but surely indicating a handicap to out-and-out royal or imperial power (*regnare*).[30]

Indeed during the early course of his campaigns against Odovacer, Theoderic was consistently described in this account as a patrician rather than a king.[31] In 490, however, when confidence in a Gothic victory was growing and all Italy was already calling him lord (*dominus*), Festus, the head of the Senate, was sent to Constantinople by Theoderic, who hoped to secure certain vestments described as "royal" (*regiam*).[32] These very well could have been imperial robes, especially given the interchangeability of royal and imperial adjectives and the fact that in 476 it had been senators who had delivered Romulus Augustus' regalia to the eastern court. Perhaps Festus was asking for them back, either suggesting that a new agreement granting Theoderic greater powers and a royal title was desired or announcing that Italy was secure and it was time for Zeno to materialize. Festus, however, failed to return with a response the following year, and Theoderic, though still described in the account as a patrician, was growing tired of laying siege to Ravenna. By 493 he reached a separate treaty with Odovacer, agreeing to share control over Italy and hence violating (though not necessarily nullifying) the terms of his original pact with Zeno.[33] Nothing, of course, would come of these new arrangements, since shortly after being admitted into Ravenna Theoderic personally slew his supposed partner for plotting against him. Nevertheless, this alliance with Odovacer had the potential to place Theoderic's loyalty to Constantinople (already questioned in the past) in doubt. It may have only been a clever ruse on Theoderic's part, but such a move could have jeopardized the secu-

---

[30] *TLL*, s.v. "praeregno," cites *AnonVal* 49, providing the definition "rule before," but suggests that the word may be a vulgarization of *proregno*, meaning "rule on behalf of."

[31] See *AnonVal* 49–54, with Ensslin (1959), 75, and Moorhead (1992), 38.

[32] For *dominus*, Jordanes, *Getica* 294, with Moorhead (1992), 36, and König (1994), 154. Both point out the weakness of Theoderic's position by the time of Festus' arrival (Odovacer had put him on the defensive), the latter even claiming that this is why the mission failed. For the embassy, *AnonVal* 53 and 64. For Festus, *PLRE* 2, 467–9 (Festus 5). On Theoderic's diplomacy with the East during his Italian campaign in general, Moorhead (1992), 37–9; Prostko-Prostyński (1994a), 131f.; and Heather (1996), 218–20. Cf. Barnwell (1992), 135.

[33] The sharing of power is not specifically referenced in the *AnonVal*, though it may be implied at 54–5. John of Antioch, frag. 206, claims that Theoderic and Odovacer both agreed to rule the Roman Empire ("tes Rhomaion arches") together ("ampho"). Cf. Moorhead (1984b), 265, who suggests that Odovacer may have accepted a position subordinate to Theoderic.

rity of his patriciate and likewise hindered ongoing attempts to secure a royal title.[34]

Zeno, however, had died in 491, while Festus was presumably in the midst of negotiating new arrangements with him, forcing a second embassy, equally fruitless, to be dispatched under the leadership of Faustus Niger in 492. After the death of Odovacer, but before the return of Faustus, the Goths, impatient for "the order of the emperor," took the initiative and confirmed Theoderic as king.[35] Why exactly Theoderic, who was already a king of the Goths, needed the approval of Constantinople to remain their king has been the subject of some debate.[36] The best explanation, however, seems to be that the position he once held was fundamentally altered by his victories in Italy. His confirmation by the Goths was hence a symbolic gesture that marked Theoderic's transition from a king of certain Pannonian Goths with a Roman title beholden to Constantinople (*patricius*), to a new role as the independent king of the Goths and Italo-Romans, *rex Italiae*.

The act was significant. Indeed, from this point forward the anonymous author consistently referred to Theoderic as a *rex*, rather than patrician, and described him in the act of ruling (*regnare*), rather than the conditional act of ruling indicated by *praeregnare*. Moreover it was a bold move with potentially serious repercussions, a flagrant violation of the original agreement established with Zeno in 488. It qualified, according to the chronicler, as *praesumptio*, a daring act of an illicit nature suggestive, in this case, of usurpation.[37] In and of itself, the feat proclaimed that Theoderic was an independent ruler who did not require the assent of Constantinople for

[34] Something like this did in fact happen during the Justinianic reconquest of Italy, when Belisarius, in order to reach a truce with the Goths, agreed to become the emperor of the West, apparently as a stratagem. The act, however, cast his loyalty in doubt and resulted in his relocation to the Persian front. See Procopius, *Wars* 6.29.18–31 and 6.30.1–4, with the Epilogue.

[35] *AnonVal* 57: "At ubi cognita morte eius antequam legatio reverteretur, ut ingressus est Ravennam, et occidit Odoacrem, Gothi sibi confirmaverunt Theodericum regem, non exspectantes iussionem novi principis."

[36] Theories range from Theoderic's being confirmed as a king over other barbarians in addition to his Goths, such as the remnants of Odovacer's army, to the suggestion that the act was a declaration of Theoderic's kingship over Goths and Romans, either as a federate king or as ruler of Italy or the western *imperium* outright. See Schmidt (1939), 407–10; Ensslin (1959), 74–9; Wolfram (1979), 22–3 and (1988), 287–8; Claude (1978a) and (1980), 155–7; Barnwell (1992), 136; Moorhead (1992), 38; König (1994), 156f.; and Wirth (1995), 253. Perhaps the best solution, however, is simply to amend *sibi* to *ibi*, allowing it to correspond with the *ante* and *ubi* occurring at the beginning of the sentence. Hence, "But before (*ante*) the return of the embassy, when (*ubi*) his death had been learned and [Theoderic] had entered Ravenna and killed Odovacer, then (*ibi*) the Goths proclaimed him king, not waiting for the new emperor's order."

[37] *AnonVal* 64 (cited later).

legitimacy. He would not be a subordinate or representative of the eastern emperor, as Odovacer had once been, but the ruler of the western Roman realm outright. And as such, he might even presume upon certain imperial prerogatives that his immediate predecessor had never dreamed of, cultivating an image that both likened him to an emperor and cast him as an imperial colleague.

Initially, and for obvious reasons, the move may not have been well received in Constantinople,[38] and a third embassy, led once more by Festus, was dispatched in 497. The *Anonymus Valesianus* provides no indication of the diplomatic maneuvering that was entailed,[39] but when the head of the Senate returned later that year, he arrived not simply with the royal vestments that had been requested seven years prior, but tellingly with the very imperial regalia sent to the East by Odovacer in 476, when he had notified Zeno that the western empire was no more. "Peace was made with Emperor Anastasius," the anonymous author records, "and he returned all the ornaments of the palace which Odovacer had sent to Constantinople."[40]

The situation in 497 was thus quite different from that in 476.[41] Regardless of its origins in an apparent act of *praesumptio* and the violation of a prior agreement (doubtless why Procopius claimed that Theoderic was a tyrant), Theoderic's position as a kind of Roman emperor had been acknowledged in the East and sealed by the return of the western empire's insignia. More importantly, this position, as will be demonstrated, was accepted with enthusiasm by a number of Theoderic's subjects, who believed that many of his qualities were imperial and provided the means for a seemingly moribund western empire to resurge. Their beliefs and his willingness to meet their expectations over the coming decades made him a

---

[38] See Schmidt (1933), 338, and Moorhead (1992), 38, who discuss possible interpretations of the standing of western consuls in the East from 494 to 497. In 495 the western consul, Viator, had no eastern colleague; in 496 the western consul, Speciosus, was not recognized in the East; and in 497 the eastern consul, Anastasius, had no western colleague.

[39] But see Duchesne (1912), 314–16; Stein (1949), vol. 2, 115–16; Burns (1982), 108; Noble (1993), 399–404; and Meier (2009), 97–8. Festus seems to have all but guaranteed that Pope Anastasius II would accept Zeno's *Henotikon*, thus ending the Acacian Schism. The pope died shortly thereafter, however, and a disputed election in Rome soon wracked the papal see with a schism of its own (the Laurentian Schism). See later discussion.

[40] *AnonVal* 64: "Facta pace cum Anastasio imperatore per Festum de praesumptione regni, et omnia ornamenta palatii, quae Odoacar Constantinopolim transmiserat, remittit."

[41] For a similar statement, but for entirely different reasons, see Demougeot (1978), 380–1, who concludes that the establishment of Theoderic's kingdom truly marks the fall/end of the western Roman Empire. On the contrary, for men like Ennodius, Cassiodorus, and others, it marked its restoration.

legitimate Roman emperor, regardless of sometimes (but not always) hostile eastern perceptions and modern preoccupations with constitutionality.[42]

AN ITALY WITH EMPERORS

The historical relationship between Italy and its emperors no doubt facilitated the acceptance of a figure like Theoderic as emperor, paradoxically allowing staunch traditionalism to inspire innovation. The earliest emperors had maintained their presence within Italy and especially at Rome, guarding their image as mere *principes* of the Senate who worked within the framework of the old republic. Increasingly, however, both Italy and Rome were abandoned in favor of the frontiers, and provincial capitals became "new Romes." Emperors could behave differently outside the empire's cradle, eventually disposing of republican niceties and becoming practically despots. The process marginalized Rome and Italy, not just politically but also ideologically. Still, many Italo-Romans continued to think of themselves and the Eternal City as central to the empire and hoped that princely emperors would one day return.[43] In the fifth century, emperors did indeed return, and not just to frontier capitals in the north like Milan and Ravenna, but to Rome itself.[44] But while potentially worthy of jubilation, this homecoming had not ushered in a golden age, but quite the opposite. The preeminence once desired came at a very disquieting price and was only partial. Italy's new emperors were not princely; they were un-republican, un-Roman, and worse still disastrously inept. Italy became central once more, but as much through the presence of emperors and the imperial administration as through the loss of surrounding provinces. Italo-Romans had wanted a Roman Empire centered on Italy, but got instead a Roman Empire that was *only* Italy. These blows to Italo-Roman prestige were exacerbated further by Constantinople's increasing challenge to Rome's status as the *caput mundi* (capital of the world). Somehow "first" Rome began to rank second to "second" Rome.

[42] As suggested in the Introduction, there are a number of such modern constitutional analyses, which tend to emphasize the absolute authority of the eastern emperor, who, it is assumed, could (and did) limit Theoderic's *imitatio imperii*. Cf. Mommsen (1889), 505f.; Hodgkin (1896), 492–4; Schmidt (1939); Stein (1949), vol. 2, 116–19; Ensslin (1959), 74–9; Jones (1962); Claude (1978b), 19–23; Chrysos (1981), 430–5; Barnwell (1992); Prostko-Prostyński (1994a); Kohlhas-Müller (1995); Haarer (2006), 79–89; and Meier (2009), 92–102.

[43] Indeed, the city of Rome remained a powerful ideology, though Romans in Italy generally did not. Cf. Wes (1967), chps. 1 and 2; Fuhrmann (1968); Cullhed (1994), 63–7; and Van Dam (2007), chp. 2. Matthews (1975), 20–3, describes some of the benefits conferred to Italian senators by the absence of a resident emperor.

[44] Gillett (2001).

The ironies may have been maddening, but the western empire's cause was not so lost that Italo-Romans abandoned completely their desire for centrality or a resident emperor. The need was powerful and long-standing, and for exactly this reason men like Ennodius and Cassiodorus had been willing to imagine Odovacer as an imperial figure, despite glaring contradictions. Though a senatorial embassy had announced Odovacer's intention of dissolving the western *imperium* and placing its remnants under the jurisdiction of Constantinople, the idea had stemmed from Odovacer himself and did not necessarily reflect his subjects' desires.[45] The world of continuity discussed in earlier chapters was thus, in part at any rate, a reflection of the wishful thinking of certain Italo-Roman patriots, but it nevertheless fulfilled a historically important need. The Romans of Italy did not want their paramount position, so recently restored, to be marginalized; nor could they accept an Italy transformed into just another province, especially of a Greek Roman Empire. The return of Romulus' regalia in 497, therefore, was especially significant in their eyes. Italy could once more be understood as a seat of imperial power, while in Theoderic they gained not only an emperor, but the kind of emperor they wanted.

EMPEROR THEODERIC

That Theoderic was in fact the emperor of the West may seem unlikely at first. Indeed, modern scholarship persists in describing him as "king of the Ostrogoths" and his realm as "Ostrogothic Italy," even though this kind of terminology is not attested in contemporary Italian sources.[46] And while convenient, terms like these, which seem so patently un-Roman, cannot help but influence modern accounts. At worst, then, Theoderic is imagined as a savage and heretical barbarian king; at best, and following the sympathetic conclusions drawn by Procopius, as a sub-Roman ruler who had technically been a tyrant: a Gothic *rex* who avoided imperial dress and titles, but was in truth a Roman emperor in his behavior.[47]

---

[45] A similar conclusion is drawn by Wes (1967), 72. Cf. Burgarella (2001), 124. Moorhead (1999), 243, on the other hand, suggests that emperors had become irrelevant to Italian senators and churchmen. This seems to go too far, though.

[46] Cf. Prostko-Prostyński (1994a), 75f. Contemporary Italians described Theoderic as a *rex* and his realm as a *regnum* but never qualified these terms with a reference to Goths (i.e. *rex*/*regnum Gothorum*). His Goths, likewise, were consistently referred to as simply "Goths" rather than "Ostrogoths," a term evidenced earlier, but that only emerges in reference to Theoderic's Goths in the mid-sixth century and in non-Italian sources. See Gillett (2000), 495–8.

[47] Procopius, *Wars* 5.1.26–9. Cf. *PLRE* 2, 1083: "He did not receive the imperial purple and never used the title 'Augustus' always calling himself 'rex.'"

The words of Procopius tend to resonate the most in modern scholarship and are valuable insofar as they hint at the imperial or quasi-imperial nature of Theoderic's reign. But again, such conclusions should be accepted with caution, for, though largely approving of Theoderic, they reflect a later Byzantine perspective. Procopius was not a contemporary Italo-Roman; nor do his sentiments duplicate their values. Likewise, preoccupations with constitutionality, ethnicity, and religion reflect modern concerns more than necessarily those of Theoderic's subjects. Though seemingly counterintuitive, for instance, Theoderic's status as a king and a Goth (as will be shown later) actually won acceptance among certain Italo-Romans, who manipulated both in ways that helped to reaffirm the rightness of his reign.[48] His status as a usurper, similarly, could be ignored and utterly fail to disqualify him from legitimate succession. Usurpation, after all, was not unheard of in Italy, while legitimacy was relative and could be acquired and lost through a number of avenues.[49] Even his status as an Arian heretic was excusable. Not only was the population of Italy mixed in its religious sympathies, including Nicene Christians, Jews, pagans, and "radical" and "soft" Arians,[50] but Italy had been ruled by heretic emperors in the past, some remembered quite fondly.[51] Moreover, for most of Theoderic's reign the eastern emperors were also considered heretics and rebuked as such on numerous occasions.[52] To Theoderic's credit, at least, he promoted a broad policy of tolerance and noninterference, quite different from the emperors in the East, and was praised in a number of contexts for his Christian piety and benign stewardship of the

---

[48] For royal manipulation, see later discussion. For Gothicness, Part V.

[49] For these avenues, Cullhed (1994), 89–93. In addition, Theoderic seems to have satisfied the criteria for "constitutional" legitimacy proposed by Jones (1964), 326–7, since his collegiality with the eastern emperor (albeit in a junior position) was recognized in the East. See later discussion, with Prostko-Prostyński (1994a), 90f.

[50] See Zeiller (1904); Cecchelli (1960); Pietri (1981), 419–23; Amory (1997), chp. 7; and Luiselli (2005). The Nicene Christians of Italy, moreover, did not constitute a unified group, since the Acacian and Laurentian Schisms promoted factionalism, the latter even violence in Rome. See later discussion.

[51] Italy had been ruled by Arian emperors for much of the fourth century. The last of these was Valentinian I, who was remembered fondly for his noninterference in doctrinal issues and neutrality during a papal schism. Cf. Cecchelli (1960), 751. His similarity to Theoderic is striking, and it is therefore tempting to see the reference in *AnonVal* 60 to Theoderic as a "New Valentinian" as an allusion to this Arian emperor.

[52] For the Acacian Schism, which rendered Zeno and Anastasius "heretics" in the eyes of many Italo-Romans, Duchesne (1912) and (1915); Charanis (1939); Pietri (1981), 444–52; Noble (1993), 399–402; Haarer (2006), chp. 5; and Kosiński (2010), 179–94. For rebukes, see the correspondence in Thiel (1868) and the *Collectio Avellana*, especially the letters of Popes Gelasius and Symmachus.

church.[53] Theoderic was, according to Ennodius, "a worshipper of the highest God from the very beginning of [his] life," and, as he informed Pope Symmachus, "Our faith is safe with him, though he himself follows another. What wonderful patience!"[54]

In spite of seeming contradictions, then, Theoderic could still pass for a Roman emperor within the confines of Italy, so long as he presented himself as such to his subjects, and they, of course, approved. Procopius might have agreed or disagreed with their assessments, but his opinions are irrelevant within a strictly Italian context, where expectations differed. Indeed, Greeks like Procopius and Italians like Ennodius and Cassiodorus generally had dissimilar ideas about Roman emperorship. In the East, emperors had been imagined from the very beginning as more or less replacements for Hellenistic monarchs; like them, the emperor was a divine king, an autocratic and despotic *basileus*. In Italy, on the other hand, it was the legacy of the late republic and principate from which imperial ideals had been derived; here emperors had always been *principes*, first citizens, the best of the senators who guarded republican notions of *libertas*.[55] Again, eastern, "basilean" despotism had prevailed in the later empire, but the traditions of the principate remained deeply ingrained within Italo-Roman society. This was the kind of emperor, a republican emperor, for which Italians longed, and it stood in direct opposition to the style of rule typical by

[53] The tolerance of the Theoderican regime has not gone unnoticed. See Giesecke (1939), 116–26; Saitta (1986), (1993), 65f., and (1999); Noble (1993); Schäfer (2001), 192f.; Rota (2001a), 235f.; and Schwarcz (2004). Luiselli (2005), 751f., sees this tolerance as a product of the "soft" Arianism to which Theoderic and many Ostrogoths had been converted. That Theoderic's mother was a Catholic probably also helped. Theoderic's benign stewardship and noninterference are best demonstrated in his actions during the Laurentian Schism. See the earlier citations, with Duchesne (1915), 221–35; Townsend (1937); Ensslin (1959), 113–27; Llewellyn (1976); Moorhead (1978b); and Pietri (1981), 455–61. For praise in a papal/Christian context, see the letters of Pope Gelasius in the *Epistulae Theodericianae Variae* 1–8, with Ensslin (1959), 100–3; *Acta Synhodorum Habitarum Romae* (portions of which are cited later); *AnonVal* 60 and 65 (cited in Chp. 8); and Ennodius' *Libellus Pro Synodo* (cited with references in Chp. 1). For tensions and the possibility of an about-face at the end of Theoderic's reign, see the Epilogue.

[54] For worshipper, *PanTh* 80: "te summi dei cultorem ab ipso lucis limine instructio vitalis instituit"; for our faith, #458.7 (*In Christi Signo*, a work replete with Christian praise for Theoderic and thought to have been directed to Pope Symmachus): "fides nostra apud eum – aliud ipse sectetur – in portu est. Mirabilis patientia." See also the discussion of Ennodius' *Life of Epiphanius* in Chp. 7, which depicts Theoderic as an ideal Christian ruler.

[55] On the *princeps-basileus* opposition in late antiquity, Wes (1967), chp. 2, and Reydellet (1981), 7f. Jones (1964), 321–3, demonstrates the preeminence of the *basileus* model in the later empire, but tempers its absolute nature with a hint of republican ideology. See also Chrysos (1980), who points out that *basileus* was not an official title until the early seventh century and suggests that it evolved from a pejorative term.

the late fifth century. Politically adept emperors had generally understood these distinctions, conforming to local expectations when in Italy,[56] and Theoderic and his image makers were no different. He too could play the role of a republican *princeps*, thereby becoming more than a mere monarch.

When Procopius claimed, therefore, that Theoderic had not usurped the title of a Roman emperor, employing instead the simple barbarian title *rex*, he was only half correct.[57] It was true that Theoderic was not a *basileus*, or as westerners would have understood the term, an *imperator*,[58] but he had also not entirely disqualified himself from Roman emperorship by being just a simple *rex*. Unconcerned with "empty titles of ostentation,"[59] as Ennodius claimed, he regularly employed the title of *princeps*, a term clearly within the imperial tradition and pregnant with meaning in Italy, but at the same time inexact enough to avoid offense in Constantinople.[60] Indeed, Theoderic actually used this title (and its derivatives) more often

---

[56] Wes (1967), 31–4, discusses the successful examples of Constantius II, Valentinian II, and Gratian I, and the lack of success of Maximinus Thrax (too barbarous) and Julian (too Greek).

[57] Procopius, *Wars* 5.1.26.

[58] Theoderic himself never adopted or used this title, though his subjects applied it to him on a few occasions, Ennodius especially. See later discussion. Even Greeks could refer to Theoderic as a *basileus*. Procopius referred to Theoderic as "a true emperor" (*basileus alethes*), despite being a *tyrannos*; John of Nikiu, *Chronicle* 47, simply called him "emperor" (though this may be an issue of translation, since his source, John Malalas, uses *rhex*). Theophanes, *AM* 5931, claimed that the Goths "ruled the Western Empire" ("tes hesperiou Basileias ekratesan") and, *AM* 5977, that Theoderic "ruled Rome and all the West" ("ekratese de kai tes Rhomes kai pases tes hesperiou"), perhaps implying some sort of imperial position. Eustathius (frag. = Evagrius Scholasticus, *HE* 3.27) records that Theoderic "placed Rome under his control" but assumed the title "king" (*rhex*), while Damascius, *Vita Isidori* (frag. 64), claims that Theoderic (his title unstated) held "the greatest power over all Italy." On Greek imperial language used to describe Theoderic's realm, Chrysos (1978), 57. Though covering a longer durée, see also the studies of Lamma (1952); Garzya (1995); and Goltz (2008).

[59] *PanTh* 81: "pomposae vocabula nuda iactantia."

[60] For the title and its potentially inoffensive nature, Cullhed (1994), 33, who asserts, "*princeps* was not a normal part of the emperor's official title, though it was used ... to address any ruler in general." Similarly and in the specific case of Theoderic, Schmidt (1939), 410, refers to *princeps* as "untechnisch" and belonging to "den Ersten in Staate," while Jones (1962), 247, writes "[Theoderic] was ... often addressed as *princeps* – as were the other German kings – But officially he used only the title *rex*." The latter assertion is incorrect, however, insofar as the *Variae* and coins are official in nature (see later discussion). Moreover, in a specifically Italian context, the connection between *princeps* and emperor was obvious, while its use by other "barbarian" kings (much less frequently attested and often not self-referential) was less obviously imperial. Cf. Näf (1990), 112. The choice of title, then, was intentional and prudent: It was within the imperial tradition, but at the same time deferential to the preeminence of the eastern emperor. For more, see later discussion.

than *rex* in his official correspondence, making its Romanness abundantly clear by occasionally modifying the term with the adjective *Romanus*.[61] As *princeps*, then, he was rightly said to rule in the manner of Roman emperors (*imperare*). Likewise, as he was the only *princeps* who ruled Italy, cherished Rome, and honored the western Senate, his realm could be referred to interchangeably as the *res publica Romana*, *imperium Romanum*, and *regnum Romanum*, all of which signified the Roman Empire in contemporary Latin, *res publica* the most traditional expression.[62] In Italy, therefore, to be *princeps* was to be emperor, yet on a model very different from and undoubtedly more authentically Roman than the model employed by the reigning Roman emperor in the East, the *basileus*.

This restoration of the principate also harmonized well with the ideas of renewal and renovation that were current in Theoderic's realm, some already encountered at the beginning of this study. The rule of the *princeps* resonated in Italy, its very terminology reminiscent of the empire's first principate, which was generally remembered fondly. This principate, under Augustus, had ushered in a golden age and the *Pax Romana* after generations of civil war and disruption. Rome was transformed from a city of brick into one of marble, and, despite one-man rule, the institutions of the old republic appeared unscathed. Now, under Theoderic, a second golden age and kind of *Pax Romana* were being proclaimed after a similar stint of misfortunes.[63] Rome and specifically Roman *Romanitas* became intrinsic components of Theoderican propaganda, linking his reign with a glorious Roman past. Traditional games, for instance, were celebrated once more in the Eternal City with a *princeps* in attendance in both 500 and 519; ancient monuments, some of which had been erected by famous late republican statesmen, were refurbished at the *princeps'* order, so that "antiquity might seem rather decently restored"; and on inscriptions and coinage, Rome-oriented themes, many harkening to the republic, were commemorated.[64]

This conscious appeal to the late republic and early principate made it possible for Italo-Romans to laud Theoderic as a new Trajan, a new

---

[61] See Reydellet (1981), 214. Theoderic (and his successors) also used this title on their coinage (see Chp. 4), while a number of Italo-Romans (as will be seen) referred to him as such. For *princeps Romanus*, *Variae* 3.16.3 (cited in Chp. 10).

[62] See Chp. 1. Doubtless the interchangeability of royal and imperial language made it all the more easy for "Theodericus Rex" to be understood as a *princeps*, *imperator*, and even Augustus.

[63] But see Chp. 10, n. 143, for the modern term, "Pax (Ostro)gothica." This peace, generally referred to as *quies generalis* in Italian sources, was understood to be Roman. See Chp. 5.

[64] For greater elaboration, Chp. 8. For decently restored, *Variae* 4.51.12: "ut ... nostris temporibus videatur antiquitas decentius innovata."

optimus princeps who often imitated one of the first.[65] It likewise helped to transform Italy from the decadent Roman Empire of the fifth century into the glorious "republic" of the first century, a period worthy of admiration and imitation in those apparently trying times. Legitimacy was thus gained for Theoderic among Italo-Romans through his princely appellation and its ideological trappings; nor was he the first late antique ruler to understand their power within a specifically Italian context. In the early fourth century, at a time when the Romans of Rome had felt particularly betrayed by their own "un-Roman" emperors, Maxentius, a usurper like Theoderic, had also become *princeps* and for a time eschewed all other imperial titles.[66] He too had found the title politically expedient and had used it as a means of signaling to the Romans in his midst his veneration for those traditions that they perceived were being threatened. He too inaugurated a renovation of the city of Rome and advertised his *Romanitas* through the use of some of the same motifs on his coinage that would later be used by Theoderic.[67] But while Maxentius did eventually become an *imperator* and Augustus and sought to become a part of the very tetrarchy that his principate had opposed, Theoderic and his successors remained content with their princely and royal titles.

IMPERIAL HARMONY

The fact that Italy's "Gothic kings" never openly declared themselves *imperatores* or Augusti should not suggest that they or their subjects understood their position to be otherwise. The rule of the *princeps* worked in Theoderic's Italy much as it had in Augustus' day, concealing before certain audiences the reality and nature of its holder's power. Just as republican *principes* were in fact *reges* in disguise, so too were "Gothic"

---

[65] On the association with Trajan, *AnonVal* 60 (cited earlier) and Fiebiger 3, #7 (two *fistulae* recording Theoderic's repair to Trajan's aqueduct in Ravenna): "D(ominus) N(oster) Theodericus / civitati reddidit." Trajan generally had a reputation for being an *optimus princeps*, explaining why "good" emperors were sometimes likened to him. Nor was Theoderic the only Amal compared to Trajan. See *Variae* 8.3.5 and 8.13.4, both regarding Athalaric.

[66] See Cullhed (1994), 21 and 32–3, who draws heavily from Lactantius' *De Mortibus Persecutorum*. The emperor Galerius had revoked Rome's tax exemption privileges in 306, transforming Rome into another "provincial" city. His Dacian origins added further insult to injury, casting the emperor as an untrustworthy barbarian, an "enemy of the Roman name" ("hostem se Romani nominis"), who wanted the empire to be "not Roman but Dacian" ("non Romanum imperium, sed Daciscum"). See *De Mortibus Persecutorum* 27.8. The idea bears a certain similarity to the claim in Orosius, *Historiae* 7.43, that the fifth-century Visigothic king Athaulf had wanted to transform "Romania" into "Gothia." See Chp. 5, n. 64.

[67] See Cullhed (1994), 46–59.

principes imperatores and *basileis* in disguise. Nowhere are these ideas better expressed than in the very first letter of Cassiodorus' *Variae*, placed thus, no doubt, so that it might serve as an ideological statement for the entire collection.[68]

Addressed to Emperor Anastasius around 508 and after a period of open hostility, this letter was replete with praise for the eastern emperor and his empire, focusing especially on their uniqueness and exceptionality. Yet, such necessary and expected blandishments aside, this missive also drew attention to the equally unique role of Italy as one of two Roman republics and Theoderic as an imperial counterpart to Anastasius. There was no mention of either Theoderic's or his realm's subservience to, or dependence on, the East. Instead, the letter staked numerous claims to an imperial status for Italy and its ruler, cunningly masking such claims with language that was complimentary to the East.[69]

These compliments began with a laudation of Anastasius as "the most beautiful glory of all kingdoms, the health-giving guardian of the whole world, [and the one] whom other rulers rightly admire."[70] The assertion clearly suggested the primacy of the Byzantine emperor but was followed by the claim of Theoderic that he especially admired Anastasius because he had learned in "your [Anastasius'] Republic how to rule over Romans in a like fashion."[71] The statement implied much. Anastasius, for instance, while extraordinary owing to his rulership over the Roman Empire, nonetheless had his empire referred to as "your Republic," insinuating that there was more than one in existence. Indeed, "your Republic" anticipated the counterpart "my Republic," a sentiment that was consistent with current principate ideologies in the West. Moreover, the comment alleged that living in this eastern republic had literally taught Theoderic how to exercise imperial power (*imperare*) over Romans in a manner similar to Anastasius

---

[68] See Suerbaum (1961), 243; Claude (1978b), 42; and Krautschick (1983), 50–1. Cf. Moorhead (1992), 44, who questions the ideological importance of this letter and argues that it was included first because of its date, imperial addressee, and subject (friction between East and West). He also claims that other *Variae* letters demonstrate the inconsistency of this letter as an ideological statement. His examples, however, simply speak to the flexibility of Cassiodorus' Latin with respect to royal and imperial terminology.

[69] Contra Suerbaum (1961), 249–52, and Azzara (2001), 246, the latter of which sees an ideology of "unquestionable subordination," coupled with an "unconcealed attempt at emulation." Cf. Heather (1996), 229, who puts it a bit more bluntly: "The deference is superficial. An iron fist is evident within the letter's velvet glove." This may go too far, though.

[70] *Variae* I.1.2: "Vos enim estis regnorum omnium pulcherrimum decus, vos totius orbis salutare praesidium, quos ceteri dominantes iure suspiciunt."

[71] *Ibid*.: "nos maxime qui divino auxilio in re publica vestra didicimus, quemadmodum Romanis aequabiliter imperare possimus." For this reading of *aequabiliter*, see the following note.

(*aequabiliter*), a Roman emperor. The flexibility of fifth- and sixth-century Latin with respect to royal and imperial terminology no doubt made the wording acceptable in Constantinople, as did the use of the adverb *aequabiliter*, which might just as easily have been interpreted to mean "with justice."[72] But even so, the implications of these statements could not have been entirely lost: However disguised with flattery, Theoderic suggested that, just like the eastern emperor, he too ruled Romans and a Roman republic.

Such ideas of parity were reiterated in other passages of the letter, again with praise for the eastern empire and its emperor attached to self-promoting claims. Shortly after the remarks just discussed, for instance, Theoderic asserted, "Our kingdom is an imitation of yours, a model of its good design, a copy of its unique imperial rule."[73] Clearly the statement marked out Anastasius' realm as special and unique, but again the ruler of Italy professed that his own kingdom bore a certain similitude to it. His was not the original, but a copy both in form and in governance of Anastasius', a Roman Empire by implication, and no one else, he claimed, could assert this.[74]

The suggestion that the western Roman Empire was now somehow a copy of the eastern Roman Empire was certainly backward and an obvious historical irony but in fact made sense within a contemporary context and had further implications for the nature of Theoderic's reign. The developments of the fifth century, as already seen, had increasingly placed Constantinople in the more senior position within the empire as a

---

[72] Given the comparisons that the letter draws between Theoderic's and Anastasius' respective realms, it would make more sense to translate *aequabiliter* as "in a like manner," as opposed to "with equity" or "justly" ("gerecht") as some, such as Claude (1978b), 42, and Heather (1996), 221, citing Hodgkin (1886), have interpreted it. The equity of Theoderic's reign, while certainly consistent with Roman values, was not the point. For this definition, Lewis and Short: "*aequabiliter*: uniformly, equally, in like manner"; also *TLL*, s.v. "aequabiliter." Cf. *Variae* 2.43.3, 4.38.1, and 7.3.2, where *aequabiliter* can be translated either way. In *Variae* 1.27.3 and 9.2.4, on the other hand, "with equity" is undeniable.

[73] *Variae* 1.1.3: "Regnum nostrum imitatio vestra est, forma boni propositi, unici exemplar imperii." This is an oft-cited passage, though Hodgkin's less than satisfactory rendering is too frequently adopted. See Hodgkin (1886), 141: "Our royalty is an imitation of yours, modeled on your good purpose, a copy of the only Empire." While technically correct, it would be more consistent with the ideas expressed in the letter for *unici* to mean "unique" and *imperii* to mean "imperial power." Combined with the prior comparison, it explains how Theoderic's *regnum* imitates Anastasius' (implied *regnum*): Both look similar and are ruled similarly, although Anastasius' is the model and Theoderic's the copy. Moorhead (1992), 45, and Heather (1996), 229, suggest that the statement implies parity, while Barnwell (1992), asserts, "[Theoderic] makes no claim to be an emperor himself, or to have parity with Anastasius." Both observations appear false, provided *princeps* is understood to be imperial. Cf. Suerbaum (1961), 249–50, and Prostko-Prostyński (1994a), 83–4.

[74] *Variae* 1.1.3: "quantum vos sequimur, tantum gentes alias anteimus."

whole, often to Italian chagrin.[75] The reigns of "Greek" western emperors appointed from Constantinople had been symptomatic of this transition, while the transfer of Romulus Augustus' imperial *ornamenta* to Constantinople in 476 had served as a final coup de grace, rendering second Rome "first Rome." The return of these insignia in 497 could thus be imagined as a *(re)translatio imperii*, reinvesting Italy with its lost imperial status, yet their very investment from the East provided a rationale for how Theoderic's Italy might be construed as a copy. Italy was reinstated, for sure, but now in a junior capacity, secondary (and to some degree beholden) to the East. It did not mean that the western empire or its ruler was a subject of the East, but it did mean that within a united Roman Empire, East and West, the eastern emperor was technically *primus inter pares*. The deference, rather than subservience, that Theoderic showed to his senior colleagues, much like what any junior Augustus or Caesar would have shown, confirms this understanding.

Indeed, as a senior and apparent investor of the *imperium*, Anastasius had encouraged Theoderic to rule in a manner becoming a proper Roman emperor, and Theoderic reminded him of these injunctions in this letter, asserting that he had done so. "You frequently urge me to cherish the Senate," he wrote, "and to delight joyfully in the laws of [former] *principes*, so that I might govern well the entirety of Italy."[76] Beyond the republican language used to describe Roman emperorship, this statement, like the others, served to reinforce the Romanness and kindredship of both realms, so important at this time of friction. Theoderic declared that such Romanness should have prevented the outbreak of recent hostilities, asking the emperor, "How can you exclude from [your] Augustan peace one whom you did not want to differ from your customs?"[77] There was no reason, he avowed, for war to occur between both Roman republics, since they were of the same quality and "things joined in the unity of the Roman name" cannot be divided from each other.[78] In fact, though Anastasius was

---

[75] For Italian chagrin, Part I. For the fifth-century rise of the East, Kaegi (1968); Williams and Friell (1999); and Millar (2006). Even in the western capital of Ravenna, the eastern emperor was often depicted in a senior position. See Deliyannis (2010), 68–70, who discusses Galla Placidia's (now-lost) mosaic in the Church of St. John the Evangelist. The same motif is repeated in eastern and western coinage, where Valentinian III is consistently depicted as Theodosius' junior. See Carson (1981), #1531 (minted at Rome) and 1544 (minted at Constantinople).

[76] *Variae* 1.1.3: "hortamini me frequenter, ut diligam senatum, leges principum gratanter amplectar, ut cuncta Italiae membra componam."

[77] *Ibid.*: "quomodo potestis ab Augusta pace dividere, quem non optatis a vestris moribus discrepare." *Pax Augusta*, again, was an ideal with roots firmly established in the principate.

[78] *Ibid.*: "Additur etiam veneranda Romanae urbis affectio, a qua segregari nequeunt quae se nominis unitate iunxerunt."

not the ruler of Rome, Theoderic claimed that he continued to be held in the city's esteem through their (imperial) collegiality.[79] This notion too was not novel and bore a certain resemblance to the ideology of concord and fraternity espoused by the tetrarchs and the eastern and western emperors of the fourth and fifth centuries;[80] there may have been multiple emperors and empires, but that there was still only one Roman Empire was an old idea.

Nor were such historical precedents lost on Theoderic, who stated most tellingly, "we do not believe that you should permit any matter of discord to endure between both Republics, whose substance is proven to have been one under ancient *principes*."[81] This was a rather frank statement: Both Anastasius and Theoderic were ruling the two Roman *res publicae*, clearly meaning eastern and western halves of the empire, and unity between the halves needed to be fostered, just as it had been under (again tellingly) ancient *principes*. Both republics were thus to be "associated with each other in peaceful delight" and to aid each other "with their mutual strength."[82] "Let there always be one sentiment," Theoderic suggested, "one desire for the Roman Empire,"[83] implying not that there was only one Roman Empire and Anastasius was *the* emperor,[84] but that both republics together constituted a greater whole, just as they had in the past, and required imperial harmony to preserve their

---

[79] See the previous note. The idea finds some echo in the statement made by Theoderic to Zeno in Jordanes, *Getica* 291: "'dirige me cum gente mea ... ut ... ibi, si adiutus a domino vicero, fama vestrae pietatis inradiet.'" Here Theoderic explained to Zeno that the fame of the emperor would beam forth in Italy, should he defeat Odovacer, though perhaps only because Zeno would be credited for having sent Theoderic in the first place.

[80] The ideology can be seen especially in fourth- and fifth-century coinage, where imperial colleagues are featured together on reverses as triumphant generals or seated magistrates, or on obverses with busts facing ("vis-à-vis") or overlapping ("jugate"). In these cases a senior emperor might also appear larger than a junior. See the examples in Carson (1981).

[81] *Variae* 1.1.4: "quia pati vos non credimus inter utrasque res publicas, quarum semper unum corpus sub antiquis principibus fuisse declaratur, aliquid discordiae permanere." Hodgkin (1886) and those who utilize his translation render the passage "between two republics," which seems to undermine the letter's point that these are the *only* two Roman republics. Cf. Prostko-Prostyński (1994a), 84.

[82] *Variae* 1.1.5: "Quas non solum oportet inter se otiosa dilectione coniungi, verum etiam decet mutuis viribus adiuvari."

[83] *Ibid.*: "Romani regni unum velle, una semper opinio sit." The use of *regni* instead of *regnorum* demonstrates the understanding that each *res publica* could constitute a greater unity. See MacPherson (1989), 82–3, and Prostko-Prostyński (1994a), 83–4. Moorhead (1992), 44–5, suggests some possible flaws based on "republican" versus "royal" terminology, but see n. 68 (earlier).

[84] Such was the conclusion of Mommsen (1889/90) and the numerous scholars who have followed him.

unity.[85] Theoderic concluded his dispatch with a final nod to Anastasius' senior position, proposing once more that his own exploits would be associated with Anastasius,[86] but doubtless as a function of their fraternity, rather than through subservience or dependence.

This first letter of the *Variae* thus provided an ideological statement that asserted Italy and its princely emperor's Roman and imperial standing, while showing due reverence to the comparatively newly won and jealously guarded primacy of the East. This was not the only instance, moreover, when sentiments of this sort were expressed in the *Variae*; nor was this language restricted to the Ostrogothic court. A series of exchanges between the emperor Anastasius and the Senate of Rome, dated to 516, provides a case in point. Seeking an end to the Acacian Schism, the emperor himself wrote in a similar fashion, claiming that the dispute required deliberation in "both Republics" and requesting that the Senate intercede with the pope and "the most glorious king Theoderic," in order to reach a solution that would "profit both [Republics] in common."[87] This solution, which favored the emperor's heretical position, would then allow "the limbs of each Republic to be healthy with desirable sanity."[88] The Senate, which was not won over, nonetheless responded to Anastasius in equally revealing ways, referring to Theoderic as "your son" (*filii vestri*) and setting his position in parallel with the emperor's. Anastasius was an "invincible emperor" (*imperator invicte*), while Theoderic was "our lord the most invincible king" (*domini nostri invictissimi regis*).[89] Concord, both political and ecclesiastical, was likewise a concern. Just as "each Republic" was "worthy of harmony," they claimed, so too was the "unity of the Church worthy of restoration."[90]

[85] Cf. Claude (1978b), 43–4. Jones (1962), 128, suggests, on the other hand, that Theoderic's Italy had ceased to be a part of the empire and was now a kingdom ruled by a king. This was certainly not what Theoderic was claiming here.

[86] *Variae* 1.1.5: "quicquid et nos possumus, vestris praeconiis applicetur."

[87] *Collectio Avellana* 113.2–3: "quotiens utrisque publicis rebus prospera voluntate consulitur … ut duabus in unum concurrentibus causis animus incitatus, quod felix et bonum partibus sit.… Non videtur absurdum tam apud gloriosissimum regem quam apud beatissimum papam almae urbis Romae patres conscriptos imperiali petitioni coniunctos ea sperare, quae et nobis et sibi deo annuente in commune proficiant." Anastasius continues by referring to Theoderic as "the lofty king to whom the power and concern for ruling you [i.e. the senators] has been committed." For more on the meaning of this letter within the context of the Acacian Schism, Charanis (1939), 67, and Haarer (2006), 180–1.

[88] *Collectio Avellana* 113.4: "in qua utriusque rei publicae membra sperata sanitate salventur."

[89] *Ibid.*, 114.1.

[90] *Ibid.*, 114.7: "ut animo quam benigno in utraque re publica concordanda fuisti, tam esse pio in ecclesiae redintegranda unitate noscaris." The letter continues with a comparison between the peace between kingdoms (*pax illa regnorum*), meaning both halves of the empire, and the

The east Roman material is admittedly scanty, doubtless because an archival source like Cassiodorus' *Variae* fails to supply relevant examples.[91] Though true, it is clear that these ideologies of unity remained a regular feature in the official dispatches sent to the emperors in Constantinople, even as Justinian's troops were busy laying siege to the cities of central and southern Italy.[92] Senators, acting as the voice of Italy, for instance, beseeched Justinian in the mid-530s to seek peace, recommending that both rulers unite their wills and counsels, "so that it may be a profit to your [i.e. Justinian's] glory, should anything prosperous be added to me [i.e. Italy]."[93] A few years later, King Witigis likewise asserted to Justinian that, despite the injury caused by the emperor's forces, peace should be established, "so that both Republics might persist with their harmony restored, and that what was once established through the praiseworthy judgment of *principes* might be exalted more with God's help under your Empire."[94] As Theoderic's empire was crumbling, then, the idea that it represented one of two Roman republics within a unified Roman Empire remained strong, as did the sentiment of fraternity and eastern seniority.[95]

A Negotiable Unity

Letters like these were nevertheless official in nature, and the ideas that they promoted were intended for a specifically Byzantine audience, an audience that, again, had agreed to Theoderic's position in Italy, but only after much

peace of the church (*haec religionis*). The former was seen as profiting subjects, the latter the one ruling (*imperanti*) along with his people.

[91] But see Prostko-Prostyński (1994a), 85f., who discusses other instances of apparent eastern acknowledgment. Priscian of Caesarea's *De laude Anastasii Imperatoris*, perhaps given in 513, may provide similar indications. The phrase "Utraque Roma tibi iam spero pareat uni / Auxilio summi, qui conspicit omnia, patris" (ln. 265–6) has sometimes been interpreted as an appeal to the emperor to invade Italy. But Coyne (1991), 181–3, places it within the context of the Acacian Schism and sees it as "an expression of the theoretical unity of the empire," going on to compare it to *Variae* 1.1 (discussed previously). Cf. Chauvot (1986), 190–2, and Haarer (2006), 102–3. See, more generally, Wirth (1995), 254f., who emphasizes Byzantine cooperation with the Ostrogothic state until the death of Amalasuentha.

[92] For Athalaric, *Variae* 8.1; Amalasuentha, *Variae* 10.8; Theodahad, *Variae* 10.9, 10.19, 10.21, and 10.23. See also the Epilogue.

[93] *Variae* 11.13.4: "iunge quin immo vota, participare consilia, ut tuae gloriae proficiat, si mihi aliquid prosperitatis accedat."

[94] *Variae* 10.32.4: "quatinus utraeque res publicae restaurata concordia perseverent et quod temporibus retro principum laudabili opinione fundatum est, sub vestro magis imperio divinis auxiliis augeatur." The *principes* in question may have been Theoderic and Anastasius.

[95] *Sub vestro imperio* (in the previous note) seems to imply the acknowledgment of Justinian's senior position within a united Roman Empire, particularly because the prior sentence fragment refers to the *concordia* of both republics.

diplomacy and more or less as a fait accompli. Dispatches to the East needed to be especially deferential and carefully composed; the fact that they still expressed Italy's independent Roman status and the (near-) parity of its rulers with those in Constantinople should suggest all the more the validity of their claims, particularly among Italo-Romans. Context and audience, again, were key. In Italy, on the other hand, Theoderic could be even less cautious in stating his position, either upholding these ideologies of imperial fraternity or disregarding them altogether according to his personal whims and his subjects' needs. Disregard could be beneficial, in fact, since it might serve to assert to Italo-Romans that they once more occupied the primary position within a greater Roman Empire, while reverence could be equally useful, since imperial harmony had, by this time, become a kind of expectation, a venerable institution.[96]

Traditional opportunities for reinforcing such ideologies of fraternity and unity reveal the flexibility of their utilization. The tendency for coins in Theoderican Italy to bear the eastern emperor's bust and name on the obverse may provide one such example. Though often assumed to have stemmed from an imperial prohibition, the practice may have actually been pragmatic and a perpetuation of earlier practices.[97] Precedents had been set during the Later Empire, when, in a show of unity, emperors intentionally minted the coinage of their colleagues, adopted their motifs, or used images and inscriptions designed to reference imperial concord.[98] Already by the mid-fifth century, however, eastern mints had ceased producing coins in the name of the western emperors, while the practice continued in the West, as seen earlier, into the reign of Odovacer.[99] More telling

---

[96] As Chp. 2 has demonstrated, this lack of harmony had been a cause for complaint against the rulers of the fifth century, particularly Galla Placidia.

[97] There seems little justification, in fact, to conclude that the Amal rulers of Italy were specifically prohibited from minting gold coins in their own name, despite the claim of Procopius, *Wars* 7.33.5, that this was an imperial prerogative (Procopius also states here, wrongly, that the Persians respected it). Clearly the image of the eastern emperor dominates Italy's gold coinage, but this might be interpreted as a sign of respect toward a senior colleague (see later discussion) or simply have been a pragmatic move for the sake of commercial regularity. Cf. Clover (1991), whose analysis of bronze coinage reforms in North Africa and Italy demonstrates the importance of such regularity at this time. Anastasius, it seems, even adopted these reforms. See also Part IV, which discusses some of Theoderic's economic policies.

[98] They also refused to mint their so-called colleagues' coinage or adopt their motifs, spurning their legitimacy. See Cullhed (1994), 35–9, for examples from the late third and early fourth centuries. For fifth-century practices, see the following note.

[99] See Kaegi (1968), 42, and Kent (1994), 123f. Valentinian III was the last western emperor to have his coinage minted in the East, while western mints produced coins in the name of Arcadius, Theodosius II, Marcian, Leo I, Basiliscus, and Zeno. They also continued producing coins that depicted both emperors together on the reverse. This was especially the case during

and unlike Odovacer, examples of coins bearing Theoderic's or his successors' image do survive in gold, silver, and bronze (albeit in very limited quantities),[100] challenging the idea of a prohibition, while a letter in the *Variae* makes plain the near-sacred significance that Theoderic attached to his own numismatic portraiture.[101] If voluntary, therefore, the minting of coins in the name of the eastern emperor could have had a propagandistic value, demonstrating the concord of both republics and signaling the western *princeps*' respect for his senior imperial colleague.[102] Anastasius' image might be featured on the obverse of a gold solidus minted in Rome, but Theoderic's monogram (in imitation of the emperor) graced the reverse and associated the two.[103]

Coins, then, might reinforce imperial harmony, but other artistic media might not be at all in keeping with this ideal. The tetrarchs, for instance, had used statues as a means of demonstrating their imperial oneness, each emperor bearing a striking resemblance to and supporting the other, while a later imperial practice was to erect an emperor's statue flanked by his respective colleague. In all known artistic representations of Theoderic, however, the *princeps* stood alone, suggesting to onlookers that the glory and *dominium* signified in his likeness were only his and did not complement the eastern emperor's, contrary to Theoderic's avowal.[104] Nor were eastern emperors entirely blind to this situation and

the reign of Anthemius. The last eastern emperor to do so, however, was Theodosius II, who depicted the western emperor (Valentinian III) as his junior.

[100] Odovacer seems to have minted his likeness in silver and bronze (without a title), while Theoderic's Roman mint produced a gold triple solidus ("Senigallia Medallion") that depicted him in an overtly imperial manner, complete with the title *princeps* (see Chp. 4). The later king Totila minted gold coinage bearing the bust of the long-dead emperor Anastasius, a statement of his lack of concord with Justinian, and silver and bronze coinage with his own bust. The bronze issues of Athalaric and Theodahad also feature their likenesses. See Wroth (1911); Kraus (1928); and Metlich (2004). Indeed, and for obvious reasons, bronze issues were far more popular (and had many more variants) in Italy than silver and gold. No known gold coins, for instance, survive from the reign of Theodahad, though certainly some must have been minted. Bronze, while perhaps less prestigious, made good economic sense and had the greatest potential audience.

[101] *Variae* 7.32.1: "tamen omnino monetae debet integritas quaeri, ubi et vultus noster imprimitur ... nam quid erit tutum, si in nostra peccetur effigie, et quam subiectus corde venerari debet, manus sacrilega violare festinet?" Gold, silver, and bronze coinages are specifically mentioned in *Variae* 7.31.2.

[102] Cf. Claude (1978b), 49.

[103] For examples, Wroth (1911), 55 (#28–9); Kraus (1928), 84 (#10); and Metlich (2004), 84–5 (#5 and 7a–b). Similar coins were minted in Milan and Ravenna, and silver issues are even more explicit, with Theoderic's monogram occupying the bulk of the reverse and encircled by the inscription "INVICTA ROMA."

[104] See the following chapter.

its implications. In the peace terms that he offered to King Theodahad, Justinian himself had included the stipulation that, henceforth, all statues of Italy's rulers would have to be accompanied by similar statues of the current eastern emperor and, moreover, that the latter would be placed in the senior position.[105] To that point, however, this had obviously not been the case.

Unity (or a lack thereof) might also be shown on an annual basis when it came time for consuls to be selected. Like his imperial predecessors, Theoderic had the power to appoint his own consuls and invest them with their curule rods, yet he often (but not always) sought confirmation of his choice from the eastern emperor.[106] Acceptance in the East was not necessary but was nonetheless a source of honor for would-be consuls and, by the early sixth century, an established tradition. There was always the potential for the western candidate to fail to win recognition in the East owing to political friction or, perhaps more admirably, to hold his consulship alone because of miscommunication or the lack of a worthy eastern colleague.[107] Neither scenario, however, weakened the validity of his consulship, especially before a western audience,[108] but the failure to secure acceptance in the East was an obvious indicator of disunity, while success implied the opposite. The consulship of Eutharic in 519 provides a special case in point. Theoderic's son-in-law and designated heir, he served as consul with the eastern emperor Justin as his colleague and

---

[105] Procopius, *Wars* 4.6.5. See, with serious caveats, Chrysos (1981) for a discussion of the various peace terms offered by Justinian and their implications for the past and (desired) future of the Ostrogothic state.

[106] There is a tendency to accept the statement of John Malalas 15.9 that Theoderic received the codicils of his chief magistrates from the Byzantine emperor, including the rods of consuls. The passage, however, is misinformed, since Malalas claimed that Theoderic received these codicils in the emperor's very presence, a ridiculous idea. *Variae* 2.1 (discussed in Chp. 10) and 6.1, moreover, make it abundantly clear that Theoderic selected his consuls and granted insignia to them of his own volition, contacting the emperor after the fact and hoping for (but not requiring) acknowledgment. Procopius, not surprisingly, provides contradictory information. Cf. *Wars* 5.6.3 and 6.6.20, with Prostko-Prostyński (1994a), 110–11. Jones (1962), 127, essentially agrees with the position taken here, while Mommsen (1889), 241; Bury (1958), vol.1, 455; Chrysos (1981), 454–60; and MacPherson (1989), 82, take more restrictive views. The art-historical analysis of Delbrueck (1929), based on consular diptychs and restrictive in its interpretation, has been challenged convincingly by Cameron and Schauer (1982).

[107] The consuls of 495–7 (cited earlier, n. 38) are obvious examples, as is Boethius, who was consul without a colleague in 510.

[108] Indeed, as Cameron and Schauer (1982), 133, so nicely put it, "There was no point in being anything but a legitimate consul." Hence, whether recognized in the East or not, Theoderic's consuls were legitimate.

was even adopted as the emperor's son-in-arms, a clear indication that Constantinople approved of his succession.[109]

Other venues proved equally negotiable in Theoderic's Italy. Inscriptions, for instance, had typically been erected in honor of both emperors or at least referred to both in passing. But in Theoderican Italy only one known inscription appears to have perpetuated this practice, possibly placing Theoderic in a role subordinate to Anastasius.[110] All others made no reference to the eastern emperor, and one series of inscriptions even referred to Theoderic as *semper Augustus*.[111] Acclamations at public and private assemblies (such as games or ecclesiastical synods) were quite similar. A synod convened at Rome in 499, for example, concluded with nearly two hundred bishops, priests, and various attendees shouting in unison thirty times, "hear us, Christ; long live Theoderic,"[112] while the pope received only twenty of the same acclamation, and the eastern emperor, Anastasius, none at all. Aside from demonstrating Theoderic's legitimacy vis-à-vis the Italian church, these minutes show just how irrelevant the Byzantine emperor could be, his absence militating against an understanding not only of Theoderic's junior status but of fraternity in general. Theoderic was not just preeminent, but unassociated. And, indeed, there is room to argue that the exclusion of the eastern emperor from such acclamations was a regular practice, given that it too appears as a grievance in Justinian's peace offer to Theodahad.[113]

---

[109] Nor was this the first time a senior emperor honored a junior emperor or heir apparent by serving as consul with him. This was the case in 425, 426, and 430, for instance, when Valentinian III served as consul with Theodosius II. In all three instances, coins were minted celebrating the event. See Kaegi (1968), 19–23, with Carson (1981), #1544, 1582, 1596, and 1599.

[110] Fiebiger 1, #187 (*ILS* 825 and *CIL* 6 1794), corrected with Bartoli (1949–50): "Salvis domi[n]is nostris Anastasio Perpetuo / Augusto et Gloriosissimo ac Triumfali Viro / Theoderico." Here both Theoderic and Anastasius are hailed as "our lord," but Anastasius is an Augustus, while Theoderic (placed second) is reduced to being a "most glorious and triumphant man." Given the connection between triumph and emperorship (discussed later), the title had some imperial connotations. Jones (1962), 128, concludes that the passage implies that Theoderic was Anastasius' colleague, while Bartoli (1949–50), 87–8, disagrees, placing the inscription between the years 493 and 497, i.e. before Theoderic's official recognition in the East. Claude (1978b), 53, interprets *Augusto* as applying to both Theoderic and Anastasius, but one would expect *Augg* or *Augustis* instead.

[111] Fiebiger 1, #193 (*ILS* 827 and *CIL* 10 6850–2): "Theodericus victor ac triumfator semper Augustus." For more of this inscription, see later discussion and Chp. 10.

[112] *Acta Synhodorum Habitarum Romae* I: "Exaudi, Christe! Theoderico vitam! / dictum XXX."

[113] Procopius, *Wars* 5.6.4. Italians were to proclaim the eastern emperor's name first whenever they acclaimed their own ruler in places like the theater and hippodrome. Prior to this point, it is not clear whether they had proclaimed him second or not at all. On the basis of Jordanes, *Getica* 304, Chrysos (1981), 468–9, suggests that westerners had honored God, then the emperor, and then Theoderic. But Jordanes' passage has nothing to do with public

Titles and Titulature

Just as the junior status of Italy's *princeps* and his fraternity with the eastern *basileus* were negotiable in Italy, so too was the style of emperorship that he adopted or had applied to him by his subjects. The language of the principate had always remained an intrinsic part of the Italo-Roman understanding of the Roman Empire and emperorship, but Italy had nonetheless experienced the empire's physical and ideological transformations over the centuries. History had initiated Italo-Romans into the cultural systems of the dominate, its language and ideas becoming a part of their conception of rulership. Theoderic and his successors were able, therefore, to draw safely from a rich heritage of Roman emperorship, and their subjects could prove rather amenable to a number of competing imperial incarnations. Indeed, since the manifestation that they held most dear, the *princeps*, remained an overriding ideology, apparent inconsistencies could become perfectly acceptable, while centuries of tradition helped to make any inconsistencies completely excusable and even necessary.

The most noticeable of these alternative images and most ironic, at least from a republican standpoint, was embodied in the specifically royal language of the era. That Italy was simultaneously presented as a *res publica* ruled by a *princeps* and a *regnum* ruled by a *rex* would have seemed absurdly contradictory centuries before. The latter terms, however, had by this time lost their first-century meaning and now served to suggest, once more, the imperial standing of Italy and its ruler. *Rex* was still antithetical to *princeps*, to be sure, but now as a synonym for *basileus*, eastern, despotic emperor, similar to *imperator*. Other titles and epithets helped to assimilate "Theodericus Rex" to this eastern style of emperorship, indicating that Italy's ruler was more concerned with "empty titles of ostentation" than Ennodius or Procopius were willing to admit. Though apparently not employing the terms himself, for instance, Theoderic was publicly acknowledged as an Augustus on a few occasions and described as an *imperator*.[114] These titles obviously had republican and principate

acclamations and should be read as further evidence for the importance of imperial unity. In this passage a dying Theoderic instructed his Goths to honor their new king, love the Senate and people of Rome, and, after God, keep the (note the choice of words) *principemque Orientalem* peaceful and favorably disposed to them always. The Synod of 499 (cited earlier), moreover, proves that acclamations in the West sometimes ignored the eastern emperor and thus provides a better rationale for Justinian's terms: he was asserting a primacy in Italy heretofore denied.

[114] For Augustus, *ILS* 827 (cited earlier) and *PanTh* 7: "augustior"; for imperator, *VE* 143: "omnes retro imperatores"; *VE* 18: "boni imperatoris"; Ennodius, *Libellus Pro Synodo* 36:

origins, but had been transformed through their constant appropriation by emperors (the former even given new meaning under the tetrarchy), unlike *princeps*. Theoderic was also, in the style of a *basileus*, referred to as *Dominus Noster* (Our Lord), regularly employing these words on his coinage and official inscriptions.[115] Early principate emperors had gone out of their way to avoid this appellation, while *dominus* itself had given its name to the late antique dominate. Theoderic was likewise associated with victory through the use of the epithets *victor* and *triumphator*,[116] and, while victory and triumphs were not completely imperial prerogatives, the two were becoming increasingly connected in late antiquity.[117]

Together, titles like these implied that Theoderic was unequivocally the Roman emperor in the West, not just some sort of quasi-imperial figure who insinuated his position with antiquated language. The association of the ruler with a plethora of typically imperial virtues reiterated this understanding. Not just a *rex*, Theoderic could be described rather imperially as *gloriosissimus, pius/piissimus, inclytus, invictus/invictissimus, clementissimus, felix/felicissimus, fortissimus, serenissimus, praecipuus, maximus, bonus/optimus, magnificus, excellentissimus,* and *eminentissimus,* among other qualities.[118] Indeed, other contemporary rulers in the West adopted some of this titulature or had it applied to them by their subjects, but never as blatantly imperial as in Theoderic's case. A series of inscriptions from central Italy proclaimed Theoderic as "Our Lord, the most glorious and famous king ... victor and celebrator of triumphs, always Augustus, born

"imperialis ... auctoritas"; *ibid.* 73: "imperiala ... scripta"; *ibid.* 74: "imperatoris nostri"; *PanTh* 17 (debatable): "inter imperatores"; and #447.5: "quando non indiget imperator." For the context of most of these, Part IV.

[115] *Dominus Noster* is ubiquitous. For coins, Kraus (1928), 99 (#98–9). Wroth (1911) and Metlich (2004) do not include Theoderican examples but demonstrate the use of DN by his successors. For inscriptions, see those cited in this chapter and Chp. 8. The phrase is also attested in *PanTh*, the *Variae*, *CassChron*, and papal letters from the *Epistulae Theodericianae Variae* and *Collectio Avellana*. Cf. Prostko-Prostyński (1994a), 59f.

[116] For *victor*, see the Senigallia Medallion and *ILS* 827 (cited later), which likewise includes *Domitor Gentium*; for triumphator (or related titles), *ILS* 827 and 825; *PanTh* 5 and 10 (a theme throughout); and *CassOratReliquiae*, p. 466, ln. 9–19 (discussed in Chp. 10). For contemporary use in Constantinople, *Collectio Avellana* 113 (the letter of Anastasius discussed earlier).

[117] See McCormick (1986).

[118] Such language is (again) ubiquitous and will be encountered throughout this study. Hence, only a few examples are cited here. For *Gloriosissimus*, *ILS* 825 and 827; *pius/piissimus*, *Variae* 1.12.4; *inclytus*, *PanTh* 14; *invictus/invicitissimus*, Senigallia Medallion and *Collectio Avellana* 114; *clementissimus*, *PanTh* 29; *felix/felicissimus* and *fortissimus*, *CassChron*, anno 489; *serenissimus*, *Acta Synhodorum Habitarum Romae A. DI* (6. *Quarta Synodus*); *praecipuus*, *PanTh* 50; *maximus*, *ibid.* 5; *bonus/optimus*, *VE* 143; *magnificus*, *Epistulae Theodericianae Variae* 2 and 5 (letters of Pope Gelasius); *excellentisssimus*, *ibid.* 4; *eminentissimus*, *VE* 147.

for the good of the Republic, guardian of liberty and propagator of the Roman name, subduer of the barbarians."[119] There was more to this phenomenon than the wishful thinking of a few die-hard Roman imperialists residing in Theoderic's Italy.[120] The best that the contemporary Frankish king Clovis could expect, for instance, was *Dominus illustris* or *Dominus Magnificus*.[121]

Theoderic's reign (and by extension his successors'), then, constituted much more than simply that of a king along the same lines as Odovacer or other "barbarian" kings in the West.[122] He was a *princeps Romanus*, or Roman emperor, acknowledged as such by his own subjects and presented as such, though in a deferential and conciliatory manner, to the East. Although he regularly employed the "barbarian" title *rex*, as a "Roman" title even *rex* could serve to associate him with emperorship, a connection that was strengthened all the more by his use of customary imperial epithets and titles, or their application to him. Theoderic promoted the traditional idea of imperial unity and fraternity with the East, yet staked a claim to the West's separate existence as one of two Roman republics. Indeed, in Italy (though not in the East), his western republic was granted primacy over its eastern counterpart, much to the delight of heretofore disappointed patriots. More importantly, the language of his reign provided Italo-Romans with the kind of emperor they wanted, a *princeps*.

---

[119] Fiebiger 1, #193 (*ILS* 827 and *CIL* 10 6850–2): "Dominus noster gloriosissimus adque inclytus rex Theodericus, victor ac triumfator, semper Augustus, bono rei publicae natus, custos libertatis et propagator Romani nominis, domitor gentium." Later the inscription refers to Theoderic as "clementissimi principis" and contrasts him with "omnes retro principes," adding that it was erected "ad perpetuandam tanti domini gloriam."

[120] Contra Jones (1962), 128. Again, this kind of language, of which the earlier citation is a rather extreme example, was pervasive, and even when produced in excess by a private individual, was manifested publicly for all to see. It was, moreover, utilized by the state, since the dedicator of the preceding inscription was an illustrious statesman, who had been given permission to undertake the work by Theoderic himself (see *Variae* 2.32 and 2.33). How much more there was to this phenomenon than just "wishful thinking" is largely the subject of Parts IV and V.

[121] *Epistulae Austrasicae* 1.1 and 2.1, respectively. A letter directed to Clovis by the bishops convened at the Council of Orleans (511) similarly referred to the Frankish king as "Dominus … gloriossimus." See the edition of Gaudemet and Basdevant (1989). Clovis is simply addressed as "rex" in the letters of Avitus of Vienne and Cassiodorus' *Variae*, though see Chapter 4 for a (probably mistaken) reference to the Frankish king being hailed as an "Augustus." A grandson of Clovis, Theudebert (r. 534–48), would later strike gold coins bearing his likeness and the inscriptions "DN Theudebertus Rex/Victor." For this, Grierson and Blackburn (1986), 115–16, with Procopius, *Wars* 7.33.5 (discussed earlier). Contemporary, non-Frankish kings employed similar (i.e. simplistic) titles. See Wolfram (1967), 32f., and Conant (2012), 44–5, who discusses the Vandals.

[122] Contra the general conclusions of Jones (1962) and, though complicating the definition of "barbarian kingship" quite considerably, Barnwell (1992) and Wolfram (1979).

The republic, the Senate, Roman *Romanitas*, and *renovatio*: These were important components of the prosperity ushered in by the first *princeps*, Augustus; by the first late antique *princeps*, Maxentius; and by the first "Gothic" *princeps*, Theoderic, who, like Augustus, inaugurated a golden age. The kind of emperor that Theoderic was perceived to be, therefore, was intrinsic to the ideologies of restoration and resurgence that so dominated his reign.

4

THE IMPERIAL IMAGE

Clothes Make an Emperor

Titles, which were flexible, had the ability to insinuate to an Italian audience that Theoderic was a legitimate Roman emperor and his reign a sort of republican principate reborn. But an imperial image, as a part of this ideology, could have even greater resonance. A ruler's image was extremely important and influenced his public reception. From the very beginning, emperors had painstakingly cultivated their public images, going out of their way to ensure that the language of their empire was legitimated through visual confirmation. Augustus, in keeping with his nonmonarchical principate, for instance, not only refused ostentatious titles and powers, but refused to behave or appear in a manner inconsistent with a mere senator. He dressed as such and was deferential to his senatorial colleagues, maintaining the charade that his reign was nothing more than a benign stewardship of the republic. His imperial iconography, likewise, emphasized his *pietas* and Roman *Romanitas* at a time when many of Rome's elite were feeling especially conservative and xenophobic.[1] Despite radical shifts in imperial ideology, the same underlying principles applied in the later empire. The behavior and public display of emperors now promoted the splendor, detachment, and divine or near-divine qualities of their titles *dominus et deus* (or for Christian emperors *theophilos*), or served to highlight the unity of colleagues in a divided Roman Empire.[2] Emperors covered themselves in sacred purple embroidered with gold and studded with gems, wore similarly adorned slippers, and employed a jeweled diadem; they appeared unapproachable,

---

[1] See Béranger (1953); Wallace-Hadrill (1982); and Zanker (1988).
[2] See MacCormack (1981) and Kolb (2001).

sublime, and statuesque.[3] Their iconography asserted their connection with Roman victory;[4] their visual association with an imperial counterpart, either through physical resemblance or perhaps clasping a shoulder, reinforced the harmony of imperial wills.

Titles, to return, could insinuate that Theoderic was an emperor, but tenuously and only for so long. Visual confirmation of his imperial standing was also necessary, for emperors had to look and behave as such, living up to their subjects' expectations. The criteria for accomplishing this had varied over time and region, and some emperors, like Diocletian and Constantine, had been quite successful in making alterations according to their own designs. But innovation could be dangerous, and while wholeheartedly accepted by one audience, it could be despised and resented by another.[5] Generally speaking, the failure to live up to such local expectations (or to modify them in a passable manner) seriously jeopardized a ruler's legitimacy, often leading to sedition, usurpation, or assassination. Those who were egregiously offensive in their lack of regard might even suffer *damnatio memoriae*, the official erasure of their existence after death, a terrifying prospect for rulers who cared about their legacy.

The situation that Theoderic inherited in Italy, therefore, made an image amenable to Italo-Romans all the more important, particularly since defeat and intolerable innovation had largely defined the preceding era. While imperial language continued to be promulgated, imperial leadership in the West had failed to give substance to its claims of victory and unity, disappointing needs deeply entrenched in Italian society.[6] Moreover, Odovacer himself had abandoned ideologies of unity altogether by announcing the dissolution of an independent western realm. Italo-Romans may have continued to believe that they lived in the western Roman Empire, but their conviction lacked a visual component in the person of their ruler, who avoided not only imperial titles but also imperial dress. For a Theoderican

---

[3] Often-cited examples include the mid-fourth-century *adventus* at Rome of Constantius II and the Avar embassy directed to Justin II at Constantinople in the mid-sixth century. See Ammianus, *Res Gestae* 16.10 and Corippus, *In Laudem Iustini Augusti Minoris* 3.191f., with the commentary of Cameron (1976), 188–93, and MacCormack (1981), 40–5.

[4] See especially McCormick (1986).

[5] Again, this was particularly the case in rather traditional Rome (and by extension Italy), where elites often took exception to certain innovations that might have been more acceptable in the provinces. Galerius' "Dacian" persona (referenced in the preceding chapter) provides a case in point.

[6] Indeed, while the East was encroaching on the West and barbarians were stripping Italy of its provinces, western coinage continued to feature legends like "Victoria Augustorum," "Concordia Augustorum," "Virtus Romanorum," and "Invicta Roma" and include "unity" and "victory" motifs. For the disappointment, Part I.

restoration and principate to have substance that extended beyond empty rhetoric, then, these grievances would have to be redressed, and visibly so. Indeed, the preceding chapter has already demonstrated instances when Theoderican language and practices reflected this altered reality, particularly in the case of Italy's regained status as an independent western realm. But while expected behavior and traditional acts of *pietas* legitimized Theoderic's imperial standing and helped to fuel sentiments of restoration,[7] a specifically imperial appearance remained important and was, owing to its absence under Odovacer, equally suggestive of a kind of restoration.

What to Wear?

Still, given the rather traditional expectations of his Italo-Roman subjects, the predominance of principate themes, and the variety of imperial incarnations available in Italy, what exactly did such an appearance entail? Cassiodorus' own comments on Odovacer's lack of imperial adornment suggest that purple robes and some sort of insignia constituted the minimal requirements for dressing as an emperor, and indeed the former were known to have been employed since the Julio-Claudians.[8] But whether Theoderic utilized such items and, if so, to what extent, is a matter of debate.[9] The Byzantine historian Procopius is the only decisively negative commentator, claiming that the king never usurped the name of Roman emperor (but see Chp. 3) and never adopted his *schema*, meaning "appearance." *Schema* is generally interpreted as clothing and insignia, a reading that would imply that Theoderic was content with both a barbarian title (*rex*) and barbarian attire.[10]

---

[7] See Part IV.

[8] See *CassChron*, anno 298 and 476, discussed in Chp. 2.

[9] Purple is generally agreed upon, but the diadem is not. See Stein (1949), vol. 2, 115; Ensslin (1959), 156; MacCormack (1981), 233–5; McCormick (1986), 270 (n. 48 especially); MacPherson (1989), 81–2; Prostko-Prostyński (1994a), 158f.; and Kohlhas-Müller (1995), chp. 4. Claude (1980), 178–80, proposes a combination of Roman and Gothic elements, seeing such a mixture in the portraits of Theoderic's successors Athalaric, Amalasuentha, and Theodahad. The extent to which these elements are "Gothic" and (more importantly) were recognizably "Gothic" to contemporary Italo-Romans is unclear, however. Cf. Amory (1997), 341–4. Regardless, the conclusions drawn in Chp. 5 will suggest that Gothicness had a place in a Roman Empire.

[10] Dewing's translation of *Wars* 5.1.26 reads, "[Theoderic] did not claim the right to assume either the garb or the name of emperor of the Romans." But *schema* may have had another intended meaning. It may have indicated that Theoderic lacked some (but not all) of the emperor's insignia, or it may have indicated a more approachable disposition. Both would have been consistent with a *princeps* but would have disqualified Theoderic in Procopius' eyes from being a *basileus*.

But if this is what Procopius had intended, other sources make it clear that he was seriously, perhaps even intentionally, mistaken.[11] The *Anonymus Valesianus* account, it will be remembered, recorded that Anastasius remitted to Theoderic in 497 the very imperial ornaments that Odovacer had sent to Zeno twenty-one years prior. And the gesture, again, was significant and unique to Theoderic. Other barbarian kings were also sent certain trappings of Roman rule from Constantinople, but Anastasius had not dispatched a consular toga or honorary chlamys, both of which insinuated their wearer's nominal status as a subject and dependent.[12] Nor, like other client kings, had Theoderic been required to travel to Constantinople to receive his regalia from the emperor himself, or been sent less ornate insignia lacking in imperial purple, an absence that would have made an important statement about Theoderic's status, since the wearing of this color was a jealously guarded prerogative.[13] Presumably Anastasius had restored to Theoderic all the trappings of imperial rule sent to the East in 476: an eagle- or cross-adorned scepter, a crown or diadem, bejeweled slippers, lances, and purple and gold-embroidered robes.[14] Of course, if these had been the actual items used by Romulus Augustus, a youth, many would not have fit Theoderic, but other accessories, such as his scepter and lances, could have been appropriated. Regardless, the very act of returning these items clearly recommended that Theoderic could adopt all of them and with the complete approval of Constantinople.

---

[11] Such irony is common in Procopius' works and would present an interesting inversion of the Justin found in the *Anecdota*: a ruler with a Roman title and Roman dress, but a barbarian by nature.

[12] Gregory of Tours, *Historiae* 2.38, records that the Frankish king Clovis received letters from Anastasius conferring upon him a consulship. He was then described donning a purple tunic, chlamys, and diadem and being hailed as "consul aut Augustus." This last reference is probably mistaken, and alternative readings, such as "Augustalis," have been suggested. At around the same time, the Burgundian prince Sigismund was apparently named a patrician and possibly even *Magister Militum per Gallias* by Anastasius. See Avitus of Vienne, *Ep.* 93 and 94, with the following chapter.

[13] The example of the Lazi ruler Tzathes is often cited. See Agathias, *Historiae* 3.15.2, with Ensslin (1959), 78; Claude (1978a), 5, and (1980), 177–8; Prostko-Prostyński (1994a), 124–9; and Kohlhas-Müller (1995), 157 with n. 88. A direct comparison is not valid, since Tzathes was invested with a diadem (or crown), scarlet slippers, and gold-embroidered robes in Constantinople, but, and this is key, did not rule over Romans and was explicitly denied the right to wear purple. For the significance of imperial purple, Avery (1940); MacCormack (1981), part 3.1; and Kolb (2001), 117–20.

[14] On late imperial dress and insignia, Delbrueck (1933), 55–66; MacCormack (1981), 184–5; Kent (1994), 42–53; and Kolb (2001), 49–54; also Alföldi (1935), whose chronological coverage is longer.

Similar ideas can be found in the *Getica*. Much as in the *Valesianus* account, Jordanes wrote that Theoderic adopted a different, more royal style of adornment after the death of Odovacer. He claimed that Theoderic, now the ruler of both Goths and Romans, "assumed clothing with royal insignia, laying aside the garb of a private citizen and the dress of his race."[15] These words cast serious doubt on Procopius' insinuation that Theoderic was content to dress like a barbarian and suggest, instead, that his royal attire was Roman by derivation. Moreover, the timing was certainly right for this royal insignia to have been the same royal (i.e. imperial) ornaments dispatched from Constantinople in 497, and Jordanes' comment that Theoderic had done this only after Zeno had been consulted hints at this relationship.[16] The statement is curious, since Zeno at this point was already dead and may not have even agreed to this kind of royal position for Theoderic in 488.[17] But it is nonetheless reminiscent of Festus' second embassy, which had succeeded in securing Romulus' imperial ornaments for the king.[18] Perhaps Jordanes assumed that Festus' first embassy had reached some sort of agreement with Zeno before his death or, better still, he may have simply (even understandably) been confused and conflated the two embassies into one. At any rate, the gist of his account was that Theoderic, with the approval of the eastern emperor, had adopted royal attire that was clearly not Gothic and possibly of an imperial nature.

The exact features of this attire are difficult to ascertain, however, owing to the survival of few pictorial representations and verbal descriptions of Theoderic. It is important, therefore, to emphasize the fact that neither Jordanes nor the *Valesianus* account provides any indication that Constantinople placed restrictions on the extent to which Theoderic could adopt an imperial appearance. Had he so desired, Theoderic could have

[15] *Getica* 295: "Zenonemque imp. consultu privatum abitum suaeque gentis vestitum seponens insigne regio amictu, quasi iam Gothorum Romanorumque regnator."

[16] This can be inferred from the grammatically bizarre "Zenonemque imp. consultu" in the prior citation, which is probably a corrupt accusative or ablative absolute, both common in Jordanes' works.

[17] See Chp. 3. According to Jordanes, however, Zeno had indeed agreed to a royal position from the very beginning. Paul the Deacon, *Historia Romana* 15.14 (also cited, but with caveats, in the prior chapter), even suggests that these royal robes, which he calls "sacred" (i.e. imperial/ purple), were given to Theoderic before he left Constantinople.

[18] See *AnonVal* 64, cited in the previous chapter. Moorhead (1992), 37–8, who reads the *Getica* as pro-Theoderican propaganda, interprets the mistake as evidence for Jordanes' having invented the entire episode. This seems too hasty, especially since Jordanes was generally Byzantine in his sympathies. Prostko-Prostyński (1994a), 134–8, on the other hand, argues that the passage refers to the first embassy of Festus in 490/1 and concludes that Festus had been successful in securing these royal vestments. The account in the *Anonymus Valesianus*, however, seems to indicate otherwise.

dressed exactly the same as the emperor, yet, if deferential to his senior position or trying to affect a more republican mien, he might have appropriated less ornate (but still imperial) decoration.[19] Denying a diadem, for instance, was a particularly republican act, a show of *pietas* recognized by, among others, Julius Caesar and maintained under the early principate emperors.[20] Likewise, men like Cassiodorus knew well enough that simpler robes, marked out as imperial only by their purple coloring, had typified the attire of a *princeps*, in obvious contrast to the bejeweled and sacred purple of the late antique *dominus*.[21] Potentially, then, Theoderic could choose the way he wanted to appear before his subjects, and while imitating his eastern colleagues, important nods were at times given to the ideals of a republican emperor.

PURPLE-CLAD

It is almost certain that Theoderic's robes were dyed with imperial purple, in stark contrast with Odovacer, who had deliberately avoided this color and its implications. Contemporary Italian sources are riddled with references to Theoderic and his Gothic successors as "purple-clad,"[22] and the second letter of the *Variae* collection is specifically concerned with the production of purple dye for Theoderic's "sacred robes" (*sacra vestis*). The positioning of this letter was again likely intentional, following directly after the dispatch sent to Anastasius that outlined Theoderic's position as an imitator and imperial colleague.[23] When originally written, it merely conveyed the official message contained within and demonstrated (via its rhetorical flourishes) its author's expert knowledge and style. But within the *Variae* collection it served a new purpose of reiterating the imperial claims of the letter preceding it, providing a kind of visual confirmation for the ideology that it had espoused.

[19] Just as one possible interpretation of Procopius' *schema* would suggest. See n. 10. In fact, Caesars (junior emperors) are never depicted wearing diadems in their numismatic portraits. See Kent (1994), 49. The solidus commemorating the joint consulship of Valentinian III, then Caesar, and Theodosius II, then Augustus, also suggests that a Caesar might wear less ornate robes. See Chp. 3, n. 109.

[20] The theme of *recusatio* (refusal to take power) is prevalent throughout imperial history but has its roots in the late republic. See Béranger (1953), 137–69.

[21] See earlier discussion, with Chp. 2.

[22] See *Variae* 4.39, 8.1 (to a Byzantine emperor, no less), 8.5, 9.24, 9.25, and 11.1. For Ennodius' use of the term, see later discussion. On the advent of *purpuratus* as a descriptor for emperors, Kolb (2001), 49. In Theoderic's Italy, just as it had been in the past, "purple-clad" was more than simply a synonym for "royal."

[23] Cf. Krautschick (1983), 51–2.

According to this letter, the production of dye at Hydron (Otranto) had been delayed for unexplained reasons, and yearly dispatches of purple cloth had not been received at Ravenna; instead, neglect had "taken away their solemn use" and "conferred an abominable lateness."[24] Rebuking the count responsible, Theoderic expressed amazement at his lack of concern for the peril he was in, maintaining that it was "sacrilegious to sin against such garments."[25] Attentiveness was required, especially in "doing royal work," and it had been rewarded in the past by increasing the count's reputation in his province and by causing him "to come to the honorable notice of the *princeps* [i.e. Theoderic]."[26] But current negligence, the letter ultimately warned, was very dangerous and would have the opposite effect. "If you have any concern for your own safety," Theoderic sternly admonished, "make haste with the purple cloth that you provide our chamber annually, coming on that day when its transporter draws nigh to you: for we will send you not an exactor but an avenger, if you are believed to delay from some sort of mockery."[27] Just as with any late antique emperor, such an outrage against Theoderic's sacred purple could not go unpunished.

Ennodius too recognized Theoderic's right and worthiness to adorn himself with this imperial color, even referring to a hoped-for son of Theoderic as a "purple-clad offshoot."[28] His treatment of Theoderic's appearance in the *Panegyric*, however, casts some doubt as to the exact nature of these supposedly purple garments. At one point in his treatment, for instance, Ennodius asserted to Theoderic that he deserved all the splendor and trappings of royalty, but likewise boasted that these were entirely unnecessary, owing to his natural regal qualities. Lauding Theoderic for the glory of his appearance, he claimed that "the purple of your royal countenance shines upon the purple of your office,"[29] suggesting that Theoderic himself

---

[24] *Variae* 1.2.1: "Comperimus sacrae vestis operam, quam nos voluimus necessaria festinatione compleri, disrupto magis labore pendere: cui usum subtrahendo sollemnem abominandam potius inferre cognosceris tarditatem. Credimus enim aliquem provenisse neglectum."

[25] *Variae* 1.2.4: "miramur tua te pericula minime cogitasse, dum sacrilegus sit reatus neglegentiae in tali veste peccare."

[26] For royal work, *Variae* 1.2.5: "cum regale opus crederis agere"; rewards, *Variae* 1.2.6: "Hoc ergo remissio tua neglegit, quod te in provincia subvexerat et ad conspectum principis honorabilem venire faciebat."

[27] *Variae* 1.2.6: "si salutis propriae tangit affectus, intra illum diem, imminente tibi harum portitore, cum blatta, quam nostro cubiculo dare annis singulis consuesti, venire festina: quia iam non compulsorem ad te mittimus, sed ultorem, si aliqua credideris ludificatione tardandum."

[28] *PanTh* 93: "sed utinam aurei bona saeculi purpuratum ex te germen amplificet!" Cf. #458.10 (*In Christi Signo*), cited in Chp. 8.

[29] *PanTh* 89: "Sed nec formae tuae decus inter postrema numerandum est, quando regii vultus purpura ostrum dignitatis inradiat."

exuded a kind of regalness that was complementary to his station and its insignia. He then addressed the people of the Far East, known for their expensive purple textiles, entreating them to send the most purple vestments they had, sparing not one drop of their ennobling dye.[30] Theoderic was thus deserving of the most overt expression of his imperial likeness, purple cloth, and in an extreme manifestation whereby he consumed all of the East's best dye, despite its local availability. The reference extended beyond the Orient as simply the source par excellence of this royal pigment and alluded to Theoderic's presumed superiority over the Byzantine emperor; it was Theoderic, after all, not the Byzantine emperor, who deserved those robes earmarked for eastern consumption.

Beyond indicating Theoderic's worthiness to wear this imperial color, this treatment also provided Ennodius with an opportunity to compare Theoderic to his senior colleague and avowed model, ultimately demonstrating that it was preferable for Italo-Romans to have their current ruler as *dominus* and *princeps*. Theoderic was superior, foremost, because it was not necessary for him to concern himself with the fancy adornments and titles with which Byzantine despots seemed so obsessed. The eastern emperor needed all the oriental purple, expensive and perilously obtained jewels, and empty titles like *Alamannicus* (conqueror of the Alamanni), *Divus* (Divine), and *Pontifex* (Chief Priest) to assert his position; but Theoderic's natural qualities and behavior made these trappings superfluous.[31] Ennodius claimed that the association of purple with his king served to ennoble the vestments themselves rather than their wearer, and that "whatever ornaments the world yields ... will shine all the more having been decorated with the splendor of your [i.e. Theoderic's] venerable body."[32] It was nature and God's own guidance that had bestowed upon Theoderic those qualities that his eastern colleague could only affect, and poorly in Ennodius' estimation, through personal adornment.[33] Theoderic

---

[30] *Ibid.*: "Exhibete, Seres, indumenta pretioso murice quae fucatis, et non uno aeno bibentia nobilitatem tegmina prorogate."

[31] *PanTh* 81: "Quid? Frustra maiores nostri divos et pontifices vocarunt, quibus sceptra conlata sunt? ... Rex meus sit iure Alamanicus, dicatur alienus. Ut divus vitam agat ex fructu conscientiae nec requirat pomposae vocabula nuda iactantia, in cuius moribus veritati militant blandimenta maiorum." For commentary, Rota (2001a), 235–42, and Rohr (2006), 53–4. Cf. Reydellet (1981), 173–5, whose interpretation of *alienus* (as a reference to Theoderic) seems unlikely.

[32] *PanTh* 89: "quaecumque ornamenta mundo obsequente transmissa fuerint, decorata venerandi genio corporis plus lucebunt." *Genius* commonly means "glory/splendor" in later Latin, as evidenced in the works of Ennodius and Cassiodorus.

[33] *PanTh* 91: "quod agunt in aliis dominis diademata, hoc in rege meo operata est deo fabricante natura." This idea echoes the Roman and Judeo-Christian understanding that rulers are selected

was lord not because of ostentatious display or fear of his imperial majesty, but because his qualities as a leader made him so. Indeed, Ennodius declared that Theoderic's "simple and unchangeable nature" made him better than the eastern emperors, who were concerned with the display of their wealth and endeavored with their finery "to obtain beauty alien to themselves."[34]

Perhaps Ennodius' words ought to be taken as an indication that Theoderic's attire was in fact less ornate than that of contemporary emperors residing in Constantinople. Such simplicity, of course, would have been consistent with current court ideologies and certainly in keeping with the practices of the principate. In a sense, then, Ennodius had described Theoderic as a perfect *princeps* who had returned to humbler, republican practices. But such a depiction had its limitations, and even Ennodius understood the difference between the simple, purple-striped toga of a high Roman magistrate, the attire of early emperors, and the sacred purple robes that Theoderic himself requisitioned annually from Hydron.[35] Indeed, Ennodius only suggested that Theoderic did not require such ornately decorated robes, perhaps in homage to the ideals of the principate or as a gentle hint to his master to remain humble; he never claimed that Theoderic did not wear them.

THE DIADEM

The diadem was another issue altogether. Its adoption by Roman emperors had been an expression of majesty as much as divinity, the splendor of its pearls and jewels intended to bedazzle and stupefy its beholder. The wearing of a diadem was the prerogative of an Augustus, and perhaps even more jealously guarded than purple-colored robes. The accessory itself had been adopted in imitation of eastern despots in the early fourth century, replacing the more republican crown of oak or laurel (*corona civica* or *laureata*), which had signified the emperor's role as a perpetually

---

by God. See Reydellet (1981), 166–8. The suggestion of Schramm (1954), 147, repeated in MacCormack (1981), 234, that Ennodius intended to reference Theoderic's long hair ("langen Haaren") is utterly ridiculous. Cf. Prostko-Prostyński (1994a), 164–5, with later discussion.

[34] *PanTh* 91: "illos faciunt tot divitiarum adiumenta conspicuos, sed hunc edidit simplex et indemutabilis figura meliorem. Quid! Cultu laborent qui cupiunt peregrinam obtinere pulcritudinem."

[35] See *PanTh* 15–16, where, in reference to Theoderic's consulship of 484, Ennodius described his wearing of something resembling a consular *toga palmata*. Similar togas, decorated with palm leaves and colored borders, are featured on contemporary consular diptyches and, while not simple, per se, were certainly less ornate than the costuming worn by late antique emperors.

triumphant commander (*imperator*) and savior. Its origins were therefore directly linked to the transition from the rule of the *princeps* to that of the more despotic *basileus*, and the eschewal of a diadem on Theoderic's part, again, might have been construed as a particularly republican or princely act by his Roman subjects. On the other hand, adopting a diadem or some variant thereof (a crown or wreath, for instance) may have been a prudent choice, despite contradictions.[36] Head insignia, after all, had been employed by emperors for centuries, and their complete absence in Theoderic's times might have caused the same kind of disapproval and confusion as Odovacer's avoidance of purple and similarly imperial trappings.

Whether Theoderic wore a diadem, however, is a great deal less certain than his use of purple. The evidence for his successors, at least, demonstrates that they employed a variety of royal head coverings, including diadems and other jeweled crowns.[37] But the evidence for Theoderic is mixed and fraught with many difficulties. In his panegyric, for instance, Ennodius called for a certain "wreath woven with different colored gems" and a "jewel guarded by a rather violent snake"[38] to accompany the garments dyed with oriental purple for his king. Though it was never explicitly called

---

[36] And there were many available styles. See Delbrueck (1933), 53–66, and Stout (1994), 83f. Earlier crowns and wreaths were still employed, while diadems themselves varied considerably and continued to evolve throughout this period. The simplest version resembled a purple headband, while more ornate styles were covered with jewels and/or pearls and included hanging ornaments (*pendilia*). By the sixth century, moreover, diadems were beginning to resemble enclosed crowns, and other types of imperial headgear, such as the *kamelaukion* and *modiolos*, were beginning to make an appearance. See Piltz (1977) and Charanis (1937), whose later written sources may be anachronistic in their treatment of fifth- and sixth-century details.

[37] For photos, Fuchs (1943) or (1944). On the diptych of Orestes (cos. 530) Amalasuentha wears ornamental headgear with what look like *pendilia*. Delbrueck (1929), vol. 1, 149, and others have identified this as a Phrygian cap or *pileus*, but see Amory (1997), 341–2. In other representations she wears a crown in the style of contemporary Byzantine empresses, though these may actually be representations of Ariadne or Theodora. While bareheaded in the diptych of Orestes, Athalaric wears a Roman helmet on some of his coins and, if Fuchs' identifications are correct, a diadem on statuary and a diptych of Amalasuentha. Theodahad's numismatic portraits, on the other hand, feature an ornamental headpiece usually identified as a late Roman or Germanic *Spangenhelm*, but possibly a *kamelaukion*, the crown of choice for later Byzantine emperors, but originally reserved for Caesars. Cf. Piltz (1977), 136, and Claude (1980), 178. Finally, Totila is depicted with both a diadem and a helmet on his coinage, the latter once again identified, unnecessarily, as a Germanic *Spangenhelm*. Procopius, *Wars* 8.31.18, describes his headgear as a wonderfully adorned *pilos*, meaning "helmet," not a fur or felt cap like Amalasuentha's supposed *pileus*. See Anderson (1970), 28–37. See also Agathias, *Historiae* 1.20, and Theophanes, AM 6044, who claims that Totila wore a jeweled *kamelaukion*.

[38] *PanTh* 89: "discoloribus gemmis sertum texatur, et quem vehementior vipera custodit lapis adveniat."

a diadem, the description certainly could be interpreted as such, especially since these items were coupled with Theoderic's robes and later described as ornaments necessary for Byzantine emperors.[39] A bejeweled wreath is consistent with the design of a diadem, a band sometimes of woven gold, decorated with precious stones and pearls, and wrapped around the forehead. Moreover, in describing such a diadem as a "wreath," Ennodius may have been alluding intentionally to the republican *coronae* described previously, rendering Theoderic's diadem all the more princely, or, given his rather ornate Latin, he may have simply been attempting to demonstrate his *eloquentia*. The "precious jewel," on the other hand, may have been a reference to an imperial fibula or to the central gem featured on many representations of Roman diadems.[40] Diadems like these were well known in Italy and beyond and were praised by Theoderic for their eye-dazzling, "fluctuating luster of gems."[41]

Regardless of this description, Ennodius later asserted that finery of this sort was unnecessary for Theoderic, casting some doubt on its actual employment. Yet just as with purple robes and ostentatious titles, their necessity and actual use were two very different matters: Theoderic may not have *needed* purple, but he clearly wore it, and by extension, despite not needing a diadem, he may have worn one of these as well. Moreover, other literary sources, while somewhat ambiguous, provide aggregative evidence in favor of a diadem's use. A brief remark in a letter in the *Variae* provides a case in point. Here, while conferring the office of urban prefect on a

---

[39] MacCormack (1981), 233, and Prostko-Prostyński (1994a), 163, interestingly (but probably erroneously) interpret the passage to refer to jewels interwoven into the fabric of the purple Oriental cloth, explaining that this was an imperial prerogative. For this to be correct, however, *sertum* would have to act as a past participle modifying *indumenta* in the prior sentence, a difficult reading given that *indumenta* is plural. It would make much more sense to see *sertum* as a noun, as rendered in the translation here. Both Rohr (1995), 261, and Rota (2002), 225, agree with this assessment, translating *sertum* as *Girlande* (wreath) and *corona* (crown), respectively.

[40] Depictions of diadems, especially on coinage, tend to feature a central jewel. In late antique mosaics, on the other hand, the jewel appears to be optional. Justinian and Theodora at San Vitale in Ravenna, for instance, wear diadems covered with jewels and pearls, while the pseudo-Justinian at Sant'Apollinare Nuovo wears a diadem with a red jewel at the center. Jeweled fibulae are also depicted in these mosaic portraits and known to have been worn by Theoderic through the Senigallia Medallion (see later discussion). See Prostko-Prostyński (1994a), 163–4, and Stout (1994), 83f.

[41] See *Variae* 2.40.13 (directed to Clovis): "ut diadema oculis varia luce gemmarum." Clovis may have understood the comment from personal experience, since two sources (admittedly later) refer to his possession of a diadem or jeweled crown. See Gregory of Tours, *Historiae* 2.38 (discussed previously), and *Liber Pontificalis* 54.10. The numismatic portraits of the Vandal kings also feature diadems, while the Lazi king Tzathes (discussed earlier) was invested with a diadem by the emperor himself. Perhaps diadems were not so uniquely imperial after all.

certain easterner who had transferred his allegiance to the West, Theoderic explained that greater offices bestow greater honor on their holders, comparing the lesser honor acquired by one who guards the wine cellar to the extreme honor acquired by an individual who "attends to the precious diadem."[42] The reference, of course, may have been entirely hypothetical or intended to demonstrate familiarity with practices in Constantinople,[43] but it is equally possible that Theoderic was referring to his own court and thus to his very own diadem.

The mid-sixth-century *Life of Caesarius of Arles*, on the other hand, provides a much more explicit reference. According to its authors, after arriving in Ravenna the bishop entered Theoderic's court and beheld the king, who "reverently rose to greet [him] after he removed the royal insignia from his head."[44] The act was intended to signify the king's utmost humility as a Christian and to cast him in the role of earlier Christian emperors, who, in accordance with biblical models, showed deference in the face of modern "apostolic" and "prophetic" men.[45] Like the Roman emperors before him, Theoderic humbled himself before the saint and removed his sacred head covering, perhaps a diadem.[46] A less specific term, "ornament/insignia" (*ornatus*), was employed, but a contemporary reader could have inferred its imperial quality from the nature and behavior of its wearer. And if not a diadem like those worn in Constantinople, it clearly served the same purpose. Less clear, however, is the trustworthiness of this account. Caesarius, of course, did travel to Ravenna and was honored by

---

[42] *Variae* 1.42.4 (to Artemidorus): "plerumque honor ex commendatis adquiritur nec tale est cellam vinariam tuendam suscipere, quale pretiosa diademata custodire." For Artemidorus, his links to the imperial family, and his eastern career, *PLRE* 2, 155–6 (Artemidorus 3), with *Variae* 1.43 and Chp. 6.

[43] Artemidorus and Theoderic, after all, had served in the eastern empire around the same time and were familiar with one another. Cf. McCormick (1986), 270, n. 48, who suggests the passage is metaphorical, and Ensslin (1959), 156, who takes it literally.

[44] *Vita Caesarii* 1.36: "Ut vero rex dei hominem intrepidum venerandumque conspexit, ad salutandum reverenter adsurgit hac, deposito ornatu de capite, clementissime resalutat."

[45] Indeed, the Theoderic depicted in this work referred to Caesarius as "angelic" and "apostolic" and gifted him handsomely, thus placing him in the company of other pious emperors (or their representatives), who had behaved similarly with earlier Gallic saints, such as Germanus of Auxerre or the Jural father Lupicinus. That the *Life* failed to reference Theoderic's Arianism is also telling, especially given its hostility to Arians elsewhere.

[46] For the precedent, Augustine, *Enarrationes in Psalmos* 65.4 and *Sermo* 61, with Vitiello (2005a), chp. 1 especially. McCormick (1986), 270, n. 48, calls Theoderic's royal insignia "some kind of headgear," which might be mistaken as a helmet or something non-Roman. He concludes that, since later Gothic kings *did* use diadems, they must have altered Theoderic's policy. But given the evidence discussed thus far (and to be discussed), it seems more reasonable to suggest that they perpetuated earlier practices.

Theoderic and others.[47] But whether the authors of his *Vita* were simply replicating a topos or received this story firsthand cannot be confirmed. The latter has much to recommend it, since the authors were confidants of Caesarius and composed his biography shortly after his death;[48] and the former, while not necessarily denying Theoderic a diadem, is still useful insofar as it reflects a Gallic understanding of Theoderic's imperial pretensions.

Despite certain ambiguities regarding the use of a diadem, these written sources nonetheless suggest that Theoderic presented himself in a way that conformed to Italian expectations of Roman emperorship, complete with sacred purple and insignia, and thus in direct contrast with Odovacer. Artistic representations, moreover, can shed further light on the extent of this imperial likeness, whether through depictions of Theoderic wearing a diadem, wrapped in purple, or through his association with traditional imperial iconography or motifs. Yet the interpretation of images from this period is also not without its own problems and is rendered additionally difficult by the nature of their transmission. Indeed, though contemporary sources refer in passing to a number of artistic representations of Theoderic,[49] only one image that is unquestionably his has survived. The remaining "known" images are of uncertain attribution or survive, in part at least, through the rather detailed observations and descriptions of later commentators. Of the latter, the *Liber Pontificalis Ecclesiae Ravennatis*, a historical work of a ninth-century priest and abbot from Ravenna, Agnellus, is undoubtedly the most important.

AGNELLUS AND THEODERIC

Agnellus' history, which consists of a series of episcopal biographies beginning in the first century AD, was intended to celebrate the autonomy and autocephaly of the See of Ravenna at a time of increased Roman (i.e.

[47] They included the deacon Helpidius, who was also Theoderic's physician, and Pope Symmachus, who granted Caesarius the *pallium* and made him papal vicar to Gaul. See *Vita Caesarii* I.38–42, with Klingshirn (1994a), 124–30.

[48] See Klingshirn (1994b), 2, who places the *Vita*'s composition within seven years of Caesarius' death in 542. The work was a collaborative project of five clerics who knew the bishop personally.

[49] Procopius, *Wars* 5.14.22, provides a strange anecdote concerning a brick portrait of Theoderic in Naples that crumbled in such a way that it divined the future. Statues of Theoderic in Rome, which were also destroyed, are mentioned in *Wars* 7.20.29 and Isidore of Seville, *Hist. Goth.* 39.

papal) dominance.[50] Though true and though focusing on Ravenna and its church, the work is replete with digressions and anecdotes, many of which include rich descriptions of the various artistic and architectural sights in and around ninth-century Ravenna. It is, hence, an invaluable source for both the history of this city and its art, and likewise relevant to the present study for its descriptions of three representations of Theoderic, one in the form of an equestrian statue and the others in mosaic.

Caution, however, must be observed in using Agnellus' work, despite its potentially enormous value. By the ninth century a number of alterations could have been made to these pieces of art, unbeknownst to their observer.[51] Worse still, Agnellus may have been confused about who had been depicted and in reality described a likeness that was not Theoderic's.[52] Either occurrence would mean that the history's descriptions themselves might be authentic, but not their association with Theoderic.[53] Moreover, even if such confusion or alterations were not a factor, the information about these works included by Agnellus was idiosyncratic, limited to his personal impression and tastes. Despite his attention to detail, he was not a technically trained art critic; nor did he always systematically examine these works, aspiring to provide as accurate a portrayal as possible, down to the tiniest minutia. His descriptions were, again, anecdotes within a greater historical opus. Certain features of ideological import, therefore, such as color or an inscription, may not have been recorded, though historically central to the piece's original message and context, and of the utmost importance for the present discussion.

These caveats aside, the mosaic representations of Theoderic as described by Agnellus are still quite revealing. The first, located at Theoderic's palace at Pavia, was simply described as a well-decorated image of Theoderic

---

[50] See Deliyannis (2004), 17–19, who also places the work within a context of securing the rights of clergymen in the face of increased episcopal oppression.

[51] Changes to the mosaics at Sant'Apollinare Nuovo are a case in point. See *LPR* 86, where only some of these (known) alterations are described. Cf. Deliyannis (2010), 6.

[52] An equestrian statue in a palace known to have been Theoderic's, for instance, might have been assumed to be a representation of Theoderic, and with good reason, yet it could have been any of Theoderic's male successors (or, for that matter, a Roman emperor, exarch, or even Lombard king). Similar confusions are known to have occurred in the Middle Ages: The equestrian statue of Marcus Aurelius now housed at the Capitoline Museum in Rome, for instance, was commonly thought to depict Constantine I owing to its placement in the Lateran. See Zucchetti (1953). See later discussion for an equestrian statue of Theoderic that may have portrayed Zeno and a surviving mosaic of Justinian that probably depicts Theoderic.

[53] Cf. Deliyannis (2004), 70f., who claims that the extant images correspond well with Agnellus' descriptions.

sitting horseback.[54] As such, it provides a good example of the problem just outlined: that Agnellus sometimes offered too little information to allow for analysis. The description of the second mosaic as similar to this one, however, suggests that there were common themes shared by them.[55] This second mosaic was located at the entrance of Theoderic's palace at Ravenna, called the Chalke on the model of the Great Palace at Constantinople,[56] and its features were described in such a way that some of its deeper symbolic meaning may be inferred. Agnellus claimed that Theoderic was depicted here holding a lance in his right hand, a round shield in his left, and covered in lorica armor.[57] These items were the trappings of both a commander and a ruler and are featured prominently in depictions of emperors as triumphant *imperatores*.[58] Though unclear, the representation may have been intended to depict Theoderic as a triumphant Roman ruler, a *princeps* or even *imperator*. More significant than this, Agnellus' description continued with the claim that Theoderic was flanked in this image by personifications of Rome and Ravenna, the principal cities of his empire, and a motif observable in other imperial iconography.[59] Rome stood near Theoderic's shield, to the

---

[54] *LPR* 94: "Ticinum ... ubi et Theodericus palatium struxit, et eius imaginem sedentem super equum in tribunalis camerae tessellis ornatam bene conspexi."

[55] *Ibid.*: "Hic autem similis fuit in isto palatio quod ipse aedificavit."

[56] *Ibid.*: "in tribunale triclinii quod vocatur Ad mare, supra portam et in fronte regiae quae dicitur Ad Calchi istius civitatis, ubi prima porta palatii fuit, in loco qui vocatur Sicrestum, ubi ecclesia Salvatoris esse videtur." This description places the image within the palace complex of Theoderic, located near his Arian church dedicated to Christ the Redeemer (Salvator), now Sant'Apollinare Nuovo. For the connection between this palace complex and the one at Constantinople, see later discussion. It is, of course, certainly possible that Chalke was a ninth-century appellation, rather than one used in Theoderic's time.

[57] *LPR* 94: "in pinnaculo ipsius loci fuit Theodorici effigies, mire tessellis ornata, dextera manu lanceam tenens, sinistra clipeum, lorica indutus."

[58] The best examples occur in coinage, which tended especially in the fifth century to feature portraits of emperors brandishing a lance, covered in lorica, and helmeted. Reverses might likewise include military scenes in which similarly dressed emperors triumphed over barbarians or received a globe from a winged victory or Roma herself. For examples of these motifs, Carson (1981); also Belinger (1958), 149f., and Bruun et al. (1964), 236f. A similar image of a "barbarian king" accompanied by many of these items can be found on the fifth-century signet ring of Childeric of the Franks. This too was intended to depict the king in a specifically Roman fashion. See James (1988), 61, and Schramm (1954), 213–17, the latter of which suggests (unnecessarily) that the use of lances is of Germanic origin.

[59] Once again the best examples can be found on coinage, where personified cities, especially Rome, were common. Such numismatic personifications of Rome served the purpose of associating an emperor with the city, demonstrating his authentically Roman and hence rather traditional *Romanitas*. For Theoderic's use of such motifs, see earlier discussion and Chp. 8. Athalaric also introduced a new bronze coin type, which featured a personification of Ravenna

left, helmeted and holding a spear, the decrepit old woman of Ennodius' panegyric rejuvenated and as fierce as ever. Ravenna stood to the right, also grasping a spear, her legs straddling the sea and land, doubtless an allusion to her status as a port and to Theoderic's claims to *dominium* over land and sea.[60]

Such imagery seems quite indicative of Theoderic's imperial pretensions and likewise to have echoed contemporary sentiments of a restoration of Rome and Italy's status. Placed in the senior position, at the actual right hand of Theoderic,[61] Rome was once more fully armored and reinvigorated, an active participant in the fortunes of the empire, while Ravenna, her subordinate, took the role occupied by Constantinople in earlier iconography as a New Rome and sister city.[62] Both, as Italian cities, represented Italy and the empire, and both were tied together in triumph through the likeness of Theoderic, located at the center. The symbolism itself is, and would have been, illuminating to be sure, but unfortunately Agnellus' description falls short of commenting beyond this. Finer details of great importance to the present discussion are left unmentioned. The mosaic itself, for instance, was described as "wonderfully adorned,"[63] indicating that the array of colors, as in surviving examples, was impressive. Yet whether there was a purple *paludamentum* tellingly wrapped around Theoderic's lorica or a flashing diadem adorning his head will never be known.

and the inscription "Felix Ravenna." See Wroth (1911), 68 (#59) and Kraus (1928), 119 (#62). Metlich (2004), 112–13 (#77–78b), suggests that the quasi-autonomous "Felix Ravenna" issues are in fact Theoderican.

[60] *LPR* 94: "Contra clipeum Roma tessellis ornata astabat cum hasta et galea; unde vero telum tenensque fuit, Ravenna tessellis figurata, pedem dextrum super mare, sinistrum super terram ad regem properans." This claim to dominance over the sea was backed up in the mid 520s, when Theoderic ordered a formidable navy constructed at Ravenna apparently ex nihilo. See *Variae* 5.16–20, with the Epilogue.

[61] It seems best to conclude that "dexter" and "sinister" are relative to Agnellus, rather than the figures in the mosaic. Not only does this place Rome within her established (and expected) senior position, but it also allows the sea on which Ravenna places her foot to be the Adriatic (also expected). It would have been perfectly natural for Agnellus to describe this image in terms of his own perspective, but perhaps, given tensions between Rome and Ravenna at this time, describing Ravenna at Theoderic's right was intentional and designed to assert a former superiority for his city. For the location protocol, Kent (1994), 56.

[62] The pairing of the "twin" Romes (new and old) in imperial iconography can be seen on both the consular diptychs of the fifth and sixth century (such as the diptych of Clementius, cons. 513) and coinage, where Constantinople, to the left of Rome, places her foot on a prow (similar to Ravenna). For Clementius' diptych, Delbrueck (1929), vol. 1, 117–21; for the coin motif, Carson (1981), #1589. See also Deliyannis (2010), 115–16.

[63] *LPR* 94: "mire tessellis ornata."

Agnellus' description of the equestrian statue of Theoderic, which had been located at Ravenna until a rather impressed Charlemagne had it shipped back to his own New Rome (Aachen), is also suggestive of his imperial pretensions.[64] As in the mosaic, Theoderic appeared with a shield in his left hand and a lance in his right, this time his arm outstretched, extending the lance forward.[65] The horse itself was magnificently wrought of copper or bronze and covered in gold, though in a state of neglect in the ninth century.[66] Agnellus additionally repeated the contemporary lore that the statue had originally been commissioned in honor of Zeno, but then (perhaps because the emperor had died) Theoderic decided to decorate it "in his own name."[67] This change may, in fact, have had something to do with Theoderic's decision to rule Italy outright (rather than *praeregnare* as a patrician). In the very least, it suggests that the statue looked imperial enough to a ninth-century audience, and, indeed, the features described by Agnellus were modeled on imperial exemplars. The outstretched right arm, the bronze and gold covering, and the general theme of dominance were motifs identifiable in other imperial equestrian statues, such as those of Marcus Aurelius and Nerva. Statues like these had a deeper ideological importance for the Roman public; they were a venue for advertising the imperial persona and its virtues, particularly valor and clemency.[68] Nor was the significance of such statues lost on Theoderic or his east Roman colleagues, for, as mentioned previously, regulations concerning them were included in the peace terms offered to Theodahad by Justinian. Theoderic's equestrian statue at Ravenna, like the others that had been erected in his empire, surely stood alone, identifying him within his capital as the undisputed and victorious ruler of the western empire.

---

[64] *Ibid.*, with Dutton (2004), 25–6.

[65] LPR 94: "ascensorque eius Theodoricus rex scutum sinistro gerebat humero, dextro vero brachio erecto lanceam tenens."

[66] *Ibid.*: "equus ex aere, auro fulvo perfusus." Agnellus' description of birds nesting in the horse's muzzle and hollow belly testifies to the statue's neglected status before Charlemagne had it relocated to Aachen.

[67] LPR 94: "Alii aiunt quod supradictus equus pro amore Zenonis imperatoris factus fuisset.... Pro isto [i.e. Zenoni] equus ille praestantissimus ex aere factus <et> auro ornatus est, sed Theodoricus suo nomine decoravit." Whether Theoderic himself had commissioned the work in Zeno's honor or simply appropriated the half-finished product is not stated.

[68] These two virtues were especially important within this medium, and it is often suggested, by inference from other imperial imagery, that a supplicating barbarian was featured beneath the rearing horse, pardoned or about to be slaughtered by the emperor. Equestrian statues were thoroughly connected to late antique imperial victory propaganda. See McCormick (1986), 64–6.

CHRIST THE REDEEMER

Beyond Agnellus' written descriptions, an actual artistic representation of Theoderic in mosaic may survive in his palace church at Ravenna, now known as Sant'Apollinare Nuovo, but originally an Arian basilica dedicated to Christ the Redeemer. This church, along with the palace complex that accompanied it, was one of the many building projects undertaken at Theoderic's command and was apparently modeled after the basilica-palace complex in Constantinople.[69] While the Ravenna complex itself does not survive, much of the church and its mosaics do. The specific mosaic in question contains the portrait of what is clearly an imperial figure: an older, heavy jawed man with white hair, dressed in the traditional clothing of imperial rule. Though it is much restored and bears a nineteenth-century inscription identifying its subject as Emperor Justinian, a number of scholars have concluded that portions of the image are contemporary with Theoderic's reign, leading to the assumption that the original portrait was either of Theoderic himself, or perhaps of Justin or Anastasius.[70] The prospect of the latter Byzantine emperors being depicted in Theoderic's Arian palace cathedral, however, seems unlikely, and not just because of theological differences or the often rocky relationship between eastern and western courts. Christ the Redeemer was Theoderic's personal church, not that of Anastasius or Justin; it connected to a palace complex modeled on the emperor's and newly renovated according to Theoderic's tastes, and its mosaic program celebrated that palace, juxtaposing its likeness with an image of Christ enthroned.[71] The church and palace, then, would seem to be a reflection of Theoderic's imperial standing, and if so, there would have been little need to show deference here to the eastern emperor.

If, therefore, Theoderic had designs on being something more than a *rex* or simple *princeps*, this was an extremely appropriate venue for expressing

---

[69] For reconstructions of this complex, its Theoderican phases, and its relationship to the "Great Palace" complex at Constantinople, Siena (1984), 526f.; Johnson (1988), 78–91; Maioli (1994), 234–7; Russo (2005), 176f.; Augenti (2007); and Deliyannis (2010), 120–1.

[70] Cf. Lorentz (1935); Fuchs (1943), 125f., and (1944), 61f.; Bovini (1956); Johnson (1988), 86–7; Andaloro (1993), 561–2; Lippolis (2000); Wood (2007), 259–60; and Deliyannis (2010), 172–4. The attribution to Justinian seems to be derived from the statement of Agnellus in *LPR* 86 (in reference to the decorations in Theoderic's church): "In ipsius fronte intrinsecus si aspexeritis, Iustiniani augusti effigiem reperietis et Agnelli pontificis auratis decoratam tessellis." Others have suggested Zeno or even Theodahad, while Deliyannis (2010), 174, maintains that the image may have always been that of Justinian.

[71] For the significance, Siena (1984), 535, and Johnson (1988), 85–6. Deliyannis (2010), 121, writes that the complex was "intended to recall Constantinople, and thus impress both friends and foes with the legitimacy and power of Theoderic's rule."

it. And at first glance, the mosaic in question seems to confirm such imperial pretensions. The figure, for instance, is depicted wearing a diadem and wrapped in purple, dispelling any doubts about their use. Moreover, his attire bears a striking resemblance to the finery featured on a mosaic likeness of the emperor Justinian located in the nearby Basilica of San Vitale, militating against the notion that Theoderic's regalia was somehow a simpler or incomplete version of the emperor's. Indeed, both rulers feature a purple *paludamentum* covering the left shoulder and attached with a golden jeweled fibula at the right; both a white tunic under the cloak; both a golden diadem spotted with multicolored jewels and hanging ornaments (*pendilia*); and both an imperial nimbus surrounding the head.

This, then, would appear to be Theoderic the *imperator*, *dominus*, and *basileus*: perhaps not the image that he could cultivate regularly in public, but certainly representative of his imperial designs. And yet, as tempting as it is to draw such a conclusion, there is a very serious problem: Most, if not all, of this imperial imagery may not date to the reign of Theoderic, constituting instead a mid-sixth-century or even later addition.[72] Only the face and hair, it seems, are genuine, while portions of the nimbus, diadem, tassels, fibula, and purple *paludamentum* seem to have been added during the era of Justinian, when the church was handed over to the Catholics and reconsecrated. In a possible act of *damnatio memoriae*, Theoderic's image was refashioned at this time to represent Justinian, while certain figures, presumably Goths, were removed from the palace scene altogether and other cycles were altered to reflect a more specifically Catholic theology.[73]

Alterations like these might suggest that the original portrait of Theoderic (and thus Theoderic himself) had lacked these trappings of imperial rule, just as Procopius had claimed. But such a conclusion is probably too hasty, not only because of the evidence discussed thus far, but also because another surviving artistic representation, this one unquestionably of Theoderic, includes both a jeweled fibula and a *paludamentum*, items supposedly added to the mosaic in the mid-sixth century. Bearing all this in mind, there is room to argue that the mid-sixth-century dating is incorrect or, alternatively, that such additions are not indicative of a prior absence. They may reflect, instead, a repair or embellishment of a preexisting image, the latter of which finds some confirmation in the history of Agnellus.[74]

---

[72] See Lorentz (1935), 339–40; Bovini (1956), 52; Andaloro (1993), 561–2; and Lippolis (2000), 465–9. Deliyannis (2010), 172–4, follows Lippolis but does not cite the two sixth-century phases. Instead, she suggests that there is simply too much damage and restoration work to date anything accurately.

[73] See Deliyannis (2010), 164–73.

[74] See *LPR* 86, cited earlier.

Perhaps the Theoderic depicted in Christ the Redeemer was simply less ornately dressed, more like a *princeps* and less like a *basileus*. And if this were the case, a simple name change would not have been sufficient to transform a princely Theoderic into a more despotic Justinian.

The Senigallia Medallion and Jewel of Bern

Thus far the discussion of images has been largely hypothetical owing to the nature of the sources involved. The purpose has been to suggest that Theoderic intentionally cultivated a public image that was indicative of his standing as an actual Roman emperor, and that this gave substance to ideological claims of his realm as a revived and restored western Roman Empire. Though perhaps not in agreement on all details, a consistently imperial image of Theoderic, which ranged from an exact copy of the eastern emperor to something more in the style of the principate, emerges. And indeed, this physical representation of Theoderic as straddling a middle course is in harmony with the official and unofficial understanding of his role as ruler of Italy. "Theodericus Rex" could appear as a new Valentinian: diademed and covered in sacred purple, a *semper Augustus*, *dominus*, and *basileus*; or as a new Trajan: a more simply adorned *pius princeps*, a mere fellow citizen and defender of the republic. Two final images, artistic representations found on the so-called Senigallia Medallion and Jewel of Bern, reiterate the reality of this situation, while adding a necessary and important complication.

Created from a commemorative triple solidus minted sometime in the early sixth century,[75] the medallion contains the only surviving likeness (or attempted likeness) that is definitely Theoderic's. The image etched into the jewel, on the other hand, which had once functioned as a signet ring, has been attributed to Theoderic through its accompanying monogram, though the identification is not entirely secure.[76] Both figures, at any rate, appear to be clothed in a Roman style, and both are accompanied by certain elements of imperial iconography, their appearance in the Senigallia Medallion being the most striking. Still, these representations also blend their Roman and imperial features with seemingly un-Roman elements, necessitating discussion.

---

[75] For the date, Chp. 10.

[76] Cf. Berges (1954), 222–6, and Breckenridge (1979), who suggests that this Theoderic is likely Theoderic II of the Visigoths.

The Theoderic found on the jewel, first of all, appears rather simply dressed, fitted in civilian attire consistent with the unadorned robes of a *princeps*: a tunic covered by a toga draped over the right shoulder.[77] Nothing explicitly imperial is featured here, though the (purple) amethyst on which the entire scene is depicted may be a statement of this Theoderic's imperial pretensions.[78] In contrast, the medallion's Theoderic is overtly imperial. The figure wears a cuirass of lorica with the customary fibula holding a *paludamentum* at his right shoulder; this kind of armament, it will be recalled, was featured in the "imperial" mosaics described by Agnellus, while the remaining items are visible in the surviving mosaics at Sant'Apollinare Nuovo and San Vitale. Here Theoderic stands at attention, his right hand raised in the imperial act of *adlocutio*, his left hand holding a globe straddled by a winged victory, which extends a laurel wreath toward him (enlarged and facing in the opposite direction on the reverse). These motifs, traditional themes symbolic of an emperor's claim of *dominium* over the entire world, are in obvious imitation of imperial models.[79] The inscriptions on the obverse and reverse conform to this, the former reading, REX THEODERICUS PIUS PRINC[EPS] I[NVICTISSIMUS] S[EMPER],[80] "King Theoderic, the pious and always most invincible *princeps*," the latter, REX THEODERICUS VICTOR GENTIUM, "King Theoderic, conqueror of the barbarians." Both highlight Theoderic's role

---

[77] The suggestion of Schramm (1954), 220, that the subject may not be dressed as a Roman, but instead in a Germanic tunic and mantel, seems unreasonable given the context. Cf. Breckenridge (1979), 12, who concludes, "The costume is … Roman."

[78] A similar jeweled signet ring is known to have been worn by the Visigothic king Alaric II; in this case, the stone was a blue sapphire. See Schramm (1954), 217–19, and Breckenridge (1979), 14, along with the discussion later regarding its authenticity. The gem portraits of the Emperors Constantine and Constantius II, discussed in Breckenridge, were carved in amethyst, though, as Spier (2007) demonstrates, other imperial portraits were carved on sapphire and both sapphire and amethyst were used for non-imperial purposes. Hence, probably too much should not be made of the choice of stone, aside from the fact that it was of high quality. The use of a monogram is simply consistent with Roman aristocratic practices.

[79] See Kent (1994), 50, for numismatic precedents. The overtly imperial (and contemporary) Barberini Diptych, discussed by Delbrueck (1929), vol. 1, 188–96, features similar iconography. Alföldi (1978) argues that the *victoriola* lacked official significance and was simply a reference to the Senate's recognition of Theoderic's dominium over Italy. This view is generally rejected, however.

[80] The meaning of PRINC I S has been debated. The I is usually interpreted as *invictissimus*, *invictus*, or *inclytus*, while the S either completes the word beginning with the I or is interpreted as *Semper*. *Invictus/issimus Semper*, however, is most commonly accepted. See Wroth (1911), 54, and Kraus (1928) 78–9. Cf. Allara (1898), who offers "PRIN(ceps) C(onsul/aesar) I(mperator) S(alutatus)."

as a triumphant *imperator*, though the term itself is eschewed and the expected *princeps* and *rex* are substituted.[81]

A Gothic Emperor?

To this point, these two portraits appear to be straightforwardly Roman and the medallion especially imperial. But in both cases, aberrant elements can be found, and these seem at first to detract from an overall Roman and imperial impression. The head on the Senigallia Medallion, for instance, appears entirely too large for Theoderic's body, almost as if he has a hydrocephalus, and the effect is exacerbated by the absence of an expected diadem, radiate crown, or helmet of a triumphant emperor.[82] In place of such headpieces, a massive, almost ridiculous head of curled hair is featured, producing a near cone-headed effect.[83] The same hair appears in the Jewel of Bern, though Theoderic's head is not misshapen, and the hair itself is a bit longer, uncurled, and parted down the middle. The faint remnants of a mustache, moreover, appear to adorn Theoderic's upper lip in the medallion, and though lacking in the Jewel of Bern,[84] the occurrence has led many to conclude that this particular style of facial hair, rather different from the Greek beard or tetrarchic stubble, was specifically Gothic and served, along with longish hair, to distinguish Theoderic as a Goth.[85]

These portraits thus produce what may seem to the modern viewer as a rather strange representation of a Roman ruler. The medallion is

---

[81] *Victor Gentium* (or more specifically over a country or specific people) was a common inscription on Roman imperial coinage. See Carson (1981), #1330, for a medallion of Constantine II bearing the phrase. *Invictissimus (Semper)* was a more florid expression of the same victory ideology. Maxentius' early coinage described him as a *Princ(eps) Invict(us/issimus)*. See Carson (1981), #1251, and Cullhed (1994), 46–9.

[82] Items like helmets and diadems are particularly prominent in the numismatic portraits of fifth- and sixth-century emperors. See Kent (1994), 46–50. For interpretations of their absence in the Senigallia Medallion, see later discussion.

[83] Some have suggested that this is not Theoderic's hair, but a fur-covered cap or helmet, citing Procopius' description of Totila's headgear as a *pilos*. See n. 37 (earlier). Cf. Fuchs (1943), 124–5, and (1944), 61; Schramm (1954), 229; Ensslin (1959), 110 and 156; and Alföldi (1978), 134–5.

[84] Despite the comments of Schramm (1954), 221; Breckenridge (1979), 12; McCormick (1986), 269; Spier (2007), 27, and countless others, the Theoderic featured on the Jewel of Bern lacks a mustache. This "mustache" is, in fact, his top lip. The absence of striae designating hair and comparisons with portraits on contemporary coinage make this abundantly clear. Cf. the rather wide-lipped numismatic portraits of Anastasius, Justin, and Justinian.

[85] See especially Ward-Perkins (2005), 73. Cf. Kraus (1928), 79; Delbrueck (1929), vol. 1, 42–3; Schramm (1954), 221; Breckenridge (1979), 12; McCormick (1986), 269; and Dutton (2004), 25.

perhaps the most bizarre: here Theoderic is dressed as an imperial figure with symbols of victory and majesty and labeled with traditional imperial epithets, yet he substitutes what seems to be an unprecedented mass of hair and mustache for a helmet or diadem, suggesting to some that he never employed the latter as part of his regalia.[86] Though striking, however, neither image is altogether inconsistent with the depictions of Theoderic discussed previously, sharing in the same symbolic language of Romanness and Roman emperorship. And regardless of certain "aberrant" or "Gothic" elements, *Romanitas* and *imperium* remain the overriding themes, serving to reiterate before an Italo-Roman audience Theoderic's imperial position. Whatever their meaning, then, Theoderic's mustache and hair were minor elements by comparison.

Moreover, and despite seeming strange to the modern eye, all of these elements may not be so novel after all. Theoderic's massive head and hair, for instance, find parallels in other numismatic portraiture, with a likeness of the emperor Olybrius (r. 472) featuring an equally colossal head and massive crop of hair.[87] Other fifth- and sixth-century depictions of Roman soldiers and officials, including consuls and emperors, betray a similar hairstyle, slightly long, sometimes curled, and with ears covered; and this style is not in keeping with the long hair associated with Germanic barbarians or Scythians in traditional iconography.[88] If Gothic in origin, therefore, which is certainly debatable, Theoderic's coiffure was as much Roman as Gothic by the early sixth century.

Though more rare, Theoderic's faint and rather kempt mustache is likewise not entirely novel. Latin, of course, lacked a technical word for mustache, but this should not be taken to mean that mustaches were unknown

---

[86] See Kraus (1928), 79; Claude (1980), 178; MacCormack (1981), 234; McCormick (1986), 270, n. 48. The suggestion is not entirely warranted, since not all imperial portraits include these "necessary" trappings. Magnentius, though a usurping Augustus, can be found without a diadem on his coins, while junior emperors (again) are never featured wearing diadems, though they might wear other imperial headgear (e.g. laurel wreaths). The later portrait of Constantine IV at Sant'Apollinare in Classe also lacks a diadem, though this may be the product of a faulty restoration. See Deichmann (1976), vol. 2.2, 273–9.

[87] See Kent (1978), #764, and Carson (1981), #1561. Other fifth-century examples of enlarged heads can be found on the coins of Honorius and Valentinian III. Coins from the house of Constantine are similarly enlarged. For these, Carson (1981), #1514, 1536, and 1561.

[88] Cf. Delbrueck (1929), vol. 1, 42, and Amory (1997), 344–6. The former suggests a Germanic origin for this particular hairstyle, the latter a Constantinian. In either case, both indicate that it was popular among fifth- and sixth-century Romans and distinct from the long hair traditionally associated with barbarians. The style is also featured on a number of late antique statues from Aphrodisias. See Smith (1999). Compare this style, worn by Theoderic, with the shoulder-length hair featured on the signet ring of King Childeric of the Franks.

to Romans or seen as specifically Gothic.[89] In fact, Romans were familiar with a host of mustachioed peoples, describing and depicting their facial hair with ease. Celtic peoples, not Goths, topped their list.[90] More importantly, some Romans actually did wear lone mustaches, despite modern claims to the contrary. As their portraits demonstrate, these individuals hailed from throughout the empire and ranged from provincials and soldiers to a number of third-, fourth-, and fifth-century emperors. Gordian III was mustachioed; so were Constantine, Honorius, and Marcian.[91] Thus, while this style of facial hair is typically taken to be Germanic, and some are even willing to see a mustache in the "Gothic beard" playfully referenced by Ennodius,[92] a strictly Gothic or even Germanic attribution is questionable.

Yet supposing such features really did have a bit of a "Gothic" flavor to them, was this really a point of friction among Theoderic's subjects? Goths like Theoderic and his followers, after all, had been instrumental in the restoration of the western Roman Empire and had ushered in a golden age. They had defeated the tyrant Odovacer, had made it possible for the western insignia to be returned to Italy, and had ruled in a style that conformed to local expectations. Soon they would even reassert Rome's dominance, despaired of in the fifth century, far beyond the confines of the Italian Peninsula. Gothicness, in other words, had not interfered with the Goths' ability, in the eyes of their Roman partisans, to rescue the Roman Empire; it had, on the contrary (and as the following chapter will show), been fundamental to its realization.

---

[89] See Arnold (2013), 155–8. Cf. Dutton (2004), 25, and Ward-Perkins (2005), 73f.

[90] Others included Parthians/Persians, Sarmatians, Thracians, Dacians, and Germans. See Arnold (2013), 166–72.

[91] *Ibid.* 172–80, with figures 10–18b.

[92] See Ennodius, #182, with Ward-Perkins (2005), 79, and Deliyannis (2010), 187. Cf. Arnold (2013), 158–60.

PART III

ITALO-ROMANS AND ROMAN GOTHS

DEFENDING THE TIBER

The idea that Goths could fit within the Roman Empire, and even become its principal defenders and restorers, was not entirely new to Romans. Before a change in imperial policy had led to their invasion of Italy in 408, Alaric and his federate Visigoths had been guardians of the Balkan frontier, commissioned to check the inroads of other barbarians in the region. Moreover, after breaking with the emperor residing in Ravenna, this king of the Goths, who doubled as a Roman *magister militum*, continued to pursue a pro-Roman policy, acquiring the support of the Roman Senate and raising one of its preeminent members, Priscus Attalus, to the purple. For roughly a year, Alaric's Goths had substituted for a senatorial army, opposing (in the name of the Senate) the emperor Honorius' "legitimate" government at Ravenna. Though these very Goths would sack the city they claimed to defend in 410, the act itself would be a last resort, following a dispute with Attalus and repeated failures to come to terms with Honorius.[1]

The sack of Rome was a significant event, but it nonetheless failed to strip the Goths entirely of their ideological role as defenders of Roman liberty. In fact, though at times rebellious, they maintained their pro-Roman policies, with some Romans being so impressed that they even used the sack of Rome as a pretense for praising Gothic *pietas*.[2] Soon, led

---

[1] See Matthews (1975), chp. 11 especially; also Burns (1994), chps. 7 and 8, and Kulikowski (2007), chp. 8.

[2] Orosius, *Historiae* 7.39, is especially kind in his depiction of the Gothic sack of Rome. He describes the Goths as showing respect for the church and doing far less damage than the emperor Nero or the Gauls. Cf. *CassChron*, anno 409 (with the comments in Chp. 2), which claims the Goths were merciful (*clementer*) in their victory.

by Alaric's brother-in-law, Athaulf, these Goths crossed into Gaul, settling there permanently. Athaulf, it was said, had begun his reign in opposition to the empire but had quickly changed his mind. At Narbonne he married the emperor's sister, Placidia, establishing a link with the imperial family that was strengthened when she bore him a son tellingly named Theodosius.[3] Though the infant would die shortly thereafter, Athaulf's transformation was complete. Once an avowed destroyer of the empire, he now wanted to "become glorious by completely restoring and increasing the Roman name using the might of the Goths, and [thus] be held by posterity as the author of Rome's restoration."[4]

In Italy, Ennodius and others had seen the situation quite differently, but in Gaul many Romans came to embrace the Goths for fulfilling Athaulf's dream. The former prefect of Rome and bishop of Clermont, Sidonius Apollinaris, eulogized the Gothic king Euric as a bona fide "defender of the Tiber" and the source from which Romans sought their salvation,[5] in stark contrast with the stereotypical barbarian encountered in Ennodius' *Life of Epiphanius*. Long before the advent of Theoderic and his Ostrogoths, then, other Goths were paving the way for their acceptance. Yet Theoderic and his Goths would fit within the Roman Empire in ways that Athaulf had never imagined. Indeed, though Goths, they were also uniquely Roman, and their perceived roles as such were of fundamental importance to the Theoderican golden age.

Here, in the two chapters that follow, the issues of Gothicness and Romanness in Theoderic's Empire will be addressed. Though once considered savage barbarians, Theoderic's Goths were embraced in Italy, just as other Goths were embraced elsewhere. They were idealized as Italy's defenders, as Rome's victorious army, and stood with Theoderic's other subjects as a united Roman front. Moreover, they were celebrated for their obedience to Roman laws (a civilizing quality) and were even proposed to the "decadent" Romans encountered in Part I as models for proper Roman behavior. In Theoderic himself, on the other hand, the Romans of Italy

---

[3] This was the name of Placidia's father, Emperor Theodosius I. On the son, *PLRE* 2, 1100 (Theodosius 5), which notes an inscription that may refer to the youth as a *nobilissimus puer*, a title that marked him as a potential imperial successor. Indeed, another son of Placidia, Valentinian III, would become emperor of the West, though Athaulf was not his father.

[4] Orosius, *Historiae* 7.43.6: "ut gloriam sibi de restituendo in integrum augendoque Romano nomine Gothorum viribus quaereret habereturque apud posteros Romanae restitutionis auctor."

[5] Sidonius, *Ep.* 8.9, ln. 42–4: "Eorice, tuae manus rogantur, / ut Martem validus per inquilinum / defendat tenuem Garumna Thybrim"; and ln. 39: "hinc, Romane, tibi petis salutem." Cf. *Carmen* 2, ln. 352–86, and *Ep.* 1.2, which praise the Goths Wallia, Ricimer, and Theoderic II.

received much more than a barbarian king, though his royal ancestry was the subject of extensive Romanizing praise that set his clan on par with an imperial dynasty. He was also a legitimate eastern Roman (or Greek), who had spent his most formative years in Constantinople and had acquired a host of Roman honors and offices in the service of the emperor. Being east Roman was not always a blessing within an Italian context, but Romans with similar pedigrees had been elevated to the western *imperium* in the past, and Theoderic, it will be argued, followed in their footsteps.

5

MEN OF MARS

A DIVERSE EMPIRE

The examples of Alaric, Athaulf, and Euric suggest that already in the fifth century Goths were filling positive niches in the Roman Empire as partners and restorers, rather than simply foes whose defeat validated imperial victory ideology and hoary notions of Roman superiority. The relationship was shaky at times, the sack of Rome being a notorious example, but the appearance of Goths and other so-called barbarians was becoming very regular in the late Roman world, and by the fifth century those living in close proximity to them were becoming desensitized to their otherness (and vice versa).[1] An inhabitant of Italy was perhaps more likely to meet a Goth than a Gaul,[2] and this potential surely rendered the former less alien, provided the Goth in question met the observer's minimal requirements for acceptability and posed no immediate threat. Acceptance, in fact, was aided by long durations of peace,[3] and much syncretism had occurred first within the frontier zones and later, after large-scale migrations, within the Roman heartland itself.[4] Such conditions meant that Gallo-Romans like Sidonius could romanticize about the attire of barbarian princes and playfully mock Ravenna as a city where *foederati* (barbarians who

---

[1] But see Whittaker (1994), 198–200, for comments on the increased opposition to barbarians in the later empire among the traditional elite.

[2] Especially given the historical reluctance on the part of Gallo-Romans to travel and participate within the empire. See Stroheker (1948), 14–28; Drinkwater (1989); and Mathisen (1992).

[3] Burns (2003), chp. 1 especially.

[4] See Geary (1988) and (1999); Whittaker (1994), 237f.; Amory (1997), chp. 8; Heather (1999); Brown (2003), 45–51; and Burns (2003), chps. 6 and 7. On the permeability of the Roman and barbarian aristocracies, Demandt (1989). For complications, Curta (2005) and Drinkwater (2007).

probably included Goths) were literati;[5] they meant that Italo-Romans, such as Ennodius' noble friend Jovinianus, could feel perfectly "Roman" sporting "Gothic" beards, just as contemporaries in Constantinople felt perfectly Roman with their long "Persian" mustaches and "Hunnic" hairstyles.[6] The more traditionally minded or elitist may have found such mannerisms aberrant, perhaps even loathsome, but they were no different in substance from emperors' affecting a Greek, Dacian, Persian, or Syrian appearance, or Gallic provincials' donning pants, all of which met with similar criticism.[7]

The very nature of the empire aided in the acceptability of such diversity, its existence an inevitable consequence of the assimilation process that radiated outward from the Roman core to its periphery (and back again). The Roman world was a heterogeneous composition of numerous ethnic and subethnic groups, all of which had adopted various Roman cultural elements to differing degrees and over different amounts of time, thus becoming "Roman," but with diverse manifestations that were constantly in flux.[8] In the fourth century, for instance, Gallo-Roman culture was still readily identifiable to outsiders as different or even bizarre,[9] and to some degree Gallic society really did maintain certain Celtic attributes.[10] Yet these differences did not disqualify Gallic provincials from self-perceived or externally perceived Romanness;[11] they could still think of themselves and be acknowledged as Roman, largely (but not exclusively) through their adoption and employment of a Roman culture system and participation

---

[5] For the barbarian prince (Sigismer), Sidonius, *Ep.* 4.20, with *PLRE* 2, 1008 (Sigismer 1). He may have been a Burgundian or Frank. Cf. Brown (2003), 100, for an alternative reading of the letter. For literati, *Ep.* 1.8: "armis eunuchi, litteris foederati." This juxtaposition of eunuchs with weapons and federates with literature inverted traditional expectations.

[6] For Jovinianus, Ennodius, #182, with Chp. 4, n. 92. For Hunnic and Persian styles in Constantinople, Procopius, *Anecdota* 7, with Amory (1997), 339–41; also Arnold (2013), 181.

[7] Procopius and Ennodius may have responded negatively to the adoption of such styles by Romans, though see the previous note for other interpretations. Anti-Greek sentiments have been encountered throughout this study and include Julian's "philosopher's" beard. For anti-Dacian sentiments, Lactantius, *De Mortibus Persecutorum* 27.8 (discussed in Chp. 3, n. 66); for anti-Syrian/Persian, *HA, Heliogabalus* 23 (ironically the clothes of a late antique *dominus*); for Gauls, Chp. 9.

[8] See Woolf (1998), chp. 1, and Curchin (2004), chp. 1; also Conant (2012), 3–9. For stricter interpretations, which imagine "static" Romanness and provincial "barbarism" or "resistance," Millett (1990); Curchin (1991); Cherry (1998); and Isaac (2000).

[9] See Part V.

[10] See Stroheker (1948), 8–9, and Van Dam (1985), 11–18, who follows him. Cf. Mathisen (1993) and Harries (1994), whose Gaul and Gauls appear thoroughly Roman.

[11] In anthropological terms, "emic" and "etic," respectively.

in the empire's cults and honors.[12] The same can be said of virtually any provincial culture and its regional manifestations. This very real diversity, visible throughout the Roman Empire, when coupled with the tendency for Romans to allow for variation along a Roman theme, provided an avenue for the eventual fitting of Goths into the Roman world. Like Gauls and other provincials before them, they could retain certain "native" characteristics and still become "Roman."

FROM SAVAGE TO SAVIOR

But, of course, the preceding should not be taken to mean that the Roman Empire was some open-minded melting pot where ethnic and subethnic groups lived harmoniously and were always tolerant of new members or external cultural elements. While tolerance existed, Romanness, so intrinsically linked with claims of dominance, was also oppositional in nature and predicated on the existence of a recognizable and perennially inferior other: the barbarian. The term itself, "barbarian," served to designate insiders from outsiders, but barbarism was not restricted to those living beyond the empire's frontiers. Every provincial culture had at one time or another fallen within its purview, and this legacy of barbarism was enduring. Indeed, it had the potential to be quite divisive, since any perceived deviance from an expected Roman norm ran the risk of being interpreted as a lapse into savagery. Old prejudices died hard in the Roman Empire, and even if forgotten, could reemerge under certain pressures and in new manifestations. The strange Gallo-Roman customs alluded to previously might find acceptance among the more tolerant, but for many, Gauls never quite gave up their status as barbarians or were, at best, semibarbarous. They could even, as later chapters will demonstrate, occupy this liminal position in the eyes of one of their own, such as the transplant Ennodius, or ironically appear as stereotypical barbarians to more traditionally "barbarian" peoples like the Goths, whose understanding of Romanness became Italocentric.[13]

---

[12] These are the general implications of the studies of Stroheker (1948); Woolf (1998); and Ando (2000), but note that Roman identity in Gaul did not necessarily require participation in the administration or its cults, and that local religion, though disguised with an *interpretatio Romana*, was nonetheless idiosyncratic. See Matthews (1975), 77–9, for the former observation; Drinkwater (1983); Wightman (1985); and Van Dam (1993) for the latter.

[13] See Part V. Burns (2003), 134, identifies a link between barbarian status and the distance a population lived from the Mediterranean, pointing out Gaul's liminal position between Italy and Germania. In addition, a Gallic stigma (*Terror Gallicus*), stemming from Rome's conflict with the Celts of Cisalpine Gaul (northern Italy), may have persisted. See Drinkwater (1989).

Much like the Gauls and other provincials, then, fifth- and sixth-century Goths became scrutinizers of barbarism at the same time as they were subject to its scrutiny. Their situation was also a bit different, however. Despite finding increasing acceptance, Goths were ultimately newcomers with a history of dictating terms through the threat and very real use of violence. Other barbarians, integrated and turned provincial, could also have bloody pasts,[14] but what separated the Goths from these was the fact that they remained proudly, perhaps even defiantly, unconquered by Rome.[15] When harnessed for the Romans (as frequently was the case), their valor and indomitability could become objects of praise, but the very existence and potentially unrestrained nature of such characteristics caused some to continue to think of Goths as dangerous and antithetical barbarians. With a little convincing from his Roman wife, Athaulf himself had even been sympathetic to this rationale, abandoning his desire to be "what Caesar Augustus had been," since his Goths "could not obey the laws" owing to their "unbridled barbarism."[16] Barbarism, accordingly, seemed to disqualify the Goths from a legitimate inheritance of Roman rule, and though the historian Orosius had placed these words in Athaulf's mouth, they nonetheless reflected the general sentiment among Romans that the wild and savage disposition of the Goths was best directed toward servile ends.

Service and a servile status, however, did not interfere with the eventual integration of the Goths and other barbarians into the Roman world. In fact, and somewhat ironically, it provided the very means through which they could win acceptance; nor should this be surprising, since service had a long history of transforming "savages" into "Romans." In the empire's early days, barbarians like the Gauls, for instance, had served as auxiliaries in the Roman army, learning Roman customs and the Latin language, earning Roman citizenship, and returning to their native communities as bona fide sources of Romanization; their children and children's children were progressively Romanized, and their descendants ultimately held some of the highest military and civil offices in the state.[17] The names and origins of the barbarians had changed, of course, but the situation remained

---

[14] The sack of Rome by the Gauls is doubtless the most infamous.

[15] Though this is not entirely the case, since the threat of internal rebellion and the memory of preconquest outrages remained burned into the Roman psyche. The life span of the *Terror Gallicus* (see the prior note), *Terror Dacicus* (visible in Lactantius' *De Mortibus Persecutorum*), and *Terror Isauricus* (see Chp. 6) provide examples.

[16] Orosius, *Historiae* 7.43.5–6: "et fieret nunc Athaulfus quod quondam Caesar Augustus, at ubi multa experientia probavisset neque Gothos ullo modo parere legibus posse propter effrenatam barbariem."

[17] See Drinkwater (1983), chps. 1 and 2; Roymans (1996); and Woolf (1998), chps. 2 and 3.

more or less the same in the fifth- and sixth-century West. In places like Gaul and Spain, barbarian kings, not just of the Visigoths but also of the Burgundians, Alani, and Franks, used their armies in defense of the empire, sometimes accompanied by Roman legions. They put down usurpers, stopped local rebellions, prevented the advance of other barbarians into and within the empire, and provided needed military backing to imperial claimants.[18] These barbarians became partners and allies of the empire, welcome solutions to contemporary problems,[19] and the relationship was remembered even after the empire's collapse. Addressing the Burgundian king Gundobad, whose warriors had recently ravaged Liguria, Epiphanius of Pavia declared, "Aren't you *our* Burgundians?"[20] They were indeed, the bishop assured him, and later Gundobad's son and successor, Sigismund, even acknowledged his subject status, though professing his allegiance to the eastern empire alone.[21]

In Italy, on the other hand, Goths and other barbarians had served in a similar military capacity for generations, and just as in the provinces, the situation provided for greater familiarity with them and their eventual integration among the local population.[22] To some degree these developments have already been discussed in an earlier chapter. They allowed the Ligurian nobility to accept the "Gothic" generalissimo Ricimer as a defender and veritable emperor, while nearly rejecting the "Roman" emperor Anthemius, who was seen as a barbarous "Galatian" and "Greekling." Similar conclusions were also drawn concerning Odovacer; again, he was not a Goth, but a military man whose barbarian origins did not disqualify him from playing the part of an emperor, though only (and tellingly) claiming to be an imperial servant. These examples demonstrate that the barbarian category was negotiable and especially subject to manipulation in the fifth

[18] Jovinus used Alani; Constantine III and his associates made use of Sueves; Burgundians were employed to check Visigoths, and vice versa; Franks tried (but failed) to prevent the mass migration of Vandals, Sueves, and Alani after the Great Rhine Crossing; Visigoths, Alani, and Franks fought alongside Romans at the Catalaunian Plains against Attila and his Huns; Wallia was contracted to destroy the Siling Vandals in Spain; Goar, the Alan king, was employed by the western empire against revolting Aremoricans; and the list goes on. These are just a few examples from the early to mid-fifth century.

[19] See Wolfram (1979), 15, and Goffart (2006), 238, who stress the financial benefits of employing federate armies.

[20] *VE* 160: "'Scimus et evidenter agnoscimus, nonne vos estis Burgundiones nostri?'"

[21] See Avitus of Vienne, *Ep.* 93 and 94.

[22] For barbarians (including Goths) settled in the north of Italy, Matthews (1975), 184; Clemente (1984), 259–60; and Szidat (1995). Their settlement is attested from the time of Constantine forward. Bachrach (1973), 34–6, discusses the example of the Alani, pointing out the comment of Claudian, *Panegyricus de quarto consulatu Honorii Augusti*, ln. 487: "Alani, you have adopted Latin customs."

and early sixth centuries.[23] And while extremely stereotypical depictions
of barbarians continued to exist, revealing their power and viability, even
the worst of archetypes, such as Ennodius' Euric, could undergo a kind
of transformation when met in the flesh. In Gaul, both he and Gundobad
were in fact mollified by the Roman eloquence of Epiphanius, while in
Pavia defenders like the Rugi, barbarians described by Ennodius as "brutal in every savagery, [men] who were incited to daily outrages with the
cruel and violent force of their minds,"[24] could become civilized partners.
The sweetness of Epiphanius' speech caused their "barbarous hearts" to
submit to his authority; "[men] whose hearts had always been dedicated to
hatred, learned to love," and "their natural perversity was transformed."[25]
It was amazing, according to Ennodius, that those who barely obeyed their
own kings now loved and feared a Catholic and Roman bishop, and a
testament to this love that they left Pavia in tears, when finally recalled to
their own families.[26]

SWEET *CIVILITAS*

Barriers, primarily ideological, were breaking down, especially when
Romans throughout the western portion of the empire were forced to
confront the barbarian bogeyman face to face. It happened in Gaul; it
was happening in Odovacer's Italy; and it continued to happen under
Theoderic. The process did not mean that all barbarians ceased to be
thought of as such, but that those who became local patrons and sources
of assistance certainly could be seen as civilized.[27] Just like Epiphanius'
Rugi, Theoderic's Goths arrived in Italy as outsiders, but soon they lost
those qualities that rendered them "barbarians" in Italo-Roman eyes, or,

[23] Cf. Geary (1983), who imagines barbarian ethnic otherness as a "situational construct," more
subjective than objective, and Amory (1997), who sees much of the language of this period as
anachronistic and the product of traditional Greco-Roman ethnography.

[24] *VE* 118: "Rugis ... hominibus omni feritate immanibus, quos atrox et acerba vis animorum ad
cotidiana scelera sollicitabat."

[25] *VE* 118–19: "quos tamen beatissimus antistes sermonum suorum melle delenibat, ut effera
corda auctoritati submitterent sacerdotis et amare discerent, quorum pectora odiis semper
fuisse dedicata cognovimus. Mutata est per meritum illius perversitas naturalis." This episode
is in many ways a replay of Epiphanius' confrontation with Euric (discussed in Chp. 1). Here,
interestingly enough, Ennodius betrays the understanding that barbarism was innate, rather
than the result of an absence of advancement or the impact of environmental factors. This is
very different from his understanding of the Gauls. See Chp. 9.

[26] *VE* 119: "Qui sine grandi stupore credat dilexisse et timuisse Rugos episcopum et catholicum
et Romanum, qui parere regibus vix dignantur? Cum quibus tamen integrum paene biennium
exegit taliter, ut ab eo flentes discederent etiam ad parentes et familias regressuri."

[27] Cf. Brown (2003), 99–101.

and even more significantly, such qualities remained, but were recast in a positive light, becoming vital to their perceived role in a restored Roman Empire.

Athaulf's fear expressed a century prior, that Goths could not obey the laws, was demonstrated to be unfounded. Italy's new Goths, the Ostrogoths, became defenders of justice and models of *civilitas*, the civilized rule of law.[28] This was a profoundly important transformation, since *civilitas* itself was at the very heart of Romanness and was said to "separate [all men] from savagery."[29] Indeed, Theoderic and his successors claimed that lawlessness was a condition of barbarians and made anyone, regardless of ethnicity, barbarous.[30] Hence, this newfound ability on the part of the Goths to obey and defend the laws rendered them not just tolerably Roman but even admirably so. Romans like Ennodius praised the "sweetness of *civilitas*"[31] in Theoderic's reign, claiming that "the law restrains characters untamed in battles: after triumphing, their necks submit to your precepts, and the decrees to which their arms should yield control them; your brave men follow your orders always."[32] Unruly provincials were similarly reminded of the fact that the Goths were modest, not bellicose, at home,[33] while administrators were instructed to "demonstrate the justice of the Goths," who had adopted the "prudence of the Romans while possessing the valor of *gentes*."[34] Justice, so intrinsically linked with

[28] This definition of *civilitas* essentially agrees with Moorhead (1992), 79, who concludes, "civilitas and its cognates ... indicate the quality of abiding by the laws," and Reydellet (1995), 285, who writes, "L'idée général est celle de respect du droit." The definition of Amory (1997), 43, "two nations living together in peace but performing different functions," is unsatisfying, since "Goths" and "Romans" were not the only nations subject to this ideology. See Part V, as well as *Variae* 1.27.1, where *civilitas* exists for the benefit of the Jews of Gerona. Cf. Ensslin (1959), 217. For an even broader reading of *civilitas*, which includes just governance, religious tolerance, and the restoration of ancient monuments, Saitta (1993).

[29] *Variae* 4.33: "Hoc [praeceptio iustitiae, i.e. civilitas] enim populos ab agresti vita in humanae conversationis regulam congregavit. Haec ratio a feritate divisit." This understanding of *civilitas* would seem to be a sixth-century counterpart of Roman *humanitas* as described by Woolf (1998), chp. 3: "*Humanitas* encapsulated what it meant to be Roman." Cf. Saitta (1993), 2, and Reydellet (1995), 285, who conclude similarly.

[30] Cf. *Variae* 4.33 (previous note), with *Variae* 9.18–19. The examples of the Rugi and Athaulf's Goths (earlier) also demonstrate the link between lawlessness and barbarism. Orosius, *Historiae* 7.43.6, may have put it best: "without these [i.e. laws] the state is not a state."

[31] *PanTh* 87: "civilitatis dulcitudini."

[32] *PanTh* 87–8: "Nam indomita inter acies ingenia lex coercet: summittunt praeceptis colla post laureas ... quibus arma cesserint, decreta dominantur. Solus es meritis et natura conpositus, cuius magnanimi iussa sectentur."

[33] *Variae* 3.24.4: "Gothos nostros, qui foris proelia, intus norunt exercere modestiam."

[34] *Variae* 3.23.3: "Gothorum possis demonstrare iustitiam. Qui ... et Romanorum prudentiam caperent et virtutem gentium possiderent."

Roman order, now became intrinsically linked with Italy's Goths: Nothing uncivilized was to be tolerated in Theoderic's Roman Empire and "the laws, not arms," were to ensure justice.[35]

These laws were Roman in origin and so too was Gothic justice, a reality that reiterated Theoderic's and his successors' claims to imperial succession and at the same time implied Gothic reverence for Roman traditions. The machinery of Roman government remained "just as it had been under [former] *principes*,"[36] while Roman law, and by extension the Roman way of life, was the model to be upheld in this Roman Empire. Theoderic asserted that there was no better condition than for mankind to live according to these laws; they were "the most certain comforts of human life" and provided for an existence that was "truly human," in obvious contrast to lawless barbarism.[37] Their restoration to others was likewise claimed as the rationale behind expelling "ignorant barbarians"[38] from newly won territories and a cause for subjects "to grieve that they had not acquired our [Roman] rule earlier."[39] Goths, then, became defenders, preservers, and even restorers of Roman law, but the relationship extended even further, since they were also expected to obey it. Though cases involving Goths might fall under a separate (military) jurisdiction,[40] those between Romans and Goths were to be decided "with consideration for [Roman] laws." "We do not permit," Theoderic explained, "those whom we wish to defend with the same purpose to live

---

[35] *Variae* 7.3.2: "Non amamus aliquid incivile.... In causa possint iura, non brachia." The use of violence instead of proper legal channels was regularly inveighed against, both in the provinces and in the city of Rome. Cf. *Variae* 1.23, 1.30, 1.31, 4.10, and 4.43 for just a few Italian examples. Some specific examples from Gaul can be found in Chp. 10.

[36] *AnonVal* 60: "Militiam Romanis sicut sub principes esse praecepit," with Mommsen (1889), 460–96, and Ensslin (1959), 160–71. Only a few offices seem to have been created with Goths specifically in mind, notably the Sajo, which was modeled on the imperial *agentes in rebus*, and various *comites Gothorum*. The latter were agents assigned to individual cities or regions who had a judicial and military function. They served as judges, for instance, in cases involving individual Goths and Romans. See also Schmidt (1925); Sirago (1986), 182–3; and Wolfram (1988), 290–1, and (1997), 116–19.

[37] For comforts, *Variae* 3.17.3: "Iura publica certissima sunt humanae vitae solacia..."; for human, *Variae* 5.39.1: "illa vita vere hominum est, quae iuris ordine continetur."

[38] *Variae* 3.43.1: "Quid enim proficit barbaros removisse confusos, nisi vivatur ex legibus?"

[39] *Variae* 3.43.3: "ut subiecti se doleant nostrum dominium tardius adquisisse." For the context, Chp 10.

[40] For this, *Variae* 7.3. These jurisdictions (civil vs. military) predate the arrival of Theoderic and his Goths. See Mommsen (1889), 526–35, with Amory (1997), 51, n. 24, and Schäfer (2001), 188–91. Some have suggested that the Goths would have adhered to a *Lex Gothica* or personal/family law (whatever this might have been), but there is no evidence for its use, let alone existence, in sixth-century Italy. Cf. Schmidt (1939), 411; Ensslin (1959), 231–2; and Sirago (1986), 194–6.

under separate laws," since matters "devoted to justice" should be judged "in common."[41]

In this way, therefore, Goths and Italo-Romans acquired the same *legal* identity and heritage, a process that contributed to the breakdown of potential barriers between immigrant and resident populations.[42] The Goths themselves praised Theoderic for his legal policies, which had "established justice," judging him "to be in all matters their most vigorous king."[43] Italo-Romans, on the other hand, fondly remembered his promise made before the Senate and people of Rome to "keep inviolate whatever prior Roman *principes* had decreed," a promise that he later engraved on a bronze tablet and posted in a public place.[44] Such practices were clearly within the Roman tradition, allowing Theoderic to refer to ancient Roman lawgivers as "our ancestors" and to provide his own interpretation of the original intent of the law, claiming all the while to preserve his imperial predecessors' judgments.[45] His grandson and successor Athalaric could likewise issue an edict deliberately divided into twelve chapters, "just as the civil law [i.e. the *Twelve Tables*] had been founded," intending "not to debilitate the remaining laws, but to strengthen them … for the sake of Roman peace."[46] Rome's new *principes*, then, styled themselves as legal

---

[41] *Variae* 3.13.2: "si quod negotium Romano cum Gothis est aut Gotho emersit aliquod cum Romanis, legum consideratione definies, nec permittimus discreto iure vivere quos uno voto volumus vindicare. Censebis ergo in commune, quae sunt amica iustitiae." Cf. *Variae* 8.3.4 and *AnonVal* 60. The status of Roman law in Ostrogothic Italy has a large bibliography, but see more recently Amory (1997), 51–2, n. 24 especially, and (more traditionally) Moorhead (1992), 75–80. The existence of a document known as the *Edictum Theoderici* complicates matters further, though not extensively for the present purposes. Its attribution and authenticity have been called into question with good reason, but if genuinely "Ostrogothic," the *Edict* reaffirms that both Goths and Romans fell under the same (Roman) legal heritage. For discussions, Rasi (1953) and (1961/2); Ensslin (1959), 220–34; Vismara (1967); Nehlsen (1969); Amory (1997), 78–84; Saitta (1999), 199; König (2000), 219–20; and Lafferty (2010). Despite claims to the contrary, the attribution of this work to Theoderic remains unsettled, and its use of the term *barbari* in reference to non-Romans (i.e. Goths) has yet to be adequately explained. Cf. Amory 79, n. 188, with Šašel (1979); Luiselli (1980), 227; and Viscido (1986b).

[42] The same could not be said for the other successor kingdoms in the West, where Roman and barbarian legal systems were in use and legal identities were often oppositional. See Amory (1993); Thompson (1969), 132–9; Collins (1983), 24–30, and (1998); James (1982), 81–92; and Fischer Drew (1991).

[43] *AnonVal* 60: "et a Gothis secundum edictum suum, quo ius constituit, rex fortissimus in omnibus iudicaretur." *Fortissimus* was an epithet applied to emperors and implied a steadfast mind.

[44] *AnonVal* 66 and 69, cited and discussed further in Chp. 8. Contemporaries associated the vow with Trajan, a model for the Amals. Cf. *Variae* 8.3.5.

[45] *Variae*: 5.14.7: "Maiores enim nostri discursus iudicum non oneri, sed compendio provincialibus esse voluerunt." Cf. *Variae* 4.26 and 4.33.

[46] *Variae* 9.19.2: "necessaria quaedam Romanae quieti edictali programmate duodecim capitibus, sicut ius civile legitur institutum, in aevum servanda conscripsimus, quae custodita residuum

traditionalists, a position doubtless appreciated by conservative Romans who feared innovation,[47] while Rome's newest Romans, the Goths, were cast as model citizens: obedient defenders and observers of Roman law.

RE-ROMANIZATION

Gothic *civilitas* and admiration for Roman values were thus important ideological components of the accommodation reached between Goths and Romans. Though Goths and Romans could prove corruptible and capable of abusing the system (often in collaboration with one another),[48] the idea, at any rate, was that the Goths had abandoned their former barbarism, ceasing to be the uncontrollable savages that Romans and even Gothic kings like Athaulf had feared. They had adopted, instead, Roman laws and virtues in a marvelous show of discipline, thereby evolving from their natural state. This imagined "civilizing process" (another way of saying Romanization) likewise fit perfectly into the understanding of the decadent status of the empire and its citizens leading up to their arrival. While the Goths had developed into models of good Roman practices, the Romans themselves had degenerated and strayed from their historic virtues. Like barbarians, Ennodius bemoaned, they preferred brute strength and the whims of chance to eloquent words and the justice of the laws, and like women, Cassiodorus complained, they had become effeminate and weak.[49]

The arrival of Theoderic and his Goths, therefore, had been well timed. They were not mere "noble savages," a concept familiar to Romans and perhaps best expressed in the *Germania* of Tacitus, but the very sources from which an uncorrupted form of *Romanitas* could be restored to the lapsed inhabitants of Italy. As a representative of this purer Romanness, Theoderic reached out to the unruly populace of Rome, enjoining it to

ius non debilitare, sed potius corroborare videantur." This letter announced to the Senate the proclamation of an edict, dated to 533/4. The last portion demonstrates the desire on Athalaric's part to prevent himself from being seen as a legal innovator, desiring instead to be viewed as a strengthener of the laws. The point is reiterated in the edict itself (*Variae* 9.18.12), where Athalaric orders all the edicts of Theoderic and the usual public laws ("omnia edicta ... domni avi nostri ... et usualia iura publica") to be upheld.

[47] Procopius, *Anecdota* 14, cites the legal innovations of Justinian, a slightly younger contemporary of Theoderic, as one of the major outrages of his reign.

[48] See Ensslin (1959), 217–20; Burns (1982), 113; and Saitta (1999), 202–3; also Castritius (1982), who claims that cases of corruption and abuse during Theoderic's reign are consistent with earlier conditions in the late Roman Empire. Cf. Sirago (1986), 184f., and Heather (1995).

[49] See Part I.

"abandon foreign customs" and to be truly Roman.[50] "There is nothing that we want you to preserve more keenly," these Romans were told, "than the discipline of your ancestors, so that you might increase under our reign what you have always, since ancient times, held as praiseworthy."[51] Senators, too, were chastised that those, "whom *gravitas* always becomes,"[52] should not commit "serious excesses" on account of "trifling causes," or use the "armed ferocity" of their slaves to "exact vengeance on the innocent, hopelessly trampling upon the prudence of the laws."[53] Later, when an anti-Semitic riot led to the burning of a synagogue in Rome, Theoderic admonished the Senate that the inhabitants of Rome should preserve the fame of their city through their good reputation and not allow a place "that has always boasted of its moral probity to seize upon alien vices."[54] "To embrace the fickleness of sedition and to burn one's own city," they were told, "is not to want what is Roman."[55] Even the Italian clergy, embroiled in the Laurentian Schism and seeking Theoderic's assistance during a series of synods, were warned repeatedly that outbreaks of violence were not in keeping with his times.[56] "It is indeed a shameful and dishonorable difference," he scolded, "that the Roman state is ruled peacefully on the border with barbarians but confused in the middle of the City, so much that *civilitas* is lacking in the citadel of Latium, though safe and sound within the vicinity of our enemies."[57] Ferocity, excess, fickleness, lack of probity, and irreverence for the laws: These were thoroughly barbarian

---

[50] *Variae* 1.31.1: "Mores peregrinos abicite: Romana sit vox plebis, quam delectet audiri." This example and the example cited later (*Variae* 1.30) involved strife at the circus. Cf. *Variae* 1.27, 1.32, 1.33, and the discussion of spectacles at Rome in Chp. 8.

[51] *Variae* 1.31.3: "Nihil est enim, quod studiosius servare vos cupimus quam vestrorum veterum disciplinam, ut, quod ab antiquis laudabile semper habuistis."

[52] *Variae* 1.30.4: "quos semper gravitas decet."

[53] *Variae* 1.30:1: "[Querela populorum] orta quidem ex causis levibus, sed graves eructavit excessus.... ut legum ratione calcata desperate persequeretur innoxios servilis furor armatus."

[54] *Variae* 4.43.1: "Urbis Romanae celebris opinio suo conservanda est nihilominus instituto, nec vitia peregrina capit, quae se semper de morum probitate iactavit."

[55] *Ibid.*: "Levitates quippe seditionum et ambire propriae civitatis incendium non est velle Romanum." Cf. *Variae* 10.14.

[56] For this schism, Chp. 3, n. 53. The relevant documents are collected in the *Acta Synhodorum habitarum Romae* and demonstrate repeatedly both the clergy's desire for princely interference and Theoderic's insistence on peace and order.

[57] *Praeceptio Regis IIII Missa Ad Synhodum* (501), p. 422, ln. 5–7: "est quidem pudenda cum stupore diversitas Romanum statum in confinio gentium sub tranquillitate regi et in media urbe confundi, ut desideretur civilitas in arce Latii, quae est sub hostium vicinitate secura." It should be noted again that this letter was not written by Cassiodorus, yet is similar in style and content, demonstrating that the ideas encapsulated in the *Variae* are indeed Theoderic's own.

characteristics. But in Theoderic's Italy the loveliness of *civilitas* demanded that truly Roman behavior be the norm.[58]

Of course, "real" Romans, upstanding individuals like Cassiodorus and the patrician Liberius,[59] assisted Theoderic in the realization of these goals and for the most part monopolized the civil offices of the state. But Gothic officials, men with names like Gudila, Bedeulf, and Arigern, played their own, complementary role, thereby helping to associate law and order with Theoderic, his times, and his Goths.[60] As agents of royal authority, these men were dispatched and assigned to places like the city of Rome in order to "look into cases with careful examination" and "settle [them] with thoughtful equity."[61] They were enjoined to "drive off violence through [their] defense" and to allow "neither the innocent to be oppressed nor criminals to evade the laws."[62] Moreover, and as a later chapter will show, they were employed throughout Theoderic's empire, in places where Gothic settlement was sparse to nonexistent, demonstrating their importance before a strictly "Roman" audience. From Syracuse and southern Italy, to the northern provinces of Rhaetia and Noricum, and later, to newly won lands in the Balkans, Gaul, and Spain, Goths "proclaimed justice to the people" and were responsible for "restrain[ing] others under the rule of law."[63]

---

[58] *Variae* 1.30.3: "civilitatis gratia reductis moribus conveniret."

[59] Liberius' career, begun during the reign of Odovacer, was exceptional. He served as praetorian prefect of Italy (493–500), patrician (500–54), praetorian prefect of the Gauls (510–34), and *patricius praesentalis* (533–4). Later he traveled with a number of senatorial elites to Constantinople in an attempt to secure peace between Theodahad and Justinian. At some point before 538 he attached himself to Justinian, serving as his Augustal prefect in Egypt (538/9–?542) and military commander against the Goths in Sicily (550) and later Spain (552–3). He also seems to have played an important role in the formulation of Justinian's *Pragmatic Sanction*. See *PLRE* 2, 677–81 (Liberius 3) and O'Donnell (1981). For more on Liberius, see later discussion and Chp. 10.

[60] For Gudila, *PLRE* 2, 521; Bedeulf, *PLRE* 2, 222; and Arigen, *PLRE* 2, 141–2. All three were sent to Rome during the Laurentian Schism to keep the peace, and Arigern appears to have remained there for quite a long time.

[61] *Variae* 3.45.2 (to Arigern): "quapropter magnitudo tua conscientiae suae probata iustitia causam diligenti examinatione discutiat et ... considerata aequitate definiat."

[62] *Variae* 4.22.4: "De qua re illustri viro comiti Arigerno praecepta direximus, ut omnium violenta defensione summota, si se occulunt, ad iudicium protrahat impetitos et vobiscum in hac causa residens nec opprimi faciat innoxios nec leges sinat evadere criminosos."

[63] *Variae* 1.18.1: "qui aequitatem populi dicere suscepistis ... qui alios creditur sub aequitatis regula continere." This letter was a response to a pair of officials (Roman and Gothic) in an undisclosed location in Italy, who had inquired into two legal questions. Other attested locations in Italy include the cities of Como, Rome, and Syracuse, and broad regions like Samnium and Liguria. For these, *Variae* 2.35, 4.43, 9.10–14, 3.13, and 5.10, respectively. Examples from outside Italy can be found in Part V.

Men of Mars

In these ways, therefore, Theoderic and his Goths had not, as Athaulf had once imagined, made *Romania* into a kind of *Gothia*;[64] on the contrary, they had recast the remnants of *Romania* into a recognizably Roman Empire, corrected and reinvigorated. As "new Romans" and guardians of *Romanitas*, moreover, Goths could (and did) function together with their Italo-Roman consorts as a united and specifically Roman front, in opposition to those who were not members of Theoderic's order.[65] Some passages cited earlier have already hinted at this possibility, demonstrating the continued relevance of the barbarian-Roman binary in Theoderican Italy. What had changed, however, was who belonged to each category: Goths and Italo-Romans were now the "Romans," while others remained or became "barbarians."

Under a Gothic aegis the western Roman Empire reasserted its Roman claims of cultural superiority and hegemony over its neighbors, speaking of itself once more as a beacon of civilization. These claims had been seriously undermined in the fifth century, not only because of perceived cultural decline, but also because emperors had been forced to behave as the equals of stereotypical barbarians or been lorded over by superiors in Constantinople. The blow to Italo-Roman prestige has already been discussed,[66] but now, once more, Franks, Burgundians, Vandals, and even Visigoths were being referred to and often directly addressed as savages, Byzantines as crafty Greeks, and Gauls, as will be shown later, as semibarbarous.[67]

As ruler of the western Roman Empire, Theoderic asserted his and Rome's special civilizing position, sending, on one occasion, a water clock to the Burgundian king Gundobad. Savage beasts, he claimed, told time by their stomachs and so this Roman gift would serve to humanize the Burgundians.[68] Burgundy, Theoderic opined, should have "what

---

[64] Orosius, *Historiae* 7.43.5: "se inprimis ardenter inhiasse, ut oblitterato Romano nomine Romanum omne solum Gothorum imperium et faceret et vocaret essetque, ut vulgariter loquar, Gothia quod Romania fuisset."

[65] Just as disparate ethnic groups in the early Roman Empire had banded together as "Romans" in opposition to other so-called barbarians.

[66] See Part I, Chp. 1 especially.

[67] Cf. Heather (1994), 188. For Franks, Burgundians, and Greeks, see later discussion and Chps. 9 and 10. For Vandals, Chp. 6. For Visigoths and Gauls, Chps. 9 and 10. See also *Variae* 11.1.10–14, with the Epilogue.

[68] *Variae* 1.46.3: "Beluarum quippe ritus est ex ventris esurie horas sentire et non habere certum, quod constat humanis usibus contributum."

you [Gundobad] once saw in a Roman city";[69] it was right for her to "put down her barbarous ways" and "desire the accomplishments of wise men."[70] Similarly, Theoderic attempted to procure a cithara and citharist for the Frankish king Clovis, suggesting to his rather blue-blooded Roman correspondent, Boethius, that the musician was "about to imitate Orpheus" and would "tame the savage hearts of the barbarians with his charming sounds."[71] To a Grecophile like Boethius, the statement might have seemed ironic, yet to others, as we shall see, the idea of the Goths brandishing the torch of *Romanitas* beyond the Alps was no laughing matter: Whatever its leader's origins, Rome was believed to have retaken its rightful, righteous position as the head of the world, *caput mundi*, its "gifts" to barbarians functioning as a statement of superiority and a form of dominance.[72]

In Italy itself, on the other hand, the Romanness of the Goths meant that there could be "a common peace for both nations" and the enjoyment of "sweet tranquility."[73] Like claims of superiority, this too had been a problem in the fifth century, when civil wars were a regular phenomenon, corruption ran rampant, and borders were objects of predation by fearsome barbarians. Peace and tranquility were therefore linked to Theoderican themes of restoration and renewal and provided an important connection with the early imperial past, when another *princeps* (Augustus) had ushered in a similar *Pax Romana* after decades of chaos and disruption. Such peaceful conditions, however, were more than just the product of the Goths' apparent Romanization and obedience to *civilitas*; specifically Gothic military might played a fundamental role as well. Barbarians, aided by ineffectual Roman leadership, had recently caused the western empire to be transformed into the "Empire of Italy," but the Goths, now Rome's soldiers, became the means by which this empire was defended, its old boundaries restored, and its claims of being a Roman (rather than Italian) Empire legitimized. Indeed, it was actually *because* of the Goths, not despite them, that Rome reclaimed its rightful place.

---

[69] *Variae* 1.46.2: "Habetote in vestra patria, quod aliquando vidistis in civitate Romana." This is generally translated as "in the city of Rome," hence Hodgkin (1886) and Barnish (1992). This translation is certainly correct, but the condescension implied in the letter makes the preceding translation (equally legitimate) too tempting to resist and possibly even preferable. Theoderic's claim to Boethius in *Variae* 1.45.2, "what is normal to us will seem a miracle to them," also seems to justify this interpretation.

[70] *Variae* 1.46.2: "per vos propositum gentile [Burgundia] deponit et dum prudentiam regis sui respicit, iure facta sapientium concupiscit."

[71] *Variae* 2.40.17: "facturus aliquid Orphei, cum dulci sono gentilium fera corda domuerit."

[72] Cf. Claude (1978b), 26, who places Theoderic's gifting within the Roman imperial tradition. On gifting as a form of dominance in general, Mauss (1954).

[73] *Variae* 7.3.2: "Sic pace communi utraeque nationes divinitate propitia dulci otio perfruantur."

Even the passages cited earlier, which demonstrate the Goths' idealized obedience to the laws, reveal the duality of their position within the empire. Ennodius praised sweet *civilitas* but hinted at the "unrestrained" temperament of the Goths in battle; Theoderic defined his Goths as having Roman prudence, but also the courage of barbarians; provincials were reminded that the Goths were modest at home, yet bellicose abroad.[74] Qualities, therefore, that had once rendered Goths susceptible to accusations of rashness and savagery, were now, since the Goths fought on behalf of the empire, transformed into familiar (and Roman) themes of bravery and military glory. The Goths were no longer barbarian raiders and marauders but Italy's protectors, guarding against external and internal acts of violence and allowing non-Goths, civilian Romans, to flourish.[75] Romans had "gained a defender at the cost of some land";[76] they were to enjoy the peaceful habitations of their cities, while the Goths "endured the toils of war for the common good"[77] and "defended the entire Republic during its wars."[78] Romans like Ennodius romantically praised young Goths who trained for battle, since they assured "the blessings of tranquility" and provided for senatorial *otium*.[79] Goths like Theoderic and his noble generals Pitzia and Tuluin, likewise, became "heroes" who fought

[74] Moorhead (1999), 253–4, reaches similar conclusions regarding the "dual character" of the Goths but sees the idea originating with Cassiodorus. The citations from Ennodius suggest a broader appeal, however.

[75] Cf. Amory (1997), chp. 5, who sees "Gothicness" as an ideological construct and reflection of one's societal role (soldier Goth vs. civilian Roman). For a more traditionally ethnic view, Burns (1984), 70–2, and Moorhead (1992), 71–5. For "Gothicness" as a political identity stemming from the Goths' land settlement in Italy, Heather (2007), 45f. The nature of this settlement, however, is a matter of debate (see the following note), while the reliability of the predominantly Greek sources that Heather uses is unclear. Cf. Sirago (1986), 188–9, who stresses Theoderic's annual giving of a donative at Ravenna as a source of "Gothic" cohesion. No doubt this kept the army loyal, but there is no evidence that it helped to promote a Gothic national identity that was antithetical to Romanness. Indeed, this was an imperial practice as well.

[76] *Variae* 2.16.5: "et parte agri defensor adquisitus est." What exactly Cassiodorus and others meant by "land" remains a matter of scholarly debate. For actual land, Burns (1978b); Barnish (1986); and Heather (2007). For tax revenues derived from the land, Goffart (1980) and (2006).

[77] *Variae* 8.3.4 (to the inhabitants of Rome): "nec aliud inter vos esse divisum, nisi quod illi [i.e. Gothi] labores bellicos pro communi utilitate subeunt, vos autem habitatio quieta civitatis Romanae multiplicat."

[78] *Variae* 7.3.3: "Vos autem, Romani, magno studio Gothos diligere debetis, qui et in pace numerosos vobis populos faciunt et universam rem publicam per bella defendunt."

[79] *PanTh* 83: "Nam illud quo ore celebrandum est, quod Getici instrumenta roboris, dum provides ne interpellentur otia nostra, custodis et pubem indomitam sub oculis tuis inter bona tranquillitatis facis bella proludere?"

on behalf of the republic and restored (rather than conquered) its lands.[80] They were "worthy to be honored forever," Ennodius claimed, winning epic victories against seemingly indomitable barbarians like the Bulgars and Franks and disgracing the haughty but weak generals dispatched by a "displeased Greece."[81] Because of them, "the Roman Republic acquired provinces" and "Roman powers were restored to their former limits," allowing Theoderic to "dictate instructions" to restored provincials "in the custom of our [western Roman] ancestors."[82] Because of them, moreover, the weapons of Rome's enemies trembled in fear;[83] their own weapons, meanwhile, established peace and secured freedom (*libertas*), preventing "the effeminate toga, now battle-ready," from "lying dead"[84] and granting substance to Roman claims of eternal victory emblematic in triumphal ornaments like the *toga palmata*, the honorary clothes of a triumphant general.[85] It was Goths who claimed the victory, but symbolically wrapped in Roman clothing, a testament to their Romanness.

The Goths, as a people but more importantly as an ideal, thus breathed new life into Italy, rescuing not only the state, but the Roman people themselves through their insertion of new, invigorating blood. These new "men of Mars" were praised for having fortuitously come to the aid of the "race

[80] For heroes, *PanTh* 87: "heroas tuos." For the restoration of land and Pitzia, *PanTh*. 62: "Pitzia ... non adquisitam esse terram credidit sed refusam," with *PLRE* 2, 886–7. For Tuluin, *Variae* 8.9–10 (discussed later) and *PLRE* 2, 1131–3. For Theoderic's restoration of the eastern and western empires, see the following chapter.

[81] For worthy, *PanTh* 68: "celebrandus saeculis Pitzia"; for Bulgars, *Variae* 8.10.4 and 8.21.3, with the lengthy ethnographic excursus and battle scene provided in *PanTh* 19–22 and 63–9 (the latter discussed in Chp. 6). For Franks, see later discussion and Part V. For the disgraced Byzantine general (Sabinianus), *PanTh* 68: "quid strages militum revolvam et Sabiniani ducis abitionem turpissimam, cum a ratione dividatur retexere exterminatis patrociniis quid evenerit indefenso?" For displeased Greece, *PanTh* 63: "Graecia est professa discordiam" and (from the reign of Amalasuentha) *Variae* 11.1.10–11, discussed in the Epilogue.

[82] For provinces, *Variae* 8.10.8 (a reference to Tuluin's later efforts in Gaul): "adquisivit rei publicae Romanae ... provinciam." For Roman powers and instructions, *PanTh* 69 (in reference to the Sirmian War): "interea ad limitem suum Romana regna remearunt: dictas more veterum praecepta Sermiensibus"; with *Variae* 3.23–4.

[83] *PanTh* 16: "quae ab hostibus sumpta fuerant arma tremuerunt." The idea is repeated often in contemporary sources. Cf. *PanTh* 53–4 (on fearful Heruli and Burgundians) and *Variae* 11.1.12 (on fearful Franks).

[84] For freedom, *PanTh* 42: "qui [Theodericus] dum munimentis chalybis pectus includere, dum ocreis armarere, dum lateri tuo vindex libertatis gladius aptaretur." On this passage, Chp. 6. For peace and the effeminate toga, *Variae* 8.10.1 (in reference to Tuluin): "auctus est enim pacis genius de ferri radiantis ornatu nec discincta iacet toga iam procinctualis effecta."

[85] *PanTh* 15–16 (cited more extensively in Chp. 6) describes the legitimacy that Theoderic granted to the *toga palmata*, the toga of a consul, but also of a triumphant general. Cf. *Variae* 6.1. Theoderic had been granted a public triumph in Constantinople in 484.

of Romulus," itself sired from the house of Mars.[86] The association gave Romans and Goths a common (divine) ancestry, perhaps not especially important to a Christian audience, but still suggestive of their imagined kinship and the importance of warfare and victory among both peoples. Ironically, violence linked Goths and Romans more than it drove them apart, martial themes being celebrated by Romans in their panegyrics, monumental architecture, inscriptions, coins, popular entertainment, and the language of emperorship itself.[87] In the late fourth century, Ammianus Marcellinus had declared that the Romans had won their empire by "fierce wars" and "valor," but that now they "owed victory to [their] name alone."[88] It was this lack of substance to Roman claims of invincibility, coupled with crippling losses, that had led to disillusionment and sentiments of decline in the fifth century. But under Theoderic, substance had been restored to these claims, fulfilling expectations of Roman victory and dominance, even if the propaganda of the day associated these old Roman virtues with Goths and Gothicness.

IDEAL AND REALITY

Though somewhat artificial, the association of victory and dominance with Goths is understandable and was fueled by the tendency for the Roman army to be staffed with provincial and barbarian recruits, rather than Italians. This was not a new development, though some in Constantinople would later suggest that it had been the very cause of the western empire's fall. According to Procopius, the barbarian element had simply grown too strong and had made demands that led to the deposition of Romulus Augustus.[89] In Procopius' classicizing mind, these barbarians were antithetical to Romans, yet the reality of the situation was much more complex. Again, many of these "barbarian" soldiers were not newcomers, but

---

[86] *Variae* 8.10.11 (directed to the Roman Senate in reference to Tuluin's patriciate): "convenit gentem Romuleam Martios viros habere collegas." Cf. *Variae* 10.31.2.

[87] The problem with violence, therefore, was not violence itself, but instances when it was turned against Rome. Hence the acceptability and praise for Athaulf and the *Gothorum viribus* found in the Orosius passage cited in the Introduction to this section. Cf. Ward-Perkins (2005), chp. 2, "The Horrors of War," who, in a reactionary move against "accommodation narratives," emphasizes the violence that typified the fifth century. There was indeed violence, but it often received praise when harnessed for the benefit of the empire. Cf. Heather (1999), 242f.

[88] *Res Gestae* 14.6.10: "ignorantes profecto maiores suos per quos ita magnitudo Romana porrigitur ... per bella saevissima ... opposita cuncta superasse virtute"; and 14.6.4: "iamque vergens in senium, et nomine solo aliquotiens vincens, ad tranquilliora vitae discessit." Ammianus was referring to only the inhabitants of Rome, however.

[89] Procopius, *Wars* 5.1.4–5.

had been settled with their families in Italy for more than a generation. No doubt, they were able to identify as both Roman and barbarian, much like the Rhineland Frank whose fourth-century epitaph read, "I am a Frank, a Roman soldier in arms."[90] Just as Frankishness became a marker for Roman soldiers stationed along the Rhine, Gothicness became a prerequisite for the soldiers defending Italy. Being labeled a Goth did not exclude such soldiers from Romanness but made a statement about their military role in society and, most importantly, suggested the bravery and might for which Goths had come to stand. Once indicative of a *Roman* army, this bravery and might now became indicative of *Rome's* Gothic army.

More importantly, the strict separation of Goths and Romans generally did not extend beyond these kinds of ideals and propaganda. There were real distinctions between newcomer and native, of course: Goths might speak the Gothic language; many (but not all) adhered to the Arian creed and worshiped in separate churches; those who lived in cities might congregate in separate quarters; and many, as already seen, were indeed liable to military service.[91] But these kinds of distinctions were not novelties in the Roman Empire; nor were they much different from those that had separated a Briton from an Egyptian or Greek, a Catholic from a heretic, pagan, or Jew, or a civilian from a common soldier.[92] And while potentially divisive, many of these distinctions had already been weakened by the conditions of the empire discussed at the beginning of this chapter, and so

[90] For the Frankish epitaph, *CIL* 3 3576: "Francus ego civis Romanus miles in armis." The association might explain why a Roman general like Aegedius in the later fifth century could be understood as a ruler of the Franks during the exile of their king, Childeric. See Gregory of Tours, *Historiae* 2.12, and *LHF* 7. For a discussion of the Frankification of the Rhineland army, Stroheker (1955) and James (1988), 38–44. Although there are no "Gothic" inscriptions that parallel this one, some scholars have suggested that a number of the names of (Roman) soldiers listed on the *Res Gestae Divi Saporis* are Gothic in origin. On the regular use of Goths as auxiliaries against Persia, Wolfram (1988), 43f.

[91] It is often suggested that Theoderic had intended to keep Goths and Romans separate and to control their integration slowly. Cf. Burns (1982), 99–102, and Schäfer (2001). If this was the case, the plan did not work; Theoderic himself admitted it (see later discussion). The use of the Gothic language by Goths and Romans is well attested, and by the time of Theoderic's death most Goths surely knew Latin. For the possibility of a "Gothic" quarter in Rome and Ravenna, Zeiller (1904), 27–9, and Deliyannis (2010), 116, who doubts its existence in Ravenna. In Rome, the supposed "Gothic" quarter was located between the Caelian and Esquiline Hills in the military quarter, underscoring the military role of the Goths. For Arian churches, Zeiller (1905); Cecchelli (1960); and Deliyannis (2010), 146f. A number were constructed in Ravenna during his reign, including Sant'Apollinare Nuovo and Sant'Eusebio. Others in Ravenna predate his arrival, but likely received his patronage. Catholic churches also received his patronage, as demonstrated by Ennodius, #458.7 (*In Christi Signo*) and *LP* 44.10–11 (a gift to St. Peter's).

[92] Cf. O'Donnell (2008), 121.

were blurring or blurred at best, growing increasingly fuzzy with time.[93] Theoderic himself was said to have wisely observed, "The poor Roman imitates the Goth, the rich Goth the Roman."[94] This was not necessarily a statement about the aristocracy giving up its military role or the ranks of the army being filled with peasants, but an affirmation of the cultural convergence that was occurring in Theoderic's Italy.[95] Gothic aristocrats, on the one hand, imitated their Roman aristocratic half brothers, as this class had been doing for generations,[96] becoming classically (and even biblically) trained in Greek and Latin and coming to possess sizable estates and senatorial titles.[97] Whether Gothic or Roman, peasant society, on the other hand, remained the same old rustic and rude rabble traditionally looked down upon by the elite as semi-, if not fully, barbarous.[98]

In spite of Theoderic's claims, however, this was no mere assimilation but a two-way process: Rich Romans were also imitating Goths, an act not nearly so fantastic when it is borne in mind that many supposedly "Gothic" traits were nothing more than Roman ones in disguise. The Roman Opilio,

[93] The near archaeological invisibility of the Ostrogoths of Italy is well known. See Bierbrauer (1975) and (1994); Maioli (1994), 238–42; Brogiolo and Possenti (2001), 272–7; and Brogiolo (2007), 116f.
[94] *AnonVal* 61: "Romanus miser imitatur Gothum et utilis Gothus imitatur Romanum."
[95] But cf. Burns (1982), 113–14, who seems to characterize this statement as an admission of failure on Theoderic's part.
[96] See the discussions of Danubian archaeology in Whittaker (1994), 178f., and Heather (1996), chp. 3. On aristocratic permeability, again, Demandt (1989) and Goffart (2006), 191f., who follows him.
[97] Heather (1994), 178–80, emphasizes the importance of Greek and Latin already among the fourth-century Goths. The most conspicuous examples from sixth-century Italy belong to the Amal clan, but others were acquiring land, adorning themselves with letters, and holding illustrious offices. Examples include Tuluin (described earlier), Theudis in Spain (Procopius, *Wars* 5.12.50–2), and the "antiqui barbari" of Sirmium (*Variae* 5.14, with the caveats of Šašel (1979) and Viscido (1986b)). Some "senators" in the *Variae* and the father of Pope Boniface II appear to have "un-Roman" names, perhaps Goths, but perhaps not. See Amory (1997), chps. 3 and 5. Cf. Sirago (1986), 189–91. Spielvogel (2002) and Heather (2007) maintain (on inferences derived largely from Procopius) that there existed a separate and proudly traditional (anti-Roman) Gothic aristocracy. There seems, however, little Italian evidence for this, and it makes more sense to see these "Goths" as a foil for Procopius. Indeed, in the same places where Procopius mentions these "traditional" Goths, he also refers to "Romanized" Goths. See, for instance, *Wars* 5.2.7–29, where three older "refined" Goths instruct Athalaric in the ways of a "Roman" prince, thereby offending "the Goths"; these same traditional "Goths" then rally to the overtly "Roman" and "unwarlike" Theodahad. The account is absurdly inconsistent.
[98] Examples of this elite understanding can be found in the works of Ennodius, Sidonius, and the *Variae*, while Whittaker (1994) demonstrates the reality of convergence along socioeconomic lines within the frontier regions. There was, however, a major exception to this pejorative understanding, which lay in the republican ideal of the citizen-soldier-farmer type, embodied in heroic individuals like Cincinnatus.

for instance, was described as both prominent for his noble character and "famous in the force of his arms." He was lauded for "upholding the virtues of the ancients," but described as "strong in body [and] a man whom peace praised, but raging war would not reject."[99] The Romans were bound to him "through his judgments," the barbarians (*gentiles*) "through his way of life."[100] This was an Italo-Roman whose virtues seemed to parallel the Goths' own (justice, physical strength, love of peace, courage in war), yet who was a Roman statesmen and a model of ancient Roman virtues. The sons of a certain Venantius, a descendant of the noble Decii, were similarly "exercised in arms and trained in letters,"[101] while those of the patrician Cyprian were extolled for "shining forth with tribal grace, having been imbued in the institutions of arms," and for being "boys of Roman stock, [who] spoke our [Gothic] language."[102] Cyprian himself was acclaimed as a valiant warrior, who helped the Goths achieve victory by pursuing fleeing barbarians during the Sirmian War,[103] while the distinguished patrician Liberius, whom Ennodius complimented for his eloquence and early role in securing Italy's "hope of restoration,"[104] was described by Cassiodorus as "a military man ... famous in his merits, notable in his appearance, but more beautiful in his wounds."[105] It was wounds, in fact, that had marked Theoderic's heroic Gothic general Tuluin as a courageous Goth; his wounds were "an inseparable source of esteem, a proclamation without an advocate, a particular language of courage, which ... adorn us for the rest of our lives."[106] Yet while Tuluin's wounds were proof that the

---

[99] *Variae* 8.17.1: "manu clarus ac summa fuit morum nobilitate conspicuus, quem nec ferventia bella respuerunt et tranquilla otia praedicarent, corpore validus, amicitia robustus aevi antiquitatem gestabat." For Opilio, see Chp. 2

[100] *Variae* 8.17.6: "Gentiles victu, Romanos sibi iudiciis obligabat."

[101] *Variae* 9.23.3: "quorum infantia bonis artibus enutrita iuventutem quoque armis exercuit."

[102] *Variae* 8.21.6–7: "Relucent etiam gratia gentili nec cessant armorum imbui fortibus institutis. Pueri stirpis Romanae nostra lingua loquuntur."

[103] *Variae* 8.21.3: "bellatorem: non te terruit Bulgarum globus.... Sic victoriam Gothorum ... iuvisti." Cf. *Variae* 8.10.4, where the Goth Tuluin is also praised as a *bellator*, his brave deeds during the same campaign serving as a testament to "the robust boldness" of the Goths.

[104] For hope of restoration, #447.3: "ad spem reparationis," with Chp. 7. In all, six letters directed to Liberius are contained within Ennodius' corpus, almost all of which comment on his eloquence.

[105] *Variae* 11.1.16: "Patricium Liberium praefectum etiam Galliarum, exercitualem virum, communione gratissimum, meritis clarum, forma conspicuum, sed vulneribus pulchriorem."

[106] *Variae* 8.10.7: "vulnera inquam, opinio inseparabilis, sine assertore praeconium, propria lingua virtutis, quae licet ad praesens periculum ingerant, reliquum tamen vitae tempus exornant."

Getic race of Mars had reinvigorated the weak toga, Liberius' proved that "he had served the Republic well."[107]

In this respect, then, there was a distinction to be made between Goths and Romans in Theoderic's empire, but its existence failed to call into question the Romanness of Goths or, for that matter, Romans who had "gone Gothic." Goths and Gothicness represented martialism, the old Roman virtue of *virtus* (the very source of the term "virtue"), meaning "manliness" or "courage."[108] *Virtus* was an ideal that the Romans had seemingly lost, becoming overly effeminate (perhaps even overly Greek), yet that until recently had been fundamental to Romanness and the existence of a Roman Empire.[109] As idealized soldiers and embodiments of manly courage, therefore, the Goths became symbolic of the restored Roman victory that other barbarians had snatched away in the fifth century, and the trappings of Gothicness (if any resisted Roman assimilation) served to complement such ideas.[110]

Indeed, Theoderic's hair and mustache may have been recognizably Gothic, after all, but, if so, their appearance would have harmonized well with the overtly Roman claims of victory and dominance depicted on the Senigallia Medallion. Theoderic, and by extension every Goth, was *invictissimus semper* and *victor gentium*, but the victory was Roman and allowed Rome, once "trembling in her slipping footsteps,"[111] to be celebrated again as unconquered.[112]

[107] For the toga, *Variae* 8.10 (cited previously, n. 84); for serving well, *Variae* 11.1.16: "ne de re publica bene meritus diu absens putaretur ingratus."

[108] Cf. Moorhead (1999), 252. On *virtus* and its association with manliness, McDonnell (2006).

[109] Martial values (ideologically speaking) had remained a constant in the Roman Empire, despite the military failures of the fifth century. Moreover, and despite complaints of feminization, Italian society in general seems to have become increasingly martialized at this time, in direct response to these crises. See Kennell (2000), 117–18; MacGeorge (2002), 170–1; Everett (2003), chp. 1; and Goffart (2006), 191. The ban on civilians' carrying arms was actually lifted over the course of the fifth century. See *CTh* 15.15.1, with *NVal* 9 and *NMaj* 8 (lost). And a number of Roman aristocrats even led private armies against barbarian invaders, including Cassiodorus' great-grandfather.

[110] These "manly" Goths would seem to be an inversion of Goffart's reading of the "happy ending" of Jordanes' *Getica*. See Goffart (1988), chp. 2 especially. If Goffart's conclusions are correct, Jordanes cleverly reversed the gender roles of Goths and Romans (as understood in Italy) and placed their union a bit later. Such a glaring reversal would seem to demonstrate the *Getica*'s value as specifically Byzantine propaganda (as Goffart, in fact, concludes). For more, see the following chapter.

[111] *PanTh* 48: "Illic vellem ut aetatis inmemor, Roma, conmeares. Si venires lapsantibus tremebunda vestigiis, aevum gaudia conmutarent."

[112] "Invicta Roma," it should be recalled, was a prevalent theme on "Ostrogothic" coinage. See Chp. 3, with the more elaborate discussion in Chp. 8.

6

REX GENITUS, VIR INLUSTRIS

GOTHS AND A GOTHIC EMPEROR

As Roman soldiers and "barbarians" Romanized much like other provincials, the Goths found a role in Theoderic's Italy, and Gothicness as an ideal became an essential component of the Roman restoration rhetoric defining the era. Gothicness complemented sentiments of renovation and republican renaissance. Just as the empire was once more the republic ruled by a modest *princeps*, its law-abiding soldiers again fought bravely and with honor, embodying those manly virtues that had granted Rome its mastery over the world and established the *Pax Romana*. Theoderic had literally become "what Caesar Augustus had been," far beyond the intent of Athaulf's wishful thinking nearly a century prior.

Yet the "Roman" heroism and valor for which the Goths had come to stand were not the only prerequisites traditionally associated with Roman emperorship, and Theoderic would have found it difficult to win acceptance in Italy if simply playing the part of a victorious Goth. Since emperors were *imperatores*, literally "commanders," such martial qualities had always played an important role in their maintenance of a loyal army and fulfillment of expectations of military supremacy. But as heads of state, emperors were held to higher standards than their soldiers, and those who failed to be more than just soldier-emperors were often unable to earn their more aristocratic subjects' respect or loyalty.[1] As discussed

---

[1] The third-century emperor Maximinus Thrax is perhaps the best example. According to the *Historia Augusta*, the nobility of Rome both hated and feared him, largely on account of his savage cruelty, ignoble qualities, and barbarous origins. Eventually the Senate rebelled, appointing the senators Balbinus and Pupienus as co-emperors. Maximinus was the prototype of the so-called Danubian/Balkan (or military) emperors of the third and fourth century. For these and their reception at Rome as "barbarous," Van Dam (2007), 35–44.

earlier, long after the ideals of the principate had all but vanished, senators had continued to imagine that the emperor would be one of their own, a first among equals, cultured, learned, and of noble blood. Such expectations had been denied throughout the course of the empire's history, but their perceived fulfillment by a late antique ruler remained a major source of praise and admiration, especially from the senatorial class. Indeed, for elites like Cassiodorus and Ennodius, the comparative lack of such finer qualities among fifth-century leaders was evidence of this period's decadence, while their presence in contemporary leadership was proof of "modern" resurgence. Cassiodorus might have praised Galla Placidia for being "distinguished by the esteem of the world and glorious in her lineage," but her lineage was no match for Amalasuentha's eloquence and splendid Amal blood.[2] Less sympathetic, Ennodius had faulted Odovacer for his ignoble origins and complained bitterly that he and his predecessors had "loved ignorance, and never did what was praiseworthy." His lack of erudition and its glaring unimportance during the late fifth century were likewise symbolic of this era in general, when "no value was given to written accounts," and eloquence, so fundamental to Ennodius' understanding of Romanness, was ignored.[3]

Such critiques nicely demonstrate how the perceived qualities of a ruler often dictated assessments and impressions of his or her reign, thereby informing the health of the republic (*status reipublicae*).[4] The presence of nobility and elite Roman culture lent legitimacy to a ruler before Roman audiences throughout the Mediterranean, but especially in Italy, where the aristocracy was tenaciously traditional and extremely proud of its republican roots.[5] Theoderic's perceived background, therefore, was extremely important. And his knowledge of high Roman culture, combined with a noble pedigree and illustrious Roman career in the East, served to transform an otherwise "barbarian" king into an acceptably senatorial man, who shared these ennobling attributes with his Italian aristocrats. Such qualities helped to reiterate before a less open-minded Italian audience that Theoderic was authentically Roman, and set him apart from his troops, who might be accepted as Romans in their own unique way, but

[2] See *Variae* 11.1, with Chp. 2.
[3] See *PanTh* 24 and 76–7, with Chp. 1.
[4] Näf (1990), 112, includes *status reipublicae* among the titles given to Theoderic by Ennodius. This would be an interesting title, but the use of this phrase in *VE* 81 (cited in Chp. 1, n. 62) makes its reference to the state, rather than its ruler, abundantly clear.
[5] This is discussed more extensively later, but see Wes (1967), chps. 1 and 2, and Jones (1964), chp. 15.

were nonetheless thought to be rude and semibarbarous, like all soldiers.[6] Moreover, this membership helped to reiterate ideas of the Theoderican era as a restoration of the principate, since the *princeps* had been ideally the *optimus vir senatus*, the best man of the Senate.

THEODERIC THE ROMAN

Given the hostility toward Greeks encountered throughout this study, it is ironic (though not entirely problematic) that Theoderic's famil-iarity with high Roman culture had been acquired in the East. He was the son of the Ostrogothic subking Theodemir, himself a federate of the eastern emperor Marcian, who had been granted lands in Pannonia in the 450s on which to settle his Goths. Theoderic was presumably born, then, on a Pannonian reservation established within the boundaries of the Roman Empire, in a locale where acculturative interaction with provincial Romans was assured.[7] Even before his birth, however, his fellow Goths had already been influenced by generations of contact and interaction with the empire's inhabitants. And during Theoderic's lifetime they persisted in their Romanizing trends, becoming "provincialized" to an extent that was recognizably Roman to other Romans.[8] Yet this "Gotho-Pannonian" var-iation on the Roman theme was not the version of Romanness to which Theoderic himself was primarily exposed. Very early in his youth, some-time around the age of eight, young Theoderic was sent to Constantinople as a hostage to ensure the conditions of a treaty established between his people and the emperor Leo I.[9] Here he remained for a decade, after which he returned to Pannonia and eventually inherited from his father the posi-tion of king.[10]

---

[6] It should be remembered, too, that even if Goths had found an ideological niche in Italy, the idea of Goths as barbarians, much like the idea of Gauls as barbarians, could continue to flourish in Italy. Its continuance, in fact, would become the ammunition of the Byzantine propaganda machine during Justinian's reconquest. See Amory (1997), 135f., and Goffart (2006), 52–5.

[7] Jordanes, *Getica* 269, places Theodemir's territory near Lake Pelso in Pannonia at the time of Theoderic's birth. The actual date, however, is uncertain. *PLRE* 2, 1078, suggests 454, while Schmidt (1925), 407, suggests 456, and Wolfram (1988), 261–2, 451. Cf. Heather (1991), 242, who places their initial settlement in Pannonia under Attila (i.e. in the 440s). The treaty with Marcian, therefore, may have placed an imperial stamp of approval on a fait accompli.

[8] See the preceding chapter.

[9] Jordanes, *Getica* 271, with Ensslin (1959), 11–13; Wolfram (1988), 262–3; and Heather (1991), 247–9.

[10] Theodemir, Theoderic's father, became king when his brother, Valamir, died. He was still king when Theoderic returned to Pannonia, though Theoderic may have been associated with his reign, perhaps as subking or co-king.

Despite the fact that few specifics are known about this time spent in Constantinople, Theoderic's contemporaries took it very seriously, and moderns would do well to follow their example. These were among the most formative years of Theoderic's life (indeed of most adolescents' lives), a time when the future king of Italy was understood by one Italian subject to have matured from the "lightheartedness of a boy" into a man.[11] As a royal hostage of the imperial court, Theoderic would have run within aristocratic circles and been reared as if the son of a Roman dignitary, exposed to all the luxury and high culture available in the eastern capital. Constantinople's ubiquitous late antique imperial monuments would have surrounded him daily with impressive reminders of Roman glory and righteousness, the emperors' names etched into these buildings perhaps serving to instill in him the importance of a ruler's reputation and legacy.[12] It was here that Theoderic proudly asserted he had learned Roman governance and justice,[13] and here that he had largely internalized what it meant to be a Roman and a proper Roman emperor. "Greece," Ennodius proclaimed in his panegyric, "raised you [i.e. Theoderic] in the lap of *civilitas*, predicting what was to come."[14]

Such, of course, had been an intended consequence of Roman hostageship, transforming former hostages into admirers and practitioners of *Romanitas* and rendering them willing allies or clients upon assuming leadership roles at home.[15] But in Theoderic's case, it is very likely that this period in Constantinople had repercussions beyond an appreciation for Roman culture and governance. His tender age upon arriving and his long stay within Constantinople's walls, isolated from his Pannonian cousins for more than a decade, surely played a fundamental role in his development as a person. Constantinople was, of course, a diverse place and there were

---

[11] *PanTh* 11: "dum adhuc de puero haberet hilaritatem." Cf. Jordanes, *Getica* 271, which refers to young Theoderic as an "infantulus" and "puerulus." Granted, human psychology and age groups are not universal and Theoderic may have been a particularly mature eight-year-old, but Ennodius' (and Jordanes') depiction implies a carefree boy who became a man imbued with Roman *pietas*. Cf. Schmidt (1939), 407, and Wolfram (1988), 262.

[12] Many of these monuments were located in and around Constantinople's city-center (Augusteum), such as the basilicas housing New Rome's senate, the Great Palace and its adjoining church and hippodrome, and Constantine's Church of the Apostles. These buildings were testaments to, and daily reminders of, the greatness of Rome, its emperors, and the empire. They doubtless instilled in Theoderic an understanding of Roman order. See Ensslin (1959), chp. 1, who goes into much more detail; also Johnson (1988) for the influence of eastern models on Theoderic's building program at Ravenna.

[13] *Variae* 1.1.2, with Chp. 3.

[14] *PanTh* 11: "Educavit te in gremio civilitatis Graecia praesaga venturi." And by this Ennodius meant *everything* that was to come, both in the East and in the West.

[15] See Braund (1984), 12–16, and Lee (1991).

Goths and other barbarians to be found in the city.[16] But even these were Romanized to some extent, while the "barbarians" with whom Theoderic generally associated, influential men like the generalissimo Aspar and his son Patricius, were so Romanized and had become so ingrained within the senatorial aristocracy that the former was offered the diadem by the Senate and the latter elevated to the rank of a Caesar.[17] When Theoderic finally left this city at the age of eighteen, therefore, he had lived more than half of his life there, surrounded by Romanness, and some of his most important, character-defining developments had occurred here. He probably developed the tastes and mannerisms of the city's elite, for instance, and received a classical education,[18] thereby acquiring a Greco-Roman worldview that would have been especially potent to an impressionable boy.[19] Modern studies of language acquisition, moreover, suggest that he could have learned to speak both Greek and Latin with a flawless local accent.[20] Doubtless, characteristics like these would have marked him not

[16] For some of these Goths, see later discussion. There was also an Arian church, where a Gothic liturgy may have been employed at least sometimes. Indeed, while Theoderic was in residence, there was even an Orthodox Church, St. Anastasia, where services were held in Gothic on certain festal days. See Zeiller (1904), 30–2; Snee (1998); and Luiselli (2005). Wolfram (1988), 135, and Burns (1994), 172–3, also discuss Gothic communities in the eastern capital, though referring to only the early fifth century.

[17] These events happened shortly before Theoderic's arrival and some time around his departure, respectively. For Aspar and the diadem, see Theoderic's *Agnosticum Regis* in *Acta Synhodorum Romae* (p. 425). For Aspar, *PLRE* 2, 164–9; for Patricus, *PLRE* 2, 842 (Julius Patricius 15). For discussions, von Haehling (1988), 98f., and Croke (2005a).

[18] For the debate concerning Theoderic's education, Cessi (1927); Schmidt (1927); Ensslin (1940) and (1959), 21–4; Riché (1976), 57–8; Baldwin (1989); and König (2000), 218. The claim in *AnonVal* 61 and 79 that Theoderic was an *illit(t)eratus* is probably not correct; the latter (rather hostile) passage is likely a mistaken reference to the eastern emperor Justin, whose lack of a formal education is well documented. Procopius' comment on Theoderic's education (*Wars* 5.2.6–17) is discussed later. Other eastern sources, including Malalas 383 (15.9), Theophanes, AM 5977, and John of Nikiu 48, suggest a formal education. Cf. Garzya (1995), 351. Theoderic's own *Praeceptio Regis IIII Missa Ad Synhodum* (cited in Chp. 5) may even prove that he could write in Latin, as it concludes with the phrase "orate pro nobis, domini sancti et venerabiles patres," written in another (Theoderic's?) hand.

[19] On Romanization and indoctrination through education, Woolf (1998), 67–76.

[20] For such modern studies (though not entirely applicable to the late antique world), Long (1990), 259f., with the introductory remarks in Flege (1999) and Stevens (1999). The age at which Theoderic relocated to Constantinople could have had a tremendous impact on his speech. Vocabulary, for instance, can double between the ages of six and eight, while proper pronunciation becomes increasingly difficult as one reaches adolescence. For Theoderic's appreciation of proper pronunciation, *Variae* 4.3. One should not rule out the possibility that he was already bilingual (or even trilingual, as Amalasuentha was) before arriving in the capital, given the importance of Greek and Latin among the fourth-century Goths. See Heather (1994), 178–80. For the roles and uses of Greek and Latin in contemporary Constantinople, Millar (2006), 20f.; Van Dam (2007), chp. 7; and Cameron (2009).

simply as a Roman, but an elite Roman, providing an important link with similarly cultured men in places like Italy.[21]

Constantinople, then, not only as a physical space but also as a way of life (a rather cosmopolitan variation on Romanness), became an intrinsic component of Theoderic's persona and had become so as he matured from an eight-year-old boy into a teen and finally young adult.[22] This made him authentically Constantinopolitan, authentically east Roman, and may have even alienated his fellow Goths, who were becoming Roman along an entirely different, Pannonian scheme and were no doubt more in tune with their Gothic heritage.[23] Much like the transplant Ennodius, whose Ligurian childhood rendered him more Italian than Gallic, Theoderic may have had developed a consciously east Roman identity with attributes that were recognizable to other Romans and other Goths. He may, in fact, have become so overtly Roman that at eighteen he seemed foreign to his kin and required a degree of reinvention in order to win their acceptance. War, and especially war at the expense of Rome, could help to reassert his Gothicness, but a Roman Theoderic would always be.[24]

BEING GRECO-ROMAN

Still, what may have seemed excessively Roman to Theoderic's Goths was, again, fundamental to winning acceptance in Italy, despite its potentially problematic acquisition in the East. Coming of age in "Roman"

---

[21] The number of contemporary references to the ennobling power of a liberal education is phenomenal. For Italian examples, Chp. 8; for Gallic, Chp. 9.

[22] Civic identities were still extremely important at this time, and individuals tended to identify more with their native city/city-community (*urbs/civitas*) than with a larger country or ethnic group. The collapse of the Roman Empire and the establishment of local cults of saints served to increase this phenomenon in the West, with Gaul the most extensively studied region. See Van Dam (1985), chp. 1, and (1993), chp. 1, and Lewis (2000).

[23] For a similar conclusion, O'Donnell (2008), 58. Cf. Procopius, *Wars* 5.2.6–17, who claims that the Gothic aristocracy was appalled at the idea that Athalaric, Theoderic's grandson, was being educated in the manner of a Roman prince. Letters, they claimed, produced cowards. The extent to which this account is trustworthy, however, is uncertain. These Goths also avowed that Theoderic himself had "never heard of letters" and had forbidden Gothic children to be educated as Romans, an assertion that is demonstrably untrue. Cf. Riché (1976), 63–4.

[24] There is some evidence that suggests that Theoderic had encountered difficulties securing the loyalty of the Pannonian Goths upon returning from Constantinople, perhaps for this very reason. The fact that there was another, non-Amal Theoderic (Theoderic Strabo) operating in the area probably did not help, though he too derived legitimacy and assistance from Constantinople. See *PLRE* 2, 1073–6 (Theodericus Strabo 5). Theoderic's early military campaigns against Strabo and the eastern empire (seizing Singidunum, for instance) may thus have been designed to demonstrate his legitimacy as a Gothic warrior. See Wolfram (1988), 267–78, and Heather (1991), 264f.

Constantinople could foster a Roman identity and a Roman understanding of the world, but even this Romanness was a variation on the Roman theme and could be questioned in the West, where eastern Romanness was regularly identified as different, complexly praised, feared, or denigrated depending on individual tastes and circumstances. It was Greece, according to Ennodius, not Rome (new or old), that had raised Theoderic, and it was the eastern empire and its customs in which Theoderic claimed he had been steeped.[25] As a representative of the East, therefore, Theoderic was either acceptably *east* Roman or foreign and Greek depending on the context. His situation thus closely resembled that of Anthemius or Julius Nepos, rather than that of the more obvious "barbarian" strongmen Ricimer and Odovacer.[26] Like these "Greeks," Theoderic ran the risk of being construed in Italy as an imperial appointee from Constantinople, selected without Italian consultation. The resentment that this kind of interference could sometimes provoke has been discussed in earlier chapters; it could be extremely divisive, reminding those in Italy of their "true" Roman pedigree and the "provincial" or semibarbarous status of others. Fear of oriental rule had a long history in Italy, but the significant role played by such oriental rulers during the perceived decline of the empire in the fifth century exacerbated such feelings.[27] Italo-Romans might have accepted Byzantium's refoundation as New Rome, but when these neo-Romans assumed control of the West and then completely botched its administration, they earned serious indignation. The blundering moved eastern and western differences, otherwise acceptable, to the forefront, causing easterners who were proudly Roman to have their Romanness called into question. Theoderic, then, as a successor to Anthemius and Nepos, inherited their "bungled" Greek legacy and was vulnerable (especially at the beginning of his reign) to rejection on account of his perceived Greekness.

But, again, this Greekness was not necessarily a burden. It could also serve as a very real source of praise and admiration, an ennobler, in fact, depending (once more) on the circumstances. Stereotypes are always two-sided and are easily inverted from negative to positive. As recently demonstrated, the savage aggression traditionally associated with barbarian Goths was transformed into Roman courage and valor in early sixth-

---

[25] The *Life of Epiphanius* likewise hints at the easternness of Theoderic. See *VE* 110–11.

[26] Cf. Jones (1962) and (1964), 245–8; Barnwell (1992), 134f.; and MacGeorge (2002), 293.

[27] As seen in Part I, it was eastern despotism that marginalized the Italo-Roman aristocracy and its Senate, eastern despots who coveted and successfully pried away Italian lands in the Balkans, and eastern appointees who failed to defend the western empire and continued it along its decadent path, an affirmation, perhaps, of their "Greek" effeminacy.

century Italy, precedents for this having been established for centuries. Greekness too was flexible. In Italy, Greeks were recognized as "men of the greatest expertise,"[28] exceedingly learned in both arcane wisdom and Christian theology. They were sophisticated, wealthy, and deeply (but at times overzealously and problematically) pious.[29] Letters in the *Variae* are replete with references to Greek learning and its awe-inspiring function. Knowledge of mathematics, music, philosophy, and natural sciences (all traditionally Greek subjects) was exceptional,[30] and, in fact, a renaissance of such learning had emerged in late fifth- and early sixth-century Italy, when educated men like Cassiodorus and Boethius began making translations and epitomes of Greek works available in new Latin editions.[31] The noblest of Italy aspired to obtain the knowledge of the East and, when they did, were loudly praised. The father of Felix, the Gallic consul of 511, was hailed for having "stuffed himself with Attic honey,"[32] while Cyprian, the son of Opilio, was celebrated for having understood during an embassy to Constantinople "the sophistry with which [Greece] exceedingly prevails."[33] In the case of the royal family, Amalasuentha, Athalaric, and Theodahad were all "adorned" with the eloquence of Attic speech,[34]

---

[28] *Variae* 5.40.5 (more of which is cited later): "talibus igitur institutis edoctus Eoae sumpsisti legationis officium, missus ad summae quidem peritiae viros." Here Theoderic praised the learning of Cyprian, who could successfully vie with the Greeks during a mission to Constantinople.

[29] For wealthy, *Variae* 8.9: "dives Graecia"; for sophisticated, *Variae* 5.40.5 (cited later). For Greek piety as problematic and overzealous, Chp. 3, n. 52 (on the Acacian Schism), along with (for instance) Gelasius, *Ep.*10.1 (to Faustus): "Graecos in sua obstinatione" or Symmachus *Ep.* 10 (*Apologeticus adversus Anastasium Imperatorem*), both in Thiel (1868). Even after the healing of the schism, there continued to be problems. Justin's anti-Arian policies were resisted by Theoderic and Pope John (see the Epilogue), while Justinian's meddling in matters of the faith earned a bit of an implicit critique from King Theodahad, who was known for his own ecclesiastical learning. See *Variae* 10.26.4. Cf. *Variae* 2.27, where similar ideas are expressed by Theoderic. Later, during his reconquest of Italy, Justinian was rebuked by Popes Agapitus and Vigilius, both of whom referred to him as "Diocletian" (i.e. a persecutor). See *Liber Pontificalis* 59.3 and 61.6.

[30] *Variae* 1.45 contains a virtual encomium of the Greek learning of Boethius that treats all these disciplines. Boethius was praised for making "Greek dogmas into Roman discipline."

[31] See Courcelle (1943), 257f., and Irigoin (1995); more broadly, Ensslin (1959), 267–78; Martino (1982), 31–3; and Polara (1995).

[32] *Variae* 2.3.4, with Chp. 10.

[33] *Variae* 5.40.5: "non tibi Graecia quod novum ostentaret invenit nec ipsa, qua nimium praevalet, te transcendit argutia." For Opilio, Chp. 2; for Cyprian, see the discussion of Romans going "Gothic" in Chp. 5. Cf. *Collectio Avellana* 137.4, where Pope Hormisdas complains of a similar kind of Greek sophistry.

[34] The Greek education of Athalaric is never explicitly mentioned in an Italian source, but the colorful story found in Procopius, *Wars* 5.2.6–17, would seem to suggest it. His mother, Amalasuentha, on the other hand, was praised for her deep learning, including "Attic eloquence" (*Atticae facundiae*). See *Variae* 11.1.6 and 10.4. Theodahad's knowledge of Greek

and it was surely no accident that Ennodius praised Theoderic for his specifically Greek education: It marked him as an exceedingly learned and refined man, validating claims that this *princeps* was a kind of "purple-clad philosopher."[35]

A Greek education thus defined an individual as outstandingly noble and served as a means of legitimizing a potential foreigner. It aided in granting the otherwise Gallic Felix a Roman pedigree before the Senate at Rome[36] and functioned similarly for a Greco-Goth like Theoderic. Indeed, even Anthemius' Greek sophistication and learning had initially provided him with a source of legitimization and esteem, eulogized by Sidonius Apollinaris in a panegyric delivered in 469.[37]

THE GREEK ROMAN EMPIRE

Just as Greekness could be laudably Roman, so too could a "Greek" Roman Empire. Indeed, Italian resentment, the product of pressure, was not necessarily the norm. East and West were clearly different, particularly with respect to the manner of emperorship expected and practiced in each region, but the eastern-style *basileus* was not denied his Roman accolades among westerners, despite glaring contradictions to republican values. Nor was Constantinople, the seat of eastern imperial power, denied its place as a second Rome. It was, in Sidonius' words, "the queen of the East, the Rome of [that] region" and had come to equal old

philosophers like Plato is mentioned in Procopius, *Wars* 5.3.1 and 5.6.10, while his learning is more generally praised in *Variae* 10.3. See also the discussions of Amalafrida and Amalaberga later.

[35] *Variae* 9.24.8: "quidam purpuratus videretur esse philosophus." This, of course, was a Platonic ideal that probably also hinted at Theoderic's Greekness. Cf. Gottschall (1997) and Hen (2007), 37–9. Vitiello (2008) sees these words, rather interestingly, as a deliberate refutation of Boethius' *Consolation of Philosophy*.

[36] Tellingly, the Greek learning of Felix's father was only referenced in the letter addressed to the Senate. It received no mention in Theoderic's announcement to Anastasius or in his congratulatory letter to Felix himself. See Chp. 10. See also Mathisen (2003), who suggests (on the basis of nomenclature) that Felix's father was, in fact, well connected in Rome and married to a member of the Italo-Roman aristocracy. If so, he was also well connected in Gaul, where Felix had established his primary residence.

[37] The panegyric was recited *before* Anthemius' falling out with Ricimer had stained his reputation. Its long-winded description of Anthemius' Greek and Latin education, full of allusions to various authors, no doubt served the purposes of both flattering the emperor and demonstrating Sidonius' own knowledge before the Romans of Rome. Ironically, then, it helped to legitimize both a "Gallo-Grecian" (Anthemius) and a "Gallo-Roman" (Sidonius) in the western capital. See *Carmen* 2, ln. 156–94.

Rome by taking up her burdens in times of need.[38] Interference might actually be welcomed, so long as it proved beneficial and a balance of power was maintained. Ideologically speaking, East and West were supposed to be separate but equal, united in their fraternity in the Roman name. Their emperors were brothers and colleagues; they shared the same governmental systems; each had its own illustrious Senate composed of officeholders and their sons; each designated a consul whose name marked the year. Such had been the case into the fifth century, at any rate, when the balance of power tipped in favor of Constantinople. Yet under Theoderic, as already seen, the eclipsing of the West by the East was far from complete, and ideologies of equality and fraternity continued to be fostered, though with the West now clearly in a junior position.

This unity of Roman Empires meant that glories achieved in the East were likewise those of the West, and vice versa, an idea that Theoderic had reiterated to Anastasius in the first letter of the *Variae*.[39] It likewise meant that an illustrious career in the East could serve as a source of esteem and honor within a specifically Italian context. It was a matter of pride, for instance, that Cassiodorus had relatives like Heliodorus holding high offices in the East.[40] The circumstance caused the Cassiodori to be celebrated before Rome's Senate as "a house glorious in either realm, one which, joined gracefully to the twin senates, has shined forth with the greatest clarity."[41] The Cassiodori of the West, therefore, were (further) ennobled by the honors won by the Cassiodori of the East (and doubtless vice versa). But even for those lacking such broad connections, offices in and of themselves were worthy of admiration, and as a consequence they allowed officials to transfer their allegiance from one empire to the other with few objections. The "Greek" emperors of the fifth century like Anthemius and Nepos provide the most conspicuous examples of this practice. Initially (and this is key), their illustrious careers in the East had not only recommended them as candidates for the western *imperium*, but had also rendered them acceptable as such to westerners like Sidonius, who expected non-dynastic emperors to have proven their worth through

---

[38] *Carmen* 2, ln. 30: "regina orientis, orbis Roma tui"; and ln. 66–7: "concordant lancis partes; dum pondera nostra / suscipis, aequasti."

[39] See Chp. 3.

[40] See *Variae* 1.4.15, with *PLRE* 2, 531–2 (Heliodorus 5). Theoderic claims to have met him personally while in Constantinople.

[41] *Variae* 1.4.15: "genus in utroque orbe praeclarum, quod gemino senatui decenter aptatum … purissima claritate radiavit."

service to the state.[42] Though less illustrious, the statesman Artemidorus provides a similar case in point for the reign of Theoderic. Appointed as prefect of Rome in 509/10, this easterner was lauded before the Senate not only for his dedication to the western republic, but also for his prior distinction "in his own country," that is, the eastern republic.[43]

In general, therefore, offices and honors were thought to be thoroughly Roman and could transcend those political and cultural boundaries that separated East and West. They served to indicate, foremost, an individual's status as a noble Roman and ultimately aided his chance of acceptance throughout the Roman world. Anthemius, Nepos, Artemidorus, and others benefited from this situation; so too did Theoderic.

VIR INLUSTRIS

As an earlier chapter has indicated, Theoderic received numerous honors in the East before going to Italy, and his credentials as an east Roman statesman were exceedingly illustrious, earning him the highest rank available in the empire, *vir inlustris*. This career had begun in 475, when the emperor Zeno was deposed by the usurper Basiliscus and Theoderic had furnished the military aid necessary to restore him to the throne. The following year, a grateful Zeno commissioned Theoderic with a high military command in the Balkans, granting him the office of *magister militum praesentalis* and making him a patrician. He likewise proclaimed him as an imperial friend (*amicus*), adopted him as his son-in-arms, and gave him many gifts. A period of intermittent hostilities, political manipulation, and open rebellion typified the close of this decade and the beginning of the next, but by 483 Theoderic and Zeno had again reached a peaceful agreement. Now the emperor promised him an ordinary consulship for the year 484 and reestablished him as *magister militum*. He was honored further with the erection of an equestrian statue in Constantinople and a triumph at public expense.[44] There was, to be sure, another period of hostility after

---

[42] This, at any rate, is a theme in all of Sidonius' panegyrics in praise of emperors. Still, it was their proven military valor that truly recommended them for the purple. For the specific case of Anthemius, *Carmen* 2, ln. 193f.

[43] *Variae* 1.43.2: "et licet esset clarus in patria, nostram tamen elegit subire fortunam." Whether this refers to the rank of *clarus* is unclear, however. The actual offices held by Artemidorus while in the East are not known, though he seems to have served in a diplomatic capacity under Zeno, treating, in one instance, with Theoderic himself while in the Balkans. See *PLRE* 2, 155–6 (Artemidorus 3).

[44] The sources for these offices and honors are primarily eastern, including Procopius, Jordanes, Theophanes, and the fragments of both John of Antioch and Malchus of Philadelphia. See, in

this, but as already seen, it was in this capacity as a patrician and agent of Zeno (and perhaps even *magister militum*) that Theoderic was understood by many to have come to Italy in 489.[45]

On the face of it, then, this was a very impressive and very Roman career, mirroring in many ways those of the "Greek" parvenu emperors of the fifth century like Anthemius, whose high offices and military glories, again, factored into their initial acceptance in the West.[46] Moreover, though the full extent and historical context of Theoderic's eastern career may not have been known in Italy in 489, his most illustrious credentials certainly were. Educated Romans throughout the empire, in fact, were aware of his time spent in Constantinople and military support of Zeno in times of need.[47] They also knew that the eastern emperor had bestowed upon him a number of honors and offices as a reward for his services, and that the holding of such offices was one possible explanation for why he had been allowed to rule in the West.[48] Italians themselves appear to have known of his patriciate and triumph, perhaps even his adoption as a son-in-arms and service as a *magister militum*.[49] But Theoderic's consulship of 484, which he served accompanied by a western colleague named Venantius, received the greatest amount of their attention, doubtless because it was the most conspicuous and distinguished of his honors.[50]

general, Ensslin (1959), 39f.; Wolfram (1988), 270f.; Heather (1991), 230–9; and *PLRE 2*, 1077–84 (Theodericus 7). For western sources, see later discussion.

[45] See Chp. 3.

[46] Anthemius' career had also been military in nature, securing him the offices of *magister utriusque militiae*, consul, and patrician during the reign of Marcian. All three were subject to praise in Sidonius' panegyric (*Carmen* 2, ln. 205–9). His marriage to the only daughter of the emperor, Euphemia, likewise made him a potential heir to the throne of Marcian, though he was denied this upon the emperor's death. Sidonius mentions this illustrious marriage and its implications in *Carmen* 2, ln. 216–18. Interestingly enough, Theoderic was also offered the hand of an imperial bride, Anicia Juliana (the daughter of Emperor Olybrius), but declined. See Malchus, frag. 17. She later married a different nobleman of Gothic descent, Areobindus, who went on to have an illustrious career and was even offered the diadem. See n. 79.

[47] Non-Italian sources that mention Theoderic's stay in Constantinople include Jordanes, *Getica* 269f.; Theophanes, AM 5977; John Malalas 383 (15.9); and John of Nikiu 48. These same sources also reference his military assistance, as do Malchus, frag. 11, 15, 17, and 18; John of Antioch, frag. 214 (206); Eustathius (frag. = Evagrius, *HE* 3.27); and *Marc. Com.* 483.

[48] See Chp. 3. Theodahad even invoked this "beneficial" relationship as relations between eastern and western courts grew strained in the early 530s. See *Variae* 10.2.3.

[49] For patriciate, *Variae* 8.9.3 and *AnonVal* 49; for triumph, Ennodius, *PanTh* 15–16 (the togas referred to here may be purely consular) and perhaps *ILS* 825 and 827 (the specific triumphs are not identified). Jordanes' *Romana* and *Getica* may also demonstrate knowledge of Theoderic's eastern offices and honors, provided that their sources are Italian in origin. This cannot be confirmed.

[50] Cassiodorus' *Chronicle* is especially interesting in this respect because Theoderic, who is listed first, is introduced as "D[omino]N[ostro] Theoderico," though not yet ruler of Italy.

Indeed, an ordinary consulship was the highest honor any Roman could receive and, in the West, had been reserved for the most noble-blooded of the empire.[51] Entered forever into the consular fasti, both consuls' names literally designated the year, which meant that Romans throughout the empire had already heard of "Consul Theoderic" years before his invasion of Italy. This consulship placed Theoderic within the highest echelon of the empire's officeholding nobility and hence legitimized him as a member of the senatorial elite. It is little wonder, then, that Italian authors gave precedence to it, either ignoring or being ignorant of his other honors.[52]

But while a consulship and the rank that it conferred could be especially ennobling and serve a legitimizing function before Italian audiences, the very means by which Theoderic was imagined to have obtained this honor could be even more prestigious. Both the *Anonymus Valesianus* account and Ennodius' panegyric comment specifically on the origin of Theoderic's consulship, and both, interestingly enough, commit the same historical error by associating it with his role during the usurpation of Basiliscus. The *Anonymus*' notice is especially terse, claiming in a single sentence that the emperor repaid Theoderic for his services, made him a patrician and consul, gave him many gifts, and sent him to Italy.[53] Despite its brevity, the passage makes clear the links imagined to have existed between Theoderic's restoration of Zeno, his offices in the East, and his eventual deployment to the West. Ennodius' panegyric, while betraying the same basic connection, went much further. As might be expected, his version was particularly elaborate, describing Theoderic's role in near-epic proportions. The result was an account that served to inscribe the affair with

---

[51] Families that traced their lineage back to the republic monopolized this office in the West, whereas parvenus often held it in the East. This difference and its implications for Theoderic's nobility will be discussed later. Noteworthy too is the fact that emperors, members of the imperial family, and emperors in the making often served as ordinary consuls. To be the colleague of an emperor was a great honor. See Chp. 8.

[52] Indeed, Italian narratives of the east Roman phase of Theoderic's life tend to be rather cursory and historically inaccurate, either out of sheer ignorance or perhaps in order to downplay those periods when Theoderic and Zeno were at odds with one another. Again, Cassiodorus did something like this in his sanitization of certain episodes in his *Chronicle*. See Chp. 2. There is, however, the strong possibility that these authors simply did not think it necessary to mention Theoderic's lesser honors, deciding that his most illustrious and traditionally Roman office (the consulship) was sufficient. Cf. Delle Donne (2001), 13. This seems to have been the case in the East, at least, where better records were surely available. Cf. Procopius, *Wars* 5.1.9–11; John Malalas 383 (15.9); John of Nikiu 47; and Theophanes, *AM* 5931. See also *Variae* 8.1.3 (Athalaric to Justin).

[53] *AnonVal* 49: "Zeno itaque recompensans beneficiis Theodericum, quem fecit patricium et consulem, donans ei multum et mittens eum ad Italiam."

meaning that extended far beyond the simple laudation of loyal service in the East. The entire episode (the revolt, its aftermath, and Theoderic's consulship) was imagined as a test for Italy's future *princeps*, one that he had passed with the greatest of distinction. It demonstrated his understanding of Roman *pietas*, honor, and justice, confirming his worthiness to rule the Roman Empire and reiterating his role as a savior of the Roman people. In Ennodius' estimation, in fact, Theoderic had rescued the eastern Roman Empire in more ways than one, foreshadowing his restoration of the West.[54]

Savior of the East

According to the panegyric, Greece had instilled Theoderic not just with an understanding of *civilitas* but also with a certain sense of obligation to the Roman Empire. When Basiliscus revolted, this obligation caused the young Goth to desire to "repay in a time of need the favor that [he] had received [in a time] of peace."[55] This time of need was a time of chaos and turmoil, described by Ennodius as disastrous to the east Roman state. The foundations of *civilitas*, law and order, had collapsed, providing a context remarkably similar to the decadent and moribund situation that Theoderic was imagined to encounter later in the West. Echoing the complaints of westerners discussed in earlier chapters, Ennodius claimed that the eastern nobility had been concerned about its favor at court and had come to fear for its livelihood shortly before Basiliscus' revolt. This terror soon turned to rage, typical of western barbarization, which "broke its chains" and "leapt forth for the testing of [Theoderic's] strength and clemency."[56] Much like Placidia's effeminate soldiers, Zeno's forces had had "their minds eviscerated by a long-lasting peace"[57] and thus failed to protect the emperor, yielding before and eventually abetting the usurper. Likewise, as in the West, reverence for the prince (Zeno) was lost, and a

[54] Cf. Rota (2001a), 227–9, and Rohr (2006), 43–8.
[55] *PanTh* 12: "aut non beneficium necessitatis tempore redderes quod pacis acceperas."
[56] *PanTh* 11: "quando aevi purpura ... promittebat sollicitis de gratiae conmutatione terrorem, cum ad probationem roboris et clementiae tuae ruptis vinculis furor emicuit." For the context, Stein (1949), vol. 1, 361–4; Bury (1958), vol. 1, 389–94; Jones (1964), 224–5; and Kosiński (2010), 79–82.
[57] *PanTh* 11: "et evisceratas diuturna quiete mentes occasionis pabulo subiugavit." Admittedly soldiers are not explicitly mentioned here, so the passage may refer to the entire population of Constantinople or to other nobles and administrators. The theme of weakness through peace, however, is unmistakable. See Chp. 2 for the Placidia reference and Chp. 5 for a discussion of the Goths' perceived role as masculine reinvigorators of the western empire.

tyrant with ignoble blood, an analogue to Odovacer, seized control and ruled through fear.[58]

Seemingly secure, Ennodius explained that Basiliscus believed that his coup had been successful and that he would continue to reign unchallenged. But Theoderic's sense of duty compelled him, unwilling to allow the nobler cause, that of *civilitas* and a legitimate emperor, to fail while in a position to act.[59] In keeping with Ennodius' overall impression of his *princeps* as a mighty general, a theme throughout the panegyric and again not un-Roman, Basiliscus was said to have yielded as soon as Theoderic arrived with his army.[60] There was no battle scene, epic or otherwise, a clear indication that Basiliscus was even more cowardly than Odovacer, who "watched, not toiled" during Theoderic's conquest of Italy. But this defeat was still powerful, transforming Theoderic into the savior of both the (eastern) republic and its rightful emperor, who was described as a fugitive uncertain of his safety.[61] Such an act, according to Ennodius, was unprecedented: "Let us breeze through the histories; let the annals be examined. In which of these has there existed the rule of a *princeps* restored from exile, purchased by a born king at the price of his own blood?"[62]

Leaving aside the important reference to royalty, these actions were envisioned as a clear demonstration of Theoderic's undying commitment to (Roman) justice and order, a fact not only highlighted by his willingness to shed his own blood for the good of *civilitas*, but also reiterated by his praiseworthy moderation following Basiliscus' defeat. Indeed, Ennodius believed that Theoderic could have exploited the situation with ease. He had become master of Constantinople, and no one denied that he had the ability to transfer the *imperium* to whomever he had wanted.[63] He had the power to back a number of imperial candidates, not just Zeno, but

---

[58] *PanTh* 12: "Pulsa est extemplo principalis urbe reverentia et in vacuam possessionem nullo adscitus sanguine tyrannus accessit. Qui aula potitus definivit, postquam metu hostes suos debellaverat." Cf. *CassChron*, anno 472 (cited in Chp. 2, n. 32) on the murder of Anthemius.

[59] *PanTh* 12: "cum animos tuos sine annorum suffragio inpulit lux naturae, ne aut causa melior te coram posito subiaceret." Such *pietas* is highly reminiscent of Virgil's pius Aeneas, and not by accident. See Rohr (1999), 276, and Rota (2001a), 221–4, and (2001b), 38–45. Ennodius not only modeled portions of his panegyric on the *Aeneid* (as was common enough), but also cast Theoderic as an epic hero, a new Aeneas who was destined to guide his people to "Ausonia" (Virgil's Italy) and found a state that would endure forever.

[60] *PanTh* 12: "in ipsis congressionis tuae foribus cessit invasor." *Invasor* refers to Basiliscus.

[61] *Ibid.*: "cum profugo per te sceptra redderentur de salute dubitanti."

[62] *PanTh* 13: "Ventilemus historias, interrogentur annales: apud quos constitit refusum exuli, quem cruore suo rex genitus emerat, principatum?"

[63] *PanTh* 15: "nemo credidit non te posse ad quem voluisses transferre quod reddideras."

had restrained his ambition, "greatest at that time when you [i.e. Theoderic] could have retained what you had acquired without harming your reputation."[64] He was even, these words implied, in a position to proclaim himself emperor and with little objection, yet had not, earning the esteem of "an especially noble man."[65] Such noble actions, moreover, had eventually paid off. Ennodius addressed Theoderic, now *princeps* of the West, with the traditional imperial epithet *inclyte domine* (glorious lord) and asserted, "Praise itself respects your giving and defending the diadem."[66] Like a certain eastern statesman and later western emperor before him, this refusal of power (*recusatio imperii*) in the East had become a useful source of honor in the West, rendering Theoderic all the more worthy of his princely office.[67]

But such moderation did not stop with his refusing to usurp the diadem or remaining the champion of the legitimate emperor. Ennodius claimed that Theoderic had been sparing in the prizes that he requested from Zeno, "as if they were sufficient," words indicating that they were not.[68] These prizes were in fact the very consular fasces associated with Theoderic's ordinary consulship of 484, again a historical inaccuracy on Ennodius' part, but a very interesting one with important implications. The ordinary consulship, as discussed, was the capstone office of the senatorial *cursus*, the most ennobling honor available to a Roman citizen and a legitimizer of Theoderic's rule in Italy for westerners and easterners alike. Somehow, however, Ennodius believed that such an honor was insufficient for the service that his *princeps* had rendered to the eastern republic. What prize remained beyond this was only the imperial purple, a tribute that Ennodius had already suggested Theoderic could have had, and now seemed to insinuate he should have had.

But if an intended point, Ennodius was more interested in attaching deeper meaning to the actual office that Theoderic had held while in Constantinople. Indeed, though illustrious in the extreme, this dignity had not conferred additional glory on Theoderic; his actions on behalf of the republic, after all, had already rendered him unequivocally glorious.

---

[64] *PanTh* 13: "illo maxime tempore, quo sine opinionis damno possis adquisita retinere."

[65] *Ibid.*: "Singularis boni fructus est ambitionis refrenatio."

[66] *PanTh* 14: "Par te, inclyte domine, laus respicit donati diadematis et defensi."

[67] The eastern statesman in mind, once more, is Anthemius. See Sidonius, *Carmen* 2, ln. 210–22, where Anthemius is lauded for refusing the (eastern) diadem, despite being worthy. As in Theoderic's case, his refusal was seen as fortuitous, since it allowed Anthemius to become emperor of the West. On the tradition of *recusatio*, see Chp. 4.

[68] *PanTh* 15: "Sed parcus in exigendis praemiis, quasi sufficerent ad vicissitudinem operum tuorum."

Instead, and in a twist of irony, the person of Theoderic now served to confer glory upon the consulship and by extension the east Roman state. Because of Theoderic, Ennodius explained, the palm-embroidered toga of a consul once more "merited its worth," and a consul "guarded the Republic through his esteem."[69] Because he had been placed in the triumphal toga, the weapons of Rome's enemies trembled in fear.[70]

Such an understanding clearly anticipated the reinvigoration of the effeminate toga in the West, an act imagined to have been afforded through the valor of noble Goths like Tuluin, a "disciple" of Theoderic.[71] By serving as consul, then, Theoderic had done more than establish useful Roman credentials; as far as Ennodius was concerned, he had rescued and restored the eastern Roman Empire for a second time, providing yet another preview of the western assistance to come.

FLAVIUS THEODERICUS

Invented, manipulated, yet based in historical reality, this understanding of Theoderic's eastern career made the ruler of Italy illustrious far beyond the rank that his offices had conferred and aided in demonstrating the rightness of his assumption of power in Italy. Though probably closer to the version found in the *Anonymus Valesianus* account, the knowledge or memory of this career nonetheless became an element of Theoderic's mystique, an intrinsic part of his legacy strong enough to legitimize even his successors. His grandson and immediate successor, Athalaric, for instance, invoked it before the Senate as a rationale for his own elevation to the purple. Because of his descent from Theoderic, Athalaric could be described as a "man most worthy of the Empire, descended from this [i.e. Theoderic's] family, his senatorial origin proclaimed as if he was born one of you [i.e. a senator]."[72] Theoderic's eastern career could be remembered, then, as thoroughly senatorial even among Italy's noblest senators, literally making him one of them. And, in true Roman fashion, it was heritable.

---

[69] For glory and worth, *ibid.*: "fasces accepisti … ut de te pretium palmata mereretur"; for guarding the republic, *PanTh* 16: "ille annus habuit consulem, qui rempublicam non tam sollicitudine quam opinione tueretur."

[70] *PanTh* 16: "quo in segmentis posito quae ab hostibus sumpta fuerant arma tremuerunt."

[71] See *Variae* 8.9.3–7, which recounts Theoderic's patriciate and instructs Tuluin to prove himself his disciple.

[72] *Variae* 8.2.3: "non iniuria, quoniam quaevis claritas generis Hamalis cedit et sicut ex vobis qui nascitur, origo senatoria nuncupatur, ita qui ex hac familia progreditur, regno dignissimus approbatur." Cf. Claude (1980), 161, who emphasizes Amal kingship, rather than Amal officeholding.

But like the "savage Galatian" Anthemius before him, whose achievements in the East were described in a similar fashion by Sidonius,[73] the
potential had remained for Theoderic to be rejected in the West because his
origins were perceived as barbarous. For men like Ennodius, Theoderic's
eastern career and upbringing had made him nobly Roman and decid-
edly patriotic, militating against any understanding of him as a barbarian.
But his name alone, despite its Latinization as Flavius Theodericus, was
a patent reminder to others of his un-Roman origins.[74] The eastern general Aspar, a Flavius like Theoderic, understood this problem firsthand.
Of mixed Gothic and Alanic origins, he chose to give the sons whom he
expected to follow in his footsteps the un-Roman names Ardabur and
Hermineric;[75] but to the son he intended to succeed to the purple, and who
again was made a Caesar, he gave the appropriately Latin name Julius
Patricius. Patricius' career had been illustrious, including a consulship in
459, and he had even married the emperor's daughter before palace intrigue
cut his ascent short.[76] But another Flavius, a contemporary equally sensitive to this issue, proved more successful: the emperor Zeno. Zeno had
originally gone by the un-Roman-sounding name Tarasicodissa[77] and was,
in fact, an Isaurian, a member of a wild tribe from Asia Minor whose
country had been walled off from the empire during the fourth century.[78]
Isaurians were as much barbarians as Goths, and although Tarasicodissa,
recast as the Roman Flavius Zeno, had married into the imperial family
and had, like Anthemius, Patricius, and Theoderic, distinguished himself

[73] Anthemius had also rescued the East from certain peril, foreshadowing his later role in the
West. Ironically, however, the people from whom he had saved the eastern empire were the very
Ostrogoths whom Theoderic's uncle, Valamir, had led. See *Carmen* 2, ln. 223–306.

[74] Cf. O'Donnell (2008), 134, who hypothesizes that if Theoderic had changed his name to
Hadrianus, he would be "remembered as the great restorer of the Roman order." On his adoption of the praenomen Flavius, Wolfram (1988), 277. Wolfram also refers to Theoderic as
"Flavius Amalus Theodericus," but the use of *tria nomina* by Theoderic does not seem to be
attested. An inscription from Rome of a relative named Theodenanda, however, makes it at least
possible. See *ILS* 8990 (Fiebiger 1, #204): "Fl. Amala Amalafrida Theodenanda c(larissima)
f(emina)"; with *PLRE* 3, 1236. Regardless, the official version of his name, "Theodericus," is
consistently Latinized, whereas other "barbarian" kings, such as those of the Vandals, are not.
Compare the "(H)ildirix" and "Geilamer" that appear on Vandal coinage and inscriptions with
the "Theodericus" and "At(h)alaricus" that appear in Italy.

[75] For Ardabur and Hermineric, both military men, *PLRE* 2, 135–7 (Ardabur iunior 1) and 549.
Both served as consuls.

[76] See later discussion.

[77] On the name and its other manifestations, *PLRE* 2, 1200–2 (Fl. Zenon 7), and Kosiński
(2010), 60–1.

[78] The *Limes Isauricus* was established after the Isaurians declared their independence from the
Roman Empire; they continued to defy imperial rule into the sixth century. See Shaw (1990);
Lenski (1999); Haarer (2006), chp. 2; and Kosiński (2010), 57–60.

with a Roman career, the Basiliscus revolt had nonetheless been inspired, in part at least, by disapproval of an "Isaurian" emperor.[79]

Zeno's lot reiterates the fact that, even if "barbarians" like the Goths or Isaurians could find niches within the Roman Empire, memories of their prior antagonism survived and under the right circumstances could become particularly divisive. The son of a known barbarian king and a barbarian king himself who at times opposed the eastern empire, Theoderic therefore ran the risk of being perceived as a leader and orchestrator of specifically anti-Roman violence, a view that threatened to cast him as an Ostrogothic analogue to the Visigothic juggernaut, Euric.

But just as holding offices in the East might be interpreted by certain Italo-Romans as especially Roman or Greek depending on the context, or Greekness interpreted as complimentary or worthy of scorn, there was also a flipside to being of barbarian stock, particularly if royal. Indeed, a royal pedigree could serve to legitimize barbarians, especially in the West, where, in contrast to the East, senators prided themselves on their (often fictitious) descent from the noblest families of the late republic and principate, like the Scipiones and Gracchi.[80] The eastern senatorial aristocracy, of which Theoderic was understood to be a member, was much different, composed virtually ex nihilo in the middle of the fourth century of the prominent and not-so-prominent families of the region. Men of particularly low origins, sons of sausage venders, for instance, rose through the administration here, eventually serving as consuls and siring houses that even included emperors.[81] So-called *novi homines* were thus typical in the East, but in the West a venerable lineage and "noble" birth continued to

---

[79] For this, Stein (1949), vol. 1, 363; Bury (1958), vol. 1, 389–90; Jones (1964), 224; Lenski (1999), 427–8; and Kosiński (2010). The coup against Aspar and his family, however, does not seem to have been racially motivated, though anti-Gothic pogroms had occurred in the East in the late fourth and early fifth centuries. Instead, members of this family fell afoul of the emperor Leo, whom Aspar had created, and paid the ultimate price. See Croke (2005b). What opposition there was to Aspar and Patricius appears to have been religiously motivated. They were Arians, and Aspar's *recusatio imperii* may have stemmed from an unwillingness to convert to Orthodoxy, contra von Haehling (1988). Indeed, Patricius seems to have agreed to convert, and later the "Gothic" consul of 506, the rather Orthodox Areobindus, was even offered the diadem in opposition to the "heretical" emperor Anastasius.

[80] See Jones (1964), 545–6, who writes that "it would be rash to deny that by adoptions or through the female line they may have been able to trace some tenuous link with the Republican nobility." The extensive prosopographical study of Settipani (2000) attempts to do just this, though invention should not be ruled out either. Obviously such republican families had never been "royal" in the same way as the Amals, but some, like the Anicii, had indeed held imperial power. For the Anicii as "princely," see later discussion.

[81] The most notorious example in the East is Philip, a notary and son of a sausage seller, who was a progenitor of the house of Anthemius. See Jones (1964), 551.

be exceedingly important, and men with claims to the most distinguished ancestries monopolized the highest offices of state.[82]

Such veneration for noble ancestries could and often did permeate ethnic boundaries, serving to assimilate all nobly pedigreed individuals into an elite clique. It allowed the Visigoth Athaulf to father through his Roman wife, Placidia, a possible heir to the Theodosian purple, aptly named Theodosius. It similarly validated before a western audience the marriage alliance struck between Ricimer and Anthemius, despite Anthemius' later cries of foul play.[83] Delivering a panegyric in the city of Rome in 468, Sidonius, in fact, lauded this marriage, drawing specific attention to Ricimer's impressive royal pedigree. The scion of two royal parents, one Gothic and the other Suevic, "two kingdoms summoned Ricimer to rule," allowing Anthemius to be "blessed through his son-in-law."[84] Ricimer's royalty was also correlated with the emperor's own, Sidonius avowing to the new Augustus, "your maiden is royal, so too is my Ricimer: both glitter with nobility."[85] These examples demonstrate the potential for nobility, and particularly a royal pedigree, to render acceptable in the minds of westerners an individual otherwise unacceptable owing to a perceived barbarian ancestry. Indeed, not only had Ricimer's royal blood made him a virtual equal of Anthemius, but it had allowed him to become the representative of the West, a west Roman, in a marriage alliance understood to have strengthened ties between both halves of the empire.

Much like the case with Ricimer, Theoderic's royal lineage could also serve a legitimizing function before certain Roman audiences. Rather than emphasizing his barbarian origins, it could complement his Greek education and illustrious career in the East, further demonstrating his authentic membership in the senatorial elite. Moreover, given the context of Theoderic's arrival, it could have certain restorative properties, restoring dignity to the western Roman Empire by reestablishing the rule of an especially noble man. The absence of such a ruler had always troubled Rome's senators, but particularly those of the early sixth century, who believed that the stewardship of the empire by exceedingly ignoble and ignorant men had contributed to its decline.

[82] Jones (1964), 545–52, and Matthews (1975).
[83] See Chp. 1.
[84] For two kingdoms, *Carmen* 2, ln. 360–2: "Ricimerem / in regnum duo regna vocant; nam patre Suebus, / a genetrice Getes"; for blessed, *ibid.*, ln. 484: "sit socer Augustus genero Ricimere beatus." In the former passage Sidonius contrasted the "double royalty" of Ricimer with the ignobility of the Vandal king Gaiseric, the current scourge of Rome, whom he depicted as a shameful bastard jealous of Ricimer's nobility.
[85] *Ibid.*, ln. 485–6: "nobilitate micant: est vobis regia virgo, / regius ille mihi."

REX GENITUS

The importance of Theoderic's royal descent for Ennodius (and by extension other Italo-Romans) has already been hinted at in the discussion of his panegyric's treatment of the usurpation of Basiliscus. Ennodius, it should be remembered, had proposed to the Romans in his audience that they "breeze through the histories" and "examine the annals," so that they might discover a time when a Roman emperor had been restored to his throne by "a born king" (*rex genitus*).[86] In his estimation the occurrence was unprecedented and Theoderic's status as a "born king" outstanding, in direct contrast to that of the very usurper, "unassociated by blood" to the imperial house, who had been thwarted. Later, in his discussion of Theoderic's consulship, Ennodius again turned to this royal descent, elaborating on its distinction. "When has there been such a consul," he asked, "as one whom the clarity of kings, tested from the very infancy of the world, has produced?"[87] The question, of course, was rhetorical, anticipating a "never," while likewise highlighting the antiquity, so important to western Romans, of Theoderic's noble line. The eastern consul and later western *princeps* was more than just a born king; he was a king descended from kings famous from the beginning of time, a pedigree of duration unsurpassed in the West. Known members of Theoderic's family tree were considered "excellent,"[88] and their historic virtues were seen as obliging Theoderic to "nobly defend the deeds of his house."[89]

This obligation, which found accord with Roman aristocratic ideals about family honor, was one that the panegyric's Theoderic understood very well, commenting on it himself in a speech directed to his mother shortly before he joined battle with Odovacer. Here the king explained that he had to enter the conflict so that he might live up to his family name, but for Ennodius' purposes these words served to highlight the laudable valor that the Amal line (and by extension its Goths) were understood to represent:

---

[86] *PanTh* 13 (cited earlier, n. 62). Cf. Delle Donne (1998), 79–82.

[87] *PanTh* 16: "Quando talis contigit sorte lectoris, qualem dedit ab ipsa mundi infantia regum examinata claritudo." For "lectoris" as "electoris," a reference to the election of prior consuls, Rohr (1995), 206. Cf. *Variae* 8.9.4.

[88] *PanTh* 17: "in tuo stemmate probati sunt qui reperti."

[89] *Ibid.*: "cum familiae tuae debeas actus generis nobiliter custodire." *Actus generis* surely refers to the race/family of Theoderic and not the Goths in general. *Hamalorum gens* appears in contemporary sources, though Ennodius never mentions the Amals by name.

Weapons must be employed, so that the glorious deeds of my ancestors do not perish on my account. In vain do we depend on our parents' glory, unless we sustain it with our own. My father stands before my eyes, a man whom fortune never mocked in battle. He acquired good fortune because his strength demanded victory. It is right for me to be compared to this leader, who was never afraid facing uncertainties, but brought success to himself.[90]

Hoping to live up to the legacy of this glorious father, Theoderic next called for exceedingly fine robes, planning to adorn himself in such a way that he might stand out before all in battle. He avowed that these holy vestments' glimmer would make known who he was to those unable to tell from his vigor, inviting the eyes of those desirous to see the "honor of what I have put on."[91] The finery, therefore, would provide visual confirmation of the splendor already associated with his noble house, both glimmering in their unique way.[92]

Already in the first decade of the sixth century, then, Ennodius was associating Amal descent with Gothic victory and valor, but again, such ideals were not oppositional or ambivalent to Romanness; these were ancient Roman virtues necessary for the restoration of the western empire.[93] Indeed, this specific episode suggested that the Amals themselves were *invictissimi*, most unconquered, an important attribute for Roman emperors that had been lost over the course of the fifth century. Romans in general, it seemed, had become feminized, but Goths like Theoderic were exceedingly manly. As Theoderic explained to his mother, "the battlefield will make known the gender of your son, since you begot a [real] man at

[90] *PanTh* 43: "telis agendum est, ut avorum per me decora non pereant. Sine causa parentum titulis nitimur, nisi propriis adiuvemur. Stat ante oculos meos genitor, de quo numquam fecit in certamine fortuna ludibrium, qui dextram sibi ipse peperit valitudine exigente successus. Hoc oportet duce contendi, qui omina incerta non timuit, sed ipse sibi secunda conscivit."

[91] *PanTh* 44: "Cultiorem me acies suscipiat, quam festa consuerunt. Qui me de impetu non cognoverit, aestimet de nitore. Invitet cupidorum oculos honor indumenti: pretiosior species feriendos exhibeat."

[92] The link between "shininess" and nobility has already been demonstrated via Sidonius' description of Anthemius' daughter and Ricimer as "shining in their nobility" (see n. 85). This terminology is ubiquitous in contemporary works and is echoed in such noble titles as *inlustris*, *clarus*, and *spectabilis*.

[93] See Chp. 5. For a different interpretation, Amory (1997), 67f., who sees the development of Amal propaganda as a departure from an "earlier" ideology that stressed *civilitas* and accommodation. Heather (2007), 45–8, accepts Amory's basic premise. But such conclusions seem misplaced given Ennodius' own unabashed (and particularly early) praise for Theoderic's royal lineage and its martial qualities. The nobility and courage that he associated with the Amal line were hardly intended to emphasize its non-Romanness. Cf. Delle Donne (1998), 82–4.

the happy time of my birth."⁹⁴ Such words clearly highlighted the *virtus* (manliness, courage, valor) that Theoderic and his clan represented and returned to Italy. The Goths themselves, moreover, were imagined as drawing inspiration from Theoderic and his noble house, claiming that their own invincibility in battle was derived from him. "Remember," the general Pitzia instructed Rome's soldiers before their epic struggle against the Bulgars, "at whose command you came to this place. Let no one believe that the eyes of our king are absent, for whose glory we must fight, or refuse to assess our people based on its *princeps*."⁹⁵ Fight, perhaps most importantly, they did, urged by "recollections of their *princeps*,"⁹⁶ until the savage Bulgars "retreated in flight, punished very severely and lamenting greatly."⁹⁷ Goths, of course, claimed victories like these, but the collective *virtus* of Theoderic and his men nonetheless served Roman ends. Even in the context of Theoderic's speech to his mother, Ennodius made it clear that his filial *pietas* and courage ultimately existed for the "happy prosperity of the Republic,"⁹⁸ describing his sword, which decorated his side along with his fine robes, as "the defender of liberty." And by this, of course, Ennodius meant Roman liberty.⁹⁹

Theoderic's royal birth thus served two very important purposes within Ennodius' panegyric. Its antiquity and fame validated his claims to rulership, much as its absence in his predecessors, immediate and not so immediate, had invalidated theirs. Second, it evoked Theoderic's Gothicness, but in a way complementary to his noble and Roman qualities. The combination made him an ideal ruler in the West: pedigreed, cultured, and, most important given the military failures of the fifth century, victorious.¹⁰⁰ Royal birth, according to Ennodius, made Theoderic

---

⁹⁴ *PanTh* 43: "scis ... quod natalis mei tempore virum fecunda genuisti. Dies est, quo fili tui sexum campus adnuntiet."

⁹⁵ *PanTh* 65: "Meministis, socii, cuius ad haec loca conmeastis imperio. Nemo absentes credat regis nostri oculos, pro cuius fama dimicandum est ... aut forte gentem nostram dedignantur aestimare de principe." The speech continues with similar comments.

⁹⁶ The epic battle is treated in *PanTh* 66–7. For recollections, *PanTh* 67: "interea dum anceps esset fortuna certaminis et pinnatae mortes sibi aethera vindicarent, superavit nostri memoria principis."

⁹⁷ *PanTh* 67: "Versa est in fugam natio punita gravius ... cum ingenti lamentatione properabant."

⁹⁸ *PanTh* 40: "et tamen candida reipublicae fortuna perurguebat, ne coepto desisteres."

⁹⁹ *PanTh* 42: "dum lateri tuo vindex libertatis gladius aptaretur." The term *vindex libertatis* cast Theoderic as a restorer of the republic. See Béranger (1953), 64–7, and Walser (1955).

¹⁰⁰ Cf. Delle Donne (1998), 78–83, and Rohr (2002), 231. The argument of Vitiello (2005b), that Ennodius was celebrating specifically "Germanic" notions of valor and honor, does not stand up to scrutiny. Not only are these supposedly "Germanic" notions derived from Greco-Roman sources, like Tacitus' *Germania* and Procopius' *Wars*, but, as demonstrated previously, they

a king, but it was his valor and judgment that asserted it.[101] Likewise Theoderic's noble pedigree won him approbation in Rome, but his conduct on behalf of the republic demonstrated that he was truly "worthy to be joined among the emperors."[102]

The Splendor of Amal Blood

Amal lineage had other functions beyond legitimizing Theoderic as a ruler through its venerability and reiteration of Gotho-Roman victory ideologies. In the *Variae* it could also demonstrate Theoderic and his family's authentic Romanness, particularly, but not exclusively, before non-Roman audiences.[103] Though already uniquely Roman through Theoderic's eastern pedigree and offices, this royal clan was increasingly transformed into an imperial dynasty that endeavored to live up to the standards of being purple-clad. Amals became custodians, not only of the Roman Empire, but of its virtues. They could represent Romanness incarnate and serve as beacons to everyone of proper and upstanding conduct.

Theoderic himself rarely emphasized his pedigree in the *Variae*, but when he did, it tended to link the Amals with the civilizing role that he had adopted as *princeps* of the West, stressing both the Romanness of his realm and the righteous and thoroughly Roman position he had assumed as its ruler.[104] He claimed to the Thuringian king Herminafrid, for instance,

are also not unique to "Germans." A read of the *Aeneid*, a source used by Ennodius, makes this all too clear.

[101] *PanTh* 88: "Origo te quidem dedit dominum, sed virtus adseruit. Sceptra tibi conciliavit splendor generis, cuius si deessent insignia, eligi te in principem mens fecisset." Cf. Reydellet (1981), 165f., who goes too far in differentiating *reges Italiae* from *principes Romani*, particularly in his assessment of Ennodius' opera. In the passage cited in this note, Ennodius does not even use the term *rex*, employing the more "imperial" *dominus* and *princeps* instead.

[102] *PanTh* 18: "Ego tibi, quod admirationem vincat, oppono principem meum ita ortum, ut eum non liceat improbari, ita agere, quasi inter imperatores adhuc precetur adiungi." Ennodius may have intended the phrase "joined among the emperors" to hint at Theoderic's imperial standing, though the context of this passage (Theoderic's consulship and rescue of the eastern empire) may suggest an interpretation more along the lines of "wishing to serve/be in the company of the emperors."

[103] There is, again, no need to see an ideological/propagandistic shift in the later reign of Theoderic, as suggested by Amory and others (see n. 93), particularly since there are no letters penned in the name of Theoderic that explicitly conform to this model. Indeed, only three of Theoderic's letters reference the Amals, and these, as demonstrated later, emphasize their *Roman* qualities, not Gothic ones. The connection between valor and the Amals in the *Variae* is a development that appears to postdate Theoderic, but it too is a reiteration of the very Roman role of "Gothicness" in Italy, a replay of the sentiments expressed by Ennodius in his panegyric.

[104] See Amory (1997), 62–72, for a different interpretation.

that his new Amal bride, a niece named Amalaberga, would cause his royalty to glitter all the more brightly "with the fame of Amal blood."[105] "Fortunate Thuringia," Herminafrid was informed, would possess "what Italy has reared: a woman learned in letters, refined in her proper behavior, glorious not just in her lineage, but also in her feminine dignity."[106] To be sure, Theoderic had not specifically used the term "Roman" to describe these qualities, but the link between Italy and Romanness was obvious, just as learning and upstanding behavior were marks of Roman civilization. Amalaberga was glorious, then, not simply because she was royal, but because she was a royal Roman; her specifically Roman splendor, the mark of an Amal bride, would hence allow Thuringian royalty, itself already brilliant as a function of being royal, to shine even more brightly. Moreover, Thuringia would become more civilized in the process,[107] allowing Amalaberga to function much as the cithara and citharist sent to Clovis or the water clock sent to Gundobad had.[108] All these "gifts" asserted a link between the Amals and *Romanitas* and served to ferry the light of Roman civilization to traditionally barbarous peoples. An Amal bride, in other words, was as much a gift and statement of Roman superiority as any other trapping of Roman civilization.

The same can be said of Theoderic's sister, Amalafrida, who was intended to complement and improve upon the noble qualities of another barbarian house, in this case, that of the Vandal king Thrasamund. Amalafrida was said to be a "unique source of celebration for the Amal race" and described as "a woman equal to your [i.e. Thrasamund's] prudence, who is not just worthy of reverence in your kingdom but can also be wonderful in her advice."[109] Again, though Romanness was not explicitly mentioned and Italy, its point of reference in the preceding example, is absent, the link between the Amals and Roman civilization is nevertheless clear.[110]

---

[105] *Variae* 4.1.1: "ut qui de regia stirpe descenditis, nunc etiam longius claritate Hamali sanguinis fulgeatis."

[106] *Variae* 4.1.2: "Habebit felix Thoringia quod nutrivit Italia, litteris doctam, moribus eruditam, decoram non solum genere, quantum et feminea dignitate."

[107] *Ibid.*: "ut non minus patria vestra [i.e. Thuringia] istius splendeat moribus quam suis triumphis." This statement makes it clear that Thuringia, like any barbarian country, might be admired for its physical strength and prowess in war (*triumphiis*), but that it lacked Roman refinement (*moribus*) in the eyes of Italo-Romans.

[108] See Chp. 5.

[109] *Variae* 5.43.1: "germanam nostram, generis Hamali singulare praeconium, vestrum fecimus esse coniugium: feminam prudentiae vestrae parem, quae non tantum reverenda regno, quantum mirabilis possit esse consilio."

[110] Cf. Claude (1978b), 28–9, and Amory (1997), 65–6, who do not make the same connection. They read this letter instead as a matter of kinship and familial honor. The Romanness, how-

Prudence and good counsel, with their obvious connection to rationality and dependability, were Roman virtues that existed in glaring opposition to the qualities of irrational and undependable barbarians.[111] Such irrationality was at the very core of what had defined traditional barbarism, and its presence even had the potential, as demonstrated in an earlier chapter, to transform an otherwise Roman emperor into an irate and immoderate savage.

Thrasamund, however, was civilized according to this letter, praised for having already obtained prudence and in proportions equal to his laudable Amal wife. On a superficial examination, then, it would seem that this Amal bride was only worthy of reverence because of her illustrious lineage and simply served as a proper match for the Vandal king, rather than as a source of improvement.[112] But one can nevertheless detect the same subtle mix of compliment and condescension here as in the other "gift" letters to barbarian kings. Gundobad had also been commended for his prudence and even hailed for helping Burgundy to put down her "barbarous ways,"[113] yet, as already seen, the Burgundians still functioned as traditionally savage barbarians who required Theoderic's (and Rome's) civilizing assistance. Similarly, Amalafrida had been intended to pacify the Vandal kingdom, her prudence and good advice aiding the king and his people in their aspiration to Roman rationalism.

It was altogether shocking to Theoderic, therefore, that Thrasamund had made a completely irrational and blatantly idiotic decision (the real crux of this letter), choosing to lend aid to the Visigothic pretender Gesalec, who was a known rival and enemy of Theoderic.[114] To be sure, the insult was personal,[115] particularly because Thrasamund's marriage

ever, is implicit, while family honor and kinship are secondary themes that do not negate Amal claims to Roman cultural superiority.

[111] Terms like *perfiditas, nimia fiducia, insania, inconstantia, furor, levitas* (and so forth) were consistently used to denigrate barbarians. See Dauge (1981), 176–7, and Heather (1999), 237–8. Such associations were inversions of typically Roman virtues like *pietas, fides, concordia, disciplina, prudentia, clementia* (and so forth).

[112] Indeed, the language here almost makes it sound as if it is the Amal bride who needs to meet the high standards of her Vandal husband. But, considering the Roman understanding of women as naturally weak and mentally unstable (*levitas et infirmitas sexus*), the likening of Thrasamund's prudence to that of a woman may not have been complimentary at all. By implication he was only the equal of an Amal woman, not an Amal man. This may be reading far too much into the passage, however.

[113] *Variae* 1.46.2: "Discat sub vobis Burgundia res subtilissimas inspicere et antiquorum inventa laudare: per vos propositum gentile deponit."

[114] For the context, Chp. 10.

[115] See Amory (1997), 65, who claims that the use of the first-person singular (*ego*) in this letter, rather than the usual first-person plural (*nos*), suggests that Thrasamund's actions were taken

to Amalafrida had entailed certain obligations that appear to have been violated by the Vandal's actions.[116] But it was equally outrageous because the gift itself, Amalafrida, and the benefits she conferred, prudence and good counsel, should have prevented such a bad policy from having been enacted.[117] Indeed, like Gundobad's clock, Clovis' citharist, or Herminafrid's Romanized bride Amalaberga, Amalafrida was supposed to be a beacon of Roman civilization, here of Roman prudence, but Thrasamund had simply not seen the light. Theoderic's hostile indignation would have to force him to yield instead, earning Thrasamund praise, when he finally complied, as the "most prudent of kings," a man who does "not favor the vice of obstinacy, which seems to befall irrational men," and who demonstrates that "wise individuals can rescue [bad] decisions."[118] Once more Theoderic showered Roman praises upon a "traditional" barbarian, but insinuated important links between himself, his family, and such praises. Amalafrida, after all, was a prudent giver of advice and doubtless had figured among those *sapientes* (wise individuals) who had changed Thrasamund's mind.

The link between Amal lineage and Roman virtues could also be expressed in Italy, both in Theoderic's lifetime and after his death. In a letter addressed to his nephew Theodahad, who would later succeed to the throne, Theoderic upbraided his relative for being accused of having wrongfully dispossessed a Roman nobleman of his land. Describing avarice as the root of all evil, Theoderic asserted, "It is not right for a man of Amal blood to make known his desire, since his race has the appearance of being purple-colored."[119] He reminded Theodahad that he needed to "shine with the splendor of [his] race [i.e. the Amals]" and that noblemen in general were supposed to live their lives according to the tenets

as a personal affront. This seems fair, though it should be pointed out that Theoderic actually slips in and out of the singular and plural in this letter and that Thrasamund himself is consistently referred to in the second-person plural (*vos*). In general, the letter has a tone of betrayal, perhaps an attempt to "shame" Thrasamund into submission.

[116] If a military alliance had been included, the lack of Vandal assistance during a recent Byzantine attack on the south Italian coast was another (unmentioned) slight. For such an alliance, see Claude (1978b), 29–31, and Goltz (1997/8), 236. This, combined with aiding and abetting a known enemy, was a serious cause for alarm.

[117] *Variae* 5.43.2: "Sed stupeo vos his beneficiis obligatos Gesalecum, qui nostris inimicis ... in vestram defensionem sic fuisse susceptum."

[118] *Variae* 5.44.1: "Ostendisti, prudentissime regum, post erroris eventum sapientibus subvenire posse consilium nec pertinaciae vitium vos amare, quod brutis hominibus videtur accidere." *Bruti homines* is virtually a synonym for *barbari homines*.

[119] *Variae* 4.39.1–2: "Avaritiam siquidem radicem esse omnium malorum et lectio divina testatur.... Hamali sanguinis virum non decet vulgare desiderium, quia genus suum conspicit esse purpuratum."

of *civilitas*.[120] Theodahad, then, was supposed to behave like the dignified nobleman his Amal lineage marked him out to be, acting as a model for that obedience to and defense of the laws that allowed all Goths to be considered neo-Romans.[121] Nor were such obligations restricted to direct members of the Amal clan, or even to Goths, for that matter. The ex-consul Maximus provides a case in point. A member of the Anicii clan of Rome, he married into the Amal family during the reign of Theodahad, thus uniting the purple-clad royalty of the Amals with an ancient Roman house "equal almost to emperors," "praised by the whole world" and "truly called noble."[122] Because of this glorious union, however, Maximus was admonished to pay more attention to his virtues: "Let your mild association be available to all; humbly attend to the business of your glory, since praise is obtained from modesty; cherish more than the other virtues patience, dear to the wise; conquer your wrath; delight in kindness."[123] Mildness, humility, modesty, patience, self-control, kindness: Such qualities were clearly antithetical to barbarism and were intrinsically linked to the ideology of Roman emperorship espoused by Theoderic and, as this example demonstrates, his successors.[124]

To be associated with the Amals, then, even if already resplendent in one's own proudly Roman or barbarian lineage, meant taking on Amal qualities and thus behaving like a virtuous Roman. This, in part, had been why Theoderic had been so shocked by Thrasamund's failure to behave according to the prudence granted by his Amal bride. Roughly two decades later, Theoderic's nephew was reiterating the same basic idea, only now to a member of one of the noblest families in Rome. Theodahad, in fact, summed up the obligation that Amal blood entailed quite nicely, claiming to Maximus, "Joined now to our family, you will be thought nearest to our glorious deeds. Hitherto your family has been praised, but they were

---

[120] *Variae* 4.39.4–5: "generis claritate fulgetis.... Generosos quippe viros omnia convenit sub moderata civilitate peragere." The passage's reference to *civilitas* demonstrates nicely the link imagined to have existed between the Amals and this ideology, contra Amory (1997), 67f.

[121] Indeed, when Theodahad became king, he too stressed the importance of civilized behavior in a letter to one of his *homines*. See *Variae* 10.5.

[122] For equal, *Variae* 10.11.2: "Anicios quidem paene principibus pares aetas prisca progenuit"; for praised and noble, *Variae* 10.12.2: "familia toto orbe praedicata, quae vere dicitur nobilis." In fact, one of the Anicii, Anicius Olybrius, had been emperor in the late fifth century. See *PLRE* 2, 796–8 (Anicius Olybrius 6).

[123] *Variae* 10.11.4–5: "Considera quid merueris et dignum te nostra affinitate tractabis.... Nunc maior opera mansuetudini detur: nunc omnibus communio benigna praebeatur.... Humilis age rem gloriae, quia de modestia laus sumitur.... Supra ceteras virtutes amicam sapientibus ama patientiam.... Iram vince: benigna dilige."

[124] For these qualities as antithetical, Dauge (1981), 428–40, and Heather (1999), 436–8.

not adorned with so great a union."[125] Indeed, whether Roman, Goth, or barbarian, attachment to the Amal line was the paramount of honors.[126]

BORN FOR THE PURPLE

As time progressed, moreover, even the most "Gothic" of the Amals, the very progenitors of the Amal clan, could take on these same Roman virtues, granting further legitimacy and Romanness to Theoderic and his kin. Cassiodorus' lost history, it seems, provides an excellent example of this, despite the availability of alternative interpretations. While, again, the contents of this history and even its date of composition are unclear, documents in the *Variae* provide important clues as to its purpose and intended message.[127] When Cassiodorus was appointed praetorian prefect of Italy in 533, for instance, he penned a letter to the Senate in the name of King Athalaric, which announced his appointment and provided a rather interesting report of his achievements. Noteworthy among these was his lost history, its inclusion a reflection of both Cassiodorus' and Athalaric's (i.e. the official) estimation of the work. From the description that follows,

---

[125] *Variae* 10.11.5: "qui nostro iungeris generi, proximus gloriosis actionibus comproberis. Laudati sunt quidem hactenus parentes tui, sed tanta non sunt coniunctione decorati."

[126] *Ibid.*: "nobilitas tua non est ultra quo crescat." This letter and some of the other letters discussed so far demonstrate the extreme nobility claimed by the Amals, which conferred unsurpassable dignity even on those already exceedingly noble through marriage alliances. Other letters in the *Variae* concerning Amal marriage ties also demonstrate the hyper-ennobling power of an Amal union. See *Variae* 8.9–10 (on Tuluin) and 9.1 (to Hilderic of the Vandals concerning the "murder" of Amalafrida).

[127] See Chp. 2. Its relationship with Jordanes' *Getica* remains a matter of debate. Earlier scholarship saw Jordanes as a simple (if careless) epitomizer of Cassiodorus' work, some going so far as to quote from his *Getica* as if quoting Cassiodorus. Cf. the introduction in Mierow (1915), 13–16; Momigliano (1955); Andersson (1963); Svennung (1969); and Wolfram (1997), 26. Jordanes himself, however, explains in *Getica* 2–3 that he was only given three days for a reread and had to write from memory. He claims that he did not remember the words, though he believed he retained their sense, and that he supplemented what he remembered using Greek and Roman histories, adding a new introduction, conclusion, and many things in the middle. Most scholars now take these claims seriously, arguing for Jordanes' independence and originality as an author. Where they differ is in their interpretations of the purpose and intended meaning of this work, as well as the extent to which certain passages depend upon Cassiodorus or other authors. Cf. Bradley (1966); Várady (1976); O'Donnell (1979), 43–54 and (1982); Baldwin (1979) and (1981); Luiselli (1980), 235f.; Martino (1982), 35–8; Krautschick (1983), chp. 2; Barnish (1984); Croke (1987) and (2005a); Goffart (1988), 20f., and (2006), 56f.; Heather (1989); Weißensteiner (1994); Gillett (2000); Søby Christensen (2002); and Festy (2003). To my mind, Jordanes' conclusion (*Getica* 315–19) makes his purpose all too clear and should be taken as seriously as his introduction (*Getica* 2–3). Here he argues that he wrote the work "not so much to praise the Goths as to praise the man who conquered them [i.e. Justinian/Belisarius]."

it becomes abundantly clear that this history was prized foremost for its thorough investigation of Amal history. It proved the extreme antiquity, so valued by western Romans, of the Amal dynasty and suggested that its ancientness was somehow complementary to Romanness and a source of honor for Romans. Cassiodorus, it was said, had "led out the kings of the Goths, obscured by long oblivion, from the hiding place of antiquity."[128] He restored to them the forgotten "splendor of their house" and demonstrated that Athalaric himself was the seventeenth in a line of Amal kings.[129] He thus made "a Gothic origin into Roman history," a sentence that has troubled scholars, but might best be understood to mean that he wrote a Roman-style history that centered on the Amal dynasty and its eventual attainment of the *imperium* in the West.[130] The letter's description closed with remarks that are consistent with such an understanding. Directly addressing the Senate, Athalaric asked its members to reflect on this work's specific value to them: "Consider how much he [i.e. Cassiodorus] valued you [i.e. senators] by praising us [i.e. Athalaric/Amals]; he showed that the family of your *princeps* was wonderful from antiquity, so that, just as you have always been thought noble through your ancestors, an ancient race of kings might thus rule you."[131] The antiquity of the Amal line, therefore, was intended to harmonize with that of Rome's venerable senators, while rendering their current emperor, the *princeps* Athalaric, worthy to rule as such, *imperare*.

---

[128] *Variae* 9.25.4: "Iste reges Gothorum longa oblivione celatos latibulo vetustatis eduxit."

[129] *Ibid.*: "Iste Hamalos cum generis sui claritate restituit, evidenter ostendens in septimam decimam progeniem stirpem nos habere regalem."

[130] *Variae* 9.25.5: "Originem Gothicam historiam fecit esse Romanam." The same theme is featured, albeit in a very cursory manner, in Cassiodorus' earlier chronicle. See Chp. 2. For a discussion of other interpretations, Croke (2003), 362–3. Despite the fact that Wolfram (1988) refers to Cassiodorus' lost history as the *Origo Gothica* throughout, *Variae* 9.25.5 neither suggests that Cassiodorus' history was some sort of *Origo Gentis Gothorum* nor explicitly entitles this history as the *Origo Gothica*. The title *de Origine Actusque Gothorum* has been inferred (problematically, it seems) from Jordanes' *Getica* and the *Anecdoton Holderi*. Cf. Luiselli (1980), 238–40, and Goffart (2006), 58f. Considering that Cassiodorus' own description of this work is rather Amal-centered (see later discussion), it would seem reasonable to assume that *origo* means "family origin" and *Gothica* is simply a reference to the Amals (who are, after all, a Gothic family). The suggestion of Goffart (1988), 35–8, that the lost history contained serial biographies of Amal rulers along the lines of the *Kaisergeschichte* does, in fact, fit with such an interpretation. Cf. Amory (1997), 68, n. 117.

[131] *Variae* 9.25.6: "Perpendite, quantum vos in nostra laude dilexerit, qui vestri principis nationem docuit ab antiquitate mirabilem, ut, sicut fuistis a maioribus vestris semper nobiles aestimati, ita vobis antiqua regum progenies inperaret." Though it might seem more natural to translate *natio* as "nation/race," as a synonym for *gens*, it seems to refer to the Amals, who are again central to Cassiodorus' final point about an "ancient race of kings."

Such an understanding of Cassiodorus' history seems at odds with modern attempts to connect this work with a late Theoderican shift in ideology that stressed Amal and Gothic exceptionalism at the expense of (presumably) earlier ideas of Romanness and *civilitas*.[132] Obviously there is little material with which to provide a complete reconstruction, but the preceding description of the history's contents and relevance suggests that the work framed Amal history in such a way that it would have been amenable to an elite Roman audience and intended for one.[133] Such an audience would not have been receptive to ideas of Gothic exclusivity that devalued its Romanness; nor would it have been prudent for Cassiodorus to praise an opus like this (or, rather, be praised for writing it) before the proudly Roman Senate. Indeed, the history was supposed to be a great honor for Cassiodorus, not just at court in Ravenna but in Rome, and Rome's senators themselves were supposed to be glorified by its contents. This was surely a "Roman" history, then, not just because it terminated with a Roman Empire ruled by a long line of Gothic kings, but also because it was Roman in essence. It proved that the Amals, despite being Goths and sometimes enemies of the empire, could be admirable and even "wondrous" in those virtues that were valued by Romans and understood to be Roman. This, in turn, helped to render the Amals worthy, perhaps even predestined, to take up the reins of Roman governance, reinvigorating and restoring the empire. Such a history would have been in keeping with the barebones narrative found in Cassiodorus' earlier *Chronicle* and, moreover, would have been remarkably similar to Ennodius' panegyric, which for all intents and purposes transformed a potentially Gothic king into a Roman *princeps* steeped in Roman values, abounding in imperial virtues, and bound to save the West from its decadence. Cassiodorus thus reinterpreted ancient Amal kings in the same way that the Goths and, more importantly, royal Goths like Theoderic had already been reinterpreted; they too were old Romans or, at least, Romans in the making.

This, of course, is a hypothetical reconstruction. However, it not only accords well with the understanding of Theoderic and his Goths found in contemporary sources, but also finds support in another document from the *Variae* collection. Here, in a similar context, Cassiodorus himself addressed the Senate, using the opportunity to provide an encomium on

---

[132] See earlier, n. 93.

[133] This elite Roman audience would have been polyethnic to some degree, including certain highly Romanized Goths. But regardless of origins, its members would have shared in the same core values discussed in Part I. For the possibility of a primarily Spanish/Visigothic audience, Diaz and Valverde (2007), 364–7, with the discussion of Eutharic's consulship in Chp. 8. Given Cassiodorus' comments earlier, an elite Italo-Roman audience seems more likely.

Amalasuentha, Athalaric's mother and acting regent. This was the same laudation in which Cassiodorus compared Amalasuentha's regency to Placidia's, the contrast placing the Amals within a succession of Roman emperors and demonstrating the perceived glory of modern times.[134] Yet Cassiodorus also appeared to draw deeply from the Gothic past in his eulogy, comparing Amalasuentha to her Amal ancestors and, in so doing, hinting at what had made them "a wonder from ancient times." To be sure, these Amals had barbaric sounding names, perhaps explaining why modern scholars tend to interpret this passage as reflective of an un-Roman, Gothic past.[135] But the audience, once more, was the Roman Senate, and the purpose of these references was to praise Amalasuentha in *its* midst.

Reiterating the venerability of Amalasuentha's house, Cassiodorus listed nine generations of Amal kings and associated each king with a virtue that had nothing to do with his Gothicness; rather, their collective virtues recommended them as civilized rulers, as precursors to the very Roman family of Theoderic. "If that royal band of her relatives were to behold her," Cassiodorus asserted, "it would see its fame reflected as if in the purest mirror."[136] Amal, he claimed, was famous for his good fortune (*felicitate*), Ostrogotha his patience (*patientia*), Athala his mildness (*mansuetudine*), Winitar his equity (*aequitate*), Hunimund his handsomeness (*forma*), Thorismuth his chastity (*castitate*), Walamer his faith (*fide*), Theudimer his piety (*pietate*), and her father, Theoderic, as the senators already knew well, his wisdom (*sapientia*).[137] These were all noble Roman virtues[138] and

[134] See Chp. 2.
[135] Cf. Luiselli (1980), 244f., and Amory (1997), 67–8. Such an interpretation rests largely on the assumptions that Cassiodorus' history contained "authentically" Gothic material along the lines of Jordanes' *Getica* (a work whose own authenticity and meaning are far from clear) and that this material was somehow oppositional to Romanness. Hence, kings with un-Roman names are assumed to be indicative of "un-Romanness," a problematic position given that many individuals with un-Roman names, including Theoderic and his immediate kin, were not excluded from Romanness (in Italy at any rate) by virtue of their names. More importantly, such a reading of Cassiodorus' history is overly naïve, denying him the flexibility and will to manipulate and even invent history for whatever purposes he or his literary patron deemed fit. In short, there was absolutely no need for this passage, or Cassiodorus' history, for that matter, to be authentic. Cf. Heather (1989) and (1995), 147–51.
[136] *Variae* 11.1.19: "Hanc si parentum cohors illa regalis aspiceret, tamquam in speculum purissimum sua praeconia mox videret."
[137] *Ibid.*: "Enituit enim Hamalus felicitate, Ostrogotha patientia, Athala mansuetudine, VVinitarius aequitate, Unimundus forma, Thorismuth castitate, VValamer fide, Theudimer pietate, sapientia, ut iam vidistis, inclitus pater."
[138] Moreover, they were *imperial* virtues regularly eulogized in panegyric. See Menander Rhetor, *Peri Epideiktikon*, with Romano (1978), 34; Ficarra (1978); Nixon and Rodgers (1994), 10–14; and Rota (2002), 86–99. Cf. Charlesworth (1937), 113f.

a source of glory for the Amal house not just in contemporary times, but all the way back to this family's very namesake, Amal. Surely this is exactly what Cassiodorus had meant when he claimed that he had made a Gothic origin into Roman history.

Amal blood, in the case of both Theoderic and his successors, therefore, could be especially useful for Theoderic and his successors because of the many ways that it could be manipulated and interpreted by men like Ennodius and Cassiodorus. The fact that it was royal, in general, could be outstanding, while its antiquity, onto which Cassiodorus' historical undertaking shed new light, was especially potent in the West, where senators prided themselves on their own venerable lineages and had been receptive to pedigreed outsiders in the past. Amals were more than just a long line of kings, however; they had internalized virtues that many claimed would have made them famous even if they lacked their noble lineage. These were qualities that first worked against an understanding of Theoderic as a barbarian, aiding in his acceptance as an elite Roman statesmen, and later extended to his successors and *even* predecessors. Amals were Roman princes, even when they were Gothic kings. Amal descent, then, not only played a role in granting legitimacy to Theoderic's principate, but also became an underlying reason for his ability to restore the western empire. His bloodline granted him the *virtus* of famous Gothic kings, valor that had come to Italy's rescue; it likewise bestowed upon him and his successors a sense of obligation to live and rule according to Amal standards, behaving in a way that further demonstrated their internalization of Roman values and their commitment to sweet *civilitas*.

A bit of a mustache and longish hair were of little consequence, then. Goths were Romans, and Theoderic and his family the most Roman of them all.

PART IV

ITALIA FELIX

Blessedness Restored

Theoderic and his Goths, prior sections have shown, could fit within the Roman Empire, not just as slaves or servants of its emperor, but as its principal leaders and defenders. Many of the developments of the later empire had made this possible, and now Italy's acceptably Roman Goths had allowed for a kind of republican renaissance to emerge. In Theoderic, Rome had a noble and outwardly imperial *princeps*; the Goths, law-abiding and valorous warriors, likewise, reinvigorated the remnants of Rome's empire, threatening its old adversaries, protecting its heartland, and extending its borders, wrapped in their Roman togas. Alone, these factors were worthy of admiration, yet they were not the only causes for the resounding adulation of this era. In fact, contemporary understandings of blessedness and imperial restoration rested on much more than the idea that Italy was safe and secure and ruled by its own emperor again. Proudly imperial, Julius Nepos had managed to secure Italy's safety, if for a limited time. But the health of his republic (*status reipublicae*), reduced to a mere "Empire of Italy," had remained in peril, persisting in its shoddy condition into the reign of Odovacer and worsening, at least initially, as a result of Theoderic's invasion.

Italy and Italo-Romans, therefore, required more than the return of Romulus Augustus' insignia and the arrival of another "Greek" emperor to wear them. These events had been of great significance, but they did not wipe clean the stains of so many fifth-century catastrophes or turn back the clock to a long departed era of Roman *felicitas*. More changes were needed and, in devastated regions like Liguria, desperately so. And while time and patience were also necessary, efforts on the part of the nascent Theoderican government could be extremely powerful, ushering in new-found prosperity in a number of cities and regions, fulfilling traditional expectations of imperial benevolence, and winning the gratitude and loyalty of uncertain subjects.

Through traditional acts of charity and *pietas* Theoderic would be hailed as a *bonus princeps* and even *imperator* long before reaching an agreement with the eastern emperor in Constantinople. And by perpetuating such postwar policies and then expanding his patronage in time-honored ways, he would assimilate Rome's glorious past to the present, earning the ultimate stamp of Italo-Roman approval and making sentiments of a golden age more than just the product of wishful thinking or empty rhetoric. Highly rhetorical though his language may have been, by 507 Ennodius was literally hailing the restored *status reipublicae* in his panegyric, providing a long list of the wondrous improvements realized through the efforts of the "greatest of kings."[1] Shortly thereafter, inscriptions proclaimed that Theoderic was "the most compassionate *princeps*" who ruled "for the good of Rome," while Cassiodorus asserted before the Senate that "ancient blessedness" had been restored to his era.[2]

Theoderic's attentive and benevolent rule gave Italo-Romans good reason to make such claims, and here, in the following chapters, case studies will be provided in an effort to understand contemporary enthusiasm. The first of these returns to the world of Ennodius' *Life of Epiphanius*, to Liguria in northern Italy. Limited to the earliest years of Theoderic's reign (c. 489–96), it looks at his patronage of this war-torn province and how his compassion and dutiful leadership assisted in its eventual recovery, helping to legitimize Theoderic as a proper Roman emperor. Such policies, it concludes, were also being applied elsewhere and, when expanded and met with tangible results, they did much to sow broader sentiments of a golden age. The second case study turns to Rome, a unique city owing to is ideological and historic significance. The Eternal City had suffered greatly as a result of neglectful emperors and declining imperial fortunes. But Theoderic pursued a pro-Roman policy throughout his reign that asserted to the Romans of Rome and all the inhabitants of his empire that Rome was again the "head of the world" (*caput mundi*). The Senate was treated with the utmost respect; there were bread, circuses, and other marvelous

---

[1] *PanTh* 5: "Salve nunc, regum maxime, in cuius dominio saporem suum ingenuitatis vigor agnovit. Salve, status reipublicae: nam nefas est, speciatim a te simul conlata narrare et unius bona temporis verborum divisione discernere."

[2] For most compassionate, *ILS* 827 (Fiebiger 1, #193 and *CIL* 10 6850–2), with Chp. 10: "clementissimi principis feliciter deserviente praeconiis"; for good of Rome, *ILS* 828a (Fiebiger 1, #191 and *CIL* 15 1665, etc.) and 828b (Fiebiger 1, #192 and *CIL* 15 1669, etc.), with Chp. 8. For Cassiodorus, *CassOratReliquiae*, p. 466, ln. 17–18: "ad saecula nostra an- / tiqua beatitudo revertitur," with Chps. 8 and 10.

spectacles for the plebs; and many decaying monuments, testaments to the greatness of Roman civilization, were saved through Theoderic's pious intervention. Moreover, and though making Ravenna his principal capital, Theoderic graced the city with his presence in the year 500, celebrating in true imperial style; and in 519, his intended successor did similarly, extending his patronage in ways that were impressive even by east Roman standards.

7

ITALY REVIVED

LIGURIA CAPUT MUNDI

Liguria, it should be recalled, played a central role in the depiction of the past recorded in Ennodius' major work of hagiography, the *Life of Epiphanius*. It was through Ligurian eyes that the Goth Ricimer had appeared a noble Roman protector and through those same eyes that the emperor Anthemius had seemed more an enraged Galatian and Greekling than the proud Roman he claimed to be. Likewise, during the reign of Nepos, it had been Liguria itself that had seemed destined to be conquered by the rapacious barbarian Euric, and it had been to the nobles of this province (*lumina Liguriae*) that this emperor had turned, hoping to establish peace and thus restore the faltering *status* of his republic. Ennodius' hagiographical work even presented the very "fall" of the western empire (or better, lack thereof) in a rather Liguro-centric fashion: The civil war between Odovacer and Orestes was described in terms of its negative effects on the Ligurian city of Pavia, while the peace and recovery that followed in this region rendered Odovacer an improvement of sorts over a number of his predecessors.

Such overt Liguro-centricity is instructive, providing important insights into the ways in which Italo-Romans thought about their world. For those hailing from Liguria, men like Ennodius, this province was home and what happened here, of necessity, outweighed developments elsewhere. Rome could always serve as the ideological head of the world (*caput mundi*), but ideology aside, Liguria, or simply a Ligurian city like Pavia or Milan, was the *real* center of the universe. Nor was such an understanding unique to Ligurians. Throughout the empire, individual loyalties mirrored those found in the *Life of Epiphanius* and were regularly predicated on a particular locale, often (though not always) centered on a specific city. Province by province and city by city, Romans formed their varying opinions of the state and its rulers based upon the happenings in their midst. As a consequence, just as emperors who neglected the city of Rome could earn the distrust and disapproval of the Romans residing in the Eternal City, so too could those neglecting Pavia or Milan lose the support of certain Liguro-Romans. The depictions of Anthemius, Nepos, and Odovacer found in the *Life of Epiphanius* bear this out, each meeting with approval or disapproval as a result of the relationship that he cultivated with Ennodius' *patria*.

The fate of Liguria, then, mattered to Ligurians, just as the fate of Lucania and Bruttium mattered to men like Cassiodorus, or the fate of Aemilia or Latium mattered to those living there. And though Liguria was the *caput mundi*, so to speak, for only a limited number of Italians, the extensively Liguro-centric nature of the Ennodian corpus, and especially the *Life of Epiphanius*, allows much to be said about this region, providing a valuable case study for the perceived impact of Theoderic and his Goths at a local level. Life in this province, as already seen, had been affected by the manifold disappointments and disasters of the fifth century, and Theoderic and his Goths had inherited this legacy of imperial failure when they arrived in 489. Moreover, though conditions in Liguria had improved to some degree under the peaceful reign of Odovacer, the advent of the Ostrogoths had inaugurated yet another series of disastrous civil wars, centering on the north, lasting for years, and leading to further devastation in the region. The situation had thus returned to its normal (and depressing) fifth-century state by the beginning of Theoderic's reign, and Theoderic himself, though a supposed liberator sent in the name of a Roman emperor, was largely responsible.

Rejection in Liguria, and by implication throughout Italy, was thus a very possible outcome in the early days of the Theoderican regime. Yet as a continued close reading of the *Life of Epiphanius* will now suggest, Theoderic's exceptional generosity and compassion, both during his invasion and in its immediate aftermath, would win for him Ligurian approval. Indeed, Ennodius would terminate his account with the death of Epiphanius in 496, the year before Theoderic's official recognition in Constantinople. Yet the kind of patronage described in his account would continue to define Theoderic's long reign, sowing in the hearts of those who benefited most sentiments of renewal and a golden age. Theoderic would cultivate meaningful relationships with a number of communities within his empire, and their transformation would render him not simply a Roman emperor, but a *good* Roman emperor.

Caught between Princes

Again, and though not the intended purpose of this work, the *Life of Epiphanius* provides many incidental details regarding the perceived condition of the empire and its rulers during the life of its principal subject, bishop Epiphanius of Pavia. In Chapter 1, the discussion of these details terminated with the reign of Odovacer, at roughly the midpoint of Ennodius' narrative. Here Odovacer had at first appeared as a benevolent ruler, granting Liguria a five-year exemption from taxation and later providing speedy assistance during the corrupt prefecture of Pelagius. Italy seemed to enjoy a period of calm otherwise absent in the account, yet Odovacer's kind assistance had required frantic embassies on the part of the story's hero, Epiphanius, and these occurrences had hinted at a lack of attentiveness and concern on the part of the ruler of Italy (shortcomings echoed in other sources). Such qualities, the concluding sentence of Ennodius' treatment makes clear, would soon define Odovacer's reign. The number of missions to Ravenna, according to Ennodius, became excessive in the lead-up to Theoderic's arrival, while Epiphanius himself had been forced to become increasingly vehement in his supplications.[1] Details beyond this are lacking, but it seems that the situation had begun to unravel in Italy, and with knowledge of changes to come, Ennodius could speak of Theoderic's invasion as an act of "heavenly dispensation."[2] God, he believed, had favored Theoderic and, in choosing to send him, had been merciful.

Having arrived in Italy, Theoderic quickly established his court at Milan, where Epiphanius, true to his established role as a peacemaker, hurried to meet him. This would be the first encounter between the bishop and the future ruler of Italy, and first impressions were important. Indeed, the description of this episode is especially revealing, for it demonstrates the extent to which Theoderic, still unknown in the West, followed in the footsteps of the "good" emperors already encountered in the *Vita*, honoring, just as they did, the holy man of Liguria. "The most excellent of kings," Ennodius wrote, looked upon the bishop "with the eyes of his heart" and

[1] *VE* 109: "Post multas tamen quas apud Odovacrem regem legationes violentia supplicationis exegit." But cf. Cesa (1988), 182, who suggests that this "violentia supplicationis" refers to the general power of his supplication rather than its vehemence. Though true, she also concludes that this passage hints at a certain coldness between Odovacer and Epiphanius.
[2] *VE* 109: "dispositione caelestis imperii ad Italiam Theodericus rex ... commeavit." Cf. Pietrella (1984), 219.

"the customary measure of his judgment," recognizing in him the existence of "all the virtues."[3] He then asserted to his followers, "Behold [here is] a man for whom there is no equal in the entire East; to have seen him is a reward; to live with him a source of security. Provided he is unharmed, Pavia is protected by the most solid of walls, which no attacking force can overwhelm."[4] Beyond hinting at Theoderic's eastern origins, these words served to highlight the preeminence of Epiphanius, not just in Italy, but in the entire world (the point of the hagiographical genre), while drawing attention to his important role as an intercessor and protector. Moreover, by placing these words in Theoderic's mouth, Ennodius tacitly approved of his king, for though other rulers had also acknowledged Epiphanius' saintly qualities (perhaps more to the bishop's credit than their own), Theoderic had not required convincing at all. His own laudable virtues, virtues that made him ideal for imperial succession, made Epiphanius' eloquent words utterly unnecessary.[5] Even more to Theoderic's credit, Ennodius' narration makes it clear that the future ruler of Italy meant every word that he had said to his followers. In fact, he believed so much in the protective powers of Epiphanius that he recommended his Goths leave their "mothers and family members in his safe-keeping," entrusting his own mother and sister to the bishop's care.[6]

Theoderic, therefore, trusted and had faith in the bishop. And though Epiphanius remained piously neutral during the coming war, to Theoderic's credit yet again, the future king persisted in his reverence, proving on more than one occasion that his esteem for this holy man could be harnessed for the good of Liguria and its inhabitants. These were tumultuous times, and Ennodius painted a vivid picture. Soldiers from both sides regularly pillaged the Ligurian countryside, generals vacillated in their loyalty, and Theoderic's own soldiers, many still qualifying as "barbarians" by Italo-Roman standards, were forced to take refuge within the walls of Ligurian cities like Pavia, often to the very great discomfort of

---

[3] *VE* 109: "Quem cum ille regum praestantissimus cordis oculis inspexisset et solita iudicii sui sacerdotem nostrum libra pensaret, invenit in eo pondus omnium constare virtutum."

[4] *VE* 110: "'Ecce hominem, cui totus oriens similem non habet, quem vidisse praemium est, cum quo habitare securitas. Fortissimo muro Ticinensis civitas incolumi isto vallatur, quos inpugnantum nulla vis possit obruere.'"

[5] Cf. the depictions of Anthemius, Ricimer, Glycerius, Nepos, and Odovacer in the *VE* (all described in Chp. 1), as well as those of the barbarian kings Euric (Chp. 1) and Gundobad (Chps. 2 and 9). Cesa (1988), 183, concludes similarly, though only using the model of Anthemius.

[6] *VE* 110: "tutum est apud istum matrem familiasque deponere." For Theoderic's mother and sister, Cook (1942), 201–2, and Cesa (1988), 184, with Pietrella (1984), 217. Ennodius does not explicitly mention them in the *VE*, but a later source that made use of his corpus (Paul the Deacon, *Historia Romana* 15.17) does.

established residents.[7] Worse than any discomfort caused by such billeting, many Romans also fell into the hands of the "enemy," whoever this might have been at any given moment, and Epiphanius, true to his calling, constantly strove to redeem them.[8] Ennodius claimed that words were not sufficient for him to relate the number of insults, attacks, and tumults the saint sustained with a brave face,[9] concluding, "He spent three years under such tormented conditions, revealing to God alone his hidden feelings of grief and begging Him to furnish him with secret aid."[10]

Caught between two "disagreeing princes,"[11] Epiphanius and all Liguria, it seemed to Ennodius, were in need of a miracle. And while the purpose of the hagiographical genre was to extol saints like Epiphanius for achieving such feats, it was Theoderic himself, aided by God, who answered the bishop's prayers. Not yet ruler of Italy and "beset by the dense battalions of the enemy,"[12] Theoderic remained exceptionally attached to the bishop, venerating him more than all the other holy men in his midst.[13] While Epiphanius endeavored to meet the different demands of "so many thousands of people at the same time," "strengthening them with his flattering words," "feeding them with his offerings," and redeeming from captivity their "children and wives with his supplications,"[14] Theoderic proved ready to assist without solicitation. Aware of the bishop's efforts to ransom captives, for instance, the future king at one point even freed from servitude every Roman who had fallen into the possession of his followers "through

---

[7] For these events, VE 109–15. The stereotypically negative description of the Rugians, encountered in Chp. 5, is from this particular episode.

[8] VE 115–16. These captives included partisans of Odovacer who had fallen into the hands of Theoderic's forces. Their ransoming doubtless provided a source of tension between the bishop of Pavia and the Theoderican side. Cf. Vita Caesarii 1.32–3 and 36, where Caesarius' loyalty is called into question for just this reason; also Klingshirn (1985).

[9] VE 117: "Iam si illa retexam, quas inimicorum sustinuit insolentias, quibus laboravit inmissionibus, quali procellas pessimorum virtute contempsit: ad haec enarranda lingua non sufficiet."

[10] Ibid.: "Sub tali cruce triennium duxit, soli deo dolorum suorum omnia secreta manifestans, a quo ministrari sibi clandestinum poscebat auxilium." Cf. Ennodius' Eucharisticon (#438.20) where, in addition to the general destruction of Italy ("cum omnia ... clade vastarentur"), Ennodius mourned the passing of his aunt and guardian. He was roughly sixteen years old at the time. See also his Dictio in Natale Laurenti Mediolanensis Episcopi (#1.17–19), where the fate of Milan is similarly described.

[11] VE 113: "inter dissidentes principes."

[12] VE 127: "quando confertissimis inimicorum cuneis urguebaris."

[13] VE 116: "Regi aptissimus et prae sanctis omnibus venerabilis existebat."

[14] VE 115: "Nam tot milia hominum uno eodemque tempore, cum diversa poscerent, reficiebat blanditiis, humiliabat adloquio, pascebat muneribus. Si cuius liberi uxorque inimicis a qualibet parte fuissent intercipientibus occupati, ilico supplicationis illius pretio reddebantur suis, quos auri redimere non potuisset effusio."

the license of war."[15] This was a pious act of charity and a gesture of great significance. Not only did it perpetuate the admirable relationship between bishop and king and reveal Theoderic's concern for the Roman population of Italy, but it did so at the expense of his own soldiers, the very backbone of his power at this time. Ennodius, quite aware of this, was again lost for words. "I could not enumerate," he claimed, "how many crowds of subjugated men he returned to their own soil, how many [people] he imposed upon, lest they [i.e. the captive Romans] be vexed."[16] Surrounded by uncertainties, therefore, Theoderic remained steadfast, proving himself a reverent and compassionate king.

YOUR LIGURIA

War, as an earlier episode in the *Vita* has suggested, could be literally hellish. But a "wretched and bloody battle"[17] finally put an end to the contest between Theoderic and Odovacer. Years of warfare, however, had been particularly hard on Liguria, causing the opening of the Theoderican epoch to be a period defined by recovery. As in the past, Epiphanius looked to the repair of Pavia, a city practically destroyed in the last of Italy's internecine struggles, but wondrously spared this time. Yet Pavia had been an exception to the rule. Epiphanius' prayers had saved this city from crippling devastation, but the rest of Liguria had not been so lucky, "ruined" and struck down by a "whirlwind of temporal commotion."[18] Adding further insult to injury, the once-kindly and charitable Theoderic had begun to

---

[15] VE 116: "ut quoscumque Romanorum bellandi licentia hominum eius fecisset esse captivos, mox illi restitueret, quem sola intellegebat aliorum libertate ditari."

[16] *Ibid.*: "Deinde enumerare nequeam, quanta ille subiugatorum agmina solo proprio reddidit, quanta ne vexarentur inposuit." Admittedly, this sentence more probably refers to Epiphanius than Theoderic. The translation in Cook (1942), 79, is ambiguous, that in Cesa (1988), 101, assumes Epiphanius. Regardless, credit would still have to be given, by implication, to Theoderic's benefaction, just as the case explicitly is in the ransoming of Ligurian captives from Burgundy (VE 175–6 and 187, discussed later).

[17] VE 120: "Postquam vero perfuncta res est misero exitialique bello."

[18] VE 121: "Et licet eam precatu illius faciente nullus in vastitatem temporalis procellae turbo dispulerat ... post ruinam omnium Liguriae." Cook (1942), 209–10, suggests that this "ruin" referenced the church and the "ruinous" absence of episcopal ordinations during the conflict, citing Gelasius, *Ep.* 14 as evidence. This is certainly possible, but given the length of the war and the later description of a destitute Liguria provided in VE 138–9 (and of northern Italy in general in #1.17, #438.20, and *PanTh* 56), it doubtless extended beyond this. Cf. Cesa (1988), 188. Beyond the dubious attempt by Brogiolo (1994), 216; (1999), 104–5; and (2007), 117–21, to connect partitioned housing with the billeting of Theoderic's soldiers at this time, referring to VE 112, little archaeological evidence has been cited for the impact of this war. Nevertheless, the attention Theoderic later gave to (re)building walls and basic infrastructure in the region may be related to its devastation. See later discussion.

alter his wartime policies, "his mind seized with a sudden resolution" to punish those Romans who, of necessity, had failed to go over to his side during the war. Soon he published an edict depriving all such individuals of the "right of Roman liberty," barring them from the ability to testify in court or make a will.[19] Once a restorer of freedom, Theoderic now desired to take it away. "All Italy," Ennodius wrote, lay "under a lamentable cessation of justice," and it seemed, through actions like these, that Theoderic might prove himself a barbarian after all.[20]

Another "public wound" was hence remitted into the "healing hands" of the saintly intercessor Epiphanius,[21] who, accompanied by Laurence of Milan, quickly hastened to Ravenna in order to plea Liguria's cause. Here they were received with due reverence,[22] and when it came time to make their case, Epiphanius was chosen for the task. Tellingly addressing Theoderic as "*invictissime princeps*," Epiphanius began by invoking the divine assistance that had allowed the Goth to become the ruler of Italy in the first place. "Sparing in your requests," he explained, "you have always received greater benefits from our God than you have wished for."[23] God had made it rain, for instance, when Theoderic needed rain and had sent the sun when he needed the sun; even the wind had fought on his behalf.[24] And despite being outnumbered and underequipped, Epiphanius explained, "an invisible power alone, sent from Heaven" had fought by his

[19] *VE* 122: "Interea subita animum praestantissimi regis Theoderici deliberatio occupavit, ut illis tantum Romanae libertatis ius tribueret, quos partibus ipsius fides examinata iunxisset; illos vero, quos aliqua necessitas diviserat, ab omni iussit et testandi et ordinationum suarum ac voluntatum licentia submoveri." Ennodius knew some of the individuals in question, many of whom would prove useful to the Theoderican regime, such as Liberius.

[20] *Ibid.*: "Qua sententia promulgata et legibus circa plurimos tali lege calcatis universa Italia lamentabili iustitio subiacebat." The use of *iustitio* here is very interesting, as Theoderic himself employed this very term in describing the condition of Gallo-Roman nobles living under Visigothic rule. See Chp. 10. The suspension of justice, therefore, was another way of indicating barbarization and injustice, the opposite of the rule of *civilitas*. But see Cesa (1988), 189, who demonstrates convincingly that Theoderic's intended policy was consistent with established punishments for high treason. He was thus upholding Roman law, not violating it, and so Ennodius' critique was a moral, rather than legal, judgment. Cf. Prostko-Prostyński (1994a), 185.

[21] *VE* 123: "Itur rursus ad illum, qui manu medica publicis consueverat subvenire vulneribus, cuius fonte aerumnarum saepe fuerat ardor extinctus."

[22] *Ibid.*: "Qui [i.e. Epiphanius et Laurentius] profecti una Ravennam etiam pariter pervenerunt, suscepti reverenter." Cf. *Vita Caesarii* 1.36, discussed in Chp. 4.

[23] *VE* 125: "'Quantus, invictissime princeps, per innumerabiles successus felicitatem tuam favor divinus evexerit, si per ordinem relegam, agnoscis te votorum parcum maiora semper a deo nostro beneficia accepisse quam optasse memineris.'"

[24] *VE* 128: "'Quotiens utilitatibus tuis aer ipse servierit, si recenses, tibi caeli serena militarunt, tibi convexa pluvias pro voto fuderunt.'" Cf. *PanTh.* 46 (cited with references in the Introduction to Part V), where the Adige River fights on Theoderic's behalf.

side, allowing him to defeat his rivals.[25] Yet the clearest indication of this divine intervention was plain for all who were present to see: "Where your enemy [Odovacer] was accustomed to rejoice in the possession of that very throne," Epiphanius claimed, "we now plead the causes of your subjects with you as the *princeps*."[26] God had given Theoderic his kingdom, while "Christ our Redeemer," he argued, had given him those very Romans "on whose behalf we beg."[27] It was right, therefore, for the ruler of Italy to "give recompense for the changes brought about through these heavenly gifts" and to devote "pity to the men [of Liguria]."[28]

Beyond invoking this divine assistance, Epiphanius provided his new *princeps* with a warning, referencing the failures of those Italian sovereigns already encountered in the *Vita*. "Think for sure about what kinds of men you have succeeded in your kingdom," he advised. "If, as is proven, wickedness expelled some of them, their plight ought to instruct those following after. The ruin of those preceding teaches those succeeding: a lapse in the past is always a warning for those remaining."[29] Theoderic, in other words, was supposed to consider why it was that these rulers, all at one time divinely sanctioned, had lost their thrones. He was to ponder "why your predecessor [i.e. Odovacer] had been ejected,"[30] lest he suffer a similar fate. And indeed the moderation of Theoderic already alluded to at the beginning of Epiphanius' speech recommended that this pious *princeps* would listen to reason. "Your Liguria," Epiphanius explained, "trusts in this and supplicates herself extensively along with us, that you might grant the benefits of your laws to the innocent and absolve the guilty."[31] "It is heavenly," Theoderic was reminded, "to forgive sins, earthly to avenge them."[32]

Though earlier rulers had missed the point of speeches like this or simply ignored them, Theoderic, according to Ennodius, was struck with reverent fear; and when the "most eminent king" finally opened his mouth, he again

---

[25] *VE* 127: "'quando armis numero adversarii praestantiores subsistere sola tecum dimicante caelitus invisibili virtute non poterant.'"
[26] *VE* 125: "'Sufficit tamen horum unum narrare sed maximum, quod apud te principem ibi servorum tuorum causas agimus, ubi solebat inimicus tuus huius solii possessione gaudere.'"
[27] *VE* 126: "'Habes plurimum Christo redemptori nostro quod debeas: pro quibus rogamus, ipse largitus est.'"
[28] *VE* 129: "'His ergo donis caelestibus vicissitudinem inpensa circa homines pietate restitue.'"
[29] *Ibid.*: "'Illud certe perpende, qualibus in regno successeris. Quos si, ut liquet, malitia expulit, casus illorum necesse est ut sequentes informet. Ruina praecedentium posteros docet: cautio est semper in reliquum lapsus anterior.'"
[30] *Ibid.*: "'Non sine exemplo militat qui respicit, qua causa decessor eiectus est.'"
[31] *VE* 130: "'His freta Liguria vestra nobiscum profusa supplicat, ut legum vestrarum beneficia sic tribuatis innocentibus, ut noxios absolvatis.'"
[32] *Ibid.*: "'culpas dimittere caeleste est, vindicare terrenum.'"

proved the extent to which he cherished the saint of Pavia, demonstrating that the piety so recently associated with him was genuine.[33] Referring to Epiphanius as a "venerable bishop," he claimed that he entertained toward him "esteem proper to his merits" and was grateful for his "many favors shown in times of distress."[34] Yet he pleaded that the "necessity of ruling" and the "difficult business of a nascent empire" precluded the pity and compassion that Epiphanius sought.[35] In fact, so Theoderic avowed, scripture even defended his actions, for the biblical king Saul had once pardoned an undeserving enemy, and God had punished him for this by inflicting upon him the very punishment that he should have exacted on his enemy.[36] "He who is lenient to his enemy when he has bested him," Theoderic opined, "either makes light of or despises the power of divine judgment ... he who lets the guilty go unpunished instigates the innocent to commit crimes."[37] But like all those rulers in the *Life of Epiphanius* who defended their actions before the bishop, Theoderic soon capitulated. As a mere "earthly" ruler, he confessed, he found it impossible "to resist your [Epiphanius'] prayers, which are approved by heaven."[38] Out of reverence for the saint and fear of God, therefore, he proclaimed a general amnesty, so that "the head of no one would be cast down with injury," and reserved only the punishment of exile for those who were "known to have been inciters of malice."[39] Such was the decision, according to Ennodius,

---

[33] *VE* 131: "At eminentissimus rex infit, quo loquente adtonita de voluntate eius corda pavor artabat." See Cesa (1988), 193, who concludes that the translation of Cook (1942), 185, is mistaken. It is not the audience that is afraid, but Theoderic himself, and this happens to the king's credit, for other rulers in the *Vita Epiphanii* (such as Anthemius) remained haughty in the face of the bishop's initial rebukes.

[34] *VE* 131: "'Quamvis te, venerabilis episcope, pro meritorum tuorum luce suspiciam et multa apud me confusionis tempore reposuisses beneficia.'"

[35] *Ibid.*: "'regnandi tamen necessitas qua concludimur misericordiae quam suades non ubique pandit accessum, et inter res duras nascentis imperii pietatis dulcedinem censurae pellit utilitas.'"

[36] This is the subject of *VE* 131–3, the scriptural passages in question being 1 Samuel 15 and 28. On the identification, Cook (1942), 213–14, and Cesa (1988), 193. That Theoderic saw fit to quote this passage is quite interesting given Philostorgius' claim (*HE* 2.15) that the Gothic translation of the Old Testament omitted these "martial" books owing to the warlike tendencies of the Goths. The verbal similarities between the tribe at war with the Israelites in these passages (the Amalekites) and the dynasty of Theoderic (the Amali) is too interesting to ignore, though the connection is probably mere coincidence.

[37] *VE* 133–4: "'Ultionem suscipit qui detractat inferre: vim divini iudicii aut adtenuat aut contemnit qui hosti suo, cum potitur, indulget.... Qui criminosos patitur inpune transire, ad crimina hortatur insontes.'"

[38] *VE* 134: "'Tamen quia precibus vestris, quibus superna assentiunt, obsistere terrena non possunt, omnibus generaliter errorem dimittemus.'"

[39] *Ibid*: "'Nullius caput noxa prosternet, quoniam potestis et apud deum nostrum agere, ut sceleratae mentes a proposita sui perversitate discedant. Paucos tamen, quos malorum incentores

of a "very excellent king," who was "most ready to show every kind of kindness."[40]

TO LIVE AGAIN

By the opening years of Theoderic's reign, then, Epiphanius had accomplished another diplomatic miracle through the use of his eloquent words, and the right of Roman liberty, to Theoderic's credit, was restored to all but a few brazen offenders. This episode, however, was far from over. As already suggested, good rulers in the *Life of Epiphanius*, men like Nepos, for instance, had been acclaimed for their diligence in taking the initiative in matters of Italian or Ligurian prosperity. Unsolicited, they sought the assistance of their fellow citizens, not requiring intercessors like Epiphanius to call local maladies to their attention. Theoderic, of course, had required Epiphanius' intervention to this point in Ennodius' account, but now, in keeping with this tradition of attentive and compassionate rulership, he pulled the saint of Pavia aside and revealed to him his own incredible concern for the well-being of Italy and specifically the province of Liguria.

This was a land, in his estimation, that was utterly ruined, and something had to be done. "You see every place in Italy devoid of its native inhabitants," Theoderic informed the bishop. "To my sadness fruitful plains bring forth thorns and useless plants, and Liguria, that mother of human harvests, for whom a numerous progeny of farmers once existed, presents to our gaze barren earth, now bereaved and sterile."[41] A personified and saddened Liguria, he claimed, voiced her objections to him; once "fruitful with vines," she now appeared wretched and "uncombed by plows."[42] It was grievous, Epiphanius was told, that "no liquid is poured out onto the lips of those whom antiquity called *Oenotrios* from their supply of wine."[43] And indeed, though the Burgundians were largely responsible for this transformation

---

fuisse cognovi, locorum suorum tantummodo habitatione privabo.'" Cf. Cesa (1988), 193, who rightly disagrees with Cook's reading of a suspension of capital punishment.

[40] *VE* 135: "praecellentissimus rex ... ad omnem benignitatem paratissimus."

[41] *VE* 138: "'Vides universa Italiae loca originariis viduata cultoribus. In tristitiam meam segetum ferax spinas atque iniussa plantaria campus adportat, et illa mater humanae messis Liguria, cui numerosa agricolarum solebat constare progenies, orbata atque sterilis ieiunum cespitem nostris monstrat obtutibus.'" This explanation is clearly Liguro-centric. Cf. Cesa (1988), 194.

[42] *VE* 138: "'Interpellat me terra, quocumque respicio uberem vinetis faciem, cum aratris inpexa contristat.'"

[43] *VE* 139: "'O dolor! nullus umor illorum labris infunditur, quos a vini copia Oenotrios vocavit antiquitas.'" Cesa (1988), 194–5, notes echoes of a number of late antique poets in these lines and suggests that this would have rendered Theoderic's speech poetic and quite solemn. Though true, the use of "Oenotrios" for the "ancient" inhabitants of Italy (and specifically Liguria) is

owing to their recent inroads and seizure of Ligurian captives, it was the ruler of Italy who would take the blame, if the problem was not corrected.[44] Valuing Epiphanius (and his powers) more than any other bishop in his realm,[45] therefore, Theoderic asked the saint whether he would, "with Christ's assistance," take up the burden of an embassy to the Burgundian king, Gundobad, and secure the release of these Italian captives.[46] The sight of Epiphanius alone, Theoderic suggested, would be a fitting ransom,[47] and he promised that, after the bishop's return, "Liguria would live again … and happiness and fecundity [would be restored] to the soil."[48]

This was an important speech within the *Life of Epiphanius*, casting Theoderic as the most caring and compassionate of all the late Roman rulers depicted in this work. In response, Epiphanius would soon undertake the second of his transalpine missions (this time with Ennodius in company), securing the release of more than six thousand captive Ligurians.[49] But his immediate response to Theoderic's words is especially revealing. Hearing that Liguria would live again, the bishop of Pavia, himself a proven master of eloquence, was left literally speechless. "Venerable *princeps*," he addressed his lord,

> if it were possible for the amount of joy that you have placed in my heart to be embraced in speech, I would pour forth an immediate and uninterrupted [stream of] words for the wealth of your merits. But what a break in the succession of my words denies, my tears of joy make clear; tears begotten of exultation, rather than the children of grief. Know, then, that I feel more than I am able to say in rendering thanks to the best king.[50]

ironic, given that the term originally referred to the inhabitants of southwestern Italy (i.e. the region of Italy from which Cassiodorus hailed).

[44] *VE* 139: "'Haec quamvis Burgundio inmitis exercuit, nos tamen, si non emendamus, admisimus.'"

[45] *VE* 136 (which introduces the private conversation between Theoderic and Epiphanius): "'gloriose antistes … cum tot in regni nostri circulo pontifices esse videantur, tu potissimum in tanta re quasi unicus eligaris.'"

[46] *VE* 140: "'Suscipe ergo Christo adiuvante huius laboris sarcinam.'"

[47] *VE* 141: "'Mihi crede, pretium captivitatis Italicae erit vester aspectus.'" Cesa (1988), 194–5, suggests that Theoderic's (unsolicited) decision to use diplomacy in this matter is reminiscent of the "bloodless victory" ideal urged by Epiphanius himself in so many of his earlier "royal" encounters. To Theoderic's credit, then, he offered exactly the solution that Epiphanius would have wanted.

[48] *VE* 141: "'Polliceor tibi redivivum statum Liguriae, polliceor soli laetitiam et post Transalpinam peregrinationem reducem fecunditatem. Ex accidenti aurum tibi commodatur pro qua talis legatus acturus est.'"

[49] For the embassy, *VE* 147–77. Ennodius mentions his participation at *VE* 171. For more than six thousand, *VE* 172.

[50] *VE* 142–3: "'Quanto, venerabilis princeps, pectus meum tripudio repleveris, si sermone posset ambiri, pro divitiis meritorum tuorum inmeditata et continua verba profunderem. Sed quam

Lost for words and teary-eyed, Epiphanius had already said so much, and when he finally turned to specifics, he remained unable to find the right words. "Is it in your justice, or your skill in battle, or, what is more excellent than both of these, your piety that I should mention that you have surpassed all prior emperors?"[51]

Concern for Liguria and its inhabitants, therefore, had rendered Theoderic not just worthy of imperial succession, but better than all those emperors who had preceded him.[52] And as far as the bishop of Pavia was concerned, there was only one model through which a worthy comparison could be made. Theoderic was no Valentinian or Trajan, but the ideal Christian ruler, King David, and when it came to sparing lives, even David was no match for the new *princeps* of the West. "Good God," Epiphanius exclaimed, "how much will You remunerate the deed of this man [Theoderic] who negotiates for the freedom of so many thousands of the oppressed, You who have exalted that man [David] for sparing the blood of one man!"[53]

Liguria's Emperor

These early events, conventionally dated to 495 and hence before Romulus Augustus' *ornamenta* had been restored to Italy, placed Theoderic firmly within the imperial tradition. There had been problems at the beginning of his reign, but the care and compassion that he showed toward Liguria and its inhabitants were powerful and legitimizing. More so than Ricimer and Odovacer, more so than even Anthemius or Nepos, the Theoderic depicted in the *Life of Epiphanius* became Liguria's patron and protector,

sermoni meo interceptus denegetur successus, monstrant lacrimae gaudiorum, quas dolorum alumnas nunc parturit exultatio. Proinde intellege, ad referendas optimo regi ... gratias plus me sentire posse quam eloqui.'"

[51] VE 143: "'Iustitia prius an bellorum exercitatione an, quod his praestantius est, omnes retro imperatores te pietate superasse commemorem?'"

[52] For a similar interpretation, Hodgkin (1896), 333, n. 1. Cf. Cesa (1988), 198, and Reydellet (1981), 170, who both suggest that "retro imperatores" in VE 143 (cited in the previous note) is oppositional in nature, rendering Theoderic something other (albeit better) than a Roman emperor. The passage is clearly intended to highlight Theoderic's superiority, but it seems not to exclude him from imperial succession, especially given the reference to his emperorship found in VE 187 (discussed later).

[53] VE 144: "'David legimus ... quod oblato minibus suis Sauli pepercit inimico.... Deus bone, in quanta remuneratione huius factum suscipis pro tot milium oppressorum libertate tractantis, qui illum pro unius servati hominis sanguine sublimasti!'" For David's "ransoming" of Saul, see 1 Samuel 24. See also Rota (2001a), 235f., who discusses Ennodius' conception of Theoderic as an Old Testament priest-king along the model of contemporary Byzantine rulers (*princeps et sacerdos*).

Liguria's emperor. Nor were these the only instances recorded in the *Vita* when the new ruler of Italy demonstrated his piety and benevolence to this region, acts that helped to contribute to nascent conceptions of a golden age.

As soon as Epiphanius returned from Gaul, in fact, yet another opportunity presented itself. Those who had just been liberated faced uncertainty at home, and the bishop of Pavia was "fatigued with concern," hoping to secure their properties.[54] He was particularly anxious about calamities befalling members of the nobility,[55] the *lumina Liguriae* and their descendents, Romans who had proven themselves useful to hard-pressed Italian monarchs like Nepos. Yet he feared, given his recent success, that approaching the king in person might be interpreted the wrong way, as a request for recompense or an act of vainglory.[56] Instead of journeying to Ravenna, therefore, he dispatched a letter expressing his concerns, and "the most pious king," consistent with prior gestures, granted the bishop everything he had asked "without hesitation."[57] Through Epiphanius' intervention and Theoderic's generosity, Ennodius wrote, those once in exile were transformed into the wealthiest of men;[58] they were "revived through the concessions of the excellent *princeps*," "bestowed with their [ancient] rights,"[59] and restored, as it were, to their prior noble condition.

Moves like this assisted Liguria in making a postwar recovery, helping to fulfill the promise of Theoderic that this region, so important to Italo-Romans like Ennodius, would live again. Following this episode, nearly two years passed without incident, and by then it seemed to those in Ravenna that this province's situation had improved. As a result, certain temporary measures were no longer deemed necessary, and among the casualties was Liguria's exemption from paying tribute. Yet, according to Ennodius' account, the move had been too hasty on Theoderic's part and the Ligurians were still incapable of making such payments. The "burden

---

54 *VE* 178: "Mox tamen ut rediit curis ex more animum fatigat, ne forte … proprii census possessione turbarentur."
55 *Ibid.*: "praecipue ob nobilium considerationem personarum, quibus inmanior … calamitas."
56 *VE* 179–80: "Ad regem … ire noluit, ne forte laboris sui vicissitudinem in relatione gratiarum … coram positus videretur exigere … aut occurrendo per adrogantiam pronuntiaretur intemperans."
57 *VE* 181: "Igitur omnia, quae a piissimo rege pro miseris per paginam petiit singularis antistes, incunctanter obtinuit."
58 *VE* 180 (Ennodius addressing a long-dead Epiphanius): "illi, quos de exulibus ditissimos reddidisti."
59 *VE* 182: "Postquam tamen omnes qui revocati fuerant indultu praeferendi principis iure suo donati sunt."

of tribute," Ennodius wrote, was "scarcely bearable to the weak Ligurians and their toiling shoulders,"[60] and the aggrieved looked to Epiphanius for assistance. "[Your] citizens were restored to their fatherland in vain," they told the bishop, "if you do not assist those now living in peril on their ancestral soil."[61] Convinced, a frail Epiphanius made straightaway for Ravenna,[62] and, although Theoderic was to blame for this embassy, to his credit the very sight of Epiphanius made it clear that he had made a serious error. Addressing a now-dead Epiphanius and speaking on behalf of his fellow Ligurians, Ennodius claimed, "Before you even spoke, you exposed our necessities through your arrival."[63] Theoderic, a "most lofty king, who had hoped eagerly to see you," was now "saddened by your presence."[64]

Epiphanius then addressed his *princeps* with his customary eloquence, demonstrating in the process the full extent to which he viewed Theoderic as a bona fide Roman emperor. "Venerable king," he began, "understand with the accustomed tranquility of your mind the prayers of your subjects ... [for] it is your condition, invincible leader, to be continuously merciful."[65] Referencing the imperial virtues of serenity and mercy, he continued by urging Theoderic to give "to your Ligurians" whatever resources might be available, explaining that "a momentary indulgence is the profit of future times."[66] Words echoing these sentiments would be penned later in Theoderic's own name,[67] but in this speech Epiphanius strove to connect such concepts with ideas of Italian resurgence and imperial stability. A "good *princeps*," Theoderic was told, "cherishes his reputation along with his virtues and arranges his kingdom as if about to pass it on to his progeny. Tottering lords delight in what they receive; but the most

---

[60] *Ibid.*: "Nam infirmis Ligurum et labantibus umeris vix ferenda tributorum sarcina mandabatur."

[61] *VE* 183 (again, addressing Epiphanius): "Doceris frustra reddidisse patriae cives, si illis in solo avito periclitantibus non adesses."

[62] Epiphanius' failing health and the obstacles that he encountered along the way are found in *VE* 183–4.

[63] *VE* 184: "Exposuisti necessitates nostras adventu tuo, antequam diceres."

[64] *Ibid.*: "Contristatus est de praesentia tui et ille eminentissimus rex, qui te videre ambienter optabat."

[65] *VE* 185: "'Solita, rex venerabilis, mentis tranquillitate famulorum preces intellege.... Lex tua est, ductor invicte, misereri iugiter.'"

[66] *VE* 186: "Liguribus tuis largire quod proferas, tribue quod reponas. Futurorum quaestus est temporalis indulgentia." For a similar (financial) reading, Cook (1942), 107. Cf. Cesa (1988), 115 and 208, who suggests that the passage refers to the contemporary glory that Theoderic will acquire from his actions and later rewards that he will receive in heaven.

[67] For such indulgences in Italy, see later discussion; for Gaul, Chp. 10.

secure in what they give away."[68] The *status Liguriae*, in other words, was a reflection of the *status reipublicae* and its ruler, and more telling still, the "wealth of the land owner," Theoderic was advised, was the wealth "of a good *imperator*."[69] With these words in mind, Epiphanius asked Theoderic to grant immunity to the province for the coming year,[70] an act that would prove, by implication, that the Goth truly was a *bonus princeps* and *bonus imperator*.

Language like this, of course, was deliberately flattering and intended to reveal to Theoderic the error of his ways, softening critiques with soothing compliments. Though true, and though Theoderic was guilty, the response that Ennodius soon placed in the king's mouth did much to exonerate him. Indeed, Theoderic's words provided a legitimate excuse for his otherwise unsettling behavior. Unlike a number of his recent predecessors, his restoration of Liguria's tributary status had not been an issue of neglect or greed, but one of genuine necessity. "The burden of massive expenses," Theoderic explained, "constantly constrains us," and as these were still uncertain times for his early regime, it was imperative that he "grant gifts incessantly to envoys for the sake of peace."[71] It was true that Liguria required succor, but the well-being of an entire realm outweighed that of a single province. All of Italy, not just Liguria, required peace and security; all of what was left of the once-proud Roman Empire needed to live again; and such a transformation could only be afforded with money and a willingness on the part of everyone to endure certain temporary hardships.

Prior obligations, Ennodius suggested, prevented Theoderic from canceling the tribute owed by the Ligurians for the coming year. But the ruler of Italy could not and did not want to disappoint his venerable friend,

---

[68] *VE* 186: "'Boni principis mos est cum virtutibus amare famam et regnum ita ordinare, tamquam ad stirpis suae posteros transiturum. Nutantes domini haec tantum quae accipiunt diligunt, firmissimi illa potius quae dimittunt.'"

[69] *VE* 187: "'Boni imperatoris est possessoris opulentia.'" It is quite surprising that Cook (1942), Cesa (1988), and Reydellet (1981) do not comment on the use of *imperatoris* in this passage. It clearly suggests, contrary to the thesis of Reydellet (adopted by Cesa), that Theoderic was being placed within an imperial mold. See Hodgkin (1896), 340, n. 2, and Moorhead (1992), 46, for similar conclusions.

[70] *VE* 187: "'Concede immunitatem anni praesentis Liguriae, qui eos ab externis.'"

[71] *VE* 188: "Ad haec princeps: 'Licet nos inmanium expensarum pondus inlicitet et pro ipsorum quiete legatis indesinenter munera largiamur.'" Nor was Theoderic making up lame excuses when it came to the number of embassies that had been (and would continued to be) necessary. One particularly mobile ambassador, Senarius, even made note of his twenty-five journeys on behalf of Theoderic in his epitaph (Fiebiger 2, #8). For Senarius, *PLRE* 2, 988–9. On "Ostrogothic" diplomacy under Theoderic, Wolfram (1988), 306–24; Moorhead (1992), 173–211; Claude (1993); Prostko-Prostyński (1994a), 103–55; Shanzer (1996/7); Pricoco (1997); and Gillett (2003), 148–219.

the friend of God, or his Ligurian flock.[72] "It is useful," he explained to Epiphanius, "to do whatever you enjoin; everything that you instruct is helpful."[73] Unable to grant the complete exemption that had been requested, Theoderic nonetheless offered a compromise in Epiphanius' favor, showing his piety and benevolence by canceling two-thirds of the tribute and stipulating that the remainder needed to be paid, "lest the constriction of our treasury create greater expenses for our Romans."[74]

As the *Life of Epiphanius* drew to a close, Liguria had been given Theoderic's special favor once more, benefiting from the patronage of this ruler and the special relationship that he had formed with its bishop, the hero of Ennodius' account. In the few years that he had reigned supreme, thousands from this province had been redeemed from captivity, countless noblemen had had their livelihoods ensured by his pious intervention, and the tribute owed by everyone had been reduced or commuted altogether. Though the Theoderic described within this work was at times far from perfect and could even err toward wickedness, he was portrayed as the best of Italy's late Roman rulers, an easterner to be sure, but also an unquestionably pious Christian, a *bonus princeps*, and even a *bonus imperator*. Because of Theoderic, Ennodius claimed, Liguria was beginning to live again. And while Epiphanius himself soon departed from this world, providing a natural terminus for his *Vita*, the tradition of Theoderican benefaction found within his biography lived on.

A MERE HAYSTACK

Epiphanius died in 496, shortly before the return of the envoy Festus and the western imperial insignia from Constantinople. As the *Life of Epiphanius* suggests, his death coincided with a period of recovery for much of Italy, when the early Theoderican regime was making the safety and prosperity of all Romans, not just Ligurians, an important priority. All of Italy, it was hoped, would recover, and sound fiscal policies mixed with compassionate (yet controlled) benefaction soon paved the way for this, providing tangible evidence of Italian restoration and renewal. As seen earlier, Epiphanius himself had once advised Theoderic to give to his Ligurians whatever resources he was storing in his coffers, suggesting that "a momentary indulgence is the profit of future times" and that "the

---

[72] *VE* 189: "'ne ... supplicatio tua expectata patriae gaudia non reportet.'"
[73] *VE* 188: "'Opus est fieri quicquid iniunxeris, iuvat omne quod praecipis.'"
[74] *VE* 189: "'Duas tamen praesentis indictionis fiscalis calculi partes cedemus, tertiam tantummodo suscepturi, ne ... aerarii nostri angustia Romanis pariat maiora dispendia.'"

wealth of the land is [that] of a good emperor." Though, as Theoderic himself had claimed, the emerging Ravenna government was still at that point too constrained by a host of other obligations to comply fully with this request, words like these did not fall on deaf ears; they would, with time, define the imperial benevolence of the Theoderican golden age.

Generosity, however, required financial stability, something that was lacking when Theoderic took up the reins of Roman government. Indeed, beyond the crippling devastation caused by years of warfare, a number of sources make clear the nearly exhausted financial resources bequeathed by the regime of Odovacer, a factor that must have rendered Italy's recovery all the more difficult. Ennodius' panegyric, for instance, decried the "fail-ure of public resources" caused by Odovacer's lavish spending and rapa-cious overtaxation,[75] while the account found in the *Anonymus Valesianus* claimed that Theoderic had "found the public treasury completely made of hay,"[76] dried up and emptied of monies. Though the latter source went on to credit Theoderic for enriching the treasury "through his own labor,"[77] assistance during this time of penury was largely dependent on local Roman notables. These men, some of whom had remained parti-sans of Odovacer to the bitter end, understood the workings of Italy and the Italian economy far better than the newly arrived Goths, and, more-over, their preeminent role in the early days of Theoderic's reign granted it additional legitimacy in the eyes of Italian onlookers. Loyal Italo-Romans became sharers in the secrets of Theoderic's counsels, guiding their sover-eign and Italy itself "towards the hope of restoration," their maintenance of power and authority making it clear that the western Roman Empire, as an institution, continued to endure.[78]

Theoderic's first praetorian prefect of Italy, for example, the noble Liberius already encountered in prior chapters, was instrumental in this regard and continued to be an asset to the Theoderican regime for decades.

---

[75] *PanTh* 23, with Chp. 1.

[76] *AnonVal* 60: "aerarium publicum ex toto faeneum invenisset."

[77] *Ibid.*: "suo labore recuperavit et opulentum fecit."

[78] For sharers in counsels, *PanTh* 51: "concutiens fecisti consiliorum participem in secretis popu-lum iam probatum." Cf. *PanTh* 57, discussed later. For the hope of restoration, Ennodius, #447.3 (a personal letter to Liberius, discussed more fully in the following note): "ad spem reparationis." Beyond Liberius, *VE* 135 credits a certain *vir inlustrissimus* named Urbicus, who "surpassed Cicero in eloquence and Cato in equity," with the drafting of the general amnesty granted to all Romans in the aftermath of Theoderic's victory over Odovacer. For Urbicus, *PLRE* 2, 1191. There were still others, such as Cassiodorus' own father (see Chp. 2) and the senators Faustus and Festus (see Chp. 3), who proved instrumental at this time, particularly when it came to Constantinople. Cassiodorus himself, however, would have been too young to participate. Cf. Schmidt (1927), 729.

In a personal letter Ennodius recalled that at the beginning of Liberius' tenure as prefect (begun in 493) "Italy was barely supported by the fatigue of public expenses," but that he had, with divine assistance, caused "royal resources to flow forth without the wickedness of private disturbance," preventing the demands of the *imperator* (and by this he meant Theoderic) from becoming detrimental.[79] Similarly, Theoderic himself eulogized Liberius before the Senate for "increasing the census revenues, not by adding to them but by preserving them, while at the same time collecting with foresighted diligence those revenues that had wrongly come to be diffused."[80] "We felt that the taxes had been increased," the *patres conscripti* were told, "but you did not know that your tribute had been enlarged. The fisc grew and private utility suffered no ruin."[81]

Diligence and careful attention, on the part of both Italo-Roman statesmen and Theoderic himself, paid off during these early years. By the turn of the century, the haystack that was once Odovacer's treasury had been replaced with glittering pieces of copper, silver, and gold. Such enrichment naturally provided Theoderic's government with greater resources with which to operate and thus more directly impact the situation on the ground in Italy.[82] Though important, the Ravenna government was not the only beneficiary of this process, a fact that served, in its own way, to endear further the new order of the day to contemporary Italo-Romans. "The resources of the Republic," Ennodius exclaimed in praise of his foresighted *princeps*, "grew along with the profits of private citizens ... there is a diffusion of wealth everywhere."[83] Italy's Romans, it seemed by the early sixth century, were getting richer, and their increased

---

[79] #447.3–5: "vix pascebatur Italia publici sudore dispendii.... Iuverunt venerabile superna consilium.... tu primus fecisti regales copias sine malo privatae concussionis effluere.... Tuta enim tunc est subiectorum opulentia, quando non indiget imperator." It is again remarkable, and a testament to the lack of attention paid to Ennodius' works (especially his *epistulae*), that Reydellet (1981); Prostko-Prostyński (1994a), 180 (n. 127); Moorhead (1992), 46 (n. 57); and others have neglected the use of *imperator* in this letter.

[80] *Variae* 2.16.4: "Is igitur infatigabili cura, quod difficillimum virtutis genus est, sub generalitatis gratia publica videtur procurasse compendia, censum non addendo, sed conservando protendens, dum illa, quae consueverant male dispergi, bene industria providente collegit." These "male dispergi" revenues were doubtless payments of tribute illicitly pocketed by those responsible for collecting them. A similar loss of revenues is recorded in *Variae* 5.14 in reference to tax collection in the province of Pannonia Savia.

[81] *Variae* 2.16.4: "Sensimus auctas illationes, vos addita tributa nescitis. Ita utrumque sub ammiratione perfectum est, ut et fiscus cresceret et privata utilitas damna nulla perferret."

[82] Cf. Ensslin (1959), 242–4; Saitta (1999), 207; and Brogiolo and Possenti (2001), 271. For a more negative view, Claude (1996).

[83] *PanTh* 58: "Creverunt reipublicae opes cum privatorum profectibus ... opum ubique diffusio est." For similar sentiments, Ennodius, #458.9 (*In Christi Signo*).

disposable income likewise helped to foster trade, which served to increase contemporary standards of living. Trade, in its simplest guise, provided a source of needed goods during inevitable times of scarcity. More importantly, it was the source from which conspicuously Roman luxury goods could be acquired, items that proclaimed Italy's prosperity and even superiority through their mere availability and consumption.[84] "Merchants from various provinces," it was said, flocked to Italy,[85] allowing "anyone to acquire whatever he needed at any hour," while the price of basic commodities like wheat and wine, once cripplingly high, was driven to historic lows.[86]

Doubtless, certain economic policies enacted by the Ravenna government encouraged such developments. The counts placed in charge of Rome's principal harbors at Portus and Ostia, for example, were told to treat all merchants justly. "A greedy hand," it was said, "closes a port and, when it clenches its fingers, it likewise confines the sails of ships."[87] The counts of Ravenna, whose port at Classe seems to have flourished at this time,[88] were similarly instructed to restrain their staffs with "equity" and to "pay attention to the tolls of merchants, neither exacting too much nor abandoning them through bribery."[89] Not all of Italy's cities were experiencing the same economic recovery, of course. Some witnessed further decline as their prior disconnection from wider trading networks increased;[90] other, better connected cities simply struggled to maintain themselves, requiring remissions of tribute or special trade exemptions in the face of

---

[84] Those trappings of civilization sent to Gaul, like water clocks and citharae (discussed in Chp. 5), are primary examples of this.

[85] *AnonVal* 72: "Negotiantes vero de diversis provinciis ad ipsum concurrebant."

[86] *AnonVal* 73: "qui<vi>s quod opus habebat faciebat qua hora vellet, ac si in die. Sexaginta modios tritici in solidum ipsius tempore emerunt, et vinum triginta amphoras in solidum"; with *AnonVal* 53, where the price of wheat during Theoderic's campaigns against Odovacer rose to "usque ad sex solidos modius tritici." See also Pferschy (1981), who argues that, while these numbers may not be correct, the basic idea of reduced costs during Theoderic's reign probably is.

[87] *Variae* 7.9.3: "Avara manus portum claudit et cum digitos attrahit, navium simul vela concludit."

[88] See Maioli (1994), 239–42, and (1995); Brogiolo (1994), 214; and Deliyannis (2010), 117–18.

[89] *Variae* 7.14.2–3: "Negotiatorum operas consuetas nec nimias exigas nec venalitate derelinquas.... Officium tuum aequitatis consideratione moderare."

[90] For a discussion of the archaeological evidence, Brogiolo and Possenti (2001), 268–71. For this process beginning in the late fourth/early fifth century, Brogiolo (1999), 100–9. Ward-Perkins (1984), 14–25, suggests that a change in aristocratic values informed it. Cf. Claude (1996) for an especially negative appraisal based primarily on the *Variae*. He concludes that, while Theoderic meant well, he inherited a bad economy and at best could only stabilize it.

unforeseeable hardships, such as bad harvests or foreign invasion.[91] But even these indulgences were important and, moreover, are indicative of the extent of economic recovery achieved over the first decade of Theoderican rule. Indeed, Liguria itself had been granted only a partial reduction in tribute in 496. Yet by 508/9 the Cottian Alps and other regions, including the newly reestablished prefecture of the Gauls, had had their entire tribute remitted, and by a self-described *providentissimus* and *benignus* (most foresighted and kind) *princeps* no less.[92]

From the Ashes of Cities

Increased and surplus revenues also made it possible for Theoderic (and other wealthy nobles in his realm) to dedicate vast sums of money to traditional acts of civic euergetism, allowing "the benevolence of our reign" to "emulate its profits, so that its kindness expands its gifts to the extent that the Republic has been improved."[93] Many of these projects of civic benefaction were quite conspicuous in their day, their number constituting as a whole a true renaissance of building, the so-called *renovatio urbium* of the Theoderican epoch. This movement, in Theoderic's own words, "preserves the reported wonders of the ancients for the praise of our clemency,"[94] while adorning "new constructions with the glory of antiquity."[95] Just as Italy was once again the republic ruled by a *princeps*, just as the empire was once more protected by valiant and virtuous soldiers, so too did its cities glimmer with their venerable monuments restored or with new constructions built in imitation of their ancient style. This was, beyond the restoration of lost provinces to be discussed in Part V, perhaps the single most important factor that contributed to contemporary conceptions of blessedness and a golden age.[96] In the aftermath of fifth-century devastation, Ennodius marveled that he now saw "unforeseen beauty" arising

---

[91] See, for example, *Variae* 2.38 (in reference to the city of Sipontum). For the same kinds of exemptions in the Gallic Prefecture, see Chp. 10. Such temporary measures were not limited to the reign of Theoderic and could apply to entire provinces. Cf. *Variae* 4.36, 9.10, 9.15, 12.7, 12.14, and 12.28.

[92] For Cottian Alps, *Variae* 4.36: "providentissimi principis"; for the Gallic Prefecture, *Variae* 3.42: "principe benigno," with Chp. 10. Similar ideas are expressed in the citations provided in the previous footnote.

[93] *Variae* 2.37.1: "Provectum regni nostri benignitas debet aemulari, ut tantum humanitas relaxet dona, quantum res publica suscepit augmenta."

[94] *Variae* 2.39.1: "audita veterum miracula ad laudem clementiae nostrae volumus continere."

[95] *Variae* 7.15.1: "ut ... nova vetustatis gloria vestiamus."

[96] Cf. La Rocca (1993) and Brogiolo and Possenti (2001), whose emphasis on the propagandistic nature and/or value of such works has the unfortunate consequence of downplaying their

"out of the ashes of cities ... and palatine roofs everywhere reddened [with new tiles] under the abundance of [Theoderic's] *civilitas*." Buildings, he exclaimed, were completed even before he learned that they had been laid out.[97] In his chronicle Cassiodorus likewise recorded that "very many cities were renewed under [Theoderic's] happy Empire ... and ancient wonders were surpassed by his great works,"[98] while the *Anonymus Valesianus* celebrated Theoderic as a "lover of buildings and restorer of cities," providing examples of the "many acts of kindness" that he had shown.[99] At Ravenna, for instance, "he restored the aqueduct, which Emperor Trajan had made," "saw to the completion of a palace," and "built porticos." At Verona "he made baths and a palace," "added a portico [stretching] from the gates to the palace," "restored the aqueduct," and "encircled the city with some new walls." And at Pavia, finally, "he built a palace, baths, amphitheater, and some walls."[100]

Indeed, it is true that only a select few (albeit important) cities are known to have received extensive royal patronage, and even then only in the form of limited prestige projects,[101] but as the *Life of Epiphanius* has already suggested, the impression that such displays of imperial benevolence

---

contemporary, Italo-Roman reception and significance. Ennodius, Cassiodorus, and countless others had not been deceived.

[97] *PanTh* 56: "Video insperatum decorem urbium cineribus evenisse et sub civilitatis plenitudine palatina ubique tecta rutilare. Video ante perfecta aedificia, quam me contigisset disposita."

[98] *CassChron*, anno 500: "sub cuius felici imperio plurimae renovantur urbes ... magnisque eius operibus antiqua miracula superantur."

[99] *AnonVal* 70: "Erat enim amator fabricarum et restaurator civitatum"; and *AnonVal* 72: "Sed et per alias civitates multa beneficia praestitit."

[100] *AnonVal* 71: "Hic aquae ductum Ravennae restauravit, quem princeps Traianus fecerat.... Palatium usque ad perfectum fecit.... Portica circa palatium perfecit. Item Veronae thermas et palatium fecit et a porta usque ad palatium porticum addidit. Aquae ductum ... renovavit et aquam intromisit. Muros alios novos circuit civitatem. Item Ticini palatium, thermas, amphitheatrum, et alios muros civitatis fecit." Two *fistulae* record Theoderic's repair to Trajan's aqueduct. See Fiebiger 3, #7. For other cities, see later discussion. On the strategic, economic, and historical importance of these (primarily) northern cities, Siena (1984) and Brogiolo and Possenti (2001).

[101] This had always been the case throughout imperial history, however, and especially after the second century. Compare Anastasius' own building program in the East as described by Haarer (2006), chp. 7. It is nonetheless largely for this reason that scholars have had mixed views concerning the impact of Theoderic's *renovatio urbium*. Some, like Siena (1984); Ward-Perkins (1984); Johnson (1988); and Pani Ermini (1995), have viewed the movement in positive terms, describing it as an inversion of certain late antique trends that led to the end of the classical city in Italy. Others, such as MacPherson (1989); La Rocca (1993); Brogiolo (1994 and 1999); Brogiolo and Possenti (2001); and Christie (2006), who either look at these developments over a longer *durée* or emphasize their propagandistic value, have been more keen to point out the limitations of this program, citing its inability to stem the tide of urban decay, its restricted range of application, and/or its failure to live up to prior imperial greatness.

could leave at a local level was powerful. And as the words of Ennodius, Cassiodorus, and the *Anonymus Valesianus* have just demonstrated, the contemporary impact of these projects had been quite significant. Northern cities like Ravenna, Verona, Pavia, Milan, Parma, Como, Aquileia, and still others received new or improved walls, palaces, aqueducts, churches, baths, and a host of other impressive and glorious buildings, all reiterating to their respective inhabitants their own importance within a newly revived and reinvigorated Roman Empire and connecting such ideas with the intervention of a caring and devoted *princeps*, Theoderic.[102] Other cities, such as Spoleto to the south, received monetary stipends for the upkeep of structures like bathing complexes, truly Roman amenities whose continued existence served both the good health and sheer enjoyment of local residents, again to Theoderic's credit.[103] In still other cities, private individuals were conceded the right to make use of public resources for the sake of civic beautification, so that "what has fallen down, decayed from old age, might stand back up, reused."[104] Though Theoderic might not have received recognition in every instance, the very transformation achieved fit into a larger picture of urban renewal at this time, fueling sentiments of restoration and resurgence.

To go through all the evidence for this *renovatio urbium*, literary, epigraphic, and archaeological, though certainly possible, would nonetheless prove overly repetitious and potentially tedious for the reader.[105] Many cities and many individuals benefited from Theoderican patronage and generally in the same basic ways.[106] One city, however, stands out before all the rest, not simply because of the extent of the benefaction granted to it, but also because of its historic significance within the totality of the Roman world. This was Rome, and it will be with Rome's restored prominence and prestige within Theoderic's Roman Empire (a final case study) that Part IV will now conclude.

---

[102] For more extensive discussions of literary and archaeological evidence for these projects, see the authors cited in the preceding note, as well as Maioli (1994); Brogiolo (2007); Marazzi (2007); and Deliyannis (2010), chp. 4 especially.

[103] For Spoleto, *Variae* 2.37. Later Lombard tradition records that Theoderic established a palace in this city, though no contemporary evidence supports this. For a discussion, Siena (1984), 524.

[104] *Variae* 4.24.1 (granting the use of public spolia to the deacon Helpidius): "rediviva consurgant, quae annositate inclinata corruerant." Cf. *Variae* 3.9, 3.49, and 4.31.

[105] Moreover, syntheses of this sort are already available via the specialist literature cited earlier (much in English).

[106] Hence the common distinction in the scholarship cited previously between "defenses" (usually walls), "sanitation and health" (usually aqueducts and/or baths), and "important public buildings" (usually palaces and entertainment complexes).

8

ROME REJUVENATED

ROMA CAPUT MUNDI

Rome gave its name to the empire and was once so essential that it was known as the "head of the world" (*caput mundi*). Though emperors spent much of their reigns along the frontiers and away from the capital, ideologies of Rome's centrality persisted, and emperors were expected, in the very least, to cultivate a deferential relationship with this city, honoring its Senate and people as a means of demonstrating their traditional *pietas* and reverence.[1] During the later empire, as already discussed, many emperors had shunned such duties, abandoning Rome altogether for new capitals and leaving the Senate to its own devices. Such actions might have been welcome in certain circumstances,[2] but the net result was the removal of useful and necessary imperial patronage, and Rome's inhabitants, as well as other Italo-Romans, grew increasingly aware of the painful consequences.[3] Rome's infrastructure was neglected, while its elevated and unique status was called into question. Long-held privileges were revoked as early as 306, much to the outrage of the city's inhabitants, and Rome's position continued to be challenged into the fifth and early sixth centuries, as it was steadily eclipsed by a "new" Rome (Constantinople).

Despite these trends, some late antique emperors understood and appreciated the value, both practical and propagandistic, of revering the Eternal City and honoring its Senate and people, and by doing so, they were able to reconcile their more traditionally minded subjects to their reigns, earning their esteem as "good" emperors. Maxentius, for instance, resided in Rome

---

[1] Such actions helped to qualify an emperor as "optimus princeps" in Western eyes. See Wes (1967), 25–51; Cullhed (1994), 60; and Chp. 3. See later discussion for late antique examples.
[2] Matthews (1975), 20–9.
[3] See Van Dam (2007), chp. 2; also Alföldy (2001).

and made specifically Roman *Romanitas* a core ideology of his epoch.[4] Constantine, likewise, made Rome his chief residence for a time, returning to celebrate his *decennalia* and *vicennalia* with games and leaving monuments as a testament to his benefaction.[5] His son, Constantius II, also made a ceremonial visit, and though awestruck by the wondrous monuments that he saw, he too left for elsewhere, never to return.[6] More significantly, the fifth century had witnessed the occasional reestablishment of imperial courts at Rome on a semipermanent and permanent basis, while senators not only worked closely with the emperors of this period, but even became emperors themselves.[7] By the time of Theoderic's arrival, Ravenna had developed into the unquestionable administrative capital of Italy,[8] but the memory of a Roman Empire where Rome was more than just an ideological capital was still fresh in the minds of his subjects.

Theoderic, of course, was well aware of the significance of Rome and worked within this late antique legacy of neglect and reconciliation. As seen earlier, he made Rome and Romanness an intrinsic part of the restorative language of his reign, employing terms that helped to link his reign with the glory days of the late republic and principate, to a time when Italy and Rome mattered most in a Rome-centered empire. Beyond his employment of terms like *princeps* and *res publica*, he used the abbreviation *SC*, *Senatus Consulto* (by decree of the Senate) on coinage and official inscriptions, honoring the senators of Rome and showing deference to notions of senatorial *libertas*.[9] The iconography chosen for his coinage, likewise, reiterated Rome's centrality, appealing to specifically Roman

---

[4] See Cullhed (1994).

[5] Van Dam (2007), 45–61.

[6] Ammianus, *Res Gestae* 16.10. Cf. MacCormack (1981), 39–45, who draws attention to the interdependence of Rome and Constantinople in the public oration given by Themistius during this same visit. Even when Rome took center stage, its rival loomed in the background.

[7] For imperial courts at Rome, Gillett (2001); for the increased importance of senators, Matthews (1975), 353–76; Clover (1978), 169–71; and Burgarella (2001). More broadly, Jones (1964), 523–62. Senatorial emperors of the fifth century included Priscus Attalus, Petronius Maximus, and Anicius Olybrius.

[8] See Deichmann (1969–89); Mazza (2005); Pani Ermini (2005); and Deliyannis (2010), chps. 3–6.

[9] For *SC*, *ILS* 8956 (Fiebiger 1, #194): "Ex p(raecepto) d. n. Theoderici et S(enatus) C(onsulto); also Wroth (1911), 57 (#73), and Metlich (2004), 100–1 (#46a–c). Some of the "quasi-autonomous" coinage minted at Rome contains this inscription and is likely Theoderican. See later discussion. Theoderic's successors also minted coins bearing the abbreviation. For Athalaric, Wroth (1911), 69–70 (#62–71); Kraus (1928), 120–2 (#67–82); and Metlich (2004), 115 (#85a–b). For Theodahad, whose issues include the inscription "VICTORIA PRINCIPUM" (rather than "AUGG"), Wroth (1911), 75–6 (#19–24); Kraus (1928), 145–8 (#28–40); and Metlich (2004), 125–34 (with plates A–F).

forms of *Romanitas. Invicta Roma* (unconquered Rome) was a common theme, usually accompanied by a helmeted and youthful personification of the city, Theoderic's monogram (an imperial practice), or a laurel wreath encircling the phrase "DN THEODORICUS REX" (Our Lord, King Theoderic).[10] Other Theoderican coins made reference to Rome's foundational myths, depicting the Roman She-wolf (*Lupa Romana*), Ruminal Fig (*Ficus Ruminalis*), and Twin Eagles.[11] In the past, such linguistic and pictorial references had been used as a means of suggesting a kind of renaissance or refoundation for the city of Rome.[12] And now, under Theoderic, another rebirth of sorts was being proclaimed. Reflecting in wonder at the rejuvenated capital of the world, once "slipping in her tracks," Ennodius himself declared, "Give us your favor, sacred rudiments of the Lupercalian genius," and asserted that Theoderic had made Rome young again.[13]

Words like Ennodius' were inspired, in part, by a genuine enthusiasm for the building and renovation projects that were under way in Rome, just as in other cities.[14] But Rome's situation was unique, and its extensive *renovatio*, when combined with the language and imagery of the day and important pro-Roman policies, served to assert that this *princeps* honored Rome above all cities.[15] Such deference did much to legitimize Theoderic as a kind of Roman emperor and, indeed, a "good" one. More importantly, it fulfilled local expectations of Roman and Italian exceptionalism. Rome

---

[10] See Wroth (1911), 57–8 (#73–81); Kraus (1928), 90–5 (#46–74) and 99 (#98–9); and Metlich (2004), 99–103 (#44a–b, 46a–c, 47–9, and 51a–d). Monograms themselves were not strictly imperial, but their use on coins was an imperial practice imitated by the "barbarian" rulers of the West.

[11] For these "quasi-autonomous" coins, which make no reference to the eastern emperor or ruler of Italy, Wroth (1911), 98–105; Kraus (1928), 212–21; Deur (1984); and Metlich (2004), 9–10. They are usually dated to the reigns of Theoderic and Athalaric, though it is not clear under whose authority (royal or senatorial) they were minted. It makes sense, however, to see them as a royal initiative, especially since emperors are known to have minted similar ("quasi-autonomous") coins in the past. For a Constantinian example, Carson (1981), #1293. The use of similar motifs on fifth-century Vandal coinage also points to a royal initiative. See Wroth (1911), 3–4, with Clover (1991).

[12] Zanker (1988), chps. 4 and 5, and Cullhed (1994), chp. 3.

[13] *PanTh* 56: "Illa ipsa mater civitatum Roma iuveniscit marcida senectutis membra resecando. Date veniam, Lupercalis genii sacra rudimenta." The Lupercal was a cave at the foot of the Palatine Hill where Romulus and Remus had been suckled by the *Lupa Romana*. The implication, therefore, was that Theoderic had refounded Rome. This is made clear in the following sentence, which compares Theoderic's act of "driving away collapse" with Romulus' "new beginnings." See Rota (2001a), 225–6. For a different interpretation, here rejected, Kennell (2001), 65. Given recent questions about the (pagan) Lupercalia, which concluded with Pope Gelasius' banning the holiday outright in 497, Ennodius' word choice may have been poor.

[14] Cf. Rota (2001a), 225.

[15] Cf. Burns (1982), 109.

was supposed to be the capital of the world. It was not just any city, but the City (*Urbs*), and Theoderic's activities, building projects being but one form, helped to validate such traditional notions, spurring on contemporary understandings of a golden age.

WHEN IN ROME

Like the majority of late antique emperors, Theoderic did not establish his court at Rome, even if (and this is significant) he did come close to doing so and hinted throughout his reign that he was entertaining the idea. From the beginning, northern Italy had been the natural and preferable choice for the location of his court, first at Milan and Pavia, and later and more permanently at Ravenna. Not only was there a preexisting administrative infrastructure here, but this region had witnessed the greatest devastation during the campaign against Odovacer and remained a vulnerable target thereafter. Provinces like Liguria simply required more guided attention than Rome, ignorant as the city had been "of the dangers of war,"[16] while Ravenna's northern and eastern orientation spoke to the strategic concerns of the nascent Theoderican government. Still, and despite favoring the north, Theoderic had been keen to develop deferential relations with the people of Rome, especially its senators, from the very beginning of his reign. Indeed, though Rome's allegiance had vacillated during the war, Rome's senators proved instrumental in the early days of the new regime, particularly when it came to Constantinople. As already discussed, Theoderic was willing to forgive and to work with these powerful elites.[17] And through their assistance he was able to secure recognition in the East, his princely position sealed when the illustrious Festus, the *caput senatus* (head of the Senate), returned from New Rome bearing the western imperial insignia.

Throughout the 490s, then, Theoderic had cultivated a relationship with Rome and its Romans from afar. In the year 500, however, this long-distance relationship was altered when Italy's new master journeyed to Rome and celebrated his *tricennalia*, or perhaps better *decennalia*, in true imperial style.[18] A number of sources record this event and its significance.

---

[16] *PanTh* 48 (addressing Rome): "quam dubia elegit nescire certaminum."

[17] Ennodius himself acknowledged this in *VE* 135 (discussed in Chp. 7) and *PanTh* 57 and 74–5 (discussed later). See also Moorhead (1978a) and (1984a).

[18] The only source that refers to this event as a *tricennalia* is the *Anonymus Valesianus*. Many, including Wenskus (1961), 482; Claude (1978a) and (1980), 153–4; Wolfram (1988), 267; and König (1994), 148, have taken this at face value and attempted to reconcile the year 500 with the thirtieth anniversary of Theoderic's reign. Their theories, however, are not entirely

The *Life of Fulgentius of Ruspe* describes the situation as "the greatest celebration, a gathering of the Roman senate and people before the delightful presence of King Theoderic," and refers to the "glorious pomp," "popular applause," and "spectacle [of] superfluous delight" that were witnessed within the Roman Forum.[19] "How much more precious can heavenly Jerusalem be," Fulgentius admonished the monks in his midst, "if terrestrial Rome glitters so!"[20] A devout ascetic, the North African monk had found the scene revolting, but the Romans participating in the fanfare seem not to have shared his sensibilities, and other, more traditional sources echo the broader appeal of this ceremonial arrival. Cassiodorus, for example, explained in his chronicle that Theoderic's presence had been "desired by the prayers of everyone," and that once in Rome he treated the Senate "with wondrous courtesy" and "gave provisions to the Roman plebs."[21] The much longer notice found in the *Anonymus Valesianus* account is similarly laudatory and adds an element of piety that even Fulgentius might have appreciated, had he known of it. Here, a rather devout Theoderic, reminiscent of the pious ruler found in the *Life of Epiphanius*, arrived outside the walls of the city and, before doing anything else, honored Saint Peter, "worshipping as if a Catholic." Following this, he paid respect to the saint's successor, Pope Symmachus, who, accompanied by the entire Senate and people of Rome, welcomed him "with the greatest joy."[22] His

---

convincing, since they have nothing to do with Theoderic's rule over Romans. Two alternative (and seemingly better) explanations are readily available. First, this visit did not commemorate an anniversary at all, but still provided an opportunity for senatorial and popular acclamation. See Vitiello (2005a), 57–71. Second, the manuscript is corrupt and *decennalia* (ten-year anniversary) is meant. Such a *decennalia* would have dated Theoderic's reign from 490 or perhaps 493. See Burns (1982), 109, and (1984), 90; and Zecchini (1993), 818. Valois himself suggested this emendation in his original edition.

[19] *Vita Fulgentii* 9: "Fuit autem tunc in Urbe maximum gaudium: Theodorici regis praesentia romani senatus et populi laetificante conventus.... memorato Theodorico rege concionem faciente, romanae curiae nobilitatem decus ordinem que distinctis decoratam gradibus exspectaret et favores liberi populi castis auribus audiens, qualis esset hujus saeculi gloriosa pompa cognosceret. Neque tamen in hoc spectaculo libenter aliquid intuitur nec nugis illius saecularibus superflua illectus delectatione consensit." The account is in harmony with that of the *Anonymus Valesianus* (see later discussion).

[20] *Vita Fulgentii* 9: "sed inde potius ad illam supernae Hierusalem desiderandam felicitatem vehementer exarsit, salubri disputatione praesentes sic admonens fratres: quam speciosa potest esse Hierusalem caelestis si sic fulget Roma terrestris!"

[21] *CassChron*, anno 500: "Hoc anno dn. rex Theodericus Romam cunctorum votis expetitus advenit et senatum suum mira affabilitate tractans Romanae plebi donavit annonas."

[22] *AnonVal* 65: "ambulavit rex Theodericus Romam, et occurrit Beato Petro devotissimus ac si catholicus. Cui papa Symmachus et cunctus senatus vel populus Romanus cum omni gaudio extra urbem occurrentes." The act imitated that of earlier "Christian" emperors. See Vitiello

ceremonial entrance then developed into a procession that culminated in the Forum, in the region beside the Senate House known as "at the Palm."[23] It was in this location, according to the *Anonymus Valesianus*, that Theoderic addressed the Senate and people, piously vowing that he would "completely preserve as inviolate whatever prior Roman *principes* had ordained" and later ordering these very words to be inscribed on a bronze tablet for everyone to see.[24]

Such accounts, especially that of the *Anonymus Valesianus*, reveal the extent to which the mere arrival of an emperor at Rome, in this case, the *princeps* Theoderic, could become a magical moment, when ruler and ruled exchanged complementary forms of legitimizing acclamation and approbation. Just as the Senate and people of Rome applauded their empire's new lord for the first time and placed their useful seal on his reign, so too did he behave according to their traditional expectations, acknowledging their sacred roles as guardians of the republic and partners in his reign. The noble lie, dating all the way back to the reign of Augustus and so essential to Rome's senatorial class, was perpetuated. When in Rome, "good" emperors acknowledged that the empire still belonged to the Senate and people and that they were simply reverent guardians, content with the honorary title of "first citizen" (*princeps*). The republic, dead for more than five centuries, lived on; and because Theoderic was so keen to make this known, the Romans of Rome cheered his arrival and welcomed him with open arms.

Theoderic's benefaction to the city of Rome, however, extended beyond the courtesy that he showed to its Senate and people during his *adventus*. An emperor's presence in any city was an opportunity for generosity on a scale reserved for the wealthiest of coffers; since this was Rome, the ideological mistress of the world, the greatest expenses (now that they were becoming available) could not be spared. Theoderic remained in the city for six months,[25] an impressive amount of time insofar as it surpassed that of

---

(2004), 75–6 and (2005a). Fulgentius may have been aware of these events, as his *Vita* places him *fuori le mura* at the time.

[23] *AnonVal* 66: "venit ad senatum, et ad Palmam populo adlocutus." Cf. *Vita Fulgentii* 10. For the Palm's location and significance, Della Valle (1959), 162–6, and Guidobaldi (1999), 52–3.

[24] *AnonVal* 66: "se omnia, deo iuvante, quod retro principes Romani ordinaverunt inviolabiliter servaturum promittit"; and *AnonVal* 69: "Verba enim promissionis eius, quae populo fuerat adlocutus, rogante populo in tabula aenea iussit scribi et in publico poni." For the practice of engraving legal documents in bronze, Williamson (1987), who writes that these tablets were "a grandiloquent statement, symbolizing imperial rule and the majesty of law" (183). See also Kohlhas-Müller (1995), 163–4, and Vitiello (2004), 106, who stress early imperial precedents.

[25] *AnonVal* 70: "Deinde sexto mense revertens Ravennam," but see later, n. 32, for a complication.

many of his imperial predecessors, some of whom had never set foot in the capital. Such an extended visit allowed this outsider to get to know Rome and its populace, and vice versa. More importantly, it provided numerous contexts for Theoderic to demonstrate his imperial *pietas* through lavish spending, exhibiting the kind of patronage that served to sow sentiments of the city's (and hence the empire's) rejuvenation and restoration. Eager to match and even surpass the feats of the ancients, Theoderic orchestrated an imperial triumph within the walls of Rome,[26] a public expression of Roman invincibility not seen here for nearly a century and a potent indication to all present (and all who heard of it) of Rome and its empire's rising fortunes.[27] Already known to have celebrated a triumph in New Rome, Theoderic transferred its awesome power to Old Rome, to the only Rome that really mattered in Italo-Roman eyes.[28] From his residence on the Palatine, the same residence once inhabited by emperors, he likewise exhibited circus games and provided for the general welfare of the city and its populace. Traditional provisions, at times despaired of in the city, were granted, and arrangements were made so that they would continue to be supplied in his absence. Moreover, "the greatest quantity of money" was set aside, so that the palace itself might be kept in good repair and various public buildings in the city might continue to function as monuments to Rome and the empire's historic supremacy.[29]

[26] *AnonVal* 67: "Per tricennalem triumphans populo ingressus palatium." Cf. McCormick (1986), 272–3, and Vitiello (2004), 80–1, who suggest that this "triumph" was simply part of the *adventus* ceremony. See also MacCormack (1981), 33–45. If a bona fide triumph, as taken here, it might have been an "empty" triumph, not unheard of in the Roman world. However, there are other, legitimate possibilities, including the defeat of Odovacer or a celebration of the dominance implied by the alliances that Theoderic had contracted with neighboring peoples. Last, if Theoderic can be placed in Rome in 504/5 (as per the hypotheses suggested in n. 32, later), the triumph might have been related to the Sirmian War.

[27] The last recorded imperial triumph in Rome dates to the reign of Honorius. See Siena (1984), 509. Consuls were known to host celebrations referred to as "triumphal," during which they generally exhibited games and granted gifts. See Vitiello (2005a), 75. Still, one should distinguish between such consular "triumphs," led by a consul, and imperial "triumphs," led by the emperor, the latter being more lavish and impressive. *Variae* 3.39 even suggests that some consuls were either financially unable (or perhaps morally unwilling) to meet such requirements.

[28] Ensslin (1959), 109, imagines Theoderic's giving of games at Rome (discussed later) as a repeat of the consular games that he celebrated at Constantinople in 484. If a bona fide triumph, it was also a repetition of his earlier "triumph" in Constantinople.

[29] *AnonVal* 67: "Donavit populo Romano et pauperibus annonas singulis annis, centum viginti milia modios, et ad restaurationem palatii, seu ad recuperationem moeniae civitatis singulis annis libras ducentas de arca vinaria dari praecepit"; *CassChron*, anno 500: "Romanae plebi donavit annonas, atque admirandis moeniis deputata per singulos annos maxima pecuniae

Such acts during this lengthy stay at Rome were so clearly within the imperial tradition that it would have been very difficult for locals to imagine Theoderic as anything other than a Roman emperor;[30] indeed, this is exactly what Italo-Romans residing elsewhere, like Epiphanius and Ennodius in Liguria, had already come to believe. But more than just acting imperial, Theoderic had exceeded local expectations in a manner befitting a *good* emperor, explaining why contemporaries saw fit to compare him with Trajan, himself an *optimus* (best) *princeps*. In keeping with late antique trends and the strategic needs of his kingdom, Theoderic would eventually depart from Rome, but his visit was nonetheless remembered fondly: The Romans of Rome remained appreciative and on more than one occasion expressed the hope that he might one day return.[31]

Theoderic, it seems, did not fulfill their wishes,[32] but he did not abandon Rome entirely as so many of his predecessors had. Instead, the pro-Roman policies initiated during this visit remained essential to a program of reconciliation and appeasement promoted throughout his long reign (and beyond). Even in absentia, Theoderic continued to make his rever-

---

quantitate subvenit." See Della Valle (1959), 157–62, who discusses how other imperial palaces in Rome were repaired and utilized by the Theoderican regime, including the Palatium Sessorianum, which had Constantinian links.

[30] Especially given the conclusions drawn in Part II. Cf. O'Donnell (2008), 57.

[31] See *Acta Synhodorum Habitarum Romae* (*Praeceptio Regis III*), p. 420, and *CassOratReliquiae*, p. 470, ln. 6–10 (cited later). In both instances (501 and 519), Theoderic sent representatives instead.

[32] But perhaps he did. A solitary six-month visit is generally inferred from *AnonVal* 70: "Deinde sexto mense revertens Ravennam, aliam germanam suam Amalabirgam tradens in matrimonium Herminifredo regi Turingorum." But there is room to argue that the *Anonymus Valesianus* account has conflated two visits into one. *Variae* 4.1 securely dates the marriage alliance with Herminafrid to 506/7–11 (507, according to Krautschick (1983), 76) and, given its association with Theoderic's return to Ravenna in the citation, it seems to indicate that Theoderic abandoned Rome in late 505 at the earliest. Such a connection may not have been intended, but one late-sixth-century chronicle (the so-called *Auctorium Hauniense*) supports the idea, recording the arrival of Theoderic at Rome in May of 504 (rather than 500) and not mentioning the fanfare described previously. If this visit in 504 lasted for sixth months, a return to Ravenna followed by the marriage alliance in 506 would be chronologically conceivable. Most scholars have concluded that the 504 dating is incorrect, citing as evidence the *Chronicle of Marius of Avenches*, which places a similar description of events in the year 500. Marius might have been just as confused, however, while the Amalaberga marriage issue remains unsolved. Cf. Vitiello (2005a), 58–79. At the very least, the common assertion that Theoderic's stay in Rome was brief and solitary is far from certain. After all, Theoderic is known to have resided in cities other than Ravenna (e.g. Milan, Pavia, and Verona), and there are large periods during which his whereabouts are unattested.

ence for Rome well known, honoring its Senate and people with laudatory language and pious generosity from afar.

A Sacred Assembly

Continuing to show deference to the Senate was perhaps the most valuable gesture of all, not simply because, as Theoderic informed its members, "what adorns the Roman name was founded by you,"[33] but because senators could be powerful men with powerful connections. As friends, they were useful allies; as enemies, a serious cause for alarm.[34] Indeed, their approval could be one of the most legitimizing forces for any Roman regime, and inversely their disapproval or disaffection could become its undoing.[35] Even Theoderic's eastern colleague, Anastasius, had been keen to point this out, and while respectful in the face of such admonitions, Theoderic made it clear to him that he did "cherish the Senate" and thus governed well.[36] Despite being absent from Rome, this esteem could be shown in a number of ways, not least through the continued employment of the republican terminology and imagery discussed so far. The consistent use of laudatory and obsequious language whenever addressing the Senate, however, was even more effective, a replay of the "wondrous courtesy" demonstrated personally in 500.

Language like this served to reemphasize the Senate and its members' unique role as leaders and guardians of the republic, as partners with its princely master. In a number of letters Theoderic reminded his senators of this position, insisting on its fundamental importance to Rome and the civilized rule of law, *civilitas*. In one instance, the senators were told that their order had once "provided for devotion in the provinces, decreed the laws for private individuals, and taught subjects in every region to yield happily before justice."[37] So important a legacy, Theoderic admonished, should not be lost, and, in keeping with their ancestors, contemporary senators

---

[33] *Variae* 2.24.1: "nam quod ornat nomen Romanum, a vobis legitur institutum."

[34] As already demonstrated, senators were key in establishing and maintaining cordial relations with the east Roman state. Their loyalty, therefore, was extremely valuable, and their disloyalty dangerous. Hence the executions of Boethius and Symmachus c. 525. See the Epilogue.

[35] This was especially the case in the more traditional and republic-minded West, where emperors were expected to be *principes* and to perpetuate ideologies of a Senate-dominated *res publica*. See Chp. 3.

[36] *Variae* 1.1.2–3, with Chp. 3.

[37] *Variae* 2.24.1: "Vos enim devotionem provinciis, vos privatis iura decrevistis et ad omnes iustitiae partes subiectos libenter parere docuistis."

were expected to act "with justice" and to be "an example of moderation" to all.[38] "You owe the Republic an exertion equal to our own,"[39] they were told, and another missive (and an important one considering that it is not derived from the *Variae*) implies that Theoderic was quite serious. Here, as elsewhere, Rome's senators were honored as *patres conscripti*, while the Senate itself was addressed, quite incredibly, as "the conqueror of the world [and] the patron and restorer of liberty."[40] These words are revealing, for they suggest just how much the Senate could be idealized, in true principate fashion, as a necessary counterpart to Theoderic himself. A mere first citizen with similar credentials, he too was hailed as a "guardian of liberty" and "conqueror of nations."[41] Equally revealing is the content of this letter, which implied that senatorial decrees, those "regulations of your sacred assembly, pleasing to our Clemency," could stand on their own with the force of law and were only strengthened by Theoderic's approval, validating current usages of the *SC* abbreviation.[42]

Respect like this doubtless played to senatorial needs, yet expressions of partnership and the (re)elevation of senatorial rank were not restricted to direct addresses to this sacred body; not mere flattery for the sake of senatorial egos, this language was ubiquitous and, owing to its traditional nature, was directly connected to perceptions of imperial renewal. The Senate was, in Theoderic's words, the "inner sanctum [and] hall of liberty," "a holy order" and "honored assembly," "most pleasing" and "glorious in its wonderful reputation."[43] Moreover, as a constituted body, senators

---

[38] *Variae* 2.24.2–3: "Et ideo non decet inde signum resultationis exire, unde exemplum potuit moderationis effulgere.... sic aequabiliter ordinate." Notice, however, that in this instance the senators were not behaving properly, but were being exhorted to do so. Also, note the translation of *aequabiliter* as "justly," though in this case it might also be translated "in a similar manner," in reference to the statement made in the following note.

[39] *Variae* 2.24.3: "patres conscripti, qui parem nobiscum rei publicae debetis adnisum."

[40] *Praeceptum Regis Theoderici* (*Epistulae Theodericianae Variae* 9): "Domitori orbis, praesuli et reparatori libertatis senatui urbis Romae Flavius Theodericus Rex."

[41] These are common themes. See, for instance, *ILS* 827: "custos libertatis" and "domitor gentium." Cf. *PanTh* 42 and the Senigallia Medallion.

[42] *Praeceptum Regis Theoderici* (*Epistulae Theodericianae Variae* 9): "nostrae mansuetudinis grata sacri coetus vestri ordinatio corda pulsavit. Et licet post venerabilem synodum ad huiusmodi decreta vestri sufficiat ordinatio sola iudicii, tamen pro vestra huiusmodi praesentibus oraculis dedimus consultatione responsum." Theoderic hence suggested that a senatorial *ordinatio* had the force of law, but that his *responsum* could strengthen its effectiveness. Such a suggestion was within the imperial tradition and lends credence to the conclusion of Prostko-Prostyński (1994a), 188, that Theoderic exercised the right to pass his own legislation.

[43] For inner sanctum of liberty, *Variae* 3.33.3: "penetralia Libertatis"; hall of liberty, *Variae* 6.4.3: "illa Libertatis aula"; holy order, *Variae* 3.33.1: "sacri ordinis"; honored assembly, *Variae*

were described to others as "a crowd of learned men," who were "joined together as first in the world" and provided "glorious visions of upstanding behavior" to those who beheld them.[44] It was splendid, prefects of the city (who doubled as presidents of the Senate) were told, to be in their midst. "Consider how great it is to say something to these learned men [i.e. senators] and to fear the shame of error."[45] Likewise, it was a great source of honor for deserving men to "radiate with senatorial luster":[46] It allowed one already "resplendent in his own merits [and] the splendor of his birth" to be "rendered even more distinguished."[47]

Indeed, the Theoderican regime had a vested interest in ensuring that the appropriate candidates were promoted to senatorial rank. Men like these were an asset to the state, but more importantly, many believed that they had been passed over during the reign of Odovacer. Ennodius, for instance, claimed that "the most eloquent man [had] seemed ignoble amid plows" and that "bodily strength [had] negated what education" bestowed, while Cassiodorus expressed frustration at the slow advancement of many noble families, including his own, during this time of inattentive leadership.[48] But now, under Theoderic, not only was the ruling family a marvel for its learning, but teachers were patronized, "skilled men [were] sought everywhere," and "he who is deserving holds a magistracy."[49]

Worthy sons, youths like Cassiodorus and Venantius, the son of the exceptional patrician Liberius, were granted senatorial offices both out of respect for their parents' achievements and in acknowledgment of their

---

6.4.3: "honoratae congregationis"; most pleasing, *Variae* 3.33.3: "gratissimum senatum"; and glorious in its wonderful reputation, *Variae* 6.4.1: "senatus ille mirabili opinione gloriosus."

[44] For crowd of learned men, *Variae* 3.33.2: "in illa turba doctorum"; cf. *Variae* 6.4.3 (cited in the following note); for first in the world, *Variae* 6.4.3: "commissos ... mundi primarios"; for upstanding behavior, *Variae* 6.4.4: "inter tot morum lumina."

[45] *Variae* 6.4.3: "Respice tot doctos viros et considera, quale sit his aliquid dicere nec erroris verecundiam formidare."

[46] *Variae* 3.33.1: "Laetamur tales viros emergere, qui senatoria mereantur luce radiare."

[47] *Variae* 2.16.2: "illustrem Venantium, tam suis quam paternis meritis elucentem ... subveximus, ut natalium splendor insitus ornatior collatis redderetur honoribus." For more on Venantius, see later discussion.

[48] See Part I.

[49] On the learning of Theoderic and his kin, Chp. 6 and König (2000), 224–7. For Theoderic and his successors' patronization of the teachers in Rome, *Variae* 9.21 and *Pragmatic Sanction* 22. Ravenna also seems to have been a center of learning, particularly scientific. See Staab (1976); Gottschall (1997), 260–2; and Hen (2007), chp. 2. For learned and worthy magistrates, *PanTh* 74: "sollers ubicumque latet inquiritur. Magistratum ... exigit qui meretur." Ennodius concludes this section with yet another comparison of Odovacer's and Theoderic's reigns: "Look at the wealth of your era: then courts did not have learned men (*perfectos*), now [even] the Church sends you a panegyrist." For Ennodius' understanding of *perfecti*, Chp. 9. Cf. #458.7–9 (*In Christi Signo*).

own ennobling pursuit of letters, traditional requirements for high status.[50] Ennodius praised his *princeps* for returning to "progeny what you owed to their sires, their good faith being well known to your mildness."[51] And in announcing his promotion of Venantius, this was exactly the rationale that Theoderic provided to the Senate. "Weigh carefully," the *patres conscripti* were instructed, "whether we ought to leave this offspring unrewarded, whose father we remember had accomplished so many excellent things."[52] Nor was Venantius undeserving of senatorial rank, for as an "attentive examiner," he pursued "the study of letters, which is worthy of its own applause in all offices, smoothly imparting to the fame of [his] family a talent for eloquence."[53] Another senatorial appointee, Armentarius, was similarly deserving, "recommended to us both for the nobility of his parents and his own talent" for eloquent speech.[54] "What is more worthy," Theoderic asked, than "for a profession already wrapped in a toga to be dressed with senatorial honor so that ... he, whom the right of eloquence exhorts to speak, may dare to utter freely his thoughts, not restrained by the fear of ignorance?"[55] The promotion of Romans like these honored and perpetuated this noble Roman institution, allowing Theoderic to wrap "the crown of the Senate," as Ennodius so eloquently put it, "with innumerable flowers."[56]

BREAD AND CIRCUSES

The Senate was only half of the equation found within the republican shorthand for Roman society, *SPQR*. The commoners of Rome, the *populus Romanus*, were also vital and, like Rome's senators, they continued to receive those customary tributes that their sovereign had granted in person during his stay. Before leaving Rome, Theoderic arranged for 120,000

---

[50] For legitimization through letters, Chp. 6. Cf. Riché (1976), 24–31. For Venantius, *PLRE* 2, 1152 (Venantius 2).

[51] *PanTh* 75: "cuius mansuetudini tuae fides innotuerit, hereditatis iure quod auctori debueras suboli mox refundes."

[52] *Variae* 2.16.6: "Perpendite, patres conscripti, si hanc subolem inremuneratam relinquere debuimus, cuius auctorem tot eximia fecisse retinemus."

[53] *Variae* 2.15.4: "Litterarum siquidem studia, quae cunctis honoribus suo sunt digna suffragio, sedulus perscrutator assequeris, addens claritati generis ingenium suaviter eloquentis."

[54] *Variae* 3.33.2: "Armentarius, qui et parentum bono et suo nobis commendatur ingenio, exigens meritis quam sperat precibus dignitatem." For Armentarius, *PLRE* 2, 150 (Armentarius 2).

[55] *Variae* 3.33.2: "Nam quid dignius, si et senatorio vestiatur honore togata professio, ut ... audeat liberam proferre sententiam, nec frenetur imperitiae terrore, quem hortantur ad vocem iura facundiae."

[56] *PanTh* 57: "Huc accedit, quod coronam curiae innumero flore velasti."

modii of grain to be supplied to these plebs on an annual basis, doubtless to be converted into bread.[57] This traditional dole, a long-established right for the Romans of Rome, had at times met with scarcity or simply neglect,[58] and though its fate under Odovacer is unknown, the *Variae* collection demonstrates that it remained a vigilantly guarded privilege under the Goths, who maintained other free provisions, such as pork.[59] Prefects of the annona were told that their office made them glorious, since they saw to the rations of the "most sacred city" and fed "so great a people."[60] Prefects of Italy, likewise, were instructed to prevent corruption and to ensure that enough grain was earmarked for local consumption before allowing any to be sold abroad.[61] There would be times of scarcity, of course, and within a decade of Theoderic's death, Rome would suffer from such want.[62] But even then, the Eternal City's elevated position was honored, and the prefect of Italy, who happened to be Cassiodorus, took great pains to provide its inhabitants with their now (re)established dole. "Our thoughts have been so troubled that these people, having grown accustomed to their ancient delights in the most blessed times of their [Amal] rulers, might rejoice with their scarcity having been removed."[63]

With bread came circuses, and Theoderic, as already seen, had offered such entertainments in true imperial style during his visit in 500. Though he occasionally condemned these games as "a spectacle that drives out the most serious of morals and invites the most fickle quarrels, a drainer of honesty, a gushing fountain of discord" and a "place that preserves

---

[57] *Variae* 6.18 demonstrates that the prefect of the annona supervised the bakers at Rome, who presumably used this grain to make their loaves. For the provisions granted in 500, see earlier discussion. The amount is considerably smaller than in earlier times. See Jones (1964), 697–9. However, it qualified in the eyes of the *Anonymus Valesianus* as generous. Perhaps, then, the 120,000 *modii* were in addition to an already established number. Cf. Barnish (1987), 161.

[58] See Marazzi (2007), 295–6.

[59] For pork, *Variae* 6.18.4, with Barnish (1987) and Vitiello (2004), 96. Beef may also have been available, though by the time of Cassiodorus' tenure as praetorian prefect of Italy the beef tribute had been commuted to cash. How long this had been the case is uncertain, and indeed the opposite (cash payments converted to payments in kind) appears to have been the case for other provinces. Cf. *Variae* 11.39, 12.22, and 12.23. For guarded privilege, *Variae* 12.11.

[60] *Variae* 6.18.1: "is certe debet esse gloriosus, qui ad copiam Romani populi probatur electus. Tui siquidem studii est, ut sacratissimae urbi praeparetur annona, ubique redundet panis copia et tam magnus populus tamquam una mensa satietur."

[61] See *Variae* 1.34.1.

[62] Cf. *Variae* 1.35 and 12.25, among others. There would also be times of plenty, referenced in *Variae* 12.25 and evident in the munificence shown to the Gauls. See *Variae* 3.41, 3.44, and 4.5, with Chp. 10.

[63] *Variae* 11.5.2: "ideo tot angusta cogitationis intravimus, ut populus ille antiquis delectationibus assuetus beatissimis regnantium temporibus explosis necessitatibus perfruatur."

excess,"[64] their importance at Rome and elsewhere was not lost on him. Indeed and despite some disdain, Theoderic claimed that he cherished such spectacles "out of obligation to the people eager for them";[65] they were a source of "happiness" and "relaxation" for the population of Rome, allowing "the multitude to know that it is at leisure."[66] Their patient acceptance, therefore, was more than just "a source of honor for *principes*,"[67] although this was significant. Tolerating and patronizing these games served to legitimize Theoderic as a proper imperial heir and reiterated the valuable role of his Goths, whose valiant labors allowed the Romans to be at ease and enjoy themselves.[68] "The blessedness of our age," Theoderic informed two illustrious inhabitants of Rome, "is the happiness of the people."[69] "Whatever [the mob] thinks is delightful," another was told, "is connected to the blessedness of the times."[70] Long after leaving Rome, then, Theoderic continued to endure "the great burden of expenses" demanded by these spectacles, the salaries paid to charioteers alone being impressive even by eastern standards.[71] The circus was "no place for a Cato," but as Theoderic wisely quipped, "sometimes is it useful to act foolishly, that we might preserve the joys desired by the people."[72]

Other entertainments in Rome also received Theoderic's largess after 500, doubtless for the same reasons. Letters in the *Variae* demonstrate that pantomimes and actors, often associated with the circus, continued to

---

[64] *Variae* 3.51.2: "Spectaculum expellens gravissimos mores, invitans levissimas contentiones, evacuator honestatis, fons irriguus iurgiorum"; and *Variae* 1.27.5: "Locus est qui defendit excessum." Beyond conventional aristocratic disdain, Theoderic had practical reasons to make such claims, since the games often engendered "un-Roman" behavior, factional strife, and violence. Cf. *Variae* 1.20, 1.27, 1.30–2, 3.51, and 6.4, with Cameron (1976), 271f.

[65] *Variae* 3.51.12: "Haec nos fovemus necessitate imminentium populorum."

[66] For happiness and relaxation, *Variae* 1.31.1: "Spectacula voluptatum laetitiam volumus esse populorum ... ad remissionem animi constat inventum"; for leisure, *Variae* 1.20.1: "quod se otiosam generalitas esse cognoscit." Cf. Ammianus, *Res Gestae* 28.4.28–31.

[67] *Variae* 1.27.5: "Quorum [i.e. spectaculorum] garrulitas si patienter accipitur, ipsos quoque principes ornare monstratur."

[68] See Chp. 5.

[69] *Variae* 1.20.1: "praesertim cum beatitudo sit temporum laetitia populorum."

[70] *Variae* 3.51.13: "Nam quicquid aestimat voluptuosum, hoc et ad beatitudinem temporum iudicat applicandum."

[71] *Variae* 1.31.1: "Ideo enim tot expensarum onus subimus." Theoderic's generosity in this regard was apparently well known in the East, given that Thomas, an eastern charioteer, chose "to favor the seat of our empire" (*nostri sedes ... imperii*) after abandoning his own country. See *Variae* 3.51.1. Cf. *Variae* 2.9 and 3.39.2.

[72] For Cato, *Variae* 1.27.5: "Ad circum nesciunt convenire catones." It is worth noting the appeal here to Cato as an exemplar, as he was a true *republican* hero. Cf. *PanTh* 30, where Theoderic himself is compared to Cato. For the quip, *Variae* 3.51: "Expedit interdum desipere, ut populi possimus desiderata gaudia continere."

receive their salaries as state employees and to be regulated by the prefects of Rome and the tribunes of entertainment.[73] More impressive still were Rome's *venatores*, who continued putting on their hunting shows at state and consular expense well after Theoderic's reign.[74] Just as with the circuses, such entertainments could insult Theoderic's personal sensibilities, the ruler of Italy decrying the games as a "detestable act," "unhappy contest," "cruel game," "bloodthirsty delight," and "human savagery,"[75] and suggesting that if there were any justice in the world, "as much wealth would be given for the life of these living men as seems to be showered for their death."[76] But, again, it was understood that there was "need to exhibit such things for the people" as much as there was an obligation to concede to the *venatores* "whatever has become a long-held custom through ancient generosity."[77] Ancient custom and popular desire trumped personal taste or moral conviction.

BEASTS OF DIVERSE TYPES

Games and entertainments, then, served as signs of *felicitas* and *beatitudo* and were a traditional expectation among the Romans of Rome that continued to be fulfilled under Theoderic's auspices. More significant still, Rome's spectacles benefited from more than one occasion of exceptional imperial generosity at Theoderic's expense. Though the elaborate circuses that he offered in person in 500 had been a remarkable tribute to the Senate and people of Rome, these games were matched, surpassed even, in 519, when he sponsored lavish hunting games in the Colosseum in honor of his son-in-law, Eutharic. The event itself was extremely significant on a number of levels. Since the "purple-clad offshoot" (a son and heir) so hoped for by Ennodius in 507 had failed to materialize, Theoderic had begun grooming Eutharic as his successor to the western *imperium*. Informed of these

---

[73] For pantomimes, *Variae* 1.31 and 1.32; for actors, *Variae* 7.10 and 9.21.

[74] And not just in Rome. See *ILS* 829 (Fiebiger 1, #203 and *CIL* 5 6418), which commemorates Athalaric's repairs to the amphitheater at Pavia.

[75] Detestable act and unhappy contest, *Variae* 5.42.1: "Actus detestabilis, certamen infelix, cum feris velle contendere"; cruel game, bloodthirsty delight, and human savagery, *Variae* 5.42.4: "Hunc ludum crudelem, sanguinariam voluptatem, impiam religionem, humanam, ut ita dixerim, feritatem."

[76] *Variae* 5.42.12: "Si esset ullus aequitatis intuitus, tantae divitiae pro vita mortalium deberent dari, quantae in mortes hominum videntur effundi." Even more so than in the case of the circuses, feelings like these (and the ones cited earlier) were in keeping with late antique Roman and Christian morality.

[77] *Variae* 5.42.11–12: "necesse est talia populis exhibere.... Et ideo quicquid in longam consuetudinem antiqua liberalitate pervenit, sine aliqua dilatione concedite supplicanti."

plans, Justin, the emperor of the East, even adopted this Goth, a "Visigoth" of (probably invented) Amal blood,[78] as his son-in-arms, repeating the gesture of Zeno made during Theoderic's consulship. Further, in 518 Eutharic was nominated as consul in the West and in the following year symbolically held this office with the eastern emperor as his colleague. Nearly a decade earlier, Ennodius had begged Christ to give Theoderic a successor from his royal line, "lest the goodness of so great a man grow old in one lifetime and what has become customary in his times be celebrated as only the memory of a golden age."[79] Now, doubtless, his prayers had been answered, for not since the days of the Theodosian emperors had Italo-Romans witnessed so stable a succession plan. The future of the resurgent western empire, along with its harmony within a greater Roman world, seemed secure. It was time, therefore, to celebrate (yet again) in the West, and Rome was an ideal place to do so.

Joint triumphal processions were thus ordered for Rome and Ravenna, commemorating the new agreement reached with Constantinople, the consulship of Theoderic's heir apparent, and perhaps, for good measure, Roman dominance over barbarian peoples.[80] Once more the populace of Rome witnessed a kind of imperial *adventus* and triumph, only now in the person of Eutharic, receiving a future *princeps* in place of the ruler whom they actually desired, who was celebrating in Ravenna. "Everyone is compelled, and rightly so, to desire your [Theoderic's] presence," Cassiodorus announced in a panegyric delivered before the Senate. "A din arises from their love of their *princeps*, and as a result you cause your subjects to grieve [at your absence], since you are obviously esteemed so well."[81] The Romans of Rome had hoped that Theoderic would attend their festivities in person, showering the Eternal City with his special patronage and remaining in their midst, perhaps indefinitely; but he had disappointed

---

[78] Cf. Burns (1984), 92–3, and Wolfram (1988), 310–11, who take Eutharic's Amal descent (recorded by Jordanes) at face value; Moorhead (1992), 200–2, is more suspicious, while Diaz and Valverde (2007), 364–7, outright deny it, suggesting that Cassiodorus' lost history was intended to legitimize Eutharic as both a Visigothic Balt and Ostrogothic Amal. See also Bachrach (1973), 97–8, who argues that Eutharic was not a Goth at all, but of Alanic descent.

[79] #458.10 (*In Christi Signo*): "Det [Christus redemptor noster] etiam regni de eius germine successorem, ne bona tanti hominis in una aetate veterescant et antiquata temporibus pro sola aurei saeculi commemoratione nominentur."

[80] For Theoderic's triumph in Ravenna, *AnonVal* 80 (alluded to in *CassChron*, anno 519). See later discussion for Roman impressions of Theoderic's absence from the festivities as well as the dominance that Eutharic's games implied over the Vandals.

[81] *CassOratReliquiae*, p. 470, ln. 6–10: "Iure ergo omnium / desideria in tuam praesentiam concitan- / tur: amore principis murmur exoritur / et ex eo subiectos tristes efficis, quia / nimium diligi conprobaris." For commentary, Romano (1978), 22–4.

their expectations. "Everyone wants you to come to them," Cassiodorus continued, for "a life is unpleasant that is not worthy of your visage and it grows weary of remaining in its own residence, when you have been compelled to abandon it for the sake of necessity."[82] Though disappointing, therefore, more pressing obligations had excused Theoderic's absence in the eyes of these Romans, much as they had excused his actions decades earlier in Epiphanius' Liguria. And while the Romans of Rome were initially saddened, Eutharic soon proved a worthy substitute.

Analogous to the events recorded for 500, this *princeps* in the making honored the Senate just as Theoderic had, while the Senate and people of Rome "happily received him with wondrous grace."[83] In the year of Eutharic's consulship, Cassiodorus' chronicle continued, "Rome saw many wonders ... and even Symmachus, an envoy from the East, was stupefied at the riches granted to both Goths and Romans."[84] Such astonishment, a clever insertion on Cassiodorus' part, served to assert Rome's equality with, and possibly superiority over, its jealous rival, the Rome of the East. Yet it was Eutharic's consular games that drew the greatest amount of contemporary awe. "Patronizing the amphitheater," Cassiodorus explained, "[Eutharic] exhibited beasts of diverse types, which the present age marveled at for their novelty."[85] Even Africa, pacified two decades earlier by the granting of an Amal bride during Theoderic's own sojourn at Rome,[86] "sent excellent delights for these spectacles in a sign of her devotion."[87] Though the Goths had not been able to restore North Africa to Roman rule, now, at least, Rome's citizens could take delight from a fitting tribute sent by its Vandal lords: beasts, worthy representatives of barbarians, viciously and symbolically cut down by Roman huntsmen.

---

[82] *CassOratReliquiae*, p. 469, ln. 21 and 470, ln. 1–6: "Hinc est, / Domine, quod te populi non patiuntur abs- / cedere, sed omnes sibi cupiunt advenire. / Ingrata vita est, quae tuos non meretur / aspectus; et taedet propriis sedibus in- / haerere, quos coactus fueris pro rerum ne- / cessitate deserere."

[83] *CassChron*, anno 518: "Eo anno dn. Eutharicus Cillica mirabili gratia senatus et plebes ad edendum exceptus est feliciter consulatum." The event must have occurred late in 518, given that Eutharic spent much of 519, the year of his consulship, in Rome.

[84] *CassChron*, anno 519: "Eo anno multa vidit Roma miracula, editionibus singulis stupente etiam Symmacho Orientis legato divitias Gothis Romanisque donatas."

[85] *Ibid.*: "Muneribus amphitheatralibus diversi generis feras, quas praesens aetas pro novitate miraretur, exhibuit."

[86] See *AnonVal* 68. This was quite important given the events of the fifth century, the sack of Rome in 455 especially. Cf. Moorhead (1992), 63–5, with Chp. 2.

[87] *CassChron*, anno 519: "Cuius spectaculis voluptates etiam exquisitas Africa sub devotione transmisit."

Although an everyday occurrence in the fourth century, such a spectacle would have been moving, "miraculous" in Cassiodorus' words, to contemporary Romans. Beasts of this sort were exceedingly rare, and knowledge of their great expense and specific origins could feed into contemporary conceptions of imperial renewal.[88] Just as the East was put in its proper place and relegated to its expected position of an equal (or even inferior) partner, so too did North Africa service Rome's populace again, providing sacrificial lambs (better, lions) for the sake of its amusement. If only for a day, it could seem as if the disasters of the fifth century had never occurred. And by the end of Eutharic's consulship, these and other unnamed gestures had served their intended purpose, instilling the citizens of Rome "with so great an amount of love [for Eutharic]" that he gained "the extraordinary approval of everyone."[89]

The succession of another *bonus princeps*, therefore, seemed secure when Cassiodorus completed his chronicle late in 519.[90] And though Eutharic would die before succeeding his father-in-law, his legacy would live on, helping to legitimize his young son, Athalaric, as a proper heir to the Amal purple.[91]

WONDERS NEVER CEASE

Entertainments, whether exhibited in person by Theoderic in 500, by his representative Eutharic in 519, or funded from afar in the intervening years, allowed the Romans of Rome to regain and maintain their historically elevated position. This helped to foster the belief that Rome truly was the undisputed capital of the world and connected such a restored position to the pious intervention of Rome's "Gothic" lords. Still, the lavish expenses of these spectacles and the wonder that they inspired were not the only means through which such entertainments could (and did) contribute to contemporary sentiments of renewal. Charioteers, huntsmen,

[88] The lack of sensitivity to this in the account of Ward-Perkins (1984), 116, who claims "all this would have been quite normal in earlier imperial times," is surprising. Indeed, it had not been "normal" for quite some time, ergo the enthusiasm expressed by Cassiodorus, who may have heard of such spectacles, but had never seen them.

[89] *CassChron*, anno 519: "Cunctis itaque eximia laude completis tanto amore civibus Romanis insederat, ut eius adhuc praesentiam desiderantibus Ravennam ad gloriosi patris remearet." The *pater* in question was Theoderic, Eutharic's father-in-law.

[90] But see *AnonVal* 80–2 for a hostile appraisal of Eutharic that casts him as anti-Catholic/Nicene. This portion of the account is untrustworthy, however. See the Epilogue.

[91] For Athalaric's official appeals to his father's legacy, *Variae* 8.1.3 (to Justin), which references his consulship and adoption as son-in-arms. Naturally, he appealed more to his "purple" Amal blood and matrilineal descent from Theoderic, whom he succeeded. Cf. *Variae* 8.1–7.

and actors required venues in which to ply their arts, and the venerable and massively monumental structures that functioned as such in Rome also received Theoderic's patronage, as did other grandiose structures.

Indeed, for Theoderic and others, Rome was a city of wonders, a miracle in and of itself, and its greatness could be deduced from the number of unique things contained within it.[92] Rome was a "wonderful forest of buildings" housing a population of statues "nearly the same in number as the one nature produced."[93] The ancient world had its seven wonders, including the Temple of Diana at Ephesus and the Colossus at Rhodes, but "who would think that these are more special," the ruler of Italy asked his urban prefects, "when in one city he can observe so many objects worthy of astonishment?"[94] Here mighty and venerable aqueducts watered the city "as if by man-made mountains ... with so great an onrush of water for so many centuries";[95] here "splendid sewers," like rivers, "so stupefy those seeing them that they surpass the wonders of other cities";[96] here, Theoderic knew from personal experience, "to see the Forum of Trajan, however recurrent, is wondrous," and "to scale the lofty Capitoline is to have seen human talent surpassed."[97] Marvels like these made Rome exceptional, and while Theoderic acknowledged that he devoted "untiring care to the entire Republic" and was keen "to recall everything to its ancient state," he vowed that he was more concerned about Rome than any other place, "since here whatever is devoted to splendor is exhibited for the joys of all men."[98]

---

[92] For city of wonders, *Variae* 7.6.1: "quia totum ad ammirationem noscitur exquisitum, quod ibi [i.e. Romae] cernitur esse fundatum"; a miracle, *Variae* 7.15.5: "universa Roma dicatur esse miraculum"; number of unique things, *Variae* 3.30.2: "hinc, Roma, singularis quanta in te sit potest colligi magnitudo."

[93] Forest of buildings, *Variae* 7.15.1: "illa mirabilis silva"; population of statues, *Variae* 7.15.3: "quas posteritas paene parem populum urbi dedit quam natura procreavit"; and *Variae* 7.13.1: "nam quidam populus copiosissimus statuarum." Cf. Procopius, *Wars* 8.21.13–14, who complains of the theft of such statues from the Greek East.

[94] *Variae* 7.15.4–5: "Ferunt prisci saeculi narratores fabricarum septem tantum terris adtributa miracula.... Sed quis illa ulterius praecipua putabit, cum in una urbe tot stupenda conspexerit?"

[95] *Variae* 7.6.2: "quasi constructis montibus ... tantus impetus fluminis tot saeculis."

[96] *Variae* 3.30.1–2: "propter splendidas Romanae cloacas civitatis, quae tantum visentibus conferunt stuporem, ut aliarum civitatum possint miracula superare. Videas illic fluvios quasi montibus concavis clausos."

[97] *Variae* 7.6.1: "Traiani forum vel sub assiduitate videre miraculum est: Capitolia celsa conscendere hoc est humana ingenia superata vidisse."

[98] *Variae* 3.31.1: "Quamvis universae rei publicae nostrae infatigabilem curam desideremus impendere et deo favente ad statum studeamus pristinum cuncta revocare, tamen Romanae civitatis sollicitiora nos augmenta constringunt, ubi quicquid decoris impenditur, generalibus gaudiis exhibetur."

The care and upkeep of so many splendid structures in Rome exacted a hefty price. And as already seen, sound policies were making the necessary revenues more readily available in Italy, with Theoderic himself able to set aside funds for just this purpose by the end of his visit in 500. Portions of the city that had welcomed him were in an obvious state of decay, making Rome as a whole seem less "eternal" and more the dying old woman described in Ennodius' panegyric.[99] Buildings, of course, were always in need of repair, not just because of the occurrence of man-made and natural disasters, of which there were many during the fifth century,[100] but also because time wreaked havoc on even the most solid of constructions. Nothing seemed immune from the devastation of rapacious old age,[101] and by the time of Theoderic's celebratory entrance, some of Rome's most impressive monumental structures had become dilapidated, been converted to other uses, or collapsed, becoming sources of spolia.[102] This was a trend empirewide that began long before the abandonment of Rome, but its progression within the city had been exacerbated as a consequence of Rome's increasing unimportance within the empire. Now, however, as an intrinsic component of Theoderic's Rome-centered program, serious attempts were made to turn back the tide.

Many emperors before him had attempted to leave their own, unique marks in this city, but Theoderic's contribution to Rome's forest of monuments was one of preservation and repair. To the modern beholder, this may seem less impressive than an arch in the manner of Constantine, but the practice was normal, and, more importantly, the gesture and its scale were quite significant to contemporaries. Ennodius expressed it best when he claimed that it was "more valuable to drive away collapse than to produce new beginnings,"[103] and this was especially the case with Rome, where so many wonders testified to the empire's lofty past. New constructions were impressive, but they mattered very little if ancient beacons of Roman

---

[99] On Rome's urban decline, Ward-Perkins (1984), 45–6; Siena (1984), 511–12; Pani Ermini (1995), 174–220; Marazzi (2007), 284–95. For Ennodius, Chp. 1.
[100] The various *Consularia Italica* record five earthquakes in Italy between 443 and 502, the earliest destroying statues and a "portica nova" in Rome. They also record a ruinous fire at Ravenna in 454. A number of fifth- and early sixth-century inscriptions commemorating repairs likewise refer to fires, earthquakes, and barbarian attacks. See Alföldy (2001), 11–12, and later discussion.
[101] *Variae* 4.51.3: "Quid non solvas, senectus, quae tam robusta quassasti?" Cf. *Variae* 1.25.3 and *ILS* 825 (both cited later). On time and the constant need for repairs, Ward-Perkins (1984), 12–13, and Alföldy (2001), 11–12.
[102] See earlier discussion; also *Variae* 2.7, 3.10, 3.31, and 7.13, which refer to the use of spolia from Rome for new constructions and/or repairs.
[103] *PanTh* 56: "Plus est occasum repellere quam dedisse principia." Cf. *Variae* 1.25.1.

supremacy and dominance succumbed to old age. "Concern for the city of Rome," Theoderic informed one prefect of the city, "always occupies our thoughts. For what ... is more worthy than to see to the repairs of that place which is known to preserve the honor of our Republic?"[104] Indeed, not simply the Romans of Rome, but Italo-Romans in general could take pride in the monuments of Rome, their continued existence a testament to all Romans' inherent and inherited exceptionalism. Their fifth-century decline and collapse had been a reflection of Rome and the western empire's loss of *status*, but now their repair and refurbishment asserted quite the opposite.

This, coupled with contemporary knowledge of the era in which many of these monuments had been erected, made their preservation a powerful component of the Theoderican golden age. A number of these structures were products of the late republic and early empire, the very period to which the revived empire of the early sixth century looked for its inspiration: a time of *principes*, when Rome and Italy were paramount, and Rome's mastery over the world was unchallenged. Venerating and repairing such monuments, therefore, provided a useful link to this idealized past and yet another opportunity for Theoderic to demonstrate the traditional *pietas* that was so legitimizing for rulers in Rome. Those grand structures that housed the entertainments described earlier provide instructive examples. In the awe-inspiring "immense mass" of the Circus Maximus onlookers could see reflected not just the "great accomplishment" and display of power of the first *princeps*, Augustus, but also "a construction wondrous even to the Romans."[105] In beholding the Flavian Amphitheater (Colosseum), likewise, it was understood that the "princely power of Titus, pouring forth a river of wealth, [had] intended this building to become the source from which the capital of cities would appear mighty."[106] And in the case of the Theater of Pompey, it was known that the ancients had "made this place suitable for so great a people, so that those who seemed to have obtained mastery over the world might have a unique spectacle."[107] It was for this reason

[104] *Variae* 3.30.1: "Romanae civitatis cura nostris sensibus semper invigilat. Quid est enim dignius, quod tractare debeamus, quam eius reparationem exigere, quae ornatum constat nostrae rei publicae continere?"

[105] *Variae* 3.51.4: "Sed mundi dominus ad potentiam suam opus extollens mirandam etiam Romanis fabricam in vallem Murciam tetendit Augustus, ut immensa moles firmiter praecincta montibus contineret, ubi magnarum rerum indicia clauderentur."

[106] *Variae* 5.42.5: "Hoc Titi potentia principalis, divitiarum profuso flumine, cogitavit aedificium fieri, unde caput urbium potuisset."

[107] *Variae* 4.51.4: "Fecerunt antiqui locum tantis populis parem, ut haberent singulare spectaculum, qui mundi videbantur obtinere dominatum."

alone, Theoderic suggested, that Pompey "not undeservedly ... had been called 'the Great,'"[108] and now, in the face of such enduring fame, it was necessary for Rome's latest patron to prove himself a worthy heir, lest he "acquire a reputation for negligence."[109]

"Would that ancient *principes* might rightly owe their praises to us," Theoderic suggested to a certain Sabinianus in Rome, "[rulers] to whose buildings we give the longest youthfulness, so that what has already been blackened with lethargic old age may glimmer with pristine newness."[110] Already a "new Trajan" in Roman eyes, Theoderic cultivated this image through his building projects, and Sabinianus, who was soon ordered to produce twenty-five thousand tiles (*tegulae*) annually, would help him in this endeavor.[111] Indeed, the modern find spots of a number of these *tegulae* suggest the full extent to which Theoderic was able to insert himself, both ideologically and literally, into the legacy of the early imperial past. More than just bearing Theoderic's name, these tiles were inscribed with the restorative language of the era; they asserted to contemporary readers that their placement within the fabric of once-decaying structures was "for the good of Rome" and allowed for a Rome that was truly "happy,"[112] while connecting such ideas of *felicitas* with Theoderic and his reign. Tiles like these were employed in the restoration of structures of great significance to the Romans of Rome. On the Palatine, for instance, they were used to refurbish the Domus Flavia, the Domus Augustana, and the so-called Stadium of Domitian.[113] These were impressive structures with solid links to the "princely" first century, and their restoration signaled to

---

[108] *Variae* 4.51.12: "Unde non inmerito creditur Pompeius hinc potius Magnus fuisse vocitatus."

[109] *Variae* 3.31.4: "Et quam miserum est, ut unde famam providentiae alii susceperunt, nos opinionem neglegentiae incurrisse videamur?"

[110] *Variae* 1.25.3: "Ut antiqui principes nobis merito debeant laudes suas, quorum fabricis dedimus longissimam iuventutem, ut pristina novitate transluceant, quae iam fuerant veternosa senectute fuscata." For Sabinianus, who may have been Theoderic's official architect at Rome, *PLRE* 2, 968 (Sabinianus 6).

[111] For the order, *Variae* 1.25.2. Actually the total number of tiles was more than twenty-five thousand, since Theoderic ordered both the Portus Licini and all the other warehouse-factories within its vicinity to produce this many. The number of other portus, however, is unknown. See Della Valle (1959), 135–43.

[112] A number of such tiles have been found. The two major variations are *ILS* 828a (Fiebiger 1, #191 and *CIL* 15 1665, etc.) and 828b (Fiebiger 1, #192 and *CIL* 15 1669, etc.). These read, "Reg(nante) D(omino) N(ostro) Theode / rico bono Rom(a)e" and "Reg(nante) D(omino) N(ostro) Theode / rico felix Roma," respectively. The practice continued under Athalaric. See *CIL* 15 1673/4 (Fiebiger 1, #201) and *CIL* 15 1675 (Fiebiger 1, #199). In Ravenna, on the other hand, Theoderic is known to have inscribed his monogram on at least four columns. See *CIL* 11 283 (Fiebiger 1, #197), with Fuchs (1944), 29–32.

[113] Siena (1984), 525, and Pani Ermini (1995), 221.

contemporary Romans that their absent *princeps* intended to return.[114] Likewise, in the Forum, such tiles were employed in the repair of the Basilica Aemilia, a massive republican building once heavily restored by Augustus after a devastating fire, and a marvel that the Elder Pliny had praised as one of the most beautiful buildings in Rome.[115] Here, in the classical heart of the city, Theoderican tiles were also used to refurbish the Temple of Vesta and lesser works near the gardens associated with the Basilica Nova (Maxentius'/Constantine's Basilica), while just to the southeast they were used to repair the marvelously vast bathing complex of Caracalla.[116] Even Rome's mighty walls were repaired and possibly strengthened with tiles bearing the words "Our Lord Theoderic, ruling for the good of Rome,"[117] and a later source records that the Senate was so thankful for these walls' restoration that it erected a golden statue in Theoderic's honor.[118]

But tiles, while revealing, provide only some of the evidence for the ideologically charged building projects funded in Rome at Theoderic's direction. Other mighty structures also received his largesse, either at the specific request of senatorial elites, out of unsolicited deference, or out of traditional or personal obligation, a further indication of Rome's centrality. Some time before 512, for instance, a specialist was sent to the "splendid sewers" of the Eternal City to see to their repair and cleaning.[119] Likewise, the upkeep of Rome's numerous aqueducts, whose "construction is a wonder and [whose] waters' wholesomeness is unique," was regularly serviced through a countship designed for the task.[120] Counts of Rome, on the other hand, were instructed to protect Rome's preexisting splendor, lest in an absence of vigilance "wicked hands" provide the "greatest of ruin ... amid [Rome's] unique beauty,"[121] while resident senators were admonished to prevent the misappropriation of funds sent "at the instigation of

---

[114] See Cullhed (1994), 60, for similar conclusions regarding Maxentius.

[115] See Pliny the Elder, *Natural History* 36.102.

[116] Siena (1984), 525, and Pani Ermini (1995), 220–2.

[117] Some of the tiles discussed earlier (n. 112) have been discovered within the Aurelian Walls, especially in its northeast circuit. For these and the possibility of Theoderican work on the walls' turrets, Pani Ermini (1995), 222–3.

[118] Isidore, *Hist. Goth.* 39: "muros namque [or: enim] eius [i.e. Romae] iste redintegravit, 'cuius rei gratia' [or: ob quam causam] a senatu inauratam statuam meruit."

[119] *Variae* 3.30.1: "propter splendidas Romanae cloacas civitatis." For this official and others, Della Valle (1959), 131–4, with the *Variae* citations that follow.

[120] *Variae* 7.6.2 (a general letter appointing an individual to the countship of the aqueducts): "In formis autem Romanis utrumque praecipuum est, ut fabrica sit mirabilis et aquarum salubritas singularis."

[121] *Variae* 7.13.1: "gravissimum damnum potest fieri in pulchritudine singulari"; and 7.13.3: "quaeras improbas manus."

many," and in addition to those already provided after 500, for the repair of the city's temples and public places.[122] Rome's prefect even had an official architect placed under his supervision, who, like the palace architect in Ravenna, was supposed to "pay attention to books and spend his free time with the teachings of the ancients," so that "we might renew the constructions of the ancients [in Rome] ... and adorn new [structures] with the glory of antiquity."[123]

PARTNERS IN RESTORATION

While a number of Roman monuments benefited from Theoderican patronage, on both a regular and an ad hoc basis, the underlying goal remained the same: for it to seem to the Romans of Rome as if "antiquity had been rather gracefully restored in our times."[124] Positive alterations like these fed into the ideological program of the era, adding to the overall feeling of Roman renaissance and renewal. But it was not always the case that Theoderic took full credit for the achievement, and the Theater of Pompey provides a notable case in point. This marvel of late republican Rome might not have been saved, according to the ruler of Italy, "had it not happened that we saw it ourselves."[125] But rather than repairing the structure himself and increasing his own reputation, Theoderic turned to a proud descendant of Pompey, the illustrious senator Quintus Aurelius Memmius Symmachus, for assistance.[126]

Symmachus' private foundations had already won him the reputation for being both an "exceptional founder and extraordinary adorner of

---

[122] *Variae* 3.31.4–5: "templa etiam et loca publica, quae petentibus multis ad reparationem contulimus, subversioni fuisse potius mancipata ... adhibite nunc studia, praestate solacia." Della Valle (1959), 179, interprets "templa" as a reference to Catholic churches in Rome. This is possible, since Theoderic is known to have patronized Catholic churches. See, for instance, Ennodius, #458.7 (cited in Chp. 5, n. 91). That said, Theoderic's repairs to the Temple of Vesta and possibly the Temple of Antoninus and Faustina (see later discussion) make the reading unnecessary.

[123] *Variae* 7.15.1–5: "ut et facta veterum exclusis defectibus innovemus et nova vetustatis gloria vestiamus.... Et ideo det operam libris, antiquorum instructionibus vacet."

[124] *Variae* 4.51.12: "nostris temporibus videatur antiquitas decentius innovata." Cf. La Rocca (1993).

[125] *Variae* 4.51.4: "Haec potuissemus forte neglegere, si nos contigisset talia non videre." Statements like these provide an excellent indication of just how useful an imperial visit might be for Rome's decaying structures.

[126] For Symmachus, *PLRE* 2, 1044–6 (Symmachus 9). That he traced his lineage to the house of Pompey has been inferred from *Variae* 4.51.3 (cited later), though see Cameron (1999), whose conclusions suggest that such a connection would have been fictive. Alternatively, the passage may refer to an early-fifth-century restoration undertaken by member of the Symmachi. See *CIL* 6 1193, with Della Valle (1959), 156–7, and Barnish (1992), 79, n. 7.

buildings" and "a most diligent imitator of ancient works."[127] This, along with his family's historic connection to the monument, was why he had been asked to oversee its refurbishment. He was supposed to help "maintain Rome in her wonders" and prevent "what has been left behind by your ancestors" from being "diminished under nobler descendants."[128] But whether accomplished "by mighty columns or devotedness to new building," he was promised the complete financial support of Theoderic's treasury, while still being allowed to acquire "the fame of good work" from the project.[129] It was hence a win-win situation. On the one hand, in striving to "restore antiquity," Theoderic was able to continue demonstrating his deference toward Rome and the Senate, establishing an important patron-client relationship with the influential Symmachus.[130] On the other hand, the monies granted to Symmachus provided the senator with a means of perpetuating his class' traditional practice of civic euergetism, in this case, refurbishing a monument of historical importance for his family. Indeed, increased senatorial impoverishment and disillusionment over the course of the fifth century had resulted in the near-extinction of such practices by the time of the Goths' arrival, but now, even if only through "secret" royal largesse, they could appear revitalized and refreshed.[131]

Nor does Symmachus appear to have been the only senator who benefited from such imperial generosity. A number of inscriptions recording contemporary building at Rome may hint at similar scenarios, some even demonstrating senatorial gratitude toward the Gothic king. The repair of the Flavian Amphitheater undertaken after an earthquake by the

---

[127] *Variae* 4.51.1–2: "fundator egregius fabricarum earumque comptor eximius... antiquorum diligentissimus imitator."

[128] For wonders, *Variae* 4.51.1: "dignum est, ut Romam, quam domuum pulchritudine decorasti, in suis miraculis continere noscaris."; for nobler descendants, *Variae* 4.51.3: "ut quod ab auctoribus vestris in ornatum patriae constat esse concessum, non videatur sub melioribus posteris imminutum."

[129] *Variae* 4.51.12: "Et ideo sive masculis pilis contineri sive talis fabrica refectionis studio potuerit innovari, expensas vobis de nostro cubiculo curavimus destinare, ut et vobis adquiratur tam boni operis fama."

[130] Symmachus was extremely well connected and had already established illustrious credentials before Theoderic's arrival. His fortunes, moreover, continued to rise during Theoderic's reign. Shortly after this commission (c. 507/12), he became *caput senatus* and (possibly) served as an envoy to Constantinople. Though true, he was later arrested in connection with the downfall of his son-in-law, Boethius, and executed on the charge of treason. See the Epilogue.

[131] On the decline, Ward-Perkins (1984), chp. 2 especially. König (2000), 222, draws an interesting parallel between Theoderic's relationship with Symmachus and the relationships that Augustus established with certain first-century senators, who were also "allowed" to renovate contemporary monuments. If correct and intentional on Theoderic's part, this would be yet another throwback to the principate.

illustrious senator Venantius Basilius, for instance, may have been funded through Theoderic's benefaction, even though its commemorative inscription claimed that Basilius "restored [it] at his own expense."[132] Likewise, a fragmentary inscription found within Rome's Forum and celebrating a restoration of the Atrium Libertatis, "which had been consumed by old [age]," famously dedicated the project to "our unharmed lords Anastasius, perpetual Augustus, and the most glorious and triumphal man Theoderic," though suggesting that a former *comes domesticorum* named Valerius Florianus was responsible for the task.[133] Finally, another fragmentary inscription from the Forum, found on a pedestal of an ornate column discovered near the Temple of Antoninus Pius and Faustina (and perhaps associated with repairs to this building), similarly dedicated some unknown project to "our unharmed lord, the most glorious king, Theoderic."[134]

Senators, then, were taking an active part in the rejuvenation of their city's historic monuments with (and doubtless without) the aid of Theoderic, complementing their *princeps'* munificence and adding to the overall sentiment of Rome's rebirth. Senatorial involvement, however, could also extend beyond the sphere of public works and monuments, ultimately serving private gain. Late antique emperors had done much to try to prevent public properties and works from being usurped through acts of private *praesumptio*, and Theoderic was no different. In one missive directed to the Senate he deplored the current misuses of the aqueducts and the theft of decorative bronze and lead from public buildings, claiming that their "general utility ought to be placed before the depraved desires of one man";[135] similarly he ordered all his *comites Romae* to exact the "fitting retribution

---

[132] *ILS* 5635 (*CIL* 6 1716 and Fiebiger 1, #186): "Deci(u)s Marius Venantius / Basilius v(ir) c(larissimus) et in(lustris), praef(ectus) / urb(i), patricius, consul / ordinarius arenam et // podium quae abomi / nandi terrae mo / tus ruina pros / travit sumptu pro / prio restituit." Admittedly the inscription may date earlier, to 484, or (as implied above) to after 508. For 484, *PLRE* 2, 218 (Basilius 13); Chastagnol (1966), 44; and Ward-Perkins (1984), 44; for 508, Ensslin (1959), 249–50; Siena (1984), 525; and Pani Ermini (1995), 221. The earthquake recorded in this inscription may be the same mentioned in Fiebiger 1, #181, which led to Theoderic's commissioning of Count Gudila to restore a podium and statue at Faenza.

[133] See Bartoli (1949–50), whose discovery of a fragment in the area around the Roman Curia allowed for a more complete version of the inscription (erroneously) recorded in Fiebiger 1, #187 (*ILS* 825, and *CIL* 6 1794): "Salvis domi[n]is nostris Anastasio Perpetuo / Augusto et Gloriosissimo ac Triumfali Viro / Theoderico Valerius Flori[an]us V C et Inl / ex com domest ex com [sacrar] larg Praef Urb / in Atrio Libertat[is] ..." For this structure and its importance, Della Valle (1959), 144–53, and Coarelli (1993), 133–5.

[134] *CIL* 6 1795 (Fiebiger 1, #189): "Salvo d(omi)n(o) [Theode]rico re[ge glorio]siss[imo]." Why "d n" has been resolved as "domino" and not "domino nostro" is unclear. The latter seems unquestionable.

[135] *Variae* 3.31.4: "Unius enim desiderio pravo generalis debet utilitas anteferri."

of the laws" on those culprits who "defile ancient beauty by cutting off its limbs and thereby do to public monuments what they deserve to suffer."[136] Rome and the Senate's special position within the empire, coupled with Theoderic's desire for "the City to be arranged with the splendor of surging constructions," however, provided for some interesting cases of imperial flexibility. In fact, Theoderic might gladly yield Rome's public resources and even property into private hands, just as he did elsewhere, provided the act did "not impede public utility or beauty."[137] Such generosity, moreover, could be seen as the act of a "good *princeps*,"[138] while providing yet another means for Rome to shed its decrepit appearance.

The *vir inlustris* and patrician Paulinus, for instance, petitioned Theoderic for the right to assume possession of certain dilapidated granaries within the city of Rome, asking for permission to repair them and pass them on as private property to his descendants. Informing the prefect of Rome, Argolicus, of his decision to grant the request and referring to it as an act of kindness, Theoderic suggested that, in pursuing his own advantage, Paulinus' "repair of ruins confers a gift to the Republic, especially in the City, where it is right for all constructions to shine forth, lest among so many adornments of her buildings there should appear an unsightly collapse of stones."[139] Such unsightliness might be sustained in other cities, the ruler of the West explained, but "in this [city], which is praised firstly by the mouth of the world, we can suffer nothing [to be] mediocre."[140] A similar rationale was provided to the *vir inlustris* and patrician Albinus, who requested (and was granted) permission to build private residences and workshops within the Porticus Curvae of the Forum. "Everyone," Albinus was told, "but especially those whom the Republic obligates with

---

[136] *Variae* 7.13.3: "ad tuum facias venire iudicium et rei veritate discussa congruam subeant de legibus ultionem, quia iuste tales persequitur publicus dolor, qui decorem veterum foedant detruncatione membrorum faciuntque illa in monumentis publicis, quae debent pati." In declaring that such wicked individuals ought to have their hands cut off, Theoderic appears to have been following the ruling of Emperor Majorian (*NMaj* 4.1), which ordered mutilation by the loss of hands for those who conspired with judges (needlessly) to destroy public works for private gain. Far from barbarous, then, Theoderic was upholding Roman law.

[137] *Variae* 4.30.3: "Unde nos, qui urbem fabricarum surgentium cupimus nitore componi, facultatem concedimus postulatam, ita tamen, si res petita aut utilitati publicae non officit aut decori."

[138] *Variae* 3.29.1: "Quis nesciat ... illud bonis principibus crescere, quod benigna possunt largitate praestare?"

[139] *Variae* 3.29.2: "quia confert magis rei publicae munus quisquis diruta maluerit suscipere reparanda, in ea praesertim urbe, ubi cuncta dignum est constructa relucere, ne inter tot decora moenium deformis appareat ruina saxorum." For Paulinus, *PLRE* 2, 847 (Paulinus 11).

[140] *Variae* 3.29.2: "In aliis quippe civitatibus minus nitentia sustinentur: in ea vero nec mediocre aliquid patimur, quae mundi principaliter ore laudatur."

the highest of honors, should rightly think of the improvement of his *patria*."[141] And since this patrician aspired to increase "the appearance of newness amid [such] ancient monuments," he proved himself "an inhabitant worthy of Roman constructions," and "his completed works" became a source of praise "for their author."[142]

What More?

Whether through direct benefaction granted to important monuments, or through the private subsidization of senatorial prestige projects, or by simply granting permission to noble Romans for the right to assume control of public works and to rebuild, the same basic outcome was achieved. More so than in generations, Rome and its decaying structures received extensive and at times lavish attention, allowing ancient constructions to be restored and providing a kind of adornment for the Senate and people of Rome, and all the inhabitants of Theoderic's realm.[143] Within this revived Roman Empire, Rome could rightly and proudly claim to be the center and capital of the world and know that there was a *princeps* who worked hard, "lest there be something desirable that the city of Rome was unable to have during our reign."[144]

But what more could Rome and the Romans of Rome have wanted? In 500 the Senate and people had been honored with an extended imperial visit, the traditional patronage and deference associated with it continuing long after Theoderic's departure. Less than a decade later, Ennodius was hailing the *status reipublicae* and claiming that youth had been restored to a once pathetically geriatric Rome. Within another decade, crumbling testaments to Rome's historic invincibility glimmered with pristine newness and even showcased wonders like North African beasts, all suggestive of the empire's renewed dominance. All that was missing, it seems, was Theoderic himself, who, though maintaining a residence upon the Palatine, was forced by "pressing need" to remain elsewhere. Regrettable though

---

[141] *Variae* 4.30.1: "Decet quidem cunctos patriae suae augmenta cogitare, sed eos maxime, quos res publica sibi summis honoribus obligavit." For Albinus, *PLRE* 2, 51–2 ((?Faustus) Albinus iunior 9). He was later accused of treason and defended by Boethius, an act that led to the latter's imprisonment and then execution. Albinus' own fate, however, is unknown.

[142] *Variae* 4.30.2–3: "antiquis moenibus novitatis crescat aspectus ... ut dignus Romanis fabricis habitator appareas perfectumque opus suum laudet auctorem."

[143] *Variae* 1.7.1: "ut redeat in decorem publicum prisca constructio et ornent aliquid saxa iacentia post ruinas." Cf. *Variae* 3.29 (cited earlier, n. 139) regarding "gifts" to the republic.

[144] *Variae* 3.53.6: "ne quid desiderabile putetur fuisse, quod sub nobis non potuit Romana civitas continere."

it was, the inhabitants of Rome were accustomed to imperial absences and, despite their disappointment, still had much for which to be grateful. Addressing his fellow senators in the Curia at the opening of his consulship in 514, Cassiodorus himself suggested the extent to which he and all senators were at a loss before so many blessings:

> Who could demand infinite things from me? Who could exact what he himself is unable to enumerate? ... Who could gather up with his efforts each thing that his [i.e. Theoderic's] generous hand has poured forth into so great an age? He fills this holy place [i.e. the Senate] with your honors; he nourishes the plebs with their established expenses; he pacifies the provinces with the serenity of his justice; he bridles proud barbarians with his *imperium*.[145]

Indeed, though able to provide a list of examples, much like Epiphanius of Pavia, what the Romans of Rome seemed at times to be lacking were the words sufficient to express their gratitude.

---

[145] *CassOratReliquiae*, p. 465, ln. 16–18: "quis a me postulet infinita? / quis exigat, quae numerare non suffi- / cit"; and p. 466, ln. 5–11: "quis enim momentis omne recolli- / gat, quod tot saeculis manus larga pro- / fundit? Hoc sacrarium vestris implet / honoribus, plebem statutis pascit in- / pensis, provincias iustitiae serenita- / te tranquillat, frenat superbas gen- / tes imperio." For the date and context, Chp. 10.

PART V

RENOVATIO IMPERII

An Empire with Provinces

Thus far this study has focused primarily on the Italian remnants of the western Roman Empire and the sentiments of Italo-Romans, who persisted in the belief that their realm was one of two Roman states and came to celebrate Theoderic and his Goths as its restorers and reinvigorators. The preceding chapters have discussed the origins and ideological framework for the celebratory language of the day, demonstrating how Roman niches could be carved for Gothic newcomers and how Theoderic could win acceptance as a good Roman emperor. Once again, it was believed, a dutiful *princeps* ruled an Italy-centered empire, and the deplorable conditions of the fifth century seemed to be swept away. "Hail, most splendid of rivers," Ennodius proclaimed while addressing the Adige in the aftermath of a major battle between Odovacer and Theoderic, "you who washes away the filth of a great portion of Italy, taking up the scum of the earth."[1] Italy had been cleansed under Theoderic's watchful eyes: inept, greedy, ignoble, and un-Roman men no longer wielded power;[2] merit mattered once more for political advancement; Roman law and order preserved justice; classical learning was revered and supported; Italian cities glimmered with refurbished, renovated, or completely new buildings; Liguria, just as Theoderic had promised, lived again; and Rome, the elderly mistress of the

---

[1] *PanTh* 46: "Salve, fluviorum splendidissime, qui ex maiore parte sordes Italiae diluisti, mundi faecem suscipiens." In true Homeric fashion, this river had literally fought on Theoderic's side against Odovacer. Cf. Delle Donne (1998), 75. Rota (2001b), 45f., and (2001a), 223–4, points out that this passage (and others from Ennodius' panegyric) borrow from Lucan's *Pharsalia*.

[2] The term "un-Roman" has been used here, as throughout, as a label for those deemed by "Romans" to be not Roman, regardless of "ethnic" labels. Hence, Theoderic, a Goth, or Ricimer, a "barbarian," can be "Roman," and Anthemius, a Roman, "un-Roman."

world, glittered with new and restored monuments, appearing not only young, but clad once more in martial attire.

Alone, these developments were worthy of jubilation, but the Theoderican golden age entailed yet another important and ideologically charged component: the reestablishment of a territorial empire that extended far beyond the confines of Italy, including long-lost lands in the Balkans, Gaul, and Spain.[3] Such an empire provided one of the most vital and obvious contributions to contemporary conceptions of imperial restoration. As a result, Theoderic and his Goths were worthy of celebration, not simply for correcting Odovacer's decadent Italy, but for restoring to it a number of its former provinces. The loss of these provinces during the fifth century had dealt a serious blow to Roman prestige and honor, nearly depriving the western empire of its raison d'être. But now their restoration served to reinforce Italy's role as the head of an independent Roman realm, reasserting its traditional standing.

Provinces, however, did more than justify the existence of Theoderic's Roman Empire. They also served, through their acquisition and proper administration, to legitimize further the position that Theoderic and his Goths were imagined to fill. More so than any of his immediate imperial predecessors, Theoderic defended the Roman heartland and extended its boundaries against its most recent encroachers, barbarians and Greeks. In so doing, he became a true *imperator*, commander in chief, whose victories lent substance to long-since-hollow imperial victory ideology. Triumphs, so intrinsically linked to the person of the emperor, asserted both Theoderic's and Italy's imperial status, and victory on such a scale exceeded Italian expectations, rendering Theoderic's subjects even more amenable to his rule. Victory, as already seen, also promoted the necessary and beneficial role imagined to be occupied by the Goths. By defeating and humiliating those who had recently humiliated Rome, Italy's Goths could be celebrated, much like Theoderic, as avengers and heroes. Once again, Rome's new soldiers were *invictissimi*, causing haughty barbarians and effeminate Greeks to cower before their Roman standards. And when the dust settled, they extended succor and benevolence to these provinces, just as they had to

---

[3] See later discussion. By comparison, Julius Nepos' "Empire of Italy" was restricted to the two dioceses of Italy, Sicily, Provence, and portions of Rhaetia, Noricum, and Dalmatia, a realm that shrank under Odovacer, who ceded Provence (476) and later abandoned Noricum (488). Odovacer is sometimes credited with restoring Sicily from Vandal rule, but see Clover (1999), 238, who claims that Gaiseric "did not occupy or otherwise dominate" the island. Cf. Conant (2012), 38. Likewise, his invasion of Dalmatia in 481 is sometimes seen as a restoration of that province. But this is a complicated issue, since to that point Dalmatia had been ruled by Nepos, and Odovacer, technically his vassal, had invaded as his avenger. Cf. Cesa (1994), 317–19.

Epiphanius' devastated Liguria. Noble Goths restored *civilitas* and *libertas* to the empire's new provincials, former Romans whose barbarian captivity had denied them their fundamental Roman rights. This too was important, for in the minds of many Italo-Romans, these provincials had been altered by decades of barbarian rule, becoming barbarized or at least appearing in danger of becoming so. Now, however, Theoderic and his Goths restored their Romanness to them and were hailed in Italy as liberators.

Provinces, therefore, mattered to Theoderic's Roman Empire, and so it is to these provinces, first to their perceived captivity and barbariza-tion, and then to their restoration and correction, that these final chap-ters will turn. But while a number of lost territories were reclaimed under Theoderic and his successors, and each was celebrated in the historical record, here the focus will remain almost exclusively on the provinces of southern Gaul, restored in the aftermath of an invasion launched in 508.[4] To some degree this emphasis is born of necessity, for the sources for other provinces are comparatively meager, while those for Gaul are rich, includ-ing numerous official documents in Cassiodorus' *Variae* and a substantial cache of personal material written by Ennodius.[5] Gaul, then, will suffice as a hypothetical model, and commonalities between this and other prov-inces, whenever apparent, will be pointed out. But caution must also be employed, and not just because of the lack of evidence needed for corrob-oration. As Ennodius, Cassiodorus, and others suggest, Gaul's relationship with Italy was unique, and the victory and subsequent restoration of it occupied an exceptional position within contemporary Italian mentalities; it was Gaul, not regions in Spain or the Balkans, that was the restored province par excellence for Italo-Romans, and, as will be shown, with good reason.

---

[4] For studies of non-Gallic provinces, including portions of Hispania, Pannonia, Noricum, and Rhaetia, see Heuberger (1937); Schäferdiek (1967), 68–84; Bierbrauer (1973), 1–10; Wolfram (1985); Prostko-Prostyński (1994a), 215–45; and Diaz and Valverde (2007); also Ensslin (1959), 172–9, who discusses the machinery of provincial government.

[5] The Italian sources for Spain are especially lacking; nor do contemporary Spanish sources, of which there are very few, provide much assistance. Pannonia is represented more completely, but both regions still pale in comparison with Gaul. Indeed, the *Variae* contains nearly fifty letters dealing with Gallic matters, but only two with Spain and thirteen with the Balkans. For Spain, *Variae* 5.35 and 5.39; for the Balkans, *Variae* 1.40, 3.23, 3.24, 3.50, 4.49, 5.14, 5.15, 5.25, 8.10, 8.21, 9.1, 9.8, and 9.9. Balkan matters are also treated in Ennodius' *Panegyric*, but Cassiodorus' later oration (admittedly fragmentary) only celebrates Gallia, tacitly referencing Spain and the Balkans in generalizations about *provinciae*.

9

BECOMING POST-ROMAN

LONG-HAIRED GAUL

While Italo-Romans had resisted the idea that the fifth century had led to the utter ruin and collapse of the western Roman Empire, their impression of the situation in Gaul was quite different. Their empire, as they imagined Italy to be, had been in dire straits and moribund, but the situation had proven salvageable, and eventually Theoderic and his Goths had come to the rescue. Gaul, however, had not been so lucky. Its fate over the course of the fifth century had been to be conquered by "real" barbarians, and by the time the Theoderican regime was strong enough to intervene, Gaul had been without direct Roman (i.e. Italian) rule for more than a generation, some regions even longer. Gaul, then, had not lapsed like Italy, but had fallen, and its long absence from imperial rule could have serious repercussions in the minds of Italo-Roman onlookers. Despite recollections of a Roman Gaul and the hope for its restoration, many believed that Gaul had been transformed, becoming a land of barbarians with few reminders of its Roman past. The claims of a young Cassiodorus were perhaps typical of his generation: "We used to only read in the annals that Gaul had once been Roman, but that was before our time and its believability wandered, doubtful."[1] By the early sixth century, words like these suggest, Roman Gaul was literally history, and its Roman past the stuff of legend.

But sentiments of this sort were not unique to this period; nor should Gaul's former Romanness be taken at face value. That Gaul was barbarous and the Gauls themselves barbarians was a traditional understanding, common knowledge throughout the empire for centuries, and a part of Gaul's pre-Roman and Roman identity. In fact, barbarian or semibarbarian

---

[1] *CassOratReliquiae*, p. 466, ln. 17–20: "Galliam / quondam fuisse Romanam solis tantum / legebamus annalibus: aetas non erat / iuncta notitiae, credulitas incerta vagabatur."

Gauls loomed large in the pages of Roman history. Before Rome had even acquired its empire, for instance, Gauls from Cisalpine Gaul (northern Italy) had been some of its greatest and most feared enemies, sacking the city in 387 BC. And though these Cisalpine Gauls had become Romanized and "Italian" by the first century BC,[2] the inhabitants of Transalpine Gaul, Gaul proper, failed to follow suit and persisted in their bogeyman status, despite generations of Roman rule. Portions in the south, to be sure, could be referred to as "more Italy than a province," and Arles, also in the south, as a "little Gallic Rome."[3] But much of Gaul continued to betray certain indigenous elements that inspired contemporary commentary. As late as the fourth and fifth centuries, "Roman" Gauls could appear as the kindred of Caesar's Gauls. The fourth-century historian Ammianus Marcellinus described Gallic women as virtual Amazons with "swollen necks," one alone able to best a whole band of foreigners with her punches and kicks "like a catapult," while their men, young and old, were depicted as warriors ferocious and hardened by nature.[4] They were "terrible for the fierceness of their eyes, fond of quarrelling, and overbearingly insolent."[5] Other sources depicted Gauls who still looked like Caesar's opponents. The fourth-century *Historia Augusta* featured a defeated Gallic tyrant, Tetricus, who was paraded in Rome as a captive Gaul wearing traditional Gallic trousers, while a panegyric by the fifth-century poet Claudian included a personified Gallia who was stereotypically "wild," with long hair, Gallic torque, and twin Gallic spears.[6]

[2] And the Senate recognized this, making Cisalpine Gaul a part of Italy in 42 BC. For the conquest and "Romanization" of northern Italy, Williams (2001a) and (2001b). Of course, "Italian" is a rather complicated concept as well. See Part I. For the memory of the Gallic sack of Rome, Ennodius, #191, and Julian, *Or.* 1.29. For northern Italy as once "Gallia," Sidonius, *Ep.* 1.5.7, and Cassiodorus, *Variae* 8.12.7–8. Both were demonstrations of historical knowledge; neither Cassiodorus nor Sidonius suggested that contemporary northern Italy was Gallic.

[3] For more Italy, Pliny the Elder, *NH* 3.31: "Italia verius quam provincia"; Gallic Rome, Ausonius, *Ordo Urbium Nobilium*, ln. 74: "Gallula Roma Arelas."

[4] For Gallic women, *Res Gestae* 15.12.1: "Nec enim eorum quemquam adhibita uxore rixantem, multo se fortiore et glauca, peregrinorum ferre poterit globus, tum maxime cum illa inflata cervice suffrendens, ponderansque niveas ulnas et vastas admixtis calcibus emittere coeperit pugnos, ut catapultas tortilibus nervis excussas." Cf. Van Dam (2007), 62, for a fourth-century depiction of Trier as an Amazon. For male Gallic warriors, *Res Gestae* 15.12.3: "Ad militandum omnis aetas aptissima, et pari pectoris robore senex ad procinctum ducitur et adultus, gelu duratis artubus et labore assiduo, multa contempturus et formidanda." Cf. Isidore, *Etymologiae* 9.2.

[5] *Res Gestae*, 15.12.1, which also includes a generalization about most Gauls' physical appearance: "Celsioris staturae et candidi paene Galli sunt omnes et rutili, luminumque torvitate terribiles, avidi iurgiorum, et sublatius insolentes."

[6] For Tetricus: *HA, DAur.* 34.2: "Inter haec fuit Tetricus chlamyde coccea, tunica galbina, bracis Gallicis ornatus." The Gallic significance, if any, of the yellow tunic is unclear, though the red

Images like these might suggest that Gaul and the Gauls had been unaffected by Roman rule, rendering sixth-century doubts about their Romanness less remarkable. But this was not the case; nor had such depictions necessarily militated against the acceptable Romanness of Gaul and its inhabitants. Representations like these were intentionally anachronistic, an expected topos, and taken with a grain of salt.[7] They were stereotypes, often failing to have substance even in the accounts that featured them. The same Gallic tyrant paraded in Rome in traditional Gallic attire, for instance, was also a former Roman magistrate and a senator, later rewarded with an additional magistracy in, of all places, southern Italy.[8] His participation as a captive Gaul in a triumph, symbolically meaningful, nonetheless struck those in attendance as bizarre and failed to strip him of his status as a Roman.[9] Similarly, Claudian's wild personification of Gaul was flanked by other indigenous caricatures;[10] despite her attire, she remained a valuable colleague of Rome, fit to recommend for the consulship a general who had protected her against the "real" barbarians, Germans and Franks.[11] Even Ammianus' Gauls, who were fond of quarreling and had terrifyingly fierce eyes, were remarkably neat and clean[12] and, most tellingly, had been "joined to our [Roman] society in an eternal compact."[13]

chlamys was the attire of a Roman general. The combination may have been intentionally Gallo-Roman. For the personified Gallia, Claudian, *de Consulatu Stilichonis* 2, ln. 240–2: "Tum flava repexo / Gallia crine ferox evinctaque torque decoro / binaque gaesa tenens animoso pectore fatur."

[7] See the introduction to Amory (1997); also Pohl (1998b) and Burns (2003), 3–5. For anachronisms in Ammianus' excursus on the Gauls (discussed earlier), Isaac (2004), 425.

[8] See *HA, TT* 24.1–5, where he is referred to as a "consularis" and "senator of the Roman people" and made "governor of all Italy" after Aurelian's triumph. Other sources, such as Aurelius Victor, *De Caesaribus* 35, suggest that Tetricus was only made governor of Lucania, an office nonetheless demonstrative of his continued Roman status.

[9] See *HA, DAur.* 34.4: "senatus (etsi aliquantulo tristior, quod senatores triumphari videbant) multum pompae addiderant."

[10] See Claudian, *de Consulatu Stilichonis* 2, where Spain appeared wrapped in olive leaves (ln. 228–30); Britain covered in beast skins, with tattooed cheeks, and wearing a sea-blue cloak (ln. 247–9); Africa sun-burned, with wheat in her hair and an ivory comb (ln. 256–7); and Italy covered in ivy and grapevines (ln. 262–4).

[11] Claudian, *de Consulatu Stilichonis* 2, ln. 243–6: "'qui mihi Germanos solus Francosque subegit, / cur nondum legitur fastis?'"

[12] Ammianus, *Res Gestae* 15.12.2 (in reference to the Aquitanians): "tersi tamen pari diligentia cuncti." Isaac (2004), 424, suggests that, since cleanliness was not part of the standard Gallic stereotype, the statement may be reflective of Ammianus' personal impression. Cf. Woolf (1998), 67f., for "neat and clean" as a form of "becoming Roman" for the Gauls.

[13] *Res Gestae* 15.12.6: "Omnes Gallias ... subegit Caesar dictator, societatique nostrae foederibus iunxit aeternis."

These, then, were not Caesar's Gauls, though they might resemble them at times. They were Rome's Gauls, *Gallo*-Romans, settled and mollified by Roman law, different, yet full-fledged members of Rome's order. As a consequence of their liminal position, they might range from nearly Italian to nearly German,[14] but diversity of this sort, as discussed earlier, was normal in the Roman Empire and did not exclude them from being Roman in their own way. Gauls could thus boast of famous Roman cities, Greek orators, refined senators, and even Roman emperors and at the same time take pride in their brutish and wild warriors who helped to make Rome's army invincible.[15] The similarities with Theoderic and his Goths are almost uncanny. Just like the Goths, stereotypical Gauls were once ferocious barbarians who had sacked Rome. Just like the Goths, they had been mustachioed savages who wore their hair long –so noticeably, in fact, that the Romans had once referred to their country as *Gallia Comata* (Long-haired Gaul). Just like the Goths, moreover, their barbarian ferocity, redirected in a Roman military capacity, had been transformed into praiseworthy and Roman *virtus*. And just like the Goths, many had adopted the culture of Rome's nobility, becoming highly educated Roman elites, complete with senatorial offices and noble pedigrees.[16] What was once recognizably Gallic, then, either conformed to or altered Roman expectations over centuries of imperial rule, becoming Roman. Just as the "Gothic" hairstyle had been internalized long before Theoderic's advent, so too had Tetricus' "Gallic" trousers.

Captured Gaul

As in most provinces, Gaul and its inhabitants had become Roman along a number of themes. But the complexities of their Romanness are important, for they had consequences for the way that Italo-Romans thought about this land in the aftermath of Roman rule. Stereotypes, even when anachronistic, remained deeply ingrained in Roman and more specifically Italo-

[14] See Burns (2003), 134, with Chp. 5.
[15] The Gallo-Romans featured in Ammianus' *Res Gestae* and Julian's opera provide great examples. Cf. *Res Gestae* 19.6 (bravery against Persians) and Julian's *Oratio* 1.34 (invincible army). This semibarbarous status was to be expected in the ranks of the army and was a useful kind of Romanness. See Chp. 5.
[16] And, indeed, unlike the Goths, there was a long-standing tradition of such officeholders, especially from Mediterranean Gaul, by the later empire. See Stroheker (1948), chp. 1. The extent to which Gaul became "Roman" largely informs the "crisis of identity" question associated with the fifth century. See Drinkwater and Elton (1992), as well as Van Dam (1985) and Mathisen (1993).

Roman society and were potent given the proper situation. Such images, as seen earlier, had provided material for exaggerated caricatures and might even be the subject of jest,[17] but under more pressing circumstances an outdated stereotype could be transformed into a kind of suppressed reality, serving to separate Gaul and Gauls from Roman fellowship.

Gallic usurpation and rebellion, which constituted yet another stereotype linking Gauls with barbarism, provide a case in point.[18] These acts had a long history of entailing in the minds of non-Gallic observers a rejection and loss on the part of Gaul, not merely of Roman rule, but of the civilizing processes that accompanied it. The very act of usurpation and rebellion, in other words, could once more transform Gallo-Romans into Caesar's Gauls, savages who were no longer restrained by Roman law and custom, but obeyed their natural instincts. Nor were even the most Roman of individuals in Gaul safe, for even the Roman senator Tetricus could, for a moment, lose his Roman veneer and become a new Vercingetorix, the Gallic archadversary of Julius Caesar, or worse still, a new Brennus, the first barbarian ever to sack the city of Rome: a foreign, overtly Gallic (and anti-Roman) nemesis.

Until the fifth century, at least, these Gallic rebellions had always been resolved and Gallic usurpers either defeated or accepted as the legitimate rulers of the Roman state. Despite sometimes decades of separation from the central empire, Gaul and its inhabitants could return with ease to their rightful Roman place.[19] Like Tetricus, they could be forgiven and corrected, and their native dispositions toward barbarism could be nullified by the reestablishment of Roman rule.

It becomes clear, therefore, that Italian sentiments toward Gaul and Gauls in the aftermath of Roman rule could draw from a rich history. The loss of Gaul was not an entirely new phenomenon, and there had been non-Roman and post-Roman Gauls in the past, both of which provided useful precedents for understanding contemporary developments. Though true, such a history of Gallic separation did not make the phenomenon any less troubling to contemporaries; nor, for that matter, were old models, however useful, completely appropriate given the specific context of the early sixth century. The Gaul of Ennodius and Cassiodorus, after all,

---

[17] The back and forth between Sidonius Apollinaris and a certain Italo-Roman named Candidianus (*Ep.* 1.8) demonstrates the ability of a Gaul and an Italian to satirize each other's respective homelands. Cf. Köhler (1995), 258.

[18] Rebellion was linked with ideas of *levitas, perfiditas, insania, furor*, and so forth, stock attributes of barbarians. See Dauge (1981), 176–7. For the link within a Gallic context, Urban (1999).

[19] See broadly, Urban (1999); on the third-century "Gallic" Empire, Drinkwater (1987).

had not rebelled but had been conquered. It was a *Gallia Capta* (Captured Gaul), taken by force by real barbarians and seemingly lost forever.[20] If no longer Roman, this Gaul had become so unwillingly, and this was a major complication that could, at times, demand deeper reflection.

Two rather different perspectives concerning post-Roman Gaul thus circulated among the inhabitants of Theoderic's Roman Empire. Gauls could, at one extreme, remain subject to the traditional understanding whereby, having left Roman rule, they reverted to their instinctual barbarism and became, once more, objects of revulsion; or, at another extreme, they could, as captives, retain their full-fledged Roman status and become, instead, objects of pity. There was room in the minds of Italian onlookers for much nuance and even contradiction, a reality that meant that either interpretation could be valid or invalid given the right circumstances. But the longer Gaul remained outside Rome's political sphere, the greater the potential grew for a barbarization model to dominate. Sooner or later parts of Gallia would become Francia, Burgundia, and Visigothia, and their inhabitants Franks, Burgundians, and Visigoths, rather than Gallo-Romans.[21] Those Romans in Gaul who seemed to be "weeping at their captivity" and struggling to maintain their Roman identities were thus slowly fading and becoming something else.[22] Nature and barbarian rule forced their transformation, but they were not alone. Time itself was driving a wedge between Gaul and Italy, while a generation reached maturity for whom Roman Gaul and Roman Gauls had little resonance or relevance.

---

[20] Indeed, the loss of Gallic provinces over the course of the fifth century was unprecedented. Though there had been earlier instances of barbarian invasion and capture of portions of Gaul (usually cities), in almost all these cases barbarian occupation had been short-lived and the barbarians easily dislodged. Some have even suggested that certain instances of capture were allowed to happen, their reconquest serving to bolster claims of Roman superiority and eternal victory. See Drinkwater (1997).

[21] Indeed, as *Variae* 1.46 (discussed in Chp. 5) demonstrates, the Italian government was already applying the term "Burgundia" to those lands in Gaul ruled by the Burgundians. In Burgundy and southern Gaul, on the other hand, the term "Gallia" was still being employed in reference to the Burgundian kingdom. Cf. *Vita Caesarii* 1.21, 1.55, and 1.60; likewise Avitus of Vienne, *Ep.* 12, 93, 94, and *Passio Sigismundi* 2. The terms *Visigothia* and *Visigoths* have been employed here despite the fact that both the Ostrogoths and the Visigoths are generally referred to as *Gothi* in fifth- and sixth-century sources. A few letters in the *Variae*, such as *Variae* 3.1.1 and 3.3.2, do distinguish between Theoderic's *Gothi* and Alaric II's *VVisigothi*, however. Moreover, and despite sharing the same Gothic appellation, real differences were perceived to exist between both peoples. See later discussion, as well as Diaz and Valverde (2007), 353–60.

[22] For weeping, *VE* 92: "ut captivitatem flerent." Though a connection with the Jewish captivity might have been implied by Ennodius, the passage bears no specific resemblance to any in the Vulgate.

THE NEW RHINE

The sentiments of Cassiodorus cited at the beginning of this chapter, which betray an utter disbelief that Gaul had ever been Roman, are easy to explain. Sheltered in the south of Italy and socially oriented away from central and northern Europe, men like Cassiodorus barely knew Gaul and, born after 476, never knew a Roman Gaul beyond the one of books and memory.[23] They could, in the wake of Theoderic's intervention in 508, be enthusiastic about a Gallic restoration, but they also may not have given Gaul much, if any, reflection before this time. Their Gaul was already a barbarian Gaul. But for Italo-Romans like Ennodius, northerners and Ligurians especially, the situation was different. Men like these were uniquely positioned with respect to Gaul.[24] Just as they were coming of age, their country was in the process of becoming the new Roman frontier, the ideological stopping point for an empire redefining itself and its Romanness.[25] The Alps, ever-present and intimidating, were the new Rhine,[26] and its soldiers, in some places an everyday sight, provided a kind of defendable gateway for Liguria, able to be closed in the face of invading barbarians, whose oaths could not be trusted.[27] This frontier status, by its very nature, served to make Gaul an "other" in the minds of Ligurians, rendering a neighboring country that was already famous for its mists increasingly clouded and dark.[28] Gaul not only seemed dangerous, but was in reality an actual source of peril and depredation for this province. When Ennodius claimed that Liguria had been brutalized in the 490s and that Theoderic had needed to resuscitate her, the cause of that suffering had been an invader from Gaul,

---

[23] See Chp. 2. In the case of books, the preceding discussion has already suggested that the Gaul found here was often stereotypically un-Roman, or at best, on the fringes.

[24] Both central and southern Gaul, in fact, as Ennodius' connections to Provence and Burgundy demonstrate. Only Francia seems to have been alien to him, and, indeed, if the letters of Sidonius are any indication, "Belgian" Gaul had long since become disconnected, even from those residing at its borders.

[25] Cf. Brown (2003), 97.

[26] For this Alpine frontier, Brogiolo and Possenti (2001), 259–64; also Christie (1991) and Azzara (2006), 14–16. For the terror (and occasional disdain) that the Alps inspired in Ennodius, see his elaborate *Itinerarium Brigantionis Castelli* (#245), with #10.4, and #31. Cf. Sidonius Apollinaris, *Ep.* 1.5.2, and Ammianus Marcellinus, *Res Gestae* 15.10.4.

[27] *Variae* 2.5.2: "qui ... quasi a quadam porta provinciae gentiles introitus probatur excludere. In procinctu semper erit, qui barbaros prohibere contendit, quia solus metus cohibet, quos fides promissa non retinet." Cf. *Variae* 7.4 (in reference to Rhaetia) and 3.48 (regarding a fort near Trento), with Cavada (1994).

[28] See Sidonius, *Ep.* 1.8.1, which suggests that mists and fog were synonymous with Lyon (and by extension Gaul) in the minds of certain fifth-century Italians.

"that savage Burgundian," Gundobad, whose followers had ravaged her.[29] Nor was this the only occasion during Ennodius' lifetime when marauding armies would come from beyond the Alps, and threats of this sort would continue to plague Italians long after his death.[30]

But while there was real danger, there were also, as might be expected along any frontier, periods of peaceful coexistence and interdependence between cisalpine and transalpine peoples, factors that fostered a kind of frontier society that straddled the Alps.[31] Social realities could belie political ones, and this was especially the case with respect to Provence and Liguria, where strong social ties had linked both regions for centuries.[32] Indeed, Ligurians like Ennodius were ideally located to be sensitive to ideas of Gallic Romanness and barbarian captivity. They traveled to Gaul on multiple occasions, conducted business there, had a number of Gallic friends with whom they corresponded frequently, played host to Gallic individuals traveling through Italy, and recommended the same Gauls to their Italian friends and patrons. They could even, like Ennodius, be born in Gaul and continue to have family ties there.[33] Yet just like Ennodius, when forced to choose, these well-connected Italians were foremost Ligurians and Italo-Romans. They could have friendly Gallic connections and be sensitive to conditions in Gaul, but as Ennodius' own correspondence will soon demonstrate, they could be shockingly insensitive and unsympathetic to Gallic Romanness. Even they, at times, found cause to invoke what seemed to be innate Gallic barbarism or barbarization. Southerners like Cassiodorus could be ambivalent, but men like Ennodius were bipolar, fluctuating between agonizing sympathy and extreme hostility.

---

[29] VE 139 (with Chp. 7): "Haec ... burgundio inmitis exercuit, nos tamen ... populatae patriae cessamus succurrere."

[30] See later discussion for a Burgundian raid on Liguria in 507. Another failed Burgundian invasion is recorded in 536. See *Variae* 12.28. Eventually the Franks would follow in their footsteps, briefly conquering portions of northern Italy during the Gothic War and continuing to be a threat thereafter until Charlemagne's conquest of the Lombard Kingdom. As will be demonstrated, then, the extension of Theoderic's empire into Gaul might best be explained as a means of protecting Italy, a traditional raison d'être for Roman Provence and doubtless the rationale behind Nepos' own willingness to relinquish the Auvergne in exchange for this region.

[31] Cf. Geary (1988); Whittaker (1994); and Elton (1996).

[32] And, in fact, would continue to do so throughout the Middle Ages and early Modern Era. See earlier discussion for northern Italy as "Gallic" and southern Gaul as "Italian."

[33] Ennodius' works demonstrate that he personally went to Gaul at least twice in his lifetime, once to Lyon and once to Briançon (see VE 147–77, with Chp. 7, and #245, cited in n. 26, earlier). For his relations with the inhabitants of Gaul, see later discussion.

The Citadel of Eloquence

Italo-Roman perceptions of post-Roman Gaul were hence complicated, but there were still "real" Romans residing in this land in the early sixth century, and for Ennodius and others, they could be recognized through their Roman erudition and Latin eloquence. This, of course, should come as no surprise. Knowledge of the liberal arts and the ability to exhibit it in a refined way could make one a member of an elite (and truly Roman) society and had even worked in the favor of certain Goths like the Amals. This understanding, in fact, had mass appeal to Latin-speaking elites throughout the empire, and its function within post-Roman Gaul had a history predating the era of Ennodius. In the 470s, for example, when no longer residing in a Roman Gaul, Sidonius Apollinaris had expressed what amounted to the same sentiment in a letter to a certain grammarian. Here he explained that the societal role of teachers had become more important than ever, providing a "safe haven for Latin speech, though Latin arms had suffered shipwreck."[34] Without the Roman Empire, he explained, "the only token of [Roman] nobility will be knowledge of [Latin] letters,"[35] and by this he meant that Latin erudition would become the only sign of (elite) Roman status in a post-Roman Gaul.

This passage, often cited in modern works,[36] illustrates the importance of Roman culture, and hence Romanness, for Gallo-Romans like Sidonius, who were coming to terms with the realities of their era; but it is also important because it was absolutely correct. A full generation later, many Italo-Romans continued to recognize the Romanness of Gaul and Gauls for this very reason, and Ennodius' own correspondence provides the clearest indication of this.[37] The learned men and women to whom he wrote were praised above all for their Roman erudition, some even described as veritable fonts of Latin eloquence. And while full of flatteries and expected

---

[34] Sidonius, *Ep.* 8.2.1: "teque per Gallias uno magistro sub hac tempestate bellorum Latina tenuerunt ora portum, cum pertulerint arma naufragium."

[35] *Ep.* 8.2.2: "nam iam remotis gradibus dignitatum ... solum erit posthac nobilitatis indicium litteras nosse." Cf. *Ep.* 5.5 to Syagrius of Lyon, who was recommended a healthy dose of Latin literature in order to maintain his noble status in the face of Burgundian Germanization. Neither of these seems to be an example of the largely "invented" idea of literary decline among the elites of fifth-century Gaul, but see Mathisen (1988) and (1993), 105–18.

[36] Cf. Van Dam (1985), 163; Mathisen (1993), 109; and Harries (1994), 246–7. Van Dam even goes so far as to suggest, 164–5, that Sidonius' ornate Latin was a coping mechanism in the face of Roman collapse.

[37] Non-Ennodian examples can be found in other Italian sources. The Ligurian poet Arator, for instance, praised the Gallo-Roman Parthenius for his eloquence in his *Epistula ad Parthenium* (cited later), and the *Variae* did similarly in the case of the father of the Gallic consul Felix.

topoi, there really was something to his language; the cosmopolitan and intellectual communities for which southern Gaul and especially Arles were renowned remained intact at this time, and Ennodius was in contact with some of their greatest participants.[38]

His letters to Firminus of Arles, a relative and perhaps the same Firminus who had published the ninth book of Sidonius' epistolary collection, are exemplary.[39] Firminus' eloquent words, according to Ennodius, were a reminder of the superiority of intellectual Romans, referred to as *perfecti* (perfect ones), and the meanness of others, whose "rough speech" and lack of talent "sowed darkness" and "engendered a kind of blindness from the ambiguity of their clouded narratives."[40] Firminus, however, was "established in the citadel of eloquence."[41] Though residing outside Theoderic's Roman Empire, he was a "learned author," who proved that "the splendor of perfectly refined speech glistens forth [in Arles], where eloquence preserves its riches with the bridle of expertise."[42] "Love of the unlearned burdens the conscience of the perfected,"[43] Ennodius explained, and even he could fail to live up to the high standards established in Gaul, despite good intentions. Firminus rightly "sought in others what you practice and love," but the meagerness of Ennodius' studies "revealed itself in far-away places," separated as he was from the "gymnasium of scholarly learning" that was Arles.[44] Ennodius even confessed upon reading Firminus' eloquent words that he was unworthy of his own Gallic lineage and thus, "like a foreigner," could only praise Firminus for his skills, not imitate them.[45] His talents were like a "parched water jug" in comparison with Firminus' "flooding ocean," a mere "oil lamp" compared to the "rays of

---

[38] See Delage (1994), 24–9, and Février (1994), 46–9. The intellectual community at Arles even made incredible gains owing to the arrival of refugees from North Africa, northern Gaul, and Pannonia.

[39] For Firminus, *PLRE* 2, 471 (Firminus 4).

[40] #12.2: "At ubi scaber sermo angustiam pauperis signat ingenii nec conceptum suum in ordinem digerendo noctem studio elocutionis interserit et nebulosae narrationis ambiguo quandam generat de ipsa explanatione caecitatem." The statement is ironic, given the complexity of Ennodius' own Latin. For *perfecti*, see later discussion.

[41] #12.2: "in eloquentiae arce constitutus."

[42] #12.1: "Iucunda sunt commercia litterarum docto auctore concepta: illa in quibus ad unguem politi sermonis splendor effulgorat, ubi oratio dives frenis peritiae continetur."

[43] #12.2.: "Gravat conscientiam perfectorum amor indocti."

[44] #40.3–4: "quaeritis nimirum in aliis quod exercetis, quaeritis quod amatis. Nos ab scolarum gymnasiis sequestrati.... Mei macies longe se monstrat studii." Cf. Sidonius, *Ep.* 1.6.2, where Rome is referred to as the *gymnasium litterarum*. By implication, Arles, once referred to as a "Little Gallic Rome," maintained its prior status.

[45] #40.4: "ego mea sum inpar prosapia, me dotibus vestris quasi peregrinum scientiae plenitudo non tetigit, ego vos tantum laudare magis quam imitari valeo."

the sun."[46] Gaul, then, was distant and remote, an "other" in this sense, to be sure. But Firminus was in a position to judge according to Roman standards, and Ennodius' highly rhetorical language, full of false modesty that begged for reciprocal praise, reiterated his correspondent's status. Such exchanges were an old game played by Roman elites for centuries, a kind of verbal badminton. That the game continued uninhibited and that a Gaul like Firminus still appeared as a star athlete is thus significant and a testament to Gaul's continued Romanness.

Nor was Firminus alone. The famous teacher of rhetoric Julianus Pomerius, another correspondent of Ennodius, was similarly gifted. North African in origin, perhaps Mauritanian,[47] Pomerius had joined the intellectual scene at Arles, becoming, in Ennodius' words, an *alumnus Rhodani*, a foster son of the Rhone.[48] His learning was exceptional, and stories of his knowledge of Greek and Latin had left Ennodius and his relations in Italy awestruck, much (apparently) to the rhetorician's surprise. In the only extant correspondence between the two, dated to the spring or summer of 503,[49] Ennodius playfully explained the situation: "Perhaps you thought you were hiding in some place, a man whom the splendor of knowledge reveals to [us] placed far off."[50] But a man so "fat with talent," who had "devoured the greatest portions of the perfection derived from the twin association [of both libraries]," could not hide, even if "most separated" and in Gaul.[51] Indeed, it was the lack of good information and the unreliability of rumors, both engendered by this distance, that had led Ennodius, perhaps a bit too rashly, to initiate correspondence in the first place.[52] "I want to be the leading addressee of your letters," he explained, "so that the wealth of Gaul may come to Italy unaltered from its travels."[53] Pomerius, then, was a master

[46] #40.3: "arentis ingenii guttis quaedam oceani fluenta provocamus, quasi lychnis contra solis radios pugnaturi."

[47] See *PLRE* 2, 896.

[48] See #39.3 (cited more fully later).

[49] For the date, Kennell (2000), 63, with *PLRE* 2, 896. For an excellent discussion, Schröder (2007), 189–95.

[50] #39.1: "An forsitan putabas te in quocumque loci delitiscere, quem scientiae lux longe positorum monstrabat aspectui?"

[51] For fat and devoured, #39.2: "utriusque bybliothecae fibula, perfectionis ex gemino latere venientis partes maximas momordisti, procurando ut tali ingenium tuum saturitate pinguisceret"; for most seperated, #39.3: "me seiunctissimus instruxisti."

[52] For lack of information, #39.2.: "et nisi me in laudibus tuis domestica quidem relatio, sed per inperitiam sui pauper angustet et amplissima meritorum tuorum praeconia relatoris artet exilitas"; too rashly, #39.1: "nolo evadere opinionem temerarii, dummodo ad notitiam possim pervenire perfecti."

[53] #39.1: "Volo esse paginarum praevius destinator, ut Galliarum bona ad Italiam migrent sine ullo formae suae translata dispendio." In other words, Ennodius did not want to receive

of Roman erudition, more impressive than many of his contemporaries, Gallic or Italian, whose knowledge of Greek was less refined or nonexistent.[54] More so than in the case of Firminus, Ennodius was thus willing to express feelings of being outclassed by his addressee, again demonstrating the occasional dominance of Gaul in the field of Latin letters (and by proxy, Romanness) in the minds of certain Italo-Romans.

Pomerius, it seems, had found merit in Ennodius' introductory letter, but Ennodius remained humble:

> You have searched everywhere in my letters, which were dictated without care, for Roman smoothness and a talent for flowing Latin. I believe an anxious and diligent scrutinizer has found, while hastening through unwrought words, what revision can refine.[55]

Ennodius was quick to admit that his writings lacked polish and required reworking, suggesting that Pomerius had been too kind. It was Pomerius and Gaul who were superior, and there was nothing wrong with this in his estimation. "Latinity strengthens those residing amid the schools of her studies, even if they are natives, since (wondrous to say) it is fond of foreigners."[56] This statement is revealing. Though Pomerius was now residing in a foreign land and no longer politically Roman, his knowledge of Latin nonetheless proved that he was still a Roman, serving (just as Sidonius had suggested) as a token of his Romanness.

There were still others residing in post-Roman Gaul whose sweet speech and Latin letters recommended them to Italians like Ennodius, but an extensive treatment would be superfluous, not least because some have already been encountered in previous chapters. Ennodius' own epistolary collection contains some fifteen Gallic correspondents with evidence for more, each explicitly or implicitly Roman through his or her education.[57] His other works betray similar individuals, while contemporary Italo-Roman sources help to fill in the picture. There was, for example, Leo, the

---

secondhand (and potentially altered) information, a common concern among letter writers. Cf. Sidonius, *Ep.* 2.11 and 7.14.

[54] See the discussion of Greek learning in Chp. 6.

[55] #39.3: "in epistulis meis sine cura dictatis Romanam aequalitatem et Latiaris undae venam alumnus Rhodani perquirebas. Sollicitus credo scrutator et diligens quid lima poliret invenit, dum per infabricata verba discurreret."

[56] #39.4: "Ergo etsi indigenas et inter studiorum suorum palestra versatos fulcit latinitas, mirum dictu, quod amat extraneos."

[57] For many of these, see later discussion.

counselor of Euric featured in the *Life of Epiphanius*, a correspondent of Sidonius and a winner of declamation contests.[58] There was also the father of the Gallic consul Felix, praised for his knowledge of Greek and Latin letters and natural science, and Felix himself, a "vestige of his paternal praises," who demonstrated while in Italy "not alien customs but Roman gravity."[59] Still others, like the priest and later bishop Stephanus, wrote to Ennodius "with such a pure stream" that he claimed his very innards "were drenched with secret passion."[60] While Ennodius' own sister, Euprepia, then residing in Gaul, was praised for pouring "twice as much honey" into an epistle, rousing, as Ennodius declared, "the depths of my heart" and causing "my captive mind, having left the residence of my body, to long for you."[61]

These examples suggest that in an empire that no longer included Gaul, the connection provided by literary culture, particularly when manifested in letter writing, could unify like-minded elites residing in separate regions. Ennodius put it best in a letter to yet another Gallic correspondent, Apollinaris: "The abundance of a vigorous pen feeds a friendship preserved in the heart: you made me, through continuing your writing, unmindful of our separation, sowing your venerable likeness within your gentle address."[62]

Writing, as in the past, fostered a society of letters that helped its participants forget about the realities of spatial separation.[63] But now, in the early sixth century, such traditional separations had been exacerbated and further complicated by new political and ideological dimensions. Though letters and their sweet words could keep Gaul very Roman for those in Italy, the situation remained fragile. Silence was devastating, and not just to those hoping to receive word from Gaul, but in its consequences.[64] Without

---

[58] See VE 85 and 89–91, with Chp. 1. Leo's eloquence was confirmed not only by his declamation contest trophies, but also through his recognition of a similar kind of eloquence in Epiphanius, who defeated King Euric with this uniquely "Roman" weapon.

[59] See *Variae* 2.3.3–5, with Chp. 10.

[60] #79.2: "Talis est vestrarum ratio litterarum ... et ita puro ditant gurgite, ut occulto ab eis viscera subfundantur incendio."

[61] #268.3: "post admonitionem meam duplicia in litteris mella fudisti, quae tota pectoris secreta concuterent et ad desiderium tui captivam animam relicta corporis sede transferrent." Cf. #313.2 (also to Euprepia).

[62] #151.1–2: "Stili frequentia vivaci pabulo insitam pectoribus nutrit amicitiam.... Aliquanto enim tempore continuando scriptionem inmemorem me sequestrationis effeceras, dum effigiem venerabilem placido inserebas adloquio." Cf. Sidonius, *Ep.* 7.14.2. For Apollinaris, PLRE 2, 115 (Apollinaris 4).

[63] Cf. Kennell (2003), 124–5.

[64] Having read Euprepia's sweet words, for instance, Ennodius entreated her not to "remove from a thirsty man the drink of affection already drunken at [her] bestowal" (#268.5). At least twenty other letters dispatched to Gallic correspondents mention silence.

knowledge, there was little to keep Gaul Roman in the minds of those beyond the Alps; without contact, men like Ennodius, with their unique Gallic connections, became disconnected and alienated from Gaul, much like Cassiodorus. To the same Euprepia who had apparently been silent for too long, Ennodius wrote, "you live again among us ... we see your love resurging as if from some kind of grave, since we believed through your disregard for us that a living person had occupied a tomb."[65]

Silence, in other words, was deadly, but continued writing was the cure.[66] As Ennodius explained to another noble lady of Arles, Archotamia, letters like hers kept Gaul in the back of his mind, even if he could not see it with his own eyes;[67] moreover, Romans like her made the prospect of a journey to Gaul, however terrifying, actually possible. "I would truly like there to be a reason for me to come to Gaul," he claimed, "so that kissing your eyes, [I] might bless you in whatever condition of suffering [you may find yourself]."[68]

NEAR THE SETTING OF THE SUN

There were real Romans residing in Gaul, men and women whom some in Italy were both highly aware of and deeply committed to. But Italo-Romans like Ennodius were not delusional. However much they accepted or regretted it, they understood that times had changed and that this was no longer Roman Gaul. Literati like Firminus, Pomerius, and Leo were relics from a bygone era: noble Romans who had resided in Gaul before its ultimate loss to the *barbaricum*. They could pass on their knowledge of Roman culture to upcoming generations, to young men like the future bishop of Arles, Caesarius, for instance; but the environment within which these youths of Gaul were maturing was changing, both in reality and in the minds of onlookers.[69] Even for well-informed Ligurians, political detachment from Italy and the Roman Empire was acting as a

---

[65] #52.1–2: "Revixisti apud nos.... Vidimus amorem quasi de quadam sepultura surgentem ... quam credebamus per contemptum nostri viventem busta conplesse."

[66] #52.5: "Poteris errata corrigere, si praesentia non vales, scriptione multiplici."

[67] #291.1: "Ego Gallias, quae totum me propter vos sibi vindicant, si oculis non inspicio, affectione non desero."

[68] #319.7: "Vere sola mihi vellem causa existeret Gallias expetendi, ut cum domno meo presbytero, utrique osculantes manus et oculos tuos, beatem te in quavis adflictione temporis redderemus." This *adflictio* was not "Gallic captivity" but simply the human condition; the kiss was intended, along with the priest's, to provide comfort.

[69] For Ceasarius' private instruction by Pomerius and eventual rejection of classical learning, see *Vita Caesarii* 1.9, with Février (1994), 52, who suggests that this was a common Christian trope. Ennodius certainly believed that Caesarius was eloquent, but the *sermo humilis* employed in

catalyst, causing Gaul and Gauls to devolve to their pre-Roman state and allowing nature to take its course. Caesar's Gauls were reemerging from the wilderness, not just as an anachronistic stereotype, but as a bona fide reality. Nowhere is this development more apparent than in the series of correspondence between Ennodius and his sister Euprepia, written during the opening years of the sixth century.

Unfortunately, not much beyond the notices provided in Ennodius' epistles is known about Euprepia. She seems, like many of the women encountered in Ennodius' letters, to have been well educated and to have shared a similar understanding of the importance of "sweet speech" for noble Romans.[70] Not only was her style at times complimented by Ennodius, as earlier, but she was also concerned that her son, Lupicinus, receive a traditional education along the same lines. Whether she was raised in Italy, like her brother, is unclear but probable considering it was from a home in Italy that she left for Gaul, placing her son in Ennodius' care. Her destination appears to have been Arles, where she hoped to secure the inheritance of certain family lands.[71] She may or may not have returned to Italy, but what is certain is that her actions during her stay in Gaul were poorly received by her increasingly estranged brother, who viewed them, in part at any rate, as a consequence of her Gallic naturalization. Long silence had already made Euprepia seem almost dead, and Ennodius and Lupicinus expressed concern. "We believed that you had endured difficulties," he explained in one letter, and "I kept going over reasons that might render you innocent."[72] But when Euprepia finally wrote and provided them with excuses, a series of rebukes followed, each demonstrating a connection between her behavior and her change in country. In Ennodius' estimation, something was amiss in Gaul, and worse still Euprepia, a classically infirm woman, had gone "Gallic."[73]

In one blunt letter, Ennodius expressed his severe disappointment with his sister's failure to correspond, an act he saw as neglectful of her familial

Caesarius' extant sermons does suggest an intentional movement away from the high style of many of his contemporaries. Cf. Bartlett (2001).

[70] The fact that she ran within some of the same lettered circles in Gaul as Ennodius suggests this, though family connections might be responsible. These individuals included Archotamia, Bassus, Viola, and Cynegia.

[71] For Arles, #319.3; for family lands, #84.4. See also #60 (to Faustus), which suggests these lands were ultimately lost, having been handed over to certain Goths in the aftermath of Gaul's "restoration." Indeed, an Italian family's ownership of land in Gaul was a more pragmatic reason to have concern for this country.

[72] #52.2: "Credimus te dura perpessam"; #52.5: "quae te innocentem faciant causas ingressi."

[73] See #109.2, where Ennodius suggested that Euprepia was mentally infirm (*mente male credulam*) and unable to flee from her vices, despite changing regions. The implication was that Euprepia was naturally weak, rather close to *infirmitas sexus*. This is made clearer in #258.4,

duties. "In what barbarous land," he tellingly asked her, "did heretofore maternal care hide? Where did what was owed to your brother wander?"[74] Answering his own question, Ennodius alleged that Euprepia's mind had retired to some place even farther away than Arles,[75] but that this was no excuse for such neglect. "If suffering, the consort of sojourning abroad, had driven you to the farthest bounds of the earth, the faith of a sister and the concern of a mother should have been in attendance."[76] Foreign travel was difficult, and Gaul was far away, but family obligations, especially to the son and brother left behind in Italy, were supposed to remain paramount.

Euprepia's behavior was thus disturbing, particularly since she had not traveled to the farthest bounds of the earth or to some barbarous land, places that might account for (but not excuse) such behavior. Instead, she had gone to Arles, where Ennodius knew there were real Romans. But were there really? In another letter to Euprepia Ennodius hinted at certain "evils of the provinces [and] onrushes of men," and claimed that his sister had not censured the excesses of those in her midst with the reprimands they deserved.[77] Even when Euprepia was not shirking her familial duties, then, the Gaul to which she had journeyed could seem a more sinister and dangerous place, a fact indicative of its perceived otherness in the minds of Italian onlookers. But when Euprepia was negligent, Gaul became even worse. "In the setting of the sun," Ennodius reprimanded, "next to which you claim to have been, you have kept your feelings of dutiful love cold."[78] This was an old understanding of Gaul, one that Caesar and others would

where Ennodius, having alleged that Euprepia had become a savage Gaul, claimed, "Again your different sex and nature promises exactly as the most wise Solomon says [Pr 27:7]: A soul, which is in abundance, mocks the honeycomb." The allusion suggests that Euprepia's sex and nature granted her a perpetually incomplete soul that was prone to error, since Proverbs 27:7 finishes with "but to a hungry soul every bitter thing is sweet."

[74] #52.2: "Ubinam gentium materna hactenus cura delituit? Ubi quod fratri debebatur erravit?" The rendering of *ubinam gentium* here is more literal than the conventional "where in the world," and seems more fitting, as it emphasizes the otherness and barbarity that are implied throughout. Cf. Gioanni (2006), 68.

[75] #52.2: "Ad longiora animus tuus quam corpus abscesserat."

[76] #52.3: "Si te ad ultima terrarum confinia peregrinationi socia dispulisset adversitas, illic sequi debuit germanae fides et sollicitudo genetricis."

[77] #109.2: "Nolo, soror Euprepia, quidquam de provinciarum malis vel, sicut dixisti, hominum inmissione causeris.... Circa propinquos tibi fuit tale propositum, ut nec benefacta ipsorum iusta interpretatione pensares nec excessus debita tantum reprehensione corriperes." To be fair, Ennodius also claimed that she had not praised those in her midst for their good deeds.

[78] #52.3: "Sed in occasu solis, cui proxima fuisse narraris, frigidum pii amoris pectus habuisti." Cf. the correspondence between Sidonius and Candidianus (*Ep.* 1.8), discussed earlier.

have recognized. From the perspective of Italy, Gaul was literally where the sun set, far to the west, and this fact impacted its climate and hence its peoples.[79] Gaul was cold and dark, and by extension so too was its population. Ennodius soon made this point clear, asserting, "You have accepted the mind-set of the provincials whom you have visited. You changed regions and renounced the practice of *pietas*."[80] "Disavowing association with Italy" and spurning in the process her friends and loved ones, Euprepia had herself become a Gaul, a coldhearted and irresponsible savage.[81] Her "change in country" had caused a fundamental "alteration of [her] personality,"[82] and such occurrences meant that Gaul was not safe for civilized individuals like Ennodius.

Indeed, it would have pleased Ennodius very much to cross the Alps and give his sister a stern reprimand in person, perhaps then visiting more dutiful correspondents like Archotamia and Firminus in the process. But the possibility was too risky. "How afraid I am," he asserted, "to reproach your carelessness with a long conversation."[83] Visiting this Gaul, in other words, was not an option.

Barbarian Gaul

Ennodius' harsh comments to his sister are indicative of Gaul's continued barbarian status before an Italian audience, even a well-connected one. But this apparent barbarization of Gaul, as discussed previously, was not simply the result of a process of regression or de-Romanization. Other barbarians, real barbarians in the minds of Italo-Romans, had largely been to blame. Barbarians like the Visigoth Euric, who spoke only gibberish and stood always armored and accompanied with weapons, had become Gaul's new masters, ruling with "cruel despotism," scorning

---

[79] See Isaac (2004), chp. 1; also Dauge (1981), 593–602.

[80] #52.4: "Suscepisti mentem provincialium, quos adisti. Mutasti regionem et propositum pietatis abdicasti." *Pietas*, of course, has a number of meanings that English terms like "responsibility" or "sense of obligation" cannot quite suggest. It was, regardless, a core Roman virtue. Gioanni (2006), 179, notes that *pietas* in this letter refers to familial piety, a sense of devotion toward one's family, but, in fact, Ennodius makes clear in the next sentence that all contacts in Italy, both family and friends, were meant. See the following note.

[81] #52.4: "Nam abiurans Italiae communionem non solum circa amicos, sed etiam circa interna pignora reppulisti." Such behavior was doubtless akin to barbarian irrationality, fickleness, and lack of compassion (i.e. *levitas, inhumanitas*, and so forth). See Dauge (1981), 176–7, and Heather (1999), 234–8.

[82] #52.4: "animae tibi mutatio adcessit cum mutatione telluris."

[83] *Ibid.*: "Quam timeo quod longis incuriam tuam incesso conloquiis!"

Roman superiority, and continually attacking the empire's borders.[84] These were the traditional enemies of the Roman Empire, stereotypical savages who were supposed to lack Roman reason, law, and morality. Some, like Gundobad, might be recognized for their prudence and as "articulate speakers," but the Burgundians were still "beasts" with "barbarous ways" in Italo-Roman eyes.[85] The same Gundobad whom Ennodius described as "trusty in his speech and rich in the wealth of eloquence" was likewise "that savage Burgundian," who had betrayed Italy, had ravaged Liguria, and was completely unapologetic about both.[86] The same Alaric, moreover, whose Visigoths had grown "unpracticed in war" and had had their "ferocious hearts softened by a long peace," had nevertheless needed to be reminded that "foresighted moderation" (an attribute of Romans) would preserve his people and that "rage" (an attribute of barbarians) should be a last resort, when justice (so important to conceptions of *civilitas*) could not be obtained.[87] Others, like the Frank Clovis, simply refused to listen to reason and provoked unjust wars.[88] His Franks had "beastly hearts" and were an "arrogant nation" that was "always the first to leap into battle."[89] Savage pagans, they created "numerous sights of cruelty," "spilling innocent blood" and appeasing "their gods with human slaughter."[90] Faced with such peoples, Theoderic could try to be a voice of moderation and Roman prudence; he could likewise actively attempt to civilize these

---

[84] See VE 85–92, with Chp.1.

[85] For an articulate Gundobad, VE 164 (cited in the following note); for beast and barbarous ways, *Variae* 1.46.2–3, with Chp. 5. Cf. Shanzer (1996/7).

[86] For trusty in his speech, see VE 164: "rex probatissimus, ut erat fando locuples et ex eloquentiae dives opibus et facundus adsertor, verbis taliter verba reposuit"; for savage and ravaging, VE 139 (cited earlier); for betraying Italy, see the (guilt-laden) speech of Epiphanius to Gundobad, VE 154–63; for Gundobad's lack of remorse, VE 165, where the king uses his own Roman eloquence to excuse his barbarous behavior.

[87] *Variae* 3.1.1–2: "Tamen quia populorum ferocium corda longa pace mollescunt.... Moderatio provida est, quae gentes servat: furor autem instantia plerumque praecipitat et tunc utile solum est ad arma concurrere, cum locum apud adversarium iustitia non potest invenire." For the context, Chp. 10.

[88] For unjust wars, *Variae* 3.3, with Pricoco (1997) and Chp. 10.

[89] For beastly hearts, *Variae* 2.40.17: "gentilium fera corda"; for arrogant and leaping into battle, *Variae* 11.1.12 (penned in Cassiodorus' name in reference to the Franks of Clovis' son, Theuderic I): "qui praecipiti saltu proelia semper gentibus intulerunt ... superba natio."

[90] Ennodius, *Vita Beati Antoni* 13–14 (in reference to Noricum, sometime after 482): "Iam Franci Heruli Saxones multiplices crudelitatum species beluarum more peragebant; quae nationum diversitas superstitiosis mancipata culturis deos suos humana credebant caede mulceri.... Innocentis effusione sanguinis." Cf. Eugippius, *Vita Severini*, where earlier episodes are recounted in Noricum involving Heruli, Thuringi, and Alamanni (but not Franks or Saxons). Rohr (2001), 26–7, argues that their inclusion was a deliberate attempt on Ennodius' part to vilify the recently converted Franks at a time when tensions between Clovis and Theoderic

barbarians through (Roman) cultural imperialism and marriage alliances. But his pleas often fell on deaf ears,[91] and despite open diplomacy and treaties, the use of brute force always remained an option, "since fear alone checks those whom sworn oaths do not restrain."[92]

The barbarians of Gaul, therefore, were not, as the Gauls had been and the Goths currently were, civilized barbarians. They had not become Roman through obedience to Roman law and custom or by defending the empire against its enemies, though all at one time or another had been praised in this capacity and some, like the Burgundians, continued to profess their loyalty to (New) Rome.[93] There was room for nuance, of course, and Ennodius could even suggest in one letter that his sister was crueler than the barbarians ruling Gaul, "inferior to dumb animals" and "surpassing the tiger in savagery."[94] But his words were more a reflection of Euprepia's lack of devotion than the barbarians' apparent kindness. In the end, Franks, Burgundians, and Theoderic's Visigothic cousins were potential enemies who had not been admitted into the Roman world. And their very existence placed Gaul's remaining Roman population, or rather its Romanness, in peril.

As a consequence, Italo-Romans like Ennodius could imagine a contemporary Gaul where Gallo-Romans were denied their customary *libertas* and the blessings of Roman *civilitas*.[95] But by the early sixth century they were also keenly aware that these same individuals had long since adapted to their new environment. The process was not only readable in the literary works emanating from Gaul, works like Sidonius', which betrayed at one and the same time staunch Romanism, feelings of captivity and betrayal, and acceptance of barbarian masters like Euric,[96] but could also be seen in the very Gallo-Romans themselves with whom individuals like Ennodius maintained ties.

were mounting. But see Shanzer (1998) for the possibility of Clovis' conversion and baptism occurring after 506/7.
[91] See Chp. 10; also Part III for the "Roman" gifts that Theoderic granted to various "barbarian" kings.
[92] *Variae* 2.5.2 (in reference to the Gallic frontier): "in procinctu semper erit, qui barbaros prohibere contendit, quia solus metus cohibet, quos fides promissa non retinet."
[93] See Chp. 5.
[94] #84.2–3: "Nulla sunt tam barbara iura populorum, quae non reddi filio debita materna patiantur.... Cuius aestimabitur esse mens illa feritatis, quae erga curam subolis posterior ab inrationabilibus invenitur.... Tigridem te inmanitate superasse."
[95] See #447.6 (to Liberius), with Chp. 10.
[96] On the availability of Sidonius, Arator, *Epistula ad Parthenium* 275, and Ennodius, #43. See also Cesa (1988), who points out echoes of Sidonius' poetry in certain passages of the *Vita Epiphanii*. These references may suggest that only Sidonius' poetry was available in Italy.

Noble and eloquent Gallo-Romans, men like Gundobad's adviser, Laconius, now collaborated with barbarian masters with few reservations. They were descended from families with a history of imperial service[97] but were now becoming Burgundians, a process that Sidonius was well aware of in the late 460s.[98] More troubling, these individuals were actual kinsmen of well-connected Ligurians like Ennodius, and some were becoming unrecognizable in their transformation. Laconius himself remained virtually untainted by his loyal service to a Burgundian master; Ennodius begged him for letters and went out of his way to secure a papal ruling on his behalf.[99] But Ennodius had other Gallo-Roman relatives who were not so lucky. The youths were especially susceptible to these changes, and Ennodius' own nephew, Parthenius, provides a notable case in point, unable to escape a barbarous future without first escaping Gaul altogether.

BLACKENING INEXPERIENCE

Parthenius, in many ways, was paradigmatic of the Italian understanding of what was happening to the youths of Gaul, the scions of noble Gallo-Roman families, in the aftermath of barbarian conquest. He was the son of an unknown sister of Ennodius and an unknown man of meaner, perhaps even barbarian origins.[100] Though alluding to correspondence with this brother-in-law,[101] Ennodius clearly felt that the match was unworthy of his family, calling it a "mixture at variance in its very differences"[102] and ironically echoing some of the same sentiments expressed by the emperor Anthemius (and then problematized) in his *Life of Epiphanius*. As demonstrated in this work, exceptions could be made, but in general

---

[97] For Laconius' officeholding ancestors, *VE* 168.
[98] See Sidonius, *Ep.* 5.5 (to Syagrius of Lyon), cited earlier. There is often an emphasis in modern scholarship on aristocratic flight to the church in Sidonius' era, but this seems not to have struck either Ennodius or Theoderic's government as the remedy sought by most noble Gallo-Romans. They imagined, instead, either continuity of offices under barbarians or stagnation and ruin. Cf. Van Dam (1985) and Mathisen (1993).
[99] For begging, #38 and #86; for the papal ruling, #252.2.
[100] See Kennell (2000), 139. Ennodius' nephew is usually distinguished from another Parthenius, a Gallic contemporary who was the son of Agricola and friend of Arator. See *PLRE* 2, 832–4 (Parthenius 2–3). However, Mathisen (1981), 101–3, argues that these two individuals are actually the same and that he was the son-in-law (not son) of Agricola. The argument is certainly appealing. See later discussion, where conclusions about Ennodius' Parthenius are drawn in reference to Agricola's Parthenius.
[101] See #368 and #369, discussed later.
[102] #94.11: "permixtio ... ipsa diversitate discordat."

nobles were not supposed to marry outside their rank nor Romans with non-Romans.[103] Such unions, which were emblematic of the synthesis occurring throughout the post-Roman West, were thought to be degrading by men like Ennodius, especially when it came to their own families. And in his estimation, his sister's marriage to an obvious "other" had tainted an otherwise noble line, spelling disaster for its offspring.

The product of this marriage, Parthenius had a future that appeared uncertain to his uncle, oscillating between Roman and un-Roman, noble and ignoble. Ennodius feared that without proper guidance his nephew would "submit to his meaner side, according to the worthlessness of the age."[104] Such fears, moreover, seemed to be well founded, for Parthenius was maturing, according to Ennodius, in a recognizably un-Roman fashion in Gaul, following in his father's footsteps and not receiving a proper education. Like many young Gallo-Romans, he still had "brightness in his blood," but the absence of erudition kept him "trapped in the darkness of rusticity."[105] Because of his mother and the "names of [her] lineage," there was still the potential for him to be recognized as a noble Roman, but without sweet speech he was doomed to barbarism, trapped in Gaul by his "blackening inexperience."[106]

Once again, a traditional education and its ennobling eloquence could provide a link between Gaul's Roman past and its continued Roman status, guaranteeing that Parthenius and his generation could retain their Roman heritage in the absence of Roman rule. But as Parthenius' example already suggests, it seemed to some in Italy that access to this legacy had been denied in Gaul and that rustification and, closely related, barbarization had ensued.[107] There were, of course, still schools in places like Arles and teachers like Julianus Pomerius, who instructed certain youths to "teach even schoolmasters" and to impart their "talents to books through

[103] Marriage to "barbarians" was in fact illegal and a capital crime (*CTh* 3.14.1), but what this meant is unclear given the fluidity of "barbarian" status and the extent of mixed marriages at this time. See Chp. 1, n. 42.
[104] #94.11: "Quam timui, ne … in deterioris iura melior victa concederet et pro vilitate temporum facilius in ipso pars indocta regnaret!" This *vilitate temporum* may be suggestive of the decline and barbarization thought to have occurred throughout the West during the fifth century, but that, at least in Italy's case, Theoderic had stopped and corrected.
[105] #94.5: "quia bonorum semper meritorum labes est habere lucem sanguinis et nocte rusticitatis includi." The glittering beauty of his Roman blood was literally imprisoned in darkness, mirroring the situation in Gaul.
[106] *Ibid.*: "prodi stemmatum vocibus et imperitia fuscante delitiscere." Darkness, once again, is at play.
[107] For the relationship, Chp 5.

recitation."[108] But these survived on entropy, and in comparison to Italy, their quality and number were diminishing.[109] In the face of such decline, Gallic youths were thus forced to look elsewhere for the learning and knowledge that were so important for their class or face the possibility of losing whatever Roman identity they still had. Naturally, they turned to Italy and especially Rome, which were renowned for their schools, unquestionably Roman, and relatively nearby.[110] Ennodius even acted as a conduit for them, recommending Gallic youths to good Italian teachers and patrons and keeping an eye on them for their transalpine parents.[111] He praised their teachers for directing "tottering [foreigners] to the glory of eloquence,"[112] and excitedly informed parents, such as his correspondent Stephanus, when their children acquired "evidence of nobility through the study of the arts."[113] He thus helped to redeem these youths from their imagined captivity, bringing to light in Italy the glittering Roman nobility that was once hidden in the Gallic wilderness. And though well on his way to becoming a Burgundian or perhaps a Visigoth, Parthenius was not an exception.

Indeed, like many of those patronized by Ennodius, Parthenius eventually pursued advanced studies in Rome and impressed others with his learning. But before doing so, he received initial instruction in Milan with a local grammarian named Deuterius, the same instructor with whom Euprepia's son, Lupicinus, later studied. When exactly he first began these studies is uncertain, but by 503 he had finished, and an impressed Ennodius dedicated a rather ornate speech in praise of his teacher as tribute.[114]

---

[108] #461.5 (to Caesarius of Arles, a student of Pomerius): "tu dum libris genium relatione concilias, et magistros informas: tibi debet quicumque ille scriptorum maximus, quod eum dote elocutionis amplificas. In te lux convenit sermonis et operis." For a different reading of "relatione," see Klingshirn (1994b).

[109] See Riché (1976), 208–9. Ennodius, #461.6, may even hint at these developments, though his comments were intended to flatter his addressee.

[110] For Ennodius' association of Rome with erudition and the liberal arts, Chp. 1.

[111] Marcellus, the son of Stephanus (see later discussion); an unnamed son of Camella (#431); and Parthenius were three Gallic youths who sought instruction in Italy and were provided with contacts through Ennodius. Beatus (#398), who is mentioned as a schoolfellow of Marcellus, may also be of Gallic descent, though a northern Italian origin is usually assumed. Cf. *PLRE* 2, 222.

[112] #227.1 (to Luminosus, a patron of young students in Rome): "Non ignari peregrinos suscipitis … dum ad eloquentiae palmam feriato ore eos qui titubant invitatis." For Luminosus, *PLRE* 2, 692–3.

[113] #357.2: "Illud ad gaudium vestrum … adiungimus, filium vestrum in studiis liberalibus ingenuitatis testimonium iam tenere."

[114] For a slightly different interpretation of this *dictio*, which does not place it within a greater understanding of Gallic decline, Kennell (2000), 50–7.

According to this speech, the transformation of Parthenius was nothing shy of a miracle, and Ennodius claimed that its architect, Deuterius, had "imitated the acts of heaven in the abundance of [his] kindness."[115] Hitherto obscured in darkness, he had made Parthenius recognizable to his uncle for his education;[116] he had, in an agricultural metaphor that both played on ideas of cultivation and hinted at his nephew's former rustic status, "dislodged from his heart the thorns and weeds with the hoe of knowledge."[117] To this point Ennodius had been afraid that his nephew's "unlearned side" would dominate his personality, but Deuterius had demonstrated to Parthenius "the things that he should learn and unlearn, two things descended from his blood."[118] And now, Ennodius claimed, "one of his kin … happily recognizes Parthenius, while the other happily does not."[119] "Now from a wintry chest and a cold heart," similar attributes developed by Euprepia while resident in Gaul, "little flowers of eloquence spring forth and laughing buds of words embroider the flower-baskets displaying [them]."[120]

Like some "benevolent furnace," Deuterius had transformed "the hidden talents" within Parthenius from their "solid-iron appearance,"[121] allowing Ennodius' nephew to emerge recast in a more Roman mold. But despite the grammarian's best efforts, this miracle only extended so far. Grammar, with its emphasis on poetic reading, had provided Parthenius with the rich vocabulary of the day, fertile with allegorical meaning and able to demonstrate, when used appropriately, his Roman learning and *Romanitas* to cultured individuals. Nonetheless, there remained irreversible consequences from his parentage and upbringing in Gaul. "Behold," Ennodius asserted, still pleased with the turn of events, "after his barbarous murmur, words are poured from his mouth that may indicate his culture."[122] It was the words themselves that mattered most, but Parthenius' *gentile murmur*, the

---

[115] #94.12: "Caelestia imitatus es ubertate beneficii."

[116] #94.9: "Uberes tibi coram multis, emendatissime hominum, grates refero, qui agnosci a me Partenium institutione fecisti."

[117] *Ibid.*: "Tu de eius pectore scientiae sarculo paliuros et lolium submovisti." For Ennodius' regular use of agricultural metaphors, Kennell (2000), 56–7.

[118] #94.10: "In una eademque persona qua arte, quod utrumque descendebat a sanguine, quid disceret et quid dedisceret, indicasti!"

[119] #94.11: "Ecce Partenium propinquitas sua ex utroque generis calle descendens alia agnoscit feliciter, alia feliciter non agnoscit."

[120] #94.12: "Ecce iam ex hiemali pectore et corde algido dictionum flosculi vernant et ridentia verborum germina depingunt calathos exhibentes."

[121] #94.6: "Fornacis beneficio de latentium fetibus venarum quod in solidi transit speciem ferro dominatur et effera hominum corda domitrice adfectione captivat."

[122] #94.12: "ecce post gentile murmur de ore eius, quae humanitatem significent, verba funduntur."

same term used to describe the Visigothic king Euric's manner of speech, remained unchanged.[123] His words, then, could help to demonstrate his learning and culture, but the way in which he spoke them continued to mark him as different from those in his midst and potentially placed his Romanness in question.[124]

Such shortcomings may explain, in part at any rate, why Parthenius chose to advance his studies in Rome, the very heart of Romanness and a pilgrimage site of sorts, where he could seek total transformation. Grammar school in Milan had been an important step in the right direction, providing welcome signs of Roman erudition. But Parthenius needed and apparently desired more. He had been motivated, thanks to Deuterius' instruction, to "strive after the ornaments of eloquence," and his newfound "love of the noble arts" had caused him to reject his "cruel disposition," a quality of barbarians acquired in Gaul.[125] Through his studies at Rome, moreover, he would endeavor to shed his remaining Gallic skin, "unlearning vices in the process" and gaining "wise judgment," a quality of Romans.[126] More simply, as Ennodius informed his nephew's newest patron, the well-connected aristocrat Faustus Junior, "Parthenius wishes, through the study of the liberal arts, to appear noble," and Faustus' wealth and assistance, it was hoped, would help to bring these desires to fruition.[127] Milan, therefore, could make the words that Parthenius spoke indicate his nobility, but Rome would take care of the rest.

---

[123] For Euric, VE 89, with Chp. 1. The *post* used by Ennodius seems to mean "after" rather than "after losing," implying that noble Roman words now accompany (and hence soften) Parthenius' still-foreign accent. See later discussion. Cf. Kennell (2000), 139, who takes the sentence to mean that Parthenius had indeed rid himself of an accent.

[124] This is alluded to through Ennodius' use of the subjunctive, *significent*, when the indicative would have been grammatically acceptable.

[125] #225.1 (a generalization, but its applicability to Parthenius is made clear in the final sentence): "Bonarum affectus artium dirum dedignatur ingenium. Ad eloquentiae ornamenta non tendunt nisi moribus instituti. His Partenius noster germanae filius incitatus stimulis Romam ... festinat invisere."

[126] #226.3 (to Pope Symmachus, regarding Parthenius' education at Rome): "sancta sunt studia litterarum, in quibus ante incrementa peritiae vitia dediscuntur. Hoc itinere cana ad annos pueriles solent venire consilia."

[127] #228.2–3: "Partenius ... per liberalis studii disciplinas ingenuus vult videri. Optat, ni fallor, peculii vestri habere testimonium. Magnitudo igitur tua ... perlatorem [i.e. Partenium] pro mea commendatione suscipiat, et qui erit per visionem vestram scribente felicior, peregrinationis non patiatur adversa sentire." For this Faustus, PLRE 2, 450–1 (Faustus 2). Cf. #368.1 (partially cited later), where fear and esteem for Faustus Niger, yet another patron, incited Parthenius to study hard, that is, until the illustrious senator left town.

A Poisoned Well

Ennodius' optimistic sentiments had been expressed when Parthenius was first arriving in the city of letters. But whether his nephew succeeded in his quest for Roman nobility is another story altogether. Judging from Ennodius' rather hostile letters to his nephew, it would seem, on the one hand, that Parthenius believed that he had, and, on the other, that Ennodius (and others) did not share his view. To Parthenius' credit, he delivered an oration in Rome, which Ennodius, in his own condescending way, found pleasing. "As far as I am concerned," Ennodius informed his nephew, "the structure of your little oration, even if it stops short of the splendor of eloquence, nonetheless radiates with a taste of Latin talent. Your words did not flow inharmoniously, but must be amplified through a wealth of reading."[128] Practice, in other words, would make perfect, and lest Parthenius persist in native vices, he was also reminded to associate with "honorable men," no doubt senatorial types like Faustus Junior.[129]

"Flee from those who soil you through their association as if a cup of poison," he was warned.[130] But the admonition fell on deaf ears, for Parthenius did fall in with "people leading him astray" and began to neglect his studies and "undertake repulsive things."[131] Word of this development traveled all the way to his father in Gaul, who begged Ennodius to intercede. Even this seemingly low-born rustic, perhaps barbarian, was distressed that his son was neglecting his studies and behaving inappropriately. He mourned "the loss of a living son in place of a dead one," for he had no confidence in Parthenius' improvement.[132] Ennodius, who had vouched for his nephew before a number of powerful individuals in Rome, including Pope Symmachus, was likewise unimpressed.[133] "You are completely unconcerned," he alleged, "about the instruction gained

---

[128] #290.2: "Ductus mihi oratiunculae tuae etsi eloquentiae nitore non subsistit, Latiaris tamen venae sapore radiavit. Fluxit sermo non absonus, lectionis tamen opibus ampliandus."

[129] #290.3: "honestorum te obsequiis indesinenter inpende."

[130] *Ibid.*: "eos qui consortio suo polluunt, debens monitis nostris reverentiam velut veneni poculum fuge."

[131] #368.1 (to Faustus Niger): "Partenium ... diu circa diligentiam litterarum ... culminis vestri metus adtraxerat. Sed nunc per absentiam vestram ... molitur obscena. Aetas illa peccatis amicior multos repperit ad errata ductores."

[132] #368.2: "Inplorat fidem propositi mei pater et incolumem filium loco deflet extincti. Sic faciunt quibus de profectu suorum fiducia nulla responderit." Cf. #369.5 (to Parthenius himself).

[133] See #226.4 (to Pope Symmachus); #225.3 (to Faustus Niger); #228.3 (to Faustus Junior); and #227.3 (to Luminosus). Portions of many of these letters are cited earlier. See also Kennell (2000), 47–50.

from reading, as if you have already obtained the pinnacle of knowledge. Know, son, that its height is not held in excess unless through practice: with nimble wings knowledge flees from those neglecting her."[134] In other letters he rebuked his nephew for his childish anger, haughtiness, feigned humility, and lazy cruelty, elsewhere threatening to physically beat him and even avowing, "I pray to God that He remove from you that which I detest."[135]

Despite an ennobling education and even studying at the very font of Latin letters, then, it seems almost as if Parthenius could never escape his un-Roman, Gallic origins. Indeed, if he was the same Parthenius eulogized by the poet Arator and mentioned in Gregory of Tours' *Histories*, his Roman education would eventually give him the appearance of "an illustrious lord" and allow him to hold Roman offices in the custom of his ancestors.[136] But by the time of his death, he was once more serving barbarian masters and perpetrating barbarisms. Even the savage Franks hated him, according to Gregory of Tours, for he had murdered an innocent wife and friend, and, far worse, was "a pig with food ... [who] used to fart loudly in public without any consideration for those who might hear."[137] Perhaps, to alter the old adage, one could take the Gallo-Roman out of Gaul, but not the Gaul out of the Gallo-Roman.

To conclude, youths like Parthenius and older individuals like Euprepia and Firminus shed important light on the complexities of Italo-Roman perceptions vis-à-vis Gaul in the wake of its loss to the barbarians. For Italo-Romans, Italy had remained the Roman Empire and they the Romans, but the situation in Gaul was not so simple. Sometimes they were keenly aware

---

[134] #369.5: "quasi arcem scientiae adeptus sis, ita nullatenus esse de lectionis instructione sollicitum. Nosti, fili, istius rei summam nisi adsiduitate nimia non teneri.... Pernicibus alis neglegentes fugit scientia."

[135] For childish anger, haughtiness, and feigned humility, #258.1: "Nisi te efflictim diligerem ... possem iniuriarum dolore provocatus, vel cum pueriliter irasceris vel cum adroganter supplicas, conmoveri. Nihil enim invenio, quod sit fabricata humilitate superbius." For lazy cruelty, #258:4: "desidem saevitiam." For threatening to beat, #369.1: "te per longum ferire debuit inclusa commotio, si tamen non ex toto ab humanitate discessisti." Here, as in the preceding examples, Ennodius continued to hint that he still had compassion for his nephew. For praying to God, #369.4: "Deum precor, ut a te quod detestor excludat."

[136] Again, this identification is disputed. See earlier, n. 100. Arator, *Epistola ad Parthenium* 267, addresses this Parthenius as "domino illustri, magnificentissimo atque praecelso Parthenio magistro officiorum atque patricio." These titles may have been conferred by the government of Italy and perhaps held in Provence. See *PLRE* 2, 833–4 (Parthenius 3). Arator also claims that Parthenius was eloquent and learned (271–5).

[137] Gregory of Tours, *Historiae* 3.36: "Franci vero cum Parthenium in odio magno haberent.... Fuit autem in cibis valde vorax ... et strepidus ventris absque ulla auditorum reverentia in publico emittebat."

that Gaul had once been Roman and had been wrested, unjustly, from their empire. In this perspective Gaul's Roman inhabitants lived in captivity and their culture and literary erudition could serve as beacons of Romanness, urging outside sympathy. Other times Italo-Romans looked askance at this former province, growing increasingly alienated from it, even if fully aware of its Roman past. This Gaul had never been quite Roman anyway, and now the absence of Roman rule allowed whatever Romanness there was to degenerate. At still other times Italo-Romans could adhere to both of these perspectives and see the addition of new barbarians as a catalyst speeding up the barbarization process. In the end, however, Parthenius and his generation provide the clearest indication of what the future had in store for Gaul. Sometimes fully Roman, other times completely not, often somewhere in between, they, like Gaul, were deprived of their Roman birthright and they, like Gaul, needed Rome in order to regain it.

The letters of Ennodius have dominated this chapter, but, as the following chapter will soon demonstrate, his views are consistent with a greater understanding in Italy. Gauls were becoming post-Roman and then un-Roman and had little choice but to accept their transformation or to flee to Italy and escape it; no choice, of course, until 508, when the Roman Empire, reinvigorated by Theoderic and his Goths, returned to them.

10

GALLIA FELIX

AN UNWANTED RESTORATION

Though certain individuals had been lamenting the developments described
in the preceding chapter, most in Italy were content with the status quo in
Gaul, provided it posed no immediate threat. There was, in fact, no ardent
desire for direct intervention in the early decades of the Theoderican regime,
despite understandings of captivity and barbarization. Instead, the Ravenna
government had looked predictably to domestic and eastern concerns and,
rather than interfering in Gaul, had taken an active interest in maintaining
peace and normalizing its ties with its barbarian rulers. A military alliance
with the Visigoths was secured as early as Theoderic's invasion of Italy in
489.[1] By the mid-490s, marriage alliances had also been formed between
the Amals and the other ruling families in Gaul. Theoderic himself married
a sister of the Frankish king Clovis, while two of his daughters married
into the Visigothic and Burgundian royal families.[2] Likewise, as already discussed, Theoderic regularly dispatched envoys across the Alps, who often

---

[1] Visigothic soldiers arrived at a key moment in 490, when Odovacer was advancing upon
Theoderic at Milan. See *AnonVal* 53, with Claude (1978b), 24–5; Wolfram (1988), 281–2; and
Moorhead (1992), 23–4. Contra Wolfram, it seems unnecessary to see this as an act of ethnic
solidarity, especially since relations between both Goths were often confrontational. See Diaz
and Valverde (2007), 356. Instead, the Visigoths may have been motivated by self-interest, while
Theoderic may have turned to them because of their presence along the (vulnerable) Alpine
frontier. See later discussion.
[2] For these marriages, Claude (1978b), 25–41; Wolfram (1988), 309–13; Moorhead (1992), 51–2;
and Diaz and Valverde (2007), 357–8. They would later allow Theoderic to invoke kinship as
a rationale for keeping the peace in Gaul, though too much has been made of the "barbarian"
elements at play here. If anything, alliances of this sort seem inspired by imperial practices, and,
in fact, *Variae* 3.2 (to Gundobad) even invokes the idea of senior and junior rulers. See later
discussion. Cf. Schenk von Stauffenberg (1938), 125–6; Schmidt (1939), 411–12; and Wirth
(1995), 256.

conveyed certain "Roman" gifts.[3] These trappings of Roman civilization, of which Theoderic was a self-proclaimed guardian, and the words that accompanied them could have manifold implications, but in their simplest form they were sent as markers of friendship and in good faith.

Gaul, then, could remain as it was, and it was only when diplomatic measures like these failed and Italy suffered the devastating consequences that the empire was forced back across the Alps. The actual outbreak of hostilities would occur suddenly in 507, catching many by surprise. Yet as sudden and shocking as they were, they had nonetheless been foreseen. After all, the oaths of these barbarians had never been particularly dependable, and the complete breakdown of peace and stability in Gaul, a patent reminder of the barbarized state into which this country had fallen, had been a long time in coming.

By 506, in fact, it had been evident to those in Ravenna for quite a while that tensions in Gaul were mounting and in danger of spilling over into Italy. To be sure, some transalpine regions had enjoyed moments of peace and security in the immediate aftermath of Roman rule,[4] but the political dynamics of Gaul were in a state of fundamental alteration as a consequence of the steady rise of the Frankish king Clovis, a process that had begun before the advent of Theoderic in Italy but that sped up significantly at the end of the fifth century. The history of Gaul (and much of Europe) would eventually become the history of the Franks, and Clovis' reign marks the beginning of this transformation. Before this energetic king, the Franks had been a minor, loose confederation of peoples largely confined to the middle and lower Rhineland. Some had been settled as federates and had been employed as Roman auxiliaries perhaps as late as the 460s, but they had never posed a serious threat to the major powers of the region, Roman or otherwise.[5] Clovis, however, changed this. He was a young, ambitious king, and though at the beginning of his reign he was outclassed by the other barbarian rulers of Gaul, brute force and brutal conquests soon made him their equal.[6]

[3] See Chps. 5 and 7; also Gillett (2003), chp. 5.
[4] For Visigothic Provence (especially Arles), Février (1994), 46–51; Delage (1994), 24–9; and Klingshirn (1994a), 69–71. For Visigothic Aquitania, Rouche (1979), 43–50, and Mathisen (2001), 105f.
[5] Indeed, as discussed in Chp. 5, their relationship with the empire was often beneficial. See Stroheker (1955); James (1988), chp. 2; and Geary (1988), 73–82.
[6] There is no denying that Clovis was outclassed at the beginning of his reign. Not only were Gundobad's and Alaric II's kingdoms more prestigious (larger, wealthier, more unified), but the two kings rested on mightier laurels. Alaric II ruled over a people who had both sacked Rome and defeated the mighty Attila (see *Variae* 3.1.1). Gundobad, likewise, had held one of the highest offices in the western Empire, had made an emperor of his own (Glycerius), and continued

Indeed, by the time Theoderic had secured his own mastery over Italy, Clovis had become a key player in Gaul and was beginning to show signs of wanting more than the respect of his royal peers.[7] The preeminent king of the Franks, who would soon become the *only* king of the Franks (and this was quite an important political development), was fast on his way to becoming the new Euric of the West, a seemingly unstoppable and cruel savage, at the very time when Euric's own son and successor, Alaric II, and his Burgundian analogue, Gundobad, were settling down and striving to consolidate their kingdoms.[8] Clovis' rise to power would bring the Franks into greater contact and thereafter conflict with the two ranking powers in Gaul. Nonetheless, caution should be observed, and a teleological, triumphalistic, and ultimately Franco-centric approach to this period (an interpretation that owes much to the writings of Gregory of Tours) should be avoided, as it is in dissonance with the realities of the day. The fact remains that neither Alaric's nor Gundobad's kingdom would be conquered decisively by the Franks in Clovis' lifetime,[9] while Theoderic and his Goths, both before and after their invasion of Gaul, would do much to forestall the transformation of Gallia into Francia.[10] As a concerned party, an in-law, and an avowed patron of all of Gaul's royal barbarians, Theoderic would do his best to keep the peace in the region, if only for the sake of Italian prosperity. And had his diplomatic maneuvering proven successful, "France" might never have been born.[11]

to derive prestige from his Roman titles. Clovis, on the other hand, inherited the sub-Roman governorship of a frontier province from his father and was in competition for rulership over his (and other) Franks from the beginning of his reign. Moreover, his position as a king was far less secure, as his father seems to have been deposed from this office for a time (and by a Roman no less). Cf. James (1988), 64–75, and Wood (1994), 38–41.

[7] The fact that Theoderic himself married into Clovis' family may be indicative of this.

[8] On these developments, Rouche (1979), 43–50; Collins (1983), 25–31; Favrod (1997), 285–91; and Kaiser (2004), 46–60. The difference is also evident in contemporary Italian sources, which, despite denigrating Gundobad, Euric, and Alaric II as traditional barbarians, are nonetheless more sensitive to their quasi-civilized status. The Franks, including Clovis, on the other hand, remain consistently fierce, savage, and even pagan. See the previous chapter and later discussion.

[9] The full extent to which Visigothic Aquitaine was conquered in the reign of Clovis is a matter of debate. See Ewig (1952), 123–8, and Rouche (1979), 49–58. Beyond Aquitaine, the Franks did not control Burgundy until 534 nor Provence until 536. Septimania, on the other hand, remained a Visigothic (and then Muslim) enclave into the early Carolingian period, when it was finally conquered by the Franks. Even then it retained its Gothic identity as the march province of "Gothia."

[10] Jordanes, *Getica* 296, declares that, so long as Theoderic lived, the Goths never yielded to the Franks. Cf. Wood (1994), 49.

[11] For an elaboration, Arnold (2012), 111–12, with the essays in Mathisen and Shanzer (2012).

PREPARING FOR THE INEVITABLE

A series of letters featured in Cassiodorus' *Variae* demonstrates the full extent to which Theoderic strove to use Roman reason and mediation in order to forestall what seems, with historical hindsight, to have been inevitable.[12] To Gundobad he pressed for peaceful arbitration, suggesting that Alaric and Clovis were youths "unable to restrain the recklessness of their wills" but who might obey the prudent advice of their elders, meaning Theoderic and Gundobad.[13] To Clovis he likewise pled for peaceful mediation and offered, if both parties agreed, to provide the necessary and impartial mediators.[14] The conflict, he asserted, stemmed from "mediocre causes," and both Alaric and Clovis were "kings of the greatest peoples."[15] Both, moreover, were flourishing,[16] but war, Theoderic eerily predicted, would utterly destroy one of them, much to the delight of certain unnamed onlookers, no doubt in Constantinople.[17] Finally, and in a similar vein, to his son-in-law Alaric Theoderic wrote that his quarrel with Clovis was trivial, calling it a matter of words, not of murdered kin or seized territory.[18] In this case, too, he urged arbitration, again sending envoys to try to work out the details. Barbarian rage, he

---

[12] For discussions of these letters, Ensslin (1959), 133–8; Pricoco (1997); and Gillett (2003), 207–12.

[13] *Variae* 3.2.2: "Nostrum est regios iuvenes obiecta ratione moderari, quia illi, si nobis vere sentiunt displicere quod male cupiunt. Audaciam suae voluntatis retinere non possunt. Verentur senes." For the anachronism of *iuvenes*, Hodgkin (1886), 197, who notes Clovis was 41 years of age in 507. See earlier (n. 2), though, for another possible interpretation.

[14] *Variae* 3.4.3: "A parentibus quod quaeritur, electis iudicibus expetatur. Nam inter tales viros et illis gratum est dare, quos medios volueritis efficere." For the style of arbitration Theoderic appears to have had in mind, Gillett (2003), 209–10. Cf. *Chronicle of Fredegar* 2.58, where Theoderic is described as personally mediating between both parties and intentionally bungling the job. Fredegar's narrative, however, is untrustworthy, not least because it seems to be relying on some sort of proto–Dietrich Saga. See Borchert (2005).

[15] *Variae* 3.4.2: "miramur animos vestros sic causis mediocribus excitatos…. Ambo estis summarum gentium reges."

[16] *Ibid.*: "ambo aetate florentes."

[17] Utterly destroy, *Variae* 3.4.3: "ubi unus ex vobis dolere poterit inclinatus." For delighted onlookers, *Variae* 3.4.2: "ut multi … de vestra concertatione laetentur" and 3.4.5: "inter vos scandala seminet aliena malignitas." Cf. *Variae* 3.1.4 (to Alaric): "qui maligne gaudent alieno certamine." For the Byzantine identification, Ensslin (1959), 139–42; Moorhead (1992), 182; and Meier (2009), 229–30. Playing one barbarian people against another was a long-standing and frequently employed tactic in the Roman Empire, one at which Anastasius, in particular, was quite adept. See Haarer (2006), chps. 3 and 4.

[18] *Variae* 3.1.3: "nos vos parentum fusus sanguis inflammat, non graviter urit occupata provincia: adhuc de verbis parva contentio est."

avowed, should yield before justice and moderation, and war should be a last resort.[19]

Peace and stability, then, which had typified Italy's Gallic policies to this point, were desired, but it remained prudent to have contingency plans should the hoped-for consensus fail. To Clovis and Alaric, therefore, a final but important comment was made. Though claiming that he found the possibility unlikely, Theoderic warned the Frankish king that "he who thinks such advice is worthy of scorn will suffer us and our friends as his enemies," while assuring Alaric that "we judge your enemy to be a common evil, since he who strives to be your opponent will rightly find me as his adversary."[20] These remarks, though somewhat vague, were nevertheless revealing. Despite seeking and serving as an arbiter for peace, Theoderic was not entirely impartial and maintained that he would side with Alaric should war break out.

This promise of support, however, should not be seen as a rare case of Gothic solidarity.[21] Though Italy's Goths did invade Gaul after Alaric's defeat, it will soon become evident that they did so out of self-interest and that their policies quickly drove a wedge between themselves and their "Gothic" allies. Besides, as already demonstrated, Theoderic presented himself as a *Roman* ruler before all western barbarians, including the Visigoths, so pan-Gothicness, while an interesting concept, fails to receive mention in the historical record.[22] More importantly, there were other factors at work in 507 that would have made the alliance with Alaric agreeable, regardless of presumed ethnic affinities. Alaric's legitimate son and potential heir was Theoderic's grandson, and Alaric's military aid in the 490s had proven particularly helpful in securing Theoderic's own rise to power. Theoderic was hence personally indebted to Alaric and had a dynastic interest in his kingdom. It also helped that ties with Visigothic Gaul represented some of

[19] *Variae* 3.1.2, cited in Chp. 9, n. 87.
[20] *Variae* 3.4.4 (to Clovis): "Ille nos et amicos nostros patietur adversos, qui talia monita, quod non opinamur, crediderit esse temnenda"; *Variae* 3.1.3 (to Alaric): "Commune malum vestrum iudicamus inimicum. Nam ille me iure sustinebit adversum, qui vobis nititur esse contrarius."
[21] Contra Moorhead (1992), 180. See n. 1 (earlier), with Wolfram (1988), 309–10, and Diaz and Valverde (2007).
[22] The closest evidence for such ethnic solidarity appears to be derived from Jordanes' *Getica*, a work that postdates the Justinianic reconquest and includes a number of instances of Goth-on-Goth violence. Such pan-Gothic solidarity, as presented by Jordanes, may have little to do with Italian perceptions during the era of Theoderic, reflecting, instead, Justinianic propaganda. Cf. Goffart (1988), chp. 2, and (2006), chp. 4. Likewise, if derived from Cassiodorus' lost history, it may be the product of Theoderic's own postwar propaganda, which sought to integrate the fallen Visigothic kingdom fully (and permanently) into his realm. See Diaz and Valverde (2007), 364–7.

Italy's most stable foreign relations at the time, even if the official position was one of disdain and distrust.[23] The Burgundians, who were poised to side with Clovis, had only too recently ravaged Liguria, while Clovis was dangerously unpredictable and a proven threat. Shortly before the outbreak of war, Theoderic himself had been keen to impress upon the aggressive Frank that he needed to show clemency in his conquests, threatening him in the case of the Alamanni, whose defeated remnants had sought refuge within the empire in 506.[24]

The survival of a friendly Visigothic kingdom, therefore, was defensively expedient, serving to impede Frankish and Burgundian access to Italy and providing all the benefits afforded to Rome by its client kingdoms in the past.[25] Theoderic knew from personal experience that there was more than one way to invade Italy, and the prospect of Franks or others sweeping down from the north or east was just as daunting as their doing so from the west. Nor were Alaric's Visigoths the only peoples whose assistance was solicited in the face of a potential invasion. The Alamannic refugees encountered earlier, for instance, were settled in Rhaetia and became "guardians of the Latin Empire," no doubt with an eye to Clovis.[26] Similarly, to their north and east, a series of alliances was formed with the lesser kings of the Warni, Heruli, and Thuringians. Like Alaric, the king of the Thuringians was wooed through the offering of an exceptionally "Roman" bride, Amalaberga, while, rather differently, the king of the Heruli was adopted as Theoderic's son-in-arms, rendering him "greatest among the *gentes*" because he had been "approved by the judgment of Theoderic."[27] Writing to these two kings and their neighbors on the eve of

---

[23] Ennodius even made this clear in one of his letters to Euprepia (#84.3), referring to the firmly rooted peace ("pace ... omni radice solidata") established between the rulers of both regions.

[24] See *Variae* 2.41.

[25] See Luttwak (1976), 24–32, and Braund (1984).

[26] See *PanTh* 72–3 (describing the peaceful settlement of Alamanni and their role as "Latiaris custos imperii"), with *Variae* 3.50. For Rhaetia, Szidat (1995), 73, and Wolfram (1988), 317–18.

[27] For Thuringians, *Variae* 4.1 and *AnonVal* 70, with Chp. 6. Cf. Ensslin (1959), 147, who places this letter after the outbreak of hostilities between Clovis and Theoderic but sees the same defensive rationale. For the Heruli and adoption, *Variae* 4.2: "largimur tibi nostra iudicia. Summus enim inter gentes esse crederis, qui Theoderici sententia comprobaris." This is an interesting letter, as it is replete with martial language and describes this adoption as "more gentium." Too much, however, has been made of Theoderic's role as a "German" in this particular episode. After all, Theoderic was the adopter, and emperors had a history of adopting warriors as their sons-in-arms. Zeno had adopted Theoderic himself, for instance, while Justin not only adopted Eutharic, but also offered to adopt the future Persian emperor Chosroes I. See Procopius, *Wars* 1.11.19–30. More importantly, *Variae* 4.2 emphasizes Theoderic's *sententia* and *iudicium*, Roman qualities that are described as greater than the *arma* he was conferring. Cf. Amory (1997), 64–5.

war, Theoderic suggested that the Visigoths had always proven themselves worthy allies in the past and, alluding to Clovis, warned that "he who is willing to act without justice will weaken the kingdoms of us all."[28] It was an ominous prediction of events to come, in keeping with Theoderic's propensity for foresightedness.[29]

VOUILLÉ AND AFTER

Clovis, then, was viewed as a "loose cannon" who could upset the modus vivendi reached in the West and pose a direct threat to Italy.[30] Still, though tensions had been mounting and Theoderic had planned for the possibility of war with alliances and strengthened defenses,[31] the actual eruption of violence in Gaul was unpredictable and swift. In the spring of 507 Clovis and his armies rapidly crossed the Loire, while allied Burgundian soldiers pressed south. Soon, on the *Campus Vogladensis,* a location traditionally associated with the modern city of Vouillé,[32] Clovis' Franks and Alaric's Visigoths engaged in a bloody contest. By the battle's end, Alaric II had been slain, and what was left of his army had fled the scene, allowing much of Aquitania to fall into Frankish hands. The military assistance promised by Theoderic had failed to appear, and a decisive battle fought without his Goths' participation had spelled the end of Gaul's Visigothic future and ushered in the birth of France; but not entirely.

Despite the suggestion in a few later sources that Theoderic had deliberately disregarded his alliance with Alaric, intending the Franks and Visigoths to slaughter one another so as to conquer Gaul more easily himself,[33] the ruler of Italy should not be blamed for failing to materialize at Vouillé. Playing one barbarian tribe off another would have been a

---

[28] *Variae* 3.3.2: "qui sine lege vult agere, cunctorum disponit regna quassare."

[29] The Franks, who had already conquered certain Thuringians under Clovis, would conquer the remaining Thuringians in 531. Ensslin (1959), 141, also sees an east Roman role in the annihilation of the Heruli and their king by the Lombards while Theoderic was busy in Gaul.

[30] Cf. Moorhead (1992),180.

[31] It is probably right to place the preoccupation with Alpine defenses described in *Variae* 1.17, 2.5, and 3.48 within this historical context, though these letters are dated conventionally to 506/11. Cf. Krautschick (1983), 73–5, and Schwacz (1993), 790.

[32] For the possibility of Voulon, Gerberding (1987), 41; Wood (1994), 46; and Mathisen (2012).

[33] See *Chronicle of Fredegar* 2.58 (cited previously). Moorhead (1992), 178, also cites Procopius, *Wars* 5.12.34–7. If this was intended as a critique of Theoderic, it was rather subtle. Cf. Procopius, *Wars* 5.12.24–32, where Theoderic intentionally delays sending troops to aid the Visigoths and Franks against the Burgundians and acquires territory in Gaul without a fight. The account is hopelessly confused but may refer to the later conquests of Tuluin, c. 523/4, which acquired new territory in Gaul "without peril" during a dispute between the Franks and Burgundians. See *Variae* 8.10.8.

tactic consistent with the policies of Roman imperial rule, but, as already demonstrated, Theoderic had little intention of conquering Gaul at this time. Instead, Clovis' invasion of Aquitaine had been sudden, so sudden that it caught those in Italy by surprise and made providing reinforcements nearly impossible from a logistical standpoint.[34] One Visigothic source (admittedly written long after the fact) even claimed that Theoderic only learned of the outbreak of hostilities through the arrival of messengers announcing Alaric's death, and that his invasion of Gaul had been launched immediately thereafter.[35] Moreover, even if there had been plenty of time to go to Alaric's aid, there were more pressing issues at home: Italy itself had been invaded, and not just by the same-old marauding Burgundians in the northwest, but by an east Roman fleet numbering two hundred warships in the southeast.[36] Theoderic's Roman Empire had been assaulted on two fronts, and it too ran the risk of crumbling with a decisive blow.

Fortunately, Clovis' allies were not intent on conquering Italy but had been dispatched to forestall Theoderic's involvement in the more important contests unfolding in Gaul, a tactic that worked. The Burgundians, though interested in Italian lands, directed most of their efforts toward Provence, while the east Roman fleet had been sent merely to "devastate the coast" in an act of "piracy."[37] Soon, it seems, the Burgundian raiders were checked, while the east Romans, with whom relations had been strained since the Sirmian War of 504, abandoned their efforts altogether.[38]

This joint invasion of Italy, however, still left its mark, providing a brilliant rallying point heretofore unavailable to Theoderic. In June of 508, the army of the *res publica* was called to arms, but making good on an alliance with the Visigoths or avenging the death of Alaric failed to receive mention. Italy had been attacked, and as always in Theoderic's Roman

---

[34] Moorhead (1992), 178.

[35] Isidore of Seville, *Hist. Goth.* 36: "Theudericus autem Italiae rex dum interitum generi conperisset, confestim ab Italia proficiscitur, Franco proterit, partem regni, quam manus hostium occupaverat, recepit Gothorumque iuri restituit."

[36] For the fleet, *Marc. Com.* 508 (cited in the following note) and *Variae* 1.16 and 2.38. For the Burgundian invasion, *Variae* 1.9, 2.30, and Avitus of Vienne, *Ep.* 1.10, with Schwarcz (1993), 790–1; also Delaplace (2000), 82, and Arnold (2012), 125–6, who accept Schwarcz's reconstruction.

[37] *Marc. Com.* 508: "cum centum armatis navibus totidemque dromonibus octo milia militum armatorum secum ferentibus ad devastanda Italiae litora processerunt et … remensoque mari inhonestam victoriam, quam piratico ausu Romani ex Romanis rapuerunt." These numbers were not enough for a serious attempt at conquest, though the ravaging necessitated a two-year relief from taxation for the merchants of Sipontum (*Variae* 2.38) and reduced tribute for the peoples of Apulia (*Variae* 1.16). Cf. Haarer (2006), 97, and Meier (2009), 230.

[38] There is no evidence for continued Byzantine aggression, and by 511 Theoderic had been able to resecure cordial relations with the emperor. See *Variae* 2.1 (discussed later).

Empire, it was Italy's safety that was paramount. Rome's Gothic soldiers, the "defenders of Italy,"[39] would be sent to Gaul, according to the official proclamation, "for the utility of all," and youths trained "in the discipline of Mars" would prove their Gothic *virtus*, the courage of their forefathers.[40] Yet just as the case had been a few years prior in the Balkans, their uniquely "Gothic" valor would serve "Roman" ends, allowing Gauls like Firminus, Parthenius, and others to "return to [their] homeland, to the Roman Empire."[41] Troops soon poured across the Alps "like a flooding river" and "rushed forth in unison for the security of all."[42] Having been attacked, then, Italy turned to Gaul in an act of defense, but Gaul's "liberation" would soon be a consequence.

Within months of the "inundation" of southeastern Gaul, a policy consistent with defending Italy was put into action. Led by the general Ibba,[43] the army began securing all of Gaul east of the Rhone and south of the Durance. Marseille fell in the autumn of 508, Arles soon after, having been relieved from a devastating Burgundian and Frankish siege. Here, it was fondly remembered more than a decade later, the noble Goth Tuluin had earned his scars, testaments to his courage, while holding Arles' famous pontoon bridge against a "close-knit throng" of Franks.[44] Other cities in the region, such as Avignon, also fell at this time, while *castella* were quickly constructed along the Durance in order to hold the emerging frontier.[45] Seemingly secured, the occupied territory was then permanently annexed to the Roman Empire, recreating the buffer province lost to Euric in 476 and leading to the eventual reestablishment of the long-defunct Prefecture of the Gauls.[46] The act, while strategically

---

[39] *Variae* 4.36.3: "Italiae defensoribus."

[40] *Variae* 1.24.1–3: "pro communi utilitate exercitum ad Gallias constituimus destinare ... quatenus et parentum vestrorum in vobis ostendatis inesse virtutem et nostram peragatis feliciter iussionem. Producite iuvenes vestros in Martiam disciplinam."

[41] *Variae* 3.18: "ad Romanum repatriavit imperium." For Magnus, the Gaul in question, *PLRE* 2, 701 (Magnus 3).

[42] *Variae* 4.36.2: "transiens noster exercitus more fluminis, dum irrigavit ... pro generali securitate frementi adunatione proruperit."

[43] For Ibba, *PLRE* 2, 585.

[44] On the siege and Tuluin's role, *Variae* 11.10.6–8, with Arnold (2012), 126–7, n. 97. For an Arlesian perspective, *Vita Caesarii* 1.28–32. For Tuluin's scars, Chp. 5.

[45] For reconstructions, Sirago (1987), 65–8; Schwarcz (1993), 791–3; Favrod (1997), 400–1; and Delaplace (2000), 83–5. For the emerging frontier, *Variae* 3.41.

[46] The exact date for the (re)establishment of the Gallic Prefecture is uncertain. *Variae* 3.17 demonstrates that there was already a *vicarius praefectorum* in Gaul in 508, and hence a prefect to whom he answered. However, none of the *Variae* letters dated 508–11 is addressed to this prefect (assumed to be Liberius), so it is generally concluded that the prefect to whom he answered was the prefect of Italy. See O'Donnell (1981), 44–6; Delaplace (2003), 481–5; and

prudent,[47] was nevertheless bold and placed Theoderic at odds with his supposed allies, the Visigoths. This was technically still their territory, and coupled with Theoderic's unwillingness to recognize Gesalec, an illegitimate son of Alaric, as a rightful successor, the move was tantamount to a declaration of war.

Indeed, by the next year, Rome's Goths and Gesalec's Goths were openly fighting, and Theoderic was now backing his young grandson, a legitimate son of Alaric, as the rightful king of the Visigoths. Carcassonne, the site to which some of the Gothic royal treasury had been relocated,[48] and Narbonne fell to Ibba in 509, forcing Gesalec to flee south to Barcelona, where he was pursued and then besieged the following year. At the same time, other contingents of Italy's army continued skirmishing with Frankish forces in Septimania and within the vicinity of Arles. By 511, however, Gesalec had abandoned Barcelona for Vandal Africa, and it was at this point that Theoderic assumed nominal sovereignty over the remnants of Alaric's kingdom, serving as regent for the boy-king Amalaric until his death in 526.[49]

Gesalec, as seen earlier, would receive aid from the Vandals and return to Gaul, continuing to pose a threat until his death in 514.[50] It was his Visigothic supporters who ambushed Theoderic's praetorian prefect of Gaul, Liberius, and dealt him a near-fatal wound along the Burgundian frontier; and indeed, as a result, Liberius too would earn his own valorous scars in Gaul.[51] Likewise, peace would continue to be strained at

---

PLRE 2, 677–80 (Liberius 3). The absence of letters directed to a prefect of Gaul, however, is not conclusive. Despite Liberius' long tenure in Gaul, only one letter directed to him survives in Cassiodorus' collection (*Variae* 8.6), and it dates to the reign of Athalaric. Likewise, the evidence for Liberius' presence in Italy from 508 to 510 is spotty. Indeed, he may have been prefect of the Gauls as early as 508, and his stays in Italy (as the case was in 512) may have been temporary or a matter of business.

[47] As suggested, Provence had protected Italy from hostile aggressors in the past. Delaplace (2000), 87, and (2003), 479, also points out the strategic value of Gaul's entire Mediterranean littoral with respect to controlling Spain. This may not have been Theoderic's initial intention, but thinking of this sort had played a role in Rome's annexation of Transalpine Gaul in the second century BC. See Ebel (1976).

[48] Though only Procopius, *Wars* 5.12.41, relates this. Gregory of Tours, *Historiae* 2.37, on the other hand, claims that all of Alaric II's royal treasure fell into Clovis' hands when he took Toulouse. But if Procopius is correct, a number of prestigious "Roman" goods, lost to the Visigoths during Alaric's sack of Rome in 410, were "restored" to Italy as a result, though only temporarily. See also Procopius, *Wars* 5.13.6, where Athalaric returns this treasure to Amalaric.

[49] For reconstructions, Ewig (1952), 124–8; Sirago (1987), 68–72; Schwarcz (1993), 793–4; Favrod (1997), 401–6; Delaplace (2000), 85–7; and Diaz and Valverde (2007), 360–1.

[50] Their support earned Theoderic's scathing and effective remonstrance. See Chp. 6.

[51] See *Vita Caesarii* 2.10, with Chp. 5. Cf. O'Donnell (1981), 48, who places these events between 512 and 526 and suggests Visigothic resistance throughout Theoderic's reign. Beyond this notice, however, the evidence points to resistance ending with Gesalec's death.

times between the empire and the other barbarians of Gaul, namely, the Franks and Burgundians, with certain southern lands in Burgundy actually being conquered, much to the elation of those in Italy, in the 520s and 530s.[52] Yet for all intents and purposes, by 511 the Roman reconquest of (southern) Gaul, and by extension Spain, was complete, and it was hence appropriate that in this year Flavius Felix, a Gallo-Roman aristocrat, was named consul.

If the Battle of Vouillé had ushered in the birth of France, no one in Italy noticed; nor was anyone claiming that a unified, Gothic superstate had arisen through Theoderic's tutelage over the Visigoths.[53] Instead, Italians were asserting that Roman Gaul and Spain had been reborn; that "Rome had gathered back to her bosom her very own nurslings"; that Gaul now paid her again with *consulares* and Spain with her ancient tributes of grain.[54]

TIRED LIMBS RESTORED

The jubilation inspired in Italy by this turn of events has already been discussed to some extent in prior chapters. Though Italo-Romans could live happily in a Roman Empire that lacked both Gaul and Spain, their restoration to the empire was, as the case had been with lands in the Balkans just years earlier, a cause for great celebration.[55] The victory, in and of itself, but especially over *real* barbarians, was significant and an obvious contrast to the triumph celebrated years before, when the Danube had been made "Roman" again. At that time, territory had been seized from other Romans, and while this fact could be sanitized with careful language, wars of this sort bore the ignominy of being fratricidal.[56] The defeat of the Franks, Burgundians, and Gesalec's Visigoths, however, lacked such connotations.

---

[52] See *Variae* 8.10 and 11.1.12–13. The latter hints at the return of certain Burgundian territories in exchange for tributary (client?) status. This may explain the strange notice in Jordanes, *Getica* 305, where Athalaric returns conquered territory to the Franks (an otherwise unattested occurrence). Perhaps Jordanes confused Franks for Burgundians, an understandable mistake given that Burgundy had fallen to the Franks by the time he was writing.

[53] See Sirago (1987), 74, and Arnold (2012). Cf. Claude (1978b), 24–5; Wolfram (1988), 309–12; and Delaplace (2000), 77.

[54] For nurslings, *Variae* 2.1.2: "alumnos proprios ad ubera sua Roma recolligat"; *consulares*, *Variae* 2.3.1 (referencing the Gallic consul Felix): "gaudete provincias ... vobis pendere consulares"; and grain tribute, *Variae* 5.35.1: "aequum iudicavimus Hispaniae triticeas illi copias exhibere, ut antiquum vectigal sub nobis felicior Roma reciperet."

[55] Cf. *PanTh* 69.

[56] For Ennodius' sanitization, *PanTh* 63–8; cf. *Variae* 11.1.10–11 and *Marc. Com.* 508 (n. 37, earlier).

As already described, these were not only stereotypical barbarians, but the very same savages who had been responsible for the loss of Gaul and Spain. Not content to keep these wrongfully wrested lands, they had even dared to attack Italy. A decisive avenging blow was thus dealt, and ideologies of Roman dominance, so intrinsic to the empire, were given additional substance, persisting from this point forward for decades.[57]

Already basking in a golden age, these victories in Gaul served to reinforce the idea that the prosperity of the Roman Empire would know no bounds, and so rightly Theoderic and his Goths, as guardians and agents of Roman power, were honored for their instrumental roles. It seems likely, for instance, that the series of triple solidi represented today by the Senigallia Medallion was minted at Rome to commemorate these very triumphs. The dating is not secure, but the message of *imperium*, dominance, and victory over multiple barbarians is unmistakable.[58] These Gallic campaigns, more than any other, made Theoderic a *princeps invictissimus semper* and a *victor gentium* who could legitimately hold the conquered world in the palm of his hand. The famous set of inscriptions erected by the illustrious ex-consul Basilius Decius was probably also dedicated at this time.[59] Their words hint at transalpine victories, applauding Theoderic as a conqueror and celebrator of triumphs, as one who had subdued the barbarians. It was these acts that made him worthy of being hailed as "semper Augustus," "guardian of liberty," "propagator of the Roman name," and "born for the good of the Republic."[60]

Other sources, with dates that are more certain, echo this same celebratory language, demonstrating clearly the links between victory in Gaul, prosperity at home, and the enthusiasm felt by a number of Italo-Romans for the Theoderican regime. In one instance their amazement and joy were expressed in the Senate House in a panegyric delivered by Cassiodorus. Here, for all the conscript fathers to see and hear, Cassiodorus referred to his *princeps* as an "untiring celebrator of triumphs" and shouted bravo,

---

[57] See Chp. 5 and the Epilogue.

[58] The coin is often thought to have been issued in commemoration of Theoderic's official visit to Rome in 500. For this, Wroth (1911), xxxii; Kraus (1928), 79; Ensslin (1959), 110; and Alföldi (1978). For 509, Grierson and Blackburn (1986), 35, and Moorhead (1992), 187–8. Not only are the coin's ideological claims more consistent with the 509 dating, but the absence of any reference to a *tricennalia* or *decennalia* (e.g. "vot/sic x/xxx") is revealing. Alternative dates have also been suggested. Cf. Metlich (2004), 15–16, who places the coin before 497.

[59] *Variae* 2.32 and 2.33, which announce Decius' project, are conventionally dated to 507–11.

[60] Fiebiger 1, #193 (*ILS* 827 and *CIL* 10 6850–2): "dominus noster gloriosissimus adque inclytus rex Theodericus, victor ac triumfator, semper Augustus, bono rei publicae natus, custos libertatis et propagator Romani nominis, domitor gentium." Cf. McCormick (1986), 278–80.

asserting, "He bridles haughty barbarians with his *imperium*; he pacifies the provinces with justice. While he fights, the tired limbs of the Republic are revived and blessedness is restored to our era. We used to only read in the annals that Gaul had once been Roman."[61] Gaul's restoration, in Cassiodorus' estimation, had been the culmination of a series of rebounds initiated by Theoderic, successes that had returned not only lost provinces to the Roman fold, but blessedness, *beatitudo*, to modern times.

Such an understanding, of course, was in keeping with the ideas expressed only a few years earlier by Ennodius, whose own panegyric had emphasized glorious victories in the East and concluded with the assertion that a golden age had dawned. Now, however, Ennodius' very own birth *patria* had been reclaimed and his own relatives and friends, dear ones whose barbarization was at times painfully obvious, had been redeemed. Writing to the prefect Liberius, who had once proven instrumental in the Theoderican recovery of Italy,[62] he could not help but express his elation:

> The Gauls agree with me in this statement: that those, to whom you con-
> veyed *civilitas* after the passing of many years and who happened not to
> taste the flavor of Roman liberty before you came, have been corrected
> through the aid of the living God Christ, and that you can now be returned
> to your Italy, since we demand it and they agree.[63]

For Ennodius, then, Gaul's restoration had been a miracle, for Cassiodorus a blessing, and for Decius and doubtless others a sign of Theoderic's exceptional stewardship over the republic. The golden age, at least in Italy, continued and even wondrously increased in its profits.

---

[61] *CassOratReliquiae*, p. 466, ln. 9–19 (partially cited in Chp. 8): "provincias iustitiae serenita- / te tranquillat, frenat superbas gen- / tes imperio.... Macte, infatigabilis triumphator, quo / pugnante fessa rei publicae membra / reparantur et ad saecula nostra an- / tiqua beatitudo revertitur. Galliam / quondam fuisse Romanam solis tantum / legebamus annalibus." The date and occasion of this oration is usually taken to be Cassiodorus' consulship of 514, based on a reference in the (rather problematic) *Anecdoton Holderi*. In truth, the reference to victory in Gaul could place the speech as early as 508. For 508/9, Romano (1978), 13–18. For 514 or even 518/9, see Traube's *MGH* edition, p. 462–3 (including n. 1 on the latter page).

[62] Ennodius' letter begins by referencing Liberius' role in the aftermath of Theoderic's defeat of Odovacer. See Chp. 7.

[63] #447.6: "mecum Galliae in hac adstipulatione conveniunt, ut Christo deo vivo disponente ordi- natis illis, quibus civilitatem post multos annorum circulos intulisti, quos ante te non contigit saporem de Romana libertate gustare, ad Italiam tuam et poscentibus nobis et illis tenentibus reducaris." For the contemporary connection between *libertas* and Romanness, Chp. 1, with Moorhead (1987) and Barnish (2003), 21–2.

The Morals of the Toga

The situation in Gaul itself, however, was different. Gaul, like other "lost" provinces, had gone its own way in the decades since imperial rule. The process, as already described in the preceding chapter, could be generalized from the standpoint of increasingly inward-looking Italo-Romans as barbarization, but for Gallo-Romans like Pomerius and Firminus feelings were probably otherwise. Life for these individuals had continued much as it had under Roman rule, and many had benefited during the reigns of Euric and Alaric II, proving themselves loyal subjects in the face of Clovis' hostile invasion.[64] Long before this, even the blue-blooded Sidonius, who seemed to pray for a new Caesar to reconquer Gaul, had accepted Visigothic rule, eulogizing the savage Euric as a near-imperial figure who defended Romanness in the face of barbarism.[65] Times, in other words, had changed along with loyalties. Ennodius could imagine a late-fifth-century Gaul where Gallo-Romans were weeping at their captivity, but by the early sixth century the lamentation was over.

There was hence a real need on the part of the Ravenna government to be sensitive in these early years of reintegration, much as the case had been in Italy nearly two decades prior. From a Gallic perspective, it was not a given that Theoderic's Italy was the reinvigorated and resurging Roman Empire that it claimed to be; nor was it obvious that a thoroughly Roman state had rescued Gaul from barbarian rule.[66] For many, Italy and Rome had continued to serve as preeminent sources of *Romanitas* in the West,[67] but the fate of contemporary Italians may not have seemed all that different from their own. Italy too had been conquered by Goths and had come to be ruled by a Gothic *rex* whose name, Theoderic, had been and would continue to be associated with the barbarian kings in their midst.[68] Well-connected Gallo-Romans might be aware of certain continuities

[64] Apollinaris, a son of Sidonius Apollinaris, is a conspicuous example. See *PLRE* 2, 114 (Apollinaris 3).
[65] For "new Caesar," Van Dam (1985), 174. For Sidonius' views on Euric, see the Introduction to Part III.
[66] Clearly some in Gaul, such as the Burgundians and Franks, recognized the Byzantines as the only legitimate Roman power at this time, if only for political reasons. For the Burgundians, Avitus of Vienne, *Ep.* 93 and 94; for the Franks, Gregory of Tours, *Historiae* 2.38.
[67] The continued desire on the part of Gallo-Romans to seek out an education in Italy and especially Rome is suggestive of this. See Chp. 9.
[68] Assuming, of course, that names like "Theodericus" had not become acceptably Roman by this point. They very well may have, since by 508 Gaul had already known three royal Theoderics (Theoderic I and II of the Visigoths and Theoderic/Theuderic I of the Franks). Moorhead

and developments, but in the end they had not been exposed fully to the Romanizing language of the day or to the benefits of Theoderican rule.

Initiation and persuasion were thus necessary, and go-betweens like Ennodius played an important, yet unofficial role in winning Gallic acceptance of their Roman restoration. Fully indoctrinated and supportive of the Theoderican regime, they proved all too willing to assure their transalpine contacts of this Roman Empire and its emperor's legitimacy, touting their blessings. A certain Aurelianus, for instance, who had been stripped of his patrimony during the course of Gaul's reconquest, was informed by Ennodius that the injury had been fortuitous. It had drawn the attention of his "most invincible lord," and the loss of substance was hence a benefit, since "the notice of a glorious *princeps* has been acquired from the expense."[69] Now, Aurelianus was assured, "the love of the highest lord" and "the greatest power" supported his roof, providing "a source of honor" for him.[70]

Similar assurances were also the main thrust of Theoderic's official dispatches, sent from the very beginning of his intervention in Gaul. In an important letter written late in 508 and directed to all his new provincials, Theoderic assumed the traditional role of a benevolent Roman *princeps* and reached out to his subjects. Once full-fledged Romans, they were told that they had fallen under the influence of barbarians and, like Parthenius or Euprepia, had developed certain uncivilized characteristics, such as cruelty and tendencies toward violence. Now, however, Rome had saved them from both the barbarians and their barbarism. They were literally welcomed back to the Roman Empire, to their birthright and to civilization, and were enjoined to become Romans once more, right down to their very togas. "Roman custom," Theoderic admonished, "must happily be obeyed by you who have been restored to it after a long time. Recalled to your ancient liberty, cast off barbarism, abandon cruel minds, and clothe yourselves in the morals of the toga. It is not right that you live like foreigners in our just times."[71]

(1992), 177, n. 13, is surely right to see no significance in Clovis' naming his son Theoderic, contra Geary (1988), 84. But see *Variae* 11.1.12, where Cassiodorus claims that Theoderic I of the Franks was unworthy of his mighty name.

[69] #270.2: "tamen sub hoc titulo invictissimi domini multum locupletem gratiam conparavit. Bona est iactura substantiae, si incliti notitia principis dispendiis invenitur."

[70] #270.2–3: "summi domini amor adquiritur ... facta est lucri mater et honorum via ... cum culmini tuo contigerit maxima iam tenere." Another letter (#412) makes it clear that Aurelianus later availed himself of Theoderic's Roman justice.

[71] *Variae* 3.17.1: "Libenter parendum est Romanae consuetudini, cui estis post longa tempora restituti.... Atque ideo in antiquam libertatem deo praestante revocati vestimini moribus togatis, exuite barbariem, abicite mentium crudelitatem, quia sub aequitate nostri temporis non vos decet vivere moribus alienis."

Words like these drew the traditional, clear-cut distinction between civilized and barbarian, Roman and non-Roman, and tried to impress upon those in Gaul that they rightly belonged with other Romans. True to ideologies current in Italy, Theoderic professed that he and the other inhabitants of his empire were still "the Romans," whether Italo-Roman or Gotho-Roman, and that the Gauls had once been, and now should want to be, Romans as well. "It is welcome," they were told, "to return to that place from which your ancestors are known to have profited."[72] Now safe, they were supposed to "enjoy what you used to only hear about" and to realize that "men are preferred not by their bodily strength but their reason."[73] Gauls were told to live peaceful lives and to rely once more on their intellect, a prerequisite of civilized men, rather than brute strength, so typical of iron-fisted barbarians.

With reason would likewise come the ability to obey and revere the laws, and this too was envisioned as a rather necessary improvement. "A restoration that is good," Theoderic continued, "should not be troublesome. Love the things from which your security is derived and your conscience profits. It is barbaric to live according to pleasure."[74] Indeed, as already discussed, lawlessness was another condition of barbarism and had once excluded the Goths from holding imperial power. It was their own defense of and obedience to Roman law that had made the Goths themselves, in part at least, tolerably Roman.[75] Now the Gauls, much like others before them, were asked to follow a Gothic lead. Gauls were told that the laws provided "assistance to the weak and bridles to the powerful" and were enjoined to "recover little by little the customs of administering justice." "What can be more favorable," Theoderic assured them, "than for men to rely on the laws alone and not fear future calamities?"[76]

Roman law, of course, had remained in effect in Visigothic Gaul under Euric and Alaric II, and Theoderic even recognized their compilations as binding.[77] The issue here was a matter of practice and application rather than straightforward existence. In a Roman Gaul where reason could now

[72] *Ibid.*: "quia ibi regressus est gratus, ubi provectum vestros constat habuisse maiores."
[73] *Variae* 3.17.5: "Fruemini quod tantum audiebatis. Intelligite homines non tam corporea vi quam ratione praeferri et illos merito crescere qui possunt aliis iusta praestare."
[74] *Variae* 3.17.3–4: "Non sit novitas molesta, quae proba est…. Amate unde et securitas venit et conscientia proficit. Gentilitas enim vivit ad libitum."
[75] See Chp. 5.
[76] *Variae* 3.17.3: "Recipite paulatim iuridicos mores … quid enim potest esse felicius quam homines de solis legibus confidere et casus reliquos non timere? Iura publica certissima sunt … infirmorum auxilia, potentum frena."
[77] For Roman law in Visigothic Gaul, Collins (1983), 25–9. For Theoderic's recognition, *Variae* 4.12, 4.17, and 5.39.

flourish, justice, so important an ideology for the Theoderican regime, was to reign supreme. "It is not right," Theoderic informed his agents in Gaul, "for those who deserved to come under our rule to accomplish anything through violence."[78] They were to have recourse to the laws, and a similar sentiment had been expressed to the inhabitants of Pannonia when Theoderic prohibited the trial by arms: "Why should you, who do not have bribable judges, have recourse to personal combat? Put down your sword, you who lack an enemy!"[79]

Reason not brawn, laws not swords, togas not furs: So far as Theoderic's newest subjects were informed, the restoration of Roman Gaul was intended to return Gaul and its inhabitants to their prior, fifth-century state, transforming contemporary, barbarized Gauls into the upstanding Romans that their ancestors had once been.[80] Noblemen like Parthenius, by implication, would no longer have to cross the Alps in order to secure their Roman birthrights; their Romanness could be acquired at home.

A GOOD RESTORATION

Transformations of this sort had always been a kind of self-appointed moral obligation for the Roman Empire and its rulers. In Theoderic's case, however, this "re-Romanization" of Gaul was especially important, as it had numerous implications for his own status, not just as a Roman ruler, but as a glorious one. Indeed, Theoderic believed that Gaul in particular had been acquired "for our praises" and that the reextension of *civilitas* to this province would "sow the fame of our name."[81] In Italy, as recently demonstrated, successes in Gaul really did earn Theoderic the adulation and fame that he sought, but the acceptance and adoration of his newest subjects, the Gauls, was likewise desired. The *princeps* of the West hoped that the Gauls would "rejoice in being conquered" and suggested to one governor that being "more concerned about those

---

[78] *Variae* 4.12.3 (a case between two Gallo-Roman litigants): "non decet per vim eos aliquid agere, qui ad nostra meruerunt regimina pervenire."

[79] *Variae* 3.24.4: "Cur ad monomachiam recurratis, qui venalem iudicem non habetis? Deponite ferrum, qui non habetis inimicum."

[80] Sirago (1987), 74–5, concludes similarly.

[81] For praises, *Variae* 3.16.2 (to Vicar Gemellus): "quos nostris laudibus specialiter credimus adquisitos"; for *civilitas* and fame, *Variae* 3.38.1 (to Wandil, a count at Avignon): "Quamvis pietatis nostrae constet esse votum, ut ubique civilia, ubique moderata peragantur, maxime tamen optamus bene geri in regionibus Gallicanis, ubi ... ipsa initia bene plantare debent nostri nominis famam." The neuter plural *civilia* is simply another way of referencing *civilitas*.

from whom an increase of triumphs [has] come" would help realize this goal.[82]

It was important, therefore, to have able administrators, referred to in official correspondence as "prudent governors," "good overseers," and "exceptional men," responsible for the situation in Gaul.[83] These men were direct agents of the emperor, his empire, and its *Romanitas*, and so they needed to behave with the utmost integrity in order to assure Gallic loyalty. The vicar Gemellus was informed as early as 508 that his duty was to "correct" the Gauls and was instructed to "hate unrest and avoid avarice so that the tired province may accept you as the kind of judge it knows a Roman *princeps* would send."[84] Likewise the inhabitants of Marseille were told that their new count, Marabad, would "bring solace to the lowly, throw before the insolent the severity of his rule, and, finally, suffer none to be oppressed by unjust presumption, compelling all to the justice by which our Empire always flourishes."[85] This was what it meant to live in a Roman Empire, and justice of this sort, afforded by able administrators, was supposed to cause Theoderic's new "subjects to grieve that they had not acquired our rule earlier."[86]

But governors served other purposes in Gaul. The mere presence of civil officials like the praetorian prefect Liberius and his vicar, Gemellus, was especially important.[87] These men were exceptional Romans, the former practically exuding *Romanitas* and proven dedication to the state.[88] Indeed, Liberius' reputation for service and eloquence was already well known in Gaul, and while prefect he continued to move seamlessly within local (and

---

[82] *Variae* 3.16.2–3 (to Gemellus): "Cara est principi gloria et necesse est de illis amplius esse sollicitum, unde sibi triumphorum venisse sentit augmentum.... Effice ut victam fuisse delectet."

[83] Prudent governors, *Variae* 4.16.1: "prudentes ... rectores"; good overseers, *Variae* 3.34.1 (to the Massilienses): "bonis praesidentibus"; exceptional men, *Variae* 3.16.3: "viros egregios."

[84] *Variae* 3.16.2–3: "quando ad illos populos mitteris corrigendos.... Turbulenta non ames: avara declina, ut talem te iudicem provincia fessa suscipiat qualem Romanum principem transmisisse cognoscat." The use of *Romanum principem* here provides undeniable proof that Theoderic wished to be seen as such in Gaul.

[85] *Variae* 3.34.2: "minoribus solacium ferat, insolentibus severitatem suae districtionis obiciat, nullum denique opprimi iniqua praesumptione patiatur, sed omnes cogat ad iustum, unde semper floret imperium."

[86] *Variae* 3.33: "ut subiecti se doleant nostrum dominium tardius adquisisse."

[87] *Variae* 3.17 states that Gemellus was vicar of the prefect and not, as Rouche (1979), 50, and Delaplace (2000), 88, claim, *Vicarius Septem Provinciarum*. Whether he initially answered to the prefect of Italy or Gaul is debated. See earlier, n. 46.

[88] Liberius' credentials have been discussed throughout this study. For Gemellus, *PLRE* 2, 499–500, with *Variae* 3.16 and 3.17. He is described as a *vir spectabilis* and identified as having already proven his integrity to Theoderic in prior (unknown) offices. There is no evidence that he was a Gallo-Roman, contra Rouche (1979), 50.

not so local) aristocratic circles.[89] Even the bishop of Burgundian Vienne, Avitus, solicited his letters.[90] His selection, then, was a characteristically prudent choice on Theoderic's part, for Roman men like him served as ready reminders to the Gauls of their reintegration into a bona fide Roman Empire.[91] Moreover, and whether available to Gallo-Romans or not, their very offices reiterated these ideas, many having vanished under Visigothic rule, not least the Gallic prefecture.[92] In more ways than one, therefore, the arrival of a praetorian prefect like Liberius announced to the Gauls that they were again part of a Roman state.

The military administrators of Gaul, mostly "Goths," also served important, complementary functions. Foremost, of course, they did exactly what they had done in Italy and earlier "restored" provinces. They were to "see to whatever pertains to security" and "defend [the Gauls] by arms" against the *real* barbarians.[93] But in Gaul, as elsewhere, Goths were also supposed to be on their best behavior and to demonstrate their own uniquely Roman obedience to the laws. While stationed at Narbonne, the famous general Ibba was exhorted to render himself "as extraordinary in *civilitas*" as he was "famous in war."[94] His prestige as a warrior was imagined as so glorious, in fact, that not even "wicked men" would resist his injunctions, demonstrating another means by which "Gothic" arms could be employed for the sake of "Roman" *civilitas*.[95] Wandil, a count residing in Avignon, was similarly informed that "whenever the army is deployed, it must be thought to defend rather than be a burden. You should suffer there to be

---

[89] O'Donnell (1981), 34 and 45, suggests that Liberius himself may have been a Ligurian and his wife, Agretia, of Gallo-Roman descent. If true, a number of preexisting Gallo-Roman contacts would be likely. While prefect in Gaul, he befriended both Caesarius of Arles (*Vita Caesarii* 2.11–13) and Apollinaris of Valence (*Vita Apollinaris* 10). He likewise built and dedicated a basilica at Orange (its dedication is recorded in the minutes for the Council of Orange). See Delaplace (2003), 497–9.

[90] Avitus, *Ep.* 35, describes himself as "thirsting" (*sitienti*) for his letters.

[91] Delaplace (2003), 481–2, concludes similarly. For a different interpretation, which nonetheless envisions Liberius as a prudent choice, O'Donnell (1981), 44–5.

[92] Cf. Sirago (1987), 68 and 74, and Delaplace (2000), 87f. There is no evidence (positive or negative) for Gallo-Romans holding high office during this period, but they doubtless continued holding local positions. For the loss of civil posts in Visigothic Gaul, Mathisen (1993).

[93] Defend by arms, *Variae* 3.43.1 (to the Spatharius Unigis): "delectamur iure Romano vivere quos armis cupimus vindicare," and *Variae* 4.12.1 (to Marabad): "Propositi nostri est, ut provincias nobis deo auxiliante subiectas, sicut armis defendimus"; whatever pertains to security, *Variae* 3.34.2 (to the Massilienses regarding Marabad): "ut quicquid ad securitatem vel civilitatem vestram pertinet." For Unigis, *PLRE* 2, 1182; for Marabad, see later discussion.

[94] *Variae* 4.17.3: "ut qui es bello clarus, civilitate quoque reddaris eximius."

[95] *Ibid.*: "Improbis enim non potuisse resistere non praevales excusare, quando omnes tibi libenter cedunt, quem gloriosum in bellorum certamine cognoverunt. Ignavus forte audacibus iubere nihil possit: nemo plus praesumentibus imperat, quam quem sua facta commendant."

no violence. Let our army live according to *civilitas* among the Romans."[96] Goths, then, were to continue leading by example, and one Goth, Arigern, was even praised before the Roman Senate for doing just this, earning a fitting eulogy, according to Theoderic, as one who had "restored the glory of *civilitas*" to the Gauls and thus repaid to the senators of Rome "what he diligently learned in your midst."[97] Gaul, to conclude, afforded the Goths yet another opportunity to demonstrate their new-found civility and Romanness, both at home and abroad, further assuring their acceptance in Theoderic's Roman Empire.

A DEVASTATED PROVINCE

But concern for new provincials extended beyond friendly rhetoric and exceptional governors, whether "Roman" or "Gothic." Regardless of its condition under Visigothic rule, this was a land ravaged by war in 508, and one that would continue to be war-torn into the next decade. Preaching to his flock in the midst of the devastation, Bishop Caesarius of Arles commented in one sermon, "our country has been left a wasteland by our enemies ... we have lost everything that we loved in this world,"[98] and in another, "dire calamity has struck our eyes ... everywhere there is great agony and grief."[99] Among Italians, likewise, Gaul was described as a "tired province," "devastated by attacks of the savage enemy," and "suffering want on our behalf."[100] The situation in Gaul, therefore, was not that dissimilar to the one confronted by Theoderic in the aftermath of Odovacer's defeat. Far beyond simply reinstilling Roman law and custom, there was a grave need for assistance and an obligation on the part of Gaul's supposed liberators to provide it.

---

[96] *Variae* 3.38.1–2: "et ubi exercitus dirigitur, non gravandi, sed defendendi potius existimentur.... nulla fieri violenta patiaris. Vivat noster exercitus civiliter cum Romanis." For Wandil, *PLRE* 2, 1149.

[97] *Variae* 4.16.1: "His rebus ad nostra vota compositis et gloriam civilitatis retulit et quod inter vos didicit diligenter ostendens et bellorum insignia reportavit." For Arigern, Chp. 5.

[98] *Sermo* 6.6: "deserta remaneret ab hostibus terra nostra ... totum quod in hoc mundo amabamus perdidimus."

[99] *Sermo* 70.2: "oculos nostros dira calamitas et tempore obsidionis percusserit ... cruciatus in utroque magnus et dolor." This particular sermon recycled much material from the *De Tempore Barbarico* of the fifth-century North African bishop Quodvultdeus, who witnessed the capture of Carthage by the Vandals. The extent to which its gory details are an accurate description of the situation in Gaul, therefore, is questionable. Cf. Klingshirn (1994a), 113–14.

[100] Tired Province, *Variae* 3.16.3: "provincia fessa," and *Variae* 3.41.2: "fatigata provincia"; devastated, *Variae* 3.40.2: "hostili feritate vastatis pro qualitate laesionis"; suffering for us, *Variae* 3.32.1–2: "qui nostris partibus ... penuriam pertulerunt."

To a large extent, this was what Theoderic had intended when he expressed the desire to show extra concern for the recently conquered, and aid packages financed by the rest of the empire were an excellent way of demonstrating this. As early as 508, such packages were being dispatched to Gaul along with pledges of future assistance and ample thanks for loyalty in the face of difficulties. Ideally such relief was designed to allow Gauls to "feel nothing in the same way that nothing was suffered when [they] asked for Rome."[101] But in reality Gaul had suffered much, and these gifts were seen as necessary "remedies" and a kind of "medicine."[102] Not only would they alleviate present difficulties, but they would link their relief with the traditional style of kindness and piety that had already legitimized Theoderic and his government elsewhere, in places like Liguria and Rome.

Throughout this period, Theoderic's agents were busy using Italian monies in an effort to ransom Gallo-Roman captives from wrongful barbarian masters. According to Caesarius of Arles, "whole provinces" had been "led into captivity,"[103] and though room must be given for hyperbole, many a southern Gallo-Roman, including Ennodius' own relatives, had succumbed to this fate.[104] Once liberated, they owed their freedom to their Roman guarantors in a way that other "liberated" Gallo-Romans could never know; and just as the case had been with Ligurian captives more than a decade earlier, their return would help to restore fecundity to a nearly dead province.[105] Though not requiring ransom money, others, like Ennodius' friend Aurelianus, his nephew Lupicinus, and a certain Magnus, still owed their livelihoods to these same imperial agents, their lost properties having been restored to them as a result of the Theoderican government's direct intervention.[106]

Beyond these individual cases, measures were also implemented to provide relief to whole communities that were struggling to survive. Provinces

---

[101] *Variae* 3.16.3: "Nihil tale sentiat, quale patiebatur, cum Romam quaereret."

[102] For remedies (*remedia*), *Variae* 3.40.1, 3.42.1, and 3.44.1. For medicine (*medicina*), *Variae* 3.40.1.

[103] *Sermo* 70.2: "totae provinciae in captivitatem ductae sunt."

[104] Ennodius (#457) solicited the aid of Liberius in an effort to secure the release of his relative (*parens*) Camella. Cf. Avitus of Vienne, *Ep.* 35, where efforts by Liberius to free captives in Burgundy are mentioned. Caesarius himself used monies acquired from Theoderic to free captives in western Gaul. See *Vita Caesarii* 1.43–4, with Klingshirn (1985), 192.

[105] See Chp. 7.

[106] For Aurelianus, see earlier discussion; for Lupicinus, #60, where Ennodius seeks Faustus' aid in securing the return of his Gallic patrimony (admittedly, he may have failed); for Magnus, *Variae* 3.18.

and provincials were supposed to provide revenues to the state, or, at the very least, pay for their own upkeep, but it was understood that this was only to be expected from "those at peace, not those who have been besieged."[107] Even Ennodius, writing to Liberius in 512, commented on the need for mercy in these trying times, urging that it was not right for those in Gaul to "provide for the nourishment of the aforementioned [i.e. Italy], while the burdens of the treasury are drawn off from their little huts."[108] Theoderic agreed, sending wheat directly from Italy in 508 to feed the soldiers stationed along the Durance, "lest the tired province become annoyed by their provisioning."[109] Later that year the entire province was exempted from paying for military expenses. "Under a benign *princeps*," the Gauls were informed, "subjects should not have to demand remedies … since it is right for a *princeps* to always decree what is more humane."[110] "The army sent for your defense," he continued, "will be nourished by our kindness," and soon both money and supplies were dispatched to Gaul so that they might think "only aid [had been granted] from so great an assembly [of troops]."[111] Similarly, in 510, a series of tax cancellations was enacted in the face of renewed Frankish aggression.[112] The entire population of Arles, which seems to have suffered the brunt of the devastation, was exempted altogether from paying a monetary tribute. The Arlesians had proven themselves "faithful" and "devoted in sorrowful times,"[113] and so Theoderic announced to the vicar Gemellus, "let those who preferred to hunger on our behalf in their difficulties take satisfaction in their freedom and be joyful. The costly tribute of their faith has already been given to us. It is unjust for those, who have shown glorious scruples, to pay us with

---

[107] *Variae* 3.32.2: "Non decet statim de tributis esse sollicitum, qui casum vix potuit declinare postremum. A quietis ista, non obsessis inquirimus." This was a standard policy in other "devastated" provinces. Cf. *Variae* 2.38, 4.19, 4.36, 11.15, and 12.28, with *VE* 186 (discussed in Chp. 7).

[108] #457.4: "Generis mei patronus quod in Italia positis praestitit, non neget in Gallia, ut vel de casellulis ipsius ordinatione vestra dum ab eis fisci onera derivantur, ad praefatae alimenta sufficiant." The use of *casellula* served to strengthen the sense of Gallic impoverishment. See later discussion.

[109] *Variae* 3.41.2: "ne fatigata provincia huius praebitione laederetur."

[110] *Variae* 3.42.1–2: "Non occurritur sub principe benigno remedia postulare subiectos … quia licet principem semper humaniora censere."

[111] *Variae* 3.42.2: "ex Italia destinavimus exercituales expensas, ut ad defensionem vestram directus exercitus nostris humanitatibus aleretur solumque auxilium provinciae de tam magna congregatione sentirent."

[112] For reconstructions, Sirago (1987), 69, and Schwarcz (1993), 796.

[113] *Variae* 3.32.1: "Constat apud nos fidelium non perire servitia, sed in tristibus impensa recipere in meliore fortuna."

worthless money."[114] The loyalty of Arles was considered payment enough, and soon other affected areas were exempted as well.[115]

Gallic Fecundity

Such indulgences were temporary expedients, pragmatic gestures necessary to ensure the loyalty of Theoderic's newest subjects and to promote recovery in a war-torn Gaul. But while underlying motives, simple recovery was not enough. Once "happy" and "prosperous," Gaul was supposed to flourish and in this way come to participate fully in the empire's golden age. Indeed, and as already seen, this land was an analogue to the devastated Italy that Theoderic had liberated at the very beginning of his reign, and just as "unforeseen beauty" had come forth "from the ashes of cities" in Italy, so too was it hoped that Roman Gaul would resurge and "live again." Such recovery, of course, would benefit Italy's coffers, a prospect not lost on the Theoderican government.[116] But the impact that this would have on Gaul's supposedly barbarized and now ravaged population was more important. Their lives would be improved significantly, while their enrichment would serve as another positive indicator, both at home and abroad, of their very real and Roman restoration.

Roman nobility, Theoderic had informed his Gallic provincials in 508, was a combination of "good morals and splendid goods."[117] Yet under barbarian rule both had suffered. Noble Gallo-Roman families like Ennodius' own had adopted "alien customs" and "hidden their riches in faraway places."[118] Consistent with this understanding of barbarization, Gaul had become an impoverished land, the squalor and pathetic "little Gallic huts" mentioned by Ennodius being typical of its imagined situation, which recent events had helped to make a reality for many.[119] The reestablishment

---

[114] *Variae* 3.32.2: "Satientur in libertate qui pro nobis in angustiis esurire maluerunt: sint laeti.... Pretiosum vectigal iam nobis dederunt fidei suae. Iniustum est ut viles pecunias exigantur qui gloriosas conscientias obtulerunt."

[115] See later discussion.

[116] See *Variae* 3.32.1 and 4.36.

[117] *Variae* 3.17.4: "quia tantum quis nobilior erit quantum et moribus probis et luculenta facultate reluxerit."

[118] For alien customs, see earlier discussion. For hiding riches, *Variae* 3.17.4: "bona longo situ recondita."

[119] For the connection between barbarism and a society's state of development, Dauge (1981), 486–91. Ennodius' depiction of the *patria* of the Alamanni, who fled to Italy c. 506, provides another example. See *PanTh* 72–3, which contrasts the "opulence" of Italy's soil with the filthy "mud" of Germany.

of Roman rule was supposed to change this, however. Now defended by Rome's valiant soldiers, now that they were "safe," the Gauls were told to "show off your wealth" and to "let the possessions of your parents be brought back into the light," acts that would turn back the clock to a pre-barbarian age.[120] Gallo-Romans, in other words, were not merely to behave like Romans, but to *look* like them as well; they were supposed to wrap themselves, figuratively, in the "morals of the toga," while wrapping themselves, quite literally, in the linens of the toga. A Roman mode of consumption, long since a prerequisite for Romanness, was thus necessary;[121] and while unearthing and then adorning oneself with "hidden" Roman heirlooms could be a step in the right direction (provided such goods existed), important economic policies were also initiated that helped to promote a Roman way of life.

As in Italy, fostering trade was key, both of subsistence goods and of more prestigious luxury items. The simple availability of commodities like wheat, wine, and oil, for instance, could allow new provincials to maintain a basic standard of living that passed for Roman.[122] Yet in a country suffering the effects of war, this could be a serious problem, and Theoderic was all too aware. Sometime between 508 and 511, he redirected Sicilian grain, normally earmarked for Italian consumption, to Gaul, a move indicative of a grave absence in the region.[123] Little more is known regarding the intended fate of this cargo, as it was lost at sea, but other sources confirm a scarcity at this time, and the situation eventually grew so desperate that rampant inflation and profiteering were a consequence.[124] Provisions were "sold at a price more lavish than their meager value (should permit)" and the Gauls, still in a state of recovery, were further impoverished.[125] Faced with this, Theoderic intervened again, turning to private merchants from Campania, Lucania, and Tuscia and instructing them to go to Gaul to sell their wares. Flooding the market, or at least giving it a needed influx of goods, it was hoped, would "promote the utility of those who are devoted [i.e. the Gauls]," while

---

[120] *Variae* 3.17.4: "Vos iam securi ostentate divitias: parentum bona longo situ recondita prodantur in lucem."

[121] See Woolf (1998), chp. 7.

[122] It helped, in addition, if these goods were shipped in conspicuously "Roman" containers.

[123] For the order, *Variae* 4.7, with Sirago (1987), 68–9. Admittedly, the grain may have been intended for the use of Theoderic's army. Cf. *Variae* 3.41 (discussed earlier).

[124] For the scarcity, *Variae* 3.32 (earlier), 4.5 (later), 3.44 (later), and *Vita Caesarii* 2.8–9.

[125] *Variae* 4.5.1: "In Gallicana igitur regione victualium cognovimus caritatem, ad quam negotiatio semper prompta festinat, ut empta angustiore pretio largius distrahantur."

providing the merchants with a ready market where they could negotiate to everyone's advantage.[126] It was hence a win-win situation, for buyer, seller, and facilitator.[127]

Similar policies were enacted in the hope of spurring on the trade of luxury goods, their possession by Gallo-Roman elites, as Theoderic claimed, being an essential component of their noble Roman standing. Sometime before 511, the *siliquaticum* (a type of sales tax) was cancelled on grain, wine, and oil. This was, in Theoderic's words, "princely foresight" and would allow "those who are worn-out" to enjoy some respite, providing for their future good health in the process.[128] The grant, of course, would reduce the cost of basic necessities, an act in keeping with those grants already discussed, but this was not exactly what Theoderic had in mind. "Let the ship coming to our ports not be afraid," he instructed Gemellus, much as he instructed the counts placed in charge of shipping at Portus, Ostia, and Classe.[129] "Right now, while we desire to be kind to our provincials, let us have regard for our lords of commerce: who would not be aroused to sell more lavish things to those whose usual expenses have been taken away?"[130] A little extra money, it was hoped, would go a long way. Doubtless the same idea lay behind Theoderic's confirmation of the "ancient privileges" of Marseille.[131] Marseille, after all, was one of the most important trade centers in Gaul and was fast on its way to becoming the preeminent emporium of the region.[132] Privileges of this sort often included reductions or exemptions from certain tariffs and, moreover, were a mark of distinction, emblematic of a special relationship between the city in question and its patronizing ruler. Marseille, then, stood to be enriched as a result of Theoderic's "unbounded kindness"; the city had been vindicated from new and unjust presumptions and now the "immunities acquired through the favor of [Roman] *principes*" had

---

[126] *Variae* 4.5.1–2: "iussiones, quae magis utilitates noscuntur extollere devotorum.... habituri licentiam distrahendi sic ut inter emptorem venditoremque convenerit." Cf. Sirago (1987), 68–9.
[127] *Variae* 4.5.2: "Sic evenit ut et venditoribus satisfiat et illis provisio nostra subveniat."
[128] *Variae* 4.19.1: "Decet principalem providentiam fessa refovere ... ut haec remissio solutionis copiam possit praestare provinciis et respirent aliquatenus fessi praesentis salubritate decreti."
[129] *Variae* 4.19.3: "Portus nostros navis veniens non pavescat." For the counts, *Variae* 7.9 and 7.14, with Chp. 7.
[130] *Variae* 4.19.3: "Quis enim ad vendendum non incitetur largius, cui solita dispendia subtrahuntur? ... nunc autem, dum provincialibus praestare cupimus, mercium dominis interim consulamus."
[131] *Variae* 4.26.1: "Libenti animo antiqua circa vos beneficia custodimus."
[132] Loseby (1992), 180f., and Delaplace (2003), 491–2.

been "restored after a long time."[133] Nor was Theoderic content with this simple restoration, for his own "princely munificence" granted, in addition, a temporary remission of taxation for the city, an act that was tellingly described as perfect *pietas*.[134]

RENOVATIO URBIUM

The inhabitants of cities like Marseille thus benefited from wartime policies designed both to address their immediate needs and to provide for their future prosperity. But re-Romanization and enrichment could also extend beyond the individual to the community as a whole. Cities, as already seen, were vital in Theoderic's empire, and building projects within Italian cities, whether restorative or new, had played an important role in the contemporary Italian understanding of a golden age even before Gaul's reconquest. Cities in Gaul, too, had witnessed their share of decay and transformation into the Late Empire, though some, like Arles and Marseille, had fared rather well.[135] Even so, there was room in Gaul for the same kind of urban patronage and renewal witnessed in Italy, and the same general implications would stem from such projects. In Arles, Theoderic saw to the rebuilding of the city's walls. These were doubtless in serious need of repair, given that the "glorious siege" lifted by Ibba and his Goths had been one in a long succession of sieges stretching back to the early fifth century.[136] "A certain quantity of money" was thus directed from Italy to be used for the project, as well as provisions to "relieve expenses."[137]

---

[133] *Variae* 4.26.1–2: "Servare quippe terminos ignorat humanitas et novellis decet blandiri beneficiis post longa tempora restitutis. Proinde immunitatem vobis, quam regionem vestram constat principum privilegio consecutam, hac auctoritate largimur nec vobis aliquid novae praesumptionis patiemur imponi, quos ab omni volumus gravamine vindicari."

[134] *Variae* 4.26.2: "Censum praeterea praesentis anni relaxat vobis munificentia principalis.... Ipsa est enim perfecta pietas, quae antequam flectatur precibus, novit considerare fatigatos." The remission, therefore, was unsolicited.

[135] For Arles, which kept much of its classical infrastructure and amenities into the sixth century, Loseby (1992) 179; Heijmans and Sintès (1994); Delage (1994), 28–32; Klingshirn (1994a), chp. 1; Heijmans (1999); and Delaplace (2003), 488–91. For Marseille, see earlier discussion.

[136] In the fifth century, Arles was besieged by Gerontius (c. 410), Constantius III (c. 411), Theoderic I (c. 425, 430, and 436/7), and Euric (475 and 476). There is no evidence that Euric had these walls repaired after his final capture of the city, but given Arles' importance as an occasional royal residence, it seems probable. Regardless, the walls must not have been very decrepit, since they proved effective in blocking the Frankish and Burgundian onslaught in the wake of Vouillé.

[137] *Variae* 3.44.2–3: "Pro reparatione itaque murorum Arelatensium vel turrium vetustarum certam pecuniae direximus quantitatem. Victualia quoque, quae vestras relevare videantur expensas, fecimus praeparari." It can be suggested in passing that this money would have included

Walls were important for defensive reasons, but they had additional meaning attached to them that extended beyond the pragmatic. Foremost, their presence could provide the community that they encircled with a sense of security, a benefit historically associated with Roman rule and one that Theoderic was keen to have associated with his times. Equally important, however, were the wonder and beauty of their construction. By their very existence, walls made a late Roman city a city,[138] but glorious, venerable, and beautiful walls made for a glorious, venerable, and beautiful city. Indeed, in his late-fourth-century *Ordo urbium nobilium*, the Gallic poet Ausonius had made it a point to describe as veritable monuments the walls of Toulouse, Trier, Milan, and Aquileia, going on to praise his native Bordeaux for its "walls so lofty with their soaring towers that their peaks penetrate the airy clouds."[139] Walls were as much an ornament as a necessity, and the former understanding was not lost on Theoderic. "It is right," he explained to the inhabitants of Arles, "for the prosperity of a city to be demonstrated by the beauty of its constructions" and for a kindly and pious sovereign to "provide a bountiful remedy to his citizens and hasten to return ancient walls to their splendor."[140] Arles, his patronage promised, would boast again of impressive and ancient walls, and the resources sent from Italy would act as yet another remedy designed to engender loyalty and to demonstrate the rightness of Roman rule. "Relieve your minds," the Arlesians were told, "and, revived by our promise and maintaining hope in future supplies, have faith in our Divine favor, since there is no less to our words than what is held in your granaries."[141] Arles and presumably other

Theoderican coinage, yet another means of Gallic indoctrination. The provisions, too, may have included building materials in addition to foodstuffs, such as bricks or tiles bearing Theoderic's monogram. See Chp. 8. No Theoderican coinage appears to have been minted in Gaul, though coinage from Italy has been found in the region. See Lafaurie and Pilet-Lemière (2003). For other instances of money being sent to Gaul, *Variae* 3.42, 3.44, 5.10, and 5.11, and *Vita Caesarii* 1.43. Likewise, no Theoderican brick stamps have been found in Gaul, though ongoing archaeological work may prove fruitful. The circus at Arles seems a likely beneficiary of Theoderican patronage, not only because this would fit his modus operandi, but also because this circus remained in use into the 550s.

[138] See Loseby (2006).

[139] *Ordo* 20, ln. 13–14: "Quadrua murorum species, sic turribus altis / ardua, ut aerias intrent fastigia nubes."

[140] *Variae* 3.44.1: "Quamvis primum sit laesos incolas refovere et in hominibus magis signum pietatis ostendere, tamen utrumque humanitas nostra coniungit, ut et largitatis remedio civibus consulamus et ad cultum reducere antiqua moenia festinemus. Sic enim fiet, ut fortuna urbis ... fabricarum quoque decore monstretur."

[141] *Variae* 3.44.3: "Relevate nunc animos et de nostra promissione recreati futurae copiae spem tenentes divino favore habetote fiduciam, quia non minus est quod nostris verbis quam quod

cities like it, then, could continue to count on Theoderic's benevolence, its monuments and privileges restored.

By 511, therefore, Gaul and its inhabitants were on their way to becoming a part of Theoderic's revived and resurging Roman Empire and were beginning to benefit from its blessings. Like the inhabitants of Pannonia Secunda and to some degree even Italy, Gallic provincials were being corrected and restored to their prior, civilized state through the imagined (and not so imagined) reimplementation of Roman customs and law. They had been liberated, both from barbarian rule and from barbarism, and were beginning to avail themselves of the empire's justice, some in places as far away as Ravenna.[142] Like all of the empire, Gaul now had Gothic soldiers, civilized heroes who had vindicated and then defended them from *real* barbarians, and Roman governors, men whose offices alone demonstrated Gaul's Roman restoration and whose integrity and assistance helped to make such a restoration welcome. Gaul even had a Roman *princeps* again, and though he was not in residence, his official dispatches, traditional acts of benevolence and patronage, and good stewardship over the entire process of reintegration acted as constant reminders of his position as a bona fide Roman emperor who ruled over a bona fide Roman Empire. Finally, as in Italy, wealth and beauty, though slow in coming, were beginning to emerge from devastated cities like Arles, and many others, including Marseille and Orange, would continue to prosper under a long Roman peace.[143] Happiness was in the air, and the glory of the Roman Empire, now including Gaul, appeared secure on both sides of the Alps.

---

horreis continetur." The use of *divino favore* comes very close to an appropriation of the imperial epithet *divus*, unless, of course, God is meant. The grain reference, on the other hand, seems to suggest that Theoderic had already gifted this city with free grain, an act that is otherwise unattested. Cf. *Variae* 3.41.

[142] For examples, *Variae* 4.12, 4.46, and Ennodius, #412 (Aetheria); Ennodius, #71, with Kennell (2000), 33–5 (Stephanus); *Vita Caesarii* 1.36–8 and Ennodius #461 (Caesarius); and n. 106, earlier (Aurelianus, Lupicinus, and Magnus). In general, traveling to Theoderic's court at Ravenna was discouraged owing to the difficulties such travels could cause the parties involved. Cf. *Variae* 4.46 and 5.15 (re. litigants from Pannonia).

[143] But cf. Klingshirn (1994a), chp. 5, and Delaplace (2003), 481, for "Pax Ostrogothica." Both focus on Arles and the evidence from the episcopacy of Caesarius. Similarly episcopal in emphasis, Schäferdiek (1967), 82, uses "Pax Gothica" for Theoderic's reign in Spain, stressing normalization and consolidation. For Marseille, Loseby (1992). For Orange, Delaplace (2003), 497–9. As mentioned in n. 137 (earlier), the state of archaeological research in this region is ongoing. New finds (it is hoped) will eventually shed further light on the matter.

THE "HAPPY YEAR" REVISITED

As mentioned at the very beginning of this book and alluded to throughout, a final, crowning achievement occurred in this very year, in 511, when, for the first time in more than half a century, a Gallo-Roman was proclaimed consul.[144] Felix, the son of a prudent and learned Gallic senator, a scion of a Gallic family said to have been "oppressed," "deprived of its honors," and "lying dead under a Gallic suspension of justice," was granted this illustrious honor, giving his meaningful name to an equally meaningful year.[145] "Let a happy year begin with this consul," it was said; "let the occasion offered by such a name pass through the gate of auspicious days!"[146] Gaul and Gallo-Romans had been restored to the empire, and Felix was put forth both at home and abroad as unquestionable proof. "What can be thought more desirable," the emperor Anastasius was asked, "than that Rome is gathering back to her bosom her very own nurslings and numbers the Gallic senate in the company of her venerable name?"[147] Gauls, the emperor of the East was informed, were in the western Senate House again, and Rome's senators would once more "recognize the splendor of transalpine blood, which not once covered [the Senate's] crown with the flower of its nobility."[148] Now, because of Rome's intervention and Felix's emblematic consulship, all the youths of Gaul, "who deserved to come into the highest honor[s] of the Republic,"[149] had reclaimed their legacy, liberated from the cold Gallic wilderness.

As Theoderic's senior colleague, Anastasius was thus asked to rejoice and to share in this triumph, an act that was likely bittersweet in Constantinople, since these very developments had been the consequence of the emperor's own hostilities and intrigues in the lead-up to 508. "We have furnished this candidate with consular insignia," he explained. "Now you, who can delight in the profits of both Republics with indistinguishable grace, unite your applause and feelings with our own: a man is worthy

---

[144] The last "Gallic" consul was Magnus Felix in 460, making the total lapse 51 years.

[145] For Felix's father, see later discussion; for deprived of honors, etc., *Variae* 2.3.2: "Iacebat nobilis origo sub Gallicano iustitio et honoribus suis privata peregrinabatur in patria. Tandem pressos divina levaverunt." For *divina*, see n. 141, above.

[146] *Variae* 2.1.1: "Felix a consule sumat annus auspicium portamque dierum tali nomine dicatum tempus introeat faveatque reliquae parti fortuna principii."

[147] *Variae* 2.1.2: "quid enim vobis credi possit optatius quam ut alumnos proprios ad ubera sua Roma recolligat et in venerandi nominis coetu senatum numeret Gallicanum?"

[148] *Ibid.*: "Agnoscit curia Transalpini sanguinis decus, quae non semel coronam suam nobilitatis eius flore vestivit."

[149] *Ibid.* (in specific reference to Felix): "nec passi sumus eum inglorium relinquere, qui ad honorem rei publicae meruit pervenire."

to be chosen by the judgment of us both, who deserves to be promoted to so great an office."[150] Not requiring Anastasius' approval, Theoderic nonetheless solicited the emperor's acknowledgment, as it would provide an additional source of honor for this "felicitous" year and place an eastern seal of approval on another fait accompli.[151] Indeed, Felix would be the first western consul recognized in the East since the Sirmian War of 504, and his recognition would do much to help normalize the heretofore strained relations between eastern and western courts. In a twist of irony, Gaul's restoration had led to the restoration of the imperial fraternity and harmony that was so important in a divided Roman Empire, neither being decisively broken until long after Theoderic's death.

In Rome, on the other hand, senators were told to rejoice and were asked for their own, validating approval. They had, as demonstrated previously, already been doing so and would continue to do so for years, celebrating Rome's newly invigorated and traditional dominance over its old adversaries. But with Felix's consulship they were likewise asked to embrace the moral repercussions that accompanied Rome's military victories abroad and to accept as Roman a land and population that had seemed anything but just a few years prior. It was too easy to write to Constantinople claiming that the western Senate once more recognized the splendor of transalpine blood. The situation, as the previous chapter has suggested, was much more complicated at home, and surely many senators required some convincing before they would refer to anything Gallic as splendid. For some, Gaul may have seemed little more than an object of conquest, a *Gallia recapta*, a source of new revenues and prestigious offices. But in his official announcement of Felix's consulship Theoderic proposed something other than the traditional spoils of war that might be expected. "A tribute of offices," they were told, "has been returned to you; provinces unaccustomed to do so for a long time now pay you with consular men."[152] Italo-Romans like Liberius, Gemellus, and others, therefore, would benefit from the availability of new offices in Gaul, but Rome's

---

[150] *Variae* 2.1.4: "Nos autem … curules infulas praestitimus candidato … atque ideo vos, qui utriusque rei publicae bonis indiscreta potestis gratia delectari, iungite favorem, adunate sententiam: amborum iudicio dignus est eligi, qui tantis fascibus meretur augeri."

[151] See Chp. 3 for Theoderic's role in selecting and investing consuls. The consulship of Felix provides a case in point. Cf. Claude (1978b), 44, who claims that in Felix's case, Theoderic presented himself as an equal partner of the emperor. For a very different interpretation, here rejected, Ensslin (1959), 150–2, who imagines that Theoderic relied on Anastasius, not only for the approval of Felix's consulship, but also for his management of western affairs in general.

[152] *Variae* 2.3.1: "Gaudete, patres conscripti, redisse vobis stipendia dignitatum: gaudete provincias longa aetate desuetas viros vobis pendere consulares."

senators were also informed that such benefits traveled along a two-way street. The Gauls, too, were Romans, and their ancestors had once participated in the glorious offices of the republic. Their "tribute," the spoil of war Italians were asked to embrace, would thus be their reclamation of these offices. "Gloriously," Theoderic announced, "they have regained Rome and plucked the ancient laurels of their ancestors from the honored grove of the Senate."[153]

Nor was Felix, a stand-in for the entire Gallo-Roman nobility, an unworthy representative of this Gallic restoration to the Senate House. Senators were reminded of his unnamed father, a man in his own time already "preeminent in the Senate for the brilliance of his prudence," though only a *clarus*.[154] He was "the Cato of our times," "truly dedicated to the study of letters," and had "stuffed himself with Attic honey."[155] Just like the other "foreigners" with whom Italian senators had been forced to come to terms, Felix too was "descended from a splendid line [and] shone forth with ancestral goods and merits."[156] And like his father, he also demonstrated before Italians "Roman gravity, not alien customs" and, as a result, had come "not unworthily into the insignia of the Senate."[157]

Doubtless a similar letter was directed to the Gauls, announcing Felix's consulship, idealizing their Roman restoration, and promising the availability of like honors to other worthy men. Cassiodorus, however, did not include this letter in his *Variae*, though a third letter, directed to Felix himself, may hint at the language that would have been employed in this missing missive.[158] Here, in a vein reminiscent of the general letter addressed

---

[153] *Variae* 2.3.2: "Romam recepere cum gloria et avorum antiquas laurus ab honorata curiae silva legerunt."

[154] *Variae* 2.3.3: "nobilissimus pater, qui prudentiae facibus ita praeluxit in curia, ut haberetur merito clarus inter tot lumina dignitatum." But cf. Mathisen (2003), 67, who does not interpret *clarus* as a reference to Felix's father's rank, taking instead *nobilissimus* to indicate his attainment of a high office. Mathisen's paraphrase of *Variae* 2.3.3, however, does not seem to catch the sense of the Latin, i.e. that Felix's father's prudence allowed a lower-ranking man to spend time with the illustrious (high-ranking) members of the Senate. *Nobilissimus*, on the other hand, seems to be a reference to Felix's father's blood, the *antiquam prosapiem* mentioned in the same sentence. Cf. *Variae* 8.17 (discussed in Chp. 2), where similar sentiments are expressed concerning the father of Opilio.

[155] Truly dedicated, *Variae* 2.3.3: "Litterarum quippe studiis dedicatus"; Cato and Attic honey, *Variae* 2.3.4: "Fuit quidam nostrorum temporum Cato ... Attico se melle saginavit."

[156] *Variae* 2.3.6: "avitis bonis cum suis meritis relucenti vestrae gratiae praestate fulgorem.... qui de speciosa stirpe descendit."

[157] *Variae* 2.3.5–6: "Vixit enim inter vos, ut scitis, non consuetudine peregrina, sed gravitate Romana.... Non impar ad curialium insignia venit."

[158] Indeed, it is most fortunate that three letters dealing with the consulship *were* included and a sign of this consul's contemporary significance.

to all the Gauls in 508, Felix was informed that he had been rescued, that Theoderic's hands had filled him up with kindness, and that the promises of a *bonus princeps* had caused him to seek out his Roman Empire.[159] A man "recommended by the fame of his race" had not been allowed to remain inglorious,[160] and with Felix's change in lords there had come a change in his familial fortune.[161] Now, Felix was told,

> through you the consulship returns to a transalpine family and you have renewed parched laurels with your green bud. Behold the Holy City striving after your desires. Stay on the path of praises, that you might surpass your ancestors, whose honor you restore, in virtue.[162]

It was an injunction that any Roman aristocrat, Gallic, Italian, Gothic, or otherwise, could appreciate.

Felix's consulship, by way of conclusion, was a sure sign that Gaul had been restored to the Roman Empire, and that the Gauls were officially Romans again. There had always been the potential for this to happen before the invasion of 508. Felix, like other Gauls, had Roman nobility in his blood and had been able to demonstrate his Roman qualities before an Italian audience even before Gaul's restoration. But families like his remained firmly rooted on the Gallic side of the Alps, and when finally forced to choose Gaul over Italy, they appeared deprived of their honors, oppressed, and slowly (but surely) barbarized. By 511, however, Felix and nearly all the once lost youths of re-Romanized Gaul, with or without Italian connections, could walk in their forefathers' footsteps over the menacing Alps and straight on to Ravenna and Rome. The frontier had shifted yet again, and the new Rhine had become a series of rivers appropriately located in transalpine territory. Now those Gallo-Romans residing within these new boundaries could benefit, like Felix and Parthenius, from Roman *civilitas* and stand a chance of surpassing their ancestors in glory. Indeed, their ability to do so was even seen as a kind of tradition, a tradition that Felix's consulship openly announced had been restored.

---

[159] *Variae* 2.2.2: "Currat quin immo honorum gratia per parentes, sub imperio boni principis omnium fortuna proficiat.... Excepit te noster affectus, implevit beneficiis manus fecitque esse votum, quod nostrum expetisses imperium."

[160] *Ibid.*: "Non enim relinqui inglorios patimur, qui generis claritate praedicantur."

[161] *Ibid.*: "Mutatur enim fortuna cum dominis." This is doubtless an allusion to Alaric II and hence an example of anti-Visigothic sentiments in the aftermath of southern Gaul's reconquest. Cf. *Variae* 5.41.6 (cited in Chp. 2), where similar statements are made regarding Odovacer.

[162] *Variae* 2.2.5: "Rediit per te Transalpinae familiae consulatus et arentes laurus viridi germine renovasti. Sacram urbem tuis votis aspice candidatam. Tende igitur ad laudum celsa vestigium, ut priores tuos, quos honore reparas, virtute transcendas."

"Frequently," Theoderic reminded his Senate, "Rome has chosen office holders from Gallic walls, lest she disregard their special qualities to her own ruin or their proven excellence cease to exist, having been dishonored."[163] It was a fitting statement, reminiscent of a speech made by another *pius princeps*, Claudius, nearly half a millennium earlier.[164] Claudius had opened the door for Gallic service in the imperial administration, and now Theoderic did so again, confident in their beneficial participation for years to come. If only for a generation, a Roman Gaul had been reborn.

[163] *Variae* 2.3.7: "Legit enim frequenter Roma fasces de moenibus Gallicanis, ne aut in damno suo praecipua contemneret aut probata virtus inhonora cessaret."
[164] Cf. the speech recorded in the so-called Lyon Tablet (*ILS* 212) and poorly reproduced in Tacitus, *Annals* 11.24.

EPILOGUE

Hindsight is 20/20. Looking back from the perspective of the early sixth century, it was easy for Italo-Romans like Cassiodorus, Ennodius, and others to find a place for Theoderic and his Goths. There were precedents for individuals just like them, equally barbarous and Roman, in the immediate and not so immediate past. There was likewise the memory of a once-mighty Roman Empire that had only recently crumbled and given way to "barbarian" successor states, had only recently had its sovereignty contested by rapacious "little Greeks," and had only recently had its time-honored values challenged from within. Traditions like the republic and the venerability of the city of Rome were powerful and, when combined with the stings and humiliations witnessed over the fifth century, provided the perfect context for a savior like Theoderic to emerge. As a traditionally *bonus princeps*, he met and even exceeded expectations and, assisted by his uniquely Roman Goths, redressed those grievances that had defined the preceding era, reasserting Rome's rightful place in the West. Hindsight, therefore, perpetuated the understanding of an Italy that remained the western Roman Empire, despite aberrations, and engendered the belief among certain Italo-Romans that a golden age had dawned.

Teleology, on the other hand, can be blinding. In 511, when Felix stood for his consulship, there was not the slightest indication that the history of Theoderic's Roman Empire would unfold as it did. Gallo-Romans did not appear fated to become Franks or Frenchmen; nor did Theoderic's empire seem destined to enter into one crisis after another and fall prey, yet again, to east Roman imperialism. The same can be said of 519, when the schism that had separated eastern and western churches for so long was finally ended. At the time, there was little concern that this might drive a wedge between Catholic Romans and Arian Goths and send

Italo-Romans into east Roman arms.[1] As with the Laurentian Schism in Rome, Theoderic had played an important role in the process, and many Catholics, not least certain popes, were grateful and continued to support him and his successors.[2] More importantly, soon thereafter Eutharic stood for his consulship with the eastern emperor as his colleague and father-in-arms, going on to honor Rome with traditional imperial splendor. In 519, in other words, succession and good relations with the East seemed secure, and the blessedness associated with Theoderic's reign appeared unchallenged.

Challenges, of course, there were, and Theoderic's final years witnessed a series of very unfortunate events. There were popular anti-Semitic riots in Ravenna and Rome;[3] Eutharic died suddenly and there was a succession crisis;[4] relations with the Vandals soured when Thrasamund died and his successor, Hilderic, not only imprisoned Amalafrida, but began to court a Byzantine alliance;[5] certain senators in Rome, including Albinus, Boethius, and Symmachus, men who had served Theoderic loyally and had benefited from his patronage, were accused of treason and arrested;[6] and finally, the eastern Roman emperor became increasingly hostile to Arian Christians,

---

[1] Cf. Giesecke (1939), 127f.; Matthews (1981), 34–5; and Burns (1982), 110–11. Noble (1993), 417–18, questions the extent to which the schism's end poisoned Theoderic's relations with Constantinople, the papacy, and the Italian aristocracy, claiming that "the early 520s were years of confusion on all sides." Indeed, the Theopascite controversy kept east-west relations strained during this period. Cf. Bark (1944) and Moorhead (1983a).

[2] For papal support, see later discussion. For Theoderic's role in ending the schism, *LP* 54.2–5, where his "consilio" is sought for three missions to Constantinople, two (failures) to Anastasius and one (success) to Justin. The two failed missions were led by Ennodius, who took some credit for healing the schism. See his epitaph (*CIL* 5 6464 = *ILS* 2952), with *Collectio Avellana* 115–16, 125–7, and 134–5. It is often suggested that Eutharic's adoption and official recognition were part of the negotiations, but this is speculative. *Variae* 8.1.3 (Athalaric to Justin) cites the emperor's desire for concord ("disiderio concordiae") as a rationale, echoing the ideologies of unity discussed in Chp. 3.

[3] See *AnonVal* 81. The events, conventionally placed around 519/20, included the burning of synagogues.

[4] The exact year of his death is unclear, though. See *PLRE* 2, 438, with Moorhead (1992), 213, n. 4.

[5] Hilderic succeeded in 523. For the souring of relations, *Variae* 9.1 (discussed later) and Procopius, *Wars* 3.9.4–5, with Moorhead (1992), 216–18, and Merrills and Miles (2010), 133–4.

[6] For reconstructions and interpretations (of which there are many), Giesecke (1939), 128; Bark (1944); Matthews (1981); Morton (1982); Burns (1982), 110–1; Moorhead (1983a) and (1992), 219–26; Barnish (1990), 30f.; Noble (1993); Heather (1996), 249–52; Gottschall (1997), 270–2; Saitta (1999), 208–10; and O'Donnell (2008), 166f. At the time, Boethius was serving as master of offices and his sons had recently held both consulships together (522), an exceptional honor for which he had given thanks to Theoderic in a (lost) panegyric.

leading to a failed papal mission at Theoderic's request and the death of an ailing Pope John while in his displeased custody.[7]

These events were potentially very damaging. And yet, and despite such reversals, contemporaries in Italy (and elsewhere) maintained their prior convictions. Whether fearing a joint Vandal-Byzantine invasion, a replay of the events that had led to his intervention in Gaul; intending to avenge Hilderic's slight to his family; or simply, and as he himself claimed, thinking of the empire's economic prosperity and future defenses, Theoderic soon ordered the hasty construction of one thousand warships (*dromones*), virtually ex nihilo.[8] This new fleet, he claimed, would place his kingdom on par with the reigning naval powers of the era. "You have adorned the revived Republic with your creation," he informed the prefect who oversaw the project. "No longer will the Greek boast or the African insult us. With envy they now see flourishing in our midst the very source from which they used to fulfill their wishes."[9] And in the case of the Vandals, he was absolutely correct.

Likewise, whether they were innocent, had conspired to place the western Empire under east Roman control, had supported the wrong successor in the wake of Eutharic's death, or had overstepped their bounds in matters of political or religious policy, Boethius and Symmachus were found guilty and executed.[10] It is true that the former denigrated Theoderic and his regime for their tyranny and corruption in his *Consolation of Philosophy*, a critique that has had a lasting impact. But it should be borne in mind that this work was written from prison and colored by its author's recent experiences.[11] Indeed, though he claimed to have been arrested for wanting "the Senate safe" and hoping for "Roman liberty," it was the Senate itself that

[7] For John's mission and death (c. 525/6), Giesecke (1939), 128–9; Ensslin (1951); Löwe (1953); Moorhead (1992), 235–42; and Noble (1993), 420–1. For his ailing health, *LP* 55.2.
[8] See *Variae* 5.16–20. For interpretations (all military), Burns (1984), 105; Moorhead (1992), 246–8; Merrills and Miles (2010), 134. But see *Variae* 5.16, where Theoderic claims these ships "will be able to convey public grain and, if it should be necessary, block hostile ships." Given the problems associated with conveying grain to and from Gaul (Chp. 10) and Spain (*Variae* 5.35), this should be taken more seriously.
[9] *Variae* 5.17.3: "Ornasti rem publicam tua institutione reparatam. Non habet quod nobis Graecus imputet aut Afer insultet. Illud apud nos invidi vigere respiciunt, unde illi per magna pretia sua vota complebant."
[10] See n. 6, earlier. The most provocative reconstruction is provided by Barnish (1990), who suggests that their treason was pro-Gothic, namely, an attempt to win eastern recognition of Theodahad, rather than Athalaric, as Theoderic's successor.
[11] Gottschall (1997) has even posited that the work may have been intended for Theoderic's ears.

had convicted him.[12] Moreover, other sources, written before and after Boethius' fall from grace, explicitly laud the virtues of the same individuals whom he singled out as corrupt.[13] And most revealingly, though a tyrant, Theoderic failed to be stripped of his imperial and Roman persona in this work. No longer a new Trajan or Valentinian in Boethius' eyes, he became instead a new Caligula or Nero.[14]

Finally, and in spite of claims to the contrary, Theoderic handled the religious tensions of the last years of his reign in a manner consistent with earlier practices. Religious tolerance and the rule of law (*civilitas*) remained paramount, and the anti-Semitic violence that rocked Ravenna and Rome could not go unpunished.[15] What changed, however, were the sources. Ennodius was dead, Cassiodorus in temporary retirement, and authors far more critical of religious difference took their place. The latter half of the *Anonymus Valesianus* provides a case in point. Its author claimed that Theoderic's defense of Jews and Arians had led to the unjust punishment of Catholics, the destruction of Catholic churches, a desire to impose the Arian rite on all Christians, and even the "martyrdom" of Pope John.[16] But this individual was so intent on casting Theoderic as a devil-inspired heretic and persecutor that he embellished his account to the point of being absurd, including such details as a Gothic woman giving birth to four snakes.[17] In fact, and despite the unfortunate timing of John's death, Theoderic continued to patronize the Catholic Church and

---

[12] *CP* 1.4.72–3: "Senatum dicimur salvum esse voluisse"; and *CP* 1.4.89–90: "libertatem arguor sperasse Romanam." For the senatorial condemnation, *CP* 1.4.130–3, with Barnish (1983), 593–4.

[13] These individuals included Basilius, Cyprian, Opilio, Gaudentius, Trigguilla, and Conigast, some of whom have been encountered in earlier chapters. See Moorhead (1978a), 608f., and (1992), 226–32.

[14] See *CP* 1.3.31–7 and 1.4.94–7, where Boethius compares himself to philosophers persecuted by these emperors, explicitly referencing Caligula in the latter.

[15] Cf. *AnonVal* 82–3 and *Variae* 4.43 (discussed in Chp. 5), where a similar case of popular violence against the Jews of Rome, dated to 509/11, is described as "detestable," "not Roman," and requiring the "severity of the laws." For Theoderic's punishment (fines and a ban on carrying arms), Barnish (1983), 586, and Moorhead (1992), 218, n. 31. It was in keeping with Roman legal practices.

[16] See *AnonVal* 82–94. The account implicitly compares Theoderic to Judas and implies that John was martyred. Cf. *LP* 55.2–6, where the term "martyr" is used explicitly, but other events are not treated.

[17] See *AnonVal* 84. Nor was this all, for this same section records that a comet shone for fifteen days and that there were frequent earthquakes. Such "wonders" were meant to foreshadow coming miseries. See Moorhead (1992), 218–19; also Barnish (1983), 584–5; König (1986); and Noble (1993), 418–20, who stress that the account of Theoderic's "persecution" is largely exaggerated and fabricated.

oversaw the election of the pope's successor, Felix IV, intending for "the religion of all churches to increase through good priests."[18] Relations may have been strained, but had he intended to "put all Italy to the sword," devout Romans like Cassiodorus and Liberius would not have persisted in their loyalty.[19]

Indeed, Theoderic's death in 526 would have provided a perfect opportunity for disaffected Italo-Romans to overthrow Gothic rule or invite the eastern emperor to intercede; but nothing of the sort transpired. Instead, Theoderic's eight-year-old grandson, Athalaric, succeeded peacefully and without "frenzied sedition, inflamed wars, or damage to the Republic," an event that says much about the strength and endurance of the Theoderican regime and the loyalties of its subjects.[20] That Athalaric was able to enjoy the support of the Gothic and Roman nobility, the papacy, and the emperor in Constantinople throughout his eight-year reign is revealing.[21] That a woman, his mother, Amalasuentha, could be the true power behind the throne is equally revealing;[22] so too the fact that both Italo-Romans and east Romans could see fit to eulogize her, citing, among other virtues, her wisdom, justice, and manliness.[23]

---

[18] *Variae* 8.15.1 (written in Athalaric's name): "quatenus bonis sacerdotibus ecclesiarum omnium religio pullularet." This letter demonstrates that there had been a disputed election following John's death and that the clergy had turned to Theoderic, as in the past, for arbitration. Cf. the various redactions of the *Liber Pontificalis* 56, which record that Felix was ordained either at the order of Theoderic (*ex iusso Theoderici*) or in a time of peace (*cum quietem*).

[19] For putting Italy to the sword, *LP* 55.2: "hereticus rex Theodoricus ... voluit totam Italiam ad gladium extinguere." Cf. *AnonVal* 86.

[20] *Variae* 8.2.2 (to the Senàte): "non protulit commota seditio, non bella ferventia pepererunt, non rei publicae damna lucrata sunt, sed sic factus est per quietem." This is not to say that the transition to Athalaric's rule was entirely without its hiccups. See Claude (1980), 162, with *Variae* 8.9.8 and 8.16. *Variae* 8.2–8, however, demonstrate that all of Athalaric's subjects acknowledged their loyalty with an oath and that he reciprocated, claiming that his actions were in imitation of Emperor Trajan's.

[21] There may have been attempts to improve relations with the family of Boethius and Symmachus, while other senatorial families continued to be promoted through the ranks. See Procopius, *Wars* 5.2.5, with Barnish (1990), 31, and Burgarella (2001), 141–8. For east Roman recognition, *Variae* 8.1 and 10.1, with *Pragmatic Sanction* 1. For the papacy, *Variae* 8.8, 8.15 (discussed previously, n. 18), and 9.15. The *Liber Pontificalis* is revealingly benign in its treatment of him. See Azzara (2001), 248–53.

[22] Ethnically motivated tensions during her reign tend to be overstated. See Chps. 5 and 6. If there was opposition to Amalasuentha, it was gender-based. *Variae* 11.1 hints at this, as does Jordanes' *Getica* 306, which cites her "weak sex" (*sexus sui fragilitate*) as a rationale for her adoption of a (male) consort.

[23] For eulogies, *Variae* 11.1, with Fauvinet-Ranson (1998), and Procopius, *Wars* 5.2.3 and 5.4.27–30. Her murder by Theodahad was even cited as a *casus belli* by Justinian (Procopius, *Wars* 5.5.1; Jordanes, *Getica* 307 and *Romana* 368; and *LP* 60.2) and, if a legitimate rationale, says much about her status vis-à-vis Constantinople.

In fact, and regardless of Justinian's "inevitable" reconquest, Theoderic's empire retained much of its original vitality during Amalasuentha's regency and then reign. Though the Visigothic kingdom went its separate way, Provence remained firmly within Italy's grasp.[24] Rome's Gothic armies, likewise, kept the Franks and Burgundians at bay, terrifying the former and causing the latter to "put down [their] arms" in order to "defend a safer kingdom."[25] Similarly, Theoderic's newly constructed navy allowed Athalaric to threaten the Vandals in the case of his great-aunt, Amalafrida, whose recent death while still in prison, it was alleged, had dishonored "the purple dignity of Amal blood," "disgraced our Goths," and "shown contempt for [Gothic] valor."[26] In the East, on the other hand, Amalasuentha, like her father before her, defied the eastern emperor and expanded Roman territory in the Balkans.[27] And like her father, she acknowledged imperial unity, supporting Justinian in his invasion of Vandal North Africa (perhaps making good on Athalaric's threats) and allowing his army the use of Sicily as a staging ground.[28] There was little indication that Italy was doomed or next on the east Roman chopping block, and when Justinian tried to claim the Sicilian port of Lilybaeum as a spoil of his Vandal conquests, Amalasuentha was in a strong enough position to resist him.[29]

Even after her murder and yet another succession crisis of sorts, even as the east Roman generalissimo Belisarius was beginning his "liberation" of Italy in 535, the fate of an independent western empire remained undetermined. Pope Agapitus, the Senate, and Italy's rulers urged Justinian to restore imperial harmony, pleading that "if Libya deserved to receive freedom from you, it is cruel for [us] to lose what [we] have always

[24] On the Visigothic kingdom, Procopius, *Wars* 5.12.50–4 and 5.13.4–13, with Collins (1983), 33–8, and (2004), 41–6. It had already fallen under the overlordship of Theudis (Theoderic's Ostrogothic agent in the region), and he would succeed as king in 531.

[25] For the Franks, *Variae* 11.1.12: "lacessiti metuerunt cum nostris inire certamen"; for the Burgundians, *Variae* 11.1.3: "tutius tunc defendit [Burgundio] regnum, quando arma deposuit."

[26] *Variae* 9.1.2: "Nam et hoc nobilitati vestrae fuisset adiectum, si … retinuissetis Hamali sanguinis purpuream dignitatem. Hoc Gothi nostri ad suum potius opprobrium intellegunt fuisse temptatum. Nam qui dominae alienae gentis intulit necem, omnino eius parentum visus est despexisse virtutem."

[27] See *Variae* 11.1.10–11 and Procopius, *Wars* 5.3.15–16, with Wolfram (1985), 315–16, and Fauvinet-Ranson (1998), 287–8. She had gone to war against the Gepids, but her armies had taken the east Roman city of Gratiana in the process. This had led to diplomatic exchanges and perhaps threats, but not war.

[28] See Procopius, *Wars* 5.3.22–6, where Amalasuentha takes partial credit for Justinian's victories in North Africa.

[29] See Procopius, *Wars* 4.5.11–25 and 5.3.27–8, with Kislinger (1994), 41–3; Goltz (1997/8), 236–7; Merrills and Miles (2010), 132–3; and Conant (2012), 38–9.

seemed to possess."[30] Cassiodorus, likewise, was steadfast, serving as praetorian prefect and busying himself with yet another panegyric in praise of a Gothic *princeps*, Witigis.[31] Amid "so many serious injuries and such shedding of blood," he remained by Witigis' side until the very fall of Ravenna,[32] editing his *Variae* and beginning the first of many spiritual *opera*, his *De anima*.[33] Not every Italo-Roman was as dedicated as Cassiodorus, of course. Liberius had already defected following the murder of Amalasuentha, and many would follow his example, not just Italo-Romans, but also Goths and members of Justinian's east Roman army.[34] Still, and despite decades of disastrous war, the legacy of Theoderic and his Roman Empire lived on. It was not by accident that Witigis described himself as the spiritual son of Theoderic, proven in the open battlefield and called to rule by blaring trumpets;[35] nor by chance that Italian resistance ended, at least for a time, when Belisarius agreed to accept the western *imperium* in his place;[36] nor, finally, a coincidence that the later Gothic king Totila invoked the memory of both Theoderic

---

[30] For Agapitus' mission, *Variae* 12.20 and *LP* 59. For the Senate, *Variae* 11.13 (from which the earlier quotation is derived): "Nam si Libya meruit per te recipere libertatem, crudele est me amittere quam semper visa sum possidere." For Italy's rulers (Theodahad and Witigis), *Variae* 10.22 and 10.32–5.

[31] See *CassOratReliquiae*, p. 473–82, with Romano (1978), 28–30. Given earlier panegyrics and the wartime context, too much should not be made of its celebration of Witigis' martial virtues.

[32] *Variae* 10.32.1: "post tot gravissimas laesiones et tanta effusione sanguinis perpetrata." Some have suggested that Cassiodorus switched sides and moved to Constantinople in the late 540s. It seems more likely, however, that he traveled to Constantinople in Witigis' train as a noble hostage. Cf. Courcelle (1948), 191; Momigliano (1955), 219f.; Wolfram (1979), 26; O'Donnell (1979), 105–7; and Krautschick (1983), 11–12.

[33] For the milieu in which he edited his *Variae*, Chp. 2. *De anima* 18.10–12 (a concluding prayer to Christ) may hint at his heartache over the conflict then raging in Italy. See O'Donnell (1979), 127–8, and Martino (1982), 39–40.

[34] For Liberius, O'Donnell (1981). Other "loyal" Romans who defected included Cyprian, Opilio, and Pope Silverius. For broader treatments, Moorhead (1983b), 588, who emphasizes "the ease with which Italian aristocrats could change loyalties in accordance with circumstances"; also Amory (1997), 165–94, with his prosopographical index. Procopius is likewise sensitive. See, for instance, *Wars* 5.8.5–5.10.

[35] For fields and trumpets, *Variae* 10.31.2: "in campis late patentibus electum me esse noveritis … tubis concrepantibus sum quaesitus"; for spiritual son, *Variae* 10.32.5: "idcirco parens illius [i.e. Theoderici] debet credi, qui eius facta potuerit imitari." His marriage to Matasuentha (Theoderic's granddaughter) made him an actual in-law.

[36] Procopius, *Wars* 6.29.26. Some have interpreted this as an attempt to make Belisarius king of the Goths, but the title *Basileus Italioton kai Gotthon* would seem to suggest an emperor, as does Procopius' later use of *basileia* in reference to his imagined position. Given that being king of the Goths and being western emperor had become more or less synonymous in Italy, the confusion is understandable. See Claude (1980), 167–70.

and Anastasius, honored the Senate at Rome, worshipped at St. Peter's, and hosted traditional games.[37]

Though Procopius and others writing in the aftermath of Justinian's conquests could insinuate that Theoderic's empire had been a barbarous deviation, a kingdom ruled by Gothic tyrants, and a regrettable mistake that had ultimately been corrected, such sentiments had not been shared by Italo-Romans living just one or two generations earlier. Teleology, again, can be blinding, and Procopius, too, it should be borne in mind, drew from the past. But as an east Roman who had never lived in Theoderic's Roman Empire, Procopius' hindsight was different. In his view, Justinian could reconquer the West in the name of Rome; but ironically, just two generations earlier, Theoderic had already done so.

[37] For the memory of Anastasius, see Totila's coins in Wroth (1911), 88f., and Kraus (1928), 185f., which depict Anastasius rather than Justinian. For the memory of Theoderic, Procopius, *Wars* 7.9.7–18 and 7.21.23. In the latter, Theoderic and Anastasius are paired and described as ruling in the imperial fashion ("bebasileukasi"). Though the invention of Procopius, letters like these are attested in the case of Witigis (see earlier discussion). For St. Peter's, *Wars* 7.20.22–5. For honoring the Senate and hosting games, *Wars* 7.37.3–5.

BIBLIOGRAPHY

Primary Sources

Acta Synhodorum habitarum Romae A. CCCCXCVIIII. DI. DII. Ed. Theodor Mommsen. MGH, AA 12. Berlin: Weidmann, 1894.

Agnellus, *LPR = Agnelli Ravennatis Liber Pontificalis Ecclesiae Ravennatis.* Ed. Deborah Mauskopf Deliyannis. CCCM 199. Turnhout: Brepols, 2006; trans. Deborah Mauskopf Deliyannis. *The Book of the Pontiffs of the Church of Ravenna.* Washington, D.C.: The Catholic University of America Press, 2004.

Ammianus Marcellinus, *Res Gestae.* Ed. and trans. J. C. Rolfe. 3 vols. Loeb. Cambridge: Harvard University Press, 1935–1940.

AnonVal = Anonymi Valesiani pars posterior. Ed. Theodor Mommsen. MGH, AA 9. Berlin: Weidmann, 1892; ed. Roberto Cessi. *Fragmenta Historica ab Henrico et Hadriano Valesio primum edita [Anonymus Valesianus]. Rerum Italicarum Scriptores* 24.4. Città di Castello: Tipi della Casa editrice S. Lapi, 1912/13; ed. Jacques Moreau. *Excerpta Valesiana.* Leipzig: B. G. Teubner, 1968; trans. J. C. Rolfe. *Ammianus Marcellinus: Res Gestae.* Vol. 3. Loeb. Cambridge: Harvard University Press, 1940.

Arator, *Epistula ad Parthenium = Aratoris Subdiaconi De Actibus Apostolorum.* Ed. A. P. McKinlay. CSEL 72. Vienna: Hoelder-Pichler-Tempsky, 1951; trans. Richard J. Schrader. *Arator's On the Acts of the Apostles (De Actibus Apostolorum).* Atlanta: Scholars Press, 1987.

Aurelius Victor, *de Caesaribus = Sexti Aurelii Victoris Liber de Caesaribus.* Ed. Franciscus Pichlmayr. Leipzig: Teubner, 1911; trans. H. W. Bird. *Aurelius Victor: De Caesaribus.* TTH 17. Liverpool: Liverpool University Press, 1994.

Ausonius. Ed. and trans. Hugh G. White. 2 vols. Loeb. Cambridge: Harvard University Press, 1949–51.

Avitus of Vienne, *Ep. = Alcimi Ecdicii Aviti Viennensis episcopi Opera quae supersunt.* Ed. R. Peiper. MGH, AA 6.2. Berlin: Weidmann, 1883; trans. Danuta Shanzer and Ian Wood. *Avitus of Vienne: Letters and Selected Prose.* TTH 38. Liverpool: Liverpool University Press, 2002.

Boethius. Ed. and trans. H. F. Stewart et al. Loeb. Cambridge: Harvard University Press, 1918.

Caesarius of Arles = *Caesarii Arelatensis Opera.* Ed. G. Morin. CCSL 103–4. Turnhout: Brepols, 1953; trans. Sister Mary Magdeleine Meuller. *Saint Caesarius of Arles: Sermons.* 3 vols. New York: Fathers of the Church, 1956; Washington, D.C.: The Catholic University of America Press, 1964–73.

Cassiodorus –

CassChron = *Cassiodori Senatoris Chronica ad a. DXIX.* Ed. Theodor Mommsen. MGH, AA 11.2 Berlin: Weidmann, 1894.

CassOratReliquiae = *Cassiodori Orationum Reliquiae.* Ed. Lud. Traube. MGH, AA 12. Berlin: Weidmann, 1894.

De anima. Ed. J. W. Halporn. CCSL 96. Turnhout: Brepols, 1973; trans. J. W. Halporn and M. Vessey. *Cassiodorus: Institutions of Divine and Secular Learning; On the Soul.* TTH 42. Liverpool: Liverpool University Press, 2004.

Institutions = *Cassiodori Senatoris Institutiones.* Ed. R. A. B. Mynors. Oxford: Clarendon Press, 1937; trans. J. W. Halporn and M. Vessey. *Cassiodorus: Institutions of Divine and Secular Learning; On the Soul.* TTH 42. Liverpool: Liverpool University Press, 2004.

Variae = *Cassiodori Senatoris Variae.* Ed. Theodor Mommsen. MGH, AA 12. Berlin: Weidmann, 1894; trans. (partial) Thomas Hodgkin. *The Letters of Cassiodorus Being a Condensed Translation of the Variae Epistolae of Magnus Aurelius Cassiodorus Senator.* London: Henry Frowde, 1886; trans. (select) S. J. B. Barnish. *The Variae of Cassiodorus Senator.* TTH 12. Liverpool: Liverpool University Press, 1992.

Chronica Gallica a. CCCCLII et DXI. Ed. Theodor Mommsen. MGH, AA 9. Berlin: Weidmann, 1892.

Chronicle of Fredegar = *Chronicarum quae dicuntur Fredegarii Scholastici libri IV. Cum Continuationibus.* Ed. Bruno Krusch. MGH, SRM 2. Hannover: Hahn, 1888.

Claudian. Ed and trans. Maurice Platnauer. 2 vols. Loeb. Cambridge: Harvard University Press, 1922.

Codex Theodosianus. Ed. Theodor Mommsen. Berlin: Weidmann, 1905; trans. Clyde Pharr. *The Theodosian Code and Novels and the Sirmondian Constitutions.* New York: Greenwood Press, 1952.

Collectio Avellana = *Epistulae imperatorum pontificum aliorum inde ab a. CCCLXVII usque ad a. DLIII datae Avellana quae dicitur collectio.* Ed. Otto Guenther. CSEL 35. 2 vols. Vienna: F. Tempsky, 1895–8.

Concilia Galliae a. 511–695. Ed. C. de Clercq. CCSL 148A. Turnhout: Brepols, 1963; trans. Jean Gaudemet and Brigitte Basdevant. *Les Canons des conciles mérovingiens (VIe-VIIe siècles).* 2 vols. SC 353–5. Paris: Les Éditions du cerf, 1989.

Continuatio Hauniensis Prosperi. Ed. Theodor Mommsen. MGH, AA 9. Berlin: Weidmann, 1892.

Corippus, *In Laudem Iustini Augusti Minoris.* Ed. and trans. Averil Cameron. London: The Athlone Press, 1976.

Corpus Inscriptionum Latinarum. Ed. Theodor Mommsen et al. 16 vols. and supplements. Berlin: G. Reimerum, 1862–.

Damascii Vitae Isidori Reliquiae. Ed. Clemens Zintzen. Hildesheim: Georg Olms Verlagsbuchhandlung, 1967.

Edictum Theoderici regis. Ed. Friedrich Bluhme. MGH, LL 5. Hannover: Hahn, 1875–89.

Ennodius –

  Epistulae; ed. and trans. Stéphane Gioanni. *Ennode de Pavie: Lettres.* 2 vols. Budé. Paris: Les Belles Lettres, 2006–10.

  Magni Felicis Ennodii Opera. Ed. F. Vogel. MGH, AA 7. Berlin: Weidmann, 1885.

  PanTh = Panegyricus dictus clementissimo regi Theoderico; ed. and trans. Christian Rohr. *Der Theoderich-Panegyricus des Ennodius.* MGH Studien und Texte 12. Hannover: Hahnische Buchhandlung, 1995; ed. and trans. Simona Rota. *Magno Felice Ennodio: Panegirico del clementissimo re Teoderico (opusc. 1).* Roma: Herder, 2002.

  VE = Vita Epiphanii; trans. Sister Genevieve Marie Cook. *The Life of Saint Epiphanius by Ennodius: a Translation with an Introduction and Commentary.* Washington, D.C.: The Catholic University of America Press, 1942; trans. Maria Cesa. *Ennodio: Vita del beatissimo Epifanio vescovo della chiesa pavese.* Como: Edizioni New Press, 1988.

Epistulae Theodericianae Variae. Ed. Theodor Mommsen. MGH, AA 12. Berlin: Weidmann, 1894.

Eugippii Vita Sancti Severini. Ed. Hermannus Sauppe. MGH, AA 1.2. Berlin: Weidmann, 1877.

Evagrius, *Historia ecclesiastica.* Ed. J. Bidez and L. Parmentier. London: Methuen, 1898; trans. Michael Whitby. *The Ecclesiastical History of Evagrius Scholasticus.* TTH 33. Liverpool: Liverpool University Press, 2000.

Fasti Vindobonenses posteriores. Ed. Theodor Mommsen. MGH, AA 9. Berlin: Weidmann, 1892.

Fasti Vindobonenses priores cum excerptis Sangallensibus. Ed. Theodor Mommsen. MGH, AA 9. Berlin: Weidmann, 1892.

Gregory of Tours, *Historiae = Gregorii episcopi Turonensis libri historiarum X.* Ed. Bruno Krusch and Wilhelm Levison. MGH, SRM 1.1. Hannover: Hahn, 1951; trans. Lewis Thorpe. *Gregory of Tours: The History of the Franks.* London: Penguin Books, 1974.

Historia Augusta. Ed. and trans. David Magie. 3 vols. Loeb. Cambridge: Harvard University Press, 1932.

Inschriftensammlung zur Geschichte der Ostgermanen. Ed. Otto Fiebiger and Ludwig Schmidt. Wien: Alfred Hölder, 1917.

Inschriftensammlung zur Geschichte der Ostgermanen. Neue Folge. Ed. Otto Fiebiger. Wien-Leipzig: Hölder-Pichler-Tempsky A.-G., 1939.

Inschriftensammlung zur Geschichte der Ostgermanen. Zweite Folge. Ed. Otto Fiebiger. Brün-München-Wien: Rudolf M. Rohrer, 1944.

Inscriptiones Latinae Selectae. Ed. Hermann Dessau. 3 vols. Dublin: Weidmann, 1974.

Isidore of Seville –
Etymologiae = Isidori Hispalensis Episcopi Etymologiarum sive originum libri XX. Ed. W. M. Lindsay. 2 vols. Oxford: Clarendon Press, 1911.
Hist. Goth. = *Isidori Iunioris episcopi Hispalensis historia Gothorum Wandalorum Sueborum ad. a. DCXXIV.* Ed. Theodor Mommsen. MGH, AA 11.2 Berlin: Weidmann, 1894.

John Malalas = *Ioannis Malalae Chronographia.* Ed. Ioannes Thurn. Berlin: Walter de Gruyter, 2000; trans. Elizabeth Jeffreys et al. *The Chronicle of John Malalas.* Melbourne: Australian Association for Byzantine Studies, 1986.

John of Antioch = *Ioannis Antiocheni Fragmenta ex Historia chronica.* Ed and trans. Umberto Roberto. Berlin: Walter de Gruyter, 2005.

John of Nikiu = *The Chronicle of John, Bishop of Nikiu.* Trans. R. H. Charles. London: Williams & Norgate, 1916.

Jordanes = *Iordanis Romana et Getica.* Ed. Theodor Mommsen. MGH, AA 5.1. Berlin: Weidmann, 1882; trans (*Getica*). Charles C. Mierow. *The Gothic History of Jordanes.* Princeton: Princeton University Press, 1915.

Julian. Ed. and trans. Wilmer Cave Wright. 3 vols. Loeb. Cambridge: Harvard University Press, 1969–80.

Lactantius, *De Mortibus Persecutorum.* Ed and trans. J. L. Creed. Oxford: Clarendon Press, 1984.

Liber historiae Francorum. Ed. Bruno Krusch. MGH, SRM 2. Hannover: Hahn, 1888.

Liber Pontificalis = Le Liber Pontificalis. Texte, Introduction et Commentaire. Ed. Louis Duchesne and Cyrille Vogel. Rev. ed. 3 vols. Paris: Éditions E. de Boccard, 1955–7; trans. Raymond Davis. *The Book of the Pontiffs (Liber Pontificalis): The Ancient Biographies of the First Ninety Roman Bishops to AD 715.* TTH 6. Liverpool: Liverpool University Press, 1989.

Malchus of Philadelphia = *The Fragmentary Classicising Historians of the Later Roman Empire: Eunapius, Olympiodorus, Priscus and Malchus.* Ed. and trans. R. C. Blockley. ARCA 10. Liverpool: F. Cairns, 1983.

Marc. Com = Marcellini v.c. comitis Chronicon ad a. DXVIII. Ed. Theodor Mommsen. MGH, AA 11.2 Berlin: Weidmann, 1894.

Marius of Avenches = *Marii episcopi Aviticensis Chronica a CCCCLV–DLXXXI.* Ed. Theodor Mommsen. MGH, AA 11.2 Berlin: Weidmann, 1894.

Menander Rhetor. Ed. and trans. D. A. Russell and N. G. Wilson. Oxford: Clarendon Press, 1981.

Orosius, *Historiae = Orose: Histoires contre les païens.* Ed. and trans. Marie-Pierre Arnaud-Lindet. 3 vols. Budé. Paris: Les Belles Lettres, 1990–1; trans. Roy J. Deferrari. *Paulus Orosius: The Seven Books of History against the Pagans.* The Fathers of the Church 50. Washington, D.C.: The Catholic University Press of America, 1964.

Panegyrici Latini = In Praise of the Later Roman Emperors: The Panegyrici Latini. Ed. and trans. C. E. V. Nixon and Barbara Saylor Rodgers. Berkeley: University of California Press, 1994.

Passio S. Sigismundi regis. Ed. Bruno Krusch. MGH, SRM 2. Hannover: Hahn, 1888.

Paul the Deacon, *Historia Romana = Pauli Historia Romana*. Ed. H. Droysen. MGH, AA 2. Berlin: Weidemann, 1879.

Pliny the Elder, *Natural History*. Ed. and trans. H. Rackham. 10 vols. Loeb. Cambridge: Harvard University Press, 1938–62.

Pragmatic Sanction = Iustiniani Imp. Pragmatica Sanctio. Ed. Fridericus Bluhme. MGH, LL 5. Hannover: Hahn, 1865–89.

Priscian, *De laude Anastasii Imperatoris = Procope de Gaza, Priscien de Césarée, Panégyriques de l'empereur Anastase Ier*. Ed. and trans. Alain Chauvot. Bonn: Habelt, 1986; ed. and trans. Patricia Coyne. *Priscian of Caesarea's De laude Anastasii Imperatoris*. Lewiston: E. Mellen Press, 1991.

Procopius. Ed. and trans. H. B. Dewing. 7 vols. Loeb. Cambridge: Harvard University Press, 1914–40.

Prosper of Aquitaine = *Prosperi Tironis Epitoma Chronicon*. Ed. Theodor Mommsen. MGH, AA 9. Berlin: Weidmann, 1892.

Sidonius Apollinaris, *Poems and Letters*. Ed. and trans. W. B. Anderson. 2 vols. Loeb. Cambridge: Harvard University Press, 1936–65.

Socrates Scholasticus, *HE = Sokrates: Kirchengeschichte*. Ed. Günter C. Hansen with Manja Širinjan. Berlin: Akademie-Verlag, 1995; trans. A. C. Zenos. In *A Select Library of Nicene and Post-Nicene Fathers of the Christian Church*. Second Series, Vol. 2: *Socrates, Sozomenus: Church Histories*. New York: The Christian Literature Company, 1890.

Tacitus, *The Annals*. Ed. and trans. J. Jackson. Vols. 2–4. Loeb. Cambridge: Harvard University Press, 1951.

Theophanes, *Chronographia*. Ed. Carl de Boor. 2 vols. Leipzig: Teubner, 1883–5; trans. Cyril Mango and Roger Scott. *The Chronicle of Theophanes Confessor: Byzantine and Near Eastern History, AD 284–813*. Oxford: Clarendon Press, 1997.

Thiel = *Epistolae Romanorum Pontificum Genuinae et quae ad eos scriptae sunt a S. Hilaro usque ad Pelagium II*. Ed. Andreas Thiel, Vol. 1: *A S. Hilaro usque Hormisdam, ann. 461–523*. Brunsbergae: In Aedibus E. Peter, 1868.

Vie de saint Germain d'Auxerre. Ed and trans. René Borius. SC 112. Paris: Les Éditions du Cerf, 1965.

Vita Apollinaris episcopi Valentinensis. Ed. Bruno Krusch. MGH, SRM 3. Hannover: Hahn, 1896.

Vita Caesarii Arelatensis. Ed. Bruno Krusch. MGH, SRM 3. Hannover: Hahn, 1896; trans. William Klingshirn. *Caesarius of Arles: Life, Testament, Letters*. TTH 19. Liverpool: Liverpool University Press, 1994b.

Vita patrum Iurensium Romani, Lupicini, Eugendi. Ed. Bruno Krusch. MGH, SRM 3. Hannover: Hahn, 1896; trans. Tim Vivian et al. *The Lives of the Jura Fathers*. Cistercian Studies Series 178. Kalamazoo: Cistercian Publications, 1999.

Vita S. Fulgentii. PL 65. Paris: Migne, 1861.

Secondary Sources

Adams, J. N. *The Text and Language of a Vulgar Latin Chronicle (Anonymus Valesianus II)*. London: Institute of Classical Studies, 1976.

Alföldi, Andreas. "Insignien und Tracht der römischen Kaiser." *Mitteilungen des Deutschen Archäologischen Instituts, Römische Abteilung* 50 (1935): 3–171.

Alföldi, Maria R. "Il medaglione d'oro di Teodorico." *Rivista italiana di numismatica e scienze affini* 80 (1978): 133–41.

Alföldy, Géza. "Difficillima Tempora: Urban Life, Inscriptions, and Mentality in Late Antique Rome." In *Urban Centers and Rural Contexts in Late Antiquity*, edited by Thomas S. Burns and John W. Eadie, 3–24. East Lansing: Michigan State University Press, 2001.

Allara, T. "Ancora sui titoli di Teoderico." *Rivista italiana di numismatica e scienze affini* 11 (1898): 67–74.

Amory, Patrick. "The Meaning and Purpose of Ethnic Terminology in the Burgundian Laws." *Early Medieval Europe* 2 (1993): 1–28.

———. *People and Identity in Ostrogothic Italy, 489–554*. Cambridge: Cambridge University Press, 1997.

Andaloro, Maria. "Tendenze figurative a Ravenna nell'età di Teoderico." In *Teoderico il Grande e i Goti d'Italia: atti del XIII Congresso internazionale di studi sull'Alto Medioevo, Milano 2–6 novembre 1992*, 555–83. Spoleto: Centro italiano di studi sull'alto Medioevo, 1993.

Anderson, J. K. *Military Theory and Practice in the age of Xenophon*. Berkeley: University of California Press, 1970.

Andersson, Theodore M. "Cassiodorus and the Gothic Legend of Ermanaric." *Euphorion* 57.1 (1963): 28–43.

Ando, Clifford, *Imperial Ideology and Provincial Loyalty in the Roman Empire*. Berkeley: University of California Press, 2000.

Aricò, Giuseppe. "Cassiodoro e la cultura latina." In *Atti della Settimana di Studi su Flavio Magno Aurelio Cassiodoro (Cosenza-Squillace 19–24 settembre 1983)*, edited by Sandro Leanza, 154–78. Soveria Mannelli: Rubettino Editore, 1986.

Arnold, Jonathan J. "The Battle of Vouillé and the Restoration of the Roman Empire." In *The Battle of Vouillé, 507 CE: Where France Began*, edited by Ralph W. Mathisen and Danuta Shanzer, 111–36. Berlin: Walter de Gruyter, 2012.

———. "Theoderic's Invincible Mustache." *Journal of Late Antiquity* 6.1 (2013): 152–83.

Augenti, Andrea. "The Palace of Theoderic at Ravenna: A New Analysis of the Complex." In *Housing in Late Antiquity: From Palaces to Shops*, edited by Luke Lavan et al., 425–53. Leiden: Brill, 2007.

Avery, William T. "The *Adoratio Purpurae* and the Importance of the Imperial Purple in the Fourth Century of the Christian Era." *Memoirs of the American Academy in Rome* 17 (1940): 66–80.

Azzara, Claudio. "Ideologia della regalità ostrogota." In *Le invasioni barbariche nel meridione dell'impero: Visigoti, Vandali, Ostrogoti: atti del convegno svoltosi alla Casa delle culture di Cosenza dal 24 al 26 luglio 1998*, edited by Paolo Delogu, 243–55. Soveria Mannelli: Rubbettino, 2001.

———. "I Goti nell'Italia settentrionale." In *Goti nell'arco alpino orientale*, edited by Maurizio Buora and Luca Villa, 9–18. Udine: Società Friulana di Archeologia, 2006.

Bachrach, Bernard S. *A History of the Alans in the West: From Their First Appearance in the Sources of Classical Antiquity through the Early Middle Ages*. Minneapolis: University of Minnesota Press, 1973.

Baldwin, Barry. "The Purpose of Jordanes' *Getica*." *Hermes* 107.4 (1979): 489–92.

———. "Sources for the *Getica* of Jordanes." *Revue belge de philologie et d'histoire* 59 (1981): 141–6.

———. "Illiterate Emperors." *Historia* 38 (1989): 124–6.

Bark, William. "Theodoric vs. Boethius: Vindication and Apology." *The American Historical Review* 49.3 (1944): 410–26.

Barnish, S. J. B. "The Anonymus Valesianus II as a Source for the Last Years of Theoderic." *Latomus* 42 (1983): 572–96.

———. "The Genesis and Completion of Cassiodorus' Gothic History." *Latomus* 43.2 (1984): 336–61.

———. "Taxation, Land and Barbarian Settlement in the Western Empire." *Papers of the British School at Rome* 54 (1986): 170–95.

———. "Pigs, Plebeians and *Potentes*: Rome's Economic Hinterland, c. 350–600 A.D." *Papers of the British School at Rome* 55 (1987): 157–85.

———. "Transformation and Survival in the Western Senatorial Aristocracy, c. AD 400–700." *Papers of the British School at Rome* 56 (1988): 120–55.

———. "The Work of Cassiodorus after his Conversion." *Latomus* 48.1 (1989): 157–87.

———. "Maximian, Cassiodorus, Boethius, Theodahad: Literature, Philosophy and Politics in Ostrogothic Italy." *Nottingham Medieval Studies* 34 (1990): 16–32.

———. "Liberty and Advocacy in Ennodius of Pavia: the Significance of Rhetorical Education in Late Antique Italy." *Hommages à Carl Deroux* 5 (2003): 20–8.

———. "Cuncta Italiae Membra Componere: Political Relations in Ostrogothic Italy." In *The Ostrogoths from the Migration Period to the Sixth Century: An Ethnographic Perspective*, edited by Sam Barnish and Federico Marazzi, 317–37. Woodbridge: Boydell Press, 2007.

Barnish, Sam and Federico Marazzi, ed. *The Ostrogoths from the Migration Period to the Sixth Century: An Ethnographic Perspective.* Woodbridge: Boydell Press, 2007.

Barnwell, P. S. *Emperor, Prefects, and Kings: The Roman West, 395–565.* London: Duckworth, 1992.

Bartlett, Richard. "Aristocracy and Asceticism: The Letters of Ennodius and the Gallic and Italian Churches." In *Society and Culture in Late Antique Gaul: Revisiting the Sources,* edited by Ralph W. Mathisen and Danuta Shanzer, 201–16. Aldershot: Ashgate, 2001.

———. "The Dating of Ennodius' Writings." In *Atti della Seconda Giornata Ennodiana,* edited by Edoardo D'Angelo, 53–74. Napoli: Pubblicazioni del Dipartimento di Filologia Classica dell'Università degli Studi di Napoli Federico II, 2003.

Bartoli, A. "Lavori nella sede del Senato romano al tempo di Teodorico." *Bullettino della Commissione archeologica comunale di Roma* 73 (1949–50): 77–88.

Belinger, Alfred R. "Roman and Byzantine Medallions in the Dumbarton Oaks Collection." *Dumbarton Oaks Papers* 12 (1958): 125–56.

Béranger, Jean. *Recherches sur l'aspect idéologique du Principat.* Basel: Friedrich Reinhardt AG, 1953.

Berges, Wilhelm. "Das Monogramm der Berner Gemme." In *Herrschaftszeichen und Staatssymbolik: Beiträge zu ihrer Geschichte vom dritten bis zum sechzehnten Jahrhundert,* 222–6. Stuttgart: Hiersemann, 1954.

Bertrand, Dominique et al. *Césaire d'Arles et la Christianisation de la Provence.* Paris: Les Éditions du Cerf, 1994.

Bierbrauer, Volker. "Zur ostgotischen Geschichte in Italien." *Studi Medievali* 14 (1973): 1–37.

———. *Die Ostgotischen Grab- und Schatzfunde in Italien.* Spoleto: Centro italiano di Studi sull'Alto Medioevo, 1975.

———. "Archeologia degli Ostrogoti in Italia." In *I Goti,* 170–213. Milano: Electa, 1994.

Bierbrauer, Volker et al. *I Goti.* Milano: Electa, 1994.

Bjornlie, Shane. "What Have Elephants to Do with Sixth-Century Politics? A Reappraisal of the 'Official' Government Dossier of Cassiodorus." *Journal of Late Antiquity* 2.1 (2009): 143–71.

Borchert, Sabine. "Das Bild Theoderichs des Großen in der Chronik des sog. Fredegar." In *Geschehenes und Geschriebenes: Studien zu Ehren von Günther S. Henrich und Klaus-Peter Matschke,* edited by Sebastian Kolditz and Ralf C. Müller, 435–52. Leipzig: Eudora Verlag, 2005.

Bovini, Giuseppe. "Note sul presunto ritratto musivo di Giustiniano in S. Apollinare Nuovo di Ravenna." *Annales Universitatis Saraviensis. Philosophie, Lettres* 5 (1956): 50–3.

Bowersock, G. W. et al., ed. *Late Antiquity: A Guide to the Postclassical World.* Cambridge: The Belknap Press of Harvard University Press, 1999.

Bradley, Dennis R. "The Composition of the Getica." *Eranos* 64 (1966): 67–79.

Braund, David. *Rome and the Friendly King: the Character of Client Kingship.* London: Croom Helm, 1984.

Breckenridge, James D. "Three Portrait Gems." *Gesta* 18.1 (1979): 7–18.

Brenot, C. "Deux monnaies d'argent aux noms d'Odoacre et de Théodoric trouvées en Provence (comm. de Saint-Etienne-du-Grès)." *Bulletin de la société française de numismatique* 52.4 (1997): 55–9.

Brogiolo, Gian Pietro. "Edilizia residenziale di età gota in Italia settentrionale." In *I Goti*, 214–21. Milano: Electa, 1994.

———. "Ideas of the Town in Italy during the Transition from Antiquity to the Middle Ages." In *The Idea and Ideal of the Town Between Late Antiquity and the Early Middle Ages*, edited by G. P. Brogiolo and Bryan Ward Perkins, 99–126. Leiden: Brill, 1999.

———. "Dwellings and Settlements in Gothic Italy." In *The Ostrogoths from the Migration Period to the Sixth Century: An Ethnographic Perspective*, edited by Sam Barnish and Federico Marazzi, 113–33. Woodbridge: Boydell Press, 2007.

Brogiolo, G. P. and E. Possenti. "L'età gota in Italia settentrionale, nella transizione tra tarda antichità e alto medioevo." In *Le invasioni barbariche nel meridione dell'impero: Visigoti, Vandali, Ostrogoti: atti del convegno svoltosi alla Casa delle culture di Cosenza dal 24 al 26 luglio 1998*, edited by Paolo Delogu, 257–85. Soveria Mannelli: Rubbettino, 2001.

Brown, Peter. *The World of Late Antiquity: AD 150–750.* London: Thames & Hudson, 1971.

———. *The Rise of Western Christendom: Triumph and Diversity, A.D. 200–1000.* 2nd ed. Oxford: Blackwell, 2003.

Bruun, P. et al. "Late Roman Gold and Silver Coins at Dumbarton Oaks: Diocletian to Eugenius." *Dumbarton Oaks Papers* 18 (1964): 161–236.

Burgarella, Filippo. "Il Senato." In *Roma nell'alto medioevo*, 120–75. Settimane di studio del centro italiano di studi sull'alto medioevo 48. Spoleto: Centro italiano di studi sull'alto medioevo, 2001.

Burns, Thomas S. "Calculating Ostrogothic Population." *Acta Antiqua Academiae Scientiarum Hungaricae* 26 (1978a): 457–63.

———. "Ennodius and the Ostrogothic Settlement." *Classical Folia* 32 (1978b): 153–68.

———. "Theodoric the Great and the Concepts of Power in Late Antiquity." *Acta Classica* 25 (1982): 99–118.

———. *A History of the Ostrogoths.* Bloomington: Indiana University Press, 1984.

———. *Barbarians within the Gates of Rome: A Study of Roman Military Policy and the Barbarians, ca. 375–425 A.D.* Bloomington: Indiana University Press, 1994.

———. *Rome and the Barbarians, 100 BC-AD 400.* Baltimore: Johns Hopkins University Press, 2003.

Bury, J. B. *History of the Later Roman Empire.* 2 vols. New York: Dover, 1958.

Cameron, Alan. *Circus Factions: Blues and Greens at Rome and Byzantium.* Oxford: Clarendon Press, 1976.

———. "The Antiquity of the Symmachi." *Historia* 48.4 (1999): 477–505.

Cameron, Alan and Diane Schauer. "The Last Consul: Basilius and His Diptych." *The Journal of Roman Studies* 72 (1982): 126–145.

Cameron, Averil. "Old and New Rome: Roman Studies in Sixth-Century Constantinople." In *Transformations of Late Antiquity: Essays for Peter Brown,* edited by Philip Rousseau and Manolis Papoutsakis, 15–36. Farnham: Ashgate, 2009.

Carile, Antonio, ed. *Teoderico e i Goti tra Oriente e Occidente.* Ravenna: Longo editore, 1995.

Carson, R. A. G. *Principal Coins of the Romans.* 3 vols. London: British Museum, 1978–81.

Castritius, Helmut. "Korruption im ostgotischen Italien." In *Korruption im Altertum,* edited by Wolfgang Schuller, 215–34. Wien: Oldenbourg, 1982.

Cavada, Enrico. "Trento in età gota." In *I Goti,* 224–31. Milano: Electa, 1994.

Cecchelli, Carlo. "L'arianesimo e le chiese ariane d'Italia." In *Le chiese nei regni dell'Europa occidentale e i loro rapporti con Roma sino all'800,* 743–74. Settimane di studio del centro italiano di studi sull'alto medioevo 7. Spoleto: Centro italiano di studi sull'alto medioevo, 1960.

Cesa, Maria. "Il regno di Odoacre: la prima dominazione germanica in Italia." In *Germani in Italia,* edited by Barbara and Piergiuseppe Scardigli, 308–20. Roma: Consiglio nazionale delle ricerche, 1994.

———. "Odoacre nelle fonti letterarie dei secoli V e VI." In *Le invasioni barbariche nel meridione dell'impero: Visigoti, Vandali, Ostrogoti: atti del convegno svoltosi alla Casa delle culture di Cosenza dal 24 al 26 luglio 1998,* edited by Paolo Delogu, 41–59. Soveria Mannelli: Rubbettino, 2001.

Cessi, Roberto. "Theodericus inlitteratus." In *Miscellanea di studi critici in onore di Vincenzo Crescini,* 221–36. Cividale: Stagni, 1927.

Charanis, Peter. "The Imperial Crown Modiolus and its Constitutional Significance." *Byzantion* 12 (1937): 189–95.

———. *Church and State in the Later Roman Empire: The Religious Policy of Anastasius the First, 491–518.* Madison: University of Wisconsin Press, 1939.

Charlesworth, M. P. "The Virtues of a Roman Emperor: Propaganda and the Creation of Belief." *Proceedings of the British Academy* 23 (1937): 105–33.

Chastagnol, André. *Le Sénat romain sous le règne d'Odoacre: Recherches sur l'épigraphie du Colisée au 5e siècle.* Bonn: Habelt, 1966.

Cherry, David. *Frontier and Society in Roman North Africa.* Oxford: Clarendon Press, 1998.

Christie, Neil. "The Alps as a Frontier (A.D. 168–774)." *Journal of Roman Archaeology* 4 (1991): 410–30.

———. "Barren Fields? Landscapes and Settlements in Late Roman and Post-Roman Italy." In *Human Landscapes in Classical Antiquity: Environment and Culture*, edited by Graham Shipley and John Salmon, 254–83. New York: Routledge, 1996.

―――. *From Constantine to Charlemagne: An Archaeology of Italy, AD 300–800*. Aldershot: Ashgate, 2006.

Chrysos, Evangelos K. "The Title Basileus in Early Byzantine International Relations." *Dumbarton Oaks Papers* 32 (1978): 29–75.

―――. "Der Kaiser und die Könige." In *Die Völker an der mittleren und unteren Donau im fünften und sechsten Jahrhundert*, edited by Herwig Wolfram and Falko Daim, 143–8. Wien: Österreichischen Akademie der Wissenschaften, 1980.

―――. "Die Amaler-Herrschaft in Italien und das Imperium Romanum: Der Vertragsentwurf des Jahres 535." *Byzantion* 51 (1981): 430–75.

Clark, Gillian. *Late Antiquity: A Very Short Introduction*. Oxford: Oxford University Press, 2011.

Claude, Dietrich. "Zur Königserhebung Theoderich des Grossen." In *Geschichtsschreibung und geistiges Leben im Mittelalter. Festschrift für Heinz Löwe zum 65. Geburtstag*, edited by Karl Hauck and Hubert Mordek, 1–13. Köln: Böhlau, 1978a.

―――. "Universale und partikulare Züge in der Politik Theoderichs." *Francia* 6 (1978b): 19–58.

―――. "Die ostgotischen Königserhebungen." In *Die Völker an der mittleren und unteren Donau im fünften und sechsten Jahrhundert*, edited by Herwig Wolfram and Falko Daim, 149–86. Wien: Österreichischen Akademie der Wissenschaften, 1980.

―――. "Theoderich d. Gr. und die europäischen Mächte." In *Teoderico il Grande e i Goti d'Italia: atti del XIII Congresso internazionale di studi sull'Alto Medioevo, Milano 2–6 novembre 1992*, 21–43. Spoleto: Centro italiano di studi sull'alto Medioevo, 1993.

―――. "Studien zu Handel und Wirtschaft im italischen Ostgotenreich." *Münstersche Beiträge zur antiken Handelsgeschichte* 15 (1996): 42–75.

Clemente, Guido. "Ticinum: da Diocleziano alla caduta dell'Impero d'Occidente." In *Storia di Pavia*, Vol. 1: *L'età antica*, 255–69. Pavia: Banca del Monte di Pavia, 1984.

Clover, Frank M. "The Family and Early Career of Anicius Olybrius." *Historia* 27.1 (1978): 169–96.

―――. "Relations between North Africa and Italy, A.D. 476–500: some Numismatic Evidence." *Revue numismatique* 6.33 (1991): 112–33.

―――. "A Game of Bluff: The Fate of Sicily after A.D. 476." *Historia* 48.2 (1999): 235–44.

Coarelli, F. "Atrium Libertatis." In *LTUR* 1 (1993): 133–5.

Collins, Roger. *Early Medieval Spain: Unity in Diversity, 400–1000*. London: MacMillan, 1983.

―――. "Law and Ethnic Identity in the Western Kingdoms of the Fifth and Sixth Centuries." In *Medieval Europeans: Studies in Ethnic Identity and National*

Perspectives in Medieval Europe, edited by Alfred P. Smyth, 1–23. New York: St. Martin's Press, 1998.

———. *Visigothic Spain 409–711*. Malden, Mass.: Blackwell, 2004.

Conant, Jonathan. *Staying Roman: Conquest and Identity in Africa and the Mediterranean, 439–700*. Cambridge: Cambridge University Press, 2012.

Courcelle, Pierre. *Les lettres grecques en Occident: de Macrobe à Cassiodore*. Paris: E. de Boccard, 1943.

———. *Histoire Littéraire des Grandes Invasions Germaniques*. Paris: Hachette, 1948.

Cracco Ruggini, L. "Ticinum: dal 476 d.C. alla fine del Regno Gotico." In *Storia di Pavia*, Vol. 1: *L'età antica*, 271–312. Pavia: Banca del Monte di Pavia, 1984.

———. "Società provinciale, società romana, società bizantina in Cassiodoro." In *Atti della Settimana di Studi su Flavio Magno Aurelio Cassiodoro (Cosenza-Squillace 19–24 settembre 1983)*, edited by Sandro Leanza, 245–61. Soveria Mannelli: Rubettino Editore, 1986.

Croke, Brian. "A.D. 476: The Manufacture of a Turning Point." *Chiron* 13 (1983): 81–119.

———. "Cassiodorus and the Getica of Jordanes." *Classical Philology* 82.2 (1987): 117–34.

———. "Chronicles, Annals and 'Consular Annals' in Late Antiquity." *Chiron* 31 (2001): 291–331.

———. "Latin Historiography and the Barbarian Kingdoms." In *Greek and Roman Historiography in Late Antiquity: Fourth to Sixth Century A.D.*, edited by Gabriele Marasco, 349–89. Leiden: Brill, 2003.

———. "Dynasty and Ethnicity: Emperor Leo I and the Eclipse of Aspar." *Chiron* 35 (2005a): 147–203.

———. "Jordanes and the Immediate Past." *Historia* 54.4 (2005b): 473–94.

Cullhed, Mats. *Conservator Urbis Suae: Studies in the Politics and Propaganda of the Emperor Maxentius*. Stockholm: Åström, 1994.

Curchin, Leonard. *Roman Spain: Conquest and Assimilation*. London: Routledge, 1991.

———. *The Romanization of Central Spain: Complexity, Diversity, and Change in a Provincial Hinterland*. London: Routledge, 2004.

Curta, Florin. "Frontier Ethnogenesis in Late Antiquity: The Danube, the Tervingi, and the Slavs." In *Borders, Barriers, and Ethnogenesis: Frontiers in Late Antiquity and the Middle Ages*, edited by Florin Curta, 173–204. Turnhout: Brepols, 2005.

Dauge, Yves Albert. *Le Barbare: Recherches sur la conception romaine de la barbarie et de la civilisation*. Bruxelles: Latomus, 1981.

Deichmann, Friedrich Wilhelm. *Ravenna: Hauptstadt des spätantiken Abendlandes*. 3 vols. Wiesbaden: F. Steiner, 1969–89.

Delage, Marie-José. "Un évêque au temps des invasions." In *Césaire d'Arles et la Christianisation de la Provence*, 21–43. Paris: Les Éditions du Cerf, 1994.

Delaplace, Christine. "La 'Guerre de Provence' (507–511), un épisode oublié de la domination ostrogothique en Occident." In *Romanité et Cité Chrétienne: Permanences et mutations intégration et exclusion du Ier au VIe siècle: Mélanges en l'honneur d'Yvette Duval*, 77–89. Paris: De Boccard, 2000.

———. "La Provence sous la domination ostrogothique (508–536)." *Annales du Midi* 115.244 (2003): 479–99.

Delbrueck, Richard. *Die Consulardiptychen und verwandte Denkmäler*. 2 vols. Berlin: Walter de Gruyter, 1929.

———. *Spätantike Kaiserporträts: von Constantinus Magnus bis zum Ende des Westreichs*. Berlin: Walter de Gruyter, 1933.

Deliyannis, Deborah Mauskopf. *Ravenna in Late Antiquity*. Cambridge: Cambridge University Press, 2010.

Della Valle, Giuseppina. "Teoderico e Roma." *Rendiconti dell'Accademia di Archeologia, Lettere e Belle Arti di Napoli* 34 (1959): 119–76.

Delle Donne, Fulvio. "Teoderico *Rex Genitus*. Il concetto della nobiltà di stirpe nel panegirico di Ennodio." *Invigilata Lucernis* 20 (1998): 73–84.

———. "Il ruolo storico e politico di Ennodio." In *Atti della prima Giornata Ennodiana: Pavia, 29–30 marzo 2000*, edited by Fabio Gasti, 7–19. Pisa: Edizioni ETS, 2001.

Delogu, Paolo, ed. *Le invasioni barbariche nel meridione dell'impero: Visigoti, Vandali, Ostrogoti: atti del convegno svoltosi alla Casa delle culture di Cosenza dal 24 al 26 luglio 1998*. Soveria Mannelli: Rubbettino, 2001.

Demandt, Alexander. "Magister Militum." In *Paulys Realencyclopädie der classischen Altertumswissenschaft*, supplement band 12, 553–790. Stuttgart: Druckenmüller, 1970.

———. "The Osmosis of Late Roman and Germanic Aristocracies." In *Das Reich und die Barbaren*, edited by Evangelos K. Chrysos and Andreas Schwarcz, 75–86. Wien: Böhlau, 1989.

Demougeot, Emilienne. "Bedeutet das Jahr 476 das Ende des Römischen Reiches im Okzident?" *Klio* 60.2 (1978): 371–81.

———. "Le partage des provinces de l'Illyricum entre la *pars occidentis* et la *pars orientis*, de la Tétrarchie au règne de Théodoric." In *La géographie administrative et politique d'Alexandre à Mahomet: Actes du Colloque de Strasbourg 14–16 Juin 1979*, 229–53. Leiden: Brill, 1981.

Deur, Charles. "The Quasi-autonomous Bronze Issues of the Ostrogoths and the Constitutional Status of the Early Ostrogothic Kings." *SAN* 15 (1984): 6–11.

Diaz, Pablo and Rosario Valverde. "Goths Confronting Goths: Ostrogothic Political Relations in Hispania." In *The Ostrogoths from the Migration Period to the Sixth Century: An Ethnographic Perspective*, edited by Sam Barnish and Federico Marazzi, 353–76. Woodbridge: Boydell Press, 2007.

Dolbeau, F. "Un nouveau témoin fragmentaire de l'*Anecdoton Holderi*." *Revue d'histoire des texts* 12/13 (1982/3): 397–9.

Drinkwater, John. *Roman Gaul: The Three Provinces, 58 BC–AD 260*. London: Croom Helm, 1983.

———. *The Gallic Empire: Separatism and Continuity in the North-Western Provinces of the Roman Empire AD 260–274*. Historia Einzelschriften 52. Stuttgart: Franz Steiner Verlag Weisbaden GMBH, 1987.

———. "Gallic Attitudes to the Roman Empire in the Fourth Century: Continuity or Change?" In *Labor Omnibus Unus: Gerold Walser zum 70. Geburtstag dargebracht von Freunden, Kollegen und Schülern*, edited by Heinz E. Herzig and Regula Frei-Stolba, 136–53. Stuttgart: Franz Steiner Verlag Weisbaden GMBH, 1989.

———. "Julian and the Franks and Valentinian I and the Alamanni: Ammianus on Romano-German Relations." *Francia* 24.1 (1997): 1–15.

———. *The Alamanni and Rome 213–496: Caracalla to Clovis*. Oxford: Oxford University Press, 2007.

Drinkwater, John and Hugh Elton, ed. *Fifth-century Gaul: A Crisis of Identity?* Cambridge: Cambridge University Press, 1992.

Duchesne, L. "L'empereur Anastase et sa politique religieuse." *Mélanges d'archéologie et d'histoire* 32.1 (1912): 305–36.

———. "Les Schismes romains au VIe siècle." *Mélanges d'archéologie et d'histoire* 35.1 (1915): 221–56.

Dutton, Paul Edward. *Charlemagne's Mustache: And Other Cultural Clusters of a Dark Age*. New York: Palgrave Macmillan, 2004.

Ebel, Charles. *Transalpine Gaul: the Emergence of a Roman Province*. Leiden: Brill, 1976.

Elton, Hugh. *Frontiers of the Roman Empire*. Bloomington: Indiana University Press, 1996.

Ensslin, Wilhelm. "Zum Heermeisteramt des spätrömischen Reiches III: Der magister utriusque militiae et patricius des 5. Jahrhunderts." *Klio* 24 (1931): 467–502.

———. "Der Patricius Praesentalis im Ostgotenreich." *Klio* 29 (1936): 243–9.

———. "Rex Theodericus Inlitteratus?" *Historisches Jahrbuch* 60 (1940): 391–6.

———. "Papst Johannes I. als Gesandter Theoderichs bei Kaiser Justinos I." *Byzantinische Zeitschrift* 44 (1951): 127–34.

———. *Theoderich der Grosse*. 2nd ed. München: F Bruckmann, 1959.

Everett, Nicholas. *Literacy in Lombard Italy, c. 568–774*. Cambridge: Cambridge University Press, 2003.

Ewig, Eugen. "Die fränkischen Teilungen und Teilreiche (511–613)." *Akademie der Wissenschaft und der Literatur Mainz. Abhandlung der geistes- und sozialwissenschaftlichen Klasse* 9 (1952): 651–715; reprinted in *Spätantikes und fränkisches Gallien*, Vol. 1, 114–71. München: Artemis, 1976.

Fanning, S. "Emperors and Empires in Fifth-century Gaul." In *Fifth-century Gaul: A Crisis of Identity?* edited by John Drinkwater and Hugh Elton, 288–97. Cambridge: Cambridge University Press, 1992.

————. "Odovacer *rex*, Regal Terminology, and the Question of the End of the Western Roman Empire." *Medieval Prosopography* 24 (2003): 45–54.

Fauvinet-Ranson, Valérie. "Portrait d'une régente. Un panégyrique d'Amalasonthe (Cassiodorus, *Variae* 11,1)." *Cassiodorus* 4 (1998): 267–308.

Favrod, Justin. *Histoire politique du royaume burgonde (443–534)*. Lausanne: Bibliothèque historique vaudoise, 1997.

Festy, Michel. "De L'Epitome de Caesaribus' à la 'Chronique' de Marcellin: l''Historia Romana' De Symmaque." *Historia* 52.2 (2003): 251–5.

Février, Paul-Albert. "Césaire et la Gaule méridionale au VIe siècle." In *Césaire d'Arles et la Christianisation de la Provence*, 45–73. Paris: Les Éditions du Cerf, 1994.

Ficarra, Rosalba. "Fonti letterarie e motivi topici nel Panegirico a Teodorico di Magno Felice Ennodio." In *Scritti in onore di Salvatore Pugliatti*, Vol. 5: *Scritti Vari*, 234–54. Milano: A. Giuffrè, 1978.

Fischer Drew, Katherine. *The Laws of the Salian Franks*. Philadelphia: University of Pennsylvania Press, 1991.

Flege, James E. "Age of Learning and Second Language Speech." In *Second Language Acquisition and the Critical Period Hypothesis*, edited by David Birdsong, 101–32. Mahwah, NJ: Erlbaum, 1999.

Freund, Walter. *Modernus und andere Zeitbegriffe des Mittelalters*. Köln: Böhlau, 1957.

Fuchs, Siegfried. "Bildnisse und Denkmäler aus der Ostgotenzeit." *Die Antike: Zeitschrift für Kunst und Kultur des klassischen Altertums* 19 (1943): 109–53.

————. *Kunst der Ostgotenzeit*. Berlin: Walter de Gruyter, 1944.

Fuhrmann, Manfred. "Die Romidee der Spätantike." *Historische Zeitschrift* 207 (1968): 529–61; reprinted in *Rom als Idee*, edited by Bernhard Kytzler, 86–123. Darmstadt: Wissenschaftliche Buchgesellschaft, 1993.

Galonnier, Alain. "*Anecdoton Holderi* ou *Ordo Generis Cassiodororum*. Introduction, édition, traduction et commentaire." *Antiquité Tardive* 4 (1996): 299–312.

————. Anecdoton Holderi *ou* Ordo Generis Cassiodororum: *Éléments pour une étude de l'authenticité Boécienne des opuscula sacra*. Louvain: Editions Peeters, 1997.

Garzya, Antonio. "Cassiodoro e la grecità." In *Atti della Settimana di Studi su Flavio Magno Aurelio Cassiodoro (Cosenza-Squillace 19–24 settembre 1983)*, edited by Sandro Leanza, 118–34. Soveria Mannelli: Rubettino Editore, 1986.

————. "Teoderico a Bisanzio." In *Teoderico e i Goti tra Oriente e Occidente*, edited by Antonio Carile, 341–51. Ravenna: Longo editore, 1995.

Geary, Patrick. "Ethnic Identity as a Situational Construct in the Early Middle Ages." *Mitteilung der anthropologischen Geselschaft in Wien* 113 (1983): 15–26.

————. *Before France and Germany: The Creation and Transformation of the Merovingian World*. Oxford: Oxford University Press, 1988.

————. "Barbarians and Ethnicity." In *Late Antiquity: A Guide to the Postclassical World*, edited by G.W. Bowersock et al., 107–29. Cambridge: Belknap Press of Harvard University Press, 1999.

————. *The Myth of Nations: The Medieval Origins of Europe*. Princeton: Princeton University Press, 2002.

Gerberding, Richard. *The Rise of the Carolingians and the Liber historiae Francorum*. Oxford: Clarendon Press, 1987.

Giardina, Andrea. "Cassiodoro politico e il progetto delle *Variae*." In *Teoderico il Grande e i Goti d'Italia: atti del XIII Congresso internazionale di studi sull'Alto Medioevo, Milano 2–6 novembre 1992*, 45–76. Spoleto: Centro italiano di studi sull'alto Medioevo, 1993.

————. *L'Italia Romana: Storie di un'identità incompiuta*. Roma: Editori Laterza, 1997.

————. *Cassiodoro Politico*. Roma: "L'Erma" di Bretschneider, 2006.

Giesecke, Heinz-Eberhard. *Die Ostgermanen und der Arianismus*. Leipzig and Berlin: B. G. Teubner, 1939.

Gillett, Andrew. "The Purposes of Cassiodorus' *Variae*." In *After Rome's Fall: Narrators and Sources of Early Medieval History*, edited by Alexander Callander Murray, 37–50. Toronto: University of Toronto Press, 1998.

————. "The Accession of Euric." *Francia* 26.1 (1999): 1–40.

————. "Jordanes and Ablabius." In *Studies in Latin Literature and Roman History*, Vol. 10, edited by Carl Deroux, 479–500. Bruxelles: Latomus, 2000.

————. "Rome, Ravenna and the Last Western Emperors." *Papers of the British School at Rome* 69 (2001): 131–167.

————, ed. *On Barbarian Identity: Critical Approaches to Ethnicity in the Early Middle Ages*. Turnhout: Brepols, 2002.

————. *Envoys and Political Communication in the Late Antique West, 411–533*. Cambridge: Cambridge University Press, 2003.

————. "Ethnogenesis: A Contested Model of Early Medieval Europe." *History Compass* 4.2 (2006): 241–60.

Gioanni, Stéphane. "La contribution épistolaire d'Ennode de Pavie à la primauté pontificale sous le règne des papes Symmaque et Hormisdas." *Mélanges de l'Ecole française de Rome. Moyen Age* 113.1 (2001): 245–68.

————. "Les élites italiennes, l'autorité pontificale et la romanité au début du VIe s. – l'engagement d'Ennode de Pavie-." In *Atti della Seconda Giornata Ennodiana*, edited by Edoardo D'Angelo, 37–52. Napoli: Pubblicazioni del Dipartimento di Filologia Classica dell'Università degli Studi di Napoli Federico II, 2003.

Goffart, Walter. *Barbarians and Romans A.D. 418–584: The Techniques of Accommodation*. Princeton: Princeton University Press, 1980.

————. *The Narrators of Barbarian History (A.D. 550–800): Jordanes, Gregory of Tours, Bede, and Paul the Deacon*. Princeton: Princeton University Press, 1988.

————. *Barbarian Tides: The Migration Age and the Later Roman Empire.* Philadelphia: University of Pennsylvania Press, 2006.

Goltz, Andreas. "Sizilien und die Germanen in der Spätantike." *Kokalos* 43/4 (1997/8): 209–42.

————. "Marcellinus Comes und das 'Ende' des Weströmischen Reiches im Jahr 476." *Electrum* 13 (2007): 39–59.

————. *Barbar – König – Tyrann. Das Bild Theoderichs des Großen in der Überlieferung des 5. bis 9. Jahrhunderts.* Berlin: Walter de Gruyter, 2008.

Gottschall, Dagmar. "Teoderico il Grande: *Rex Philosophus.*" In *Mutatio rerum: Letteratura, filosofia, scienza tra tardo antico e altomedioevo*, edited by Maria Luisa Silvestre and Marisa Squillante, 251–72. Napoli: Città del sole, 1997.

Grierson, Philip. *The Coins of Medieval Europe.* London: Seaby, 1991.

Grierson, Philip and Mark Blackburn. *Medieval European Coinage: With a Catalogue of the Coins in the Fitzwilliam Museum, Cambridge*, Vol. 1: *The Early Middle Ages (5th–10th centuries).* Cambridge: Cambridge University Press, 1986.

Guidobaldi, F. "Palma (ad Palmam)." In *LTUR* 4 (1999): 52–3.

Haarer, F. K. *Anastasius I: Politics and Empire in the Late Roman World.* Cambridge: Francis Cairns, 2006.

Harries, Jill D. *Sidonius Apollinaris and the Fall of Rome AD 407–485.* Oxford: Clarendon Press, 1994.

Heather, Peter. "Cassiodorus and the Rise of the Amals: Genealogy and the Goths under Hun Domination." *The Journal of Roman Studies* 79 (1989): 103–28.

————. *Goths and Romans.* Oxford: Clarendon Press, 1991.

————. "The Historical Culture of Ostrogothic Italy." In *Teoderico il Grande e i Goti d'Italia: atti del XIII Congresso internazionale di studi sull'Alto Medioevo, Milano 2–6 novembre 1992*, 317–53. Spoleto: Centro italiano di studi sull'alto Medioevo, 1993.

————. "Literacy and Power in the Migration Period." In *Literacy and Power in the Ancient World*, edited by Alan K. Bowman and Greg Woolf, 177–97. Cambridge: Cambridge University Press, 1994.

————. "Theoderic, King of the Goths." *Early Medieval Europe* 4.2 (1995): 145–73.

————. *The Goths.* Oxford: Blackwell, 1996.

————. "The Barbarian in Late Antiquity: Image, Reality, and Transformation." In *Constructing Identities in Late Antiquity*, edited by Richard Miles, 234–58. London: Routledge, 1999.

————. *The Fall of the Roman Empire: A New History of Rome and the Barbarians.* Oxford: Oxford University Press, 2006.

————. "Merely an Ideology? – Gothic Identity in Ostrogothic Italy." In *The Ostrogoths from the Migration Period to the Sixth Century: An Ethnographic Perspective*, edited by Sam Barnish and Federico Marazzi, 31–60. Woodbridge: Boydell Press, 2007.

Heijmans, Marc. "La topographie de la ville d'Arles durant l'Antiquité tardive." *Journal of Roman Archaeology* 12 (1999): 142–67.

Heijmans, Marc and Claude Sintès. "L'évolution de la topographie de l'Arles antique. Un état de la question." *Gallia* 51 (1994): 135–70.

Hen, Yitzhak. *Roman Barbarians: The Royal Court and Culture in the Early Medieval West.* New York: Palgrave Macmillan, 2007.

Herrmann-Otto, Elisabeth. "Der spätantike Bischof zwischen Politik und Kirche: Das exemplarische Wirken des Epiphanius von Pavia." *Römische Quartalschrift für christliche Altertumskunde und Kirchengeschichte* 90 (1995): 198–214.

Heuberger, Richard. "Das ostgotische Räten." *Klio* 30 (1937): 77–109.

Hodgkin, Thomas. *Italy and her Invaders*, Vol. 3: *The Ostrogothic Invasion.* 2nd ed. Oxford: The Clarendon Press, 1896.

Irigoin, Jean. "Les textes grecs circulant dans le Nord de l'Italie aux Ve et VIe siècle." In *Teoderico e i Goti tra Oriente e Occidente*, edited by Antonio Carile, 391–400. Ravenna: Longo editore, 1995.

Irmscher, Johannes. "Das Ende des weströmischen Kaisertums in der byzantinischen Literatur." *Klio* 60.2 (1978): 397–401.

Isaac, Benjamin. *The Limits of Empire: the Roman Army in the East.* Oxford: Oxford University Press, 2000.

———. *The Invention of Racism in Classical Antiquity.* Princeton: Princeton University Press, 2004.

James, Edward. *The Origins of France: From Clovis to the Capetians, 500–1000.* London: MacMillan, 1982.

———. *The Franks.* Oxford: Blackwell, 1988.

———. "The Rise and Function of the Concept 'Late Antiquity.'" *Journal of Late Antiquity* 1.1 (2008): 20–30.

Johnson, Mark J. "Toward a History of Theoderic's Building Program." *Dumbarton Oaks Papers* 42 (1988): 73–96.

Jones, A. H. M. "The Constitutional Position of Odoacer and Theoderic." *The Journal of Roman Studies* 52.1&2 (1962): 126–30.

———. *The Later Roman Empire 284–602: A Social, Economic and Administrative Survey.* 2 vols. Norman: University of Oklahoma Press, 1964.

Kaegi, Walter Emil. *Byzantium and the Decline of Rome.* Princeton: Princeton University Press, 1968.

Kaiser, Reinhold. *Die Burgunder.* Stuttgart: Kohlhammer, 2004.

Kennell, S. A. H. *Magnus Felix Ennodius: A Gentleman of the Church.* Ann Arbor: University of Michigan Press, 2000.

———. "Style and Substance in the *Libellus pro Synodo*." In *Atti della prima Giornata Ennodiana: Pavia, 29–30 marzo 2000*, edited by Fabio Gasti, 57–67. Pisa: Edizioni ETS, 2001.

———. "Ennodius the Epistolographer." In *Atti della Seconda Giornata Ennodiana*, edited by Edoardo D'Angelo, 109–26. Napoli: Pubblicazioni del Dipartimento di Filologia Classica dell'Università degli Studi di Napoli Federico II, 2003.

Kent, John P. C. "Julius Nepos and the Fall of the Western Empire." In *Corolla Memoriae Erich Swoboda Dedicata*, 146–50. Graz-Köln: Hermann Böhlaus Nachf., 1966.

———. *Roman Coins*. London: Thames and Hudson, 1978.

———. *The Roman Imperial Coinage*, Vol. 10: *The Divided Empire and the Fall of the Western Parts AD 395–491*. London: Spink and Son, 1994.

Kislinger, Ewald. "Zwischen Vandalen, Goten und Byzantinern: Sizilien im 5. und frühen 6. Jahrhundert." *Byzantina et Slavica Cracoviensia* 2 (1994): 31–51.

Klingshirn, William. "Charity and Power: Caesarius of Arles and the Ransoming of Captives in Sub-Roman Gaul." *The Journal of Roman Studies* 75 (1985): 183–203.

———. *Caesarius of Arles: The Making of a Christian Community in Late Antique Gaul*. Cambridge: Cambridge University Press, 1994a.

Köhler, Helga. *C. Sollius Apollinaris Sidonius Briefe Buch I: Einleitung, Text, Übersetzung, Kommentar*. Heidelberg: C. Winter, 1995.

Kohlhas-Müller, Dorothee. *Untersuchungen zur Rechtsstellung Theoderichs des Großen*. Frankfurt am Main: Peter Lang, 1995.

Kolb, Frank. *Herrscherideologie in der Spätantike*. Berlin: Akademie, 2001.

König, Ingemar. "Theoderich der Große und die Kirche S. Stefano zu Verona." *Trierer Theologische Zeitschrift* 95 (1986): 132–42.

———. "Die Herrschaftsbestätigung Theoderichs des Großen durch die Goten im Jahre 493: Ein spätantikes Rechtsproblem." In *E fontibus haurire: Beiträge zur römischen Geschichte und zu ihren Hilfswissenschaft*, edited by Rosamarie Günter and Stefan R. Rebenich, 147–61. Paderborn: F. Schöningh, 1994.

———. "Theoderich der Große und Cassiodor: Vom Umgang mit dem römischen 'Erbe.'" In *"Das Wichtigste ist der Mensch": Festschrift für Klaus Gerteis zum 60. Geburtstag*, edited by Klaus Gerties et al., 211–28. Mainz: P. von Zabern, 2000.

Kosiński, Rafał. *The Emperor Zeno: Religion and Politics*. Cracow: Historia Lagellonica, 2010.

Kraus, Franz F. *Die Münzen Odovacars und des Ostgotenreiches in Italien*. Halle: A. Reichmann, 1928.

Krautschick, Stefan. *Cassiodor und die Politik seiner Zeit*. Bonn: Dr. Rudolf Habelt GMBH, 1983.

———. "Zwei Aspekte des Jahres 476." *Historia* 35 (1986): 345–71.

Kulikowski, Michael. *Rome's Gothic Wars: from the Third Century to Alaric*. Cambridge: Cambridge University Press, 2007.

La Rocca, Cristina. "Una prudente maschera 'Antiqua'. La politica edilizia di Teoderico." In *Teoderico il Grande e i Goti d'Italia: atti del XIII Congresso internazionale di studi sull'Alto Medioevo, Milano 2–6 novembre 1992*, 451–515. Spoleto: Centro italiano di studi sull'alto Medioevo, 1993.

Lafaurie, Jean and Jacqueline Pilet-Lemière. *Monnaies du Haut Moyen Âge découvertes en France (Ve-VIIIe siècle)*. Paris: CNRS Editions, 2003.

Lafferty, Sean D. W. *The* Edictum Theoderici: *A Study of a Roman Legal Document from Ostrogothic Italy*. Toronto: PhD diss., University of Toronto, 2010.

Lamma, Paolo. "Teoderico nella storiografia Bizantina." *Studi Romagnoli* 3 (1952): 87–95.

Leanza, Sandro, ed. *Atti della Settimana di Studi su Flavio Magno Aurelio Cassiodoro (Cosenza-Squillace 19–24 settembre 1983)*. Soveria Mannelli: Rubettino Editore, 1986.

Lee, A. D. "The Role of Hostages in Roman Diplomacy with Sasanian Persia." *Historia* 40.3 (1991): 366–74.

Lemerle, Paul. "Invasions et migrations dans les Balkans depuis la fin de l'époque romaine jusqu'au VIIIe siècle." *Revue Historique* 211 (1954): 265–308.

Lenski, Noel. "Assimilation and Revolt in the Territory of Isauria, from the 1st Century BC to the 6th Century AD." *Journal of the Economic and Social history of the Orient* 42.4 (1999): 413–65.

Lewis, Carin M. "Gallic Identity and the Gallic Civitas from Caesar to Gregory of Tours" In *Ethnicity and Culture in Late Antiquity*, edited by Stephen Mitchell and Geoffrey Greatrex, 69–81. London: Duckworth and Classical Press of Wales, 2000.

Lippolis, Isabella Baldini. "Il ritratto musivo nella facciata interna di S. Apollinare Nuovo a Ravenna." In *Atti del VI Colloquio dell'Associazione italiana per lo studio e la conservazione del mosaico: con il patrocinio del Ministero per i Beni e le Attività Culturali (Venezia, 20–23 gennaio 1999)*, edited by Federico Guidobaldi and Andrea Paribeni, 463–75. Ravenna: Edizioni del Girasole, 2000.

Llewellyn, P. A. B. "The Roman Church during the Laurentian Schism: Priests and Senators." *Church History* 45.4 (1976): 417–26.

Long, Michael H. "Maturational Constraints on Language Development." *Studies in Second Language Acquisition* 12 (1990): 251–85.

Lorentz, Friedrich von. "Theoderich –nicht Iustinian." *Mitteilungen des Deutschen Archäologischen Instituts, Römische Abteilung* 50 (1935): 339–47.

Loseby, S. T. "Marseille: A Late Antique Success Story?" *The Journal of Roman Studies* 82 (1992): 165–85.

———. "Decline and Change in the Cities of Late Antique Gaul." In *Die Stadt in der Spätantike –Niedergang oder Wandel?* 67–104. Stuttgart: Franz Steiner, 2006.

Löwe, Heinz. "Theoderich der Große und Papst Johann I." In *Zwischen Wissenschaft und Politik. Festschrift für Georg Schreiber*, edited by Johannes Spörl, 83–100. München: K. Alber, 1953.

———. "Theoderichs Gepidensieg im Winter 488/9. Eine historisch-geographische Studie." In *Historische Forschungen und Probleme. Peter Rassow zum 70. Geburtstage dargebracht von Kollegen, Freunden und Schülern*, 1–16. Wiesbaden: F. Steiner, 1961.

Luiselli, Bruno. "Cassiodoro e la storia dei Goti." In *Passaggio dal mondo antico al Medio Evo da Teodosio a San Gregorio Magno*, 225–53. Roma: Accademia Nazionale dei Lincei, 1980.

―――. "Dall'arianesimo dei Visigoti di Constantinopoli all'arianesimo degli Ostrogoti d'Italia." In *Ravenna da capitale imperiale a capitale esarcale: atti del XVII Congresso internazionale di studio sull'Alto Medioevo, Ravenna 6–12 giugno 2004*, 729–59. Spoleto: Centro italiano di studi sull'alto Medioevo, 2005.

Lumpe, Adolf. "Die konziliengeschichtliche Bedeutung des Ennodius." *Annuarium Historiae Conciliorum* 1 (1969): 15–36.

Luttwak, Edward. *The Grand Strategy of the Roman Empire from the First Century A.D. to the Third*. Baltimore: Johns Hopkins University Press, 1976.

Maas, Michael. "History and Christian Ideology in Justinianic Reform Legislation." *Dumbarton Oaks Papers* 40 (1986): 17–31.

Macbain, Bruce. "Odovacer the Hun?" *Classical Philology* 78.4 (1983): 323–7.

MacCormack, Sabine. *Art and Ceremony in Late Antiquity*. Berkeley: University of California Press, 1981.

MacGeorge, Penny. *Late Roman Warlords*. Oxford: Oxford University Press, 2002.

MacPherson, Robin. *Rome in Involution: Cassiodorus' Variae in their Literary and Historical Setting*. Poznań: UAM, 1989.

Maioli, Maria Grazia. "Ravenna e la Romagna in epoca gota." In *I Goti*, 232–51. Milano: Electa, 1994.

―――. "Rapporti commerciali e materiali di Ravenna e Classe in epoca teodericiana." In *Teoderico e i Goti tra Oriente e Occidente*, edited by Antonio Carile, 227–36. Ravenna: Longo editore, 1995.

Marazzi, Federico. "The Last Rome: From the End of the Fifth to the End of the Sixth Century." In *The Ostrogoths from the Migration Period to the Sixth Century: An Ethnographic Perspective*, edited by Sam Barnish and Federico Marazzi, 279–302. Woodbridge: Boydell Press, 2007.

Marcone, Arnaldo. "A Long Late Antiquity? Considerations on a Controversial Periodization." *Journal of Late Antiquity* 1.1 (2008): 4–19.

Markus, R. A. "The End of the Roman Empire: A Note on Eugippius, *Vita Sancti Severini*, 20." *Nottingham Medieval Studies* 26 (1982): 1–7.

Martindale, J. R. *The Prosopography of the Later Roman Empire*, Vol. 2: A.D. 395–527. Cambridge: Cambridge University Press, 1980.

―――. *The Prosopography of the Later Roman Empire*, Vol. 3: A.D. 527–641. Cambridge: Cambridge University Press, 1992.

Martino, P. "Gothorum laus est civilitas custodita." *Sileno* 8 (1982): 31–45.

Mathisen, Ralph W. "Epistolography, Literary Circles, and Family Ties in Late Roman Gaul." *Transactions of the American Philological Association* 111 (1981): 95–109.

―――. "Patricians as Diplomats in Late Antiquity." *Byzantinische Zeitschrift* 79.1 (1986): 35–49.

———. "The Theme of Literary Decline in Late Roman Gaul." *Classical Philology* 83 (1988): 45–52.

———. "Leo, Anthemius, Zeno, and Extraordinary Senatorial Status in the Late Fifth Century." *Byzantinische Forschungen* 17 (1991): 191–222.

———. "Fifth-Century Visitors to Italy: Business or Pleasure?" In *Fifth-century Gaul: A Crisis of Identity?* edited by John Drinkwater and Hugh Elton, 228–38. Cambridge: Cambridge University Press, 1992.

———. *Roman Aristocrats in Barbarian Gaul: Strategies for Survival in an Age of Transition.* Austin: University of Texas Press, 1993.

———. "The Letters of Ruricius of Limoges and the Passage from Roman to Frankish Gaul." In *Society and Culture in Late Antique Gaul: Revisiting the Sources*, edited by Ralph W. Mathisen and Danuta Shanzer, 101–15. Aldershot: Ashgate, 2001.

———. "'Qui Genus, unde Patres?' The Case of Arcadius Placidus Magnus Felix." *Medieval Prosopography* 24 (2003): 55–71.

———. "Vouillé, Voulon, and the Location of the Campus Vogladensis." In *The Battle of Vouillé, 507 CE: Where France Began*, edited by Ralph W. Mathisen and Danuta Shanzer, 43–61. Berlin: Walter de Gruyter, 2012.

Mathisen, Ralph W. and Danuta Shanzer, ed. *Society and Culture in Late Antique Gaul: Revisiting the Sources.* Aldershot: Ashgate, 2001.

———, ed. *Romans, Barbarians, and the Transformation of the Roman World: Cultural Interaction and the Creation of Identity in Late Antiquity.* Aldershot: Ashgate, 2011.

———, ed. *The Battle of Vouillé, 507 CE: Where France Began.* Berlin: Walter de Gruyter, 2012.

Matthews, John. *Western Aristocracies and Imperial Court AD 364–425.* Oxford: Clarendon Press, 1975.

———. "Anicius Manlius Severinus Boethius." In *Boethius: His Life, Thought and Influence*, edited by Margaret Gibson, 15–43. Oxford: Blackwell, 1981.

Mauss, Marcel. *The Gift: Forms and Functions of Exchange in Archaic Societies.* Translated by Ian Cunnison. London: Cohen & West, 1954.

Mazza, Mario. "Ravenna: problemi di una capitale." In *Ravenna da capitale imperiale a capitale esarcale: atti del XVII Congresso internazionale di studio sull'Alto Medioevo, Ravenna 6–12 giugno 2004*, 3–40. Spoleto: Centro italiano di studi sull'alto Medioevo, 2005.

McCormick, Michael. "Odoacer, Emperor Zeno and the Rugian Victory Legation." *Byzantion* 47 (1977): 212–22.

———. *Eternal Victory: Triumphal Rulership in Late Antiquity, Byzantium, and the Early Medieval West.* Cambridge: Cambridge University Press, 1986.

McDonnell, Myles. *Roman Manliness: Virtus and the Roman Republic.* Cambridge: Cambridge University Press, 2006.

Meier, Mischa. *Anastasios I. Die Entstehung des Byzantinischen Reiches.* Stuttgart: Klett-Cotta, 2009.

Merrills, Andy and Richard Miles. *The Vandals.* Malden, Mass.: Wiley-Blackwell, 2010.

Metlich, M. A. *The Coinage of Ostrogothic Italy*. London: Spink, 2004.

Millar, Fergus. *A Greek Roman Empire: Power and Belief under Theodosius II (408–450)*. Berkeley: University of California Press, 2006.

Millett, Martin. *The Romanization of Britain: an Essay in Archaeological Interpretation*. Cambridge: Cambridge University Press, 1990.

Mitchell, Stephen. *Anatolia: Land, Men, and Gods in Asia Minor*. Oxford: Clarendon Press, 1993.

Mitchell, Stephen and Geoffrey Greatrex, ed. *Ethnicity and Culture in Late Antiquity*. London: Duckworth, 2000.

Momigliano, Arnaldo. "Cassiodorus and Italian Culture of His Time." *Proceedings of the British Academy* 41 (1955): 207–45; reprinted in *Secondo contributo alla storia degli studi classici*, 191–229. Roma: Edizioni di storia e letteratura, 1960.

———. "Gli Anicii e la storiografia Latina del VI sec. D.C." *Rendiconti Accademia dei Lincei, Classe di Scienze morali, storiche e filologiche*, ser. 8, 11 (1956): 279–97; reprinted in *Secondo contributo alla storia degli studi classici*, 231–53. Roma: Edizioni di storia e letteratura, 1960.

———. "La caduta senza rumore di un impero nel 476 d.C." *Annali della Scuola Normale Superiore di Pisa, Classe di Lettere e Filosofia*, ser. 3, 3.2 (1973): 397–418; reprinted in *Sesto contributo all storia degli studi classici e del mondo antico*, Vol. 1, 159–79. Roma: Edizioni di storia e letteratura, 1980.

Mommsen, Theodor. "Ostgotische Studien." *Neues Archiv* 14 (1889): 225–49; 453–544; and *Neues Archiv* 15 (1890): 181–6; reprinted in *Gesammelte Schriften*, Vol. 6, 362–484. Berlin: Weidmann, 1910.

Moorhead, John. "Boethius and Romans in Ostrogothic Service." *Historia* 27 (1978a): 604–12.

———. "The Laurentian Schism: East and West in the Roman Church." *Church History* 47 (1978b): 125–36.

———. "The Last Years of Theoderic." *Historia* 32 (1983a): 106–20.

———. "Italian Loyalties during Justinian's Gothic War." *Byzantion* 53 (1983b): 577–96.

———. "The Decii under Theoderic." *Historia* 33 (1984a): 107–15.

———. "Theoderic, Zeno and Odovacer." *Byzantinische Zeitschrift* 77 (1984b): 261–6.

———. "*Libertas* and the *Nomen Romanum* in Ostrogothic Italy." *Latomus* 46.1 (1987): 161–8.

———. *Theoderic in Italy*. Oxford: Clarendon Press, 1992.

———. "Cassiodorus on the Goths in Ostrogothic Italy." *Romanobarbarica* 16 (1999): 241–59.

———. "The Word *modernus*." *Latomus* 65 (2006): 425–33.

Morton, Catherine. "Marius of Avenches, the 'Excerpta Valesiana' and the Death of Boethius." *Traditio* 38 (1982): 107–36.

Musset, Lucien. *Les invasions: les vagues germaniques*. Paris: Presses universitaires de France, 1965.

Näf, Beat. "Das Zeitbewusstsein des Ennodius und der Untergang Roms." *Historia* 39 (1990): 100–23.

Navarra, Leandro. "Contributo storico di Ennodio." *Augustinianum* 14 (1974): 315–42.

Nehlsen, Hermann. "Review of Giulio Vismara, *Edictum Theoderici.*" *Zeitschrift der Savigny-Stiftung für Rechtsgeschichte, Germanistiche Abteilung* 86 (1969): 246–60.

Noble, Thomas F. X. "Theodoric and the Papacy." In *Teoderico il Grande e i Goti d'Italia: atti del XIII Congresso internazionale di studi sull'Alto Medioevo, Milano 2–6 novembre 1992*, 395–423. Spoleto: Centro italiano di studi sull'alto Medioevo, 1993.

Noyé, Ghislaine. "Les Villes de Provinces d'Apulie-Calabre et de *Bruttium*-Lucanie du IVe au VIe siècle." In *Early Medieval Towns in the West Mediterranean*, edited by Gian Pietro Brogiolo, 97–120. Mantova: SAP, 1996.

———. "Social Relations in Southern Italy." In *The Ostrogoths from the Migration Period to the Sixth Century: An Ethnographic Perspective*, edited by Sam Barnish and Federico Marazzi, 183–202. Woodbridge: Boydell Press, 2007.

O'Donnell, James. *Cassiodorus.* Berkeley: University of California Press, 1979.

———. "Liberius the Patrician." *Traditio* 37 (1981): 31–72.

———. "The Aims of Jordanes." *Historia* 31 (1982): 223–40.

———. *The Ruin of the Roman Empire.* New York: Ecco, 2008.

O'Flynn, John M. "A Greek on the Roman Throne: The Fate of Anthemius." *Historia* 40 (1991): 122–8.

Pani Ermini, Letizia. "*Forma urbis* e *renovatio murorum* in età teodericiana." In *Teoderico e i Goti tra Oriente e Occidente*, edited by Antonio Carile, 171–225. Ravenna: Longo editore, 1995.

———. "Lo spazio urbano delle città capitali." *Ravenna da capitale imperiale a capitale esarcale: atti del XVII Congresso internazionale di studio sull'Alto Medioevo, Ravenna 6–12 giungo 2004*, 1003–57. Spoleto: Centro italiano di studi sull'alto Medioevo, 2005.

Paschoud, François. *Roma aeterna: Études sur le patriotisme romain dans l'Occident latin à l'époque des grandes invasions.* Rome: Institut Suisse de Rome, 1967.

Pferschy, Bettina. "Das Problem der Getreidepreise unter Theoderich: Zur Beurteilung des Anonymus Valesianus." In *Siedlung, Macht und Wirtschaft: Festschrift Fritz Posch zum 70. Geburtstag*, edited by Gerhard Pferschy, 481–5. Graz: Steiermärkisches Landesarchiv, 1981.

Pietrella, Egidio. "La figura del santo-vescovo nella 'Vita Epifani' di Ennodio di Pavia." *Augustinianum* 24 (1984): 213–26.

Pietri, Charles. "Aristocratie et société cléricale dans l'Italie Chrétienne au temps d'Odoacre et de Théodoric." *Mélanges de l'Ecole française de Rome. Antiquité* 93 (1981): 417–67.

Piltz, Elisabeth. *Kamelaukion et mitra: insignes byzantins impériaux et ecclésiastiques.* Stockholm: Almqvist & Wiskell, 1977.

Pocock, J. G. A. *Barbarism and Religion*, Vol. 3: *The First Decline and Fall*. Cambridge: Cambridge University Press, 2003.

Pohl, Walter. "Introduction: The Empire and the Integration of Barbarians." In *Kingdoms of the Empire: The Integration of Barbarians in Late Antiquity*, edited by Walter Pohl, 1–12. Leiden: Brill, 1997.

———. "Introduction: Strategies of Distinction." In *Strategies of Distinction: The Construction of Ethnic Communities, 300–800*, edited by Walter Pohl and Helmut Reimitz, 1–15. Leiden: Brill, 1998a.

———. "Telling the Difference: Signs of Ethnic Identity." In *Strategies of Distinction: The Construction of Ethnic Communities, 300–800*, edited by Walter Pohl and Helmut Reimitz, 17–69. Leiden: Brill, 1998b.

Polara, Giovanni. "La letteratura in Italia nell'età di Teoderico." In *Teoderico e i Goti tra Oriente e Occidente*, edited by Antonio Carile, 353–66. Ravenna: Longo editore, 1995.

———. "Ennodio fra chiesa, politica e letteratura." In *Atti della Terza Giornata Ennodiana*, edited by Fabio Gasti, 19–41. Pisa: ETS, 2006.

Pricoco, Salvatore. "Cassiodore et le conflit franco-wisigothique, rhétorique et histoire." In *Clovis: histoire & mémoire*, edited by Michel Rouche, 739–52. Paris: Presses de l'Université de Paris-Sorbonne, 1997.

Prostko-Prostyński, Jan. *Utraeque res publicae: The Emperor Anastasius I's Gothic Policy (491–518)*. Poznań: Instytut Historii UAM, 1994a.

———. "Fu Armato fratello di Odoacre?" In *Studia Moesiaca*, edited by Leszek Mrozewicz and Kazimeirz Ilski, 173–8. Poznań: Instytut Historii UAM, 1994b.

Rasi, Piero. "Sulla paternità del c. d. Edictum Theodorici Regis." *Archivo Giuridico* 145 (1953): 105–162.

———. "Ancora sulla paternità del C.D. Edictum Theodorici." *Annali di storia del diritto* 5/6 (1961–6): 113–36.

Ravenna da capitale imperiale a capitale esarcale: atti del XVII Congresso internazionale di studio sull'Alto Medioevo, Ravenna 6–12 giungo 2004. Spoleto: Centro italiano di studi sull'alto Medioevo, 2005.

Reydellet, Marc. *La Royauté dans la Littérature Latine de Sidoine Apollinaire à Isidore de Séville*. Rome: École française de Rome, 1981.

———. "Théoderic et la *civilitas*." In *Teoderico e i Goti tra Oriente e Occidente*, edited by Antonio Carile, 285–96. Ravenna: Longo editore, 1995.

Riché, Pierre. *Education and Culture in the Barbarian West: Sixth through Eighth Centuries*. Translated by John J. Contreni. Columbia: University of South Carolina Press, 1976.

Roberts, Michael. "Rome Personified, Rome Epitomized: Representations of Rome in the Poetry of the Early Fifth Century." *The American Journal of Philology* 122.4 (2001): 533–65.

Rohr, Christian. "Überlegungen zu Datierung und Anlaß des Theoderich-Panegyricus." In *Ethnogenese und Überlieferung: angewandte Methoden der Frühmittelalterforschung*, edited by Karl Brunner and Brigitte Merta, 95–106. Wien: Oldenbourg, 1994.

————. "Nationalrömisches Bildungsgut im Reich der Ostgoten. Zur Rezeption von Q. Aurelius Symmachus bei Ennodius." *Römische historische Mitteilungen* 40 (1998): 29–48.

————. "La tradizione culturale tardo-romana nel regno degli Ostrogoti –il panegirico di Ennodio a Teoderico." *Romanobarbarica* 16 (1999): 261–84.

————. "Ennodio panegirista di Teoderico e il conflitto tra Ostrogoti e Franchi." In *Atti della prima Giornata Ennodiana: Pavia, 29–30 marzo 2000*, edited by Fabio Gasti, 21–9. Pisa: Edizioni ETS, 2001

————. "Das Streben des ostgotenkönigs Theoderich nach Legitimität und Kontinuität im Spiegel seiner Kulturpolitik: Beobachtungen zu imperialen Elementen im Theoderich-Panegyricus des Ennodius." In *Integration und Herrschaft: ethnische Identität und soziale Organisation im Frühmittelalter*, edited by Walter Pohl and Maximilian Diesenberger, 227–31. Wien: Verlag der Österreichischen Akademie der Wissenschaften, 2002.

————. "Byzanz und die oströmischen Kaiser im Spiegel der Werke des Ennodius." In *Atti della Terza Giornata Ennodiana*, edited by Fabio Gasti, 43–57. Pisa: ETS, 2006.

Romano, Domenico. "Cassiodoro Panegirista." *Pan: Studi dell'Istituto di Filologia Latina* 6 (1978): 5–35.

Rota, Simona. "Teoderico il Grande fra *Graecia* e *Ausonia*: La rappresentazione del re ostrogotico nel *Panegyricus* di Ennodio." *Mélanges de l'École Française de Rome: Moyen Âge* 113.1 (2001a): 203–43.

————. "Ennodio anti-Lucano. I modelli epici del *Panegyricus dictus clementissimo regi Theoderico*." *Atti della prima Giornata Ennodiana: Pavia, 29–30 marzo 2000*, edited by Fabio Gasti, 31–55. Pisa: Edizioni ETS, 2001b.

Rouche, Michel. *L'Aquitaine des Wisigoths aux Arabes 418–781: Naissance d'une région*. Paris: L'École des hautes études en sciences sociales, 1979.

Roymans, Nico. "The Sword or the Plough. Regional Dynamics in the Romanisation of Belgic Gaul and the Rhineland Area." In *From the Sword to the Plough: Three Studies on the Earliest Romanisation of Northern Gaul*, edited by Nico Roymans, 9–126. Amsterdam: Amsterdam University Press, 1996.

Russo, Eugenio. "Una nuova proposta per la sequenza cronologica del Palazzo imperiale di Ravenna." In *Ravenna da capitale imperiale a capitale esarcale: atti del XVII Congresso internazionale di studio sull'Alto Medioevo, Ravenna 6–12 giugno 2004*, 155–90. Spoleto: Centro italiano di studi sull'alto Medioevo, 2005.

Saitta, Biagio. "'Religionem imperare non possumus.' Motivi e momenti della politica di Teoderico il Grande." *Quaderni Catanesi* 8 (1986): 63–88.

————. "La Sicilia tra incursioni vandaliche e dominazione ostrogotica." *Quaderni Catanesi* 9 (1987): 363–417.

————. *La Civilitas di Teoderico: Rigore amministrativo, "tolleranza" religiosa e recupero dell'antico nell'Italia ostrogota*. Roma: "L'Erma" di Bretschneider, 1993.

————. "The Ostrogoths in Italy." *POLIS* 11 (1999): 197–216.

Šašel, Jaroslav. "*Antiqui Barbari*: Zur Besiedlungsgeschichte Ostnoricums und Pannoniens im 5. und 6. Jahrhundert nach den Schriftquellen." In *Von der Spätantike zum frühen Mittelalter. Aktuelle Probleme in historischer und archäologischer Sicht*, edited by Joachim Werner and Eugen Ewig, 125–39. Sigmaringen: J. Thorbecke, 1979.

Schäfer, Christoph. "Probleme einer multikulturellen Gesellschaft. Zur Integrationspolitik im Ostgotenreich." *Klio* 83 (2001): 182–97.

Schäferdiek, Knut. *Die Kirche in den Reichen der Westgoten und Suewen bis zur Errichtung der westgotischen katholischen Staatskirche*. Berlin: Walter de Gruyter, 1967.

Schenk von Stauffenburg, Alexander Graf. "Theoderich der Grosse und seine Römische Sendung." In *Würzburger Festgabe: Heinrich Bulle dargebracht zum 70. Geburtstag am 11. Dezember 1937*, edited by Reinhard Herbig, 115–29. Stuttgart: Kohlhammer, 1938.

Schmidt, Ludwig. "Die comites Gothorum. Ein Kapitel zur ostgotischen Verfassungsgeschichte." *Mitteilungen des Instituts für Österreichische Geschichtsforschung* 40 (1925): 127–35.

———. "Cassiodor und Theoderich." *Historisches Jahrbuch* 47 (1927): 727–9.

———. *Die Ostgermanen*. München: C. H. Beck, 1933 (1969 reprint).

———. "Theoderich, römischer Patricius und König der Goten." *Zeitschrift für Schweizerische Geschichte* 19 (1939): 404–14.

Schramm, Percy Ernst. *Herrschaftszeichen und Staatssymbolik: Beiträge zu ihrer Geschichte vom dritten bis zum sechzehnten Jahrhundert*, Vol. 1. Stuttgart: Hiersemann, 1954.

Schröder, Bianca-Jeanette. *Bildung und Briefe im 6. Jahrhundert: Studien zum Mailänder Diakon Magnus Felix Ennodius*. Berlin: Walter de Gruyter, 2007.

Schwarcz, Andreas. "Die *Restitutio Galliarum* des Theoderich." In *Teoderico il Grande e i Goti d'Italia: atti del XIII Congresso internazionale di studi sull'Alto Medioevo, Milano 2–6 novembre 1992*, 787–98. Spoleto: Centro italiano di studi sull'alto Medioevo, 1993.

———. "*Beato Petro devotissimus ac si catholicus*. Überlegung zur Religionspolitik Theoderichs des Großen." *Mitteilungen des Instituts für Österreichische Geschichtsforschung* 112 (2004): 36–52.

Settipani, Christian. *Continuité gentilice et continuité familiale dans les familles sénatoriales romaines à l'époque impériale: mythe et réalité*. Oxford: Unit for Prosopographical Research, 2000.

Shanzer, Danuta. "Two Clocks and a Wedding: Theodoric's Diplomatic Relations with the Burgundians." *Romanobarbarica* 14 (1996/7): 225–58.

———. "Dating the Baptism of Clovis: The Bishop of Vienne vs the Bishop of Tours." *Early Medieval Europe* 7.1 (1998): 29–57.

Shaw, Brent. "Bandit Highlands and Lowland Peace: The Mountains of Isauria-Cilicia." *Journal of Economic and Social History of the Orient* 32.2 (1990): 199–233; and 33.3 (1990): 237–270.

Siena, Silvia Lusuardi. "Sulle tracce della presenza gota in Italia: il contributo delle fonti archeologiche." In *Magistra Barbaritas: i barbari in Italia*, edited by Maria Giovanna Arcamone et al., 509–58. Milano: Libri Scheiwiller, 1984.

Sirago, Vito A. "I Goti nelle Variae di Cassiodoro." In *Atti della Settimana di Studi su Flavio Magno Aurelio Cassiodoro (Cosenza-Squillace 19–24 settembre 1983)*, edited by Sandro Leanza, 179–205. Soveria Mannelli: Rubettino Editore, 1986.

———. "Gli Ostrogoti in Gallia secondo le *Variae* di Cassiodoro." *Revue des Études Anciennes* 89 (1987): 63–77.

Smith, R. R. R. "Late Antique Portraits in a Public Context: Honorific Statuary at Aphrodisias in Caria, A.D. 300–600." *The Journal of Roman Studies* 89 (1999): 155–89.

Snee, Rochelle. "Gregory Nazianzen's Anastasia Church: Arianism, the Goths, and Hagiography." *Dumbarton Oaks Papers* 52 (1998): 157–86.

Søby Christensen, Arne. *Cassiodorus, Jordanes and the History of the Goths: Studies in a Migration Myth*. Translated by Heidi Flegal. Copenhagen: Museum Tusculanum Press, 2002.

Southerland, C. H. V. *The Roman Imperial Coinage*, Vol. 6: *From Diocletian's Reform (A.D. 294) to the Death of Maximinus (A.D. 313)*. London: Spink and Son, 1967.

Spielvogel, Jörg. "Die historischen Hintergründe der gescheiterten Akkulturation im italischen Ostgotenreich (493–533 n.Chr.)." *Historische Zeitschrift* 274 (2002): 1–24.

Spier, Jeffrey. *Late Antique and Early Christian Gems*. Wiesbaden: Reichert Verlag, 2007.

Staab, Franz. "Ostrogothic Geographers at the Court of Theodoric the Great: A Study of Some Sources of the Anonymous Cosmographer of Ravenna." *Viator* 7 (1976): 27–64.

Stein, Ernst. *Histoire du Bas-Empire*. 2 vols. Paris: Desclée de Brouwer, 1949–59.

Steinby, Eva Margareta, ed. *Lexicon topographicum urbis Romae*. Roma: Quasar, 1993–2001.

Stevens, Gillian. "Age at Immigration and Second Language Proficiency among Foreign-Born Adults." *Language and Society* 28 (1999): 555–78.

Stout, Ann M. "Jewelry as a Symbol of Status in the Roman Empire." *The World of Roman Costume*, edited by Judith Lynn Sebesta and Larissa Bonfante, 77–100. Madison: The University of Wisconsin Press, 1994.

Stroheker, Karl F. *Der senatorische Adel im spätantiken Gallien*. Darmstadt: Wissenschaftliche Buchgesellschaft, 1948 (1970 reprint).

———. "Zur Rolle der Heermeister fränkischer Abstammung im späten vierten Jahrhundert." *Historia* 4 (1955): 314–30; reprinted in *Germanentum und Spätantike*, 9–29. Zürich: Artemis, 1965.

Suerbaum, Werner. *Vom Antiken zum frühmittelalterlichen Staatsbegriff. Über Verwendung und Bedeutung von res publica, regnum, imperium und status von Cicero bis Jordanis.* Münster: Aschendorff, 1961.

———. "Zu Cassiodor und Jordanes." *Eranos* 67 (1969): 71–80.

Szidat, Joachim. "Le forme d'insediamento dei barbari in Italia nel V e VI secolo: sviluppi e conseguenze sociali e politiche." In *Teoderico e i Goti tra Oriente e Occidente*, edited by Antonio Carile, 67–78. Ravenna: Longo editore, 1995.

Tamassia, Nino. "Sulla seconda parte dell'Anonimo Valesiano." *Archivio storico italiano* 71.2 (1913): 3–22.

Teoderico il Grande e i Goti d'Italia: atti del XIII Congresso internazionale di studi sull'Alto Medioevo, Milano 2–6 novembre 1992. Spoleto: Centro italiano di studi sull'alto Medioevo, 1993.

Thompson, E. A. *The Goths in Spain.* Oxford: Oxford University Press, 1969.

Townsend, W. T. "Councils Held under Pope Symmachus." *Church History* 6.3 (1937): 233–59.

Urban, Ralf. *Gallia rebellis: Erhebungen in Gallien im Spiegel antiker Zeugnisse.* Historia Einzelschriften 129. Stuttgart: Franz Steiner, 1999.

Usener, Hermann. *Anecdoton Holderi: ein Beitrag zur Geschichte Roms in ostgothischer Zeit.* Bonn: C. Georgi, 1877.

Van Dam, Raymond. *Leadership and Community in Late Antique Gaul.* Berkeley: University of California Press, 1985.

———. *Saints and Their Miracles in Late Antique Gaul.* Princeton: Princeton University Press, 1993.

———. *The Roman Revolution of Constantine.* Cambridge: Cambridge University Press, 2007.

Vandone, Gianluca. "*Status* ecclesiastico e attività letteraria in Ennodio: tra tensione e conciliazione." In *Atti della prima Giornata Ennodiana: Pavia, 29–30 marzo 2000*, edited by Fabio Gasti, 89–99. Pisa: Edizioni ETS, 2001.

Várady, László. "Jordanes-Studien. Jordanes und das 'Chronicon' des Marcellinus Comes – Die Selbständigkeit des Jordanes." *Chiron* 6 (1976): 441–87.

Viscido, Lorenzo. "De ordinis generis Cassiodororum excerptis ab Alfredo Holder Inventis." *Hermes Americanus* 3 (1985): 6–16.

———. "De textus critici 'Ordinis generis Cassiodororum' excerptorum quaestione quadam." *Vita Latina* 104 (1986a): 32–4.

———. "Sull'uso del termine barbarus nelle 'Variae' di Cassiodoro." *Orpheus*, n.s. 7 (1986b): 338–44.

Vismara, Giulio. *Edictum Theoderici.* Mediolani: Giuffrè, 1967.

Vitiello, Massimiliano. "Teoderico a Roma. Politica, amministrazione e propaganda nell'*adventus* dell'anno 500." *Historia* 53.1 (2004): 73–120.

———. *Momenti di Roma ostrogota: adventus, feste, politica.* Historia Einzelschriften 188. Stuttgart: Franz Steiner, 2005a.

———. "Motive germanischer Kultur und Prinzipien des gotischen Königtums im Panegyricus des Ennodius an Theoderich den Grossen (Die drei ‚direkten Reden')." *Hermes* 113 (2005b): 100–15.

———. "Cassiodorus Anti-Boethius." *Klio* 90 (2008): 461–84.

von Haeling, Raban. "'Timeo, ne per me consuetudo in regno nascatur': Die Germanen und der römische Kaiserthron." In *Roma Renascens: Beiträge zur Spätantike und Rezeptionsgeschichte*, edited by Michael Wissemann, 88–113. Frankfurt am Main: Verlag Peter Lang, 1988.

Wallace-Hadrill, Andrew. "Civilis Princeps: Between Citizen and King." *The Journal of Roman Studies* 72 (1982): 32–48.

Walser, Gerold. "Der Kaiser als Vindex Libertatis." *Historia* 4 (1955): 353–67.

Ward-Perkins, Bryan. *From Classical Antiquity to the Middle Ages: Urban Public Building in Northern and Central Italy, AD 300–850*. Oxford: Oxford University Press, 1984.

———. "Continuists, Catastrophists and the Towns of Post-Roman Northern Italy." *Papers of the British School at Rome* 65 (1997): 157–176.

———. *The Fall of Rome and the End of Civilization*. Oxford: Oxford University Press, 2005.

Weißensteiner, Johann. "Cassiodor/Jordanes als Geschichtsschreiber." In *Historiographie im frühen Mittelalter*, edited by Anton Scharer and Georg Scheibelreiter, 308–25. Wien: Oldenbourg, 1994.

Wenskus, Reinhard. *Stammesbildung und Verfassung: das Werden der frühmittelalterlichen Gentes*. Köln: Böhlau, 1961.

Wes, M. A. *Das Ende des Kaisertums im Westen des Römischen Reichs*. 's-Gravenhage: Staatsdrukerij, 1967.

Whittaker, C. R. *Frontiers of the Roman Empire: A Social and Economic Survey*. Baltimore: Johns Hopkins University Press, 1994.

Wickham, Chris. *Early Medieval Italy: Central Power and Local Society 400–1000*. Ann Arbor: University of Michigan Press, 1981.

———. *Framing the Early Middle Ages: Europe and the Mediterranean 400–800*. Oxford: Oxford University Press, 2005.

Wightman, Edith M. *Gallia Belgica*. London: B. T. Batsford, 1985.

Williams, J. H. C. *Beyond the Rubicon: Romans and Gauls in Republican Italy*. Oxford: Oxford University Press, 2001a.

———. "Roman Intentions and Romanization: Republican Northern Italy, c. 200–100 BC." In *Italy and the West: Comparative Issues in Romanization*, edited by Simon Keay and Nicola Terrenato, 91–101. Oxford: Oxbow, 2001b.

Williams, Stephen and Gerard Friell. *The Rome That Did Not Fall: The Survival of the East in the Fifth Century*. New York: Routledge, 1999.

Williamson, Callie. "Monuments of Bronze: Roman Legal Documents on Bronze Tablets." *Classical Antiquity* 6.1 (1987): 160–83.

Wirth, Gerhart. "Zu Justinian und Theoderich." In *Panchaia: Festschrift für Klaus Thraede*, edited by Manfred Wacht, 251–60. Münster: Aschendorff, 1995.

Wolfram, Herwig. *Intitulatio I: Lateinische Königs- und Fürstentitel bis zum Ende des 8. Jahrhunderts.* Mitteilungen des Instituts für Österreichische Geschichtsforschung, Ergänzungsband 21. Graz –Wein – Köln: Hermann Böhlaus, 1967.

———. "Gotisches Königtum und römisches Kaisertum von Theodosius dem Großen bis Justinian I." *Frühmittelalterliche Studien* 13 (1979): 1–28.

———. "Westillyrien unter gotischer Herrschaft (490/493–537)." In *Lebendige Altertumswissenschaft: Festgabe zur Vollendung des 70. Lebensjahres von Hermann Vetters*, edited by Manfred Kandler et al., 315–17. Wien: A. Holzhausen, 1985.

———. *History of the Goths.* Translated by Thomas J. Dunlap. Berkeley: University of California Press, 1988.

———. *The Roman Empire and Its Germanic Peoples.* Translated by Thomas Dunlap. Berkeley: University of California Press, 1997.

Wolfram, Herwig and Falko Daim, ed. *Die Völker an der mittleren und unteren Donau im fünften und sechsten Jahrhundert.* Wien: Österreichischen Akademie der Wissenschaften, 1980.

Wolfram, Herwig et al., ed. *Typen der Ethnogenese unter besonderer Berücksichtigung der Bayern: Berichte des Symposions der Kommission für Frühmittelalterforschung, 27. bis 30. Oktober, 1986, Stift Zwettl, Niederösterreich.* 2 vols. Wien: Verlag der Österreichischen Akademie der Wissenschaften, 1990.

Wood, Ian. *The Merovingian Kingdoms: 450–751.* Harlow: Longman, 1994.

———. "Theoderic's Monuments in Ravenna." In *The Ostrogoths from the Migration Period to the Sixth Century: An Ethnographic Perspective*, edited by Sam Barnish and Federico Marazzi, 249–63. Woodbridge: Boydell Press, 2007.

Woolf, Greg. *Becoming Roman: The Origins of Provincial Civilization in Gaul.* Cambridge: Cambridge University Press, 1998.

Wroth, Warwick. *Catalogue of the Coins of the Vandals, Ostrogoths and Lombards and of the Empire of Thessalonica, Nicaea and Trebizond in the British Museum.* London: Trustees of the British Museum, 1911.

Zanker, Paul. *The Power of Images in the Age of Augustus.* Translated by Alan Shapiro. Ann Arbor: University of Michigan Press, 1988.

Zecchini, Giuseppe. "Il 476 nella storiografia tardoantica." *Aevum* 59.1 (1985): 3–23.

———. "L'Anonimo Valesiano II: genere storiografico e contesto politico." In *Teoderico il Grande e i Goti d'Italia: atti del XIII Congresso internazionale di studi sull'Alto Medioevo, Milano 2–6 novembre 1992*, 809–18. Spoleto: Centro italiano di studi sull'alto Medioevo, 1993.

Zeiller, M. J. "Les Églises ariennes de Rome à l'époque de la domination gothique." *Mélanges d'archéologie et d'histoire* 24.1 (1904): 17–33.

———. "Étude sur l'arianisme en Italie à l'époque ostrogothique et à l'époque Lombarde." *Mélanges d'archéologie et d'histoire* 25.1 (1905): 127–46.

Zucchetti, Giuseppe. "Marco Aurelio." *Capitolium* 28 (1953): 328–32.

INDEX

Acacian Schism, 70 n. 39, 73 n. 52, 82,
   295–6
acclamations, 87
adventus, 205–6, 207 n. 26, 216
Agapitus, pope, 300
Agnellus of Ravenna, 104–10, 112
Alamanni, 267, 284 n. 119
Alani, 125
Alaric, Visigothic king, 117–18
Alaric II, Visigothic king, 252, 264–9,
   275, 277
Albinus, patrician, 227–8, 296
Alps, 241–2, 293
Amalaberga, 166, 267
Amalafrida, 166, 296, 300
Amalaric, Visigothic king, 271
Amalasuentha, 48–51, 143, 149, 173,
   299–300
Amals, 42, 143, 162–5, 171, 216
   Romanness of, 165–74
Anastasius, emperor, 70, 78–82, 87, 95, 97,
   109, 209, 265 n. 17, 290–1, 302
Anecdoton Holderi, 41 n. 16
Anicia Juliana, 153 n. 46
Anicii, 169
Anonymus Valesianus, 65–70, 199, 205, 298
Anthemius, emperor, 16–20, 45, 125, 148,
   150–3, 157 n. 67, 159, 161, 179
Apollinaris, 247
aqueducts, 200, 219, 223, 226
Arator, 260
Archotamia, 248
Arians, 73, 109, 138, 146 n. 16, 160 n. 79,
   295–9
Arigern, 132, 281

Arles, 21, 236, 244–5, 249–50, 255, 270–1,
   283–4, 287–9
Armentarius, 212
army, 125, 142, 182–3, 280–1, 283
   east Roman, 155, 301
   of Odovacer, 34–5
   Roman, 49, 137–9, 155, 238, 269–70
Artemidorus, 152
Aspar, 146, 159
Athalaric, 129, 149, 158, 170–1, 218,
   299–300
Athaulf, Visigothic king, 118, 124, 161
Augustus, emperor, 28, 76–7, 91–2, 206, 221,
   225 n. 131
Aurelianus, 276
Ausonius, 288
Avignon, 270, 280
Avitus of Vienne, 280

Balkans, 2, 117, 152, 232, 233 n. 5, 270,
   272, 300
barbarians, 121–2, 124, 241, 253, 263, 272–3
   fall of Rome and, 2–5, 17, 44, 125–6, 134,
      137–8, 141, 235, 239–40, 272–3
   marriage with Romans, 19, 161, 254–5
   stereotypes, 13, 18–19, 24–5, 121, 123,
      125–7, 131–4, 160, 167, 236–9, 251–3,
      258, 273, 277
Barcelona, 271
basileus, 30, 74–5, 101, 111, 150
Basiliscus, 152
   coup of, 154–6, 160
Basilius Decius, 273
baths, 200, 223
Belisarius, 64, 69 n. 34, 300–1

benevolence, imperial, 175–7, 180, 191,
 194–5, 197–200, 206–7, 215, 223–8,
 232, 282–4, 286–9
Boethius, 134, 149, 296–8
building projects, 109, 198–200, 203, 220–8,
 231–2, 287–9
Bulgars, 136, 164
Burgundians, 21, 125, 188–9, 240, 252–3,
 267, 269–70, 272, 300

Caesarius of Arles, 103–4, 248, 281–2
Capitoline, 219
captives, 29, 183–4, 189, 194, 282
Carcassonne, 271
Cassiodori, 40–1, 55–6, 151
Cassiodorus, 1, 7, 10, 38, 94, 97, 132, 149,
 151, 172–4, 176, 199, 205, 216–17, 233,
 241, 273–4, 298
 career of, 38–9, 46–7, 170, 213,
  229, 301
 chronicle of, 42–6, 172
 De anima, 301
 education of, 38–9
 fall of Rome and, 39, 41–2, 46, 48, 51–4
 Greeks and, 40, 50
 lost history of, 42–3, 170–2, 216 n. 78
 Variae, 46–8, 54, 78, 82, 97, 265, 292, 301
Celts. *See* Gauls
Charlemagne, emperor, 108
Christ the Redeemer. *See* Sant'
 Apollinare Nuovo
churches, 138, 200, 224 n. 122, 298
circus, 207, 213–14, 287 n. 137
Circus Maximus, 221
civilitas, 127–8, 130–5, 145, 155–6, 168–9,
 172, 174, 199, 209, 233, 252, 274, 278,
 280–1, 293, 298
Classe, 197, 286
Claudius, emperor, 294
clientage, 64, 95, 145, 267
Clovis, Frankish king, 90, 95 n. 12, 102 n. 41,
 134, 252, 262–9, 275
coinage, 62, 76–7, 84–5, 89, 111, 202–3,
 287 n. 137
collegiality, imperial, 58, 78–82, 87, 90, 92,
 151, 290–1
Colosseum, 215, 221, 225–6
Constantius II, emperor, 202
Constantine, emperor, 93, 202
Constantinople, 71, 79, 106, 144–7, 150–3,
 156, 201, 202 n. 6

consuls, 63, 70 n. 38, 86–7, 153–4, 157–8,
 207 n. 27, 216, 290–1
corruption, 32, 34, 36, 40, 130, 213, 297–8
Cottian Alps, 198
Cyprian, 54–6, 140, 149

Dalmatia, 62
damnatio memoriae, 93, 110
Danube, 2, 51
Deuterius, 256–7
diadems and crowns, 92, 97, 100–4,
 101 n. 36–7, 110, 113–14
Diocletian, emperor, 93
diplomacy, 166, 193, 253, 262–8
 with Burgundians, 133–4, 189, 262, 265
 with Constantinople, 61–2, 68–70, 204,
  216, 290–1, 296–7, 300–1
 with Franks, 134, 262, 265–7
 with Heruli, 267–8
 with Thuringians, 166, 267–8
 with Vandals, 166–8, 217, 300
 with Visigoths, 262, 265–7
Durance, 270

eastern Roman Empire, 43, 54, 150–2, 265,
 275 n. 66, 299
 acceptance of Theoderic, 59, 64, 70, 80, 82,
  86–7, 95–6, 296
 fall of Rome and, 62, 137
 primacy of, 78–80, 83, 85–6, 97,
  99–100, 151
 tension with, 50, 68–70, 78, 80–2, 217,
  269, 272, 290–1, 300
east Romans, 74, 296–7, 299
 foreignness of, 17–18
 Greekness of, 10, 72, 144, 148–50
 religion and, 73, 149, 296
Edictum Theoderici, 129 n. 41
education, 13–14, 36, 44, 139, 146–7,
 149–50, 211–12, 231, 243, 249, 255–8
Ennodius, 7, 10, 37, 74, 98–102, 115, 122–3,
 174, 176, 198, 203, 212, 215, 233, 241,
 261, 274, 283, 296 n. 2, 298
 career of, 11
 education of, 11–14
 fall of Rome and, 14–15, 27, 37, 179
 Gallic ties of, 11–12, 242–51, 254–60,
  276, 282
 importance of Rome to, 14
 Italian identity of, 12, 37–8, 179,
  241–2

Life of Epiphanius, 15–26, 29–33, 118, 176, 179–94, 199. *See also* Epiphanius of Pavia
Panegyric to Theoderic, 15, 28, 33–6, 98, 154–8, 162–5, 172
entertainments, 176–7, 213–18, 228
Epiphanius of Pavia, 125, 180, 183–4
  embassy to Anthemius, 18–20
  embassy to Euric, 23–5
  fall of Rome and, 29–30
  Odovacer and, 31–3, 181
  Theoderic and, 181–94
ethnogenesis, 4
euergetism, 225–6
Eugippius, 26 n. 81
Euprepia, 247–51, 253
Euric, Visigothic king, 21–5, 118, 179, 251–2, 258, 275, 277
Eutharic, 43, 86, 215–18, 296

Faustus Junior, 258
Faustus Niger, 69, 258 n. 127
Felix, 247, 292–3
  consulship of, 1–2, 8, 272, 290–5
  father of, 149, 247, 290, 292
Felix IV, pope, 299
Festus, 68–70, 96, 204
Firminus of Arles, 244–5, 248
Flavian Amphitheater. *See* Colosseum
fleet, 297, 300
Forum
  Roman, 205–6, 223, 226–7
  of Trajan, 219
Franks, 125, 138, 237, 240, 242 n. 30, 252–3, 260, 263–4, 268, 270–2, 283, 300
frontier, Roman, 4, 71, 117, 121, 123, 241–2, 270, 293
Fulgentius of Ruspe, 205

Gaiseric, Vandal king, 44–5
Galla Placidia, 48–51, 118, 143, 155, 161
Gallo-Romans, 1, 121–3, 238–40, 248, 253–4, 275–6, 284–6, 292–3, 295. *See also* Gaul; Gauls
games, 87, 213. *See also* entertainments
Gaul, 5, 8, 118, 191, 232, 263–4, 281, 300
  barbarization of, 1, 235, 240, 242, 243 n. 35, 249–51, 253–5, 260–1, 263, 274, 276, 284, 290
  end of Roman rule in, 9, 20–1
  personifications of, 236–7

prefecture of, 198, 270, 280
provisioning of, 283, 285, 287
re-Romanization of, 276–9, 284–5, 287, 289
restoration of, 1, 233, 241, 261, 270–2, 274, 277–8, 284, 289, 292–3
Romanness of, 23, 235–40, 242–8, 253, 255, 260–1, 292–4
Gauls, 121, 124, 235–9
Gemellus, 279, 286
gender, 48–50, 163–4
Gesalec, Visigothic king, 167, 271
Glycerius, emperor, 20, 31, 67
Gothicness, 6, 8, 113–15, 118, 135 n. 75, 137–42, 147, 164, 165 n. 103, 173, 266, 270
Goths, 6, 8, 44, 49, 57, 69, 110, 115, 121, 138 n. 91, 147, 214, 238, 275, 299, 301
  as barbarians, 124, 130
  as defenders, 118, 127–8, 132, 134–5, 175, 270, 280, 289
  as restorers, 117–18, 121, 128, 134–6, 158, 164, 175, 232
  Romanness of, 7, 118–19, 123–4, 127–30, 133–9, 141–2, 144–6, 164, 169, 273, 277, 280–1, 295
  as soldiers, 125, 134, 138, 141–2, 232, 270, 289
Greek culture, 149–50, 238, 245–6, 292
Gundobad, Burgundian king, 125, 133, 189, 242, 252, 264–5

hair, 113–14, 122, 141, 174, 238
Heliodorus, 151
Herminafrid, Thuringian king, 165–6
Heruli, 267
Hilderic, Vandal king, 296–7
Honorius, emperor, 117

Ibba, 270–1, 280, 287
iconography, imperial, 92–3, 104, 106–8, 111–14
ideology, imperial, 169, 201–4, 221–2, 224, 232, 241, 273, 277–8
Illyricum, 50–1
imperator, 75
inscriptions, 76, 87, 89, 176, 202, 273
Isaurians, 159–60
Italo-Romans, 1, 37–8, 56, 58, 71–5, 88, 93–4, 101, 104, 129, 135, 139–41, 148–50, 153–4, 180, 184–5, 187–8, 191,

Italo-Romans (*cont.*)
　199–201, 207–8, 216, 252, 272, 275,
　　277, 296, 299, 301
　barbarization of, 36, 41–2, 130–2
　fall of Rome and, 9–10, 26–8
　Gaul and, 233, 235, 238–43, 246,
　　248–51, 253, 255, 260–2, 272–5, 281,
　　291, 293
　partisans of Theoderic, 10, 58–9, 76–7, 84,
　　88–91, 99, 115, 143–4, 158, 175–6, 180,
　　195–7, 220–1, 231–2, 273–4, 276, 278,
　　287, 295, 297, 299, 302
Italy, 1, 194, 269–70, 275, 289
　east Roman reconquest of, 8, 47, 66,
　　83, 300–2
　economy of, 34, 39, 195–8, 220, 297
　emperors and, 71–2, 74–6, 88
　as Roman Empire, 53–4, 56, 58, 78–82, 84,
　　90, 193, 195, 216, 232, 260, 275, 289,
　　293, 295
　See also Northern Italy; Southern Italy

Jewel of Bern, 111–13
Jews, 73, 127 n. 28, 131, 296, 298
John, pope, 297–8
Jordanes, 64–5, 96, 141 n. 110, 170 n. 127,
　266 n. 22
Julius Nepos, emperor, 20–6, 31, 53, 62–3, 67,
　148, 151, 175, 179
Julius Patricius, 146, 159
Justin, emperor, 83, 86, 109, 146 n. 18,
　216
Justinian, emperor, 2, 86–7, 109–10,
　300–1

Laconius, courtier of Gundobad, 254
late antiquity, 3–4
Laurentian Schism, 74 n. 53, 131, 296
law, 128 n. 40, 129 n. 42
　Roman, 118, 127–30, 185 n. 20, 210,
　　227 n. 136, 238–9, 277–8, 280, 289
Leo, courtier of Euric, 23, 246–8
Leo, emperor, 144
letter writing, 247–8
Liberius, 132, 140–1, 195–6, 211–12,
　270 n. 46, 271, 274, 280, 283, 301
libertas, 13, 22, 74, 117, 136, 164, 185, 188,
　202, 210, 233, 274, 276, 297
Liguria, 8, 12 n. 5, 16, 33, 125, 175–6,
　179–86, 188–94, 198, 241–2, 252, 267
　nobles of, 17, 23, 125, 179, 191

Lilybaeum, 300
localism, 147 n. 22, 179–80, 193

Marabad, count, 279
Marcian, emperor, 144
Marseille, 21, 270, 279, 286–7
Maxentius, emperor, 77, 91, 201–2
Maximus, ex-consul, 169
Milan, 12, 16, 57, 179, 181, 204, 256, 258
monuments, 177. *See also* building projects
mosaics, 105–7, 109–11
mustaches, 113–15, 122, 141, 174, 238

Narbonne, 271, 280
North Africa, 39, 44–5, 217–18, 271, 300
Northern Italy, 57–8, 176, 180, 204,
　236, 241–2
　cities in, 200
　emperors and, 12–13
　frontierization of, 13, 241–2
　See also Liguria

Odovacer, 2, 10, 66, 125, 143, 148, 162, 181,
　232 n. 3
　coup of, 26, 29, 52
　criticism of, 33–6, 54–6, 64, 101, 211
　position of, 30–1, 52–4, 58, 61–3, 72,
　　90, 93
officials, 279
　Gothic, 40 n. 12, 128 n. 36, 132, 280–1
　Roman, 132, 151–2, 195–6, 279–80,
　　289, 291–2
Olybrius, emperor, 20, 114
Opilio the Elder, 54–6, 139–40
Opilio the Younger, 54–6
Orestes, patrician, 26, 29
Ostia, 197, 286
Ostrogothic Italy, 2, 5–8, 72
　as Roman empire, 7
Ostrogoths, 2, 72, 240 n. 21. *See also* Goths

palaces, 105–6, 109, 199–200, 207
Palatine, 207, 222–3, 228
Pannonia, 144, 278, 289. *See also* Balkans
papacy, 14, 38, 82, 87, 205, 254, 296–9
Parthenius, 254–60
Paulinus, patrician, 227
Pavia, 12, 16, 29, 32, 57, 105, 126, 179, 182,
　184, 199, 204, 215 n. 74
Pelagius, prefect of Italy, 32, 181
Pitzia, 135, 164

Pomerius, 245–6, 248, 255
Pompey the Great, 222, 224
Po, 13
Portus, 197, 286
princeps, 13, 30, 58, 71, 74–8, 88, 97, 101, 111, 202, 206
Priscian of Caesarea, 83 n. 91
Priscus Attalus, emperor, 117
Procopius, 64–5, 70, 72–5, 94–6, 137, 302
purple, 52, 92, 95, 97–100, 110.
    See also regalia, imperial

Ravenna, 12, 57, 68, 103–8, 121, 177, 196–7, 199, 202, 204, 216, 222 n. 112, 224, 293
    personifications of, 106–7
recusatio, 97, 101, 157
regalia, imperial, 52–3, 58–9, 62, 68, 70, 72, 80, 92, 94–104, 107, 110–11
Rhone, 270
Ricimer, 17–20, 45–6, 125, 148, 161, 179
Roman Empire. *See* eastern Roman Empire; Italy; western Roman Empire
Romanitas. See Romanness
Romanization, 124–5, 130, 144, 238
Romanness, 76–7, 80, 114–15, 118, 122–3, 125–7, 130–2, 137–41, 143–5, 148, 152, 163, 166–7, 171–2, 200, 202–3, 231 n. 2, 233, 253, 257–8, 275, 278–9, 284–6
    eloquence and, 13–14, 25, 36, 146–7, 243–4, 249, 255, 258, 279
    imperial terminology and, 31, 75–6
    personal names and, 159–60, 173, 275
Rome, 2, 8, 57–8, 71, 76–7, 87, 176–7, 197, 200–29, 231–2, 256, 258, 272, 293, 302
    as *caput mundi*, 14, 134, 176, 179, 201–4, 218–24, 227–8
    emperors and, 201–2, 206–7, 220
    Gallic sack of, 236, 239
    neglect of, 35, 71, 176, 201, 220
    personifications of, 35, 106–7, 203, 237
    prefects of, 211, 219, 224
    provisioning of, 207, 212–13
    Romans of, 130–2, 176, 180, 201, 204–6, 208, 212–18, 220–4, 228–9
    Theoderic in, 177, 204–9, 208 n. 32, 228
    Vandal sack of, 45
    Visigothic sack of, 2, 44, 117, 271 n. 48
Romulus Augustus, emperor, 26, 54, 62
royalty, 27–8, 30–1, 43–4, 79, 88, 118–19, 160–2
Rugi, 63, 126

San Vitale, 110, 112
Sant' Apollinare Nuovo, 109–12
Senarius, 193 n. 71
Senate, 2, 82–3, 131, 160–1, 170–2, 202, 204–5, 209–12, 217, 223, 225, 229, 238, 273, 281, 290–2, 294, 296–8, 300
Senigallia Medallion, 111–14, 141, 273
sewers, 219, 223
Sicily, 39, 41, 44, 58, 300
Sidonius Apollinaris, 1, 5, 9, 17, 19, 118, 121, 150, 159, 161, 243, 246, 253, 275
Sigismund, Burgundian king, 125
Sirmian War, 136 n. 82, 140, 269, 291
Southern Italy, 39–40, 241
Spain, 232, 233 n. 5, 272
Spoleto, 200 n. 103
statues, 85–6, 108, 152, 219, 223
Symmachus, east Roman envoy, 217
Symmachus, pope, 74, 205, 259
Symmachus, senator, 224–5, 296–7
synods, 87, 131

taxation, 32, 191–8, 282–4, 286–7
tetrarchs, 77, 81, 85
Tetricus, Gallic emperor, 236–7, 239
Theater of Pompey, 221–2, 224–5
Theodahad, 86–7, 149, 168–70, 297 n. 10
Theodemir, king, 144
Theodenanda, 159 n. 74
Theoderic
    appearance of, 94–115, 141
    as barbarian king, 2, 63, 65, 69, 72–3, 90, 94, 113, 118–19, 143, 156, 159–61, 164–5, 184–5, 275
    career in the East, 63–4, 67, 143, 152–8
    childhood of, 144–7
    as east Roman, 119, 147–8, 150, 182
    invasion of Gaul, 264–6, 268–72
    invasion of Italy, 56–8, 68–9, 180–4, 231, 266
    religion and, 72–4, 87, 103, 109, 186–7, 194, 205, 296, 298–9
    as Roman emperor, 7–8, 58–61, 70–92, 100, 103–4, 106, 110–13, 128–9, 157, 164–5, 174–6, 180, 182, 190–6, 200, 203, 208, 214, 227, 232, 273, 276, 278–9, 283, 287, 289, 293, 295, 298
    Romanness of, 7, 47, 75–6, 96, 113–15, 130, 133–4, 143–8, 155, 174, 252, 265–6, 267 n. 27, 273
    sent by the East, 58, 63–8, 153

Theoderic (*cont.*)
    titles of, 2, 75–6, 88–90, 99, 288 n. 141
    as Trajan, 58, 76, 111, 129 n. 44
    as usurper, 64, 69–70, 72–3
    as Valentinian, 58, 73 n. 51, 111
Theodosius II, emperor, 67
Thrasamund, Vandal king, 166–9
tiles (*tegulae*), 222–3, 287 n. 137
Titus, emperor, 221
tolerance, 73. *See also civilitas*
Totila, 301–2
Toulouse, 21
trade, 197–8, 213, 285–7
Trajan, emperor, 199
triumph, 89, 152, 207, 237
Tuluin, 135–6, 140–1, 158,
    268 n. 33, 270
Tzathes, Lazi king, 95 n. 13

unity, imperial, 80–7, 90, 92–3, 151–2, 216,
    291, 300
usurpation, 53

Valentinian III, emperor, 50–1, 67
Vandals, 39, 44–5, 296–7

Venantius, 140, 211–12
venationes (hunting shows), 215, 217–18
Verona, 57, 199–200
virtues, 140–2, 174
    Gothic, 117, 124, 126–7, 135, 162
    imperial, 49 n. 45, 89, 108, 142–4, 163,
        173 n. 138, 182, 192, 207, 221
    Roman, 55, 137, 163, 165, 167–70, 172–3,
        209–11, 251 n. 80, 258, 284, 292
Visigoths, 117–18, 125, 262, 266–9, 271–2
    barbarism of, 21–4, 133, 240, 251–3,
        272–3
Vouillé, Battle of, 268–9, 272

walls, 199–200, 223, 287–8
Wandil, 280–1
Warni, 267
western Roman Empire, 2, 53
    decadence of, 28, 41–2, 48–50, 93, 130,
        133–4, 137, 141, 143, 155–6, 161
    as Empire of Italy, 22, 43, 71, 134, 175
Witigis, 83, 301

Zeno, emperor, 26, 53, 61–9, 96, 108, 152–7,
    159–60, 216